PRAISE FOR GOD,

A must read for sceptics. Roy Williams brings a lawyer's careful attention to evidence and strength of inference to life's (and death's) most important questions. He respectfully, but effectively, cross-examines the case against Christianity as propounded by its recent atheist advocates. Like C.S. Lewis and other authors who came to faith late in life, Roy Williams understands the issues that trouble atheists and agnostics and gives thoughtful, convincing responses.

Robert F. Cochran, Jr., Louis D. Brandeis Professor, Pepperdine University School of Law

Full marks go to Roy Williams, who has written an antidote to Richard Dawkins and Christopher Hitchens ... This is a well-argued and sensible approach to Christianity.

Bruce Elder, The Sydney Morning Herald, 19-20 July 2008

Of course the entire book is a piece of proselytising, albeit of the lowest key, the humblest kind you may experience... That's Williams' advantage. We have heard many of the messages before, but this time the tone is respectful and correct, though he is never apologetic for the faith that has transformed him.

Jill Rowbotham, The Weekend Australian, 12-13 July 2008

[I]t's time for believers to stand up and be counted. That's what former legal eagle and author Roy Williams does in this very sane, well argued book... Williams mounts a passionate but tightly reasoned defence of religious faith in the 21st century... [H]e sifts through the evidence and confidently deconstructs the debate.

Phil Brown, Brisbane News, 2-8 July 2008

Williams has not only done a lot of hard thinking and reading, he has the literary skills to do justice to his views. In one sense, this book is a reply to the trenchant critiques of religion by writers such as Christopher Hitchens and Richard Dawkins. It is also the story of Williams' own journey from atheism to Christianity. While informed by this personal perspective, Williams argues his case like the lawyer he is... The value of the book, whether you agree with it or not, is that it forces you to take up the challenge and justify your own views on God's existence.

Fiona Capp, The Age (Melbourne), 19 July 2008

You don't need blind faith to enjoy this book. Nor does it browbeat sceptics. Instead, *God, Actually* is a long-overdue, highly invigorating enquiry into Christianity and the debates surrounding the existence of God. If you're sick of hearing that religion doesn't work because it's not rational, you can draw a breath of relief.
Doubleday Australia Book Club, August 2008

There are few things in *God, Actually* with which I would quarrel... I am encouraged that an intelligent Australian has risen to the challenges posed by the 'New Atheists' and responded with such an articulate and reasoned defence of Christian faith. I hope that *God, Actually* will be read with as much attentiveness as *The God Delusion*.
Bishop Tom Frame, Director, St Mark's National Theological Centre, Canberra

Williams [writes] ... wittily ... wisely ... ably.
Kevin Hart, The Australian Literary Review, 2 July 2008

[A] painstakingly honest and thoughtful book. And wherever you sit on the believer-nonbeliever spectrum, it demands close attention for the respect demonstrated by the author for his readers... *God, Actually* is a book that will stir ferocious argument and debate. It is erudite, wide-ranging, reasoned and reasonable, and asks only that its observations and arguments be approached with an open mind.
Diana Simmonds, Sydney Alumni Magazine, Spring 2008

[The] book is a very considerable achievement. It is exceptionally well-written, and carefully nuanced on all the crunch points.
Graham N. Stanton, Lady Margaret's Professor of Divinity Emeritus, University of Cambridge (Letter to the author, 22 July 2008)

I thought that *God, Actually* was one of the best statements of reasoned faith that I have read. I loved it.
Tim Costello, Chief Executive, World Vision Australia

GOD, ACTUALLY

Why God probably exists,
Why Jesus was probably divine,
and
Why the 'rational' objections to
religion are unconvincing

ROY WILLIAMS

MONARCH
BOOKS
Oxford, UK, and Grand Rapids, Michigan, USA

First published in the UK in 2009 by Monarch Books
(a publishing imprint of Lion Hudson plc),
Wilkinson House, Jordan Hill Road, Oxford OX2 8DR.
Tel: +44 (0)1865 302750 Fax: +44 (0)1865 302757
Email: monarch@lionhudson.com
www.lionhudson.com

First published in Australia by ABC Books 2008.

ISBN 978-1-85424-920-3 (UK)
ISBN 978-0-7459-5391-5 (USA)

Distributed by:
UK: Marston Book Services Ltd, PO Box ...59,
Abingdon, Oxon OX14 4YN.
USA ... Trafalgar Square ... N. Franklin Street,
Chicago, IL 60610.

This book has been printed on paper ... and independently
certified ... from sustainable forests.

British Library Cataloguing Data
A catalogue record for this book is available
from the British Library.

Printed and bound in Malta by Gutenberg Press.

I want you to know, brothers, that the gospel I preached is not something that man made up.

St Paul, Galatians 1:11

A little philosophy inclineth men's minds to atheism, but depth in philosophy bringeth men's minds about to religion.

Francis Bacon, *Of Atheism*

For Suzanne, Hope and Violet,
with love

CONTENTS

NOTE TO INTERNATIONAL EDITION

The first edition of *God, Actually* was published in Australasia in June 2008. Already that feels like a very long time ago. It seems an eternity since the day, early in March 2008, when I gave up my baby and submitted the final version of the manuscript to ABC Books in Sydney. A great deal has happened in the interim, both internationally and for me as an individual.

Over the past year the world has witnessed, among other significant events, the deepening of the 'Global Financial Crisis', an appalling act of terrorism in India, and the heavy and sustained bombing of Gaza by Israel. The myriad threats posed by climate change and nuclear weapons have not gone away, and nor have the culture wars. On the positive side, Barack Obama succeeded George W. Bush as President of the United States. Obama's inspirational oration on election night – and John McCain's gracious words of concession – gave the world some cause for hope. In his inaugural address, President Obama hit the nail on the head when he quoted from St Paul: it is time for all of us to 'put childish ways behind' (cf. 1 Corinthians 13:11).

At a personal level, I have enjoyed a giddying twelve months. The publication and promotion of *God, Actually* was a richly satisfying experience – yet also, in many respects, a surreal one. Sometimes I still shake my head and smile, to think that it has really happened.

I have learned an enormous amount and have been blessed in so many ways. For a start, in Australia at least, the book has sold a respectable number of copies – a relief, let it be admitted frankly, for any self-respecting writer, to say nothing of his dependants and his publisher. The book has also (for the most part!) been kindly and intelligently reviewed in the local media.

Even more gratifying – and illuminating – have been the unsolicited private letters and emails which I have received from readers. A few came from as far afield as Britain and North America. Not all of them were wholly favourable – far from it – but almost without exception the authors exhibited wisdom and sincerity. The faith of many people is already strong, and the spiritual hunger of many others is patent and uplifting. It is extraordinarily touching to learn that your book has helped someone to take a step or two in their spiritual journey.

To date, the only people who have exhibited a degree of hostility toward me – as well as almost total closed-mindedness about the issues – were certain contributors to Richard Dawkins' official website. In late May 2008, one gentleman posted an item about *God, Actually* entitled 'A New Flea'. (The term 'flea' is used by Dawkins' supporters in reference to non-entities like me; people who have had the temerity publicly to disagree with their hero. Like fleas, we are annoying – but can be effortlessly flicked away.) Following this gentleman's post, there ensued a running blog of over 100 entries. Perhaps unwisely, I entered the debate myself. So did a close friend of mine from Sydney who holds rather more fundamentalist views than me. I was humoured but dismissed; my friend was pilloried. With one or two honourable exceptions, no-one seemed to be seriously interested in tackling the key issues.

The more I look at the arguments for atheism, the weaker they seem. I do not say that pejoratively, or to boast: that is genuinely my opinion. And I can truthfully say that I have done my best to understand the case against God's existence. I have tried mightily to educate myself in Darwinian evolutionary theory, the keystone of the modern atheist's arch. Most other serious Christian apologists have done the same. On the other hand, I can discern little evidence to suggest that the likes of Richard Dawkins, Christopher Hitchens or Sam Harris have made a real effort to educate themselves about Christianity, or any religion. I am talking here, not of straw man arguments or lazy stereotypes, but of the real thing – the truly hard questions and the concrete evidence that Man has to go on. That evidence is scientific, philosophical, psychological and – perhaps most important of all – historical.

As a result of the publication of *God, Actually*, I have had the honour of meeting, conversing and/or corresponding with a good number of eminent people, both here and overseas. These have included several authors, broadcasters and public figures who, in one way or another, inspired and nurtured – or challenged – my own developing Christian faith. I will name just a few, as a mark of gratutude to them. From overseas: Graham N. Stanton, John Shelby Spong, Jim Wallis, John Lennox and – a blissfully talented singer/songwriter from Canada – Jane Siberry. Here at home: Thomas Keneally, Gough Whitlam (prime minister of Australia from 1972–75), Tim Costello, Frank Brennan, John Cleary, Geoff Gallup and Australia's best-selling Christian author, John Dickson. Through the kindness of John's charming wife, Buff, I am now honoured to be a member of their weekly Bible-study group.

The release of this international edition of *God, Actually* affords me a priceless opportunity, one not extended to many first-time authors. I have been able to hone my original manuscript, so as to make corrections and to take account of events subsequent to publication. In some chapters – particularly those about Jesus – I have tried to bolster and/or improve my arguments. I learned a lot in 2008 from the constructive feedback of readers and reviewers, and from reading many additional books, both Christian and secular. Some of these books were new releases; others were classics which had previously escaped my attention. Among those which I found especially valuable were J.I. Packer's *God Has Spoken* (Hodder & Stoughton, 1979), Josh McDowell's *Evidence for Christianity* (Thomas Nelson, 2006), Francis S. Collins' *The Language of God* (Free Press, 2006), Garry Wills' *What Jesus Meant* (Viking, 2006) – a little gem, and Craig

L. Blomberg's *The Historical Reliability of the Gospels* (Intervarsity Press, 2007). I also re-read several old favourites in 2008, including substantial sections of the Bible itself.

As a result of all this reading, and a lot more hard thinking, my faith has deepened. On a few issues, my beliefs have changed – not radically so, but not insignificantly either.

Another book which I discovered during 2008 was written by my great-great-grandfather on my mother's side, an Englishman named Frederick Smith (1845–1931). I had known since childhood that my great-grandfather on my *father's* side, a gentleman called Thomas Evans (1865–1935), had served as a Presbyterian minister in rural New South Wales. I had not been aware, until my mother told me last year, of the existence of Rev. Smith. He was the author of several books, including one entitled *The Boyhood of a Naturalist*. Published in 1900 by Blackie & Son Ltd, a Glasgow firm, it was in its day both a modest best-seller and a school textbook. I am now the proud owner of a pristine copy.

My great-great-grandfather was a fascinating man. He was educated at St. John's Choir School in Cambridge and became an accomplished geologist, botanist and science teacher. In 1889 he was ordained a clergyman of the Episcopal Church of Scotland. He served at St. Ninian's Cathedral, Perth (1888–90); St. Luke's Church, Glasgow (1890–95); Cromlix (1895–1901); and the Priory Church of St. Mary's at South Queensferry (1901–18). During the Great War (1914–18), he was Priest-in-charge and Chaplain to the Royal Navy's forces stationed in the Forth. He was commended by the Admiralty in 1919 for his services ministering to officers and seamen, including at the Naval Hospital. His obituary in *The Times* described him as 'an author of some distinction'. As regards his work for the Royal Navy, he was lauded as having been 'extremely popular with the men and … known among sailors in every port in the world'.

I mention these things because learning about them was, for me, an almost spiritual experience. It seems that I had at least two direct ancestors, one on each side of my family, who shared a good number of my own interests, traits, skills and sensibilities, especially as regards matters religious. My own mother (affectionately, if wistfully) has called me a 'throwback'. I expect that Richard Dawkins would attribute my wrongheadedness to an unlucky combination of genes and memes. As for Rev. Frederick Smith, Dawkins would doubtless include him among the legion of well-meaning, but hopelessly mistaken, scientists down the ages who 'let down the side' by believing in God.

I had another uncanny experience in 2008, which is also, I think, sufficiently relevant to mention. In the course of my further readings, I came across two books which were – in content, tone and method, if not so much in style – distinctly similar to *God, Actually*. I found myself in agreement with the authors on almost everything, a rare experience for me. Both books were written by men in middle age, of cerebral bent. The goal of each, as I discerned it, was to explain Christianity in a holistic, rational way to the educated lay reader.

The more recent of the two books is well-known: *The Reason for God: Belief in an Age of Skepticism* (Dutton, 2008) by Timothy Keller. It was published in the US in February 2008, almost simultaneously with my completion of *God, Actually*. I now know that Rev. Keller is a prominent and eminent figure in American Christian circles, but I must confess not to having heard of him until mid-2008. But reading his book was like finding a kindred spirit.

The second book resonated even more strongly with me. A copy was lent to me by the father of a close friend. Very few people will have heard of it, but it deserves to be read. Written by an eminent Australian, Sir Warwick O. Fairfax, and published in 1965 by Godfrey Bles of London, it bears the somewhat grandiose title *The Triple Abyss: Towards a Modern Synthesis*. Sir Warwick's evident aim was the same as mine: to synthesise his knowledge of the world, derived from all sources on all subjects, and to reconcile that evidence with the existence of the Christian God, as revealed by and explored in Scripture. (Sir Warwick, unlike me, was also strongly influenced by Hinduism. He died in 1987.)

From a personal point of view, it is quite weird that Fairfax should have been the author of this book and, in many ways, such a kindred spirit. For almost 150 years, his family owned and ran *The Sydney Morning Herald*, Australia's oldest newspaper, and the one I have read almost every weekday and every Saturday of my life since the age of seven or eight. My father began his career in journalism at the Herald in 1951, and worked there continuously until 1970. Dad remembers Sir Warwick Fairfax clearly. Dad also remembers that, while working in the mid-1960s at the *Herald*'s London office in Fleet Street, he was directed from 'on high' to collate copies of any and all reviews of *The Triple Abyss* in the English press.

When reading Fairfax's book, and Keller's too, I was struck by the frequency with which the author framed issues and/or reached conclusions in almost precisely the same way that I had. Time and again, after reading a particular passage, I found myself smiling in quizzical astonishment. I have had the same sensation when reading other books, including the Bible itself: most of the authors of Scripture did not collaborate, or know each other; the Old Testament authors were, of course, entirely ignorant of what the New Testament authors would write. Yet their exegesis is *consistent*.

John D. Barrow is a contemporary British science-writer, and another of my favourite authors. In *New Theories of Everything* (Oxford University Press, 2007), he makes this astute observation about the difference between mathematics and the creative arts:

> Mathematics exhibits simultaneous discovery, whereas the arts do not; indeed, intuitively, we might feel that they cannot. Independent mathematicians working in different cultures, feeling different motivations, using different notations and methods, often produce the same final discoveries or 'theorems'. Such coincidences do not happen in literature or in music. The independent recovery of *Macbeth* or a Beethoven symphony would be inconceivable, because … [t]heir uniqueness is a reflection of the uniqueness of the individual.

Is theology properly to be regarded as a science or an artform? Clearly enough, it is a hybrid; but I have come to believe that in one key respect it closely resembles a science. Independent thinkers – such as Keller, Fairfax and me – scrutinised much of the same evidence, pondered many of the same problems, and arrived at essentially the same conclusions. Not merely in some general way ('Yes, there is a God!') but in many detailed particulars as well. Obviously, the analogy is not exact. For one thing, there is no way of empirically proving that the three of us are right. We may all be totally wrong. But I believe that possibility is unlikely.

Why? For the reason Barrow gives as regards the phenomenon of 'simultaneous discovery':

> The fact that simultaneous discovery occurs in mathematics, as well as the sciences, points towards some objective element within their subject matter that is *independent of the investigator*. (My emphasis)

In other words: if God really does exist, and if Jesus really was divine, then they are objective facts about the Universe. One would expect them to be discoverable by minds grappling conscientiously with the relevant questions.

Sydney, April 2009

PREFACE

The advantage of knowledge is this:
that wisdom preserves the life of its possessor.

Ecclesiastes 7:12

The liberally educated person is one who is able to resist the easy and preferred answers, not because he is obstinate but because he knows others worthy of consideration.

Allan Bloom, *The Closing of the American Mind*

In the first decade of the twenty-first century there has been an upsurge in public discussion of the 'religion question'. This phenomenon has occurred throughout the Western world, and many factors have contributed to it. 9/11 and other jihadist atrocities, the 'war on terror', the invasions of Afghanistan and Iraq, natural disasters such as the 2004 Boxing Day tsunami, the looming threat of climate change – all these have generated widespread existential angst. But a number of other, quite disparate influences have also been at play, including – in the West – unprecedented material affluence coupled with worsening inequality. In 2008, the 'Global Financial Crisis' came upon us, adding more fuel to the fire.

In this fraught and unsettled atmosphere, popular 'debate' about religion has tended to be conducted by zealots and opportunists on all sides – posturing politicians, commercially motivated proselytisers, radical atheists, and high-profile 'leaders' of the main faiths. The resultant discourse has left many ordinary citizens angry and confused, or – worse – indifferent and uninformed. Not nearly enough light has been shed on the underlying theological issues, which remain fascinating and vital. The questions 'Is there a God?' and 'What does God expect of me?' are the most important questions of all. Grappling with them is, or should be, what religion is *actually* about.

Deep down, most people understand this – even people who live in overwhelmingly secular countries such as Australia. The key issues are rarely done justice here by our mainstream electronic and print media, and they are scarcely taught at all in our public schools. Since those are the two sources from which most Australians derive their knowledge of the world, it is not surprising that apathy about matters spiritual runs deep. Nowadays you are unlikely to know much about Christianity unless you were instructed in it by your parents or sent to a church school. And yet, according to public opinion surveys, a large majority of Australians still profess to believe in God. In the 2006 Census, only 18.7 per cent of people classified themselves as having 'no religion'.

What these surveys are truly measuring is, I suspect, a state of uncertainty. A good many Australians must realise at some level that they do not know enough about Christianity, or any religion, to dismiss the notion of a deity out of hand; and they are reluctant to profess atheism. Many such people might sense instinctively that they *ought* to learn more about this most seminal of subjects – but they do not want to go to church to do it, and most choose to stay away. That circumstance gives rise to a big practical problem: ignorance, even among those who are otherwise well-educated.

In many ways I am a most unlikely person to write a book defending Christianity. A decade ago the idea would have struck me as preposterous.

I was born in 1963 and grew up on the North Shore of Sydney. Religion was not a subject much discussed in our family home. My parents were, and are, virtuous people – ethical, compassionate and learned – but they have never been practising Christians. Even so, they saw to it that I was baptised as an Anglican, and sent me to Sunday school as a young child. At the age of ten or eleven, at the urging of a school friend, I attended a Bible study group. As a teenager I went occasionally to church services with my grandmother, whose own father, my great-grandfather, was a Presbyterian minister.

But none of these experiences made any enduring impression upon me, at least not noticeably at the time. My boyhood was sheltered and contented. I went to a state primary school and a state high school, experiences for which in many ways I remain extremely grateful. However, there was one huge gap in my education. The few 'Scripture' classes at school were taught by hapless outsiders, most of them elderly women. No doubt they were doing their best in a tough situation, but their efforts were generally regarded as a joke – by our regular teachers no less than most of the students. I can recall feeling rather sorry for them, and also for the rare kids who were identified as 'religious types'. My preoccupations at school were study, sport and girls, in roughly equal measure.

At university in the early 1980s I learnt about many things, but theology was not one of them. When the subject sometimes came up it was evident that many of my fellow students, whether churchgoers or not, knew much more than I did about the doctrines and customs of the Christian religion. Among these people was the vivacious young woman who became my wife. She had been to a private church school, and regarded my ignorance as surprising. But even then, my spiritual curiosity was not much aroused. For whatever reason, my thirst for knowledge about other things did not then extend to religion.

The position remained much the same for another decade. My twenties were years of discovery of the world, but not of myself. After getting married and starting work as a lawyer – events that occurred almost simultaneously for me at the age of twenty-three – many things changed. Marriage in those early years was joyful and exciting, and legal practice at a large Sydney firm of solicitors was challenging and frenetic. I knew little about the real world when I started out. Cooking a meal, buying a house, running a file for a paying client who was relying on me – almost everything was new, and each day required energy and concentration. Life was variously stressful, fun, and enlightening. But my mindset remained relentlessly secular.

By the time I turned thirty, I imagined that I knew a good deal about the world – enough to appreciate the practical wisdom of the basic moral teachings laid down in the Bible. In fact, my knowledge of those teachings (and to a lesser extent of the world) remained awfully superficial. In any case, most of the time I did not think in those terms. I was a disinterested sceptic when it came to God and the afterlife. To the limited extent that my thoughts turned in that direction, the notion of faith in a supernatural power struck me then as outmoded, even somewhat absurd. I suppose that like a great many people living today in Western countries such as Australia – people who by the standards of human history are healthy, well-educated, law-abiding and, above all, stupendously affluent – the serious practice of any religion seemed irrelevant to my daily life. I was an agnostic leaning towards atheism.

The turning point in my spiritual life was the birth of our first child. We named her Hope. Quite suddenly the world seemed a different place, and I seemed in myself a rather different person. Reason no longer gripped me so strongly. I became more emotional (at least in my own heart), more attuned to the power of love, and both more critical of and more thankful for the world around me. This change did not immediately manifest itself in an interest in theology. That came a few years later, when my wife and I decided to send Hope to Sunday school. We fronted up one morning at the local Presbyterian church – St Luke's at Roseville – and were welcomed warmly. The church's policy was to frown upon parents who did not themselves stay for the morning service and, like the conformist I then was, I complied. I now thank God that I did.

The path towards belief has been slow and fitful. At first, during those early services, I was aware of little more than a disconcerting sense that there were, after all, some serious questions at stake. Occasionally, something in particular would resonate. I remember becoming interested in a sermon about Ruth – the story was just so touching – and I remember a number of times picking up a Bible in the pew, opening it at random, and becoming engrossed.

Gradually, what began to strike me was the Bible's relevance to 'everyday' issues. My interest at first was not predominantly in the bigger questions but in the smaller ones: what, for example, Jesus had said about lawsuits, what St Paul had said about marriage. My curiosity was whetted. I began to read books about theology and books about science. I began to connect up much of what I was learning about those subjects with my pre-existing knowledge about the world. Certain things said or done by people close to me, who I knew were believers, began to assume significance.

Even now, I sometimes wonder whether I am yet quite there. At least, my frequently recurring doubts and insecurities remain such that, when I hear accounts of the steadfast faith of others, it is hard to accept that my own state of mind merits the description 'belief'.

Nor can I honestly say that my faith is often a source of joy. It is, however, consistently a source of wonderment. It is also – as it seems to have been for the Old Testament author of Ecclesiastes – a source of solace. But just as often my belief is a source of uneasiness, even of fear: as the truth as I see it becomes clearer, I am reminded ever more forcefully of my own unworthiness and of the great responsibilities that any Christian faces. Bertrand Russell, perhaps the most famous agnostic of the mid-twentieth century, once contended that '[r]eligion is based … primarily and mainly upon fear'.[1] He exaggerated, but he was not wholly wrong.

My own current position might best be summed up by Julia Flyte's reply (in Evelyn Waugh's *Brideshead Revisited*) to Ryder's hopeful question: 'You do know at heart that it's all bosh don't you?' To which she answered: 'How I wish it was!'[2]

At all events, my belief is real. Some years ago it became a part of me. And once that happened, there began to weigh upon my conscience a compulsion to get absolutely clear in my own head the reasons why I believed in Christianity. I felt it was necessary to undertake that exercise before I would be in a position to explain those reasons cogently to others. I was anxious to begin doing so because of the responsibility I felt – and still feel – to the people I love most. For the Bible suggests that you must seek God 'while he may be found' (Isaiah 55:6); in other words, before it is too late.

Engagement in the process of trying to explain the reasons for your own belief is also of immense benefit to the believer himself. It is one thing to be aware of emotions and ideas stored somewhere in the recesses of your own mind. It is quite another to examine them systematically and truthfully and then to try to articulate them to others. To do so in a spirit of seriousness and sincerity is to force yourself truly to *think*. There can never be any guarantee that your arguments will convince others, but the chances of doing so will be much improved if you have put some work into their preparation and genuinely believe them yourself. Earnest fishers of men can be attractive bait.

Originally, I did not set out to write a book for publication. But I knew that the best way to hone my deductions would be to attempt to write them down. My original effort began as little more than an essay to myself. Over the course of months, and then years, I kept adding to and tinkering with the manuscript. It happened in fits and starts. Eventually I had written so much that the idea of turning it into a book began to take hold.

Everyone is a product of their upbringing. During the process of writing down my ideas I became increasingly conscious that my faith had developed via a strange route. My education, as I have indicated, was almost exclusively secular-humanist rather than overtly religious; my taste in the arts was, and still is, strongly biased toward the worldly. Even my secular education was far from rounded. I did not develop any serious interest in science until well into adulthood, though it then became a rich source of fascination.

Yet despite or even *because* of these influences, I had come to the Christian faith. It occurred to me that people with similar backgrounds to mine might relate to a discussion of Christianity written by someone like them.

Of course, there is a huge amount of Christian and other religious literature. It seems, however, that few Australians are much interested in seeking it out. One reason for that is the shortage of books written for today's open-minded agnostic, let alone the convinced or half-convinced atheist. Most contemporary Christian books are aimed at the converted, assume a lot of biblical knowledge on the part of the reader, and rely principally on citations from Scripture. Very few tackle the central issues of theology by reference to current *secular* thinking about science, politics, the arts and society.

These considerations may partly explain the recent commercial success of a number of well-written books advocating atheism, such as *The God Delusion* by Richard Dawkins. It is as if many smart people with a pre-disposition to mock Christianity knew in the back of their minds that they had never engaged with the issues, conscientiously or at all. Here was a book that purported to do the job for them. Better yet, it showed that the whole 'religion thing' is bogus. Having read the book and confirmed their prejudices, some people may have felt they could put the whole subject out of their minds. Once upon a time I would likely have bought and read *The God Delusion* myself for just that purpose.

Perhaps naively, I hope that my book may appeal to a previously untapped readership. But it is to be stressed that what follows is an explanation of the reasons for *my own* personal hope. I do not pretend to cover all of the possible arguments 'for' or 'against' Christianity, or any religion. I am frankly unacquainted with a good deal of theological learning. My purpose is to attempt to explain the matters that, for me, have been and still are decisive.

The insights of a number of Christian and non-Christian authors have assisted me greatly, and in many places I will refer to them. The same two dozen or so names recur quite frequently: C.S. Lewis, Martin Luther King, Paul Davies, John D. Barrow, D.A. Carson, Mary Eberstadt, Herbert Butterfield, Frank Morison, Marcus Braybrooke, A.N. Wilson, Garry Wills, Richard Dawkins, Andre Comte-Sponville, Jim Wallis, G.N. Stanton, John Polkinghorne, Warwick Fairfax, Paul Johnson, John Dickson, Alister McGrath, Jack Miles, Robert Winston, Timothy Keller, Christopher Hitchens, M. Scott Peck, Lee Strobel, Joachim Kahl, G. Campbell Morgan and John Shelby Spong. Some of them are long dead. Of those who are still alive, some are famous, some are not; each would disagree strongly with the others on at least a few issues, and in some cases on almost all issues. But I have found each person's work extremely useful. In any event, through accident or design, or God's grace, these are the authors who have informed my religious consciousness.

But religious inspiration cannot be derived solely from the written word. Experience and memory play a big part too. Accordingly, I will refer to certain incidents in my own life that made an impression upon me at the time or which, looking back, have assumed significance.

I will also refer to political causes that are important to me, and past and present political leaders whom I admire. Politics has been a lifelong interest, inspired initially by my father. Dad had the honour of working as press secretary to E.G. (Gough) Whitlam, the Labor prime minister of Australia from 1972–75. For the last thirty years he has advised numerous premiers and senior government ministers in Australia's largest state, New South Wales. Dad's influence upon me has been enormous, and for most of my life left-wing politics were the prism through which I saw the world. Especially in its early stages, my developing belief in Christianity coincided with a belated but life-changing realisation: some of the socio-political principles that I held most passionately were to be found elucidated with the greatest eloquence in the Bible – in particular, in the Gospels.

This came as a surprise to me. It ought not to have, of course, but I was still then in the grip of hopelessly shallow views about religion. Now, I look at politics through the prism of Christianity. Principally for this reason, while deploring some of its recent manifestations, I welcome the increasing emphasis upon 'values-based' politics. As commentators such as John Ralston Saul have observed, the West's narrow obsession with economics in the last generation or so has contributed significantly to the coarsening of political discourse and the mediocrity of politicians.

I refer to numerous works of art, especially novels, poetry and films. Joseph Haydn wrote that he composed music so that 'the weary and worn, or the man burdened with affairs, may enjoy a few moments of solace and refreshment'.[3] So, often, has it been for me, with all of the arts. They are a refuge from the world, but also – the written word, in particular – the principal medium through which my knowledge of the world has been acquired. Many ideas that are central to my religious belief are conveyed in or by works of art far more lucidly than I can express them myself. Moreover, I share Noam Chomsky's sentiment that 'we will always learn more about human life and personality from novels than from scientific psychology'.[4]

Inevitably, my legal background has also been a strong influence. Lawyers trained in the Anglo/American legal system are expected to think in a certain way. The emphasis is not upon being creative or open-minded but upon being analytical and partisan, and this sort of training ingrains in lawyers certain skills and attitudes.

I am a fairly typical product of that training. In writing this book, and more generally in contemplating Christianity, some lawyerly skills and attitudes have been useful. Indeed, there is a noble tradition in theological writing of the 'legal apologetic', especially as regards certain issues that lend themselves to a diacritical kind of analysis: Darwinism, the reliability of the Gospels as historical documents, and the evidence for Jesus's physical Resurrection, to name three. The tradition of the legal apologetic can be traced back to such historical giants as Hugo Grotius (*On the Truth of the Christian Religion* [1645]) and Simon Greenleaf (*An Examination of the Testimony of the Four Evangelists* [1846]),[5] and even to Paul himself, who was a rabbinic lawyer of evident skill.

On the other hand, the legal approach has its limitations. The modern lawyer's inclination toward scepticism can easily turn into cynicism, and this tendency must constantly be fought against. My principal aim in this book is to encourage readers to refrain from cynicism and to engage in serious, tolerant thinking.

If anything in this book causes just one person to begin to think more closely or more clearly about even one issue, then it will have served a valuable purpose. My hope, though, is that many readers will be persuaded that the likelihood of the Christian God's existence lies well above 50 per cent on what Richard Dawkins has called the 'spectrum of probabilities'.[6] At least, some might reassess the all-too-common attitude that Christianity is a refuge for charlatans, killjoys and well-meaning dopes, and is certainly not something for 'sophisticated people'.[7] In fact, the more sophisticated you think you are, the more carefully you may need to consider it.

A DEDUCTIVE APPROACH TO CHRISTIANITY

We accept man's testimony, but God's testimony is greater because it is the testimony of God.

1 John 5:9

If we could solve all the mysteries of the Universe, we would be co-equal with God. Every drop of ocean shares its glory but is not the ocean.

Mohandas K. Gandhi

This book is intended for people who are in any of the following states of mind about Christianity.

- You know next to nothing about it, and cannot imagine how it could be relevant to contemporary life.
- You resent being told what you should and should not do by a bunch of moralists and fuddy-duddies. The presumptuousness is absurd; civilisation has gone past all that. So long as others do not harm you, you will not harm them. You just want to make your way in the world and enjoy yourself.
- You cannot understand how any intelligent person could fall for such nonsense. It is largely fable and superstition, long discredited by modern science. And all the different religions contradict each other. Believers of every stripe are 'the victims of fraud'.[1]
- You regard Christianity – indeed religion in general – as a malign and dangerous force.

It has always held back human progress. Any God who would permit such dreadful suffering as occurs in the world must be repudiated. Religion provides an excuse for human beings to do nothing to alleviate suffering in the here and now.

- You have some respect for the more liberal churches, but in the main you associate Christianity with right-wing politics. It seems to be a belief system that helps keep many odious and reactionary governments in power. Being of the Left yourself, you do not want a bar of it.
- You can admire some – though certainly not all – of the ethical teaching in the New Testament. Jesus was evidently a fine person, but nothing more. The Old Testament is utterly outdated and often incomprehensible.
- You sense that something is lacking in your life, and would like to be able to believe in God. Sometimes you think that you might already sense His presence. But for whatever reason, you cannot get any further than that.
- You incline to the view that there is a higher force than Man, but remain sceptical about many of the claims of Christianity. In particular, you struggle with Creationism, the idea of miracles, the afterlife, and the divinity of Jesus. These issues are too hard to fathom, so you are inclined to let them go as 'unknowable'.
- You would call yourself a Christian, but it is not a major part of your life. In fact, on reflection, you really do not know a great deal about Christianity, or any religion. You would like to learn more and to try to develop a stronger, more meaningful faith, but you just never seem to get around to it.
- You are a Christian, and your faith is important to you, but even so you have never taken the time to analyse rigorously why you believe what you do. Nor could you honestly say that you have tried to obey the seminal injunction of St Peter, who urged that every believer must 'always be prepared to give an answer to everyone who asks you to give the reason for the hope that you have' (1 Peter 3:15). You are content to leave that job to the churches, or at any rate to people more eloquent and knowledgeable than you.

At various stages of my life I have held one or more of these views in some combination, so I can empathise with anyone who is currently of a like mind. Nevertheless, I have come firmly to the belief that Christianity is *true*. To varying degrees, each of the states of mind set out in my list is the product of confused, lazy or wishful thinking.

Any decision that you make about Christianity should be informed. This book is not a comprehensive treatment of the subject; indeed, people more schooled than me in Christian theology may find much of it rather elementary, even heretical. But I hope that for some readers the book will provide a useful starting point for further investigation. At the least, I hope to challenge the increasingly fashionable idea that 'most religious claims … are not so much false as incoherent'.[2]

The nature of faith: do not expect a cast-iron 'answer'
The attempt to explain one's belief has been made by many millions of Christians during the last 2,000 years, among them theologians of remarkable eloquence, erudition and wisdom. Yet no believer has ever come close to succeeding fully in the attempt, if

'success' is to be measured by the effect of the believer's explanation upon his or her contemporaries, and the human race in general. Of course, countless people have been guided to faith by the spoken and written words of others. But countless other people have *not* been persuaded and – a fact that must be confronted – countless people have never been exposed to any explanation at all.

Certainly, no believer has ever proffered an explanation that is irrefutable. The famous attempts to construct logical proofs of the existence of God – those advanced by St Thomas Aquinas, St Anselm of Canterbury, Georg Hegel and others – are fascinating and valuable. Indeed, some of the arguments advanced in this book are variations on their themes. But none of these proofs hold up in any *definitive* way. Aquinas was well aware of the fact: he called his proofs viae – paths or roads – 'by following which a believer might arrive at some sense of transcendent presence'.[3]

The challenge of giving an irrefutable explanation of God is, literally, impossible. As I conceive it, the task is not merely extremely difficult yet theoretically achievable, like counting the number of grains of sand on a beach. Rather, it just cannot be done; and its very impossibility is a fundamental concomitant of God's Creation, and of the uniquely simple but simultaneously intricate nature of Christian belief. It could not be any other way. If anyone were ever capable of articulating the basis for their personal belief so persuasively that anyone hearing the explanation would *necessarily* also be convinced, and thus believe, then there would be no such thing as Christianity, or any religion. Yet more fundamentally, everyday life as we all experience it simply could not be. One of the arguments I will make in this book is that the world 'works' as well as it does only because, in almost all things, there is an element of uncertainty involved. Religion is no exception to that principle; indeed, it may be the best and most important example of the principle in action.

In the Acts of the Apostles, St Paul's efforts to preach to the people of Rome are movingly described. On one occasion:

> [T]hey came in even larger numbers to the place where he was staying. From morning till evening he explained and declared to them the Kingdom of God and tried to convince them about Jesus from the Law of Moses and the Prophets. Some were convinced by what he said, but others would not believe.
>
> (Acts 28:23–24)

So even St Paul, at the height of his powers, had only mixed success.

It is significant that St Peter, Christ's chosen apostle, spoke in terms of the duty to explain one's own 'hope'. In this choice of words, St Peter recognised implicitly that even the most ardent believer can vouch only for his or her own state of mind. That state of mind may, for that individual, rise to the level of complete certainty; indeed, one definition of faith is 'being sure of what we hope for and certain of what we do not see' (Hebrews 11:1). But faith would not be faith if the basis for it were capable of unanswerable demonstration; it would be mere knowledge.

Faith is a much more challenging thing and – for that reason – correspondingly more precious if it is attained. This truth must have been appreciated by St Peter. He had witnessed the occasions of disbelief of the Disciples themselves, and he knew intimately of his own.

Jesus of Nazareth articulated this idea profoundly. Of all Jesus's aphorisms, one of the most resonant is that towards the end of John's Gospel, in the passage recording His appearance before Thomas after the Crucifixion: 'Because you have seen me, you have believed; blessed are those who have not seen and yet have believed' (John 20:29).

The key point, as I now understand it, is that those who require definitive proof of Christianity as a precondition to taking it seriously are missing the key point. The greatest benefits of religion come to those who genuinely do not need such proof, but who are prepared to open their hearts and minds to the ineffable. St Paul grasped this vital concept, and expressed himself with his usual candour:

> For God in his wisdom made it *impossible* for people to know him by means of their own wisdom. Instead, by means of the so-called 'foolish' message we preach, God decided to save those who believe.
>
> (1 Corinthians 1:21–22; GNB. My emphasis)

The version of this passage in the Good News Bible comes closest to capturing the essence of what St Paul was saying. His basic point was that there is a critical difference between the knowledge of God of which Man is capable – which is both limited and finite – and faith. Faith cannot be attained solely by a process of reasoning: there is an extra step involved, which is subtle and personal. Soren Kierkegaard, the great Danish philosopher, famously called it 'The Leap'. To those who have not taken that leap, faith can seem incomprehensible or foolish – even downright evil, like Abraham's putative sacrifice of Isaac. Faith can also seem arrogant: some outspoken religious people give the impression of claiming 'to know *everything*'.[4] That is unfortunate when it happens, because such an attitude is not typical of most believers. Speaking for myself, faith began to come when I realised how very little I knew about anything, compared with what there is to know.

In the end a Christian must 'live by faith, not by sight' (2 Corinthians 5:7). But that does not mean that faith is blind. True faith begins with knowledge: it is only when we understand something of the world around us, and something of the conscience residing inside us, that it is possible to begin to arrive at an informed opinion about how those things came to be. As W.H. Griffith-Thomas, an early twentieth-century theologian, once insisted, faith 'commences with the conviction of the mind based on adequate evidence'.[5]

The metaphorical passage in Genesis in which Adam and Eve disobey God and eat the fruit of the tree of knowledge is not, as some atheists would have it, a 'ban on intelligence'.[6] It is a warning against hubris. The earnest Christian must try, within the limits of his or her capabilities, to grapple with life's many mysteries. And in the course of that exercise the utmost intellectual rigour should be employed.

God's existence cannot be demonstrated conclusively, but believers should still do their best to try. There is one passage in Richard Dawkins' *The God Delusion* with which I completely agree. Dawkins comments on the strict agnosticism of T.H. Huxley, the nineteenth-century English scientist:

> [H]uxley, in his concentration upon the absolute impossibility of proving or disproving God, seems to have been ignoring the shading of *probability*. The fact that we can neither prove nor disprove the existence of something does not put existence and non-existence on an even footing … God's existence or non-existence is a scientific fact about the universe, discoverable in principle if not in practice.[7]

This is good, vigorous stuff – and as relevant for believers as for unbelievers. The ultimate issue is not whether Christianity is a good or a bad influence on individuals or society, but whether – on the probabilities – it is true. One of the most useful things that any believer can do for others is to try to convey, as lucidly and as vividly as possible, his or her own insights as to the likely truth. Those insights may seem unexceptional or unoriginal. But the believer can, and should, hope that someone of like mind, situation or temperament may find in them something of merit – perhaps even of inspiration.

The primary emphasis of any evangelist should, I think, be upon the basal *supernatural* claims which undergird their faith. Like the contemporary American scientist Steven Weinberg, a Nobel Prize winner for physics, 'I wonder how long religion can last without a core of belief in the supernatural, when it isn't about anything external to human beings.'[8] That 'core' is crucial; without it, you are left with a hotch-potch of philosophy, psychology, sociology, history and politics. Of course, those subjects are important, just as science is important: it is essential that you be able, in good conscience, to bring *all* of your knowledge into 'harmony' with your faith.[9] But for the purposes of evangelism, supernatural bait will attract the most fish.

The evangelist must be careful not to overreach. Dawkins is right that it is a matter of asking people fairly to assess the probabilities. It is rarely if ever desirable to claim that your beliefs are immutable, or unimpeachable, as though you were presenting strict proof of a mathematical equation. St Peter was careful to note the importance of proffering your explanation gently and respectfully, or, as it is put in the King James Version, 'with meekness and fear'. Interestingly, the same injunction appears in the Qur'an. Muslims must 'bear with patience what [non-believers] say' and 'deal gently with [them]' (*sura* 73:10, 86:17).[10]

In short, dogmatism must be avoided. Dogmatism, a manifestation of pride, is a sin perpetrated all too often by religious advocates of every faith. In general, it is counter-productive; it tends to alienate people by belittling their own doubts and insecurities; further, it tends to cause people to try to justify their own disbelief, rather than to encourage them to question it. Dogmatism by believers thus discourages many people from pursuing, or even from beginning, their own personal search for spiritual enlightenment.

Albert Schweitzer remarked of Jesus's methods of teaching:

> He does not think dogmatically. He formulates no doctrine. He is far from judging any man's belief by reference to any standard of dogmatic correctness. Nowhere does he demand of his hearers that they shall sacrifice thinking to believing.[11]

Jesus, in fact, usually took the opposite approach. He preferred to employ what Kierkegaard called 'indirect communication'. He told parables, and allowed His listeners to draw their own conclusions.

Mine is a deductive approach to Christianity. I reject the fashionable notion that 'faith of … the sort that can stand up at least for a while in confrontation with reason … is now plainly impossible.'[12] I want to encourage people to gather the relevant evidence and – ignoring preconceived notions and prejudices in either direction – truly think through all of its implications. That is how Christianity got started. When the Apostles began to preach in Jerusalem seven weeks after the Crucifixion, and at all times subsequently, their appeal 'was not to the emotions but to the intellect'. They presented the evidence and challenged 'the minds and judgments of their hearers'.[13]

That said, it is necessary to be precise about what 'reason' actually is. For a start, it is not an absolute virtue. Moreover, I do not believe that reason can be detached from emotion. As Warwick Fairfax observed, the notion of entirely disinterested reason is a myth, because it ignores or conceals 'two contingent or hypothetical considerations'. First, someone must want to know the particular conclusion which is sought. Second, someone must care that the conclusion be true.[14] Presumably, Richard Dawkins and other atheists would not bother writing books about God's non-existence unless they cared deeply, even passionately, about the issues.

I will admit to those emotions myself. Even so, I will also strive not to be excessively dogmatic, because dogmatism is an ineffective method of evangelism. But dogmatism should be regarded suspiciously for an even more basic reason. Christian belief – and life itself – is predicated at many levels upon the existence of some degree of doubt, some element of uncertainty or unpredictability. I reject the idea that 'in the sphere of theology, doubt is acknowledged only as a challenge that has to be overcome'.[15] Doubt should not merely be candidly acknowledged, it should be respected, and doubt's important place in God's Creation should be analysed carefully. It should also be acknowledged on both sides that '[a]ll doubts, however skeptical and cynical they may seem, are really a set of alternate beliefs'.[16] As Timothy Keller has pointed out, an atheist is making a leap of faith too: he or she 'is betting his or her life that no God exists who will hold you accountable for your beliefs and behaviour if you didn't feel the need for him'[17].

In *The God Delusion*, Richard Dawkins derides the notion expounded by British theologian Richard Swinburne that too much evidence of God's existence 'might not be good for us'. 'Read it again,' Dawkins insists incredulously.[18] But despite his supercilious tone, it is Dawkins who fails to recognise the profundity of Swinburne's point. If Man knew with 100 per cent certainty that God exists, free will would be replaced by fearful and slavish obedience to our perception of God's wishes, and atheists' legitimate concerns about the dangers of theocracy[19] would soon be realised. On the other hand, if Man knew with 100 per cent certainty that God does *not* exist, life would truly become the survival of the fittest. Think about both of those scenarios for a while.

Either way, Man might cope. But the world would be very different, and I believe those differences would mostly be for the worse. It may not be overstating things to say that 'it would be a disaster – would be the very work of Beelzebub – for God's existence to be proved'[20]. Or, I would add, disproved.

The same point applies not merely to evidence of God's existence or non-existence, but to evidence of how the world works. Too much knowledge would transform everything. If Man understood every aspect of every natural process, every cause and effect, then the future would be entirely predictable. Man would become co-equal with God.

Dawkins' attitude is, though, a common one. Why doesn't God just make Himself obvious to everyone? It would be an easy thing for God to do, if He exists, and would put paid to all fancy theological arguments. The fact that God does *not* blatantly reveal Himself is treated as proof that God cannot exist. But my view is that the opposite is closer to the truth, and it is reassuring that Jesus of Nazareth addressed the point directly. When once asked by a group of supercilious sceptics to produce an unimpeachable 'sign' of His divinity, He answered as follows: 'How evil and godless are the people of this day!' (Matthew 12:39 (GNB)). There was another adjective which He might have used – lazy. Rightly, Jesus resisted the temptation to make things too easy.[21]

I have begun with these observations because grasping a central concept – the futility of any search for demonstrable and certain proof of Christianity – did not come easily to me. The strange paradox is that when eventually I did understand *and accept* the concept, belief in God did not become harder but easier. Elsewhere in this book I will try to explore this notion further, as regards such key issues as the timing of Jesus's life on Earth, the Resurrection, the nature and incidence of human suffering, and the existence or otherwise of the afterlife.

It is never too late, or too politically incorrect, to start thinking about God

Another popular misconception is that there reaches a point in your life when it is too late to start 'bothering with religion', if you have not been steeped in it since childhood or, at least, since your young adult years. Some people seem to regard 'late' conversions as bizarre, even hypocritical. Those on the Left of politics are especially likely to take that view.

There are advantages as well as disadvantages in coming to religious belief in an unconventional way later in life. Some of those who are raised from birth as practising Christians may experience throughout their lives a sense of comfort – of moral certainty – that is wonderfully reassuring. But others whose beliefs as children were perhaps never thoroughly thought through – because they were more the product of habit or parental expectation – often seem to drift away from religion when they enter adulthood, or even earlier, as they begin to confront the harsh realities of the world. Those who are converted, not in spite of but because of their experience of those realities, may, at least sometimes, be surer in their faith.

Another possible disadvantage of coming to faith too early is the risk of being indoctrinated in a one-dimensional version of the Christian religion, that discourages searching and ongoing appraisal of your beliefs. It is human nature to cling to reassuring 'certainties', religious or otherwise. But Christianity is anything but an easy set of doctrines – easy truly to live by or easy to categorise in worldly political terms. As someone who has come relatively late to the faith, I am frequently surprised, and sometimes appalled, by the wide disparity between fact and fiction. The wise principles espoused by Jesus in the Gospels bear but a passing resemblance to the hollow caricatures of Christianity portrayed in the secular media and advocated by some denominations of the Church itself. There is a fascinating gulf between what C.S. Lewis called 'mere' Christianity – the real thing – and certain contemporary images of it. The very existence of that gulf seems to me highly suggestive: the fact that Christ's lessons do not conform to any commonly professed or commonly practised worldview (at least in the West) indicate to me their universal rightness.

The more I come to understand the faith, the more wrong it seems that either the Right or the Left of politics should try to claim exclusive 'ownership' of it. In recent decades the Right has made by far the more concerted attempt to do so, and it is encouraging that the Left, especially in the United States, has begun to make an effort to engage in religious discourse. Indeed, in early 2009, there are good grounds for thinking that '[w]e have now entered the post-Religious Right era'[22]. This is a welcome development, not because the Religious Right is wrong about everything (far from it), but because any attempt to target 'religious' voters poses a fundamental problem for both sides of politics. Some of the causes most fervently espoused by each are quite antithetical to any fair-minded interpretation of Scripture – a theme I will explore in Chapter 8.

There is another unhelpful notion that many people hold today, especially tertiary-educated professionals. It is an idea that, even if there is a slim prospect of Christianity being true, it would be necessary to do a lot of work in order to understand it properly and to faithfully practise its tenets. That much, these people assume, is surely a prerequisite to qualify for any God's 'approval': it cannot be enough just to 'believe' in God or in Jesus. A related notion is that the only 'religious' people who might be worth listening to are those with impressive academic or ecclesiastical credentials. Your average God-botherer is most likely an ignorant airhead.

It is certainly true that there is a vast body of theological and other learning devoted to Christianity. But you do not become a Christian in the same way that you become a doctor or a lawyer or an architect. Likewise, in my view, to be an effective evangelist you do not need to be 'qualified' in Christianity in the same way that a university lecturer must be qualified in his or her field of study.

Consider the implications of the following passage:

We must deprecate the idea that God has been so unjust as to locate himself at the end of a long course of academic study … God is not so unloving, so unjust, as to have weighed faith in favour of intellectuals … After all, if the Christian faith is true, we are not in the kind of world in which men have to grope their private way to truth through darkness.[23]

The author's ultimate point must be right, but I would express the argument somewhat differently. No one should be discouraged from embarking upon a long course of study of the literature of Christianity, or of other religions. For *some* kinds of people – I include myself – that may well be a possible way to faith. Jesus said that God's house has many mansions: if Christianity is true, then there must necessarily be places in that house for every sort of person, including those of cerebral bent. But if Christianity is true then the intellectual way to God certainly cannot be the *only* way, or even an especially common way, because even in today's relatively literate world most people do not have the opportunity, let alone the capacity, to take it. To be valid, Christianity must be accessible to people in the most ordinary and the most desperate of human circumstances.

As Erasmus put it back in 1516, did Christ teach such complex doctrines that only a handful of theologians can hope to attain salvation? Certainly not: faith 'does not require a mighty intellect'[24]. On the other hand, Christ's doctrines, if valid, must also be explicable to the most searching of questioners. But if you choose to ask a lot of questions you should not expect the whole truth to be simple. As Warwick Fairfax observed: 'There is nothing simple about [Einstein's theory of] relativity or other explanations of the material universe; why should the spiritual side be simple?'[25]

In short, it may be right that 'the vast majority of religious people are not religious because they have rational grounds for their belief'[26], in the sense of having come to faith by a process of careful reasoning. Most people's reasons are 'much more likely to be intuitive, instinctive, visceral, emotional' or 'the product of indoctrination, upbringing or environment'[27]. However, that does not mean that belief in God is irrational. Most people believe that the woman they know as their mother gave birth to them. Although that belief is usually held unthinkingly – and must invariably be based on trust – it is neither irrational nor (at least in most cases) any the less true. We are entitled in many things to rely on our hearts as well as our minds.

The same principles apply to Christian evangelism. If Christianity is true, then it strikes me as unthinkable that only those formally trained or published in theological matters should be considered qualified to advance their views. To the contrary, each and every person's reasons for believing are worth considering, however humble the believer's circumstances, and every believer should in any case make the effort to explain them. St Peter's injunction that *every* believer should be ready with an answer is the epitome of egalitarianism. St Peter assumed that any believer might have something worthwhile to say, at least to the ears of someone.

This was not only fair, but far-sighted. The basic truths of Christianity must be universal or they are worth little. However, any given *explanation* of Christianity may be more or less influential, depending upon the circumstances in which the explanation is given. An explanation that may resonate with, say, an affluent fifty-five-year-old doctor in the eastern suburbs of Sydney may be all but meaningless to an impoverished twenty-year-old rice-farmer in rural Thailand – and vice versa. It is surely horses for courses.

Of course, some people's reasons may lack any logical credence, and it may be sensible to accord special deference to the views of a cardinal or an archbishop. But nobody's reasons should be ignored, just as nobody's reasons should be regarded as infallible.

Reading the Bible

The Bible is *the* primary source for anyone interested in Christianity, and therein lies a problem.

Even in its contemporary translations, the Bible's form, language and tone are quite unfamiliar to most modern readers. Where once the Bible was seen 'as a social, economic, and political text', and as having established rather than followed literary trends[28], the position in 2009 is quite different. Nowadays people are used to assimilating news and other 'public' information from television, radio, movies and the Internet. A shrinking number of people read novels, works of non-fiction, newspapers and magazines. At work people read emails, letters, memoranda, reports, briefing papers and (in some cases) scholarly articles pertinent to their field of expertise.

Lawyers also read legislation, textbooks and court judgments; and they read and draft countless legal documents. One thing that any good lawyer must be able to do is to organise his or her thoughts in a clear and logical way – or, at least, in a way that *appears* clear and logical to a client, an adversary or a court. One thus develops a tendency to compartmentalise ideas, in order to present them in a form that is convenient to the reader or listener, even if the various ideas are, in truth, complex, diffuse, and interconnected. This tendency is not unique to lawyers: increasingly, in the Western world, many forms of oral and written communication are so presented.

The Bible is not presented in that way. As a result it is a hard book to read for many uninitiated people, including (perhaps especially) those who are tertiary-educated. Unfortunately, man-made intellectual systems 'can be a screen between oneself and reality'[29]. Many people today approach the Bible as though it is, or should be, an instructional textbook in the modern style, and not surprisingly they are bored, baffled or disappointed by it. Some take a kind of weary offense at the unflinching tone which is sustained throughout. As a contemporary American intellectual, Jack Miles, has astutely observed: '[The Bible] is morally serious to the virtual exclusion of charm'.[30] Although not often remarked upon, I believe that these factors have contributed significantly to the waning of the Christian faith in many Western countries. It is not so much that the *concerns* of the Bible appear irrelevant to many people; rather, even among people who wish to grapple with those concerns, the Bible is not a simple and convenient starting point for doing so. Not only are its form and style unfamiliar, and its tone confronting. Let it be said frankly: a good deal of the writing in the Bible is of pedestrian quality, especially in those parts of the Old Testament that were probably composed in committee by professional scribes.[31] In between the sublime poetry and captivating narratives there are many dull lists and formulaic recitations of dogma.

For these and other reasons, the Bible is not read as much as it should be. Many people, if they read serious books at all, are rather more likely to read and digest a recent critique of Christianity than the Bible itself. Furthermore, even if an unbeliever does start to read the Bible, he or she will employ all of their modern-day training and sensibility. This tends immediately to cause problems, especially if the reader starts with the book of Genesis. A lot of 'sophisticated' people today cannot get past the story of Adam and Eve.

How is this problem to be solved? One suggestion is that secular people should be encouraged to read and appreciate the Bible purely as literature. Jack Miles has written two engrossing books in which the Old and the New Testaments are analysed in this way.[32] By adopting Miles' approach, the reader need not constantly be asking himself whether a particular passage of Scripture, or the Bible as a whole, is consistent with 'extra-textual' evidence. He can proceed 'in serene indifference to all that religious commentary has made of it'[33] and respond to the text as a self-contained work, in the same way he would a play or a novel. That experience may well, but need not, lead to spiritual insights.

This approach may work for some, but I doubt it would have worked for me. It is not the approach I will take in this book. Art, of which fictional literature is but one form, has always had a role to play in religion. Some objective truths – be they historical, theological, even scientific – can be conveyed effectively by imagery, allusion or other literary devices. But none can be tested that way. Ultimately what most people want to know is whether the central claims of Christianity as laid down in the Bible – and especially in the New Testament – are true. As I see things, that requires the Bible to be assessed, to the extent reasonably possible, for its historical and other factual correctness, including 'its reliability as a testimony to ancient events'.[34]

The Bible was written by scores of people over the course of well over a thousand years; roughly, from 1300 BC to 150 AD.[35] In essence, 'it describes the growth of the monotheistic faith of the Jews sequentially'[36]. It recounts certain seminal events in Jewish history, and represents the accumulated wisdom of centuries. But every passage in it was written in a certain context, and each author had his or her own purposes. It also helps to remember that every version of the Bible we read today is a *translation*. The ancient Jewish scriptures which became the Old Testament were originally written in two languages, Hebrew and Aramaic. Even before the time of Christ they had already been translated into Greek, with a number of original Greek insertions – a massive exercise reputedly understaken by a team of some 72 scholars.[37] The New Testament was written almost entirely in Greek, which was 'the international language' of the first century.[38]

Today, most of us read the Bible in the current 'international language', English – or in Spanish, or German, or French, or Korean, or Chinese. Indeed, the Bible is now available in some 2,200 languages.[39] That is an amazing thing in itself, and perhaps the best possible evidence of the obdurate appeal of the Christian religion. Moreover, there are strong grounds for confidence that most modern translations of the Bible are of high quality, and faithful to the original texts. The Hebrew Scriptures were meticulously copied, generation after generation, for centuries before Christ; and, after His death, every effort was made to pass down both the Old *and* the New Testament texts with scrupulous accuracy.[40] Nevertheless, the process of transmitting and translating any text written in an ancient language cannot possibly be an exact science. And in the case of the Bible, there are additional complications, arising from the fact that many of its translators down the ages were required to heed the wishes of the secular or ecclesiastical leaders of their time.[41]

There is a charming and sensible book called *The Bible and the Common Reader*, written in 1946 by the American novelist Mary Ellen Chase. It helped me greatly in learning how to approach the Bible. Perhaps the simplest but most important point which Chase made was that the Bible contains many different kinds of writing: stories, fables, proverbs, prophecy, allegory, typology, song, poetry, treaties, history, biography, autobiography, law, letters and theology. To read any passage from the Bible intelligently you must have some idea which genre it belongs to. You do not read Aesop's fables in the same way as a contemporary history of the Vietnam War. You do not read the poems of T.S. Eliot in the same way as an email from your colleague at work. The same principle applies to the Bible: 'we learn God's message through finding out what [its] human writers meant'.[42]

The Bible's many authors and translators were, I now believe, divinely inspired. At least a few of them may have been conscious of the fact. But, whatever their state(s) of mind in that respect, it is indisputable that their *methods* differed hugely. Granted they were inspired: how did they each go about articulating the substance of that inspiration? Divine revelation in its basic form is verbal, and 'thus of necessity propositional; God reveals Himself by *telling* us about Himself'.[43] But even *God's* words must be read, interpreted and mulled over by individual human beings. That is the very nature of language.

I have come to believe that the Bible is 'wholly reliable in its own terms, making no false assertions, claims or promises on its own account'.[44] In short, Scripture can be trusted as 'God-breathed' (2 Timothy 3:16). I take this expression to mean that God noted and approved all of *the words* chosen by the Bible's human authors (cf. 2 Peter 1:21), and that those authors were utterly sincere.[45] However, I prefer not to employ either of the terms which are often employed to convey these concepts – 'inerrant' and 'infallible'. They are too often invoked by modern-day biblical literalists to justify what are, in fact, uninformed and/or unhistorical propositions.[46]

A good number of sincere Christians fall into the trap. Inadvertently, they do the Christian religion a huge disservice, in two ways. First, unwittingly or not, they disparage the faith of the majority of believers who, to a greater or lesser extent, cannot accept interpretations of Scripture that fly in the face of contemporary knowledge of the world. The ratio of the circumference of a circle to its diameter is pi, not 3:1 (cf. 1 Kings 7:23–6; 2 Chronicles 4:2–5). Obscurantism – consciously 'shutting one's eyes to God's facts', in the name of fidelity to Scripture – is a sin.[47] As St Augustine observed, writing way back in the early fourth century, obscurantism is counter-productive: '[T]he people outside the household of the faith think our sacred writers held such opinions, and ... the writers of our Scripture are criticised and rejected as unlearned men'.[48] The dangers of obscurantism were also recognised by Origen of Caesarea, another intellectual giant of the early church. Origen stressed to his students that the Scriptures often had to be read allegorically, and preferably in conjunction with the best human teachings of philosophy, dialectics, science and ethics.[49]

Second, and perhaps more important, literalism trivialises religion. It allows agnostics and atheists an easy way out of tackling the most important questions. The Disciples themselves fell victim occasionally to dull-witted literalism (see, e.g., Luke 22:35–8). Many people today seem to think that dismissing Christianity is as simple as denying that Man has lived on the Earth since the sixth day after its creation (cf. Genesis 1:26–31) or as simple as asserting (with a smirk) that people nowadays should not be executed for blasphemy (cf. Leviticus 24:16). Eloquent atheist authors such as Christopher Hitchens and Sam Harris have utilised this approach cleverly. But people like Hitchens and Harris make the same mistake as the fundamentalists, only in reverse. They throw the baby out with the bathwater. Just as I once did.

There are certain parts of the Bible that must be read literally, even though they contain quite amazing assertions, because clearly enough they were written with that intention. But there are many other parts that cannot be read literally, or which admit of more than one possible interpretation. Sometimes it is genuinely unclear which genre of writing a particular passage belongs to.[50] I would include in this category a number of verses in the New Testament dealing with Heaven and Hell.

Sometimes the Bible's authors were concerned with metaphysical concepts that are not capable of definitive expression in human language. Jesus's exchange with Nicodemus in Chapter 3 of John's Gospel is a clever exposition of the dangers of literalism in such a context. Sometimes a biblical passage contains allegory, simile or metaphor. For example, in order to make a point to some of his fellow apostles, St Paul once invoked the Law of Moses: 'Do not muzzle an ox while it is treading out the grain,' he implored them. He then asked them rhetorically, in an indignant tone that always makes me chuckle: 'Is it about oxen that God is concerned? Surely he says this for us, doesn't he?' (1 Corinthians 9:9–10).

There is another reason why literalism is misguided. The Bible is full of references to ancient customs, rituals, and social practices that are no more valid as 'universal truths' than are our own customs, rituals and social practices today. Bearing this in mind should enhance rather than detract from your reading of the Bible. Those parts that were intended by their authors to be understood literally or as conveying universal truths are all the more compelling when they are distinguished from other parts that are more allusive in style or that merely set the scene.

But reading the Bible well is not only a matter of informing yourself about what sort of book you are reading. It also requires a certain state of mind. Jesus told his followers that they should be child-like: 'I tell you the truth, anyone who will not receive the kingdom of God like a little child will never enter it' (Mark 10:15).

Jesus surely did not mean that, in contemplating religious claims, we should abandon our adult intelligence and our reason. Such an attitude would have been quite contrary to Judaic teaching: 'Fools despise wisdom and discipline,' declared Solomon (Proverbs 1:7). To this day, Orthodox Jews take the view that every word of the Torah (the first five books of the Old Testament) is holy, but that it is a person's *duty* 'to interpret the text … to turn it and turn it again, to examine nuances, to reflect on various shades of meaning'[51]. I take the same view as regards the whole of the Bible. What Jesus meant when He urged people to be childlike was that we should approach religion with an inquiring mind. Furthermore, we should do so with an overriding attitude of open-mindedness, and of wonderment, rather than of cynicism. That is how children the world over learn from their parents and their teachers. That is how St Paul asked that his message be received (cf. 2 Corinthians 6:11–13). In the forthright words of J.I. Packer, 'the Bible … does not reveal its secrets to the irreverent and censorious'.[52]

To put it another way, in a lawyer's terms: you should give God the benefit of the doubt. This may sound trite, but I have found it most helpful to approach all issues in that spirit, requiring the case against God to be proved beyond a reasonable doubt. I am now quite convinced that it cannot be done; indeed, I agree with Mary Eberstadt that 'three centuries of debunking, scepticism, criticism, revolution, and scorn … by secularists not only have failed to defeat religious belief, but have actually enhanced its self-defense'[53]. But, equally, the case *for* God cannot be proved irrefutably either. And my suggestion is this: try to assume that God means it to be that way. If you take that suggestion as a working hypothesis, then many, many things could begin to fall into place; in particular the words of the Bible may begin to make more sense.

But before being able to give God the benefit of the doubt, and then to read the Bible in that spirit, many people may first find it necessary to do some serious preliminary thinking. Unorthodox as it may sound, the Bible for most unbelieving people today is probably not the best place to start. The genius of the Bible – its extraordinary depth, beauty, subtlety and richness – is likely to be better appreciated once you have read other far less challenging books and listened with care to the views of other believers and unbelievers. Certainly, that has been my own experience.

I would also suggest that, when you do turn to the Bible, you should start with a modern translation. In this book I have cited from the New International Version, except when I have formed the view that a different version more clearly conveys the essence of a particular passage. I have adopted this approach for reasons of pragmatism. For many people, myself included, the King James Version is the most beautiful and the most profound translation of the Bible that there is[54], and it has certainly been the most influential in terms of shaping human history. But it is also a product of its time (1604–11). Move on to it when you have grasped the guts of an issue from a more accessible source.

Please 'pick the eyes' from this book

All readers should be as selective as they please. Each individual comes to faith via a unique set of influences.

Walt Whitman wrote:

Logic and sermons never convince;
The damp of the night drives deeper into my soul.[55]

In trying to come to grips with Christianity, it is frequently the little, unexpected things that impress the most. Thus, an incident in your life suddenly remembered when a vast amount has been forgotten; an intriguing new fact that connects in your mind with something else; a rhapsodic piece of music; a dappled sunset; a pithy passage from the Bible that conveys a deep truth – these are the kind of things that have tended to strike me most forcibly in a 'religious' sense, and to start me thinking about the ultimate questions. On the other hand, you may sit through long sermons or read whole books without gaining any new insight.

In other words, a gradual understanding of the whole may well be more likely to come in fits and starts, from a variety of sources and personal epiphanies, rather than 'in one hit'. Eventually, some time after making a conscious decision to try to reach God, you become convinced. This is one of the key beliefs of the Quakers.

My own journey toward belief might be compared with solving a difficult cryptic crossword puzzle. At first, the task can appear formidable, even impossible. You may lack the urge even to try. The hardest part is getting started. However, once you have solved even a few clues, the whole exercise begins to get easier. Because everything in the puzzle is interconnected, a clue solved in one place gives you a lead to solving a number of other clues. Your mind begins to think in the right way, which is not the normal way of the world. At the same time, it is essential to call upon all of your stored knowledge of the world: every place you have visited, every person you have met, every experience you have had, every fact you have learned. You begin to surprise yourself, and your enthusiasm to complete the puzzle is heightened as more and more of it makes sense. Some clues may remain stubbornly hard to solve, but by then you will be extremely reluctant to give up. You will know that you have solved most of the puzzle, and you will have faith that, given enough effort or some further inspiration, it is only a matter of time before everything is clear.

In this book I will identify the matters that have been particularly influential for me. However, it may well be that some, or most, or all, of the matters that have gradually persuaded me will not impress others. So be it: that certainly does not discredit Christianity; nor does it discredit my own explanation of my hope, because that is personal to me. But I would urge any reader impressed by even one point in this book to concentrate on that point, and to consider its implications fully. If you think about that single point hard enough, you may find that it is like completing the first clue in the crossword puzzle, and achieving that may enable you to move on to and solve other clues that previously seemed impenetrable.

On the other hand, if and to the extent that any of my points do not assist, put them aside. You may find, as I did, that you will eventually be inspired to come back to them when other matters have become clearer. And do not feel constrained to start at

Chapter 1, which is quite technical – especially if there are subjects in other chapters that hold greater immediate interest for you. But I would urge you to return later to any chapter that you initially might skip.

Three stages to faith

This book is divided into three parts.

Part One is an examination of certain fundamental features of our world that, to me, suggest the existence of God. They are: the scientific laws underlying the physical Universe, and in particular life on Earth (Chapter 1); the unique properties of the human mind – cognition and conscience (Chapter 2); and love (Chapter 3). My central thesis is that these phenomena cannot have come into being by accident, and that it is insufficient simply to say that they 'are as they are'. God is the best explanation; and in using the term 'God' I am happy to adopt the conventional definition insisted upon by Richard Dawkins: 'a supernatural creator that is … appropriate for us to worship'[56]. In Chapter 4, I tackle various arguments that are often raised against the existence of such a Designing God, and religion in general.

Part Two is about the central figure of Christianity, Jesus of Nazareth. Chapter 5 covers certain aspects of His life and His death. I try to explain why I believe (literally) in the Incarnation, including the reality of at least some of the miracles, and how I understand the significance of the Crucifixion. Chapter 6 is devoted to the Resurrection, which I am now convinced was a real historical event – the most important of all time.

Part Three seeks to address certain issues frequently raised by atheists and other sceptics of religion. For a long time, many of these issues were stumbling blocks to my own faith. Gradually, if with difficulty, I overcame them. In Chapter 7, I deal with what may be the hardest issue, the existence of suffering. Chapter 8 examines the oft-assumed association between Christianity and right-wing politics, a huge turn-off for many people of the Left. My own view is that Christianity is more left-wing than right-wing in emphasis, but that ultimately it defies any such labelling. Chapter 9 is a discussion of other religions, and the 'problem' of reconciling them with Christianity. Chapter 10 is about the afterlife: the factors that persuade me it is a reality, and my conceptions of Heaven and Hell.

There is, of course, a significant degree of overlap between each of these issues and each of the others (like the clues in my crossword puzzle). In places I will remark upon that overlap. Further, my attempts to refute certain common arguments against religion – including some of those made by the likes of Richard Dawkins, Christopher Hitchens and Sam Harris – are not confined to Part Three. Some are addressed earlier in the book as, logically, they arise from the subject matter under discussion. For example, it is frequently asserted by atheists that religion 'wholly misrepresents the origins of man and the cosmos'[57]. Science now fully explains these issues, it is said, so there is no need to invoke God.[58] A milder version of the argument is that 'between science and religion there is, if not an incompatability, [then] at least … a tension'[59] Because these claims run counter to one of my central reasons for belief – the ordered complexity of the physical Universe – I address them in Chapter 1.

Throughout the book I have used quotations from the Bible to try to explain my thinking. I have done so even in the first four chapters, which do not relate specifically to Christianity, either because those passages were formative in my own journey toward belief or because they express an idea much better than I can in my own words. Another of my aims is to explain and contextualise these passages for the sceptical reader. I would urge you to have a Bible by your side when reading this book, so that you can check the cross-references to those biblical passages which I have not quoted verbatim.

Finally, it is only right to acknowledge that already in this introduction I have assumed such things as the existence of God and the divinity of Jesus Christ. I have not, I hope, already conveyed a tone of superiority or presumptuousness – a fault frequently to be detected in a lot of theological writing. I am quite aware that my task in this book is to try to convince the reader of the probable but not certain truth of those very things.

PART ONE

REASONS TO BELIEVE IN GOD

CHAPTER 1

THE PHYSICAL UNIVERSE

You alone are the Lord. You made the heavens, even the highest heavens, and all their starry host, the earth and all that is on it, the seas and all that is in them. You give life to everything, and the multitudes of heaven worship you.

Nehemiah 9:6

Order is Heaven's first law.

Alexander Pope

The Universe exists. That brute fact of itself – banal when written down, but astounding when truly pondered – is one of the keys to my belief in God. It seems the logical starting point for serious theological enquiry.

Broadly speaking, there are two issues to consider. The first is the *how* of existence. How did the Universe begin? How did it get to its present state? How does it work? In this sphere of discourse, which will be the focus of this chapter, science has a major – but not exclusive – role to play. Learning about science has been crucial in my path *toward* Christianity.

The second aspect of this enquiry is the why of the Universe. In this sphere of discourse, science has only a peripheral role. This is pre-eminently the realm of theology and philosophy. Much of the rest of my book is an attempt to come to terms with the 'why' side of things.

This dichotomy – between the 'how' and the 'why' of the Universe – seems to me a critical one to recognise. That is why I have laid stress upon it at the outset. When atheists like Richard Dawkins make large claims about the ambit of scientific knowledge, they can be talking – *at most* – about the 'how' of the Universe, not the 'why'.

Often, even their claims about the 'how' are exaggerated. In general, these exaggerations fall into two categories. The first is the presentation of inference and opinion as scientific 'fact'. In *Letter to a Christian Nation*, Sam Harris declares bluntly that 'Nature offers no compelling evidence for an intelligent designer'[1]. That is an opinion, not a fact. There is a lot of evidence capable of leading a reasonable person to the very opposite opinion. Speaking for myself, the more I read of physics, chemistry and biology, the more strongly I believe in God. The discoveries of science – and especially the more recent discoveries – point towards, rather than away from, God's existence. The Universe is just too extraordinary to be a unique and happy accident.

Of course, this is an ancient debate. It has been pointed out many times that there are dangers in inferring the existence of God (i.e. a supernatural, intelligent 'Designer') by reliance upon the apparent design of things in Nature. Over the ages many people have sought to refute the argument from Design, even though it has moved Man to religious belief since the beginning of recorded history. The finest minds of ancient Greece grappled with this conundrum, and there were then, just as there are now, brilliant minds on each side of the theological fence. Anaxagoras, Emphedocles, Socrates, Plato, Epicurus, Aristotle, Zeno – all of them, from about the fifth century BC onwards, put in their ten cents' worth.[2]

Today's New Atheists contend that, whatever the situation may have been in the past, the argument from Design has now been refuted – definitively – by modern science. But, to put things charitably, they overstate their case. The Design argument is still available, and – as I shall try to demonstrate – it may well be stronger than ever. This may surprise readers who have, until now, been exposed to only one side of this debate. As Sir Antony Flew has written, Richard Dawkins' worst sin as an academic is his consistent tendency to distort or ignore both counter-evidence and counter-arguments. Too often, Dawkins and his supporters present the theistic case in its weakest forms, the opposite of sound intellectual practice.[3]

There is a second way that atheists exaggerate their 'scientific' case. Sometimes, they will assert that science explains the 'how' of a given process more fully than it really does, or they treat scientific theories that are at best descriptive of a given process as explanatory of it.[4] More often, in areas of acknowledged uncertainty, they assert with total confidence that science will in future come up with complete answers. It is just a matter of time, they say, because there are no truly unsolvable mysteries anymore. This is faith in another guise.

My own emerging belief is that science as understood and articulated by Man will never explain everything – or anything like it. But I suspect that many laypeople in the West think otherwise, consciously or unconsciously. It would be understandable if they did, because much of what they read, see and hear in the secular media is predicated on the assumption that 'religion is now completely superseded by science'[5]. That assumption is false, but it is indisputable that science has made astonishing advances in recent times, and that a few of those discoveries have undermined orthodox religious teachings. Famously, the development of the Darwinian theory of evolution is blamed for the general decline of religious faith in the Western world since the mid-nineteenth century. I will come to Darwin presently, but in some ways that whole subject strikes me as less important, or at any rate no more important, than a number of others. In my view, Darwinism is a prime example of a little knowledge being a dangerous thing – for experts as much as laymen.

In this chapter I will examine four issues, all of which have obvious theological implications. They are:

- the origin of the Universe
- the organised complexity of the Universe
- the origin of life on Earth
- the organised complexity of life on Earth

Many people may be surprised to learn that science is nowhere near providing an explanation of the first and third of these issues. Science has gone some way to explaining the second and fourth, but there are still many, many mysteries inherent in both. As regards all four issues, science has revealed some astonishing things. But none of these discoveries disprove the existence of God. Far from it. To the contrary, as I will argue, at least some of the natural phenomena disclosed by modern science are strongly suggestive of a Designer.

Setting the parameters

I do not want sceptical readers to put aside my book at this early stage, so before going further it is as well to state clearly the parameters of the discussion that follows. Some Christians will strongly disagree with what I have to say, but I would ask them to persist also.

First, I do *not* believe that the Universe as we see it today was created in six days, i.e. over a period of 144 Earth hours. Nor do I believe that the Earth is only a few thousand years old or that Man, i.e. the species *Homo sapiens*, has lived on the Earth since its formation.

As far as the age of the Universe is concerned, I see no reason to quibble with the best estimate of modern cosmologists, 13.7 billion years. Measurements of the wavelengths of light from distant galaxies prove that all galaxies are moving away from us at speeds directly proportional to their distance from us (Hubble's law). What is more, all the galaxies are moving away from each other. At some finite moment in the past, then, the whole Universe must have been compressed at a single point – a so-called 'singularity', with no radius and infinite density. If scientists have correctly measured the current rate of the Universe's expansion, and the distance from us of the furthest galaxies, then the calculation of the Universe's time of origin is relatively straightforward. In any event, the exact figure is not terribly important. Let us say it was certainly more than ten billion years ago.[6]

As far as the history of the Earth is concerned, I also see no reason to doubt the views of the vast majority of scientists. It is hard to see how the fossil record and the results of radiocarbon dating* can be explained away. I cannot accept the somewhat desperate suggestion that God must have made the Earth with 'apparent age'. This theory was first proposed in the nineteenth century by one Philip Gosse, and it is still mooted today by some 'young Earth' Creationists. The theory holds that the entire Universe came into existence just a few thousand years ago 'with all its complex features ready-made, but bearing all the features of having already existed for millennia'. In short, God has made the Universe appear old, in order to test the faith of modern Man.[7]

It seems to have been proved beyond reasonable doubt that the Earth is about 4.55 billion years old, and that it existed for several hundreds of millions of years before the emergence of life. Single-celled organisms (prokaryotes) have lived on the Earth for about 3.85 billion years. The first multi-celled organisms (eukaryotes) appeared about one billion years ago. There was a sudden 'explosion' of complex life some 545 million years ago, during the so-called Cambrian era. Countless species of plants and animals followed, before the appearance of the hunter/gatherer species *Homo sapiens* about 200,000 years ago.[8] It was not until about 9000–8000 BC, following the end of the last Ice Age, that 'modern Man' emerged. It was only then that our species began to harvest crops, keep domesticated animals and congregate in larger settlements. These key developments led to others, such as time-keeping and the invention of writing. The first truly complex societies seem to have been the city-states of Mesopotamia, which were founded around 3000 BC[9], though there were not insubstantial settlements much earlier than that.

It follows that certain passages in the book of Genesis cannot be read literally on all points of detail. To do so is to fall into the trap of dogmatism; it is too easy for

---

* In brief, Man can estimate the age of an object if it contains a measurable amount of a certain radioactive substance: carbon-14 and/or potassium-40 in the case of once-living objects; uranium, potassium and/or strontium in the case of inanimate objects, such as rocks. Each of these substances 'decays' over time, at a fixed rate. For example, it takes 5,730 years for *half* of a given sample of carbon-14 to decay into nitrogen. The half-life of uranium is 704 million years (it decays into lead) and the half-life of potassium-40 is 1.3 billion years. Other substances do not decay over time – for example, 'normal' carbon, otherwise known as carbon-12. This is what makes radiocarbon dating possible. In the case of a relatively 'young' once-living object, say of less than 60,000 years, its age can be determined by ascertaining the ratio of the amount of carbon-14 to carbon-12, and comparing it with the ratio of carbon-14 to carbon-12 in an equivalent-sized living object. See David S. Kidder and Noah D. Oppenheim (eds), *The Know-It-All Book: 365 Steps To Being Very Clever Indeed*, Hodder & Stoughton (2007), p.116; Francis Collins, *The Language of God*, Free Press (2007), pp. 88–9.

both blinkered Christians and blinkered atheists to sidestep the real mysteries inherent in this controversy, rather than to ponder them with care. It is neither necessary nor desirable for Christians to defend 'young Earth' theories; and atheists do not disprove the existence of God by erecting such flimsy arguments as straw men to be demolished. The questions underlying the 'how' of Creation are much more profound than either camp allows, though, that said, I believe 'young Earth' Christians are much closer than atheists to the *ultimate* truth. In the end, it is a secondary consideration whether God created the Universe 6,000 years ago[10] or 13.7 billion years ago. The core issue is whether or not the Universe was created by a supernatural Being.

Genesis remains one of the most important books of the Bible. It deals metaphorically with these deep and vital issues, and points the way to the truth. The great Jewish theologian Moses Maimonides expressed this view way back in the twelfth century[11] – as, much earlier still, had St. Augustine – and it should not be an especially difficult concept to grasp today. Christians should not feel guilty if, consciensciously, they feel compelled to accept strong scientific evidence for the Big Bang, an ancient Earth, and/or the basics of Darwinism. Nor need they resort to a strained semi-literal reading of Genesis. I agree with 'young Earth' advocates to this extent: the so-called 'gap' and 'day-age' theories are extremely unconvincing.[12]

The first three chapters of Genesis must be read as *poetry*, (just like the equivalent sections in the Zend-Avesta and the Upanishads, which are unequestionably symbolic and which pre-date Genesis by many centuries.[13] In the modern jargon, Genesis lays down a 'literary framework' for contemplating Creation: '[it] is not describing what happened but is establishing an intimate theological connection between the created world and the creative power that underlies it'.[14] Hard scientific evidence of that 'creative power' may be discerned, in my opinion, from a number of sources.

The origin of the Universe
Ludwig Wittgenstein wrote: 'Not *how* the world is, is the mystical, but *that* it is.'[15] Wittgenstein thus identified the cardinal fact of the Universe: there is something rather than nothing. And that fact gives rise to a basic question: How did something (the Universe) come from nothing? This is surely among the most important questions of all. The traditional religious answer is that nothing is caused by itself; every effect has a prior cause. The Universe itself must have been brought into existence by something, and that 'First Cause' is what is called God.

Many an atheist declares blithely at this point in the argument that the Big Bang theory now explains everything![16] But the Big Bang theory does not purport to explain the initial moment of Creation, the 'how' or the 'why'. It deals with what happened *after* the initial moment of Creation, albeit in its unimaginably early phases.[17] The theory does, however, postulate two things of fundamental importance, each of which is strikingly consistent with the existence of a supernatural Designer and with the account of Creation in Genesis.

First, the Universe had a finite beginning. *Something came from nothing.* Specifically, what first came from nothing were the four fundamental forces of Nature: gravity, electromagnetism, and the weak and strong nuclear forces. As Paul Davies has written, 'The laws of physics [were] somehow already there, underpinning everything'[18]. It is estimated that gravity emerged first, at one ten-millionth of a trillionth of a trillionth of a trillionth of a second in the history of the Universe. The other three forces followed a similarly infinitesimal time later[19] and, together with gravity, have governed the Universe ever since.

The fundamental forces generated matter.* In the earliest micro-moments there was an enormous amount of energy. That energy was converted into heat (at one stage, a thousand trillion trillion degrees of it) and from that heat protons, neutrons and electrons were produced.[20] Shortly after, there emerged enormous quantities of helium and hydrogen, and a comparatively tiny amount of lithium.[21] As well as matter, it seems that time itself also came into being at the moment of the Big Bang – or, more precisely, space-time.

It is noteworthy that the proposition that the Universe had a finite beginning was not generally accepted as a *scientific* fact until the 1960s, when American astronomers identified the existence of 'background' radiation emanating from the Big Bang. Before this discovery, some scientists had theorised that the Universe had always existed and would always exist (the so-called 'Steady State' theory). At that time, atheists such as Bertrand Russell could sneer that '[t]here is no reason to suppose that the world had a beginning at all'. Such a notion was, he asserted, 'really due to the poverty of our [i.e. the religious] imagination'.[22]

The discovery of background radiation from the primeval Universe, and the subsequent development of the Big Bang theory, strike me as prime examples of science tending to confirm an essential claim of religion, rather than the reverse. Indeed, many scientists resisted the Big Bang theory for some time because of its unwelcome theistic implications. Apart from the conclusion that the Universe had a finite beginning, the Big Bang theory was also consistent with St Augustine's speculation many centuries earlier that the world was made *with* time and not in time.

Interestingly, also, the Big Bang theory holds that the creation of most of the matter in the Universe happened very quickly. It is estimated that 98 per cent of all of the matter that there is or will ever be was created in the first three minutes.[23] That conclusion is also broadly consistent with the description of Creation in Genesis, which suggests that God did His initial work rapidly.

There is a second key aspect of the Big Bang theory. It holds that from the very ear-

---

* There is a very strange 'chicken and egg' paradox here. Initially the four fundamental forces generated matter, yet those forces cannot operate independently of matter. They are not instantaneous, but are 'mediated' by the exchange of elementary particles between the two bodies which are in interaction. Gravity is mediated by gravitons, electromagnetism by photons, the weak nuclear force by so-called massive W or Z particles, and the strong nuclear force between quarks by the exchange of gluons. See Barrow, *New Theories of Everything*, Oxford University Press (2007), pp. 96–7.

liest moment of Creation measurable by Man, the four fundamental forces of Nature were *fixed*. Ever since, they have remained the same (or virtually so) everywhere in the Universe. Gravity is by far the weakest of the four, and it governs effectively only in the realm of large objects; in the micro-world, gravity is overwhelmed by the other three forces. In combination, the action of the four fundamental forces – acting simultaneously at both vast and microscopic levels – is sufficient to explain almost all of the things that we see around us.[24] Crucially, each of the forces diminishes in strength with increasing distance away from its source: this explains the phenomenon of 'locality', whereby events are caused primarily by 'nearby' sources rather than those on the other side of the Universe.[25] Thus is the world intelligible.

But even these four forces do not constitute the absolute bedrock of Man's understanding of the physical Universe. That honour seems to belong to the so-called 'constants' of Nature. These are the pure numbers, first postulated in the 1920s by the great British cosmologist Sir Arthur Eddington, that describe some of the most basic features of the Universe. They account for the logical consistency of physics; why, for instance, 'every electron seems to be same as every other electron'[26]. Examples of such numbers are the ratio of the masses of the proton and the electron (1/1836), the ratio of the gravitational force to the electromagnetic force between an electron and a proton (10 to the power of 40) and the number of protons in the visible Universe (10 to the power of 80).[27] Another example is the so-called fine structure constant (1/137). It describes mathematically the equilibrium in Nature that permits the existence of *all* stable entities in the Universe (from elementary particles to the largest galaxies). Insects can coexist with the Moon because there are 'stable balancing acts between competing forces of attraction and repulsion'.[28] The magic number 1/137 (sometimes described by its inverse value, 137) represents that interaction.

All of this may seem abstruse, but there is a key point of relevance. The constants of Nature – like the four fundamental forces – did not 'evolve' in the way that living organisms have evolved. They have existed at (or very near[29]) their current values *from the very beginning*.

This, then, is the position as articulated by modern science. Approximately 13.7 billion years ago, from nothing, there suddenly emerged the finely calibrated laws of physics, which have remained more or less constant ever since. The working out of those laws has produced, over eons, the magnificent phenomenon that Man now observe. Are we not entitled to conclude that, on the face of things, something extraordinary – something greater than the Universe itself – must have caused that process to begin?

John D. Barrow has described as 'worrying' the fact that modern discoveries of physics and cosmology reveal 'just refined images of rather traditional human intuitions'.[30] His use of the word 'worrying' says a great deal. Barrow resists the conclusion that such discoveries tend to support the existence of God, an attitude shared by many contemporary scientists. For instance, the proposition that the Universe had a finite beginning (i.e. came into existence a finite time ago) is not logically equivalent, they say, to the proposition that 'something came from nothing'. Their argument is that the 'came from' is meaningless, because time itself did not exist before the Big Bang.

Other scientists reject the contention that only a supernatural cause can account for the initial moment of Creation. They say that the laws of quantum physics do admit of the possibility that – in the micro-world of electrons and other subatomic particles – something can come from nothing. The moment of Creation can thus be explained as a 'quantum fluctuation'. There is a concise discussion of this line of thinking in Paul Davies' book *The Mind of God*.[31]

Quantum theory is an extraordinarily arcane branch of science, which few people claim fully to understand. Nevertheless, two things about it seem to be reasonably well established. First, to the extent that the laws of quantum physics admit of the possibility that matter can come into existence from nothing at all, there is a crucial proviso. That proviso is that the matter in question 'disappears again with sufficient haste'[32]. But the matter that came into being at the moment of the Big Bang has not disappeared; it still exists, 13.7 billion years later. Second, the laws of quantum physics primarily operate in the micro-world. (They operate in the macroworld too, but there we see only their averages.) The amount of matter that came into being at the moment of the Big Bang was not tiny but gigantic, albeit that initially it was highly compressed.

For these reasons I am unpersuaded that quantum physics provides a good explanation for the 'how' (let alone the 'why') of Creation. As Paul Davies has observed wryly, there is '[an] astonishing extrapolation involved in applying a theory of subatomic particles to the whole cosmos'.[33] In any event, it seems to me that the use of this sort of terminology ('singularity' etc.) is, from a theological perspective, beside the point. It begs the question where the laws of quantum physics themselves came from – as well as the four fundamental forces which govern the behaviour of matter, and the constants of Nature. The truth is that, as a matter of science, 'the cause of the Big Bang remains unknown even today'[34]. According to Barrow, who has investigated the matter as thoroughly as anyone: 'It may well be that we can never know how (or if) the Universe began.'[35] Thus, these issues 'will remain always partially within the realm of philosophy and theology'.[36]

The organised complexity of the Universe

As we have seen, Wittgenstein argued that 'the mystical' was to be discerned from the mere fact that there is *something*. I agree, but would not stop there. The mystical is also to be discerned from the nature, the quality, of that something.

I am what used to be called a natural theologian. When I contemplate the Universe, what seems to me most significant is its organised complexity. The Universe not merely 'is' – it is a particular kind of universe. Many of its observable workings 'can be reduced to the presence of very simple patterns, described by short formulae and small equations'[37]. Happenstance or fluke might be a barely adequate explanation for certain kinds of universes – random, featureless and dead – but not for the exquisitely ordered Universe in which we live. Consider the fact that in our Universe there are three dimensions of space and only one dimension of time. According to contemporary physicists this *one* combination, of all the many combinations theoretically available, seems to have special properties that are necessary if structures as complex as living beings are to exist.[38] That, of itself, is suggestive.

Another highly suggestive phenomenon is the process by which carbon is created. Carbon atoms are the basic building blocks of all life. Their unique chemical property is their capacity to link together to form complex molecules, such as proteins.[39] Without carbon, Man would not exist; we are all partly made of it. Yet I venture to suggest that very few people, including most unbelievers, have any idea how carbon is made and why it is that carbon is capable of being made. I was ignorant on the subject until I read John D. Barrow's fascinating book *The Constants of Nature*. Barrow's remarkably erudite explanation[40] of the process of the creation of carbon got me thinking fiercely about God.

Carbon is made inside stars. The process requires the interaction in one place of three nuclei of helium. A simultaneous triple collision of three helium nuclei is an extremely rare event in Nature, and very little carbon would exist were it not for what Barrow calls a 'finely balanced sequence of apparent coincidences'. That sequence '[makes] carbon-based life a possibility in the Universe'[41].

The first step in the process is the collision of two helium nuclei, a relatively common event. This collision produces a nucleus of beryllium. Beryllium has an unusually long atomic lifetime – much longer than helium – and this is the first crucial 'coincidence'. The beryllium nucleus exists for a sufficiently long time to make it probable that it (the beryllium nucleus) will at some point collide with a third nucleus of helium.

At that stage there is a second 'coincidence'. The combined energies of beryllium and helium (7.3667 MeV) – when boosted by the additional thermal energy existing inside a star – produce what is called a 'resonant' nuclear reaction. When this happens the nuclear reaction is much faster than usual. The critical thing is that the 'resonance' level of carbon occurs at 7.656 MeV – *exactly* the level of thermal energy produced by the interaction of beryllium and helium nuclei *inside* (but not outside!) a star. Accordingly, huge amounts of carbon are produced.

Then there is a third 'coincidence'. Some of the carbon inside the star immediately gets burned up into oxygen, because there are still many helium nuclei inside the star and the interaction of carbon and helium nuclei produces oxygen. But this reaction is *not* resonant, so only a relatively small amount of oxygen is thereby produced, and a relatively huge amount of carbon 'survives'. The amazing thing, though, is that the interaction of carbon and helium inside a star only just fails to be resonant. The oxygen nucleus is resonant at 7.1187 MeV, fractionally less than the combined energy level of carbon and helium (7.1616) when it is boosted by the thermal energy inside the star.

Contemplating these remarkable facts in 1959, the eminent English cosmologist Fred Hoyle – who had previously been an agnostic – reached this conclusion:

> I do not believe that any scientist who examined the evidence would fail to draw the
> inference that the laws of nuclear physics have been deliberately designed with regard

to the consequences they produce inside stars. If this is so, then my apparently random quirks have become part of a deep-laid scheme. If not then we are back again at a monstrous sequence of accidents.[42]

Hoyle, it should be noted, played a key role in discovering the process of carbon-creation inside stars. He correctly predicted the resonance level of the carbon nucleus *before* it was confirmed by objective experiments. Yet this brilliant man is frequently derided by atheists – some of whom are lacking any scientific qualifications – for having become 'infatuated' by the Design Argument.[43]

The reasons for Hoyle's conversion to Design still hold up today. Yet it is important to stress that the three 'coincidences' inherent in the process of carbon creation inside stars are not – even in a strict scientific sense – truly coincidences. The resonance levels of carbon and oxygen nuclei are, as John D. Barrow explains, 'a consequence of the fine structure constant and [the] strong nuclear force constant taking the values that they do with high precision'. The real 'coincidence' is that those values are – and always have been – precisely as they are:

> If they are altered from their actual values we end up with large amounts of carbon or large amounts of oxygen but never of both. A change of more than 0.4 per cent in the constants governing the strength of the strong nuclear force or more than 4 per cent in the fine structure constant would destroy almost all carbon or almost all oxygen in every star.[44]

The process whereby carbon is created inside stars is but one of many such examples of fine tuning in Nature. I will mention five others, chosen because they were important ones for me in coming to understand this phenomenon. The first two examples arise from the fact that the Universe is expanding (and has been expanding since the Big Bang).

The first remarkable thing about this phenomenon is the *rate* at which it happens – it is very delicately poised. If the expansion rate were any faster, the matter in the Universe would not have aggregated into galaxies, stars and planets; if the rate were any slower, the Universe would have collapsed back into itself within the time required for stars to have created carbon. In either case, the conditions for life would not exist. The actual expansion rate is extraordinarily close to the 'critical divide': it is the same in all directions to one part in 100,000.[45] Still more extraordinary ('quite fantastic', in Barrow's words) is that it remains so close to the divide after 13.7 billion years of expansion, since any deviation from the divide would tend to be accentuated over time.[46]

The second remarkable thing about the expansion of the Universe is its uniformity. The matter in the Universe is spread out in all directions in a virtually symmetrical way. But the symmetry is not quite exact: the Universe has just the right amount of 'lumpiness'. This, too, is crucial for life. If matter had accumulated not in the form of galaxies and stars but in larger clumps, then the Universe would soon have consisted of black holes (areas where the force of gravity is so strong as to prevent light from escaping) and planets could not have formed. On the other hand, if the accumulation of matter were any less 'lumpy', there would be no galaxies or stars.[47] Barrow observes that this trait of the Universe has always struck cosmologists as mysterious, since 'there are so many more ways to be disorderly than to be orderly that one would have expected a universe pulled out of a hat at random to be a very asymmetrical and disorderly one'.[48]

It is worth mentioning here that, in a different context, the same point has been made by Richard Dawkins himself. Referring to complex biological systems such as the eye, Dawkins wrote in 1996:

> Almost all random scramblings of the parts of the eye would fail ... There is something very special about the particular arrangement that exists. But of all particular arrangements, those that aren't useful hugely outnumber those that are. *Useful devices are improbable and need a special explanation.*[49]

Scientists have proposed a credible special explanation for the eye: Darwinian evolution. I will come to that subject shortly. For present purposes, I would simply observe that there are many basic features of the Universe which, by the same reasoning as Dawkins applied to the eye, also need a 'special explanation'. But, as we will see, scientists are unable to propose any which are even remotely credible.

A third example of fine-tuning in the Universe is the fact that gravity obeys the so-called inverse square law. Discovered by Newton, this law holds that every particle in the Universe that possesses mass attracts every other particle in the Universe that possesses mass, and does so with a force *exactly* proportional to the product of the two masses and inversely proportional to the square of the distance between them.[50] This law has operated since the earliest moments of the Universe and has an infinite range. It too is crucial to the formation of galaxies, stars and solar systems – and habitable planets, such as the Earth.

A fourth example is the existence in the Universe of *water*. Water, like carbon, is essential for life.* Water exists only because about 90 per cent of the nuclei in the Universe are hydrogen nuclei. Hydrogen exists because the repulsive force of electromagnetism was just strong enough in the primordial Universe to prevent hydrogen nuclei (protons) from colliding with each other and forming 'di-protons': if that had happened, all of the hydrogen nuclei in the Universe would have been converted into helium. The key point, again, is that di-protons only *just* failed to exist. If the strong nuclear force binding protons together were only a few percentage points stronger, the

---

* A notable property of water is the way in which it cools. Water condenses until its temperature falls to about 4 degrees Celsius but then, unlike most other liquids, it expands as it freezes. As a result, ice forms first at the top of an ocean, lake or river rather than at the bottom. And the ice does not sink. This phenomenon is crucial for survival of marine life but, despite frequent claims to the contrary, I do not think it is especially strong evidence of intelligent design. It is consistent with intelligent design (see Michael Behe, *The Edge of Evolution*, Free Press (2007), p. 208), but it is also explainable as an example of life adapting to the environment.

nuclear force would have prevailed, there would be no hydrogen, no water, no life, and (in Paul Davies' words) 'the universe would probably have gone unobserved'[51].

My final example of fine tuning in Nature is of a somewhat different character to the other four, because it relates specifically to the Earth and is not, strictly, concerned with the any of the fundamental forces of Nature. It is a natural phenomenon essential for life. It is not of itself a living thing, though some have compared it to a living thing. I refer to the Earth's atmosphere. One of the most amazing things about it is how finely balanced are its constituent parts. Nitrogen, oxygen and argon comprise some 99.95 per cent of the air that Man breathes. Yet the other 0.05 per cent is also crucial for life. The Earth's moderate and life-sustaining average temperature (14 degrees Celsius) is brought about only because of the presence in the atmosphere of three parts of carbon dioxide per 10,000. The presence of even tinier amounts of ozone is equally crucial. Ozone accounts for only ten parts in the atmosphere per one million, but, the salient point, again, is that the amounts of both carbon dioxide and ozone are just right: human beings would not exist if the proportionate amount of either gas were, to any significant extent, greater or smaller.[52] (That, of course, is why the increased level of man-made carbon dioxide and other greenhouse gases is such a serious danger to the planet.)

These examples could be multiplied many times over, and there are a number of useful and accessible books which draw them all together and explain them in greater detail. In late 2007, British octogenarian Anthony Flew caused great controversy in certain academic circles when he published *There Is a God: How the World's Most Notorious Atheist Changed His Mind*[53]. For Flew, a distinguished professional philosopher and long-time trenchant atheist, the scientific arguments I have touched upon were decisive. They convinced Flew that there is 'an intelligence that explains both its own existence and that of the world', and his book has been described as 'perhaps the handiest primer ever written on the science … of religious belief'[54].

Another highly sophisticated analysis of these issues, from a scientific standpoint, is to be found in Paul Davies' 2006 book *The Goldilocks Enigma: Why Is the Universe Just Right for Life?* Davies is not a theist, but he accepts that there are more than 30 known instances in physics and cosmology of extraordinarily precise fine-tuning.[55] The 'biggest fix' of all*, he says, relates to so-called dark energy, the anti-gravity force that permeates space. That force is almost but not completely counteracted by negative dark energy: the cancellation effect is complete to one part in ten to the 120th power. Life would not be possible if the net force were different by a single power of ten. The odds of the right value having arisen by chance are akin to tossing heads 400 times in a row.[56]

These examples of fine-tuning in the laws of Nature give rise to an obvious question. Where did the laws come from? More specifically, where did the constants of

---

* John D. Barrow's nomination for the biggest fix of all in Nature is '[t]he fact that Nature displays populations of *identical* elementary particles'. (My emphasis) All electrons in the Universe are the same, all protons are the same, all gravitons are the same, and so forth. Barrow judges this to be 'the 'fine tuning' that surpasses all others': Barrow, *New Theories of Everything*, op. cit., p. 95. See also pp. 228–9.

Nature come from? If happenstance is ruled out as just too far-fetched, what explains such organised complexity – the fact that these laws 'work' to sustain the Universe, *and only just*? Like Anthony Flew, I am driven to the view that there must be a supernatural force behind it all, the mind that set it up. Sir Isaac Newton thought so. He ascribed the 'frame' of the Universe to an 'Intelligent Mechanic' – God.[57] So did Galileo, Copernicus, Kepler, Brahe, Cuvier, Harvey, Dalton, Faraday, Kelvin, Pasteur, Maxwell, Planck and Mendel – to name just a few of the truly great scientists down the ages who were practising Christians.[58]

You will search science books in vain for a credible alternative explanation. Considering the disdain with which many scientists dismiss God, there are remarkably few explanations even attempted. Those that have been attempted are skilfully dissected by Paul Davies in *The Goldilocks Enigma*. Davies shows convincingly that none of the main non-theistic explanations survive scrutiny, and the fact that Davies is not a Christian makes his analysis the more telling.

The most common non-theistic explanation for the bio-friendliness of the Universe is that we do not live in the *only* universe. It is postulated that there are many other universes, perhaps an infinite number of them, all slightly different: the known Universe just happens to be the one that we are in. It should not surprise us that the laws of the known Universe are such as to seem tailored for our existence, because if those laws were not as they are, we would not be here to comment upon the fact.

This explanation (sometimes called the 'multiverse' theory) has the advantage of being logical. If it were true it would explain a great deal. There is, however, no tangible evidence whatsoever for the existence of any universe other than our own, and speaking for myself the suggestion that there must be many other universes smacks of glib desperation. In the words of Paul Davies:

> Invoking an infinite number of other universes just to explain the apparent contrivances of the one we see is pretty drastic, and in stark conflict with Occam's razor (according to which science should prefer explanations with the least number of assumptions). I think it's much more satisfactory from a scientific point of view to try to understand why things are the way they are in this universe and not to invent imaginary universes to do the job.[59]

And elsewhere, Davies has written:

> My conclusion is that the many-universes theory can at best explain only a limited range of features, and then only if one appends some metaphysical assumptions that seem no less extravagant than design. In the end, Occam's razor compels me to put my money on design.[60]

My money is also on design. If you reject the multiverse theory, as many eminent scientists have done[61], there looks to be no other credible naturalistic explanation for the underlying laws of the Universe – for the fact that those laws exist at all and for the fact that they seem specially calibrated to sustain life, and, in particular, human life. Atheists are fond of invoking Occam's razor for their own purposes[62], but many seem unaware of its relevance to this critical issue. Perhaps some choose to ignore it.

Paul Davies, it should be noted, has proposed another possible explanation for the Goldilocks enigma; that is, why, like Goldilocks' porridge, the Universe is 'just right' for life. The explanation is ingenious, and displays a reverence for life and the human mind. Davies suggests that the Universe may be 'self-explaining' by recourse to notions of time travel or a 'causal loop'. Under one scenario, the physical laws underlying the Universe were set in motion by highly evolved and super-advanced beings *from the future* who were (or will be?) able to use information from the distant future in order to shape the distant past. Those beings will be capable of creating a Universe fit for the evolution of beings such as them. This is an interesting idea, but personally I do not buy it – and Davies himself laments that his suggestion seems, like all the others that have been made, 'either ridiculous or hopelessly inadequate'[63].

Davies, though, lumps in God with all the other ridiculous and inadequate theories. He rejects God as the 'Great Designer' – 'unless there is already some other reason to believe in [His] existence'.[64] That, however, is a huge 'unless'. Millions of Christians believe that there *are* other reasons to believe in God – conscience, love and Jesus among them – and my purpose is to use them to build a cumulative case for God and Christianity.

But before moving to those subjects, it is instructive to examine other possible pointers to God in the physical Universe. It is a constant source of surprise to me to discover just how many such pointers there are.

The origin of life on Earth

Apart from the origin of the Universe itself, the origin of life is among the most basic theological issues. Paradoxically, I will say a lot less about this issue than many others, for the simple reason that there is a lot less that can sensibly be said. As John Horgan has pointed out, the origin of life 'is by far the weakest strut of the chassis of modern biology … It abounds with exotic scientists and exotic theories, which are never entirely abandoned or accepted, but merely go in and out of fashion'[65].

Darwinism assumes the pre-existence of life. It is concerned with the process of diversification of life *once life exists*. Darwinism is problematic enough, but the question of how any living thing came into being in the first place is, from the perspective of an atheist, much more difficult to answer. As Paul Davies has written:

> Unless life ha[s] always existed, at least one species – the first – cannot have come to exist by transmutation from another species, only by transmutation from non-living matter … Yet in the absence of a miracle, life could have originated *only* by some sort of spontaneous generation.[66]

Charles Darwin himself wrote that he had 'met with no evidence that seems in the least trustworthy, in favour of so-called Spontaneous Generation'[67]. Nearly 150 years later the evidence remains exceedingly thin, but that does not stop many contemporary Darwinists from treating the issue lightly. In *Life's Grandeur*, the late Stephen Jay Gould was content with this throwaway line: 'Life *presumably* began in primeval oceans as a result of sequential chemical reactions based on original constituents of atmospheres and oceans, and regulated by principles of physics'[68]. This from a man who, but a dozen or so pages earlier in the same book, had made this statement: 'I do confess great discomfort when I see words such as ..."presumably", attached to conclusions stated without compelling logic or evidence'[69].

Most scientists, if pressed, will acknowledge that the origin of life remains a deep mystery.[70] Even Richard Dawkins allows that it was 'an extremely improbable event', but he is content with the explanation that the Earth enjoyed 'an initial stroke of luck'[71]. Such a stroke of luck seems all the more incredible when the geological history of the Earth is taken into account. If life somehow originated on Earth without God's intervention, then the process must have happened with quite amazing speed. As earlier noted, life (in the form of single-celled prokaryotes) first appeared on Earth about 3.85 billion years ago. But the surface of the Earth did not become solid until about 3.9 billion years ago.[72] That leaves a tiny 'window' of time available for the spontaneous generation of life from non-living matter.[73]

All life on Earth is based on DNA, which contains the genetic code. DNA is like 'an instructional script, a software program, sitting in the nucleus of the cell'[74]. It is, of itself, a staggeringly complex substance. The DNA in a typical human cell contains some ten billion nucleotides[75], arranged in sequence along the rungs of the 'ladder' of the double helix. The amount of information stored in DNA is extraordinary – 'if written out in ordinary language [it] would occupy one hundred thick volumes'[76]. Some people regard the existence of DNA as the single most compelling piece of evidence for the existence of a supernatural Designer. Francis Collins, the director of the Human Genome Project, bases his faith on other grounds. Nevertheless, Collins has acknowledged that he is 'in awe of this molecule'[77] and that 'DNA ... seems an utterly improbable molecule to have "just happened"'[78]. He has dubbed DNA 'God's instruction book'[79].

The odds of DNA having spontaneously emerged by sheer accident – the random shuffling of molecules – are astronomical. They have been calculated at one in ten to the power of 40,000.[80] (To give some notion of the vastness of this number, remember that the number of protons in the visible Universe is only ten to the power of 80.) Even allowing for the estimated age of the Universe, about 13.7 billion years, and its huge size, most scientists agree that DNA could not have originated in that way anywhere in the Universe, even once. Famous comparisons have been made with the prospects of a monkey, left in a room with a typewriter, punching out the plays of Shakespeare; or a tornado blowing through a junkyard assembling a jumbo jet.

Some atheists will respond by asserting that DNA itself evolved from much less complex beginnings – 'one day, quite by accident, a molecule arose that was able to make crude copies of itself'[81], and life followed more or less inevitably from that. But the exact process is left unexplained, and there are many, many mysteries to explain.

DNA cannot replicate itself nor make proteins without the help of enzymes, which are themselves a kind of protein. And proteins cannot be synthesised without DNA. This raises a chicken and egg issue: which came first, DNA or proteins?[82] Evolutionary biologists are stumped. After decades of research by some of the most brilliant scientific minds on Earth, there is nothing near to a settled account of the origin of DNA. This was a key factor in Sir Antony Flew's 'conversion'.[83]

Blind chance seems to me a less than satisfying explanation for life's beginning. Some atheists are prepared to say that it must have happened that way. Others insist that, in time, science will find another solution. One theory is that non-living matter may itself be subject to a 'self-organising' force that eventually leads to life. The American biochemist Stuart Kauffman is one who has speculated along these lines.[84] Other theories are that life somehow emerged from beneath the surface of the Earth or from tiny crystals of clay. (Genesis 2:7, it will be recalled, says that Man was made from 'the dust of the ground'.) Still another suggestion – made by, among others, Francis Crick, the joint discoverer of DNA – is that life must have come to Earth from outer space, via meteorites ('panspermia') or as a deliberate result of alien colonisation.

Ultimately, however, these speculations remain just that – speculations. The fact remains that no one knows how life first began, and it may be that the truth will never be known. In the absence of any received and proven scientific truth I am quite prepared to believe that God intervened at some early stage in the process: in other words, that it was a miracle. Of course, this is a 'God of the gaps' argument (a notion I will discuss in Chapter 4), and I am not wedded to it. But atheists need to understand that their own case will not be 'proved' even if, eventually, scientists in a laboratory somehow contrive to create life – real, self-replicating life – from inanimate matter. This, in Warwick Fairfax's words, 'is not life coming from a lifeless world, it is life producing life'[85]. Scientists working in the twenty-first century and beyond will have a massive body of knowledge to help them. Four billion years ago, lightening bolts, lava, and pools of stagnant water were not nearly so well equipped.

I suppose it is barely possible that, one day, scientists may discover a self-replicating molecule, of a kind which could be proved to have existed on the primeval Earth, or expound some other purely physical explanation for the origin of life. Even then, I very much doubt that my belief in God would be shaken. I feel certain that any such explanation would, of itself, be astounding enough. It would necessarily be based upon the outworkings of the fundamental laws of the Universe, which must themselves – in my view – have been designed. It would not truly be an explanation based upon blind chance.

The organised complexity of life on Earth

This subject demands treatment at some length, and not only because of the heavy emphasis placed upon it by atheists such as Richard Dawkins. In some Christian circles, *anti*-Darwinism has become a sort of litmus test of sincere belief. This attitude is most regrettable, because belief in God is not inconsistent with belief in some form of Darwinian evolution; indeed, there are aspects of the process of Darwinian evolution that strongly suggest the existence of God.[86] Sir Antony Flew has gone as far as suggesting that 'if [the Design] argument is applicable to the world of physics then it must be hugely more powerful if it is applied to the immeasurably more complicated world of biology'[87].

Again, it seems best to lay out clearly the parameters of the discussion that follows.

The case for gradual evolution by natural selection *within* species, including *Homo sapiens*, appears overwhelming. Over time, a species as a whole will change in some characteristics as a result of its environment cumulatively 'selecting' those characteristics that best promote the species' survival. Individual organisms that possess an advantageous characteristic will, on average, produce more offspring than those organisms that do not possess it. The offspring so produced will pass on that advantageous characteristic to its own offspring, and so on. This process (sometimes called 'micro-evolution') convincingly explains why, say, a certain kind of horse may, over time, change into a somewhat different kind of horse. Or, to cite a famous example, known as 'industrial melanism', the colour of the wings of a particular species of moth can change from light to dark in response to altered environmental conditions.*

We then come to more controversial territory. Does Darwinian theory adequately explain the emergence of *all* complex organisms from a 'simple' primeval beginning? Mainstream Darwinism holds that all life on Earth is the result of the accumulation over eons of slight, successive, favourable variations. These variations, it is postulated, occur *randomly*, being brought about from time to time by mutations of DNA in individual organisms. Such mutations 'create' the new advantageous characteristic for which the organism's environment then 'selects'. By this process, which began over three billion years ago, one species can 'transmute', over time, into another species – such as man from ape. This is sometimes called 'macroevolution'.

I used to accept such propositions unthinkingly. But the more I have read about evolution, the more doubts I have developed about the truth of some of the wider claims that are made for it. Let me be clear: I am *not* suggesting that Darwinism is entirely bogus, the product of some kind of mass secular conspiracy. Some of my initial doubts were resolved by further reading. But I suspect that even the *scientific* truth is far more 'nuanced' than many evolutionary biologists claim it to be. In the words of two Australasian experts, there remain 'conceptual and empirical tasks [which] are daunting'[88]. Above all, I am sure that the existence or otherwise of God does not hang on the truth or falsity of macro-evolution. That debate is important, but it is not the be-all-and-end-all of theology. With that caveat, it is instructive to survey the claims and counter-claims.

---

* Soot from nearby factories discoloured the flora in which the moths lived, thereby conferring upon the previously rare dark-coloured moths a better camouflage and, thus, an advantage in evading predators; the dark-coloured moths survived and reproduced in ever-greater proportion to the total population of the species in that geographical area: see Richard Dawkins, *Climbing Mount Improbable*, Penguin Books (2006), pp. 77–8. I remember this example from science class in high school. In fact, there has been some controversy in the scientific literature even about this example: see Judith Hooper, *Of Moths and Men*, W.W. Norton & Company (2003).

Intelligent Design theory

My introduction to this burgeoning subject came a few years ago, and quite by chance. A friend lent me a copy of Phillip E. Johnson's groundbreaking 1993 book, *Darwin on Trial*[89]. I started reading it with very low expectations, but quickly became intrigued. Johnson, an American lawyer, elucidated a number of arguments against macro-evolution in clear and accessible terms. Those arguments seemed to me surprisingly cogent, so much so that I sought out and read two other seminal books on the subject: Michael Denton's *Evolution: A Theory in Crisis*[90] and Michael J. Behe's *Darwin's Black Box*[91], both first published in 1996. Denton and Behe came at the issues from the perspective of molecular biology, and they too argued their case well. I formed the opinion that Intelligent Design (ID) theory could not be dismissed out of hand. These three authors, at least, did not seem to be fundamentalist kooks.

The general idea of Intelligent Design in biological systems is not new. Perhaps its most eminent exponent before Darwin was the eighteenth-century theologian William Paley, who invoked the famous metaphor of a watch lying in a field. Anyone finding the watch – as opposed to, say, a stone – would infer, quite justifiably, that it was a contrivance: i.e. the outcome of deliberate design, rather than chance. In Paley's view, complex life forms were to be compared with watches rather than stones. Modern ID theory is a more sophisticated variation on this theme. It is an attempt to reconcile Paley's underlying premise – that organised biological complexity must, at some level, be the product of design – with the hard evidence for Darwinism.

Opponents of Intelligent Design theory in the scientific establishment dismiss it as 'pseudo-science'. They often impugn the motives and credentials of those who propound it, displaying in the process an unbecoming arrogance. Richard Dawkins in *The God Delusion* denounces Michael Behe as, in effect, a charlatan; and it is true that Behe's expert evidence was rejected in strong terms in a court case in Pennsylvania in 2005 concerning a school science curriculum. But judges are not infallible; and most of them, being human, are prone to allow their personal ideology to guide their decision-making, even if only subconsciously. In any event, one judge's view 'is not enough to decide scientific truth'[92]. In 2007, Behe published a second book, *The Edge of Evolution*[93], in which he defended his position and expanded some of his arguments. Having reviewed the critiques of Behe's work by Richard Dawkins and others[94], I am not persuaded that all Behe's arguments are done justice.

I will come to Behe's arguments presently. First, it is important to understand that not all proponents of ID are believers in God, and that not all of them agree on everything. Most accept that Darwinian processes account for variations *within* species (i.e. micro-evolution). Most contend, however, that there are limits to the amount of variation that natural selection can have produced on Earth in the finite time available, acting upon slight, successive, *random* mutations in individual organisms. Most agree that the 'time' problem is especially acute as regards species with relatively small populations and relatively slow rates of reproduction (e.g. elephants, tigers and Man, as compared to insects, bacteria and viruses).

So, most proponents of ID share certain opinions. But there are also clear points of departure among them. Proponents of ID fall into two main camps:

- Those who argue that all species cannot have descended from a common ancestor. New species must, they claim, have been deliberately designed and 'introduced' to the Earth from time to time by an intelligent agent (God, or something else).
- Those (most notably Behe) who accept that all species *did* descend from a common ancestor, by a process of natural selection acting upon slight, successive mutations of DNA. They contend, however, that not all of those mutations can have occurred *randomly*. Some of the *mutations themselves*, they insist, must have been brought about deliberately by an intelligent agent (God, or something else).

It helps clarity of thought to consider these two lines of argument separately. They are not mutually exclusive in all respects (people in the first camp are happy to adopt some of Behe's points about the limitations of random mutation), but they are significantly different.

The main arguments against common descent, as propounded by those in the first camp, may be summarised as follows.

First, Nature is full of examples of classes or groups of organisms (e.g. mammals) that are separated from all other classes or groups in fundamental ways – each is isolated from all others and unlinkable by any *existing* 'transitional' forms. Second, an argument related to the first, it is wrong to regard the similarities between different species (such as the pentadactyl limb) as evidence of a common ancestor; such similarities may only reflect the fact that there are a limited number of design solutions for a given problem. To establish a common ancestor, what is needed is proof of the existence of *workable* intermediate life forms, i.e. a pathway from one form of life to the other. Third, the fossil record contains virtually no evidence of any such 'intermediates'. Fourth, it is hard to conceive how certain 'irreducibly complex' features of existing species – such as the human eye, or a bat's radar – could have evolved gradually: take away any single component of such a feature, and it is rendered useless. An intermediate organism (say, a fish with half a 'leg') might even be at a disadvantage, not an advantage.[95] How, then, would such organisms have survived, let alone prospered and reproduced in greater numbers than then-existing species? Fifth, scientists have failed to construct such intermediates *even in theory*, using sophisticated computer models: such creatures just do not 'work'.

There are answers to each of these arguments, and I will come to those answers presently. But before doing so, it is necessary to stress again that arguments against common descent are not the be-all-and-end-all of ID theory. Far from it. The weightier arguments focus upon two specific subjects:

- the 'building block' of complex life, the cell
- the phenomenon of mutation of DNA – when and how it happens, and whether it is truly random.

These two issues are Michael Behe's specialities. They present, to my mind, the most serious complications for mainstream Darwinian theory. As I have noted, Behe falls into the second (smaller) camp of ID proponents, because he has come to accept, readily, that all species are descended from a common ancestor. '[A]ll creatures on earth are biological relatives,' he states bluntly in *The Edge of Evolution*.[96] Behe seems to be a person who is prepared to follow the evidence wherever it leads, and his two main points deserve consideration.

The cell

The cell is the base component of complex living organisms. For a long time scientists assumed that cells were no more than tiny lumps of amorphous goo. But recent discoveries of molecular biology have revealed that each and every cell is, of itself, a thing of astounding complexity, akin to a highly sophisticated machine. As Paul Davies has written, '[t]he living cell contains miniscule pumps, levers, motors, rotors, turbines, propellers, scissors and many other instruments, … all of them exquisite examples of nanotechnology'[97].

Michael Behe came to prominence in 1996 by highlighting these undoubted facts and considering their implications. He drew the conclusion that the cell exhibits telltale features of Design:

> There is an elephant in the roomful of scientists who are trying to explain the development of life. The elephant is labeled 'intelligent design'. To a person who does not feel obliged to restrict his search to unintelligent causes, the straightforward conclusion is that many biochemical systems were designed. They were designed not by the laws of nature, not by chance and necessity; rather, they were *planned*. The designer knew what the systems would look like when they were completed, then took steps to bring the systems about. Life on earth at its most fundamental level, in its most critical components, is the product of intelligent activity.[98]

A key strength of Behe's thesis was, and still is, that it does not depend on speculative arguments about anatomy (such as how the eye could have evolved) or the fossil record. It is concerned with known and discrete phenomena that can be studied under a microscope at their lowest (i.e. most basic) molecular level. Such phenomena can more credibly be categorised as irreducibly complex – incapable of operation at all except as a unified whole.

Behe points to a number of fascinating examples from the human body, including the cilium (used by some cells to swim), blood-clotting, and cellular self-defence. He maintains that there is, and always has been, a dearth in the scientific literature of any attempt to explain the *detail* of the evolution of these or any other like phenomena. There was such a dearth in 1996 when he published *Darwin's Black Box*, and, according to Behe, there remains such a dearth today, despite a decade of carping outrage by his Darwinist critics.[99]

Mutations of DNA

As we have seen, Darwinists claim that all evolutionary processes are driven by *random* mutations of DNA – 'random' in the sense that they are never the product of any conscious planning. This is sometimes called the 'mutational assumption'.[100] Proponents of ID such as Behe challenge that assumption. They accept that mutations are critical to evolution, and that *some* mutations are genuinely random, but contend that not all or even most evolutionary change happens that way.

What are the *facts* on which these differing opinions are based? I will try to summarise those which seem to me to be the most important.

The first thing to understand is the 'how' of mutation. It occurs when DNA, in the process of replicating itself, fails to do so *exactly*. Amazingly, on the vast majority of occasions, DNA does replicate itself exactly.[101] Mutations are highly unusual, but they do happen – in a number of varieties*, and at rates which vary from gene to gene, across and within lineages and for different kinds of mutation[102]. On average, mutations occur at the rate of about one for every hundred million nucleotides of DNA copied in a generation.[103] Even then, most such mutations (those known as 'snips') do not affect the organism one way or the other.[104] Occasionally, a mutation does have a material effect. Far more often than not it is a deleterious effect, and as a result is filtered out by natural selection. *Favourable* mutations of DNA are much rarer still, and even most of those are lost by chance before they can spread in the relevant population.[105] It is only on extremely rare occasions that favourable mutations occur and are preserved by natural selection.[106]

The next thing to understand about 'favourable' mutations of DNA – at least, those that have been identified and studied in laboratories – is that most are destructive not constructive. They cause *damage* to the design and functionality of the relevant organism, but it is damage of a kind that happens to be useful in the particular and peculiar circumstances in which it occurs. Behe uses the analogies of burning a bridge to stop an invading army and breaking a lock to slow down a burglar[107]. The best-known example from Nature is the gene that causes sickle-cell disease in humans: it is harmful of itself, but effective in counteracting malaria. For this reason, the gene has been 'selected' for in some tropical populations during the 10,000 years since the original mutation occurred.[108]

Likewise, the malaria virus itself has twice selected for 'favourable' mutations. In each case, the relevant mutation counteracts the effect of a man-made anti-malarial drug, atovaquone or chloroquine. Both these mutations are, in that limited sense,

---

* The main types of mutations are: substitution (switch of one kind of nucleotide for another), (omission of one or more nucleotides), insertion (addition of one or more nucleotides), inversion ('flipping' of a segment of DNA double helix), gene duplication (doubling of a region of DNA containing a gene), and genome duplication (doubling of the total DNA of an organism). By way of specific example, the mutation that led to chloroquine-resistance in maleria involved a switch of the amino acids in a particular protein at positions 76 and 220 (among 424 sequenced amino acids). The relevant protein is but one of 5300 proteins that the maleria cell's DNA encodes. See the table in Behe, *The Edge of Evolution*, The Free Press (2007), p.67; see also pp. 48–50.

advantageous, but they are harmful in the broader sense that they cause damage to an integrated biological system.[109]

These kinds of 'favourable' mutations are properly described as random. They are also properly described as 'simple', in the sense that they involve only *one* or at the most *two* changes to the structure of pre-existing DNA. Even then, the odds of the exact mutation or double-mutation occurring are staggeringly high: one in a trillion in the case of malarial resistance to atovaquone and one in a hundred billion billion in the case of malarial resistance to chloroquine.[110] The latter mutation eventually occurred only because a truly gigantic number of malarial cells have existed in the decades since chloroquine was invented; by contrast, there have not been as many mammals, let alone humans, in the entire history of the Earth.[111]

These known examples of 'favourable' mutations are extraordinary enough. But they are to be contrasted with genuinely *constructive* mutations, those which are non-harmful, specific and useful, i.e. those which change the overall design of the organism in some significant and beneficial way. Such mutations occur much more rarely than those of the kind which led to chloroquine resistance in malaria. Behe points to the HIV virus, which has undergone about a hundred billion billion copies in just the last few decades. 'Yet through all that,' Behe observes, 'there have been no significant basic biochemical changes in the virus at all.'[112]

On the basis of all this evidence, Behe reaches two firm conclusions. First, on the statistical probabilities, *random* mutations can account only in small part for the development, over eons, of complex life. Second, 'since common descent with modification strongly appears to be true'[113], evolutionary change must in large part have been caused by *non*-random mutations. In Behe's words, '[t]he overwhelming number of mutations may be due to chance (to little constructive effect), numerically swamping those due to design'. However – and this is the key point – 'the comparatively few [mutations] due to design … [are] nonetheless inordinately significant'.[114]

The Darwinian response to Intelligent Design

Thus far, I hope to have demonstrated that ID theory is, at least, worthy of consideration. Yet a recurring problem in the literature is the vindictiveness of the hard-core Darwinists. Many of them assert that ID should not be dignified by the word 'theory', and that Darwinism (being as they see it unimpeachable fact) should not be belittled by the word. The debate has become unnecessarily bitter and has spilled over into politics, and in particular into education policy. Many supporters of Darwinism argue that under no circumstances should ID theory be taught in schools, at least if it is taught 'as science'. In the United States, the debate is complicated by the no-establishment clause in the Constitution, but similar arguments are now being advanced in countries throughout the West. For example, in Australia, a coalition of 70,000 scientists and teachers stated in an open letter in October 2005 that to permit the teaching of intelligent design in science classes 'would make a mockery of Australian science teaching and throw open the door of science classes to similarly unscientific world views – be they astrology, spoon bending, flat Earth cosmology or alien abductions'.[115]

This struck me at the time as a considerable overreaction, and still does. To equate Intelligent Design theory with astrology or flat Earth cosmology looks a fatuous exaggeration, and to trivialise the possibility of alien life in the same breath also reveals an unfortunate lack of perspective. It seems to me, speaking as a layman, that ID raises some perplexing questions. Why should schoolchildren be denied an opportunity to consider the strengths and weaknesses of the arguments on both sides? A possible compromise is to restrict the teaching of Intelligent Design to 'religion' or 'philosophy' classes only. This seems a fair solution, though it is hard to understand why it ought not to be taught – as a set of *arguments* – in science classes as well.

A policy which encourages open-minded analysis would be welcome, because to date too many people, in responding to ID theory, have resorted to scorn and bluster, rather than allowing their own counterarguments to do the talking. And they do have some decent arguments. Although none of the seminal texts that I have read contain any entirely convincing refutation of ID theory, there are some serious objections to many of the key claims underpinning it.[116]

As far as I can judge, the Darwinists are at their strongest when rebutting the claim that all species did not descend from a common ancestor. The Darwinists point out, for a start, that many of the alleged 'gaps' in the fossil record are explainable by the natural imperfection of that record, because most organisms do not get buried in aquatic sediment. Further and in any event, they argue, the fossil record *does* contain quite abundant evidence of 'intermediate' organisms connecting major groups (such as fish with tetrapods, dinosaurs with birds, reptiles with mammals and land mammals with whales).[117] (It is almost universally conceded that, at the *species* level, fossilised intermediates are very rare.) Darwinists also point out that some existing organisms contain apparently useless 'vestigial' features (such as the kiwi's tiny wings or Man's appendix) and that these point strongly toward their descent from an ancient ancestor.

Another argument advanced in favour of common descent is that derived from biogeography, the study of the distribution of plants and animals. Darwin himself was strongly influenced by the phenomenon of 'oceanic islands', such as Hawaii and the Galapagos, being islands that were never connected to a continental land mass but which arose, lifeless, from underneath the sea. These islands (unlike so-called continental islands, such as Britain, which were once connected to a continental land mass) are missing many types of plants and animals. The plants and animals that do inhabit oceanic islands are present in profusion. They bear the greatest similarity to species living on the nearest mainland that can most easily get to the island.

These facts suggest that all species on oceanic islands were not created suddenly, but descended from organisms that came from the mainland to the island. One of the pioneers of 'speciation' theory, Ernst Mayr, contended just before his death in 2005 that the origin of new species has been observed to be allopatric (geographical) in most studied groups of organisms, and always in birds and mammals.[118]

Opponents of Intelligent Design theory also seek to refute the arguments based on 'irreducible complexity'. They contend – persuasively, in many instances[119] – that features such as the human eye only *appear* to be irreducibly complex: in fact, they say, there is a viable pathway from a very primitive feature (such as the pigmented eye-spot found in flatworms) to the human eye. They concede that it is more difficult to trace the evolution of biochemical systems (such as blood clotting) than of anatomical structures, but express confidence that answers will eventually be found. One biologist, Kenneth R. Miller, claims to have demonstrated how the bacterial flagellar motor could have evolved from known functional intermediates, though Miller's arguments too are disputed.[120]

What to believe?

It difficult to know who or what to believe in this debate.

At least a few of the arguments in support of Intelligent Design theory appear to have force – especially Michael Behe's thesis about life at the tiny level of the cell, and his analysis of the incidence of mutations in DNA. On the other hand, if you are a Christian, you must be careful not to fall into the trap of believing what you want to believe in the face of the preponderance of mainstream scientific opinion. And you must also be careful to scrutinise the motives and credentials of ID proponents, not a few of whom display the same intemperance and intolerance as some hard-core atheists. Many disaffected anti-intellectual people in the West are fixated with the Creation/evolution debate. Often, as Richard Hofstadter has pointed out, this fixation is more a product of deep disgust with modernity than reasoned study of the scientific and theological issues.[121]

After much reading and thought, I am persuaded by the evidence for common descent. In short, it seems probable that all life on Earth evolved by a process of slight, successive mutations of DNA. The 'choice', then, would seem to lie between the Darwinian view that all mutations are truly random, and the view that most of the important mutations down the ages were not random, but deliberately planned and brought about.

But is that the real choice? For people trying to weigh up the likelihood of God's existence, I do not believe it is as stark as that. True, if Intelligent Design theory is sound – whether the Behe version or the more radical alternatives – then the case for the existence of God becomes almost overwhelming. Behe properly concedes that 'if one wishes to be academically rigorous, one [cannot] leap directly from design to a transcendent God'[122]. Still, if you are persuaded by the case for design in biological systems, the most obvious inference is that an all-powerful supernatural being must have been responsible. That supernatural being, i.e. God, must have brought about mutations of DNA at various times during the history of the Earth, so as to introduce new species (or, if Behe is wrong about common descent, simply introduced new species in toto). This may be the explanation for the mysteriously rapid emergence of multi-celled life 545 million years ago and, perhaps, for the emergence of Man.

But what if modern Intelligent Design theory is plain wrong? Is that the end of the matter, as far as rational belief in God is concerned? Certainly not. For one thing, there are still all of the arguments based on the finely tuned laws of physics and chemistry. But even putting those matters aside, there remain powerful arguments for God based on the evidence of earthly biological systems. In my view, the existence of a Designing God is sufficiently indicated by the objective facts upon which mainstream Darwinian theory is based. It is a question of assessing the *implications* of those facts.

A possible stance for believers in God, adopted consciously or unconsciously by countless millions of people since the late nineteenth century, is so-called 'Theistic Evolution'. This is the idea that Darwinian natural selection was simply God's chosen mechanism for creating all the different forms of life. God, on this view, 'produced the universe by a single creative act', which involved 'implanting' in it at the very beginning all natural laws necessary to create life, including Man. God could then 'step back' and – without any further interference on His part – observe the 'natural development' of every living thing.[123] Pope John Paul II held to this view.

My personal belief is a variation on the theme. Unlike many people who believe in Theistic Evolution, I am not uncomfortable with the notion of periodic interference by God in natural processes which He originally set in train.[124] But nor am I wedded to the notion. When it comes to reconciling Darwinian evolution with God – or, rather, finding a strong pointer *towards* God in Darwinian evolution – there are three other considerations which loom larger for me.

First, there is the long-recognised fact that 'natural forms embody mathematical regularities'[125]. This is one of the points made by Sir Anthony Flew. Think, for instance, of the hexagonal cells in a beehive or the nautilus spiral shape of a sea-shell. Think of Phi (1.61803398874989...), also known as the 'Golden Ratio' or the 'Divine Proportion'. Numerous features of the human body – including the DNA molecule itself – are modelled on Phi, which recurs very frequently in Nature. So does the so-called Fibonacci series of numbers (0, 1, 1, 2, 3, 5, 8, 13, 21, 34, 55...) – for example, in flower petals. Thus, it can be seen that the laws of mathematics, physics and chemistry – which themselves point to Design – permeate the living world as much as the inanimate world. Indeed, in the living world, they operate at much higher levels of complexity.

Second, as we have seen, the evolutionary process depends upon there occurring from time to time a sufficient number of favourable 'random' mutations of an organism's DNA. The mutation thus 'creates' the new advantageous characteristic for which the relevant species' environment then 'selects'. This crucial aspect of the process of evolution, rather than being inherently antithetical to the existence of God, is highly suggestive. On reflection, it points – perhaps counter-intuitively – towards Design. Why? Because the process is like the creation of carbon atoms inside stars: it works, *but only just*. I am not contending that mutations are biased towards improvement; they do not somehow 'anticipate the needs of the organism'. Most mutations are harmful.[126] What I am contending is that the *overall* process is tuned to an extraordinary level of precision.

The main point is this. If mutations were significantly more common, complex life could not exist, because the process of reproduction would be too unstable: 'too many copying errors and the genetic message would get diluted and eventually lost'.[127] But likewise, 'natural selection has to have alternatives to choose among'.[128] If there were no mutations at all, or if mutations were significantly less common than they are, complex life would never have evolved: all species would be vulnerable to adverse changes in their environment, and would eventually become extinct.[129]

One of modern cosmology's foremost atheists, Carl Sagan, summarised the position this way:

> Evolution works through mutation and selection. ... If the mutation rate is too high, we lose the inheritance of four billion years of painstaking evolution. If it is too low, new varieties will not be available to adapt to some future change in the environment. The evolution of life requires *a more or less precise balance* between mutation and selection. When that balance is achieved, remarkable adaptations occur.[130]

And it seems that there could be a kicker to this state of affairs. Recent research suggests that, as well as mutation and selection, there is another key aspect of the evolutionary process – 'co-operation'. In biology, this is the idea that 'someone or something gets a benefit because someone or something else pays a cost'[131]. Dr Martin Nowak of Harvard University has postulated the theory that biological co-operation arises only in certain conditions and – amazingly – that those conditions can be identified in terms of an exact mathematical equation.*

Assuming Sagan and Nowak to be correct, I cannot escape the conclusion that these phenomena constitute yet further aspects of Fred Hoyle's 'deep-laid scheme'. Nowak's formula suggests Design, and so too does Sagan's observation – echoed by many others – about the need for 'a more or less precise balance between mutation and selection'. If Nature were truly random, then – even assuming DNA existed at all – one would expect mutations of DNA to be much more common or much more uncommon. It would be an astounding coincidence that they should occur just frequently enough to ensure the continued existence of stable, complex, interactive species in workable numbers.

Darwinists would, no doubt, dispute this reasoning. They insist that all mutations of DNA are genuinely random.[132] They lay stress on the fact – which I see no reason to dispute – that mutations have been shown to be caused by one or more physical events, such as exposure to x-rays, cosmic rays, radioactive substances, various chemicals, and other genes known as 'mutator genes'.[133] There are also 'hot spots' on certain chromosomes which are more prone to mutation than others.[134] These 'natural' events, it is said, sufficiently explain the occurrence of mutations; there is no need to invoke God.

Significantly, however, even Richard Dawkins has conceded that '[i]t is not necessary that mutation should be random in order for natural selection to work'. 'Selection,' he admits, 'can still do its work whether mutation is directed or not.'[135] However, Dawkins shies away from the idea that mutation *is in fact* directed.[136] That would not fit his atheistic worldview.

---

* Nowak's equation is: B/C>K. 'That is, cooperation will emerge if the benefit-to-cost (B/C) ratio of cooperation is greater than the average number of neighbors (K).' See Carl Zimmer, 'In Games, an Insight Into the Rules of Evolution', *The New York Times*, 31 July 2007.

I remain unpersuaded. For the sake of argument, I am prepared to accept – contrary to Michael Behe's thesis – that *all* mutations necessary to account for the development of life came about in the ordinary statistical course of things, as a result of 'natural processes'. However, that still does not make mutations truly random. The cause of a given mutation may be *effectively* random (i.e. as a practical matter, unascertainable by human beings). But that does not make the mutation, in John D. Barrow's phrase, *intrinsically* random (i.e. untraceable even in theory to any definite local cause, as are fluctuations in the quantum world).[137] Left unanswered, in particular, is the question why *more or fewer* mutations are not brought about by x-rays, mutator genes and other like causes. A phenomenon such as the exposure of a cell to radioactivity is no more than the *proximate* cause of the relevant mutation. It does not explain how and why events converged to ensure that a particular cell at a particular time came to be exposed to radioactivity (nor how cells came to exist in the first place).

That leads to my third reason for detecting God in evolution. Favourable mutations of DNA are necessary, but far from sufficient. At least two other fiendishly clever processes are at play in driving and maintaining workable biological change: one inhibits change and one promotes it.

The phenomenon of 'generative enrichment' ensures that once certain basic features of an organism have evolved – and are functionally interconnected – they become increasingly *resistant* to change. Significant genetic alteration of any part of the 'system' just will never be selected for, even if the 'right' mutation came along, because it would be 'likely to have some appalling consequences somewhere'[138]. That is why, for instance, no six-limbed vertebrates have ever evolved from four-limbed ancestors. However, at least *some* genetic mutations must be 'available' for selection, otherwise no organism could adapt to environmental change. But which mutations, and when, and how?

The 'hottest of hot topics' in evolutionary developmental biology today is so-called modularity, 'the idea that certain characteristics of organisms develop independently of other traits'[139]. So, for example, a given mutation may affect one organ in the body – say, the stomach. There must be a mechanism – *other than genetic mutation* – which enables other closely-related organs (such as the kidney, liver, intestines, etc.) to 'adjust' appropriately in response to the original change. The organism must not have to 'wait', as it were, for another (random) genetic mutation affecting each associated organ. That must be so 'even when *both* organ systems must change for *either* change to be adaptive'[140]. Amazingly, according to modularity theory, this appears to be the position. Genetic change affecting a 'quasi-independent' trait triggers a 'cascade' of appropriate changes in other traits.

Of course, this is not proof of God. But it is yet more evidence that life on Earth owes its existence to processes which are ordered, complex and – at best – only partially understood by Man. Those processes are staggering, and I am quite convinced they had to have been set in train by a supernatural being. That is a personal opinion; no doubt the likes of Richard Dawkins would disagree. Dawkins has suggested, rather hopefully, that 'evolvability' itself may have evolved – that Nature has selected for embryology which 'may be more evolutionarily promising than the kinds of variations thrown up by other types of embryology'.[141] There is an argument that developmental modularity itself has an evolutionary history.[142] But all these suggestions are speculative and, in any event, my point is made.

It is relevant that Charles Darwin himself remained a believer in God. As Alistair McGrath has remarked, 'If everything altered after Darwin, it is clearly important to determine what Darwin himself believed to have changed as a result of his new ideas'[143]. There are disagreements about this issue too, but the essential position seems clear. Darwin's faith waxed and waned appreciably, and he cannot be described as having been an orthodox Christian. He was shattered by the death of his daughter at the age of ten, an event that seems to have had a greater effect on his faith than his work on evolution. Nonetheless, towards the end of his life, in his autobiography, Darwin affirmed his belief in a Deity. Darwin's reasoning process was fairly straightforward. He thought it impossible to conclude that 'blind chance or necessity' could account for 'this immense and wonderful universe, including man'. He conceived of God as 'having an intelligent mind in some degree analogous to that of man'[144].

Conclusion

The first reason for my belief in God is that the physical Universe is too delicately contrived to be a glorious accident. Rather, it gives every appearance of having been designed and constructed by a 'mind' of unfathomable genius. In the words of James Jeans, the great British physicist and astronomer: 'Mind no longer appears to be an accidental intruder into the realm of matter ... [W]e ought rather to hail it as the creator and governor of the realm of matter.'[145]

Jeans concluded that the Universe 'look[s] more like a great thought than a great machine'[146]. And that is how it appears to me: the product of conscious planning. My instinct tells me that this is not a *false* appearance, and there is rational confirmation of the fact in unexpected places. It is there in the mathematical constants of Nature and the four fundamental forces of Nature, which make possible the existence of stars, planets, water and life-giving carbon. It is there in the discoveries of modern biochemistry, which have revealed the astonishing organised complexity of the tiniest forms of life, at the level of the cell. It is there, I suggest, even in conventional Darwinian theory. It is certainly there in the Big Bang theory, which holds at its core that the Universe had a finite beginning – that something came from nothing.

With these thoughts in mind, go back to the opening of the book of Genesis. Does it make better sense? I hope so. For as the Italian novelist and thinker Umberto Eco has pointed out, 'once you say that the seven days of Creation are an expression of poetic license and can be taken figuratively, Genesis seems to allow Darwin everything': an initial explosion of light; the formation of stars and planets; geological upheavals on Earth; the separation of the land from the oceans; the beginning of life in the water; the emergence of birds and animals. Man, it will be noticed, appears last, created not out of nothingness but from pre-existing matter.[147]

All of these considerations discredit the notion, frequently advanced by atheists, that 'the maintenance of religious dogma *always* comes at the expense of science'[148]. To the contrary, modern science tends to confirm the uninstructed, commonsense view of primitive Man: the grandeur of the physical Universe requires a special explanation. In short, both the beginning of the Universe, and the continued existence of the Universe since its beginning, must have a supernatural cause.

God, I believe, is that cause. In the words of the Prophet:

> He made the earth by his power; he founded the world by his wisdom and stretched out the heavens by his understanding.
>
> (Jeremiah 51:15)

CHAPTER 2

THE HUMAN MIND: COGNITION AND CONSCIENCE

Test me, O Lord, and try me,
Examine my heart and my mind.

Psalm 26:2

The mind is its own place, and in itself
Can make a heaven of hell, a hell of heaven.

John Milton, *Paradise Lost*

I am hopeful that the reader may regard my arguments so far as, in the main, convincing. But even if they seem unconvincing, or at best inconclusive, I would ask you to suspend any disbelief. Do not put the book aside at this early stage. Instead, I would ask you to ponder – really ponder – the ramifications, for Man, of there being a God who designed and created the physical Universe. If that state of affairs is even a *possibility* in your mind, then questions of the utmost seriousness should arise. For as Richard Dawkins rightly states in *The God Delusion*:

> [A] universe in which we are alone except for other slowly involved intelligences is a very different universe from one with an original guiding agent whose intelligent design is responsible for its very existence …They are close to being irreconcilably different.[1]

One of the things that now strikes me most forcibly is this. If such a Designing God exists – all-powerful, all-knowing – then there is nothing to be gained by wishing away His existence, or to complain about it as somehow cramping your style here on Earth. To do so amounts to an attempt to put off facing something that you do not want to face. Almost always, like ignoring a bad toothache, or an upcoming examination, such an approach is dangerous.

It is likewise wrong-headed to regard the apparent flaws of Creation – the prevalence of suffering and evil, for instance – as somehow invalidating God's existence. That is a natural human attitude even among believers (sometimes, still, it is mine), but logically it is perverse. God, *as your Creator*, is an infinitely greater being than you are. If and because such a God exists, and because the Earth is as it is, you must try instead to understand why God made things as they are and, even more importantly, what it is that God wants of you as an individual. And, however difficult it may seem, to do it.

To use an imperfect analogy from childhood, if you are stuck with a teacher who is especially strict, it does not really do you any good to whinge about his or her methods or to wish for another teacher. If you want to help yourself, you have to accept the fact that Mrs X is your teacher – whether you like it or not – and to try to obey her strictures as best you can. That is the only way to survive and to prosper.

This may seem a basic point, but it took me a long time to grasp. Yet it is an utterly crucial point, one of the key concepts that any believer must accept and come to terms with. Christopher Hitchens has asserted that one of the four 'irreducible objections' to religious faith is that 'it manages to combine the maximum of servility with the maximum of solipsism'[2]. Many atheists seem exasperated by '[t]he worshipper's tedious refrain about the greatness of God and the feebleness of Man'[3]. But – and Hitchens, to his credit, understands this – once you accept the proposition that a Creator God exists, no other mindset is logical. Criticism of God (a very different thing to criticism of organised religion) becomes pointless.

The prophet Isaiah conceived the issue in these terms:

> You turn things upside down, as if the potter were thought to be like the clay! Shall what is formed say to him who formed it, 'He did not make me'? Can the pot say of the potter, 'He knows nothing'?
>
> (Isaiah 29:16. See also Isaiah 45:9; Isaiah 64:8; Romans 9:20–22)

I would ask the reader to keep in mind this image – of God as the moulder of a clay pot – in reading this next chapter.

Now, if there is such a God, it seems fair to assume that the Universe was created for a purpose. One of the keys to theology, then, must be to try to discern what that purpose was, and is. How are we to go about doing so? My own view is that the answer is to be found in a careful consideration of the nature of Man. What, exactly, has God created in Man? By distilling the essence of what it is to be a human being (as opposed to a ray of light, or a rock, or a tree, or a fish, or a dog) we can begin to lead ourselves towards the probable truth.

It must be acknowledged that, physiologically, human beings are similar in many respects to a lot of other organisms. We share 96–98 per cent of our DNA with chimpanzees (estimates vary).[4] Even so, the genetic differences between Man and the rest of the animal kingdom are, in practical reality, very significant indeed. A prominent Australian atheist, Robyn Williams, has conceded as much. In his admirably witty words: '[T]he 2 per cent or less separating us from chimpanzees … [is] enough to put one creature in the jungle threatened with extinction and the other in Wall Street trying to take over the solar system'[5].

Man seems to be unique among all living things on Earth in at least two remarkable respects. First, Man has the capacity to think things through. Man is able to ponder his surroundings, to understand some of the underlying laws governing those surroundings, and thereby to contemplate his own place in the Universe. This is what I will call cognition. (Deliberately, I do not use the term 'consciousness', which is a somewhat broader concept, for reasons which I will come to.) Second, perhaps even more significantly, Man is possessed of an 'inner voice' that tells each of us how we should behave, even though each of us frequently does not *in fact* behave according to the dictates of that inner voice. This, of course, is conscience.

Before turning to the specifics of these two issues, cognition and conscience, it is appropriate to address a related issue that is frequently raised by atheists and other sceptics of religion. It is an issue that lies at the heart of all religious and anti-religious discourse, whether the protagonists realise it or not.

Is Man special?

It can credibly be argued that a person's fundamental attitude to life is determined by the view he or she holds, consciously or unconsciously, about the qualities of the human mind.[6] Atheists seem to swing between two extremes in addressing this question – or they adopt both positions simultaneously.

At one extreme is the belief that Man is the be all and end all of everything, a state of mind sometimes labelled humanism. Herbert Butterfield, an eminent professor of Modern History at Cambridge University in the mid-twentieth century, thought it a subtle form of intellectual pride. To adopt humanism as your creed amounts to making a decision that the material welfare of the human race is always paramount; or, as Butterfield put it, that 'we [i.e. Man] will see ourselves as gods or kings of the universe (as absolute ends in ourselves)'.[7] Of course, some of the causes which are fervently espoused by humanists – or humanitarians – are extremely worthy. The relief of poverty is a prime example. But poverty can be relieved without abolishing religion; and, in any event, Man's material welfare is not the only thing that matters. Moral, ethical, cultural and spiritual values are also important – many would say more important. Man's physiology (including our cranial capacity) has changed relatively little in 100,000 years. For much of that time, sheer survival was Man's highest goal. Today, we live on a far higher plane.

Humanism, then, 'is not so much wrong but … inadequate'[8]. There is a better alternative. We can decide that there *may* be something greater than ourselves, that 'the things which inside us are most lofty and most luminous [could be] … the broken reflections of a greater light"[9]. That is the position I will advocate in this chapter, by focusing on the two aspects of the human mind that I consider the most lofty and the most luminous.

Before doing so I will try to address the other main atheist argument – the notion that Man is not special at all. According to this view of the world, Man is merely a species of animal like the millions of others that now live on Earth and the far greater number of species that are extinct. Man just happens to be a recently evolved species, with a large brain size relative to body size, and is for that reason more than usually intelligent. But that is all. The human genome is of only moderate size and complexity, compared to those of other species.[10] It follows, so the argument runs, that Man is a trivial and insignificant part of the history of the Earth, let alone of the Universe. Accordingly, any 'God' constructed by the mind of Man that accords Man a unique place in the grand scheme of things is an egocentric pretence.

It is difficult to refute this argument without falling into the trap of dogmatism. But to me the matter is straightforward. For a start – theology aside – '[t]here is a consensus in evolutionary biology that the complexity of life has increased over time'[11]. And of all the forms of life which exist today, Man is the most complex in terms of *morphology*. The human brain is easily the most complicated object in the known Universe. It is more sophisticated by far than the best modern computers and is capable of feats of reasoning and of imagination way, way beyond any animal.[12] It is also worth noting that, according to Darwinian theory, no more complex species than *Homo sapiens* can ever evolve in the future, *unless* it is through us.[13]

Are these facts not highly suggestive, in and of themselves? I think so. Indeed, the conclusion seems to me inescapable that Man *is* relevantly unique among living things on Earth and (most probably) among all living things that have ever existed on Earth. To argue otherwise is little more than sophistry.

Shakespeare wrote, through the voice of his greatest character:

What a piece of work is a man! how noble in reason! how infinite in faculty! in form,
in moving, how express and admirable! in action how like an angel! in apprehension
how like a God! the beauty of the world! the paragon of animals![14]

Later in the same play, in one of finest of the soliloquies, Hamlet identifies more specifically the nature of Man's uniqueness (and incidentally assumes the existence of God). He muses:

What is a man
If his chief good and market of his time
Be but to sleep and feed? A beast, no more.
Sure he that made us with such large discourse,
Looking before and after, gave us not
That capability and god-like reason
To fust in us unused.[15]

The author of the Eighth Psalm, celebrating Man's dominion over all of the other living things on Earth, made essentially the same point. In his words, Man has been placed by God 'a little lower than the angels' (Psalm 8:5, KJV).

Man's dominion over the Earth is simply a fact. It is evidenced more forcibly all the time by advances in our knowledge and our technology. It is also evidenced by the uneven but inexorable spread of human civilisation. These achievements are a concomitant of our unique intellect and our ability to reason.

Of course, Man's dominion over the Earth has not always been wisely exercised. Put to one side the proliferation of nuclear weapons. More generally, it is undeniable that Man has already caused considerable harm to the Earth's ecosphere: the degradation of arable land into desert; the cutting down of forests; the pollution of streams and rivers; the hunting to extinction of some species of animals and birds; the destruction of the natural habitat – and subsequent extinction – of many more species of animals, birds, fish and insects.

Then there is the huge issue of climate change, caused by global warming. The evidence seems increasingly compelling that this phenomenon is real, and virtually all politicians now at least pay lip service to it. For present purposes, the key point is that global warming has been brought about *by Man*. It is a result of the burning of fossil fuels since the Industrial Revolution, at a rate that increases each year. This has caused an increase in the proportion of greenhouse gases in the atmosphere, principally carbon dioxide. The scope of the long-term harm that has thereby been done to the Earth is still, it appears, difficult fully to assess, but no one denies that for over 150 years Man has caused massive volumes of noxious fumes to be released into the atmosphere.[16]

There is an ongoing scientific and geo-political debate about the environment. I will consider that controversy in Chapter 8, but it is irrelevant to the current discussion. So, even, are the ethical issues as to the extent of Man's *right* to exploit the Earth for our own ends. The only point I am making at the moment is that – for good or ill – it is a fact that Man exercises dominion over the Earth. We hold its fate in our hands, subject (so Christians say) to the grace of God.

How far beyond the Earth does Man's dominion extend? The possibility of extraterrestrial life has always fascinated me. For many years I would have said without hesitation that there must be many, many other civilisations such as ours in the Universe, including a considerable number that are more advanced. My opinion would have been based on little more than the sheer number of stars in the sky and some vague notions about the laws of probability. Now, having read fairly widely on the subject of extraterritorial life, as well as on the origins of life on Earth, I am far less sure. The argument from probability has been exposed as statistically 'bogus'[17]. It seems likely that intelligent living beings such as Man are *extremely* rare in the Universe[18], and possibly unique to the Earth.

It is still conceivable that other habitable planets exist elsewhere in the Universe, perhaps (in absolute terms) in large numbers, but the current evidence suggests that such planets are very much the exception rather than the norm. Any such planets upon which there in fact exists life of the kind that exists on the Earth must be much rarer still. Given the staggeringly vast distances of space, and the absolute constraint upon any form of travel or other communication imposed by the speed of light, it strikes me that Man (as a self-conscious, conscience-possessing being) is for all practical purposes alone.[19]

The fact, if it be the fact, that Man is *effectively* alone in the Universe is, of itself, highly suggestive. If there are intelligent beings like Man elsewhere in the Universe, as technologically advanced as us or more so, then there can be little doubt that our isolation from them has been an invaluable blessing. The recent history of the Earth tends to demonstrate that when two advanced civilisations encounter each other for the first time, the result is disastrous for at least one of them. Consider the fate of the Aztecs, the Incas, the Native American tribes, and Australia's Aboriginal people, to name but four civilisations decimated by contact with a more 'advanced' (i.e. more technologically sophisticated) society. If extra-terrestrial beings did ever make contact with the Earth, or Man with them, I fear that the result would be much more like *Aliens* or *War of the Worlds* than *E.T.* or *Close Encounters*. The fact that no such contact has happened and seems most unlikely ever to happen leads me to believe that God means it that way. It is evidence of His grace. More prosaically, this may be another reason for the vast size of the Universe: we are left 'unperturbed'.[20]

If I am correct, and Man is an extremely rare thing in the Universe – perhaps unique – then we *are* entitled to regard ourselves as special. At all events, it is legitimate to say that Man is special among all of the creatures on Earth. From that starting point, it follows that the quest for God must involve a consideration of the nature or quality of Man's specialness. The two key attributes that set Man apart are cognition and conscience. Both of those attributes are strong pointers to the existence and the nature of God.

Consciousness

The phenomenon of human consciousness has always intrigued philosophers, and it intrigues me. Warwick Fairfax rightly described consciousness as being *both* 'the key to our behaviour' and 'a baffling phenomenon; not merely how we know, but our emotional life, our aesthetic feelings, our persistent belief in the validity of knowledge and in our awareness of right and wrong'.[21] These are all huge subjects in themselves, but only certain aspects of consciousness (the subsets that I will call 'cognition' and 'conscience') are directly relevant to my belief in God. I will come to those subjects presently. First, however, in order to put the issues in context, it seems necessary to make some general observations about what is sometimes called the 'mind/body' problem.

A simple definition of consciousness is the capacity to experience awareness, most particularly an awareness of one's 'Self'. When, and because, you are aware of this 'Self', you will have desires and intentions.[22] How is this phenomenon to be explained? Among scientists and philosophers there seem, broadly speaking, to be two schools of thought.

The first holds that consciousness is a purely physical phenomenon: that it is a function of the stuff of our brains, no more and no less. Our sense of self, our free will, is 'no more than the behaviour of a vast assembly of nerve cells and their associated molecules'[23]. Or, to put it another way, everything that that we do – everything that happens – is causally determined; the sensation of free will is the result of our ignorance of most of the causes.[24]

The other school of thought is that consciousness 'exists independently of its physical substrate'[25]. The sixteenth-century French philosopher Rene Descartes famously observed that our ability to think is absolutely certain. We can 'know', beyond doubt, that we have had a thought. The thought exists in our own consciousness – it may be a delusion or hallucination, and other people may interpret it differently if we try to put it into words – but this thought unquestionably 'happened' as a conscious experience.[26] 'I think, therefore I am.' On the other hand, as Descartes also pointed out, the nature and even the existence of one's body is *not* certain. Our perception of it may be a delusion or a hallucination. Therefore, Descartes reasoned, mind and body must be distinct.

That argument may or may not be sound. What is, I think, incontestable is that the properties of consciousness are deeply complex and mysterious. They remain way beyond explanation in a material, determinist way, by any laws of chemistry or physics, including quantum theory. In short, science cannot explain subjective experience. The problem is encapsulated in the age-old truism that no person can ever know that any other person (or creature) has a subjective experience of the world.

Even the memories of *our own* experiences of the world are deeply mysterious. Our memories are what make us who we are, yet they relate to only a tiny fraction of our past; we quickly forget most of the things that happen to us in our lives. Neurologists cannot 'locate' memories in any particular part of the brain[27] and, more remarkable still, the brain that 'stores' your memories today is not the same brain as the one that existed when you had most of the experiences which you now remember. Consider this quite extraordinary insight:

> [Think] of an experience from your childhood. Something you remember clearly, something you can see, feel, maybe even smell, as if you were really there. After all, you really were there at the time, weren't you? How else would you remember it? But here is the bombshell, you *weren't* there. Not a single atom that is in your body today was there when that event took place.[28]

Thus, a childhood memory is genuinely 'yours' (i.e. of and relating to yourself) even though the body which that Self inhabited as a child no longer exists. The body which your Self now inhabits is a different body.[29]

My instinct is that consciousness exists, in some sense, independently of matter. C.S. Lewis approached the issue by melding both the physical and metaphysical explanations: Man, he argued, must be a 'composite being – a natural organism tenanted by, or in a state of *symbiosis* with, a supernatural spirit'[30]. I tend to agree. My own guess is that the mind cannot operate in the absence of a body; the two are, in that sense, inseparable. However, the mind can, under some conditions, act *outside* the body, i.e. other than through the five senses. Knowledge itself – i.e. memory – cannot be purely material, for the reasons discussed. The mind, then, is 'immaterial, though bound up with matter'.[31] There really is a ghost in the machine!

Fascinating as these questions are, their resolution is not central to my belief in God. Or, perhaps more accurately, I did not come to believe in God as a result of considering the mind/body problem. Whether or to what extent human consciousness is a by-product of purely physical phenomena, the stark fact is that Man possesses it. As Soren Kierkegaard recognised, the most certain thing that each of us knows is that there is an 'I' experiencing that sensation. My father believes that the greatest mystery of all is why each of us is who we are; why 'I' inhabit this body and no other. He calls this the question of unique personal identity. My father's view is shared by the American philosopher and lawyer Thomas Nagel, who doubts that the natural sciences will ever go close to explaining our sense of self.[32] My own view is that the likely position is encapsulated in these wise words of Warwick Fairfax: '[T]here is not the slightest need for a clash between science and religion as regards the nature of the individual. The clash only comes if the scientist believes that what he knows is the whole truth, instead of a part of it.'[33]

These are deep questions, but as I have said they were not central to my emergent belief in God. I will now turn to the two particular aspects of human consciousness that seem to me especially salient.

Cognition

It is a remarkable fact that Man, alone of all creatures, can 'decode' Nature. Man has discovered, and applied for selfish purposes, at least some of the objective laws that govern the Universe. This is a key feature of the capacity that I have defined as cognition.

Paul Davies' ruminations on this subject – in his books *Are We Alone?* and *The Mind of God* – played an important part in my passage toward belief in Christianity. No doubt Davies did not have evangelism in mind, but the theistic implications of his arguments seemed to me inescapable, and still do.

The key point made by Davies is this. Man is capable not merely of observing the physical things that surround us and the actual behaviour of those things; Man is also capable of devising theories to account for the *underlying* laws that govern those things. Thus, many animals are capable of observing the fall of an apple from a tree, but only Man understands that the apple falls because of the force of gravity, and that the force of gravity is capable of expression in precise mathematical terms. Moreover, only Man understands, when he cogitates further still, that the apple and the tree and the air itself each exists in the form in which we find them because of the complex interaction of the other fixed forces of Nature. Only Man understands (albeit most imperfectly) the issues that I have sought to tackle in Chapter 1.

Now, the heart of the matter for Davies – and for me – is that there seems no good explanation merely in terms of 'survival value' why Man should be able to understand any of these things. It ought to be enough that Man, like many other animals, is capable of seeing and dodging out of the way of the falling apple. Anything else looks like a huge case of 'overkill'. As Davies has observed, 'many communities, for many thousands of years, have made a perfectly satisfactory living on this planet without having such underlying theoretical knowledge'. It appears, then, that 'latent in the human brain lay a mathematical ability to decode Nature and discern the hidden linkages between the rules on which the universe runs'. I agree with Davies that this is 'an extraordinary thing'.[34]

Thomas Nagel has made a similar point, more didactically:

> Darwinism may explain why creatures with vision or reason survive, but it does not explain how vision or reasoning are possible. These require not diachronic but timeless explanation … The possibility of minds capable of forming progressively more objective conceptions of reality [i.e. decoding nature] is not something the theory of natural selection can attempt to explain, since it doesn't explain possibilities at all, but only selection among them.[35]

Nagel and Davies here put their fingers on one of the most puzzling things about Man, not explicable readily or at all in Darwinian terms. If Man's capacity to decode Nature has lain dormant in our brains for hundreds of thousands of years, as many scientists assert, then how was this capacity 'selected' for in the first place? How can a 'hidden quality' gain any breeding advantage for the organism that possesses it? On the other hand, if our capacity to decode Nature has evolved only very recently (in the last few thousand years) where is the evidence that this capacity has *of itself* given rise to a breeding advantage? Practical intelligence is one thing, but cognition is quite another.

In this vein, Davies has also observed:

> The most striking product of the human mind is mathematics. This is the baffling thing. Mathematics is not something that you find lying around in your backyard. It's produced by the human mind. Yet if we ask where mathematics works best, it is in areas like particle physics and astrophysics, areas of fundamental science that are very, very far removed from everyday affairs. In fact, they are at the opposite end of the spectrum of complexity from the human brain. In other words, we find that a product of the most complex system we know in nature, the human brain, finds a consonance with the underlying, simplest and most fundamental level, the basic building blocks that make up the world.
>
> That, I think is an astonishing and unexpected thing, and it suggests to me that consciousness and our ability to do mathematics is no mere accident, no trivial detail, no insignificant by-product of evolution that is piggy-backing on some other mundane property. It points to what I like to call the cosmic connection, the existence of a really deep relationship between the minds that can do mathematics and the underlying laws of nature that produce them …[36]

Paul Davies is not the only scientist to have called attention to this strange 'connection'. It was Einstein who remarked that '[t]he eternal mystery of the world is its comprehensibility'.[37] The distinguished British particle physicist and Anglican clergyman, John Polkinghorne, has also written eloquently on the theme. In Polkinghorne's view, the 'rational transparency, the deep intelligibility of the physical world' cannot be explained by natural selection. Quantum physics and cosmology – to mention two fields of human discourse – are a long way removed from everyday experience.[38] Yet the human mind can grapple with them, *as well as* attend to the basic activities of daily life.

Naturally enough, as men of science, the focus of Davies and Polkinghorne is upon the capacity of the human mind to perform mathematics. I would emphasise another – our capacity to understand abstract concepts, and to communicate those concepts by way of the spoken and written word. In short, our use of language. I am attracted to Robert Winston's suggestion that primitive Man's emergent ability to use language could have 'predisposed us to morality'. As Winston says, '[y]our brain needs a level of abstraction to come up with a moral supposition such as "I wouldn't like this if it was done to me" – one only possible with the fluidity lent to us by language'[39].

Samuel Johnson called language the dress of thought. The ability of Man to use language precisely to *articulate* the underlying laws of Nature – and philosophical issues such as where those laws came from – seems to me another fundamental aspect of Davies' 'cosmic connection'. Many great writers have experienced this sense of 'connection' with peculiar intensity. Agatha Christie was perhaps the most popular (and critically under-rated) author of the twentieth century. She was also a quietly devout Christian. In her autobiography she identified one or two favourite books which she had felt compelled to write, and mused openly about 'where these things come from'. For Christie, the act of using language could, in rare moments, stir 'kinship with the Almighty'. Why? '[B]ecause you have been allowed to feel a little of the joy of pure creation. You have been able to make something that is not yourself'.[40]

(One of the many reasons for the greatness of John's Gospel is the use of the concept of 'the Word' (*Logos*) – it goes to the essence of all these notions. The author seems to have understood the Word as being equivalent to Creative Wisdom – 'the expression of mind in reasoning and speech'[41]. Man of all living creatures has unique access to the Word and hence to knowledge of his surroundings. That idea is also touched upon in Genesis 2:19–20 – it is Adam who names each species of animal – and in Job 39:17 – God did not endow animals with wisdom nor give them a share of Man's 'good sense'.)

Paul Davies has made another point about Man's capacity to think and to learn. The average lifespan of any individual human being is just the 'right' length to allow a certain amount of knowledge and wisdom to be acquired, and to be communicated through language to others – long enough to allow for the many years of education necessary to get a young adult to 'square one' in respect of any given field of knowledge, and then to develop and expand that knowledge, but short enough to ensure that no single individual can possibly hope to master more than one or two fields. Even then, the prime of any person's life is sufficiently short as to ensure that even when a field of knowledge is mastered, there is only a fairly limited amount of time available in which that person can make further discoveries.[42]

A related point is that Nature imposes limits upon the sensitivity of Man's eyes and ears. This 'prevents us from being overloaded with information about the world ... [and] ensure[s] the brain receives a manageable amount of information'. If our senses could discern everything – over vast distances and/or at the quantum level – our brains would need to be much bigger and more complex, and this would inhibit everyday survival.[43]

In short, for these and other reasons, no one person can know it all, or anything like it. In this way, the laws of the physical Universe (which dictate the lifespan and sensory capabilities of each human organism) themselves ensure that the human race, collectively, is limited to a gradually expanding understanding – generation by generation – of the whole. Thus, there always remains a degree of uncertainty as to the limits of human knowledge.

The practical tools of cognition: an extraordinary feature of the Moon

Another point made by Paul Davies is that the laws of the physical Universe are such that Man is provided with the 'tools' to make the possession of cognition meaningful. This is a subtle but profound insight. Thus, for example, at the most basic level, there are things to count – such as the fingers on each of our hands. This makes mathematics possible.[44]

Consider another phenomenon: the relative sizes of the Sun and the Moon, and their respective distances from the Earth. The diameter of the Sun is about 400 times the diameter of the Moon. However, the Sun is about 400 times further away from the Earth than the Moon is. This means that, seen by human observers from the Earth, the Sun and the Moon appear roughly the same size in the sky. It also means that during a solar eclipse the Sun is almost *exactly* obscured by the Moon. There is, however, no physical law of Nature to account for this. There is no law of physics or cosmology (like, say, the inverse square law) that requires the size of a planet's satellite to be proportionate to the planet's distance from its sun. In the Earth's case, say cosmologists, this is merely a curious coincidence – a 'happenstance of history'[45]. We were just lucky, they would have it, that there was a 'just so' collision of the nascent Earth with another large celestial body of exactly the right size, at exactly the right point on the Earth, and at exactly the right time in the Earth's formation.[46]

I have always found this explanation hard to accept. Even before I became a believer in God, it had always seemed to me rather eerie that this arrangement of celestial bodies should be unique to the Earth *by accident*, the one place in the Universe that we know to be inhabited by conscious living beings who are able to observe an eclipse. However, for some years I did not connect this strange fact with any theological issue.

One day, however, I learned something that startled me, because it tended to confirm my long-held intuition that there might be something significant about this supposed coincidence. In 1907, Albert Einstein made an important personal breakthrough in the formulation of what was to be called his general theory of relativity. It is a theory explaining the behaviour of gravity in all circumstances throughout the Universe. In some respects, Einstein's theory supplanted Isaac Newton's laws of gravity, which had stood since the middle of the seventeenth century. Einstein considered that Newton's laws could not accurately predict certain phenomena when the force of gravity is extreme, such as occurs near the surface of the Sun. Most of Einstein's contemporaries resisted his new ideas, which he had not been able to prove by observation, only to construct 'on paper'. It was not until 1919 that Einstein was able to prove that he was right and that Newton (and almost everyone else) was wrong.

Einstein conceived an experiment. The experiment involved measuring the effect of gravity upon light itself. Newton's laws already predicted that light is 'bent' by the gravitational pull of another object, but Einstein's theory held that the effect of gravity upon light is substantially stronger than Newton's laws allowed. Testing this proposition was impossible using objects on Earth, because no object is big enough to exert a gravitational pull upon light that is measurable. Einstein's idea was to measure the effect upon starlight of a massive celestial object – the Sun itself. If a distant star is *in fact* behind the Sun on a direct line of sight from the Earth, then we would not expect to be able to see it (because it will blocked out by the Sun). However, if the star is in fact only just behind the rim of the Sun, then the huge gravitational force exerted by the Sun deflects the light emanating from that star toward the Earth. The star then can be seen from the Earth, even though it is in fact still 'behind' the Sun. It appears from Earth to be just barely beyond the rim of the Sun. By measuring from the Earth the distance that the star appears to be from the rim of the Sun, it is possible to ascertain precisely the effect of the force of gravity on light.

Einstein still faced a huge problem in conducting his experiment. In his excellent book *The Big Bang*, Simon Singh has explained how Einstein proceeded:

> But there was a problem: a star whose light was deflected by the Sun so that its position was apparently shifted just to the side of the Sun would still be impossible to see because of the overwhelming brilliance of the Sun. In fact, the region around the Sun is always sprinkled with stars, but they all remain invisible because their brightness is negligible in comparison with the Sun. There is, however, one circumstance when the stars behind the Sun do reveal themselves…
>
> When the moon obliterates the Sun during an eclipse, day temporarily becomes night and the stars emerge. *The Moon's disc fits over the Sun's so perfectly* that it ought to be possible to identify a star just a fraction of a degree from the rim of the Sun – or rather a star whose light has been warped so that it *appears* to be a fraction of a degree outside the solar disc.[47]

And that is how Einstein eventually proved the general theory of relativity*. An expedition was sent to Madeira in 1919 (headed by Arthur Eddington) to observe a solar eclipse. The measurements taken there were consistent with Einstein's predictions and quite inconsistent with those based on Newton's laws. Man's knowledge of physics was

---

* Einstein had a second major stroke of 'luck' without which he could not have formulated the general law of relativity. His old friend, Marcel Grossmann, possessed expert knowledge about the mathematical objects known as tensors, and explained the relevant concepts to him. These were indispensable tools: Barrow, *New Theories of Everything*, p. 220.

advanced enormously, in ways that led later in the twentieth century to, among other things, the development of the Big Bang theory. I have already tried to explain the significance of that theory in the shaping of my own religious beliefs. More fundamentally, this was an instance where a physical feature of the Universe enabled the gift of cognition to be realised in a profound way.

When I first read about Einstein's experiment in Simon Singh's book, it occurred to me immediately that this might be the real explanation for the relative sizes of the Sun and the Moon. Did God make the Moon with Man in mind?

I learned subsequently that this suggestion has been made by numerous creationist Christians, including those of the 'young Earth' school. Apart from the value of eclipses, they point to many other 'purposes' of the Moon – it is a source of night light, the cause of the ocean tides, and a 'shield' from meteors, asteroids and comets.[48] These features can plausibly be regarded as further evidence of Design[49], but the atheist's response is also logically open: if these features were *not* present then life would not have evolved on Earth in the form in which it has, or at all. Man would not be here to speculate about the matter.

But solar eclipses are in a quite different category: their occurrence is not a necessary pre-condition of Man's existence. Why, then, do they happen only on Earth? There are but two possibilities. The first is sheer fluke; the second is Design – solar eclipses are another tool with which Man has been provided in order that we might more fully exploit the faculty of cognition. In that connection, it is noteworthy that eclipses have served several other useful purposes: for precisely dating events in the ancient past that coincided with an eclipse; for providing information about the Sun's outer atmosphere; and for measuring its diameter.[50]

If the relative sizes of the Sun and Moon are the outcome of design, then they are properly understood as a divine miracle. I will deal with the issue of miracles in more detail in Chapter 5. For present purposes it is enough to plant the suggestion that miracles *can* happen. As far as the relative sizes of the Sun and Moon are concerned, a miraculous explanation seems to me considerably more likely than sheer fluke.

Cognition: my conclusions

What conclusions can be drawn from Man's possession of cognition? Paul Davies' conclusion is as follows:

> [F]ar from being a trivial accident, [it] is a fundamental feature of the universe, a natural product of the outworking of the laws of nature to which they are connected in a deep and still mysterious way.[51]

In my view, it is legitimate to go a step further than this. The unique properties of Man's cognitive ability point to the existence of God.

The laws of Nature – and the physical outworkings of those laws – are calibrated in such a way that Man is able to contemplate the grandeur of his own existence, and of the Universe as a whole. In short, only Man has the capacity to experience awe.

The possession of that capacity – one of the basic differences between intelligence and understanding – is one of the things that distinguishes Man from everything else in the known Universe. It seems, however, that Man does not need to possess that capacity in order to survive and prosper as a physical species on Earth. Why, then, do we possess it?

The answer seems to me to be this. It is that capacity which inevitably causes Man to ask the most fundamental of questions: How and why are things as they are? And once we begin to think in that way, we are drawn to consider the possible existence of a supernatural Creator who caused all of these things to be: i.e. God, a First Cause. Throughout the recorded history of human civilisation, it has always been so. As John Polkinghorne has observed, it is natural for Man to seek an explanation for the fit between 'the reason within and the reason without'. The most natural explanation is that 'there is some deeper rationality which is the ground of both, linking them together'. Of course, on the Christian view of things, that link is 'the Creator who is the ground of both our mental life and our physical life'[52]. In short, the reason that Man can understand something of the laws that govern the Universe is that God made both our minds and those laws.

Now, I have said that Man's capacity to reason leads to contemplation of, at least, the possibility of God's existence. Yet there are, and always have been, many people in the world who have cogitated on the matter intensely and reached the conclusion that God does *not* exist. Where does that leave my argument? Is it not just as likely that the unbelievers are right and the believers wrong?

In some ways it would be comforting to be able to agree with the unbelievers. If there is no God, and Man exists as a strange aberration in a Universe governed solely by accidental physical laws, then none us will ever have to answer for our failings to a higher power. But such a state of affairs seems contrary to the evidence. The bare fact that Man is capable even of *contemplating* the underlying order of the Universe – and the possible existence of God – is difficult to explain away. As Timothy Keller has observed, Man's other innate desires – for food, sex, sleep, companionship – 'correspond to real objects that can satisfy them'[53]. Why not our innate desire for God? Or, if you prefer, for beauty, transcendence, immortality?

As I have said, if there is no God, there seems to be no plausible explanation in evolutionary terms for why Man should possess the capacity to conceive Him. Religious observance must always have been a significant distraction from other more 'practical' activities that would better have ensured the survival of the species. I will tackle this issue more fully in Chapter 4, but if 'survival value' is ruled out there must be another reason why Man possesses these capacities. Only one credible reason occurs to me. God does, *in fact*, exist and we have been granted – by God – the capacity to speculate about Him and His works.

In other words, the very fact that Man is able to ask himself the ultimate question – is there a God who created me? – is powerful evidence that the question has an affirmative answer. Crucially, though, we have the capacity only to speculate about God – we cannot know definitely. That seems to me to be a part of the grand scheme.

Conscience

If Man's possession of the faculty of cognition points to the existence of God, then our possession of another unique attribute – conscience – seems to me further to increase its likelihood. At all events, I agree with English agnostic John Humphrys that '[t]he notion of conscience is central in the debate about the existence of God' because 'it is difficult to understand the existence of conscience without accepting the existence of something beyond ourselves'[54]. The arguments are simple and compelling.

The starting premise is that Man understands innately that there is such a thing as right and such a thing as *wrong*. This faculty is what I will refer to as 'conscience'.

Of all my theological reading, none has had a greater impact than C.S. Lewis's introductory discussion of conscience in *Mere Christianity*. It influenced me in the very early stages of my emergent belief in God, because it made sense of thoughts and feelings that had affected me powerfully all my life, and still do. In the writing of the section that follows I have drawn a great deal from Lewis's work.

One point needs be stressed at the outset. I am *not* contending – and nor did C.S. Lewis – that only the religious person is capable of sincere goodness. Bertrand Russell rightly decried self-satisfied people down the centuries who have insisted that 'we should all be wicked if we did not hold to the Christian religion'[55]. There are, and always have been, good-natured people who are atheists and mean-spirited people who are (or profess to be) Christians. The argument that belief in God is necessary for moral conduct is a red herring. Atheists who lead decent and useful lives justifiably prickle at the contention. Nor even am I contending that, on the whole, people who practise religion live worthier lives than those who do not. The opposite may be closer to the truth, because many people are drawn to religion precisely because their sins lead them into desperation and despair. Their consciousness of guilt eventually compels them to reassess the meaning of life, with a higher degree of insight and sincerity than that which is frequently displayed by contented and successful people. Nonetheless, there have also been countless Christian saints. Bertrand Russell went to a ludicrous extreme by his assertion that 'the people who have held to [Christianity] have been for the most part extremely wicked'[56].

All that said, morality and religion are inextricably connected, and not merely in theory. At the level of individual lives, I believe (like the Methodists) that a person who truly believes in Christianity should behave *better* than he would otherwise have done if he did not believe. In short, true faith should improve your behaviour, whether you are coming off a low or a high base. As the American theologian D.A. Carson has observed, Christians 'are still contaminated by failures, sin, relapses, rebellion, self-centeredness; we are not yet what we ought to be'. However – and anyone who calls himself or herself a Christian must sincerely believe this – 'By the grace of God, we are not what we were.'[57]

But my main purpose in this section is not to discuss the moral benefits of practising Christianity. It is to analyse the phenomenon of conscience, as it manifests itself in believers and non-believers alike. Few non-believers who live good lives appear to consider why they lead such lives – why, more often than not, they obey the dictates of their conscience. And even fewer consider where their conscience comes from.

The universal standard of right conduct

Each of us knows, or feels, that there is such a thing as right and wrong. It is not an illusion, but very real.

Moreover, when stripped down to essentials, Man's notions of what is right and wrong do not differ fundamentally across different societies and cultures; nor have they fundamentally differed for (at least) several thousands of years. St Paul's injunction that we should all 'be careful to do what is right in the eyes of everybody' (Romans 12:17) is notable for its implicit assumption that all people do agree, at core, upon what is good. Modern anthropological and psychological studies point to the same basic conclusion: '[D]espite our diverse languages, religions, social practices, and expressed beliefs … [there is] a vast terrain of common ground'[58].

Thus, everybody knows (and has always known) that truthfulness is better than deceit, courage is better than cowardice, loyalty is better than treachery, generosity is better than selfishness, compassion is better than cruelty, and love is better than hate. It is hard to conceive of a world in which even one of these truths could be different, let alone all of them. These are the 'core values' that underlie the judgements, big and small, that each of us makes daily – including agnostics and atheists.

In one of his early sermons, Martin Luther King took up this theme:

[S]ome things are right and some things are wrong. Eternally so, absolutely so. It's wrong to hate. It always has been wrong and it always will be wrong. It's wrong in America, it's wrong in Germany, it's wrong in Russia, it's wrong in China. It was wrong in 2000 B.C., and it's wrong in 1954 A.D. It always has been wrong and it always will be wrong.[59]

Of course, real life is rarely black and white. Each of us must try continually to strike a balance between competing virtues and competing evils. Is it right, for example, to tell a 'white lie' in order to spare someone's feelings? To betray a confidence in order to expose an injustice? Is killing justified in war in order to avoid the suffering of the innocent? To say that there is such a thing as right and wrong is not to say that it is always easy to know what to do. In the words of D.A. Carson, 'the pursuit of [moral] excellence does not turn on transparent distinctions between right and wrong. It turns, rather, on delicate choices that reflect one's entire value system.'[60]

But however delicate the choice may be in a given situation, the fact remains that the moral task for each individual is, always, to try to make the *right* choice. Moreover, that choice is never between our 'intellectual' preference on the one hand, and our 'emotional' preference on the other. Both the emotions and the intellect are involved throughout the process.[61] Everyone is aware of these strange facts. Everyone, each day of their life, feels the pull of conscience. We each of us struggle many times a day with questions of right behaviour, big and small. This is so whether or not you know or believe anything about Christianity, or any religion. It is a universal reality of human life.

St Paul touched upon this notion in his letter to the Romans, during a discussion about the doing of right and wrong by both Jews (who were educated in the Law of Moses) and Gentiles (who were not):

> For it is not those who hear the law who are righteous in God's sight, but it is those who obey the law who will be declared righteous. (Indeed, when Gentiles, who do not have the law, do by nature things required by law, they are a law for themselves, even though they do not have the law, since they show that the requirements of the law are written on their hearts, *their consciences also bearing witness*, and their thoughts now accusing, now even defending them.)
>
> (Romans 2:13–16. My emphasis)

In short, it was possible for Gentiles ignorant of Jewish law to obey it 'by nature', through the pull of conscience.

St Paul was surely speaking about the fundamentals of good behaviour. There is a basic difference between, on the one hand, notions of right conduct that are truly fundamental to all human societies and, on the other hand, mere customs, rituals or codes of manners that are the product of a particular time or place. There is a most unfortunate tendency among many 'religious' people mistakenly to elevate the latter into the former, so that religion seems to become to many unbelievers a rigid and often obscure set of rules.

The Bible contains both fundamental moral injunctions and (because it was written by many different people each of whom lived at a particular time and place in history) numerous references to local and/or contemporary laws, customs and rituals. It is important to distinguish intelligently between the two. Thus, the Ten Commandments clearly enough were intended to be understood as fundamental moral injunctions, and most of them 'are present in virtually every form of human society'[62]. On the other hand, the many references in the Old Testament to such things as diet, dress, animal sacrifices and circumcision are not, it seems to me, to be regarded as 'binding' in the present day. Other Old Testament pronouncements (for example, 'an eye for an eye') are explicitly 'overruled' in the New Testament.[63]

Jesus of Nazareth was highly conscious of the distinction between the mere keeping of rules – outward appearances – and the doing of good. He was trenchant in his criticism of the Pharisees on this account, frequently accusing them and other religious leaders of hypocrisy. He denounced their insistence upon adherence to fussy man-made rules of personal behaviour as though they were God's edicts (cf. Mark 7:1–8; Matthew 15:1–9)[64]. Jesus also taught that adherence even to God's true commandments is not enough if it is done only for public show, or for the wrong motives, or in a grudging spirit (Matthew 5:27–30; 6:1–4). It is hardly an exaggeration to say that 'there can be no such thing to Christ as doing "good" for the wrong reasons'[65]. The Beatitudes are notable for the emphasis placed by Jesus upon the state of mind – and not merely the objective conduct – of the truly good and devout. What matters most are not our achievements but our intentions. Provided we have the right intentions, and genuinely strive to achieve them, God will excuse our failures of execution.

The same point is made in the Old Testament. Martin Luther King once based a sermon[66] upon the passage in the first book of Kings in which David is praised by God for merely having wanted to build a great temple in God's honour. The temple was not constructed during David's reign, because God willed that it be built by Solomon, his son. But God told David that 'because it was *in your heart* to build a temple for my Name, you did well' (see 1 Kings 8:17–19).

Jesus too understood that the measure of virtue is what is 'in your heart'. Jesus also understood that for certain kinds of people, virtue comes more easily than it does for others. We do not all have the same temperament or the same material advantages; we enjoy varying degrees of good and bad fortune. How well each of us measures up to the universal standard of right conduct is not to be assessed merely in absolute terms but (at least in part) by reference to the amount of effort that we put into it. The congenitally timid man who performs one apparently modest act of bravery may surpass in moral merit the popular hero who was born with an instinct for valour and who routinely performs audacious deeds, expecting and receiving adulation for doing so. The timid man's conduct may be more meritorious because he must really force himself to do it, expecting nothing in return but the doing of the right thing.

Such inner struggle is usually not known to other people, but it is real nonetheless. I certainly feel it, constantly. Thus, for me, one of the seminal (and comforting) messages of the Gospels is the importance of sincere good conduct: in other words, the primacy of conscience.

As I have said, views may reasonably differ as to what is the right or the wrong thing to do in a given situation. And the subtle balancing act which is morality must, to some extent, be taught: one of the key roles of the established churches is to assist people in developing a properly *informed* conscience. But the curious fact remains that at a basic level each of us is aware that everything we do is, to a greater or lesser extent, either right or wrong. St Augustine's view, with which I agree, was that 'there is no soul, however perverted … in whose conscience God does not speak'[67].

I now come to a critical issue. Granted, each of knows at some level that the rightness or wrongness of any given conduct is to be judged against a certain standard. Granted, too, that as a matter of practical reality all human beings acknowledge much the same standard – and that many people, in significant part, manage to live by it. But there remains a vital question. Is the standard relative or absolute? By 'relative', I mean something ultimately grounded in the personal or fortuitous judgment of each individual. By 'absolute', I mean something like the laws of physics or mathematics, 'a powerful objective element behind the scenes that is discovered rather than invented'.[68]

If the standard is merely relative, then no one ever truly asks themselves, 'What ought I ought to do?' The second 'ought' is just a number of alternative 'oughts' (even if, in practice, most people apply roughly the same one).[69] Strictly, on this view, there is no such thing as 'right' conduct, just an individual's sincere feeling that certain conduct feels right to him.[70] In those circumstances, there is no valid basis for judging anyone else's conduct; indeed, there is no basis for any system of ethics at all, as most people understand the term.

On the other hand, if the standard of proper conduct is objective – i.e. an unchangeable fact about the Universe, and hence truly universal – then it cannot be an invention of any man or woman, or of any group collectively. It must exist, like the laws of physics and mathematics, 'outside us and beyond us'.[71] If so, it must emanate from God. On this view, which is the one I hold, God is the source of our conviction that 'some things ought not to be done regardless of how a person feels about them within herself, regardless of what the rest of her community and culture says, and regardless of whether it is in her self-interest or not'.[72] So too as regards things which ought to be done. To encapsulate these notions, theologians sometimes use the term 'the Moral Law'.

The content of this Moral Law was distilled by Jesus into two basic commandments: to love God with all your heart and soul and mind, and to love your neighbour as yourself (Matthew 22:36–40; Mark 12:28–31). Most people, religious or not, seem more consciously attuned to the second injunction than they are to the first; but both injunctions are critical, and both are capable of being grasped by everyone, however imperfectly.

In the next chapter, about love, I will attempt to explain my understanding of these injunctions in more detail. However, the key point, for present purposes, is that an objective or absolute standard of right conduct exists. It resides in the conscience of each one of us.

Man does not meet the standard

That leads to my second main point about conscience, which is that the standard to which I have referred is *not* derived from what Man in fact usually does. Indeed, we can recognise or imagine what is incontestably 'right' conduct – by ourselves and others – even when we have rarely, if ever, come close to such conduct ourselves.[73] In brief, each one of us continually falls far short of the universal standard of right conduct, *and yet we are aware of that fact*. Bertrand Russell was an implacable agnostic, but he allowed that 'the soul of man is … a battleground of two natures, the one particular, finite, self-centred, the other universal, infinite, and impartial'[74]. A contemporary Australian writer on religion, Margaret Symons, has written that she ceased to be an atheist partly as a result of 'the realisation that, particularly when gardening, I was sometimes conducting an internal conversation with a person who did not seem to be me'.[75]

St Paul grappled with this strange aspect of human behaviour. He wrote:

> So I find this law is at work: When I want to do good, evil is right there with me. For in my inner being I delight in God's law [i.e. right conduct]; but I see another law at work in the members of my body, waging war against the law of my mind [i.e. conscience] and making me a prisoner of the law of sin at work within my members.
>
> (Romans 7:21–23)

Thus, what St Paul called 'the law of my mind' (or his conscience) was frequently in conflict with the impulses and desires of his body. Man's natural condition, according to him, was sinfulness; the only way that Man can save himself is by deliberately making the effort to follow the dictates of conscience.

In his letter to the Galatians, St Paul was even more explicit:

> So I say, live by the Spirit, and you will not gratify the desires of the sinful nature. For the sinful nature desires what is contrary to the Spirit, and the Spirit what is contrary to the sinful nature. They are in conflict with each other, so that you do not do what you want.
>
> (Galatians 5:16–17)

St Paul's words are applicable not merely to sexual desire, but sexual desire is an excellent example of what he meant. Almost anyone who is married, or in any other serious personal relationship, will have felt the temptation of illicit sex. The overwhelmingly 'natural' thing to do is to submit to that temptation. It is only an ideal of right conduct – monogamy, or loyalty to your sexual partner – that may hold you back. Animals, which do not possess a conscience, do not hold back (though there are, charmingly, a handful of species that practise monogamy). Animals simply do what their bodies wish them to do. Man – at least some of the time – does not.

Even when the pull of conscience is not strong enough to hold us back from conduct that we know to be wrongful, it can still operate powerfully after the event. The Bible warns that 'you may be sure that your sin will find you out' (Numbers 32:23), and this does not necessarily mean that we will be punished, formally or informally, by other people. Everyone knows what a miserable feeling it is to have a guilty conscience. This phenomenon, too, serves a number of vital purposes: it may act as a deterrent against similar wrongful conduct in the future or, at least, as a punishment for the wrongdoing itself.

In other words, our consciences are an instrument of God's justice. As Lady Macbeth lamented during her descent into madness:

> Nought's had, all's spent,
> Where our desire is got without content:
> Tis safer to be that which we destroy
> Than by destruction dwell in doubtful joy.[76]

Another way of looking at the notion of conscience is that of the Quakers. They do not believe that everyone is inherently sinful, or that the primary role of our conscience is to guide us away from sin. Rather, they teach that each person has a small part of God's Spirit within them. That part of our soul, the 'Inner Light', may in many people lie dormant; the spiritual challenge facing each one of us is to nurture it to the maximum extent. The rewards of doing so are faith and righteousness. In other words, the role of our conscience is to guide us *toward* God's way. I find this idea both shrewd and attractive.

Whichever way you look at conscience, two things about it seem highly significant.

First, the fact that Man's experience of the pull of conscience is unique; together with the faculty of cognition, our possession of a conscience is one of the main things setting us apart from animals. (I am not prepared to say that animals do not possess some other attributes of consciousness – clearly enough, to varying degrees, many animals do.[77]) Second, the phenomenon of conscience – the dichotomy between the good conduct that each of knows to be right, and the wrongful conduct that each of us knows we should guard against – helps in inferring the existence of God. Why? I have come to believe this: the *source* of our inner voice (conscience) must be something separate from, and greater than, Man. In other words, our conscience cannot merely be a construct of the human brain – i.e. of Nature. That must be so because the universal standard of right conduct is not based on what, much of the time, each of us actually does or would wish to do. What our conscience does is to enable us, sometimes, to rise above our natural instincts. In Shakespeare's words, 'Our bodies are gardens to which our wills are gardeners'[78].

At this point I find myself compelled to quote at some length from two theologians. First, there is C.S. Lewis, because this is the passage that caused the penny to drop for me:

> The position of the question, then, is like this. We want to know whether the universe simply happens to be what it is for no reason or whether there is a power behind it that makes it what it is. Since that power, if it exists, would be not one of the observed facts but a reality which makes them, no mere observation of the facts can find it. There is only one case in which we [i.e. Man] can know whether there is anything more, namely our own case. And in that one case we find there is. Or put it the other way around. If there was a controlling power outside the universe, it could not show itself to us as one of the facts inside the universe – no more than the architect of a house could actually be a wall or staircase or fireplace in that house. The only way in which we could expect it to show itself would be inside ourselves as an influence or a command trying to get us to behave in a certain way. And that is just what we do find inside ourselves [i.e. conscience]. Surely that ought to arouse our suspicions?[79]

Paul Johnson, a contemporary English historian and writer, has expressed the same idea in a slightly different way. In another passage that has made a profound impression upon me, Johnson explains why, in the history of human civilisation, atheism has been very much a minority creed:

> I suspect the reason why atheism has so little attraction is precisely our awareness of a desire in ourselves to do good. All of us have a conscience, whatever we may call it. We know we have this thing inside us, this nagging inner voice which tells us not to be so selfish or to help those in need or to prefer right to wrong ... The conscience can never quite be killed. And because it exists *and we know it exists*, we are periodically driven to ponder – or half-ponder – the question: how did it get there? Who put it there? ... The agnostic cannot shake off conscience as easily as he shakes off positive

belief in God, and because conscience remains, there is always in the background of the agnostic's mind the suspicion that some agency put it there. What other explanation can there be? So the shadow of God is never quite dispelled.[80]

Johnson poses the rhetorical question: What other (naturalistic) explanation can there be for the existence of our conscience? None is readily apparent to me.

Some people suggest that conscience may be accounted for in terms of Darwinian selection.[81] Thus, so a typical version of the argument runs, the earliest living creatures, including primitive man, like most animals now, had no conscience; they behaved completely instinctively and selfishly. But at some time in the distant past Man realised that there were advantages in behaving with greater restraint, with less violence, with a greater disposition for sharing. Such forms of behaviour increased the chances of survival by reducing destructive conflict and allowing a more equitable distribution of food and resources. Gradually, the species might select for those of a milder, more tolerant, more submissive nature.

This argument does not persuade me, for a number of reasons. For one thing, it seems to run counter to the basic tenets of Darwinism itself, as well as Mendel's discoveries about genetic inheritance. Physical characteristics (including those affecting mental processes) are not acquired or learned during the life of an organism and then handed down to offspring; they are embedded in DNA.[82] Moreover, Darwinian natural selection 'operates on the individual, not on the population'[83]. To assert that primitive man 'realised' the advantages of cooperative behaviour without any intervention by God is in fact to assert that a random mutation of DNA, occurring initially in one organism, somehow conferred a propensity to engage in such behaviour in that organism, *and that this trait was subsequently selected for by primitive man's environment.*

Even if such a mutation had occurred, it is hard to see how it could have been a favourable mutation, conferring an advantage on the organism in question. Cooperative behaviour is advantageous when most people are prepared to engage in it; if most people are acting selfishly and instinctively, then the mild and tolerant person would seem – in terms of survival prospects – to be at a distinct *dis*advantage. Darwinian processes – which 'will always favour short-term benefit'[84] – would quickly weed out such a trait, before it could take root. I see that problem in the postulated case of primitive man, and similar doubts have been expressed by numerous distinguished scientists, including the head of the Human Genome Project, Francis Collins.[85]

On the other hand, there are also numerous distinguished scientists who contend that Darwinian processes must account for morality. Not surprisingly, Richard Dawkins is one of them. He covers this issue in *The God Delusion*, suggesting that genes ensure their survival not only by programming individual organisms to be selfish, but also (in certain situations) by programming them to be altruistic. He claims there are two 'well understood' examples: genes promoting altruism towards an organism's offspring and genes conferring a propensity to altruism towards those in a position to do the organism a reciprocal favour. He also suggests that genes might confer altruism because altruism assists an organism to acquire a reputation for goodness and/or to assert its superiority by overt displays of generosity.[86]

But even Dawkins accepts that the many subtle nuances of human morality cannot be explained solely by natural selection.[87] Dawkins argues that Nature confers instinctive 'rules of thumb', such as a mother's protectiveness toward her children. The more noble aspects of morality – pity for the stranger in distress; honesty in the face of temptation, even when we are unlikely to be found out – are, Dawkins asserts, 'misfires' of our basic instincts, which were formed when Man lived in small tribes and villages. Those instincts still govern our behaviour today, 'even where circumstances make them inappropriate to their original functions'. In short, the urges to generosity and other noble conduct are 'blessed, precious mistakes'[88].

There is a fundamental problem with these arguments. The very notion of conscience is concerned with what we *ought* to do, not with what we in fact do, or desire to do, or are instinctively driven to do. Our instincts and our impulses, which attach themselves to primal ends such as food, sex, physical safety, feelings of pleasure[89] – these are the things conferred by our DNA. Our conscience comes into play when two or more impulses – two or more possible courses of conduct – are in conflict, and a *decision* is required as to which impulse to follow. Indeed, as I have already suggested, the reality is rather more complicated than that. Man often ponders, not merely what he ought to do, but what ought he ought to do! 'The second ought,' Fairfax explained, 'asks me whether, being the individual that I am, I should not constitute myself into somethings different and better. And of course it will be found that I can.'[90]

So where does that leave us? With this conclusion: science cannot explain either morality or aesthetics. As Einstein wrote, reflecting upon the limits of science:

> The scientific method can teach us nothing beyond how facts are related to and conditioned by each other … [K]nowledge of what *is* does not open the door directly to what *should* be. One can have the clearest and most complete knowledge of what is, and yet not be able to deduce from that what should be the goal of our human aspirations.[91]

Warwick Fairfax made the same point, invoking the example (among others) of Einstein himself:

> If morality and aesthetics are no more than biological derivatives, if the urge to do something men call great has a simple psychoanalytic explanation, then the title to fame which we give Einstein, Beethoven and Plato vanishes, and the ends they believed themselves to be following become phantoms.[92]

C.S. Lewis, who accepted the basics of Darwinism, was alive to these arguments also. Lewis concluded that any decision we make in life about the 'should' or the 'ought' must involve more than physical matter, even though such decisions are effected by and through physical matter. '[W]henever we think rationally,' Lewis suggested, 'we are, by direct spiritual power, forcing certain atoms in our brain and certain psychological tendencies in our natural soul to do what they would never have done if left to

Nature.'[93] In the language of modern psychiatry, we exercise free will in a 'good' way when the ego (the self) is aware of a conflict between the animal urges of the id and the ideals and controls of the super ego, and chooses to follow the latter. For present purposes, the main point is that The id and the super ego 'contain forces which, as it were, come into the self from regions *outside* it'.[94]

Another naturalistic explanation for conscience is that it is no more than a set of societal rules learned from our parents, or others in authority. We obey them because we fear the wrath of society and/or our parents. I think this idea, too, is unsound. Of course, many of the dictates of good conduct are learned that way. But that does not explain conscience. For a start, it 'does not explain why society, as a *group* of persons, should ever have erected a moral structure which its members as individuals did not understand or believe in, but simply feared'.[95] It also confuses the ultimate source of morality with the process by which an individual is 'induced to accept' it.[96]

Why does the parent teach the child the dictates of good conduct? Because the parent's own conscience requires it, and he or she recognises the universal validity of those dictates. Why – if the parent is lucky! – does the child obey those dictates? Not, I submit, from fear of disapproval or hope of approval and reward (at least, not always or exclusively for those reasons). The child does so because '[a]ffection for others, that is to say, a desire for their welfare, comes naturally to most people as soon as they begin to think of others as "people" at all'[97].

Yet more fundamentally, why are the dictates of good conduct more or less universally agreed? Because, as I have argued, they are more than a construct of Man, which might have been different. The laws of proper conduct seem to be fixed, in much the same way as the laws of mathematics. This suggests to me that they emanate from a source outside of Man. This is not a new idea: the nomadic peoples of ancient Persia believed that truth and decency were fundamental laws of Nature (*asha*), 'akin to the rising and setting of the sun and the passage of the seasons'[98]. One of the earliest-appearing and most basal themes of the Old Testament is that morality is 'God-given'[99].

Some atheists are aware of the mystery of conscience. Christopher Hitchens is eloquent on the subject, but abruptly concludes that 'those who believe that the existence of conscience is a proof of a godly design are advancing an argument that simply cannot be disproved because there is no evidence for or against it'[100]. For me, it is not a matter of strict proof or disproof. Rather, the traditional religious explanation for the phenomenon of conscience is the most satisfying. The existence of universal moral laws, the pull of which we experience through our conscience, implies the existence of a universal law*maker*. Moreover, it implies the existence of a universal law *enforcer*; otherwise we might be conscious of the laws but feel no compunction about breaching them. In the words of John Henry Newman:

> If, as is the case, we feel responsibility, are ashamed, are frightened, at transgressing the voice of conscience, this implies that there is One to whom we are responsible, before whom we are ashamed, whose claim upon us we fear.[101]

To reiterate, there is an 'inner voice' in each one of us, and it is extremely difficult to find any satisfactory explanation for its presence there, other than a supernatural explanation: God. Science is incapable of providing an explanation, because the force of conscience is concerned with an ideal: what *ought* to be rather than what is.

Free will

The notion of an 'ought' leads to the next key consideration – the third in the sequence of my argument – namely, the phenomenon of free will. Unavoidably, I have already alluded to free will several times. The notion of conscience is predicated on the assumption that our behaviour is our own – that the person who decides what 'I' do is, in a real and not notional sense, me, my-Self. This conviction is deeply ingrained in the human psyche.

Free will is one of the most important concepts in theology – and for good reason. In order to believe in God, you must believe that Man's possession of free will is not an accident – that free will is not a mere incidental by-product of the outworking of random physical laws, but a necessary feature of a moral world. As Soren Kierkegaard observed, Man is distinguished by his capacity to experience 'dread', the fearful awareness of moral freedom. This, Kierkegaard argued, is an important theme of the story of Adam and Eve: 'Once Adam knows he can disobey God, he desires to do so, and he dreads his own desire, because he knows that as a free being there is nothing but himself to stop him from sinning.'[102]

In order to believe in God you must also believe that free will is not an illusion. Free will would be a mere illusion if each of us only *appears* to have a choice whether or not to behave in a particular way. Indeed, the problem is stranger still. Before we make any choice, we must come to realise that there is a choice to be made, and identify the possible choices. Are those experiences also illusions?

I cannot bring myself to believe that free will is either an accident or an illusion. It does not look like an accident because it is hard to envisage how Man's possession of conscience can be attributed to random physical processes; the standard by which each of us judges right and wrong is not based upon what (much of the time) we actually do or would wish to do, but what we ought to do. Accordingly, it seems most unlikely that such a thing as conscience could have 'evolved' in the Darwinian sense, through a process of random mutation and natural selection. Even if I am wrong about that, and our consciences are somehow the product of evolution, it is inconceivable to me that this is merely a happy accident. I explained in Chapter 1 why the *process* of Darwinian evolution appears to me to have been designed; if that process is also responsible for conscience, then the argument for Design seems stronger still.

Nor can I accept that free will is an illusion. That would mean that each one of us is compelled by fixed forces of Nature to live our lives in a particular way, without being aware of it. The seventeenth-century Dutch philosopher, Benedictus Spinoza, held to this view. Freedom, as he conceived it, is simply 'ignorance of necessity'[103]. Think about the implications of that proposition. They are deeply disconcerting.

You may be bored now with this book. If there is no such thing as free will, you do not really have a choice whether to put it down (with relief) or to read on (perhaps out of some sense of duty); what you end up doing will *not* be the result of a conscious weighing of alternatives and a decision on your part, even if you perceive that such a process has occurred. Similarly, when you eat a meat pie for lunch rather than a sandwich; when you apologise to a friend for forgetting their birthday rather than staying quiet; when you summon the courage to ask a woman to dance – none of these acts are decisions at all, but are pre-determined by the chance position of atoms. Likewise, too, the 'decisions' of other people. If free will is an illusion, then no one else has any genuine control over their conduct either. You may imagine that your wife is making up her mind which dress to buy, or whether to have sex with you tonight, but in fact her 'choices' will not be made by her.[104]

To me, all of these notions are not only profoundly repugnant; they are contrary to common sense. Each of us perceives that our choices are real. Each of us perceives that other people's choices are real (and we judge them accordingly). The best explanation for these perceptions is that everyone's choices *are* real. The alternative is a morally barren world of automata.

Man's possession of free will is, I believe, neither an accident nor an illusion. Rather, like cognition, it is another fundamental feature of the Universe. What we now call 'civilisation' is the cumulative result of many, many centuries during which Man has gradually realised the wisdom of not *always* following our selfish instincts, or man-made laws, or even formal religious teachings. This has happened as a result of the exercise of free will by countless individuals, rather than Darwinian processes. It is our conscience that produces 'love, joy, peace, patience, kindness, goodness, faithfulness, humility and self-control' (Galatians 5:22). It is free will that makes the outcome of listening to our conscience (or not) something that is meaningful.

The Holy Spirit and the notion of 'primacy of conscience'

Some of the ideas articulated in this chapter have been developed with much more sophistication in the Christian concept of the Holy Spirit – the Third Person of the Holy Trinity – and in the notion of the 'primacy of conscience'.

As to the Holy Spirit, I conceive it as the force which assists and encourages me to love God and to obey His commandments. (Most imperfectly, of course.) This conception is shared by many Christians. I believe that the Spirit operates on and through my conscience, helping me to recognise moral problems, big or small, and guiding me in deciding what to do in response to those problems. The Spirit is present in every human being. Indeed, it is present throughout the cosmos as the ultimate life force.[105] You may not always be aware that the force is operating upon you at any given moment. But the force is real, and I believe that the force is God, who, in St Paul's words, 'works in you to will and to act according to his good purpose' (Philippians 2:13).

As I have said, the task of deciding what is the right thing to do in a given situation is frequently a difficult one, and that can be so even if the Spirit is operating within you. But the key point is that such a decision is there to be made; and *only you* can truly know whether any decision you make is consistent with your conscience. You can and should listen to advice from others, and especially from religious authorities, but ultimately – in a real sense – the decision is yours. You can and should override everyone and everything else, if you really believe it right to do so; and if enough people behave in the same way in a given situation, the teachings of the relevant religious authorities may come into question and, ultimately, be changed. Thus were the Christian Church's edicts about usury and slavery overturned.

So, only you can know what your conscience is telling you. But – and this too is significant – only you can know whether you have tried in good faith to *educate* your conscience. The concept of 'informed conscience' is an important one.[106] Many people seek to discredit religion by insisting that they feel no sense of guilt as to the way they live their lives, and in particular as to their lack of curiosity about God: they say that their 'conscience is clear'. This phenomenon has led some prominent Catholic thinkers to question the very notion of the 'primacy of conscience', for fear it encourages people intent on 'doing their own thing' to rely on their own laziness and ignorance. There is a danger, they believe, that among people with an unformed and under-educated conscience 'clear thinking and past wisdom will be repudiated and ridiculed'[107]. St Paul recognised the same problem (see Ephesians 4:18–19).

These are entirely valid concerns, but I do not believe they are insoluble. The doctrine of the primacy of conscience can prevail 'without abandoning a commitment to clear thinking and past wisdom'; moreover, it 'gives no consolation to the uninitiated'[108]. The doctrine protects people who genuinely wrestle with their conscience and decide in good faith to follow a course of conduct that is contrary to orthodox church teaching – they do not offend God even if their decision is erroneous. But the doctrine does not protect people who just do not bother to think about religion or morality, those whom Kierkegaard identified as having opted for a life of moral 'neutrality'. Nor does the doctrine protect people who, while holding themselves responsible to an ethical code of some sort, make up their own rules as they go along. Your conscience is real just as your muscles are real – it is your fault if you choose not to exercise and look after them.

Even if you do not believe in God, imagine for the sake of argument that God *does* exist. Then imagine that, on Judgment Day, God were to ask why you rarely if ever took the trouble to seek Him out or to understand what He wanted of you. Do you honestly believe that 'I didn't get around to it' or 'It didn't interest me' would be a satisfactory answer? No – your conscience can certainly tell you that much.

It is incumbent on everyone, then, to educate their conscience. Many Christian people today are assisted in the process, on a day-to-day basis, by asking themselves the question, 'What would Jesus do?' (If you see a bumper sticker or a t-shirt bearing the letters 'WWJD'*, that is what they stand for.) The approach of asking oneself

---

* The WWJD technique originated from Charles M. Sheldon's classic book, *In His Steps*, first published in 1897. It is a work of fiction, depicting a small church community in small-town America. Everyone is challenged by their pastor to live for a year by applying the WWJD technique to *every* decision in their lives. The concept is fascinating, though I find Sheldon's characters and situations somewhat trite. Millions of people think otherwise, however.

what Jesus would do in a given situation is consistent with the well-known passage in St John's Gospel in which Jesus is recorded as having told the disciples that the Spirit 'will take from what is mine and make it known to you' (John 16:15). But, of course, in order to make the WWJD technique effective it is necessary to become familiar with the Bible, and especially with the Gospels.

Another way of educating one's conscience is through prayer. St Paul stressed this theme with characteristic vigour. Famously, he taught that the Spirit may do its work on our conscience even when we are so unsure that we do not know what to pray for:

> [T]he Spirit helps us in our weakness. We do not know what we ought to pray, but the Spirit himself intercedes for us with groans that words cannot express.
>
> (Romans 8:26)

The Holy Spirit is, then, a fundamental aspect of Christianity. So fundamental, indeed, that Jesus told the woman from Samaria: 'God is spirit' (John 4:24). This is the *only* instance in the whole of the New Testament where Jesus is recorded as having made an explicit statement about the nature of God.[109] But my contention is that you do not need to know anything about Christian theology to work out that the phenomenon of conscience ('Spirit') is one of the keys to existence.

Cognition and conscience: my conclusions

The key point, then, for present purposes, is that Man possesses the amazing gifts of cognition and conscience. These faculties are fundamental to what it is to be human, and it seems that Man's possession of them is an exceedingly rare (if not unique) phenomenon in the Universe. My belief is that, for the reasons I have tried to explain, they point the way to an understanding of the nature and purposes of God.

Admittedly, there are still mysteries inherent in this approach, not least the question of when, precisely, Man acquired these distinct attributes. Did the species *Homo erectus* have a conscience? When did individual souls first become subject to God's judgment? I suspect that no one will ever have definitive answers to these questions, because Man is not meant to know. But the story of Adam and Eve may usefully be regarded as the ancients' poetic conception of a finite moment in history – the moment when consciousness first emerged in a living organism.

In any event, the phenomena of cognition and conscience are crucial to any appreciation of God. They make sense of the asseveration in the Old Testament that God created Man in His own image (Genesis 1:27). This notion has nothing to do with 'physical anatomy'[110]. Rather, in the words of Martin Luther King:

> [T]he 'image of God' … is the idea that all men have something within them that God injected. Not that they have substantial unity with God, but that every man has a capacity to have fellowship with God. And this gives him a uniqueness, it gives him worth, it gives him dignity.[111]

Music

Man's sense of 'fellowship with God', about which Martin Luther King preached so eloquently, is made possible by cognition and conscience. But in concluding this chapter, mention needs also to be made of a third faculty that is unique to humans – our ability to create and respond to music.

Many animals have much more powerful hearing than Man, and many animals communicate by way of sound. But only Man makes and enjoys music. This is very suggestive, when you consider the profound effect that music can have on the human psyche. As Lawrence Kramer has written, music 'grips or grasps us, almost with the electricity of touch'[112].

Of course, music can be analysed in technical terms. Paul Johnson's thesis is that tonality – the relationship between pitches – is central: 'a modulation in key or a chord in exactly the right place can linger in our memories for the rest of our lives'[113]. But such technical explanations are beyond the comprehension of most people; and no one really needs them in order to feel music's power. Even the greatest composers may not be entirely conscious of what they are doing; Beethoven's letters, for instance, give no clue as to his motives or his methods.

Down the ages, attempts have been made to account for Man's relationship with music in scientific terms. It was Pythagoras who discovered the fundamental mathematical basis of the octave. A contemporary expert, Daniel J. Levitin, has argued that Man's capacity to appreciate music was wired into the human brain by evolutionary processes.[114] That may well be so; but for present purposes I am not focusing on the how of music, rather on the why. Paul Johnson believes that the why is beyond Man's comprehension. 'All we can do,' he suggests, 'is rejoice in the felicity which divine providence has provided by such mysterious means'[115].

I would go a step further. The existence of music challenges our intellect. Music seems to me like the gift of cognition, and the silent pull of conscience: each inclines and enables Man to speculate about the existence of God. Moreover, music is yet another example of organised complexity in Nature, 'an image of cosmic harmony'[116]. It is wondrous and magnificent, yet it hangs by a thread. How likely is it that music is but another freak accident of Nature? Music works because of the laws of mathematics, and those laws were wired into the Universe from the beginning.

Even more significantly, music stirs our emotions. At a purely materialist level, music is just 'vibrations in the air, impinging on the eardrums'[117]. But at an emotional and spiritual level, music 'is our premier embodiment of the drive for attachment' because it 'enlarges [our] capacity … to attach [ourselves] … to whatever we care about'[118]. This drive for attachment extends beyond the strictly material and even beyond the glories of love. It has a spiritual dimension. For many people, listening to music – in their genre of choice – is the closest thing there is to a religious experience. It can take us into another realm of being. Like gazing at the ocean, or watching over a sleeping child, listening to music can move us to a state of transcendence. The modernist composer Arnold Schoenberg may have had these notions in mind when he described music as 'a prophetic message revealing a higher form of life towards which mankind evolves'[119].

In most of the great religions, music plays a vital role in worship. Christianity has an extraordinarily rich tradition in this regard, rooted in the creations of David the psalmist. J.S. Bach believed that '[b]esides other arrangements of the worship service, music too was especially set in order by God's spirit through David'[120]. For Bach, and many other classical composers, all music was dedicated *ad maiorum gloriam Dei*, to the greater glory of God.[121]

In the twenty-first century, music is still central to faith. For many modern-day worshippers the communal singing of hymns or spiritual songs is the most affecting part of the service. Others prefer the more passive experience of listening, of just letting the sounds flow over them. Tastes in music vary widely, of course, but the common denominator is the sense of exaltation and sublimity that music can produce, particularly in a congregational or other group setting. St Paul was alive to this phenomenon 2,000 years ago (see Colossians 3:16), and, while hard external evidence is scant, it seems likely that the earliest Christian communities regularly wrote their own hymns and songs (e.g. Philippians 2:5–11) and/or adapted traditional Jewish music for their purposes.[122] It is certain that medieval Christian monks recorded written music as an aid to the celebration of Mass. I doubt that either those monks or St Paul would have approved of much of today's music, religious and secular, but the essential points remain: the capacity to use harmonised sound to convey abstract concepts, and to evoke emotion, is both unique to Man and integral to transcendent religion. I agree with J.I. Packer that '[t]heologies that cannot be sung … are certainly wrong at a deep level'.[123]

Music looks to me like another part of Paul Davies' 'cosmic connection'. The connection is perhaps most palpably apparent in song, the art form that combines no less than three of Man's unique abilities: to imagine concepts, to use words and to make music. E.Y. 'Yip' Harburg, the man who wrote the lyrics of 'Somewhere Over the Rainbow', described song's cosmic connection in these terms:

> Words make you think a thought. Music makes you feel a feeling. A song makes you feel a thought.[124]

Songs of all kinds often make me feel thoughts of God – sometimes directly, more often indirectly. This appears to be a universal phenomenon. Songs can give rise to the sensation that almost all believers will say they have experienced: the sudden 'flash' of understanding that this world is not all that there is.

In short, song – music in general – is another thing that draws us to God. Music is also the food of love, and love is the subject of my next chapter.

CHAPTER 3

LOVE

We love because he first loved us. If anyone says, 'I love God', yet hates his brother, he is a liar. For anyone who does not love his brother, whom he has seen, cannot love God, whom he has not seen. And he has given us this command: Whoever loves God must also love his brother.

1 John 4:19–21

Love, love, love – that is the soul of genius.

Wolfgang Amadeus Mozart

Love is such a grand phenomenon that any defence of Christianity, or any religion, must take account of it. Yet the subject is so gloriously multi-faceted as to be elusive. So much human creativity has been devoted to love – by philosophers and poets, by novelists and songwriters, by theologians and film-makers – that it is hard to know where to begin.

My chosen starting point is to advance this contention: love has a fundamental place in the scheme of the Universe. For the reasons advanced in Chapter 2, human beings have a genuinely special place in that Universe. But our specialness is not entirely attributable to the faculties of cognition and conscience. The capacity to give and receive love – in all its forms – is also central to our conception of what it is to be human. Our lives are sustained and made meaningful by love.

Now contemplate a remarkable thing. Almost everybody, whatever their circumstances, is able to find substantial comfort and joy (i.e. love) in something or someone. The Earth provides Man with an abundance of things upon which to bestow love (living and non-living, tangible and conceptual) and an abundance of living things (human and non-human) from which to receive love.

This seems to me an extraordinary state of affairs. And it gives rise to some critical theological questions. Might love have been different? Might Man – or the Universe itself – exist without it?

Atheists and other unbelievers tend to concentrate their attention on the most obvious features of the physical Universe. At the level of cosmology, they try to explain the existence of galaxies, stars and planets (and, in part, they succeed). At the level of earthly biology, they try to explain how species evolve (and again, in part, they succeed). But few even begin to try to explain (as opposed to describe) the *existence* of the phenomenon of love, in all its intricacy. Yet love is just as basic a feature of Man's Universe as light or oxygen or blood. Without love, no one can hope to allay the 'dreadful loneliness of his personal consciousness, the feeling that in the last resort there is nothing but his own puny body and limited mind to care for him'[1].

Love, then, requires explanation. But what, exactly, is meant by 'love'? Spinoza defined it as 'a pleasurable state, joy, accompanied by the idea of an external cause'[2]. As a general proposition, that seems to me prosaic but profound. But love comes in various forms, and it is instructive to consider some of them in a little detail.

The forms of love

In the following discussion I have adopted the structure used by Andre Comte-Sponville, a French professor of philosophy, in his superb book *A Short Treatise on the Great Virtues*. In the chapter about love he considers, in turn, *eros*, *philia* and *agape* – the three main types of love in the context of human relationships.[3] I will do the same, and then look briefly at certain other forms of love.

What emerges is that love is not merely a 'many-splendoured thing', serving a multitude of essential purposes. Love itself exists in an ordered hierarchy. Love of neighbour – *agape* – is ultimately the greatest and the most important form of human love, but *agape* is made possible only because of the existence – and the wondrousness – of the other two (*eros* and *philia*). Grasping the interconnectedness of these and other types of love is integral to an understanding of Man, and in particular of conscience. Love is also central to the concept of truth.

All of these considerations point to the existence of God.

Eros

When many people think of 'love', their first thought is of romantic passion, what the Greeks called *eros*. Modern culture (and especially popular music) is dominated disproportionately by veneration of this form of love, a fact that contributes to a great deal of unhappiness for both sexes. I say 'modern' culture, but it seems that things may well have been this way for a very long time. *Eros* has always been one of the principal and abiding concerns of artists of most genres. I am as much a product of that artistic tradition as anyone, probably more so than most. To attempt to explain my arguments about *eros*, and the other forms of love, I will call in aid many references to films, plays and novels.

To be in love is a dizzying, disconcerting feeling. It is much more than being sexually aroused. Lust is a quite different thing to *eros*. Lust is about the sexual act alone. It is an instinct rather than an emotion – an amazingly potent instinct, it is true, and an instinct that is, of itself, another example of the genius of Creation. Most of us – to a greater or lesser extent, and whether we will admit it to ourselves or not – cannot live properly without periodically satisfying this instinct. It is a truism, but the survival of our species (indeed, almost all species) depends, literally, on this unchallengeable fact.

However, because the sexual instinct is (necessarily) so powerful and so insidious, and also because the sexual act is capable of being so transcendentally sweet, lust frequently wreaks havoc upon people's lives. Although lust can always, at least potentially, be controlled or redirected[4], it is rarely an easy thing to do. There are two films that depict lust in ways that resonated for me: Louis Malle's *Damage* (1992) (seen from the perspective of male lust) and Adrian Lyne's *Unfaithful* (2003) (seen from the woman's). These are really frightening – and for that reason, highly moral – films. Each has as its central character an essentially decent married person who is drawn, irresistibly, into a torrid affair. In each case that decision has dreadful unintended consequences: not only the ruination of the person's marriage and the inevitable breakdown of the affair, but the violent death of a third party. Guilt, despair and disgrace follow for all involved.

But lust is not to be distinguished from *eros* on the basis that lust may often be destructive and that *eros* is not. *Eros*, too, may be highly destructive. The real point of distinction is that *eros* is truly a form of love, whereas lust is not. Indeed, the sexual act when divorced from love (marital *philia*, or *eros*) is a base and tawdry thing. Most people in some sense know this to be true, when they listen to their conscience. Sophocles called sexual desire his mad and savage master[5], and St Paul seems to have been fixated with the same idea (cf. 1 Corinthians 6:12–20). So was an early Christian apologist of some influence, Tatian, who lauded the virtues of celibacy. Tatian was an extremist, but two thousand years later there is more evidence than ever that he was not wholly misguided.

Seeking sex for its own sake is dangerous, and the purely physical dangers (AIDS, herpes, etc.) are not always, or even usually, the most serious. Nor even the dangers posed to inter-personal relationships (by adultery, other infidelity, unwanted pregnancies and so on). So-called 'recreational sex' is dangerous *precisely because* these risks can, up to a point, be minimised. In any case they are risks that many people are prepared to run, for the obvious reason that sex can be so intensely pleasurable. Accordingly, sex 'without strings attached' easily becomes a way of life, an addiction, a distracting and corrupting force. Stanley Kubrick's last film, *Eyes Wide Shut* (1999), was a meditation on the theme. So was Shakespeare's blackest of black comedies, *Measure for Measure*. In real life, Bill Clinton's second term as president was, and is, a modern-day cautionary tale.

Eros is quite different. It rarely seems to begin as lust. It is true that sexual consummation with the beloved often, though not always, becomes one of the lover's aims. And, certainly, *eros* in its fullest and most sublime form must involve sex – which, at its best, is a form of 'human communion'[6]. But at least in the earliest and most intense stages of *eros*, lust may be altogether absent. *Eros* at this stage is a form of worship. It is the feeling that nothing is more important than the approval of one's beloved, that almost any sacrifice (of time, effort, reputation, money, dignity, safety, sex itself) is worth the receipt of that approval.

Eros is the form of love that encourages the fulsome declaration of adoration – as Juliet's to Romeo, when she realises with joy that her love is requited:

And yet I wish but for the thing I have:
My bounty is as boundless as the sea,
My love as deep; the more I give to thee,
The more I have, for both are infinite.[7]

Eros, too, is the feeling that makes marriage possible. It is the feeling, sublime while it lasts, that causes people to make life-long promises. Again, Juliet says it perfectly:

If that thy bent of love be honourable
Thy purpose marriage, send me word tomorrow,
By one that I'll procure to come to thee,
Where, and what time, thou wilt perform the rite;
And all my fortunes at thy foot I'll lay,
And follow thee my lord throughout the world.[8]

Eros is capable of transforming the personal behaviour of anyone under its influence. Because someone in the grip of *eros* desires above all else the approval of the beloved, he will want desperately to do good things vis-à-vis the beloved. Moreover – and this seems to me most important – some of that goodness may also flow to other people. The lover will find himself (perhaps for the first time) being generous, kind, courteous, loyal or brave. *Eros* teaches us – involuntarily – what it feels like to wish to practise many of the virtues. It is a stepping stone to the higher forms of love, because the lover has 'within him … the feeling that he matters for some other reason than just himself, and that therefore life matters'[9].

But, of course, *eros* is not always, or even most of the time, a wholly pleasurable feeling. Partly this is because *eros* is a form of love that cannot be readily controlled: it just happens. No one can command this sort of love, either to begin or to cease.

Eros can give rise to debilitating anxiety. Unless and until it is requited, *eros* spawns tiny thrills and many miseries, self-delusion and procrastination. When Orlando first meets the luminous Rosalind, he finds himself unable to speak to her: 'What passion,' he wonders, 'hangs these weights upon my tongue?'[10] Perhaps even more important than obtaining the beloved's approval is avoiding the beloved's *disapproval*. Often, for this reason, a person in the power of *eros* chooses to love at a distance, rather than to declare his or her love and risk its refusal, for unrequited love – as Goethe's Werther for Lotte – is a terribly bittersweet thing. The victim of unrequited love may feel 'in some inexpressible way that his own personality has ceased to be present'[11]. For a time, he does not care about anything – including whatever the beloved may do or say. (I do not know of any Western author who has succeeded in conveying this feeling more accurately or more vividly than the Australian novelist Martin Boyd. I am thinking of the scene in his best novel, *Lucinda Brayford* (1946), when Tony Duff is rejected by Lucinda.

She has loved him as an older brother since she was a girl, and still feels that way; but his love has turned into *eros*. This doleful exchange near the end of their conversation encapsulates the mental agony of each of them: ' "We mustn't quarrel, Tony," she said after a while. / "It doesn't matter now." / "That's a horrid thing to say." '[12] In effect, their relationship is over forever, and they both know it.)

The overwhelming fear of failure is another reason why sex may not be, at least at first, one of the lover's principal aims, or an aim at all, because any sexual advance carries with it (and should) the high potentiality for rejection. So the uncertain lover waits, sometimes forever. As Somerset Maugham so rightly remarked, 'the love that lasts longest is the love that is never returned'[13].

Even when *eros* is requited, happiness does not necessarily follow. Adulterous love, for example, must almost inevitably cause pain for someone, and not infrequently for everyone concerned, because it tends to undermine other more enduring forms of love. This is the central theme of Tolstoy's *Anna Karenina* and another of Goethe's great masterpieces, *Elective Affinities*.

One of the greatest joys in life comes when it is *not* necessary to suppress *eros*. In Ang Lee's film of *Sense and Sensibility* (1995), there is a superb scene in which the central character, Elinor Dashwood, experiences both of these emotions (the agonising suppression of *eros* and the guiltless surrender to it) within a few minutes. Elinor believes that Edward Ferrars, the man she loves, has come to tell her that he has recently been married. Elinor is despondent but (because she is such a good person, perhaps Austen's most decent heroine) she is resigned to be stoic. Eventually it transpires that it is not Edward who has married, but his brother. Elinor weeps with relief and joy. The scene is magnificently performed by Emma Thompson. Somehow she conveys a sense of the dual quality of Elinor's rapture. Thompson's performance in this scene is one of the best evocations in modern art of the ecstasy that results when you are permitted to submit to the pull of *eros*. Warwick Fairfax described it as 'feel[ing], as it were, alive for the first time'[14].

Why does *eros* so often end not in happiness but in disappointment or even despair? Partly it is because *eros* is an inherently selfish form of love: the lover wants what he lacks, namely the beloved, to the exclusion of all others. If the beloved finds happiness with someone else, or even with some*thing* else, the lover is not pleased; on the contrary, he is miserable and jealous. The general happiness of the beloved is not paramount in the lover's thoughts. *Eros*, accordingly, can be a negative force.

This spiteful aspect of eros – as well as its rapture – is one of the principal subjects of *Othello*. It is *the* principal subject of *The Winter's Tale*. But many centuries before Shakespeare it had been explored in one of the most underrated books of the Old Testament, the Song of Songs, as in this passage:

Place me like a seal over your heart, like a seal on your arm; for love is strong as death, its jealousy unyielding as the grave. It burns like blazing fire, like a mighty flame.

(Song of Songs 8:6–7)

But for all its potency, eros is ultimately a fragile and ephemeral form of love. It is not based upon practical reality, but upon an idealised conception of the beloved. The power of *eros* is so strong as initially to blind the lover to any faults or imperfections of the beloved; indeed, it sometimes converts those same faults and imperfections into virtues. For this reason, eros can frequently beget disillusionment, when (as is inevitable) *eros* fades and the beloved's true nature becomes evident. Robert Frost's short poem, 'On Being Idolized', evokes this truth:

> The wave sucks back and with the last of water
> It wraps a wisp of seaweed round my legs
> And with the swift rush of its sandy dregs
> So undermines my barefoot stand I totter
> And did I not take steps would be tipped over
> Like the ideal of some mistaken lover.[15]

There is another situation in which *eros* may beget sadness. *Eros* can be mutually felt and declared by the two lovers but then consciously forsaken: eros remains unconsummated. David Lean's beautiful black-and-white film, *Brief Encounter* (1946), is a terribly moving portrayal of this kind of love. Douglas Sirk's *There's Always Tomorrow* (1956) and Todd Haynes' *Far From Heaven* (2003) are two others. In all three of these films, there is an emphasis upon the nobility of the characters for their knowing sacrifice of personal happiness.

Sadder still, perhaps, is reciprocal but *undeclared* romantic love. One of the best evocations of this phenomenon is to be found in *Shane* (1952), a classic American film directed by George Stevens. Much of the emotional depth of the film, ostensibly a Western, is derived from the skill with which the feeling between the Alan Ladd and Jean Arthur characters is conveyed by visual imagery alone: 'Every gesture and every glance in every scene tells us of their impossible and unrealisable love'[16].

The dilemma of the characters in *Shane* is real, because Jean Arthur is married (and to a good man), but in James Ivory's film *The Remains of the Day* (1993) the dilemma is sadder still because it is merely *apparent*. The potential of the relationship between Anthony Hopkins and Emma Thompson (both of whom are unmarried) is stunted not even by societal convention but by emotional detachment, and by Hopkins' excessively developed sense of duty. The causes and implications of the situation are conveyed with tremendous power in a scene where Hopkins resists Thompson's playful attempt to get a look at a book he is reading. The acting during this exchange is of the highest quality. On the surface, there is very little 'action', but the scene is entirely compelling and achingly sad. These characters – so desperately in need of each other – do not even experience the consoling pleasure of hearing *eros* reciprocated.

Why are these situations so sad but, at the same time, uplifting? Partly it is the realisation of lost potential: the filial love that might in different circumstances have sprung from *eros*. But principally it is because of the element of self-sacrifice: the recognition of the duty to put other forms of love ahead of *eros*. Thus, adulterous lovers who submit to *eros* may well know a kind of joy, perhaps sublime; but they will also still know at heart that what they are doing is wrong, because of its effect on other people: spouses, children, mutual friends. 'Emotional sincerity does not entitle people to come together irrespective of the consequences as in the romantic melodrama.'[17] *Eros* is thus demonstrated as the least of the three forms of love, because the dictates of conscience most frequently require its subordination.

Philia

Under this heading are the (loving) feelings generated by many of the most fundamental interpersonal relationships. Or, as Andre Compte-Sponville has expressed it: 'philia is love in all its forms when it flourishes between human beings, whenever it is not reduced to want or passion'[18].

Thus, *philia* is the love of a husband for his wife, or of a wife for her husband, when the spouses have passed through the stage of *eros* to the much higher state of wise and joyful intimacy. This is the love not of an ideal but of the real, fallible person, the love that gives rise to (or is evidenced by) easy familiarity, trust, shared confidences, a similar sense of humour, mutual support and a common sensibility about the world. It undoubtedly has a sexual element as well. That element is, ideally, a state best described as indulgent compatibility, reflected not in equivalent frequency of desire (which seems to be rare), but in a mutual preparedness to be generous with the other. (St Paul's admonition to husbands and wives in 1 Corinthians 7:3–5 may be regarded today as the height of political incorrectness. Nevertheless, I am convinced the advice is sound, particularly if it is read together with Ephesians 5:25–34. Sex bonds a marriage. It should be treated as a precious way of expressing love and promoting intimacy, not an optional form of recreation. Interestingly, some post-feminist writers in the United States have recently expressed not dissimilar views[19], as have the leaders of the fastest-growing denomination in Australia, the Pentecostals[20].)

Montaigne called the successful combination of these elements – the emotional, the sensual and the practical – 'marital friendship'. It is a priceless gift, if attained and maintained. The Jews have a special word for the person who is 'destined' to bestow this gift, i.e. the man or woman who is, or should be, your life long soul-mate and bed-mate: *bashert*. Strangely, and perhaps tellingly, it is not easy to think of many examples from literature or cinema that are intricately realised. The vast majority of plays, novels and films about marriage seem to explore either the events leading up to it ('journeys end in lovers meeting') or aspects of the marriage's dysfunction or collapse. And those portrayals that there are of good marriages often work by allusion. Such marriages may be suggested, rather than depicted in any detail, by reference to the sacred memories of a widow or widower or by the intensity of a single scene of reunion. Alternatively, good marriages may be sketched only briefly. Two or three incidents are made to suggest the whole. But it is rare indeed to discover a credible and fully actualised treatment in art of a successful lifelong marriage. Anyone who has ever been in one, however, will understand its immeasurable worth.

Philia is also the love of a parent for his or her child. This is a very potent love indeed. It is common for marriages to fail, but it is far less common for parents to stop loving their children. Parental love is the golden thread of Nature. For present purposes, I do not distinguish between the love felt and given by a father and the love felt and given by a mother. Both forms of love are, quite clearly, similar in nature though they are not, in my view, identical. A father's love for his son is likely to be rather more critical (though no less intense) than his love for his daughter; likewise, a mother's love for her daughter as compared to her love for her son. A mother's love for her son (as Gertrude's for Hamlet) may be the strongest and most unconditional form of human love that there is.

A key point is that most parents' love is *resilient*. It has to be, in order for the parent to fulfil his or her vital function, namely the nurturing of the child to physical and emotional maturity. At the most basic level, a parent's duty is to protect. As Mary Eberstadt has observed, '[a]ll men and women fear death; but only mothers and fathers, and perhaps some husbands and wives, can generally be counted upon to fear another's death more than their own'[21]. Beyond watching out for their children's health and safety, parents' most critical task is to teach each of their children how to love; they do that, principally, by the example they set themselves in loving the child, and especially in overcoming potential barriers to that love. It is remarkable and significant that parents derive intense pleasure from things said or done by their own children (especially when very young) that they would otherwise consider boring or even offensive. Similarly, most parents will tolerate from their own children a huge amount of inconvenience and suffering – sleeplessness, physical discomfort, anxiety, tedium, expense. These are burdens that the parents would not lightly inflict upon themselves in any other circumstances.

Parental love is like *eros* in that often one loves in spite of, not because of, the conduct of the beloved. Any parent who has struggled with the behaviour of a difficult child – indeed, any child – will recognise this truth. Most parents battle on in these situations not merely because it is their duty to do so, but also because they cannot stop themselves from *wanting* to do so. They will keep on loving even after it is too late to influence the child's development. Parental love may often appear selfless, but really it is not: it is a need inside the parent, requiring fulfilment.

Philia is, next, the love of a child for his or her parents. The child learns how to love principally from its parents (and, by a sort of flow-on effect, from its siblings). However, even before that process of education begins, the infant child's love for (or, at least, *need* for) its mother seems to be more or less instinctive. The mother's love for the infant child is the same. But as the child gets older, and develops a mind of its own, a process of mutual estrangement is at risk of occurring – especially from the point of view of the child, and especially toward the parent of the same sex. It can continue into adulthood.

Why is this so common? Putting aside situations of parental abuse, the phenomenon of estrangement highlights what can often be the fine line between love and hate. There is also a strong parallel with *eros*. From the child's point of view, and especially from the point of view of the son vis-à-vis the father, or the daughter vis-à-vis the mother, the parent begins as the supreme role model – and often as a hero or heroine. But everyone, of course, is highly fallible. As the child matures and begins to learn this about the parent, a phase of disillusionment seems frequently to take place: the parent can be transformed swiftly in the child's eyes from hero to villain, even enemy.

This phase is, perhaps, *the* most important of the child's life, and often, unfortunately, it turns out for the worse. The child who escapes harm from this process must (by grace) either have an exceptionally loving – and forbearing – parent or be of an unusually mature – and forgiving – disposition. If the relationship survives this phase, however, it usually remains strong and nurturing for both parent and child, and for any grandchildren.

Philia is also the love that exists between siblings. In many ways, this is the closest of all human relationships, especially during childhood. And frequently a close sibling relationship is carried well beyond childhood. Indeed, potentially, the love for and from a brother or a sister is the most enduring of one's life, lasting as it may from infancy to old age. In Gillian Armstrong's charming film of *Little Women* (1994), Amy March says sternly that 'a sister is far more important than marriage'. The remark is intended to be understood ironically, and yet it also contains more than an element of truth.

The nature of the bond between siblings is reflected in our language. The words 'brother' or 'sister' may be employed not merely as a description of the blood relationship itself but also to suggest a solidarity, a common purpose, a sense of love that is divorced from the vagaries of eros or the complications wrought (in either direction) by the generation gap. The founders of the trade union movement, modern-day feminists, the Apostles themselves – to mention three disparate examples that come quickly to mind – all thought of and addressed each other in terms of brotherhood or sisterhood.

It is not coincidental that the first murder described in the Bible is Cain's of Abel: to murder your brother (or sister) in cold blood is, perhaps, the gravest crime of all. It has, as Claudius confesses in *Hamlet*, the primal eldest curse upon it. Why should that be so? Because to kill your sibling is, almost, to kill oneself – and yet it is a far worse thing than killing oneself. Necessarily, each of us knows more about ourselves than any other living thing; but the next closest living thing (in terms of genetic make-up, environmental influences and, frequently, temperament and worldview) is a sibling. To kill a sibling is thus to kill the living thing that we have the capacity to know the best: the killer, because of this knowledge, this capacity to identify with the victim, ought to realise more forcefully than in any other situation the enormous evil of the act of taking a life. St John in his first letter said that Cain killed Abel because 'his own actions were evil and his brother's were righteous' (1 John 3:12). That is so, but it is because Abel, a good man, was Cain's brother – the closest thing to Cain himself – that Cain's murder of him appears so heinous. Cain had the potential to be the good Abel.

Other 'extended' or 'intermediate' forms of *philia* are worth noting. Many people's lives are enriched by the love of, and the love given to, relatives outside the nuclear family: grandparents, aunts and uncles, cousins. Before modern medicine – for most of human history – it was common for orphans to be raised by their next-closest relatives. Today this happens much less often, at least in the West, and these secondary forms of love provide an opportunity for people to enjoy the more congenial aspects of filial love without all of its responsibilities. Thus, grandparents and aunts and uncles can pass on their wisdom and give freely of their time to grandchildren, nieces and nephews, but they do not endure the day-to-day grind that parents must. This fact can enlarge the experience of love for both the giver and the receiver. Similarly, cousins can sometimes share the indelible bond that emanates from the blood tie – a quirk of personality, a shared sensibility about the world – without the regular squabbles and rivalries that (at least during childhood) are an inevitable by-product of the sibling relationship.

Last in this exegesis, *philia* is the love between friends. True friendships are fairly rare. Unworthy of the name are the many minor relationships, more or less civil, that most of us maintain with work colleagues and social acquaintances. These relationships are critical to any stable society, but friendships are something quite different. They are the close and vital unions that contribute so much to our everyday happiness and which sustain us in times of unhappiness. Our friends are the people to whom we feel comfortable confiding some of our most personal thoughts; the people with whom it is unnecessary to pretend.

Besides family – and putting God to one side – having real friends is the most important thing in anyone's life. Long after achievements are forgotten, or with hindsight seem unimportant, friendships endure. (Sometimes, it may be the memory of friendship that endures – for some friends may have belonged to an earlier, now-closed, section of one's life. That does not make such a friendship any the less important or even any the less a still-current source of comfort and joy.)

The vital importance that most people (consciously or unconsciously) place upon friendship is demonstrated by what happens when a friendship is betrayed. The emotional pain caused by the betrayal of a friend can be extremely acute, sometimes *more* acute even than in the case of (say) a spouse. Why should that be so? Because, I suggest, whereas the relationship with one's spouse (or child, or parent, or sibling) is consecrated upon and/or complicated by the ties of blood or sex or law or other formal duty, the tie of friendship is based solely upon (assumed) mutual goodwill, respect and loyalty – or, in short, of love. To betray a friend – especially a friend in need (cf. Psalm 41:9) – is thus the basest act of withdrawal of love, and this is why it hurts the victim so.

Friendship is, perhaps, the purest form of *philia*, because at its best it is unadulterated by any forces other than love. Jesus gave extremely high priority to filial friendship: it was an emblem of much that he stood for. Perhaps the most moving verse in the Bible, for me, is John 13:34. Shortly before His death, Jesus explained to the Disciples that one of his greatest concerns was for and about *them* – in particular, how they were going to treat each other in His absence, and how the persistence of their friendship (or lack of it) would impact upon the task they would have of teaching His message.

Jesus thus, at the eleventh hour, imposed upon them the New Commandment:

A new command I give you: Love one another. As I have loved you, so you must love one another. By this all men will know that you are my disciples, if you love one another.

(John 13:34–35; see also John 15:9–17)

The vital words are 'as I have loved you' – with the emphasis on 'as', meaning 'in the same way'. The love that Jesus gave to the Disciples – the love that He exhorted them to give to each other – was the most constructive form of friendship: not uncritical (far from it) but true, enduring and deep.

But even such friendship is not the highest form of love. Jesus taught this too. He said during the Sermon on the Mount:

[God] causes his sun to rise on the evil and the good, and sends rain on the righteous and the unrighteous. If you love those who love you, what reward will you get? Are not even the tax collectors doing that? And if you greet only your brothers, what are you doing more than others? Do not even pagans do that? Be perfect, therefore, as your heavenly Father is perfect.

(Matthew 5:45–48)

How, then, in accordance with Jesus's injunction, is one to aspire to being perfect? The answer lies in the highest form of love.

Agape

Agape is the word that the Greeks gave to the concept of neighbourly love, or charity: the love not merely of those dearest to you, or of friends, but of acquaintances, strangers, even of enemies. The earliest Christian communities appropriated the word from the Greeks (it had, until then, been little-used) and made it their own.[22] *Agape* is the subject of St Paul's justly famous discourse about 'love' in 1 Corinthians 13, perhaps the best-known and most often-read passage in the New Testament.

Agape is the form of love that emanates not from the hypnotic thrill of *eros* or the strong bonds of *philia*. They are forms of love that usually do not need to be forced. It is difficult not to be kind to the person with whom you are in love; and most of us (at least most of the time) want to do the right thing by our families and close friends. On the other hand, *agape* is the product of fulfilling not a wish but a duty; it begins with an act of will. That, it seems it me, is the key to understanding its nature; and that is why *agape* is the greatest form of love, because it is selfless.

Iris Murdoch, the English novelist, once articulated this idea:

Love is the extremely difficult realisation that something other than oneself is real.
Love, and so art and morals, is the discovery of reality.[23]

For most of my life I associated the word 'love' only with the feelings generated by *eros* and *philia*. It took me a long time to grasp the notion that charity (*agape* by another word) is best understood as a form of love. *Agape* requires you to act toward others *as though* you loved them, as though they were your lover or your daughter or your brother or your best friend. You must behave – with kindness, courage, generosity, etc. – as though you were motivated by love that is personally felt, when in fact you are not.

These observations may seem trite, but reaching an understanding of the moral and spiritual nature of *agape* was an important part of my gradual acceptance of the tenets of Christianity.

A key feature of the history of human civilisation is the increasing influence of *agape* in the shaping of public policy. Indeed, what is civilisation but the product of *agape* – the slow, difficult but essential attempt to bring the greatest happiness to the greatest number of people? The seminal principles that sustain Western society are best understood as manifestations of *agape*, the treating of other people in the way that you would wish to be treated yourself.

Five civilising principles stand out: freedom of religion, equality under the law, freedom of speech, the universal franchise and the alleviation of poverty. In the Western world, the outstanding religious and political leaders of the last 200 years were those who furthered or protected these causes in some critical way, often when to do so was dangerous or unpopular: William Wilberforce, Abraham Lincoln (perhaps the greatest political leader ever to be democratically elected – and re-elected too), Benjamin Disraeli, Gandhi (he is included as being of the West), Franklin Delano Roosevelt (with some reservations), Winston Churchill (with grave reservations), Clement Atlee, Konrad Adenauer, John and Robert Kennedy, Martin Luther King, Nelson Mandela, Mikhail Gorbachev, Pope John Paul II. They form a disparate group indeed, but all were motivated by a desire to implement a practical vision of *agape*. (So, too, were a number of other heroes of mine who might fairly be classified as noble failures: William Jennings Bryan[24], George McGovern[25], Lord (Tom) Denning[26]. The first two were losing Democratic Party presidential candidates in the United States, Bryan in 1896, 1900 and 1904 and McGovern in 1972; Lord Denning was an idiosyncratic English judge of the mid-twentieth century.)

Robert Kennedy, in his justly famous impromptu speech on the night of the death of Martin Luther King, a speech that I much admire and will consider in more detail in Chapter 7, distilled the essence of the matter. He abjured his fellow citizens to dedicate themselves to a plain goal: 'To make gentle the life of this world'.

There is a good way to test whether, in a given situation, the dictates of *agape* have been fulfilled. Think of a situation in which a person who is truly fearful or in trouble receives from another person – a stranger – the help he seeks. Then observe the reactions of the two people involved. The person who is helped rarely forgets. His gratitude is genuine and sincere, and frequently it is bounteous. That gratitude is, in fact, the manifestation of his conscience: he 'knows' that the person who helped him is deserving of thanks. The person who did the good deed may also feel, for a little while, uplifted; at the least, he could at any time happily look the other person in the eye, knowing he had done the right thing by him. Generally speaking, however, it is the person who is helped who remembers the episode the more intensely, and for longer. And the larger the act of charity, the greater the sense of gratitude (cf. Luke 7:41–3).

Recall the scene in Harper Lee's *To Kill a Mockingbird* when the Negroes stand as Atticus Finch leaves the courtroom.

Now imagine the same situation in reverse. When people who are fearful or in trouble do *not* receive the help they crave, often it comes as no surprise. Such people often may hope for help, but they do not necessarily expect it. So if help is refused or they are otherwise ignored, they will often quickly forget. On the other hand, the person who has refused to help will know, at some level, that he has done the wrong thing. His conscience will tell him that. He may try to justify his conduct by excuses ('I couldn't help because …') or by misrepresenting the situation ('You didn't really need my help because …'). He will certainly not relish a face-to-face meeting with the other person. Probably, he would prefer never to have much to do with the person again or, if that is impossible, never to have the subject mentioned again. Occasionally, he may apologise. Interestingly, however, he is most unlikely to argue that helping people in need *per se* is wrong. He knows as well as anyone, through his conscience, the dictates of *agape*. All of these ideas, and many more, are inherent in one of the greatest of Jesus's parables, that of the Good Samaritan (Luke 10:30–37).

But even giving a generous helping hand to a stranger is not the highest form of *agape*. The ultimate test is how we treat our enemies. Perhaps the most radical aspect of Jesus's philosophy was his total opposition to physical violence, even in the face of provocation or attack. The passage in the Sermon on the Mount rejecting 'an eye for an eye' and advocating 'turning the other cheek' is, perhaps, the most challenging in the Gospels. It is *not* a call for supine inaction in the face of evil, but for principled 'non-violent realism'[27]. It requires courage of a high order to stand up to bullies without resorting to their methods. Only a very few other great leaders – such as Gandhi and Martin Luther King – have genuinely tried to live by that creed.

During the height of the Cold War and the civil rights movement, King exhorted his supporters to love their enemies. This they could do, he said, by eschewing violence and, instead, analysing themselves in a spirit of honest self-criticism; seeking to discover the element of good in others; and refusing to inflict humiliating defeat upon the enemy even if the opportunity presented itself. King emphasised that to do so was to practise *agape*, which he described as 'something of the understanding, creative, redemptive goodwill for all men'. But the wisest aspect of King's advice was his explanation of *why* we should love our enemies. It is not so much a question of altruism, as good sense:

> I think the first reason that we should love our enemies, and I think this was at the very center of Jesus's thinking, is this: that hate for hate only intensifies the existence of hate and evil in the universe. If you hit me and I hit you back and you hit me back and so on, you see, that goes on ad infinitum. Somebody somewhere must have a little sense, and that's the strong person.[28]

King gave his followers two other reasons for loving their enemies: hate distorts the personality of the hater, and love 'has within it a redemptive power' that is capable not merely of sustaining the person who loves but – ultimately – of transforming the behaviour of the enemy.[29]

This is, then, the ultimate test of human love: whether it can tame the basest aspects of our nature.

Other forms of love

It is not only in the context of human relationships that love wields its extraordinary influence. There can, for instance, be love between people and animals.

For a considerable number of people, especially the elderly, domestic pets may be the main, perhaps the *only* source of emotional consolation. Speaking for myself, I have felt toward several cats an attachment that merits no less a description than love, and am proud to think that my cats (in their own way) also loved me. And having recently become the master of a spirited border terrier*, it is hard to think of a finer tribute than that accorded to Sir Walter Scott: 'He was a gentleman even to his dogs'.[30]

Love between animals and human beings is a recurrent theme in art, and especially in children's books and the cinema. Some of the most moving films ever made explore this theme: *Lassie Come Home* (1943), *National Velvet* (1944), *Au Hazard, Balthazar* (1966) and *Dances With Wolves* (1990) are among my own favourites of a rich genre. These films say as much or more about the greatest of the virtues – courage, generosity, gratitude, fidelity, gentleness, compassion – than many other, far more ambitious works of art. Their popularity reflects a deep truth about the potential for mutuality between Man and at least some kinds of animals.

The Bible, while far from sentimental as regards animals, recognises this potential. The story of Noah's Ark, so treasured by painters and children, highlights the need for co-existence between all living things. The image of the shepherd and his flock is repeatedly invoked in both the Old and the New Testaments. St Thomas Aquinas regarded animals – every living creature – as a *vestigium Dei* (trace of God) and the life and teachings of St Francis of Assisi are so universally admired because, in part, of his love for animals. Bellini's gorgeous painting of St Francis, which hangs in the Frick Museum in New York, depicts him standing amidst a number of gentle creatures.

The objects of love are not confined to living things. It is possible to love a non-corporeal object: a house or a mountain or a piece of furniture. It is possible to love an avocation. Most people's lives are immeasurably enriched by at least one avocation (or, more usually, a number of them). Music, gardening, reading, fashion, sport, cooking and dining, home maintenance and renovation – these are a few of the most popular pastimes in contemporary Australia, but the list is almost infinite.

It is possible to love a concept. Patriotism, for instance, is one of the most powerful forces operating in the world today. The love that most people feel for their country is real and personally sustaining – if too often at risk of being channelled toward unworthy purposes. (As Reinhold Niebuhr once observed: 'Patriotism transmutes individual unselfishness into national egotism.'[31] Love of country means different things to dif-

---

* Her name is Tricky-Woo, a choice inspired by a canine character of the same name – but quite different disposition – in the English television series, *All Creatures Great and Small*.

ferent people, but it is no less potent for that. Indeed, for some kinds of men it seems to be one of the strongest forms of love of all. One of the most moving books that I have ever read is Roger Scruton's *England: An Elegy*.[32] Scruton traverses many weighty subjects – history, government, the law, sociology – but what comes through most strongly are not so much the intellectual arguments as a dominant emotion: the author's *love* for his country, or at least for his conception of what his country once was.

Honesty

It may seem strange that I should choose to discuss truth in the context of love, but they are intricately related. The Christian conception of the world, as Warwick Fairfax recognised, involves 'not so much a progression from love to wisdom, but their harmony and union as twin aspects of truth'.[33]

The concept of truth is, or should be, fundamental to any right-thinking civilisation. There is nothing novel about that observation, of course, nor the incidence of dishonesty. Individual human beings have always been, and will always be, dishonest from time to time; and, on a larger scale, most of the butchers and other monsters of history were also masters of propaganda. 'A wicked man puts on a bold face' (Proverbs 21:29). In that sense, there is nothing new under the sun.

What, I fear, *is* novel is the way that dishonesty seems increasingly to have become an accepted – sometimes even a lauded – feature of everyday life. Puffery or worse in advertising; euphemism, spin or outright deceit in politics, business and the professions; gamesmanship or worse in sport – these practices are commented upon from time to time but are not sufficiently denounced for what they really are: dishonesty. Too often they are justified as 'the way of the world', and their perpetrators even praised for being 'wily' or 'realistic' or of a 'can do' frame of mind. The Australian writer Don Watson, among others, has documented how these odious trends have manifested themselves in the misuse of language itself.[34] Of course, there are many honourable exceptions to this complaint, in all walks of life. And truth is not an absolute virtue – there is such a thing as a kind white lie. But, in general, the distortion of truth happens far too often.

But *why*, exactly, is dishonesty wrong? It is wrong because it is inimical to all three forms of human love – *eros*, *philia* and *agape*.

Eros when mutually felt begets honesty: the desire to tell all *to* the beloved, and the desire to learn as much as possible *about* the beloved. When two people are truly in love with one another, each person is both willingly candid and intensely curious. There must be no secrets. That is the core reason why infidelity is the gravest sin a lover can commit.

Likewise, unusual honesty is the hallmark of our other closest personal relationships. With spouses, parents, siblings, our children and friends, there is – or should be, if the relationship is to be healthy – a much greater candour than with mere acquaintances or strangers. In *Sense and Sensibility*, Marianne Dashwood becomes furious with her sister Elinor for failing to confide in her; Marianne is hurt because, justifiably, she equates lack of candour with lack of love.

D.H. Lawrence took up another aspect of this theme in a poem called 'Courage':

What makes people unsatisfied
is that they accept lies.

If people had courage, and refused lies
And found out what they really felt and really meant
and acted on it,

They would distil the essential oil out of every experience
and like hazel-nuts in autumn, at last
be sweet and sound.

And the young among the old
Would be as in the hazel-woods of September
Nutting, gathering nuts of ripe experience.

As it is, all that the old can offer
Is sour, bitter fruits, cankered by lies.[35]

Lawrence's message was that the harmful effects of deceit are not confined to the misleading of the victim on the matter immediately at hand. If people are less than honest in their personal relationships, especially with those who ought to be closest to them, true love is impossible. Honesty can be painful (cf. Job 6:25) but dishonesty sickens the soul.

Neighbourly love, too, demands a certain level of honesty – other people are entitled, not to know the truth about everything (because there is such a thing as privacy), but certainly not to be actively misled. The Prophet Jeremiah warned of a society in which truth is not respected:

> They make ready their tongue like a bow, to shoot lies; it is not by truth that they
> triumph in the land. They go from one sin to another; they do not acknowledge me
> … Beware of your friends; do not trust your brothers. For every brother is a deceiver,
> and every friend a slanderer. Friend deceives friend, and no-one speaks the truth. They
> have taught their tongues to lie; they weary themselves with sinning.
>
> (Jeremiah 9:3–5)

Jeremiah's point was that calculated and ingrained deceit is the antithesis of neighbourly love, and that it harms those who perpetrate it as much as its victims. If there is a single theme to be distilled from the writing of George Orwell, it is that respect for truth is critical to civilisation; on the other hand, routine dishonesty – and routine *acceptance* of dishonesty – is a sure sign of its corruption. Alexander Solzhenitsyn regarded dishonesty as the benchmark of oppression in the Soviet Union: 'In our country the lie has become not just a moral category but a pillar of the State'.[36]

Finally, truthfulness is not mere candour and the non-telling of lies. It is also the recognition that there is such a thing as objective truth, that 'which stands above and outside the mind of the individual'.[37] One man's 'truth' is *not* as valid as another's. Pilate's rhetorical question at Christ's trial – 'What is truth?'* (John 18:38) – betrayed his cynicism and his slothfulness, and those same attitudes are still at work in Western society today under the banner of postmodernism.

In contemporary Australia, the most unfortunate consequences of postmodernism are felt in the education system.[38] Regulated external examinations, in which every student competes against every other student on the basis of a uniform curriculum, are no longer routine. At the primary and junior secondary levels, it is no longer a given that every student will, or should, be taught a basic set of skills (reading, spelling, grammar, punctuation, mental arithmetic) and a basic body of knowledge (civics; the Bible; historical names, dates and events; geographical features, placenames and landmarks). Time-worn techniques such as phonic reading and rote-learning are out of vogue. At the senior secondary and tertiary levels, the overwhelming emphasis nowadays is on 'outcomes' – training a student for a specialised vocation, as a means of enabling him or her to earn money – rather than on educating the student to *think* in a discriminating way. In the humanities, students are offered greater 'choice' of texts and subjects. But this sometimes comes at the expense of their acquiring compulsory knowledge of the Western canon and of post-Enlightenment history and philosophy, without which any efforts at 'deconstructive' or 'comparative' analysis will be lame.

Most of the people who defend these trends are well-meaning. But they do not seem to appreciate the problem, which is that too many students emerge from the education system ill-equipped to seek out *objective truth*. Not only are they incapable of serious theological enquiry; they are vulnerable to the facile claims of unscrupulous people in positions of power: politicians, financiers, marketers, employers, trend-setters and – it must be admitted plainly – religious zealots. Students from low socio-economic backgrounds suffer most, because often they do not have family wealth, security or influence to fall back on if and when they are led astray.

Instilling in the young a thirst for objective truth, and providing them with the skills to seek it out, is best understood as an act of love. Love of truth, in all its manifestations, nurtures the emotional, intellectual and material well-being of Man. As St Augustine wrote: 'Nothing conquers except truth and the victory of truth is love'[39].

Conclusions about love

It is necessary to draw together these thoughts and to tie them back to God. Everyone can agree that earthly human love is an extraordinary and precious thing. I must explain why I am dissatisfied with the atheist's conception that 'there is nothing higher'[40].

My strong conviction is that the phenomenon of human love is as intricate and finely calibrated a thing as the physical Universe itself. It too is part of what Fred Hoyle

---

* I subscribe to the so-called 'correspondence' theory of truth. Truth consists of the correspondence between an independently verifiable fact about the world and a sentence. Note, again, the crucial importance of Man's capacity to use language, an issue discussed in Chapter 2. Compare Fairfax, *The Triple Abyss*, pp. 120–1.

called the 'deep-laid scheme'. It did not just happen by accident: it is too complex, too beautiful and too *right*. Love is the creation of a genius. God is that genius, and the forms of love that God has given Man point the way to how we should love God and how God loves us.

The following (abbreviated) passage from St John's first letter contains a neat distillation of my belief:

> No one has ever seen God; but if we love one another, God lives in us and his love is made complete in us. We know that we live in him and he in us, because he has given us of his Spirit … God is love. Whoever lives in love lives in God, and God in him.
>
> (1 John 4:12–13, 16)

What St John was saying, it seems to me, is that the best evidence we have for the existence of God is the phenomenon of love. Love is something that we have all, to a greater or lesser extent, experienced. And love is (with fear) the most powerful force in human relations.

Accordingly, love is one of the keys to understanding God, and God's wishes for Man. But in order to understand these things, we must understand the different forms of love – not merely in isolation, but how they interact.

The hierarchy of love

Eros is the least of the three forms of love. It can be inexpressibly wondrous, but it remains inferior to the other forms of love, because *eros* is essentially selfish – and ephemeral. It has to be ephemeral, or normal life would be impossible. Imagine a world in which everyone was always in love. Little would get done. Imagine a world in which everyone, whenever they wished, surrendered to the power of *eros*. Family life would not function. Thus, *eros* is also the form of love that must most often be suppressed – or, much better, sublimated to other pursuits.

Philia is a higher form of love than *eros*. It manifests itself in various critical relationships: husband and wife, parent and child, siblings, friendship. What do all of these forms of *philia* have in common? An obvious point of commonality is that all are longer-lasting than *eros* – few would dispute, for instance, that you should love your children for the rest of your life or that, at least ideally, marriage should be 'for keeps'. However, the durability of *philia*, at least a good deal of the time, is only made possible by another curious feature of it. *Philia* can be like *eros* in that one loves in spite of, not because of, the conduct of the beloved. Try to imagine a world in which we each received from our parents (or from our children, or our spouse, or our siblings, or our friends) only our just deserts – not sympathy or forgiveness. It would be an intolerable place.

Philia makes human society possible because at an individual level it affords everybody (or nearly everybody – and the exceptions are instructive) the protection, the consolation and the encouragement of loved ones.

But human society could not function well *as a whole* if everyone's highest duty was exclusively or even predominantly to family and friends. A society based primarily on the defence of existing privilege or the amelioration of existing deprivation at the level of the family (or clan) would be brutal, backward and unjust. To a considerable extent still, human society is run along those lines. Families, corporations, political parties, countries all seek to further their own position, at the expense of other people who are not included in the relevant group. Conduct which would be quickly condemned in an individual acting for personal motives may be praised to the hilt if done to further some collective interest. It can be a short step to long-running family feuds, à la the Hatfields and the McCoys; price-gouging and monopolistic trade practices; pork-barrelling and election-rigging; crass displays of nationalism. This kind of selfishness is often camouflaged by appeals to loyalty, 'team play', 'the good of the party', and/or love of country. But when it is carried to the worst extremes, we get the Mafia; systematic exploitation of Third World labour; military dictatorships; genocide; and savage wars of conquest. Curiously, as Warwick Fairfax observed, 'all this may be done with comparative sincerity.'[41] The person who listens to his or her conscience is aware that *philia* must frequently give way to – or operate in conjunction with – a higher form of love: *agape*.

A key point is that *agape* begins as an act of will. At core it involves doing the right thing by someone for whom you may feel no loving feeling at all – perhaps indifference, perhaps even animosity. This is the form of love that makes human society possible, and also ensures that the other forms of love – *eros* and *philia* – are able to survive.

Another curious thing about *agape*, however, is that when by an act of will you behave toward a person *as though* you loved them, you often find that in time you really do come to love them (i.e. in the sense of *philia* or even *eros*), or (in cases of estrangement) to begin to love them again. The other person, too, after a time, may respond by loving you. Many friendships and romances begin in most unpromising circumstances, often at a time when you may not be in the mood to meet a new person. Likewise, when people who dislike or even hate each other are forced by circumstances to work together, and to go through the motions of civil conduct, a finer feeling may soon develop. Spouses, parents and children, siblings, friends – often they can resolve the most wounding of disputes by forcing themselves to behave toward the other person as though they loved them. The only thing that will certainly doom the relationship is a failure even to try to pretend.*

---

* This truth was expressed astutely by, of all people, Ian Fleming (the creator of James Bond) in a short story entitled 'Quantum of Solace'. The Governor of Jamaica, late at night after a cocktail party, tells Bond a sad tale about marital breakdown. Towards the end, the Governor muses thus: 'You're not married, but I think it's the same with all relationships between a man and a woman. They can survive anything as long as some kind of basic humanity exists between the two people. When all kindness has gone, when one person obviously and sincerely doesn't care if the other is alive or dead, then it's just no good. That particular insult to the ego – worse, to the instinct of self-preservation – can never be forgiven. I've noticed this in hundreds of marriages. I've seen flagrant infidelities patched up. I've seen crimes and even murder forgiven by the other party, let alone bankruptcy and every other form of social crime. Incurable disease, blindness, disaster – all these can be overcome. But never the death of common humanity in one of the partners. I've thought about this and I've invented a rather high-sounding title for this basic factor in human relations. I have called it the Law of the Quantum of Solace.' From 'Quantum of Solace', in *For Your Eyes Only*, first

Marriage is the bridge between all three forms of love – it has been a near-universal phenomenon throughout human history[42], and may be the best example of love's hierarchy. Marriage usually begins with *eros*, and often develops into *philia*. But it is also a manifestation of *agape*. Every spouse at least sometimes behaves irresponsibly, proudly, selfishly. That is when *duty* must prevail. The marriage vows that husbands and wives have taken – and the societal expectations that even today still go with marriage – become all-important. In blunt terms, they play a role in keeping the couple from hurting each other more, and they serve to deter both partners from ending the relationship whenever it happens to suit.

Of course, marriage itself is far from being a perfect institution. Like democracy, marriage is highly problematic – but much less so than any of the alternatives. And the very difficulty of sustaining marriage, at both the societal and individual levels, is the best reason for having strict rules aimed at preserving and protecting it. That is why St Paul urged that 'marriage should be honoured by all' (Hebrews 13:4).

This is one of the teachings of Jesus that receives heavy emphasis in all three of the Synoptic Gospels. Jesus was trenchant in His opposition to divorce, partly because of the hurt it caused to women, but fundamentally because it flouts the Creation principle that husband and wife 'will become one flesh' (Genesis 2:24; see also Malachi 2:14–16). In Mark's Gospel, Jesus's opposition to divorce is total (see Mark 10:10–11), but in Matthew's Gospel He is said to have allowed an exception for 'unchastity' by the wife (Matthew 5:32, 19:1–9; see also Luke 16:18). It has been argued persuasively that the blanket prohibition in Mark represented Jesus's true position – which was stricter than that allowed under Mosaic law.[43] By twenty-first century standards, Jesus's views on divorce may appear uncompassionate. But in the circumstances of first-century Judea, His views were considerably *more* compassionate than the then-prevailing orthodoxy. In those days divorce was exclusively a male prerogative, and any divorce was almost certain to cause great harm (financial and reputational) to the woman. That consideration is not so pertinent today, and I think it must now be allowed that in some cases – especially if no children are involved – divorce may be the best thing. As St Paul considered, it should be 'permitted reluctantly for marriages between believers and unbelievers'[44] as well as for marriages between two unbelievers.

I doubt that anyone, whatever their religious views, takes the decision to seek a divorce lightly. That too is best. Marriages ought not to be broken up unless the differences between the spouses are truly momentous, and irreconcilable. The dictates of the hierarchy of love will usually require that the spouses stay together, if not for their own sakes then for the sake of others. In the story of the woman caught in adultery (John 8:1–11), it is significant not merely that Jesus declined to condemn the woman, but that, having forgiven her, He sent her back to her husband. Otherwise, an isolated lapse caused by lust or *eros* would have prevailed over *philia* and *agape*.

published by Jonathan Cape Ltd. (1960), Pan Books (1965), p. 100. This passage made a deep impression on me when I first read it, and I have gone back to it many times. This is, I think, a good example of how important insights can 'come' to you from the unlikeliest of sources.

Love and conscience

It is instructive to tie the three forms of love back to individual conscience. Remember that Man's possession of a conscience seems to be unique among all living things in the known Universe. Thus, what our conscience tells us – and when, and *why* – is a matter of the highest importance.

It has been rightly said that we have need of morality only because we cannot (most of the time) love others: morality asks us to perform out of duty what love causes us to perform out of compulsion. Thus, morality is that which we would do simply out of love – *eros* or *philia* – if we in fact loved. Morality is made possible by the love that we have experienced, when the memory of love – and its transforming effect upon our conduct – is preserved.[45] In this sense, love is both 'the gateway' to morality and morality's 'immediate motive force'[46]. That is why people who do not know what it is really like to love and be loved – often because of their experiences in childhood – are more likely to behave immorally.

The key to an understanding of morality is the hierarchy of love.

To follow the dictates of *eros* is easy; in fact, there is nothing easier. You crave to do good for the beloved. Our conscience does not force us to obey *eros*, though it is exquisitely pleasurable when our conscience tells us (as it tells Elinor Dashwood at the conclusion of *Sense and Sensibility*) that there is no impediment to doing so. More often than not, however, our conscience tells us that there *is* such an impediment. To follow the dictates of *philia* is a mixed bag. Sometimes it is easy to do good for our family or our friends: we want to, and our conscience does not try to stop us. Sometimes we do not want to do good – it is easier to be lazy, though our conscience is telling us that the right thing to do is to make the effort. Sometimes (and this to me is the strangest thing about *philia*) we want to do good by our family or friends, but our conscience tells us not to, because someone or something else has a higher call on our love. The dictates of *agape* – our duties to acquaintances, strangers, enemies, the community – prevent us. It is in this sense that love may properly be defined as 'the antithesis of laziness'[47].

Thus: *eros*, *philia*, *agape*; but the greatest of these is *agape*.

Why love points to the existence of God

Having outlined my conclusions in relation to the nature of love, it remains to explain how those conclusions strengthen my belief in God.

Love is not an accident

The many forms of love are so magnificent, and so finely interwoven, that they bear comparison with the most extraordinary features of Nature – the laws of physics, DNA, the unique capacities of the human mind. Love gives every appearance of having been designed, with the survival and overall well-being of Man in view. The very existence of love suggests to me the existence of a supernatural designer, God.

John Shaw Neilsen, an early Australian poet whose work is increasingly a revelation to me, seems to have shared this intuition. In 'Surely God Was a Lover' he not merely employed symbols from Nature to evoke various aspects of *eros*. He went further and explicitly equated God's creations in the natural world with His creation of romantic love:

> Surely God was a lover when He bade the day begin
> Soft as a woman's eyelid – white as a woman's skin.
> Surely God was a lover, with a lover's faults and fears,
> When He made the sea as bitter as a wilful woman's tears.
> Surely God was a lover, with the madness love will bring:
> He wrought while His love was singing, and put her soul in the Spring.
> Surely God was a lover, by a woman's wile controlled,
> When He made the Summer a woman thirsty and unconsoled.
> Surely God was a lover when He made the trees so fair;
> In every leaf is a glory caught from a woman's hair.
> Surely God was a lover – see, in the flowers He grows,
> His love's eyes in the violet – her sweetness in the rose.[48]

Shaw Neilsen's insight was that both Nature and human love are equally God's *creations*. But it is necessary to go back a step. Why are we justified in inferring that human love is something created by God, rather than an incidental by-product of Nature? My answer is this. If a pre-existing God created the Universe, as a lot of other evidence suggests, then God Himself must first have experienced love. Divine love must have come first; nothing else provides a sufficiently credible reason for the creative act. It has been justly said that 'the world is like a work of art, since God created it out of love rather than need.'[49] Moreover, we find that, in the world which God created, love has a fundamental place. Love makes the living world 'work'. All forms of earthly love are glorious, and human love is the most glorious – it is Nature's masterpiece. But experience on Earth tells us that no artist creates a masterpiece in, as it were, a vacuum. Think of painters, sculptors, composers, writers. Especially writers. An author (if he aspires to be any good) must first acquire a great deal of knowledge about his subject; he must 'eat, sleep and breathe' it in some way. Could Shakespeare have written *Romeo and Juliet* – or *Anthony and Cleopatra*, or the Sonnets – without his first having loved, and been loved? No. I believe the same principle must apply even to God. The creation of earthly love would not have been possible for a God who had not experienced love for Himself, and become intimately knowledgeable about it.

In short, God needed both a motive and a precedent.

If that reasoning is sound, then the fact that Man is capable of love is strong evidence of God's love, and thus of God. It is in that sense that God *is* love – or 'God is love *to us*'[50]. Julian of Norwich, the fourteenth-century English anchoress, grasped and developed this notion:

> You want to know our Lord's meaning in this thing? Know it well: love was His meaning. Who showed it to you? Love. What did He show you? Love. Why did He show it?

For love. Hold onto this and you will know and understand love more and more ... So it was that I learned that love was our Lord's meaning.[51]

This insight – that love is God's meaning – underlies the Christian doctrine of the Trinity (the three-personed God). I will come to the Trinity later, in Chapter 9. For present purposes, the main point is that God must have experienced love *before* the act of Creation – the Father loved the Son, the Son loved the Father, and (I would speculate) both the Father and the Son loved the *concept* of the physical Universe before it was actualised. A contemporary English theologian, Keith Ward, has developed this point very well. The reason that God bothered to create the Universe and populate it with human beings, Ward has suggested, is that 'the divine nature [is] essentially loving, which involves some form of relationship to other persons'[52]. By creating Man, God both expanded His own opportunities for loving and increased the number of beings capable of experiencing love for themselves. (Since writing those words, and publishing them in Australia, I have been pleased to learn that very similar views were once expressed by the great American preacher and theologian, Jonathan Edwards. He relied on John 17:20–4, among other passages from Scripture.[53])

Are any of these ideas undermined by Darwinism? Some atheists assert that human love (like altruism in general, and religious belief itself) can be explained in Darwinian terms. On this view, 'the experience of love ... is merely a biochemical state in the brain'[54], and solely the product of nearly four billion years of mindless, remorseless evolution. Personally, I am far from satisfied that all forms of human love can be so explained[55], any more than religion can; but even if such theories about love were ultimately proved correct, that would not alter the primary fact that love *exists*. If God created human love by evolutionary means that would neither detract from the splendour of love nor diminish the need for God to explain love's creation – or, if you prefer, to explain the process of the evolution of love. Nor would it weaken my conviction that love must have been God's motive.

The impossibility of perfect love

Love is not merely an intricate and fundamental natural phenomenon. It is also an ideal – the basis of morality.

To love perfectly is *always* to act according to the dictates of conscience, if you are truly listening to your conscience. The dictates of *agape* are paramount. Occasionally you can submit to *eros* consistently with *agape*. Much more often, but certainly not always, you can practise *philia* consistently with *agape*. In these situations, your 'neighbour' is the beloved (in the case of *eros*) or (say) your wife or child or sister or friend (in the case of *philia*) – and no one else has any higher claim to your love.

Of course, Man cannot completely live up to these ideals. Every individual fails in some way to adhere to the dictates of love. As St Paul insisted, 'All have sinned and fall short of the glory of God' (Romans 3:23). But those sins manifest themselves in different ways in different people. Furthermore, each of us is inclined to regard our own failures as much less serious than those of others. To a greater or lesser extent, we all resemble the 'sanctimonious pirate' of *Measure for Measure*, who 'went to sea with the ten commandments but scraped one out of the table': in the pirate's case the one that he himself serially transgressed, thou shalt not steal.[56]

Similarly, each generation of human beings tends to value its own virtues more highly than those of earlier generations, and to look askance at the failings of earlier generations while underplaying its own. Those of us alive in the West today, who enjoy all the luxuries of modern medicine and technology, of political stability and material abundance, tend to forget the sheer physical courage which must have been required in everyday life in centuries past. We dwell on our own civility and compare that with the relative brutality of earlier peoples, while forgetting the circumstances which gave rise to each.[57] It is another form of sanctimony.

This ingrained trait in human beings is, of itself, another pointer to the reality of God. Putting to one side the special case of Jesus of Nazareth, the perfect human being has never existed, except as an ideal. That ideal is capable of realisation only by perfect adherence to God's injunction to love others as you loves yourself. Indeed, according to some prominent biblical scholars of the late nineteenth century, this is the ideal that Jesus was alluding to when He spoke of the 'Kingdom of God': 'human society organized through action inspired by love'[58].

Of course, such a society remains only an ideal. No single human being is, or has ever been, perfect – let alone any group of people of significant size. But the fact that human beings are, and have always been, capable of conceptualising such an ideal is highly significant. That ideal (Kant's *summum bonum*) must itself emanate from some-thing – and to my mind the best, the only, explanation of that something is God.

Human love as the bridge to God

The third conclusion to which I have come after contemplating human love is that it can help us to understand the way that God loves Man, and the way that we should try to love God.

Spinoza conceived of God as the experience of love. His was not a conventional Christian conception of God, but Spinoza went some of the way to articulating the mystical connection between human love and the divine. Spinoza's views have been summarised as follows:

> You need not be in fear of this God because He will never punish you. Nor should you work hard in the hope of getting rewards from him because none will come. The only thing you may fear is your own behaviour. When you fail to be less than kind to others, you punish yourself, there and then, and deny yourself the opportunity to achieve inner peace and happiness, there and then. When you are loving others there is a good chance of achieving inner peace and happiness, there and then. Thus a person's actions should not be aimed at pleasing God, but rather at acting in conformity with the nature of God. When you do so, some kind of happiness results and some kind of salvation is achieved.[59]

Bertrand Russell expressed similar views as a young man[60] and so too, more recently, has the liberal American bishop, John Shelby Spong. In Bishop Spong's judgment, we experience God when we 'share with all people the life-giving power of love that always enhances human life'[61]. Buddhists believe something similar.

The notion that giving and receiving human love draws you toward God is one lesson to be distilled from the passage in St John's first letter which I earlier quoted. There are also obvious parallels between Spinoza's ideas of right conduct and the Christian doctrine of conscience. The man was a remarkable thinker, and so is Bishop Spong. Still, I believe that their conception of God – and of love – is badly incomplete. God is not the mere experience of human love. God, I have argued, must have created human love. God is love, but love is not God.

Mary Eberstadt has come closer, in my view, to distilling the theological significance of love. She argues that modern history demonstrates a clear statistical correlation between, on the one hand, a society's rate of fertility and family-formation and, on the other hand, the prevalence of religious belief. In short, on the whole, 'having larger families ... mak[es] people more religious'[62], as much as the other way around. Why? Eberstadt suggests various factors, including the 'transcendental' effect that the event of birth has upon most parents and 'the primal fact that the motherchild and fatherchild bond, as no other, appears to push at least some people toward an intensity of purpose they might never otherwise have experienced'[63] – feelings that I, for one, most certainly can vouch for.

Eberstadt also argues that many people do not come to faith via 'an atomistic decision' based on careful reasoning, but as a result of a 'holistic response to family life ... mediated through the elemental connections of husband, wife, child, aunt, great-grandfather, and the rest'[64]. This is surely right, and is consistent with my own view – mentioned in the Introduction – that if God exists the 'cerebral' way to faith cannot possibly be the only way, or even an especially common way. There must be a route accessible to all. So, as Eberstadt puts it:

> [I]t appears that the natural family as a whole has been the human symphony through which God has historically been heard by many people – not the prophets, not the philosophers, but a great many of the rest ... [It is] the totality of family through which many people derive their deepest opinions and impressions of life – including religious opinions and impressions.[65]

The metaphor of family as 'human symphony' (note the allusion to music, another of God's principal means of communication) seems to me exquisitely apt.

But even Eberstadt's analysis is incomplete. I would not confine God's 'human symphony' to *family* love, important though it undoubtedly is. Other forms of filial love, such as friendship, as well as *eros* and *agape*, must also move many people to religious belief. All the forms of love are capable of speaking to people in a transcendental way. Martin Luther King said it best:

I know now that Jesus is right, that love is the way. And this is why John said, 'God is love,' so that he who hates does not know God, but he who loves at that moment has the key that opens the door to the meaning of ultimate reality.[66]

I believe that one of God's main purposes in creating human love was to help Man understand how we should love God; or, to put the matter another way, to help Man understand what 'loving God' really means. This is the most important way in which love, to use King's phrase, opens the door to the meaning of ultimate reality. The Puritans used to say that they could 'taste' God in all their pleasures.

One of the crucial breakthroughs for me was to understand that the love of God is nothing like *eros* or even – at least at first – much like *philia*. It is necessary to put out of your head the idea that one is expected to 'fall in love' with God, or even to 'like' Him. In other words, it is necessary to ignore most contemporary obsessions about love. Rather, love of God begins with an act of will. It is a discipline. In this sense it is like *agape* – you must force yourself, as it were, to behave as though you loved God. You do so by obeying the Commandments (cf. Matthew 5:19), and the other dictates of conscience, just as a young child obeys a parent's rules.

If you do that for a time, you should eventually realise the genius of the rules themselves. In the words of the psalmist:

The law of the Lord is perfect,
　　Reviving the soul.
The statutes of the Lord are trustworthy,
　　Making wise the simple.

(Psalm 19:7)

If and when you reach that state of mind, you may become increasingly convinced that God is watching you. You have then become aware of God's reality, and what began as mere obedience may well evolve into understanding, respect for wisdom, awe – and then empathetic love.

Once you believe in the reality of God you may come more realistically to recognise the limits of human love. As great a thing as human love is, it is not perfect. Like any other inherently good thing – work, education, physical beauty, good health – each and every form of human love can become an object of idolatry if it is pursued as an *ultimate* thing.[67] The danger of basing your whole sense of self-worth on a person (or on wealth or career or reputation, or the cultivation of a particular talent) is that all people, and all worldly things, are flawed and transient. Inevitably, you will feel let down, disappointed, disillusioned – perhaps utterly crushed. This happened to me at around the age of 40, and it is an affliction which I continue to fight against. Only God is ultimate and perfect.

Once you have truly grasped that concept – and perhaps even before – you will want to communicate with God and reveal yourself to Him. Love of God is, in this sense, something like the desire we sometimes have to lay ourselves bare to the few people who are really close to us. But it is an even stronger desire than that, because it is impossible to be *totally* candid even with people extremely close to us, however much we love them or they love us. On the other hand, communication with God is predicated upon the belief that God already knows – for 'nothing in all creation is hidden from God's sight. Everything is uncovered and laid bare before the eyes of him to whom we must give account' (Hebrews 4:13).

In short, only 'God's eyes' see all. Accordingly, with God, there is no point whatever in being anything less than fully candid. Love of God thus becomes love of truth, or of that small part of 'the Truth' that any single individual can ever definitely know, namely the thoughts in our own head.[68] This notion was, I believe, the one that Soren Kierkegaard sought to convey in extolling the virtues of 'subjective' or 'existential' truth.*

As to God's love for Man, there are strong clues as to its nature in various manifestations of human love. God has not left us groping around hopelessly in the dark as to His love for us. He has shown each of us the way, if we look around us, or just take notice of our own feelings. In this regard, both *eros* and *philia* are analogous.

Eros is a largely involuntary form of love; it just happens, and (at least in many instances) it is not predicated upon the beloved having done anything 'deserving' of that love. So it is with God's love of Man: we do not deserve it, but God feels love for us anyway. Moreover, when God's love is not returned, He feels all the miseries of the unrequited lover to which I alluded earlier.

The analogy with *eros* breaks down there, however, because *eros* is ephemeral. A better analogy is with parental love. It too is involuntary, but it is also resilient. In part this is because the parents have – literally – created the child, by their act of physical love; in the same way, God created Man, and feels pleasure in His creation. Love springing from an act of creation – especially of so extraordinary a piece of work as Man – is not apt to fade away lightly. So it is with human parents and perhaps especially with mothers. As Mary Eberstadt has suggested, commenting upon the disproportionately high rate of church attendance by women: 'Perhaps women who are mothers tend to be more religious because the act of participating in creation, i.e. birth, is more immediate than that of men'[69].

Above all, parental love is forgiving. The good parent is sympathetic when the child tries and fails, but is disappointed and angry – largely for the child's sake – when the child behaves improperly or dishonourably. The good parent wants the child to succeed, but not at any cost, because the parent understands that in the long run the child is unlikely to get away with, or to be fulfilled by, a life of misconduct. Most parents will give their children an unlimited number of chances, however badly they may have

---

* It was unquestionably Evelyn Waugh's ultimate point in *Brideshead Revisited*. Julia Flyte, the real hero of the novel, tells Ryder that she cannot marry him when, and because, she finally faces the truth. Her conscience has been screaming at her for months. 'I can't marry you, Charles; I can't be with you ever again … I saw today there was one thing unforgivable … the bad thing I was on the point of doing'. She characterises her decision as 'a private bargain between me and God, that if I give up this one thing I want so much, however bad I am, he won't quite despair of me in the end'. (Ryder was married already, and, at that stage, an unbeliever as well.) See *Brideshead Revisited*, Penguin Books (1981), pp. 386–7.

behaved in the past, at least until the child becomes an adult. It is the same with God – until we die, He gives us an unlimited number of chances to repent. That is the lesson of the parable of the barren fig tree (Luke 13:1–9).

This may be one of hardest things for many people to grasp about God; it took me a long time. The misconception is to think of God, if as a parent, then as a cold or even tyrannical parent, obsessed with imposing harsh and impossible rules, as though He wished to make life hard for us and to watch us struggle. But the opposite is the case. Yes, life can be hard and, yes, there are rules – laws of Nature and norms of proper conduct. But the purpose of those rules is not to 'establish death on earth for the sake of eternity in heaven'[70]. When Adam disobeys God, life becomes *harder*. The purpose of God's rules is to make life on Earth as happy and harmonious as possible for as many people as possible, while still maintaining a meaningful Universe in which Man has the gift of free will. It may be that not even God had any choice in imposing them.

Likewise, parents do not, by and large, make up the rules of good morals or society. The parent's task is to teach the child how to survive and prosper according to those rules. That is the essential point of the biblical injunction that children should honour their parents (Exodus 20:12): it is largely a rule for the benefit of *children*, not for the pleasure of parents.

It is the same with the biblical injunction that people should obey God's rules (Deuteronomy 13:4). The injunction is for Man's own good. Although God originally imposed the rules, they are now 'set' in place, and they are the same for everybody. God is like an indulgent, devoted and loving parent, 'committed to changing you for the better, and [whose] very persistence … is really an affirmation of you'[71]. God wants to help us succeed by learning to *understand* the rules, as much as to comply with them (cf. Proverbs 23:19). But understanding of the rules begins with compliance, and compliance with the rules begins with respect for the authority which imposes them. Just as a child will never truly learn from its parent unless and until the child believes in the authority of the parent, so Man must believe in the authority, the legitimacy of God. This is what St Paul meant when he wrote that 'without faith it is impossible to please God'. Love of God requires that you 'believe that he exists and that he rewards those who earnestly seek him' (Hebrews 11:6).

At some time after the moment arrives when a person truly believes in the reality of God, that person may begin to experience a feeling towards God that is something more easily recognizable as a form of human love. The closest thing I can think of (related to personal experience) is a boy's love for his father. (A girl's love for her mother is, I expect, the same.) First, there is the sense of sheer physical dependence, for the physical being that can effortlessly lift you up off the ground. Second, there is the feeling of awe for that powerful presence which created you in its image and that is now harnessed for your own protection (but that, in your nightmares, could also destroy you). Third, there is the desire to avoid disapproval. Fear of a parent's disapproval is analogous to fear of God, in this utterly crucial way: it tends to promote right behaviour towards others, that is, the practice of *philia* and *agape*. That is one reason why, as Solomon believed, 'The fear of the Lord is the beginning of knowledge' (Proverbs 1:7).

Once you are in a loving relationship with God, you will feel compelled more and more to extend love to other people. Experiencing divine love compels you to obey the dictates of conscience, to practise *philia* and *agape*, and not merely because you believe you must do so, or to avoid punishment for not doing so. Fear of the Lord is merely the *beginning* of knowledge. Sin, on this view, is not so much the breaking of rules but 'a wrecked relationship with God, one another, and the whole created order'[72]. Sooner or later you will find yourself obeying the dictates of conscience because, in a real sense, you *want* to, in order 'to live [a life] worthy of God' (1 Thessalonians 2:12).

CHAPTER 4

TACKLING ARGUMENTS AGAINST A DESIGNING GOD

Will the one who contends with the Almighty correct him?

Job 40:2

I believe a leaf of grass is no less than the journey-work of the stars,
 And the pismire is equally perfect, and a grain of sand, and the egg of the wren,
And the tree toad is a chef-d'oeuvre for the highest,
 And the running blackberry would adorn the parlours of heaven.

Walt Whitman

Three remarkable features of the world strongly suggest to me that God must exist: the ordered complexity of the physical Universe; the unique faculties of the human mind; and love. There are solid grounds for thinking that these glorious phenomena are not accidental by-products of mindless natural forces, but were designed.

In concluding Part One of this book, it is now time to address some of the major atheistic objections to the concept of a Designing God. A few of them have already been touched upon, but all need to be examined more fully. It is not my contention that there are completely clear-cut refutations of these arguments, though all are logically flawed in one way or another and none of them move me. My base contention is that the issues are much more complicated than atheists would have us believe.

Moreover, except in some of the technological details, few if any of these issues are genuinely new. There were eloquent atheists in ancient Greece. As far as Christianity is concerned, the first non-Jewish critique of serious note was written by one Celsus, a resident of Alexandria, in or about AD 177. Though not strictly an atheist, Celsus was an educated sophisticate of his day, and a few of his arguments bear a striking similarity to those of Richard Dawkins. And, of course, there were many successors to Celsus over ensuing centuries. Dawkins' arguments are no more original than Bertrand Russell's were in 1927, when he penned his anodyne but vastly influential monograph, 'Why I Am Not a Christian'. As Herbert Butterfield wrote in 1949:

I am not sure about the existence of any modern obstruction to religious belief which, when we come to the essential point, does not resolve itself into a fundamental difficulty of which the world was already cognisant two or three thousand years ago. Neither the difficulties nor the options before us are as modern as many people think.[1]

Yet, as Butterfield added, the issues are 'not any less important for that'[2]. They must be addressed.

The God of the gaps

It is often objected by atheists and sceptics that God is invoked by believers whenever science cannot explain something: we are left with a God 'of the gaps'. A corollary of this argument is that as science becomes more and more sophisticated, those gaps will be further and further narrowed, perhaps to a stage where there is no room left for God at all.

The Christian Church largely has itself to blame for such superficial strength as these arguments carry. It 'has so often imagined the gospel to be tied to the science of a particular epoch … that men have felt that the one must stand or fall with the other'[3]. St Augustine was alive to these dangers in the early fourth century[4], but his warnings went largely unheeded. Far too often the Church, and/or individual Christians, have tried to defend entrenched orthodoxies in the face of strong contrary evidence, such as that produced by Galileo and Darwin.

Nevertheless, the 'God of the gaps' argument is weak. The fact that too many religious leaders down the ages have been needlessly antagonistic towards science does not disprove the existence of God. As I sought to argue in Chapter 1, there are key instances where science supports rather than discredits certain basic tenets of Christianity. The Big Bang theory is a good example. More generally, the discoveries of science tend increasingly to reveal the wonderful complexity of the Universe, and in particular of life on Earth, making luck or happenstance less and less credible as explanations for why things are as they are. So many things must come together in just the way that they do; the slightest difference in any of countless ways and the whole would not merely be different – it would not exist, meaningfully or perhaps at all.

The great Australian chess player and analyst, C.J.S. Purdy, once remarked of Bobby Fischer's best games that they often seemed to 'hang by a thread'[5]. Purdy's insight was that the mind's greatest and most profound creations are not simple but astoundingly complex: that is the way of deliberate genius. It is the same in Nature – many of its essential features hang by a thread.

In this context I would make another observation. Often, it is only when you have acquired considerable expertise in a particular field – like Purdy in chess – that you are in a position to appreciate just how extraordinary a certain achievement is, and thus to try to explain its significance to others. Paul Johnson has made this point with respect to naturalistic painting. (I gather that he is a reasonably gifted amateur.) The point he makes is that in order to paint any scene, person or object well, the artist is required really to see – perhaps for the first time – precisely how the relevant thing is constructed. In Johnson's own case, he says, painting has more and more opened his eyes to the ordered splendour of the physical world. For this reason, he believes that God must approve of his pastime.[6] (I am sure that God does approve of it, and many other artistic pursuits too, for the reason given by Warwick Fairfax: 'In art we learn what is good in the divine creation, we learn to create ourselves, we learn to create our powers of creation.'[7])

Many of the greatest painters have sought to venerate God. Speaking for myself, those who best succeed are *not* those who set out to convey explicitly 'religious' images. Rather, they are those who, by their genius for verisimilitude, and whether consciously or unconsciously, convey a sense of the beauty and mystery of the physical world, together with a sense (sometimes spooky) that something greater exists outside of that world. The great German Romantic, Caspar David Friedrich, was perhaps the best-ever exponent of this skill. Georges La Tour and Jan Vermeer are two others whose works have had that effect upon me. Viewing their paintings evokes a heightened sense of reality, together with a feeling that the artist – as the observer and magical recorder of even a commonplace scene – is like God Himself, watching and understanding. It may not be coincidental that my own interest in painting as a genre of art coincided with an emergent belief in God as the designer of the physical world.

My main objection to the 'God of the gaps' argument is this. It is a grave mistake to regard God merely as a convenient explanation for what cannot be explained by science. God as I conceive Him is the explanation for *everything* – both things that cannot be explained by science and things that can be explained by science. To put it colloquially, God 'invented' science: He invented gravity, electromagnetism, DNA, cognition, natural selection and so forth. Science is *possible* only because we assume that there exists an underlying order which is objectively discernible and explainable – 'that things are governed by a logic that exists independently of those things'[8]. The things that can be explained by Man's current knowledge of science are sufficiently numerous and extraordinary to point towards God's existence. That is why many scientists believe in God: they have an informed sense of awe for the stupendousness of Nature. They have drawn what look to me to be the logical conclusions from the 'seemingly biophilic features of basic physics and chemistry'[9]. These scientists – contemplating such amazing things as the rate of expansion of the Universe, the creation of carbon atoms inside stars, the inverse square law, and the existence of water – are forced to believe in a Creator.

Sir Martin Rees, the Astronomer Royal of Great Britain, is not one of those scientists. However, he has conceded that 'these features [i.e. the laws of physics and chemistry] cannot be as readily dismissed as the old claims for design in living things'. Why? Because 'the basic laws governing stars and atoms are a given, and nothing biological can react back on them to modify them'[10]. This is one of the points that sways me: these laws have *always* existed, and everything ultimately emanates from them.

The British particle physicist and Anglican clergyman, John Polkinghorne, has written eloquently on this theme. For Polkinghorne, the 'scientifically discerned regularity of the world' is a sign that there is something about the Universe of deeper significance than mere matter. The finely tuned laws of Nature are a 'reflection of the steadfast will of a Creator', who continuously upholds and sustains the physical world in which we live.[11]

It is surprising that more scientists – and more laypeople who are well educated in science – do not think in this way. Richard Dawkins, in his introduction to *The Blind Watchmaker*, reveals a passionate reverence for the organised complexity of life. He says that if he had lived before 1859 (when Darwin published *The Origin of the Species*) he could not imagine having been an atheist.[12] My question to Dawkins would be this: What, really, does Darwinism change? The theory provides a plausible explanation of the mechanism by which is brought about, in Dawkins' own words, 'the sheer hugeness of biological complexity and the beauty and elegance of biological design'[13]. The question still remains whether the process of evolution came about as a result of mere happenstance, or whether *the process itself* was designed. The arguments for design persuade me, principally because the process appears to be anything but random.

To repeat: God is not to be invoked merely to fill the gaps in Man's scientific knowledge. God must be invoked in order to *make sense* of our scientific knowledge, the things that science can explain. That may be one reason why God has imbued Man, alone of all creatures, with the ability to comprehend such things.

The limits of science

Apart from the things that science can explain, there are those things that science cannot presently explain. In this context, there is an important distinction to be drawn between (on the one hand) the current status of scientific knowledge in the continuum of what is knowable and (on the other hand) the ultimate limits of scientific enquiry.

As to the first issue, there are respectable arguments both ways. John Horgan's thesis in *The End of Science* is that empirical science may well *already* have reached, or almost reached, its practical limits. In other words, there are no more truly ground-breaking discoveries (like those of Newton, Darwin, Einstein and Crick) to come. Many of Horgan's arguments are persuasive. On the other hand, it is undeniable that similar claims have often been made before: infamously in 1894 by Albert Michelson, a Nobel prize-winning physicist, who opined that 'it seems probable that most of the grand underlying principles have been firmly established'[14]. What would Michelson have said in 1994?

It may be, then, that science has further major breakthroughs in store. But I am convinced that even if, in time, those breakthroughs come, the total store of human knowledge will remain a meagre portion of all that there is. In John Horgan's words, 'our imaginations can always go farther'[15]. My guess is that, even today, despite all of the astounding discoveries of science to date, Man understands considerably less about most things than even the most humble among us may like to assume, let alone the most complacent scientists. Horgan has coined the term 'ironic science' to describe the search for what are, he believes, unanswerable questions. It 'reminds us', he says, 'that all our knowledge is half-knowledge; it reminds us of how little we know'[16]. Socrates was close to the mark when he admitted that he knew nothing except the fact of his ignorance.

My own belief is that God *for our own good* has deliberately set some kind of limit upon our capacity to understand certain things – such as the initial phase of the Big Bang[17]. A degree of uncertainty seems to be wired into the laws of the Universe. A famous example is Gödel's theorem, which postulates that certain mathematical propositions can neither be proved nor disproved. Another example, from quantum physics, is Heisenberg's Uncertainty Principle, which holds in substance that it is *impossible* to predict where an electron will be at any given moment, because the momentum and the position of an electron cannot both be ascertained simultaneously. Unless and until an electron is observed, it is indeterminable – 'at once everywhere and nowhere'[18]. And the act of observation itself interferes with any prediction as to where the electron will be in future.

Apart from quantum physics, it seems that God has limited our capacity to predict the future course of certain other events, not necessarily because the relevant laws of Nature are too complex in theory, but because their outcomes are too uncertain in practice.[19] The exact time, place and manner of each of our deaths is one example, which will be discussed more fully in Chapter 7; another example, less morbid but no less important, is the weather. John Polkinghorne has noted this remarkable feature of 'structured openness' in the Universe, which is the subject of chaos theory – the idea that systems of any significant complexity 'rapidly acquire an exquisite sensitivity to circumstance'. Polkinghorne argues that chaos theory is consistent with the theistic notion that Man does not live in an entirely determinist Universe. Despite the fixed laws of Nature, the future is not fixed – Man can affect it by his conduct, and so can God.[20]

I believe that there is another, related, reason for this 'hidden flexibility' in the Universe. God has ensured that many phenomena are inherently uncertain and unpredictable, in order to protect Man from the consequences of his own evil. Evil is an inevitable by-product of the gift of free will. But by leaving some things beyond the knowledge or control of any individual person or organised group of persons, there is at play in the world a kind of equalising factor that prevents even greater evils from being perpetrated. (Man's discovery of nuclear fission and nuclear fusion, and the subsequent invention of nuclear weaponry, appears to defy this suggestion. Yet despite the existence of such weaponry for sixty years, the human race has not been exterminated by nuclear holocaust. That seems to me to indicate more strongly than anything else the reality of God's *grace*, another topic to which I will come later.)

For present purposes, my point is this. The fact that there are – and most probably always will be – gaps in Man's scientific knowledge is not merely, or at all, a useful convenience for those who argue in favour of the existence of God. The *nature* of at least some of those gaps is significant and revealing. In my judgment, the gaps in our knowledge are a further pointer to the existence of a grand scheme for the Universe – a scheme that centrally involves Man. I cannot shake the conviction that there are some things we are not meant to know.

The argument from imperfection

Another argument against a Designing God is that the Universe is not 'perfect'. Bertrand Russell advanced this contention in 'Why I am not a Christian'; he regarded it as 'astonishing' that anyone could believe 'that this world, with all the things that are in it, with all its defects, should be the best that omnipotence has been able to produce in millions of years'[21]. In 2006, the eminent Australian science journalist Robyn Williams based an entire book on this theme. He called it <u>Unintelligent Design: Why God Isn't As Smart As She Thinks She Is</u>. In Williams's words: 'If God was really on your case, I think you might quite reasonably expect perfection. As it is, there's much to be cross about.'[22]

There are various dimensions to this argument. The weightiest is the existence of evil and suffering – what C.S. Lewis called 'the problem of pain'[23]. That deep conundrum is addressed as best I can in Chapter 7. For present purposes, it is convenient to tackle the narrower point that Nature contains all kinds of creatures, and parts thereof, which would seem to have been designed in a less than optimal way.

Robyn Williams and others point to a host of examples from the human body: the useless appendix, pain in childbirth, poor drainage from our sinuses, weak backs, bad breath, disparate sexual desires, and our jerry-built optical system. The same complaint is made against Nature more generally: the koala's downward-opening pouch, flesh-eating parasites, germs, viruses and other nasties.[24] Some of these examples are contentious[25], but for the sake of argument let us take them at face value. Why, it is argued rhetorically, would an all-powerful Designer permit such shoddy merchandise to leave the factory?

One aspect of this complaint may be dismissed quickly: the notion that, if the Universe was designed, things ought not to exist in Nature which human beings find displeasing or revolting, such as flesh-eating parasites. (Darwin's own example was the *Ichneumonidae*, which feeds inside the living body of caterpillars.) But this, of course, is a non sequitur. The existence of such things may tell us something about the nature of any Designer. It certainly tells us something about the nature of Man. (Notably, even Darwin applied human standards of morality to the natural world, and felt disgust and pity. This is something we have all done; it is another indicator that morality is more than a product of Darwinian forces and that Man is special.) But the fact that something in Nature offends the sensibilities of Man is irrelevant to the question whether the thing itself was designed.[26] In any event, creatures such as parasites serve useful purposes in the ecosystem, and are themselves extremely complex organisms.[27] It is necessary to think more deeply than this.

Some Christians – those who take a literal view of the opening chapters of Genesis – attribute all the flaws in Nature to the Fall. God, on this view, created Nature to be perfect; it was Adam's disobedience which brought on, not only the Fall of Man, but Nature's own 'bondage to decay' (see Romans 8:21; Genesis 3:17-19).

Here, then, are two possible explanations for the presence of 'design flaws' in Nature. From the atheist's perspective we have no right to expect anything better, because Nature is mindless and purposeless. By contrast, on the Biblical literalist's view, we once *did* have something better, but it was spoiled as a result of Adam's original sin. Personally, I find neither of these competing explanations at all satisfying. An entirely literal reading of Genesis is unjustified: as I have said, the opening chapters are surely allegorical. And St Paul's main point in Chapter 8 of Romans was, as I read it, a rather different one: that Christians should look beyond their current sufferings, to a time in the afterlife, following bodily resurrection, when even Nature will hold no fears.

For the present, however, Nature produces physical hardships to be endured by all living creatures. Must we therefore conclude that God, if He exists, 'got things wrong'? Or, more likely, that God does not exist? No and no. For the reasons set out in Chapters 1 to 3, I hold firm to the belief that the Universe must be the creation of an intelligent and loving mind. Furthermore, God knew exactly what He was doing. Any and all 'flaws' in Nature exist for a reason.

Already in this book I have invoked the Prophet Isaiah's metaphor of God as the moulder of a clay pot (see Isaiah 29:16, 64:8). St Paul himself also employed this device. In Chapter 9 of Romans, he sought to counter any argument that God was somehow 'to blame' for the imperfect devotion of some of His children, as compared to that of others:

> But who are you, O man, to talk back to God? 'Shall what is formed say to him who formed it, 'Why did you make me like this?' Does not the potter have the right to make out of the same lump of clay some pottery for noble purposes and some for common use?
>
> (Romans 9:20–1)

St Paul assumed, of course, that God is Man's Creator – and, what is more, he assumed that even people who were lax in their religious devotions accepted that much. Paul's point was that, given the fact that God is Man's Creator, it is futile for Man to complain about God's methods. God is entitled to create things as he likes. It is no use blaming God; all you can do is try to understand Him as best you can.

The modern argument from imperfection is a somewhat different argument to the one Paul was answering. The modern argument does not proceed on the assumption that God created Man – or any part of Nature. What it does assume is, first, that Nature is less than perfect and, second, that anything that any God would create would necessarily be perfect, because God is supposed to be perfect. Because Nature is less than perfect, the argument runs, God cannot have created it.

I do not quibble with the assumption that God is perfect. I do quibble with the sweeping assumption that Nature is not perfect. My belief is that even if individual components of Nature, viewed in isolation, are imperfect, Nature *as a whole* is perfect – or, more precisely, as perfect as anything that is not itself God can possibly be. Man should not be misled by the imperfections in Nature. As Francis Bacon observed, 'The subtlety of Nature is greater many times over than the subtlety of the senses and understanding.'[28] Our focus should be upon the overall greatness of Nature: the existence of imperfections does not detract from that greatness nor from its divine meaning.[29] As the author of John's Gospel wrote, trying to suggest this notion in poetry: 'The light shines in the darkness, but the darkness has not understood it' (John 1:5).

Does that explanation sound a bit grandiose? Let me suggest another. God permits imperfections in individual *components* of Nature, because Nature is the balance between competing imperfect organisms, each with strengths and weaknesses. Nature works as an integrated whole. And human life is made meaningful by the inevitability of death. It is a positively good thing – an essential thing – that the human body, like all living organisms, is vulnerable to a thousand natural shocks. Otherwise we would all live forever.

In short, a perfect physical world is a contradiction in terms. God would not have bothered creating it.

Man's alleged 'insignificance' in the physical Universe

Many scientists dispute that Man has any special place in the Universe. This is another frequent objection to Christianity, and religion in general, that I used to make myself. Stephen Hawking epitomises this mindset; he once asserted flatly that 'the human race is just a chemical scum on a moderate-sized planet'[30].

The objection is usually along these lines. The Universe is billions of years old and hundreds of millions of light years in size. The Sun is but one star and the Earth is but one planet among billions of stars and (probably) billions of planets in the Universe. Man has lived on the Earth for only a tiny fraction of the time that the Earth has existed. Of what possible significance, then, is Man, which is but one species, albeit an unusually intelligent species, among the millions that have inhabited the Earth? In short, why would any God bother with us? More particularly, if God's special concern is Man, why did He 'wait' until extremely recently in the cosmic scheme of time before bringing Man into existence? And why is there all that 'wasted' space in the Universe?[31]

Various aspects of this conundrum have already been touched upon in Chapters 2 and 3. Man is genuinely special, in my view, because we possess certain unique faculties: cognition, conscience, the multi-faceted capacity to love. These seem to me powerful philosophical objections. Another is that there is no logical correlation between mere size and intrinsic moral worth. Why does it matter that the Earth is a moderate-sized planet? Which is more beautiful, a diamond or a slagheap?

All other arguments aside, there is an entirely satisfying practical explanation for why the Universe is now as large as it is and why Man has appeared in it only at this very recent stage of its history. The educated modern person should not be intimidated by the size and age of the Universe into rationalising God away.

Again, I draw upon John D. Barrow:

> In order for a Big Bang universe to contain the basic building blocks necessary for
> the subsequent evolution of biological complexity it must have an age at least as long
> as the time it takes for the nuclear reactions in stars to produce those elements. This
> means that the observable universe must be at least ten billion years old and so, *since
> it is expanding*, it must be at least ten billion light years in size. We could not exist in a
> universe that was significantly smaller.[32]

The point is gloriously simple, and once stated seems almost self-evident. Nevertheless, until I read this passage I had not understood that the immense size and age of
the Universe are prerequisites to Man's existence, rather than curious incidental facts.
In Barrow's words:

> Modern cosmology shows that these features are not random accidents. They are part
> and parcel of the whole interconnectedness of the universe. They are, in fact, neces-
> sary features of any universe that contains living observers.[33]

It may still be objected, and often is: Why would any God have gone about things in
such an odd way? Tentatively, I proffer three answers, which are not mutually exclusive.

The first is that there may well be very few ways, perhaps only one way, to make a
complex universe with rational, self-conscious, conscience-possessing beings in it. Can
anyone suggest another way, let alone a better one? As Einstein famously asked, did
God have any choice? There are compelling reasons to suspect that the answer to all
these questions is 'no'.

Everything about the Universe, from Man's perspective, seems so perfectly integrated – in ways obvious and not so obvious. I have already detailed some examples in
Chapter 1, but there are many others. Barrow points out, for instance, that life could
not exist on Earth unless the stars were so far away and so relatively few in number,
compared to the space between them. It is not simply that if the Earth was any closer
to the Sun, or in comparable proximity to more than one star, the temperature of the
planet would skyrocket. The vast distances between the stars guarantees the darkness
of the night sky: we do not look up and see a star at the end of every line of sight, as
one sees a tree at the end of every line of sight when looking into a thick forest.[34] I
would ask the reader to think hard about that concept for a minute or two. It strikes me
as yet another facet of Fred Hoyle's deep-laid scheme.

(It does not follow, by the way, that if God Himself was subject to certain con-
straints, or 'laws', in the construction of the Universe then He cannot be 'the ultimate
law-giver'. This was another of Bertrand Russell's arguments[35], but I think it is fallacious. It is akin to saying that Leonardo da Vinci was not the ultimate creator of the
Mona Lisa because it could not have been painted in any other way (for if it had, it
would be a different painting) – therefore da Vinci *had* to paint it that way. Contemporary physics shows that in theory there are many other ways to make a universe – just

as there are many other ways to paint a painting. And just as the vast majority of theoretical paintings would be awful, the vast majority of theoretical universes would not sustain life, let alone Man. Yet the 'laws' of the actual Universe – which are, as Russell understood, just a description of how things *in fact* behave – do sustain life, and Man. Is that just lucky happenstance, or was it brought about?)

My second answer to the apparent 'problem' of God's methods is to suggest that God's attitude to time and space must be very different from Man's. If God exists, then He created time and space. Moreover, as I conceive things, God is not encumbered with or constrained by either, at least not in the same way that Man is. A billion years, in other words, is not for God an unimaginably long time (cf. Psalm 90:4; 2 Peter 3:8)[36]; nor a billion light years an unimaginably long distance. Furthermore, although Man may legitimately regard himself as special, we are far from being God's *only* concern. I agree with John Polkinghorne that it is a mistake to regard the Universe as no more than 'a backdrop for the human drama, which is lately begun after an overture lasting 15 billion years'[37]. That may, understandably, be the way that Man looks upon the eons that preceded us, but I do not believe that it has ever been God's attitude. Even today, God is vitally interested in all aspects of His Creation; not one sparrow escapes His attention (Luke 12:6).

Man, however, is God's *highest* concern (cf. Luke 12:7). And this consideration leads to my third answer to arguments about 'wasted space' and 'wasted time'. The vast size and age of the Universe seem to me to be crucial to preserving Man's sanity. They are also necessary concomitants of faith of any kind – and of the right *not* to have faith, if that is what you choose in exercise of the gift of free will.

The enormity of the Universe has tended over the course of recorded history *not* to cause Man to doubt the existence of God – that seems to be a fairly recent phenomenon – but rather instinctively to assume it. The people of many ancient civilisations inferred the presence of a deity primarily from the world around them, and in particular from the night sky. That conclusion was and remains open, but it is not axiomatic. Now consider the alternative. Imagine if the Universe was much smaller, of a scope 'manageable' to the human imagination. Imagine, say, that there were a 'border' of the Universe in a fixed position, like the domed roof in Peter Weir's 1998 film *The Truman Show* – a border actually or at least potentially within Man's reach. You need only to begin to conceive such strangeness to realise some of the troubling implications. For one thing, Man would know for certain whether or not he was alone in the Universe; and if we were not alone, the likely consequences would be dire, for the reasons I suggested in Chapter 2.

Similar considerations apply as regards the vast age of the Universe. As C.S. Lewis observed, 'God, from the first, created [Nature] such as to reach her perfection by a process in time'[38]. The fact that God went about things in this way was extraordinarily wise, and it is surprising that neither atheists nor young-Earth proponents can see why. Try to imagine a world in which it were received *scientific fact* – and not merely the sincere though mistaken belief of a minority – that the Earth and Man were only a few thousand years old, a 'sensible' age. Would there then be much, if any, room for doubt that both the Earth and Man had been created from nothing by a supernatural being?

What role, if any, could faith play in human affairs? How would the psyche of modern Man cope with such knowledge?

Many of the technical and metaphysical arguments concerning cosmology and evolution are the product of the vast timescales involved. I suggested in Chapter 1 that it was not inconceivable to me that God may have intervened from time to time in the evolutionary process. Many people on both sides of the debate baulk at the idea of a 'hybrid' process of Creation involving the outworking of natural laws *and* periodic tinkering by a deity. Some religious people object that an omnipotent God would not need to work that way: He would either create everything in an instant, or create natural laws sufficient to allow Nature to take its course without further intervention by Him.

Atheists regard the idea of periodic theistic intervention as absurd. No 'rational' God, they say, would have created species from time to time over billions of years, and observed them become extinct – especially if Man was always the ultimate point of the exercise. Such a God would be a 'fumbling fool' and a 'blunderer'[39]; therefore, God cannot exist. This is one of the reasons why Darwinists scoff at Intelligent Design theory. In most of its variants, ID posits intervention by God not only at the initial stage (the origin of life) but at many other stages as well (the origin of individual species), either directly, by God creating new species from scratch, or indirectly, by God causing a favourable mutation of DNA that leads to a new species by Darwinian processes.[40] Darwinists will not countenance any such ideas. They insist that speciation theory (natural selection acting upon *random* mutations) is quite adequate to account for the emergence of new species from time to time. That may be right. Personally I am doubtful, for the reasons discussed in Chapter 1, but in any event it is hard to see how the proposition can ever be definitely proven – or disproven.

The possibility remains open that God actively intervened at various stages in life's ancient past, as part of an ongoing process of Creation. Why would God have gone about things that way? My own view is that there is at least one quite plausible reason. Perhaps God wished to leave hints to modern Man as to the fact of His existence. The currently unexplainable 'jumps' in the history of life – such as the Cambrian explosion – might be further instances of St Thomas Aquinas' *viae*, paths or roads by which some people may be led toward that truth. But this is a possibility only. It may well be that God did *not* intervene in the evolutionary process once He had set it in motion. I do not think it is possible, let alone necessary, to answer that question one way or the other. My present point is that the possibility of God's intervention cannot be ruled out, and that there is uncertainty about the matter because of the huge timescales involved. Accordingly, if God exists, He did not 'waste' time any more than He 'wasted' space, or matter, or energy. There was method in His apparent madness.

In the elegant and insightful words of Warwick Fairfax, which I urge the reader to mull over with care:

> Things happen with devastating certainty, but so gradually, so logically and so methodically that when the miracle is finally accomplished it appears perfectly natural and is called a scientific fact.[41]

Naturalistic explanations for religion

We have seen that, with varying degrees of cogency, Darwinian explanations have been postulated for the complexity of life on Earth, for human conscience, and for love. In recent years scientists have attempted, by similar means, to explain religious faith itself. Richard Dawkins devotes a chapter to this issue in *The God Delusion*.

For Dawkins and a number of other leading evolutionary theorists (including Daniel Dennett, E.O. Wilson, Scott Atran and David Sloan Wilson) accounting for Man's *belief* in a Designing God is a perplexing issue requiring a complex answer. On the face of it, Darwinism is incompatible with 'the time-consuming, wealth-consuming, hostility-provoking rituals, the anti-factual, counter-productive fantasies of religion'[42]. Atheists have to find a way of explaining how a gene conferring a propensity toward belief in a *non-existent* God could have provided Man's ancient ancestors with a competitive advantage over organisms not possessing such a gene. In the words of Francis Collins: 'Why would such a universal and uniquely human hunger exist, if it were not connected to some opportunity for fulfilment?'[43]

Various Darwinian explanations have been proposed, and Dawkins provides a useful road-map of the territory.[44] Broadly speaking, the competing explanations fall into two categories: the 'adaptationist' theories and the 'by-product' theories.

The adaptationists argue that a gene conferring a propensity towards religious belief must have had (and perhaps still has) direct advantages for the survival of *individual* organisms. It has been suggested, for example, that the consolation and reassurance afforded by religion may help to protect people from stress-related illnesses. Other contentions of this sort are that religion satisfies human curiosity and/or assists the powerful to subjugate the weak. Or consider this rather sweeping suggestion:

> [P]eople gain a selective advantage from believing in things they can't prove [because] those who are occasionally consumed by false beliefs do better in life than those who insist on evidence before they believe and act.[45]

I find these arguments exceedingly thin. For many conscientious believers, religion is as much a source of anxiety, guilt and misery as it is confidence, consolation or reassurance.[46] There are, too, a number of strictly Darwinian objections to this line of argument, which have been enunciated by Richard Dawkins himself and other experts in the field.[47] In my judgement, it is fair to conclude that 'religion does not seem to be produced by a specific part of our psychological make-up'[48].

Another adaptationist explanation is founded on the idea of so-called 'group selection': religion advantages certain groups of people against other groups because it fosters collective loyalty, solidarity and sacrifice. The 'religion gene', it is surmised, confers an advantage not upon individual organisms but upon groups in which the gene is found more often in individuals within the group than it is in other groups. But, again, Dawkins provides sound reasons for rejecting this notion as an explanation for religious belief and observance.[49]

The theory favoured by Dawkins is that religion is an incidental by-product of a gene which confers some other 'legitimate' biological advantage. Christianity, like all religions, is 'a misfiring by-product of a normally useful compass'[50]. Dawkins employs the analogy of moths flying into a flame. They do so not to deliberately commit suicide, but because they are 'wired' to fly towards light: moths evolved at a time long before man-made fires were prevalent on Earth and, much more often than not, sources of light (such as the Moon) were an aid to navigation at night. Human beings, he speculates, must be drawn to religion for some analogous reason from our distant past: perhaps because much more often than not it was (and still is) advantageous for a child to obey those in authority. Other possibilities are that religion is a by-product of Man's deeply ingrained psychological tendencies to ascribe a purpose to things, to infer the presence of agents that might do harm, to recognise that other people have minds of their own, and to fall in love.[51]

A similar idea, originally proposed by Stephen Jay Gould, is that religion is like a spandrel. The word 'spandrel' is an architectural term for the V-shaped structure that forms between two rounded arches. It is a feature that is not *itself* there for any particular purpose, but which 'comes with' a feature that does. In such circumstances the apparently useless feature may sometimes be made functional or develop functionality of its own.[52]

My own view is that while the 'spandrel' analogy is useful in accounting for certain incidental physical features of Nature, such as the colourful patterns on butterflies' wings and tropical fish[53], it is quite inadequate as an explanation for religion. Even most proponents of such theories concede that the exact genetic 'advantage' of which religion is a by-product remains unproven. Nevertheless, they press the idea that religion is 'a wholly natural phenomenon'[54] for which Man is 'psychologically primed'[55].

A related notion is that religion may be the product of the natural selection of units of information – 'memes'. The theory of 'memetics' is an attempt to explain, in quasi-Darwinian terms, the development of many aspects of human culture. In the language of proponents of this theory, a meme is a 'cultural replicator', analogous to a gene, which enables the transmission of information across time and space. Certain units of information – alone or in combination with others – are more likely to have 'survival value' and to be passed down. Memes can thus be replicated, says Richard Dawkins, 'like viruses in an epidemic'[56].

Dawkins argues that memetics, in combination with conventional genetic evolution, may explain the existence of both religion in general and specific religions in particular. His thesis is that '[i]n the early stages of a religion's evolution, before it becomes organised, simple memes survive by virtue of their universal appeal to human psychology … The later stages, where a religion becomes organised, elaborate and arbitrarily different from other religions, are quite well handled by the theory of memeplexes – cartels of mutually compatible memes'.[57]

So there you have it. Christianity and all the other great religions of the world are 'viruses of the mind'. If you want to read a scholarly rebuttal of this patronising notion, read Alister McGrath's compelling book, *Dawkins' God*.[58] McGrath identifies four major difficulties with the 'virus' theory, not the least of them being that Dawkins' own belief system, atheism, is susceptible to exactly the same 'explanation'. Even some atheists have been quite dismissive of Dawkins' musings on these issues.[59]

My own untutored view is that there are several serious flaws in Dawkins' approach. Perhaps the most fundamental is this: a purely Darwinian view of our cognitive abilities compels the conclusion that we cannot trust them for *any* purpose. If Man's ability to reason is itself no more than a convenient aid to the reproduction of our DNA, i.e. the product of natural selection in a godless universe, then how can we place faith in pure reason? In the words of Timothy Keller: 'If we can't trust our belief-forming faculties to tell us the truth about God, why should we trust them to tell us the truth about anything?'[60]

Another problem with Dawkins' thesis is that it is founded upon the very conclusion he is trying to prove: God does not exist, so some other 'rational' explanation must be found for why people waste their time thinking about Him. In McGrath's parody: 'People do not believe in God because they have given long and careful thought to the matter; they do so because they have been infected by a powerful meme.'[61]

Somewhat different ideas have been propounded by both John Shelby Spong and an Australian philosopher, Tamas Pataki. Bishop Spong's contention is that the notion of a theistic God was invented by primitive man as a kind of coping mechanism. Ever since, he suggests, that mechanism has assisted Man to deal with the 'trauma of self-consciousness', our search for meaning in the face of knowledge of the inevitability of death.[62] Pataki's thesis is along similar lines. He argues that many people's religious beliefs are best understood as a product of psychological *dis*order – in particular, unfulfilled needs for 'infantile narcissistic satisfactions'[63]. In this vein, the founder of modern psychiatry, Sigmund Freud, equated God with a child's image of an ideal father.[64]

All of these theories amount to the same thing: religion is a form of conscious or unconscious wish-fulfilment. It is a way of defending one's identity and self-esteem, achieving certainty, and/or controlling sexual impulses. The monotheistic God has all the attributes craved by an infant in its parents.

As someone who has suffered from mental illness, I would be the last person to dismiss the role of psychological factors in any sphere of life, including religion. It seems probable that psychological disorder is one reason for religious extremism. But Pataki's wider thesis – like Spong's – proves too little and too much. The over-developed ego or super-ego, the hated father-figure, the pull of societal convention – 'as motives for such a tremendous force as religion they are little short of grotesque'[65]. Psychological factors no doubt partly account for many people's interest in religion. But if God exists and (as Christians believe) made Man in His own image, why would you expect anything else? God needed to find ways to mediate with Man in a 'language' accessible – but not obvious – to everyone. I have argued that two of God's chosen ways are of a 'psychological' kind: the pull of conscience and the experience of human love, including, in particular, parental love. One might add the fear of death. The points made by Pataki and Spong are not inconsistent with my arguments.

Spong admits openly that his purpose is to discredit the concept of a theistic God. I do not think he succeeds. Pataki, on the other hand, aims to ascertain the 'underlying motives' for some people's belief in God and for the intensity with which such beliefs are held. The truth or falsity of any given religious belief is, he concedes correctly, a quite different issue.[66] The same point applies to Dawkins' theory of memes and other bio-evolutionary explanations for religious beliefs. Ultimately, they beg the key question: are those beliefs *true*? In Alister McGrath's words, 'The way in which ideas spread has no necessary relation to their validity'[67].

Finally, to return to a central theme of Chapter 2, Dawkins does not explain (at least to my satisfaction) why it is that Man possesses the gift of cognition. I emphasise the word *why*. Like Paul Davies, I simply cannot accept that Man's extraordinary capacity to discover and understand the underlying laws of the Universe, and to speculate about our origins, is a mere *incidental* by-product of a favourable genetic mutation affecting the human brain.

This is not to say that religion may not one day be explained in Darwinian terms. Personally, I find the current scientific explanations unconvincing, but, regardless of their correctness, all of them still beg the ultimate questions. Does God exist? Which religious beliefs are true? Consider these observations of Justin Barrett, an American psychologist. He is another strong proponent of the Darwinian 'by-product' theory, and he is also a practising Christian:

> Christian theology teaches that people were crafted by God to be in a loving relationship with him and other people. Why wouldn't God, then, design us in such a way as to find belief in divinity quite natural? Suppose science produces a convincing account for why I think my wife loves me – should I then stop believing that she does?[68]

In other words, the most important question is not how Man acquired the capacity to speculate about God, but *why*.

Who designed the Designer?

Who or what made God? This rhetorical question is often posed by genuine agnostics[69], and is the last string in the bow of many an atheist. John Stuart Mill and Bertrand Russell both fell back upon it, without proffering anything substantial by way of logical or theological reasoning. Russell did little more than invoke a childhood epiphany.[70] Among moderns, Richard Dawkins seems to regard this point as decisive. And he, at least, has fleshed out a coherent argument.

Dawkins's starting point is that the biological complexity of life on Earth is the result of Darwinian processes. So much may, for the sake of argument, be conceded; but as we saw in Chapter 1, biological complexity is not the only, or even the most significant, example of fine-tuning in Nature. Dawkins accepts that Darwinism cannot account for the appearance of design in physics, chemistry and cosmology, but he argues that invoking a Designer just compounds the conundrum. The ability to design, he asserts, comes *after*, not before, a very long period of biological evolution has resulted in the development of intelligence. Any God capable of designing the Universe from scratch and monitoring every aspect of it continuously from then on would be, he reasons, much more complex than anything in the Universe *now*, 13.7 billion years since the Big Bang; and such a God 'is going to need a mammoth explanation in its own right'[71].

I have a number of problems with this argument. The first is that it is inconsistent with other aspects of Dawkins' thesis, and with his insistence upon reason and scientific rigour. In order to account for the Goldilocks enigma – Why are the physical laws which underlie the Universe just right for life? – Dawkins is happy to adopt the so-called multiverse theory, which I discussed in Chapter 1. This, it will be recalled, is the idea that there must be many universes, perhaps an infinite number of them. Dawkins claims that the multiverse theory, for which there is no objective evidence at all, is 'simple' and only 'apparently extravagant' – '*if* each one of those universes is simple in its fundamental laws'[72]. That is a gigantic 'if' (how could anyone in our Universe ever possibly know?), and in any case begs the question where the fundamental laws of all of those gazillions of other universes came from – a question that, on Dawkins' thesis, must necessarily have a naturalistic answer. I fail to see how any such naturalistic answer could reasonably be described as simple. According to some variants of the multiverse theory, many or even most of the universes in it must be fakes; you and I may well be 'brains in a vat', à la *The Matrix*. If the number of universes is infinite, there must also exist an infinite number of 'freak observers', intelligent beings like us who strictly speaking ought not to exist, according to the laws of the relevant universe, but do! You and I could be such freak observers, who only imagine that we perceive 'reality'.[73]

In my opinion, there must be a simpler and more rational explanation for the fine-tuning that is evident in the Universe, an explanation that permits Man to 'have confidence that what one perceives with one's senses is generally a reliable reflection of reality'[74]. I believe that the best explanation is God.

But how, then, to explain God? This, ultimately, is Dawkins' challenge to believers. I think that his challenge is misconceived, however, because the premise on which it is based (that God requires a naturalistic explanation) is misconceived. *Does* God require any explanation, let alone a naturalistic Darwinian explanation? Why cannot God – the First Cause – be accepted as something unexplainable (unexplainable in the sense of not itself having had a cause)? In other words, God must be taken as a given. The concept of God is none the less coherent for that, at least for me.

Dawkins accuses religious people of misunderstanding what it means to explain something.[75] In fact, it is Dawkins who misunderstands what religious people believe about the nature of God.[76] God is indeed unexplainable if conceived of in earthly terms, like some kind of ultra-sophisticated living creature. One is driven to a supernatural conception of God precisely because any other conception is far-fetched in the extreme. As I conceive it, the Universe simply '[would] not work without 'outside' forces, the nature of which must postulate planning, designing, teleological, even moral qualities'[77]. But those 'outside forces' (God), while real, are ultimately indefineable and probably unimaginable. This is the first principle of one of the oldest religious texts known to us today, the Rig Vedas of the ancient Hindus.[78]

Theists are quite prepared to admit that they cannot 'explain' God in the way that Dawkins demands.[79] We regard the demand as illogical, because it skirts the key issue: Why – if there is no God – does anything exist at all? Dawkins and fellow atheists cannot answer that question, except to say that 'science' will eventually do so. But that is a non sequitur, because *science itself* is one of the things that needs an ultimate explanation. In the words of G.K. Chesterton, which I think are devastating:

> [It] is absurd … to complain that it is unthinkable for an admittedly unthinkable God to make everything out of nothing, and then pretend that it is more thinkable that nothing should turn itself into everything.[80]

If Chesterton's retort does not satisfy you, then consider certain words of Martin Luther King. They are the words I now go back to whenever I hear the Dawkins argument expounded, or some version of it. King derived his message from the Old Testament description of Moses' encounter with God, the occasion when God assumed the form of the burning bush (Exodus 3:1–22). In particular, King reminded his congregation about God's instructions to Moses as to the name Moses should give God, when speaking of Him to the Israelites. The name that God proposed was *Yahweh* – which in Hebrew meant 'I Am'.

King explained:

> God is the only being in the universe that can say 'I Am' and put a period [i.e. full stop] behind it. Each of us sitting here has to say 'I am because of my parents; I am because of certain environmental conditions; I am because of certain hereditary circumstances; I am because of God.' But God is the only being that can just say 'I Am' and stop right there. 'I Am that I Am.' And he's here to stay. Let nobody make us feel that we don't need God.[81]

Put to one side the incidental question whether there was, literally, such an encounter between Moses and God. (I am not sure.) The vital point is that the ancients' very conception of God was as something that does not require explanation; the First Cause; the *necessary* Being.

PART TWO

REASONS TO BELIEVE IN CHRISTIANITY

CHAPTER 5

JESUS

Who, being in very nature God, did not consider equality with God something to be grasped, but made himself nothing, taking the very nature of a servant, being made in human likeness. And being found in appearance as a man, he humbled himself and became obedient to death – even death on a cross!

Philippians 2:6–8

[H]istory as we know it now began with Christ, and ... Christ's gospel is its foundation.

Boris Pasternak, Doctor Zhivago

So far in this book I have postulated the existence of a loving God who conceived and created the Universe, in all its splendid intricacy, with a special place in it for Man. In short, I believe that there exists, in Hamlet's phrase, a divinity that shapes our ends.

It is now necessary to analyse the more particular claims of Christianity. These are the beliefs that distinguish Christians from people of other faiths. Some of those beliefs have already been touched upon; as I noted in the Introduction, there is a substantial degree of overlap between each of the issues under discussion. In the chapter about love I drew upon several of Jesus's teachings. What I have not done so far is to grapple with the specifics of Jesus's life on Earth and, in particular, the evidence for His divinity.

This is an unavoidable challenge for any Christian. To this point, there may have been at least a few arguments that would elicit qualified agreement from educated secular humanists. But the task now becomes more challenging. A good number of Christ's teachings are not exclusive to Christianity, and it may readily be conceded that the world would be a better place than it is today if more people acted consistently upon of the tenets of Buddhism or Hinduism, or the teachings of Confucius, or the ideas of the best atheistic thinkers.[1] There have been, after all, a considerable number of great moral philosophers throughout human history. Why should the teachings of Jesus be accorded any higher status than theirs?

This chapter and the next represent my answer to this entirely valid question.

For a start, it is important to acknowledge the difficulties inherent in any serious consideration of theology. My conception of God is as the explanation of everything: everything that Man understands and everything that Man does not understand. The majority of the human race through the ages, and still today, has likewise had some roughly similar conception – an invisible, all-powerful supernatural force, or multitude of forces, that made and monitors the Universe. Indeed, until the nineteenth century, traditional Christian teaching had always taken as its starting point the concept of God the Creator. That is how the Bible begins, and I have done so myself in this book.

However, any attempt to articulate the basis for religious belief in such abstract terms tends to be problematic – and often seems less than convincing to the unbeliever or the sceptic. As Robert Winston has observed, the seminal passage in the Old Testament in which God responds to Moses (Exodus 3:14) reads more like a rebuke than an explanation, an expression of God's 'essential beyondness, His separateness from the world, the inability of men to know Him'[2]. Warwick Fairfax was a tremendous theologian, but I doubt he would have made many converts by reciting his conception of God: '[A] single reality with forms of activity which can be either transcendental or immanent, supracosmic or cosmic, or to us unmanifest or manifest'[3]. That is accurate enough, in my view, but bordering on the obtuse.

On the other hand, the notion of 'the perfect man' is something that everyone can understand. Surprisingly, to me, it was not until the late seventeenth century that defenders of Christianity began to study the New Testament as an historical text, to seek to demonstrate the central tenets of Christianity primarily by reference to actual events in the life of Jesus, and from those events to argue for – or, in some cases, against – His divinity. As I have said, this 'quest for the historical Jesus', a phrase coined by Albert Schweitzer, did not begin in earnest until the Enlightenment; but it had its roots in the Reformation. Protestants acquired a motive to search for evidence that might be used to undermine the authority of the Roman Catholic Church. But there were unintended consequences. The quest, which continues apace to this day, became increasingly rigorous and sophisticated. Doubts began to be raised in the public mind about the objective truth of key aspects of the New Testament, not all of them easily dismissable. This led, in turn, to 'redoubled effort' by Christians to 'create [or, as I would argue, to discover] a religiously usable history'.[4]

Some have argued – both believers and unbelievers among them – that this quest is futile and/or mendacious. I am unable to agree. There is no doubt that it is difficult, and will probably never produce definitive answers. But Jesus – the real Jesus, not merely the 'character' – was and is the linchpin of Christian faith. The twentieth-century Swiss theologian Karl Barth went so far as to say that it is *impossible* for human beings to come to God any other way than through the words and example of Christ as recorded in the Gospels. By reason of the 'wholly otherness' of God, Barth argued, it is beyond mere human beings to arrive at any proper sense of His nature by metaphysical speculation, of the kind attempted so far in this book. The only hope for Man is that God has condescended to reach us.[5]

Barth's thesis was rather extreme, but his underlying insight was astute. One of the best ways to attempt to explain Christianity to an unbeliever or a sceptic, especially in the twenty-first century, is to appeal to the example of Jesus as the perfect man, and to challenge people to think hard about the implications of such a man really having lived on the Earth. The notion of 'the perfect man', moreover, assumes the existence of a set of behavioural standards applicable to Man that no reasonable person can argue with. As I argued in Chapter 2, the very existence of those standards is a pointer to the existence of God as the 'setter' of those standards.

Understood in this way, Karl Barth's idea helps to make sense of one of the most frequently quoted verses in the Gospels: 'I am the way and the truth and the life. No-one comes to the Father except through me' (John 14:6). I used to hear Christians say these words and think them no more than a rather trite, hollow-sounding slogan. But they express a deeply profound, as well as strictly literal, truth. Jesus – His conduct, His teachings, and His death on the Cross – represents the notion of God that is most readily explicable in human terms, 'a vision that we should be capable of comprehending'[6]. To quote a young member of the congregation at Sydney's Hillsong (Pentecostal) church, Jesus is 'God in a form we can cope with'[7].

Later, in Chapters 9 and 10, I will attempt a fuller discussion of John 14:6. It is the verse most often invoked by Christians who insist – mistakenly, in my view – that the *only* way to God and salvation is to practise the Christian religion. For present purposes, it is convenient to put that controversy aside. My purpose now is to argue that Jesus is, at the least, *a* way – and very probably the *best* way – to God and salvation.

Let me come at the point from another angle. I would ask the sceptic or unbeliever to adopt my introductory suggestion and to take as a starting premise the existence of God. Assume, also, that this God is loving and just. He wishes desperately that every person's soul may be saved, with the minimum amount of attendant suffering, but has decided to create a world in which each individual must, by the exercise of free will, *choose* to save it. Then ask yourself a further question. What would be the most effective way for such a God to lead Man towards the truth, without 'giving it away' so obviously as to render the gift of free will meaningless? The best way, I suggest, would be to send into the world, at a carefully chosen time and place in history, a perfect man. This man would not merely be a gifted teacher: by his unarguable and unique perfection *as a human being*, He would provide Man with a living example of the nature of God.

That, of course, is what Christians believe did in fact happen. In C.S. Lewis's phrase, Jesus was God 'becoming local'[8] or, as St Paul put it, 'the image of the invisible God' (Colossians 1:15). The concept is straightforward enough when stated in such bald terms, but it took me a long time fully to appreciate all of its implications. The central idea is that God wanted to help us understand Him – the values God holds dear and His wishes for Man. God knew that most human beings are followers; we are most effectively taught by example. A practical demonstration of an idea is almost always the clearest and most persuasive way of convincing people of its rightness. And we all love heroes.

These precepts apply, in human affairs, even in relation to God – perhaps especially so in relation to God. Jesus was the ultimate instance in history of someone leading by example. He was, as the author of John's Gospel conceived Him, 'the Word made flesh': God's moral laws manifested. He was also the instrument of God's plan for humanity. St Paul explained it this way:

> For God was pleased to have all his fullness dwell in him [i.e. Christ], and through him to reconcile to himself all things, whether things on earth or things in heaven, by making peace through his blood …
>
> (Colossians 1:19–20)

Many theologians over the centuries have tried to articulate these concepts in accessible terms. The great German theologian, F.D.E. Schleiermacher, hit the nail on the head. He regarded Jesus as 'the ideal *representative* of religion' (my emphasis). The man Jesus, Schliermacher thought, personified in its fullest form the powerful sense of 'absolute dependence' which is, at core, the basis of all religious experience.[9] He was, in the words of Herbert Butterfield, 'a human being more human than we are'[10], and thus uniquely recognisable as a revelation of God's presence.

At this stage there are a number of possible objections that need to be considered and a number of aspects of my argument that need to be further developed.

The historical Jesus
The first possible objection is that Jesus of Nazareth was not a real person, but an invention of human minds. This is not a common assertion even among atheists, but a few self-styled 'ultra-rationalists' have made it from time to time. Michel Onfray, for instance, describes Jesus as a 'construction', a 'forgery reaching down to the smallest details'. In Onfray's view, Christianity was originally the product of anti-Roman, messianic hysteria rife in first-century Palestine. The character of Jesus, he alleges, was created by Mark, embellished by the authors of the other Gospels, and perpetuated by second- and third-century apologists in texts (or passages therefrom) which are recognisable as 'fabrications'.[11]

To put it mildly, Onfray's is a minority view. One of the harshest critiques of religion ever written is Joachim Kahl's *The Misery of Christianity*. Kahl was a disillusioned German pastor who, in 1967, quit the Protestant Church in fury and despair; but even he did not claim that Jesus was a fictional character. Kahl squarely accepted the fact that the man named Jesus had actually lived and died. He rejected the alternative proposition (that what was in the first place a myth was subsequently made into an historical figure) as 'giv[ing] rise to more problems than it solves'[12]. That must be right. It is impossible to read St Paul's letters, most of which pre-date the Gospels, without forming the conclusion that the Jesus of whom he wrote was a real man who had been crucified. The attempts to 'prove' otherwise, by G.A Wells and others, strike me as too clever by half.

Let us start, then, with the relatively uncontroversial facts.[13] Put to one side for the moment the reality or otherwise of the miracles and the Resurrection. It seems to be generally accepted that Jesus was born in or about 5 BC, shortly before the death (in 4 BC) of King Herod the Great, the Roman-appointed ruler of Palestine. Jesus's father was named Joseph and his mother was named Mary. He had four brothers (James, Joseph, Judas and Simon) and at least one sister. The family lived in the small but prosperous Galilean village of Nazareth (population about 1,000–1,500). Jesus was raised in the Jewish faith and trained as a carpenter (a vocation requiring both considerable physical strength and a broad range of technical skills).[14] He worked in the family business for most of his life. At the age of about thirty, until his death a few years later, he established a following as an itinerant religious teacher. His supporters were small in number (perhaps only a few hundred people out of a total population in Palestine of about two million[15]), but his activities generated some controversy. He came to the unfavourable notice of both the local Jewish authorities and the occupying Roman powers. He was put to death by crucifixion in or about AD 30, in Jerusalem, by order of the procurator Pontius Pilate during the reign of the Emperor Tiberius. It is also generally accepted that Jesus was a man who kept unusually high moral standards, who was regarded by his followers as a divine figure, and to whom miracles were ascribed.

These are historical facts at least as well established as others from the same or earlier eras of human history. As John Dickson has observed, if the evidence for the historical Jesus is to be set aside as inadequate 'then we would have to start erasing countless other figures from the pages of the textbooks'[16]. Yet, for most of my life, I did not think of Jesus in historical terms. Julius Caesar (say) was real history; Jesus was shadowy religion. This was a fundamental mistake on my part and a mistake that many people make today, wittingly or unwittingly. To overcome this kind of faulty thinking it is necessary to go back to basics. How do we 'know' about Julius Caesar and his achievements or, going back much further into the past, how do we know about the Athenian and Spartan civilisations or the lives of the Pharoahs? The answer is straightforward: from the usual sources of historical evidence. These include historical writings (most of which were *not* written exactly contemporaneously with the relevant events, but reasonably shortly thereafter) and the discoveries of archeology.

Now that I have read into the subject, it seems almost glib to say that the life and death of Jesus of Nazareth (I am still not talking about his divinity) is solidly established in fact. The key evidence bears mention: for most of my life I was quite unaware of it, and just seeing it in print may help others, as it helped me, begin to come to grips with the fact that Jesus really lived. This was for me the first step in accepting Christianity, as opposed to a more general belief in God. I will list the categories of evidence in ascending order of importance.

The first category is near-contemporary Greco-Roman and Jewish literature.[17] Thallus (writing in about AD 52), Pliny the Younger (AD 110-113), Tacitus (AD 114-117) and Suetonius (AD 120) each refer, albeit briefly, to Christ and/or Christianity. There are more extensive references in the work of Lucian of Samasata, a second-century Greek writer. But the most important evidence in this category is to be found in the writings of the pro-Roman historian, Flavius Josephus (who was Jewish). In his magnum opus, *Jewish Antiquities*, Josephus refers variously to John the Baptist, to the stoning to death in AD 62 of James ('the brother of Jesus the so-called Christ'), and to the circumstances surrounding Jesus's crucifixion during Pilate's tenure in Judea. The most famous passage (deleting certain parts that were most likely added later by Christian apologists) was written by Josephus in or about AD 90, and has been translated as follows:

> About this time lived Jesus, a wise man, a teacher of those who delight in accepting the truth (*or* the unusual). He attracted many Jews, and also many from the Greek world. He was the so-called Christ. On accusation of our leading men Pilate condemned him to the cross, but those who were attracted to him from the first did not cease to love him. The race of Christians named after him has survived to this day.[18]

The second category of evidence is later rabbinical writing, dating from about AD 200 onwards.[19] These include the Palestinian and Babylonian Talmuds – written collections of secondary teachings on the Torah based upon oral tradition and recorded for posterity. In this material, Jesus is criticised, even condemned. But, importantly, his existence is taken for granted. Indeed, as Graham N. Stanton has observed, it is highly significant that even the most vehement opponents of the early Christians all accepted that Jesus lived, taught, had disciples (including an 'inner core' known as the Twelve), and was put to death on a Roman cross. A good number also accepted that Jesus had performed miracles. According to the Sanhedrin, 'Jesus the Nazarene practised magic and led Israel astray'. Josephus had earlier referred to Jesus's 'surprising feats' – an expression translated from the Greek *paradoxa erga*, literally 'baffling deeds'[20]. The debate, then, while frequently violent and bitter, was not about Jesus's existence. It centred upon his true nature and significance.[21]

The third category of evidence is geographical. Many of the towns and villages in which key events in the New Testament reportedly took place – Jerusalem, Cana, Nazareth, Jericho, Bethlehem and the rest – are there to be visited in 2009. Some individual buildings, and other significant landmarks, still exist today. So, of course, does the Sea of Galilee and the fertile countryside surrounding it – the inspiration for so much of Jesus's imagery.[22]

The fourth category of evidence is archeological.[23] This evidence is important in various ways. '[M]ost of the events of Jesus' life have left no physical traces'[24], but many ancient manuscripts containing accounts of his words and deeds have been unearthed in the Middle East and elsewhere. Among other things, these help to confirm that modern-day translations of the New Testament are faithful to the original first-century texts. There are over 6,500 full or partial copies of the New Testament preserved in Greek-language manuscripts alone, all originally written out by hand between the second and fifteenth centuries. By the standards of ancient history – indeed, even relatively modern history – this is a great deal of evidence.[25]

Of course, the most valuable manuscripts are the oldest ones. An especially precious find was made in 1904, with the discovery in Armenia of a copy of a previously unknown work by Iranaeus of Lyons. Entitled *Demonstration of the Apostolic Preaching*, it is a second-century summary of all the basic teachings of the Apostles.[26] There are extant fragments of the Gospels dating back to the mid-second century: the oldest known piece of any Gospel text is the so-called Rylands Fragment, dated at about AD 125–130. It was discovered in Egypt in 1920 and contains two brief excerpts from John (18:31–3 on the front and 18:37–8 on the back).[27] The earliest *complete* copies of the New Testament in existence today are of the fourth century, i.e. they were created some 250–300 years after the events recorded in them. But, again, by the standards of ancient history, that is a relatively short interval.[28]

The significance of the manuscript evidence is this. We know with substantial certainty what Jesus's first-century biographers actually wrote about Him. According to Craig L. Blomberg, 'almost no-one' now denies this. 'The controversy today centres on whether or not what they wrote was *true*.'[29]

Other archeological evidence underscores the fact that places mentioned in the Gospels which are no longer there today – such as the fishing village of Capernaum – did really exist. Luke's Gospel and Acts, in particular, have been proven time and again to be extremely reliable historical documents. And not only as regards places and placenames, but myriad other details as well, including the Roman census, the exact titles of officials, major transport routes, army units, and numerous local customs.[30]

There was an especially significant archeological discovery in 1968. A first-century ossuary was found in Jerusalem containing the remains of a young man named Yohanan who had (according to the inscription inside it) been crucified. Examination of the remains suggested that nails had been driven through his ankles and into wood. This confirmed that a previously-disputed feature of the crucifixion of Jesus was consistent with objective evidence of first-century practices.[31] Similarly valuable archeological finds have included: the site of Jacob's Well (John 4:5–6); the likely remains of the Pools of Bethesda and Siloam (John 5:2, 9:7); brittle glass perfume jars of unusual shape (cf. Luke 7:38; John 12:3); the court in which Pilate tried Jesus; first-century Roman and Palestinian coins (cf. Matthew 22:17–21, 26:14–15; Luke 21:1–4); ancient stone winepresses (cf. Luke 6:38); and a first-century fishing boat – which surfaced in the Sea of Galilee – large enough for twelve or thirteen people.[32] (There is, it may here be noted, a great deal of similarly powerful archeological evidence as regards the Old Testament – people, places, objects and events.[33])

The fifth category of evidence about Jesus is the non-canonical Christian literature – surviving documents of the Church founders, or of other Christian or quasi-Christian apologists, which were not subsequently included in the New Testament.[34] Most of these texts were never seriously proposed for inclusion in the canon; a few were proposed, but were excluded as being insufficiently reliable. This is, I think, a significant thing of itself. It highlights the confidence which the compilers of the canon must have had in the texts which were included, and the toughness of the criteria which they applied. For at least some of the non-canonical texts are of significant value.

Of modest interest are the so-called 'Gnostic' or 'alternative' Gospels, such as those attributed to St Thomas, St Philip and St Peter. These were written in the second and third centuries (or later still) and do not carry anything like the authority of the four canonical Gospels. Nonetheless, a few of the sayings of Jesus recorded in the Gnostic gospels are generally regarded as authentic.[35]

Of much greater historical value are seven documents written between about AD 90 and AD 150. This collection, known as 'the Apostolic Fathers', is comprised of 'the Didache' (an instructional handbook for practising Christians), the *Shepherd of Hermas* (a sort of extended parable), and the letters of St Clement (two), St Ignatius, Polycarp of Smyrna and St Barnabas.[36] These documents are important for various technical reasons, chief among them that they 'speak strongly against the notion that the early church felt free to invent teachings Jesus never really uttered' [Blomberg, p. 263]. They also include original material about Jesus which cannot have been derived from Matthew, Luke or Q. But, for me, their greatest value lies in the steely passion of their authors. I consider it inconceivable that these men were lightweights or phonies.

Ignatius was the Christian bishop of Antioch. He was personally acquainted with the Apostles and a disciple of Polycarp (who was, probably, a student of the Apostle John).[37] Ignatius was executed by the Romans in about AD 107. Shortly before his death – he was thrown to ravenous beasts in the Colosseum – Ignatius wrote to the Christian community at Tralles (in Asia) in these terms:

> Close your ears then if anyone preaches to you without speaking of Jesus Christ. Christ was of David's line. He was the son of Mary; he was *really* born, ate and drank, was *really* persecuted under Pontius Pilate, was *really* crucified … He was also *truly* raised from the dead.
>
> (Trallians 9. My emphasis.)

Was Ignatius lying, or deluded, when he wrote those words?

The sixth category of evidence is the earliest post-Crucifixion literature, the famous epistles of St Paul, St Peter (the first letter) and St James. James was Jesus's brother, and the leader of the early Church in Jerusalem. His letter was most likely written in the mid-to-late 40s AD – i.e. within fifteen years of Jesus's death. If that dating is correct then this document is almost certainly the oldest in the New Testament.[38] Another candidate is Paul's first letter to the Thessalonians. It was written in AD 50 or 51, still only about twenty years after Jesus's death.[39]

Contemporary letters are regarded by all historians as an especially valuable form of evidence.[40] Usually, their authors were not conscious of writing for posterity. Whatever else they are – and whatever one may or may not believe as to their theological content – the New Testament letters are genuine historical artifacts. They were written by real men, two of whom (Peter and James) claimed to have known Jesus intimately and to have seen many of his deeds. Although St Peter probably did not write the second letter attributed to him, I am convinced that the author accurately reconstructed what must have been a common retort by the Apostles to those who doubted their veracity:

> We did not follow cleverly invented stories when we told you about the power and
> coming of our Lord Jesus Christ, but we were eye-witnesses of his majesty.
>
> (2 Peter 1:16. See also 1 John 1:1–3)

St Paul, in his first letter to the Thessalonians, had earlier expressed a similar sentiment:

> The appeal we make does not spring from error or impure motives, nor are we trying
> to trick you. On the contrary, we speak as men approved by God to be entrusted with
> the gospel. We are not trying to please men but God, who tests our hearts. You know
> we never used flattery, nor did we put on a mask to cover up greed – God is our wit-
> ness. We were not looking for praise from men, not from you or anyone else.
>
> (1 Thessalonians 2:3–6)

The epistles incidentally record numerous details of events, people and places, including the Last Supper and Jesus's betrayal (cf. 1 Corinthians 11:23–5).[41] It is indisputable that the people to whom St Paul and St Peter wrote were in the process of establishing new Christian communities, often in harsh circumstances. At a bare minimum, the epistles constitute evidence that a man known as Jesus had lived and taught and inspired his followers. He had inspired them to such an extent that St Paul would write, within a generation or two after Jesus's death, that the Church was 'built on the apostles and prophets, with Christ Jesus himself as the chief cornerstone' (Ephesians 2:20).

The seventh and most important category of evidence about Jesus's life is that provided by the canonical Gospels themselves, together with the book known as the Acts of the Apostles (or 'Acts'). There is, of course, a mountain of scholarship about these texts. Views differ as to the identity of their authors, though it is fairly certain that the same man – a Greek physician who accompanied St Paul on his travels (see Colossians 4:14) – wrote both Luke's Gospel and Acts. Mark's Gospel was most likely written by a close confidant of St Peter.[42]

The authorship of the other two Gospels, each attributed to a disciple of Jesus, is more controversial. There is at least an arguable case that Matthew's Gospel really was written by Jesus's disciple of that name, a former tax collector also known as Levi.[43] As for John's Gospel – the most eloquent and profound of the four – the scholarly consensus[44] is that it was probably *not* written by the 'beloved disciple' John (son of Zebedee), even though it is named for him. Nor, it is generally agreed, was John's Gospel written by an eyewitness – a view to which I somewhat reluctantly incline. However, there is excellent evidence that John the Apostle was the original source for much of the information. The author(s) state clearly: 'We know that [John's] testimony is true' (John 21:24). It is likely that 'his' Gospel was completed shortly after he died.

Views also differ as to precisely *when* the Gospels were written. The rough consensus seems to be some time between AD 60 and AD 90, though both earlier and later dates have been proposed.[45] A few scholars have suggested that Mark's Gospel may have been written as early as AD 45[46], though that appears to me unlikely. At any rate, it is generally accepted that Mark's was the earliest Gospel and John's the latest, though there are dissenters from this orthodoxy too. For instance, a tenable case can be made that Matthew's Gospel rather than Mark's was the first in time.[47]

There is scope for honest debate about many details. However, what is largely undisputed is that all four of the Gospels – though probably not direct eyewitness accounts – constitute the work of dedicated first-century evangelists. These men compiled their information from first-century sources and materials, written and oral, including credal snippets which had been current in the early 30s AD. One is quoted at Luke 24:34: 'It is true! The Lord has risen and appeared to Simon [i.e. Peter].'[48]

We now come to a particularly important point in assessing the claims of the first Christians. Many of the evangelists' human sources had become followers of Jesus during His lifetime or shortly after the Resurrection (i.e. in the 30s AD). These were real people. Quite a few are specifically named in the Gospels and the Epistles, and were still alive when they were 'published'. So too numerous 'bystanders, officials, and opponents who had actually heard [Jesus] teach, seen his actions, and watched him die'.[49] (See, for example, Mark 15:21 and Acts 2:22.) If the Gospel and/or the Pauline accounts had been invented, or were factually inaccurate in significant respects, there was no shortage of people with the capacity, and/or the motive, systematically to demolish them.[50] But that did not happen. Opponents of Christianity usually resorted to more brutal methods.

One of the more hyperbolic claims made by Richard Dawkins in *The God Delusion* is that the Gospels are 'as factually dubious as the stories of King Arthur'. Dawkins further asserts that the Gospels 'were in no sense an honest attempt at history' and, more sweepingly still, that 'reputable biblical scholars do not in general regard the New Testament … as a reliable record of what actually happened'[51]. For Dawkins, apparently, a 'reputable biblical scholar' must be an atheist like him.

Each of the four Gospel authors had his own theological preoccupations, and wrote 'at various levels of symbolization'[52]. But none of them was writing fiction from scratch. The three Synoptic Gospels, at least, were intended principally as 'reportage'[53] and were written too soon after Jesus's death to have survived as legends.[54] Whichever Gospel came first (let us assume it was Mark's) it had to have been based on the memories of Jesus's followers, at least some of whom may have kept private handwritten notes of things they had heard and witnessed.[55] (I read John 21:24 in that way.) In any event, the recollections of these witnesses were relayed to the Gospel author(s) either directly or through third parties. Subsequent Gospels may then have been based on the first. Many scholars believe that Matthew's and Luke's Gospels were based in significant part upon Mark's, and also upon another written source (known as Q) that was not used by the author of Mark. That hypothesis would account for the numerous textual similarities between the three 'Synoptic' Gospels. The significant textual *differences* between Matthew's, Luke's and John's Gospels are similarly explicable, on the basis that each author relied upon at least one source unique to him (those known as M, L and SQ respectively).[56]

An alternative or supplementary idea, recently propounded by the eminent American scholar Richard Bauckham, is that the Gospels were not primarily based on a patchwork of written sources, or on oral traditions passed down through early Christian communities. Bauckham's thesis is that the Gospels were sourced from, and perhaps even written by, certain individuals whose names appear throughout the New Testament, many of whom were eyewitnesses to key events. Taken to its logical conclusion, Bauckham's research suggests that the Gospels may have been grounded in 'decisive personal contributions by recognized and authoritative eyewitnesses'[57].

There are still many uncertainties about the composition of the Gospels and the relationship between them. But three things seem tolerably clear to me.

First, the Gospels should not be disregarded merely because they were based, to a greater or lesser extent, on an oral tradition. It is important to remember that in first-century Palestine only 10–15 per cent of the population could read[58], and that the practice of passing on information orally was far more widespread and sophisticated than it is today. Two important Swedish historians of the mid-twentieth century, Harald Riesenfeld and Birgir Gerhardsson, proposed that the early Christian communities used rigid techniques employed by first-century Jewish rabbis. The relevant information about Jesus was recorded in a certain 'standard' form, learned by rote, and passed on as 'memorized text'[59]. This thesis is now regarded as somewhat extreme; it is likely that the methods used were not always, or even often, so robotic. But nor was it *ever* a case of 'make it up as you go along'. The dominant theory among experts today is one of 'flexible translation within fixed limits'[60]. Jesus's followers 'carefully preserved accurate information about him without necessarily memorizing it word for word'.[61] A contemporary scholar, Kenneth Bailey, has lent further weight to this view. Bailey points out that a tradition of community storytelling still survives today in parts of the Middle East: 'The storyteller [is] bound to reproduce the essentials of the narrative, and at crucial points the exact wording, but [is] also … expected to bring something of his own style and recollection to give new life to the recital.'[62]

Second, it is a mistake to become too fixated on the *differences* between the Gospels. This supposed 'problem' was raised by Celsus way back in the mid-second century, and has been trotted out routinely by sceptics ever since. But the argument does not improve with repetition. For a start, 'the similarities far outweigh the differences'[63]. The differences are explainable by the authors' use of varying sources, their differing literary and theological preoccupations, and the natural lapses and divergences of witnesses to the same events. It is probable that Jesus repeated the same message many times to different audiences, using slightly different language each time[64] – like a politician during a long election campaign. Luke certainly changed some of Mark's imagery to make certain points more intelligible to his non-Palestinian readers.[65] It is also important to remember that the Gospel authors – indeed, the authors of all the texts which were later included in the New Testament – did not collaborate. Although some were acquainted personally, by and large they were unaware of each others' writings.[66]

This whole argument about 'inconsistency' is really very thin. No two biographies of Julius Caesar are identical – does anyone thus dispute that a successful military leader known by that name was the ruler of Rome from 49–44 BC? The writing of history and the reporting of events are necessarily selective. All historians and journalists are *editors*, and so were the authors of the Gospels.[67]

It may also be granted that down the years there must have been inaccuracies of copying and translation. But that does not disprove the essential facts. Indeed, in a strange way, examples of possible textual errors in the Gospels tend to point to their overall reliability. For instance, it has been suggested that one of the most famous statements attributed to Jesus – 'It is easier for a camel to go through the eye of a needle than for a rich man to enter the Kingdom of God' (Matthew 19:24) – may well be based upon a mistranslation of Aramaic.[68] The Aramaic word for 'camel' was almost identical to the word for 'rope'. The metaphor seems much more appropriate – though still powerful – if the word rope was the one actually used. I am persuaded that the use of the word camel was probably the result of a mistranslation. I am also persuaded – because it is highly unlikely that anyone would have deliberately concocted such a natural slip – that there must have been an original statement of Jesus on which this line was based.

The third main reason to trust the Gospels is perhaps the most important. The Gospel authors were men of evident integrity and sincerity. Even a radical atheist like Michel Onfray cannot bring himself to contend that they were consciously fraudulent[69], and for an obvious reason. These men had nothing worldly to gain from their labours; on the contrary, they faced the prospect of persecution and violent death. With the notable exception of St John they were not possessed of great literary genius (like some of the Old Testament authors), but they had a definite purpose and 'were able to place upon their rolls of papyrus an undying ardour which has made their literature peculiarly beautiful and their messages to mankind immortal'[70]. The straightforward aim of all four Gospels was 'to acquaint those whose knowledge was lacking or insufficient with the facts of the life of Jesus [and] with His teachings'[71]. St Luke said so plainly enough at the outset of his Gospel (see Luke 1:1–4).

On the objective evidence Jesus was a real historical person who made a huge impact on those who knew him. At the core of all four of the Gospels is the central historical fact that Jesus lived and died in a remarkable way, and left behind a band of devoted followers. The Gospels and Acts were inspired by events that had actually happened, and were an attempt to make sense of those events – especially the tumultuous last week of Jesus's life. It is notable that at this point in the narrative (the 'Passion') all four Gospels become more detailed and less divergent, another indication that Jesus's arrest, trial, crucifixion and resurrection were the critical events in the birth of Christianity. That is why these texts came to be written, that is why people took notice of them, and that is why they are still read today. In this crucial sense, the Gospels are 'self-ratifying'[72].

Even John Spong, a man who denies the miraculous, and who regards the Passion narratives as 'liturgy' rather than 'history'[73], has grasped the essential force of this argument. Why were the Gospels and the Epistles written at all, if not because there was something very special about Jesus? In Spong's words: '[W]e need to recognise that it was the movement brought into being by this Jesus that has preserved for us any portrait whatsoever of the Jesus of history … [I]t is only because his was a life that demanded interpretation then and demands it still that he remains alive for us.'[74]

Jesus, the man

Enough, for the moment, of historical methodology. The next step on my own path to belief in Christ was accepting that Jesus was a real person at a *subjective* level; in other words, coming to a positive state of mind about what Jesus must really have been like as a man. In this regard, close reading of the Gospels was crucial. Beyond the central events recorded in them, there emerges something altogether more compelling, something that confirms in my mind the fact that Jesus really lived and that he was utterly special. It is particularly hard to put this idea into words. I can express it no better than by falling back on the old chestnut that truth is stranger than fiction.

When I read the Gospels, the overall effect is one of verisimilitude. In particular, the character of Jesus as revealed by many of his deeds, and by at least some of the words attributed to him, seems to me too singular, and yet at the same time too 'real', to have been capable of having been wholly or even mainly invented. Rather, I can 'see' Jesus in my mind's eye, not merely as one imagines an especially vivid character in literature (though Jesus can usefully be considered in that way[75]), but as unmistakably a real and particular man.

I reached this state of mind before I read A.N. Wilson's fascinating book *Jesus*. Wilson is an exceptionally accomplished modern writer, and a sceptic as to many aspects of Christianity. He questions the authenticity of many events described in the Gospels, especially in John's Gospel, which was almost certainly the last of the four to be written. (The author referred to many incidents which are absent from the Synoptics, and his theological preoccupations were quite different to those of the other three. For these and other reasons, John's Gospel was traditionally regarded as the least reliable of the four Gospels as a literal historical record, though nowadays that is far from a universal view.[76]) Wilson is alive to all these issues. He is a million miles away from being a biblical literalist. For him, there is nothing sacrosanct in the Gospels. And yet, he confesses, 'there remains that figure at [their] centre who haunts us'[77].

Wilson points to passages in John's Gospel in which 'we overhear little exchanges which are at variance with the generally high tone which is supposedly being maintained'[78]. Among the examples Wilson cites are Jesus's curt treatment of His mother during the wedding banquet at Cana; His lecturing of Nicodemus, a member of the Jewish ruling council, during a night-time visitation; and His strange conversation with the Samaritan woman at Jacob's well. On the last occasion, upon being told by the woman that she had no husband, Jesus quipped: 'You are right … The fact is, you have had five husbands, and the man you now have is not your husband!' (John 4:17–18)

Wilson asks rhetorically: 'Does not this have the mercilessness and the directness which we meet in other dialogues in other Gospels?'[79] Wilson also draws attention to one of Jesus's distinct verbal mannerisms: 'Verily, verily, I say unto you'. It appears in all four Gospels, including John's, and its presence is highly significant, 'like the tiniest clue in a detective story'[80]. This little phrase could not have been made up. 'It is not an idiom, it is an idiolect. We do not find it anywhere else in Greek nor its equivalent anywhere else in Hebrew or Aramaic.'[81]

Wilson concludes that Jesus was a real – and thoroughly intriguing – historical figure:

> The cumulative effect of reading his words is to be confronted by a wholly distinctive view and voice – distinctively Jewish, distinctively of its time, but distinctive. But it is more than the teachings of Jesus that make us want to blink our eyes and wish that we could adjust the focus a little more on that figure who is one moment transfigured in glory on a mountainside, and the next is squatting on the ground frying fish … It is the fish that lures us on. It is those little details – a man irrationally losing his temper with a tree. It is someone remembering that a little girl, when she recovers from a fever, will be extremely hungry … These little novelistic details could all, of course, have been fabricated, though it is hard to see what purpose would have been served in inventing them.[82]

Like Wilson, I do not believe these details were invented. In the first century there was no such thing as realist fiction (the novel did not become an established art form until a few hundred years ago). In any case, many of the details in the Gospels ring too true, and help to persuade me that such things really happened. They are the fish that lure me on.

This, however, is the point beyond which many sceptics will not be lured. Even Christopher Hitchens admits that some parts of the Gospels have the quality of verisimilitude, because not a few show Jesus in a less than obviously flattering light (e.g. Matthew 15:21–8). Hitchens grudgingly allows that 'an idiosyncratic story like this is another oblique reason for thinking that some such personality [as Jesus] may at some time have lived'.[83]

But that is as far as Hitchens – and many others – will go in taking the Gospels seriously. Why? One of the main reasons they cite is 'inconsistency'. A lot is made of real and apparent discrepencies between the four texts (and, although much more rarely, of discrepancies between the Gospels on the one hand and historical evidence from other non-Biblical sources on the other[84]). It is argued that if the authors of the Gospels could not agree among themselves, and/or could not get basic things 'right', then what they wrote must mostly have been invention; at the least, no one else can or should be expected to uncover the truth.

I have already pointed out various weaknesses in this line of argument, but it is worth expanding on a few points. As to theological matters, we have seen that each author interpreted the traditions passed down to him in somewhat different ways. For instance, it appears that the author of John's Gospel, the last of the four, 'may well [have] believe[d] that he ha[d] better expounded [the] significance' of many of Jesus's speeches than had the authors of the Synoptics.[85] I suspect that is right, but it does not undermine the other three Gospels in any relevant way. It is merely a truism that some writers are better than others.

As to strictly 'factual' matters, it may be conceded that the four Gospels are not capable of being reconciled on all points.[86] Many of the differences are explainable on an entirely 'innocent' basis, but, if necessary, I am quite prepared to accept that the authors paraphrased some of the sayings attributed to Jesus and, perhaps, made educated guesses about certain details of times, places and events. I am ambivalent as to whether all aspects of the birth narratives should be taken literally: it is at least plausible that these were written in the light of the Resurrection.[87] The hard historical evidence for Bethlehem as the place of Jesus's birth is inconclusive[88], and the other Nativity-related events described in Luke's and Matthew's Gospels are even less suceptible to forensic 'proof'. Similar considerations apply as regards the accounts of Jesus's trial in the desert[89] and the Transfiguration.

But despite all those qualifications, I am convinced that at the core of all of the four Gospels lies a solid kernel of truth. Many scholars have devoted their lives to 'proving' this by redaction criticism, literary form criticism, and other intricate methods. Graham N. Stanton, Professor of Divinity at Cambridge University, has usefully summarised the four main criteria used to test the authenticity of a given passage: those of 'dissimilarity', 'coherence', 'multiple attestation' and 'backwards translation'.[90] Without grasping all the details, I find it reassuring that such meticulous experts have performed these analyses and have concluded that the Gospels may be regarded as generally reliable.[91] And surely that should be enough, because 'the conditions for a universal religion would not be satisfied by a religion which demanded that men should be experts in New Testament criticism … before they were in a state to make the essential choice between belief and unbelief'[92].

It may be objected, however, that to concede Jesus lived, and was a person whose distinctive speech and exemplary conduct were accurately 'captured' by the authors of the Gospels, is a very different thing to conceding his divinity. There must be better reasons for making the essential choice between belief or unbelief in Christ. That brings me to the next strand of my argument.

Many, indeed most unbelievers are prepared willingly enough to say that Jesus's teachings provide a fine model for how Man should conduct himself. Such people will concede that the world would be a better place if everybody took to heart the precepts which He laid down in the Sermon on the Mount. (See chapters 5 to 7 of Matthew's Gospel.) And believers and unbelievers alike may often be heard to say that Western civilisation owes a great deal to its 'Judeo-Christian' tradition.

To bring the point back to Jesus: very few people ever say that his example was a *bad* one that ought not to be followed. Among unbelievers or sceptics, the most common line is that although Jesus's example was in many ways admirable, he was merely a remarkable *man*. Talk of miracles and the Resurrection is dismissed as unrealistic fantasy. Michel Onfray calls such people 'Christian atheists', those who generally approve of the values espoused in the New Testament but who reject the supernatural mumbo jumbo.[93] That, indeed, used to be my own way of looking at things.

During the last 175 years there have been three major schools of 'Christian atheism', each one more radical than its predecessor. The first two flourished in the mid-nineteenth and mid-twentieth centuries respectively; each was instigated by a German scholar (D.F. Strauss in 1836 and Ernst Kasemann in 1953) and each was highly influential in certain circles. But the conclusions which were drawn never convinced a majority of scholars, let alone practising Christians. Then, in the mid-1980s, came the so-called Jesus Seminar. A group of about 70 or 80 scholars, mostly liberal Christians, met twice a year well into the 1990s. Their frank aim was to identify – by a process of open voting – the 'authentic' sayings or deeds of the historical (secular) Jesus. They concluded in their wisdom that there are, in fact, very few such sayings or deeds – no more than about 16 per cent of those voted upon, and perhaps as few as 2 per cent.[94] The Seminar's activities enjoyed extensive media coverage, especially in North America. But among most New Testament experts its methods and conclusions were regarded as 'more aberrant than mainstream'[95] – in my view, justly so.

As I stressed at the outset of this book, there is no way that anyone can prove definitively that the wider claims made by believers about Jesus are true. Faith must play a role. Garry Wills has contended that '[i]f you reject the faith, there is no reason to trust anything the gospels say'.[96] I would not go that far, though I agree with Wills that the shredded Gospels of the Jesus Seminar would make dull and platitudinous reading. For the Seminarists, 'anything odd or dangerous or supernatural is prima facie suspect'[97]. But, in my view, that very presumption is empirically suspect. There are reasons for contending that it is the unbelievers and the sceptics who may well have the harder, *more unrealistic* side of the argument. As C.S. Lewis remarked, 'The historical difficulty of giving for the life, sayings and influence of Jesus any explanation that is not harder than the Christian explanation, is very great.'[98]

The miracles

The Gospels record some thirty miracles as having been performed by Jesus during his lifetime on Earth. (Put to one side the Resurrection, to which the next chapter is devoted.) The miracles are a favourite target of sceptics and atheists, and even many Christians seek to downplay their significance or explain them away. But it is hard to reconcile that approach with the probabilities.

According to David Hume's classical definition, a miracle is 'a transgression of a law of Nature by a particular volition of the Deity or by the interposition of some invisible agent'. Similarly, St Thomas Aquinas defined a miracle as a thing 'done by divine power apart from the order generally following things'.[99]

The problem with both of these definitions, for present purposes, is that they define the term (miracle) by reference to a supernatural force (God) which cannot, at the end of the day, be *proven* to exist. What we are trying to decide is whether there is good reason to believe that God does exist. Thus, it is preferable to leave God out of the definition of the term 'miracle' itself and instead (borrowing from the English philosopher Brian Davies) to define a miracle as an event that cannot be explained in terms intelligible to the natural scientist or observer of the regular processes of Nature.[100]

The miracles are important because the authors of the Gospels laid considerable stress upon them. For example, St Luke attests that, at one time, even John the Baptist was in doubt about Jesus's divine nature. John relayed a question to Jesus through two messengers – 'Are you the one who was to come, or should we expect someone else?' Jesus responded to His mentor by invoking the miracles. He told the messengers to return to John and tell him what they (the messengers) had seen and heard: 'The blind receive sight, the lame walk, those who have leprosy are cured, the deaf hear, the dead are raised' (Luke 7:20–2).

Similarly, in John's Gospel, Jesus is recorded as having challenged His persecutors by reference to the miracles:

Do not believe me unless I do what my Father does. But if I do it, even though you do not believe me, *believe the miracles*, that you may know and understand that the Father is in me, and I in the Father.

(John 10:37–38. My emphasis).

A similar statement is attributed to Jesus in the account of the Last Supper (see John 14:11), and, towards the end of John's Gospel, the author states plainly:

Jesus did many other miraculous signs in the presence of his disciples, which are not recorded in this book. But these are written that you may believe that Jesus is the Christ, the Son of God, and that by believing you may have life in his name.

(John 20:30–31)

Thus, we must ask ourselves about the nature of the miracles of Jesus as recorded in the Gospels. Did any of them really happen?

It seems to me highly significant that most of the miracles cannot be explained by the application of modern-day science. Arthur C. Clarke famously said that any sufficiently advanced technology is indistinguishable from magic. Thus, for example, if a man alive at the time of the Norman Conquest in 1066 were to be transported forward in time to the twentieth century (the scenario of one of my favourite television shows as a child, *Catweazle*) he would regard such everyday things as a car or a struck match or a telephone as supernatural. But few if any of Jesus's miracles are susceptible to any such prosaic explanation. It is just as impossible today as it was 2,000 years ago for a man – merely by an act of will – to turn water into wine, or to heal the terminally ill instantaneously, or to turn five loaves of bread and two fish into a meal for 5,000 people.

If the miracle stories had been originally based upon an honest but mistaken interpretation of now readily explicable events, which had later assumed the status of legend, then at least a few of the stories would by now – 2,000 years later – be so explicable. Thus, for instance, if there had been a Gospel story to the effect that Jesus gave a potion to a man suffering from nausea, and that a few minutes later the man said that he felt better, one might fairly conclude that, even if the legend had some original basis in fact, what happened was not miraculous. Rather, Jesus was a man who had acquired some expertise in medicine. Christopher Hitchens, by his assertion that '[m]ost of the 'miracles' of the New Testament have to do with healing'[101], is one of many 'realists' to have advanced that suggestion. Behind it is a notion, express or implied, that common people in the ancient world were hopelessly gullible and naïve.[102]

There are a number of major difficulties with this line of argument. For a start, people of the first century were not imbeciles. As Craig L. Blomberg has wryly observed, '[o]nly a moment's thought is required ... to realize that people of every age have known that two human parents are needed for conception and that death is irreversible!'[103]. Likewise, while it is true that 'miracle-workers' (faith healers and exorcists) were not uncommon in Jesus's era, it is *not* true that people were easily duped by them. To the contrary, as G.N. Stanton has pointed out, 'there is plenty of evidence to confirm that in antiquity miracles were by no means accepted without question'[104]. The Romans and the Jews were hard-headed people. Most of them remained hostile to Christianity until the third century and beyond. Yet, as we have seen, a number of their most eminent historians accepted, explicitly or implicitly, that Jesus had performed miracles.

The realists' position has other flaws. A good number of Jesus's reported feats were of a completely different character to those performed by faith healers and exorcists – calming a storm, walking on water, conjuring a huge catch of fish, and so on. Few if any of these miracles are plausibly explainable in a naturalistic way. (In saying this, I discount certain feeble suggestions that have been made from time to time – for example, that when Jesus walked across the water of the Sea of Galilee, he used stepping stones of which no one else was aware.)

Similar considerations apply as regards the healing miracles. It may be granted that some of the people Jesus cured were suffering from psychosomatic rather than 'physical' illnesses. But what of that? Psychosomatic illnesses usually take a long time to heal, even with the use of modern-day drugs and therapies. They certainly cannot be treated 'on the spot'. The same is true of lameness, deafness, dumbness and blindness – and miraculous cures of these conditions were virtually unheard of in first-century Palestine.[105] The possibility that Jesus was just another faith healer must, on the evidence, be ruled out.

So we arrive at this position: either these things happened as described – *and were miraculous* – or they did not happen at all.

At this point in the argument, Hume would have said flatly that Jesus's miracles cannot have happened, whatever anybody may have claimed at the time or since, because there is no such thing as a miracle. Even if there were 'a cloud of witnesses' attesting to a miracle, all those witnesses would simply be wrong, because miracles are 'an absolute impossibility'. 'And,' wrote Hume, 'this surely, in the eyes of all reasonable people, will alone be regarded as a sufficient refutation.'[106]

Hume elaborated as follows:

[N]o testimony is sufficient to establish a miracle unless the testimony be of such kind, that its falsehood would be more miraculous, than the fact, which it endeavours to establish; and even in that case there is a mutual destruction of arguments, and the superior only gives us to that degree of force, which remains, after deducting the inferior.[107]

Hume gave four specific reasons for his assertion that no human testimony can ever be enough to establish a miracle: no such testimony has ever been given by enough people of adequate learning and intelligence; people are naturally gullible and untrustworthy; reports of miracles tend to emanate from 'ignorant and barbarous nations'; and different religions report different miracles, and this invalidates all such reports.

These are not convincing answers, and they were thoroughly refuted during Hume's own lifetime in a number of books and essays.[108] Indeed, Hume admitted to a friend that one of his ablest contemporary critics, a 'Scotch theologue' named George Campbell, had got the better of the argument.

Campbell's dissertation is well worth reading in full, but I will briefly attempt my own. Hume's fourth argument – the one about different religions – is addressed in Chapter 9. As for the others, they amount to saying that no human observer can ever be completely trusted, at least in circumstances where the phenomenon in question has no present-day analogue. This seems to me a cynical generalisation. Of course, any miracle must at first seem to any observer of it to be impossible. But if there are such things as miracles, that sort of reaction is inevitable. That must be the point of them – to astonish.[109]

One may also readily concede that any report of a miracle should be treated with extreme scepticism. However, as a lawyer, my preference is not to set up an irrebuttable presumption that there is no such thing as a miracle. As Josh McDowell has observed, this 'presupposition of antisupernaturalism' underlies a great deal of modern thinking about religion. It is, as McDowell says, a 'crucial and often misunderstood topic … in which ignorance abounds'[110]. The Jesus Seminar, for instance, operated on the pre-determined assumption that God has never intervened miraculously in human history.[111]

A more rigorous and open-minded approach is to look at the evidence in each individual case. This is the approach of all competent litigation lawyers as regards any contestible issue of fact. True, some facts are much harder to prove than others. In criminal matters, when the accused's liberty is at stake, the standard of proof is 'beyond a reasonable doubt'. A judge will require extremely compelling evidence before concluding, or permitting a jury to conclude, that an (apparently) incredible event has occurred – such as the vicious murder of a total stranger by a citizen of previously blameless reputation. These legal safeguards are absolutely right and proper. Nevertheless, such conclusions *are* drawn from time to time, when the evidence is thought to be there – and justifiably so.

In my view, the same principles should be applied to reports of the miraculous. As Brian Davies has written:

But does it follow that we can never reasonably say that there has occurred a violation of a natural law? Initially we might have very good reason for doubting that a particular natural law had been violated; and confronted with what appears to be good testimony that it has in fact been violated we might therefore attempt to account for the phenomena appealed to in some way that does not contradict the principle that laws of nature are not violated… *But it is not inconceivable that such a way of proceeding could land us in more difficulties than we would solve.*[112]

The emphasis placed upon the final sentence is mine, and I would ask the reader to bear Davies' point in mind.

What, then, is the evidence in respect of Jesus's miracles? What are the arguments?

The turning point for me in considering this issue was a developing belief that the physical Universe must be the product of a divine intelligence, a Creator. I had gradually come to the view that God must exist for this reason. However, for some time afterwards it did not occur to me that the miracles of Jesus might also be considered in this light. The thought eventually struck me that if Jesus was (in human form) God, the Creator of the Universe, then it should not be especially difficult to believe that Jesus performed the miracles. The miracles were tiny feats by comparison. I have since learned that this is a standard argument in Christian apologetics.[113]

But it is not enough to argue by analogy. It is necessary to deal with the miracles in isolation. Preposterous as it may sound, there are a number of cogent reasons to believe in them.

To test the matter, I have tried to assume that Jesus did *not* perform any of the miracles. If that were so, it would follow – because it is hard to see how the miracle stories could have been based on an honest but mistaken interpretation of real events – that each and every one of the miracles was invented a generation or so after Jesus's death by the authors of the Gospels. That was essentially the thesis of Rudolph Bultmann, a German theologian of the mid-twentieth century. Bultmann's ideas are less in vogue today than they once were, but they still have prominent supporters. Among them is John Spong, who contends that the miracles and other supernatural elements of the Gospels were 'a late-developing part of the Jesus story'[114]. The Gospel authors, he claims, adopted the then-familiar language and imagery of the Old Testament to convey a sense of the specialness of the man Jesus. The miracle stories, in his view, were interpretive rather than descriptive.[115] Others have speculated that the Gospel authors must have drawn upon an already-existing stereotype of the 'divine man' in Greco-Roman mythology or Middle Eastern folklore.

I have pondered all these arguments, but in the end they strike me as overly contrived and essentially unconvincing. Certainly, they are rejected by most professional New Testament scholars today, including many of quite liberal bent.[116] To be sure, there are some puzzling aspects of the miracle stories, not least why they are not mentioned in St Paul's letters (most of which pre-date the Gospels), and why some of the most astonishing of the miracles (especially the raising of Lazarus) are not highlighted in all four Gospels.[117] However, a number of considerations lead me to conclude that the scenario which Bishop Spong postulates is more unlikely than the reality of the miracles themselves.

For a start, if all of the miracle stories were concocted, there is a similar difficulty as besets any suggestion that the miracles were an honest but mistaken interpretation of real events. It must be probable that someone would have 'tripped up' somewhere and invented a story that would by now be susceptible to a naturalistic explanation. There would exist 'the presence of an analogy to something already known to be unhistorical' – in the same way that UFO sightings have usually been attributable to air balloons, shooting stars and the like.[118] But, as I have argued, few if any of the miracles may be so explained.

If the miracle stories were concocted, what is remarkable is that they were concocted so brilliantly well. The events described in the Gospels almost 2,000 years ago still hold up as miracles.

The character of the miracles is also important. The most common miracle story of Jesus's time and culture involved a holy man somehow procuring rainfall, but such an act was *never* attributed to Jesus.[119] Indeed, it has proved difficult to find any convincing parallels with Jesus's recorded feats amongst all the myriad myths and legends of antiquity. In the words of A.E. Harvey, one of the world's leading scholars in this area, and generally a *sceptic* as regards the miraculous: 'We … come to the remarkable conclusion that the miraculous activity of Jesus conforms to no known pattern'[120].

Jesus's miracles were not merely unprecedented in a literary-historical sense. Their character was otherwise consistent with the character of Jesus Himself, and this strikes me as another pointer to their genuineness. Jesus did not conjure up great riches or mighty armies. Atheists such as Christopher Hitchens complain that many of the miracles seem 'petty'[121], but, along with millions of other Christians, I see them differently. In performing most of the miracles, Jesus demonstrated His humility and compassion. His overriding concern was for the sick, the weak and the powerless. The miracles were grounded in the everyday travails of Man and, often, the beneficiaries of them were people who had already demonstrated faith in God. In the Synoptic Gospels, in particular, the evangelists are concerned to emphasise how 'the individual's faith in God elicits the *response* of Jesus'[122].

But the miracles were not merely a 'reward' for the faithful. I am attracted to a dominant theme of John's Gospel, that the miracles are to be regarded as 'signs' – though not proof – of the reality of God. In the process of performing them, Jesus showed Man a glimpse of God's awesome supernatural powers. This combination – of uniquely potent power harnessed for humble good – was what must have made Jesus such a charismatic figure. Jesus preached and practised neighbourly love in a compelling way. He was 'signalling that the *future* kingdom [of God] was somehow present *right now*'[123]. His miracles were both actual and symbolic.[124]

C.S. Lewis made a related point about the character of Jesus's miracles. He observed that they did 'close and small' things that (according to Christians) God does all the time on a much grander scale, but which often pass unappreciated. Thus, for example, the miracle of the loaves and fishes was but a tiny illustration of the way in which God has provided Man's material needs. (It is worth noting here that Lewis regarded the miracles of Jesus as quite distinct from the Old Testament miracles, many of which

– such as the story of Jonah and the whale – he thought were not to be understood literally but as divinely inspired myths.[125]

The next consideration relates to Jesus's notoriety during His life. If Jesus did not perform any of the miracles, then it is hard to imagine how he could have attracted, so quickly, such a significant following among the common people – and the fierce hostility of the Jewish and Roman authorities, religious and secular. Jesus's circumstances were humble, and his moral teachings, although admirable, and uniquely expressed, were in many respects not novel.[126] Apart from His exhortation to love one's enemies, which was a truly ground-breaking idea, it was Jesus's claims to *divinity* which really set Him apart. And without the miracles, those claims would most likely have been dismissed by Jesus's contemporaries as the ravings of an eccentric (cf. Mark 3:21) if, indeed, anyone had taken notice of him at all.

My point is this. Without the miracles, or at least some of them, it is difficult to imagine how Jesus would have got his 'start'. It seems unlikely that we would know of Jesus today if at least some of the miracles had not been performed.

It appears that Jesus performed just enough miracles, of just the right sort, in order to attract a sizeable following for His ministry. Significantly, Jesus did not behave like a 'capracious magician'[127], performing miracles on demand (Matthew 4:1–7, 12:38–9; Mark 15:29–32). It might be objected that a truly 'good' man possessing miraculous powers would have gone for broke and alleviated the suffering of everybody he encountered.[128] But if Jesus had done that, His divinity would surely have been obvious to all and sundry during His lifetime. It seems that Jesus was anxious to avoid that happening. He is recorded in the Synoptic Gospels as having told the Disciples 'privately' that they were in an extremely privileged position ('Blessed are the eyes that see what you see' [Luke 10:23].) and He often urged other witnesses to the miracles to keep them secret (though these urgings were usually disobeyed and news of Jesus's gifts spread quickly).

Likewise, the Pharisees and chief priests feared that 'if we let him go on like this [i.e. performing miraculous signs], *everyone* will believe in him' (John 11:47–8). But that fear was misplaced, because evidently it was not part of God's plan that Jesus should perform miracles indefinitely and indiscriminantly. *Faith* had to be left with a substantial role to play in human affairs. In the words of Warwick Fairfax, the miracles 'were not meant to relieve man of his responsibilities, to give him short cuts, to deprive him of his most precious gift of choosing good or evil'[129]. Moreover, as I will seek to argue in Chapter 7, it is not God's way to 'protect' people continuously from any and all suffering caused by the outworkings of Nature or by evil wrought by Man. The world 'works' because everyone is mortal and has free will. It would have been incongruous, even for Jesus, to have overturned this natural order of things *completely*. He said as much at a synagogue in Nazareth (see Luke 4:23–30).

I am more puzzled by a different issue. Despite the miracles that Jesus *did* perform, it seems that – but for the Resurrection – He might well have been forgotten by history. An issue that still perplexes me to some degree is why the Disciples, at least, were not totally convinced of Jesus's divinity during His lifetime. They saw many extraordinary things, including the raising of Lazarus, yet the extent of their personal doubts remained considerable. Does their equivocal conduct up to and immediately following Jesus's death (i.e. before the Resurrection) cast doubt on the reality of the miracles?[130] It is a valid question, but all things considered I think the matter is explicable.

The position appears to be that, during Jesus's lifetime, the Disciples and others were impressed and even astounded by the miracles (or such of them as really happened). But, despite occasional protestations of individual belief (such as Peter's at Luke 9:20), their state of mind fell short of unequivocal acceptance that Jesus was divine. Why? As we have seen, sceptics are fond of pointing out that Jesus lived in age when spiritualists, sorcerers and faith healers were numerous. 'Tricks' of the kind Jesus performed were, they say, not novel. But surely that is an argument *in favour* of Jesus. He is remembered and revered 2,000 years later while most of the mystics and conmen of His day are entirely forgotten. One whose name survives – a 'sorcerer' known as Simon Magus, or Simon the Magician, who had enjoyed fleeting fame in Samaria – could recognise the real thing. He was converted by an Apostle, Philip, and was 'astonished by the great signs and miracles he saw' (Acts 8:9–13).

So what is the explanation for the prevarication of the Disciples, and others, during Jesus's lifetime and immediately following the Crucifixion? Why were the miracles which Jesus had performed not regarded as decisive, at least by those who had witnessed many? I suspect that Jesus Himself provided the best answer. It is implicit in the parable of the rich man and Lazarus: there will always be some people on Earth whose pride prevents them from taking notice of even the most striking of God's signs (see Luke 16:27–31). Miracles are 'always susceptible to another interpretation'[131]. And as far as the Disciples are concerned, there was a special factor at play. Jesus's death – especially the degrading manner of it – shocked and demoralised them. It seemed to convince them that Jesus was mortal after all. Their reasoning seems to have been (notwithstanding Jesus's address to them at the Last Supper and on earlier occasions) that the real Messiah would not have allowed himself to be crucified. According to the Torah, anyone 'hung on a tree' was cursed by God (Deuteronomy 21:23). No doubt – without Jesus to lead and embolden them – they also feared for their own safety. It took the Resurrection to finally persuade them.[132]

There is another reason why I believe in the miracles. It is a personal reason. Some of the details included in the various descriptions of them have that uncanny quality of verisimilitude. Scholars have pointed to various obscure matters, such as consistency with local customs[133], and often these are telling. But I would make a more general observation. The people for whom and in whose presence Jesus performed the miracles were a disparate lot: young and old, common and privileged. Especially thought-provoking are the accounts of the various miracles that swayed people in authority. These were people who, on the face of it, should have had a natural 'bias' *against* belief in a Jewish Messiah, at least one of the sort that Jesus claimed to be. Every time I read about them I am moved by the miracles of the Roman centurion's servant (Matthew 8:5–13; Luke 7:1–10), the royal official's son (John 4:46–54) and the daughter of Jairus, one of the synagogue rulers (Mark 5:22–42). In each case, an apparently 'unlikely' man came to Jesus begging for help – not for his own benefit, but on behalf of a person dear to him who was very ill. Jesus acceded to each plea because the person making it demonstrated humility, compassion and faith in Jesus's healing powers. Another especially powerful miracle story is the healing of the man at the pool of Bethesda (John 5:1–9). Like a number of the miracles, it was performed on the Sabbath day, a fact which aroused the ire of religious purists – a detail that rings true.

A number of the miracles are recorded in more than one of the Gospels. It is useful to compare the various accounts. A good case study is the miracle of the feeding of the 5,000, the only miracle described in all four Gospels: Matthew 14:1–21; Mark 6:35–44; Luke 9:12–17; John 6:5–15. In this and other like instances, there are just enough *differences* between the various accounts to suggest that what was being described was a real event, differently recalled by various witnesses down one or two generations, to the time when the Gospels were written. In real life, that is how *truthful* witnesses to the same events, and conscientious historians, in fact behave. If the practice of law has taught me anything, it has taught me that. It is deliberate fabricators who tend to get their stories suspiciously straight. I quite realise that this is not an original argument[134], and that elaborate attempts have been made to refute it, but for me, as a lawyer, it has considerable force.

There is another argument, only in part related to the miracles, which I have not seen advanced by anyone before. It requires you to assume that Jesus was sent by God. Then ask: Why did this event occur at that particular time and place in history? Why did not God do it sooner or wait until, say, the twentieth century?

St Paul remarked (in Galatians 4:4) that God sent Jesus 'when the time had fully come'. But St Paul was commenting upon the long wait *before* Jesus's appearance – the intricate steps which God took to prepare Man for that event, including the laying down of prophecies in what became the Old Testament.[135]

Paul, however, did not anticipate the next 2,000 years or more of human civilisation. And my point in this regard is that God seems to have chosen things especially carefully. Uncannily so. Jesus was born into 'the most highly developed and completely self-centred ego-group in the world'[136], the Jews of the first century. Theirs was a deeply religious society – much more so than those of Greece, Rome or Byzantium – so that Jesus's conduct and teachings were bound to attract serious attention and fierce resistance. Furthermore, by the standards of the ancient world, it was a society which was quite advanced technologically and sociologically. A modest, but not huge, number of eyewitnesses were able to comprehend that there was something very special about Jesus – and to leave an eloquent record of the fact. It is also worth noting that Jesus and the Apostles lived during the so-called *Pax Romana* (27 BC– AD 180). Roman rule was oppressive – as the Christian martyrs found – but it was also a period of relative peace. Importantly, land and sea transport were uncommonly safe and easy throughout the Mediterranean diaspora, a situation which would not repeat itself until the nineteenth century.[137] This must have been a contributing factor in the success of the early Christians, who were peripatetic and managed to spread the Gospel with remarkable speed.

Now consider some alternative scenarios.[138] If, for instance, Jesus had been sent in the Stone Age, it is hard to imagine that anyone would have had the capacity to understand properly what He was saying or to record His deeds satisfactorily, or at all, for future generations. Even if they had, the lack of any efficient modes of transport and communication would have hindered evangelism to a hopeless degree. On the other hand, things were not so far advanced when Jesus came that His nature must inevitably have become 'obvious' to everyone. If He came today, his miracles would be videotaped and televised around the world; his shroud and tomb forensically examined. Definite proof (or disproof) of his divinity, or at least of his uniqueness, would almost certainly be available. And that, as I have tried to explain, seems to me the very thing that God had to avoid in order to ensure that free will remains a meaningful gift, and faith the ultimate prize.

There are two last points worth making about Christ's miracles. The first is that there is about them a pleasing symmetry. One reason for my belief in God is that certain laws of the physical Universe are fixed, predictable and finely tuned. Those laws are the basis of order. It is that very order that suggests the existence of a Designer who created and maintains the conditions necessary for order. But another reason for belief in God is the occurrence of extremely rare events which contradict that order. No being of the known Universe which emanates from the fixed and predictable laws of that Universe can flout those laws – as Jesus said, 'with man this is impossible, but with God all things are possible' (Matthew 19:26). In other words, God's hands are not 'in chains' – a point made by the great twelfth-century Islamic philospher, Abu Hamid al-Ghazzali. He objected to the very notion of 'the laws of Nature' as somehow impinging upon God's freedom of action.[139] But it is not necessary to go so far. If it be granted that there are laws of Nature, it follows that *only* a supernatural being somehow 'outside' of Nature (i.e. God, the Designer) can be capable of flouting or suspending those laws, or (another way of saying the same thing) performing miracles. Thus, if Jesus did cause miracles to occur, as the evidence suggests He did, then He must have been the Designer or somehow controlled by the Designer – in short, divine.

This thought may well have haunted the Jewish leaders who engineered Jesus's death. That is my final point about the miracles. I agree with Frank Morison[140] that these otherwise ruthless men appear to have been *afraid* of Jesus. In the four vital days before Jesus's arrest they 'behaved as men under the compulsion of some secret fear' and seem to have been 'apprehensive of something happening which they did not care to define'. Then, late on Thursday night, Judas reported to them that Jesus was 'waiting' in the Garden of Gethsemane. They hastily concocted a plan to execute Jesus within twenty-four hours, and sent a heavily armed posse of soldiers to effect His arrest. Despite these precautions, they 'seem to have been in some doubt whether even a considerable force would be adequate to take Him, and that in the last resort He might even prove to be unarrestable'.

Why did the chief priests harbour these fears? Garry Wills draws attention to the fact that, shortly before Jesus returned to Jerusalem, the chief priests had also plotted to kill Lazarus (the man from Bethany in Judea whom, according to reports, Jesus had raised from death a few weeks earlier). The priests were agitated because 'on account of [Lazarus] many of the Jews were going over to Jesus and putting their faith in him' (John 12:10–11). Lazarus' dead body had been entombed for four days, and for this reason his restoration to life seems to have been even more startling to onlookers than the other healing miracles. Moreover, the performance of this miracle had, much more than any other, deeply affected Jesus Himself. He had explained to Martha, Lazarus' sister, that it was 'a Messianic act', a precursor of His own Passion.[141]

For the author of John's Gospel, the raising of Lazarus was the primary cause of the chief priests' fears, and of their decision to order Jesus's arrest. But, as I have noted, this miracle is not recorded in the other three Gospels, all of which treat Jesus's threats against the Temple building as the activating cause of His arrest. That does not discredit the account in John[142] – which, to me, bears every stamp of verisimilitude – but it suggests that news of the Lazarus miracle cannot have come to the chief priests as a bolt from the blue. Rather, it was one of many; and the straw that broke the camel's back. This means that the miracles were *notorious*. So, in Frank Morison's words:

> Whether the reader believes that the 'miracles' of Christ were actually performed or are merely the legendary ascriptions of a superstitious and unscientific age, the fact remains that the personal ascendancy and repute of Jesus during His own lifetime was immense. The stories of His cures of the blind, the paralytic and the possessed were widespread. They came from all parts of the country and were apparently implicitly accepted even in high quarters in Jerusalem…[143]

In short, the chief priests knew about the miracles, and believed in them (Acts 2:22).

Other considerations about Jesus

Now, put aside the miracles. There is also the conduct and character of Jesus himself. I have already touched upon this issue, but there are other things to be said.[144]

The first thing worth noting is Jesus's sublime self-assurance. It was other-worldly. As G. Campbell Morgan, an eminent English Congregationalist preacher of the late nineteenth and early twentieth centuries, once pointed out:

> The greatest human teachers have always been reticent as to the ultimate authority of their teaching. They have always admitted that there is room for interpretation, for question, for further investigation. That note is entirely absent from the teaching of Christ.[145]

Why was doubt entirely absent from Christ's teaching? In order to answer that question, it is instructive to recognise why doubt is *not* absent from the best human teaching: it is because the wisest people are conscious of how much they do not know. Only the deluded, the arrogant and the stupid presume to know it all. The Jesus of the Gospels was certainly not deluded or arrogant or stupid; one is driven to conclude that His self-assurance sprang from ultimate knowledge and authority.

It appears that Pontius Pilate feared as much. The man who ordered Jesus's death by crucifixion did so most reluctantly. Pilate was 'a matter-of-fact unreligious man', and he remains, arguably, 'the only completely impartial witness of Jesus that we have'.[146] After conversing with Jesus at some little length, Pilate was 'amazed' by His calm and His courage. He told the Jews more than once that he could find no basis for a valid charge (see Matthew Luke 23:1–25; John 18:28–19:16). Pilate's wife also regarded Jesus as an 'innocent man' (and, by an urgent letter, pleaded with her husband to spare Him) (Matthew 27:19). In the end Pilate bowed to political pressure, but his true feelings seem plain. I agree with Warwick Fairfax that Pilate 'was completely convinced of Jesus's uprightness as a man and ... persuaded that Jesus's extravagant statements were not mere paranoia'[147].

A similar argument was made by C.S. Lewis. Taken on its own, and at first blush, the argument seems simplistic[148], but it offers much food for thought. Lewis' basic point was that, if Jesus was not sent by God, then his conduct as a man in *claiming* to be the Son of God, and specifically to his having the power to forgive sin, can only be regarded as silly and conceited. But the notion of Jesus as a silly, conceited man just does not square with the picture painted of him in the Gospels. Even sceptics and unbelievers do not regard him that way; most concede that he was at least a great moral teacher, a man of courage and wisdom. So we are left with a weird sort of paradox. As Lewis put it:

> A man who was merely a man and said the sort of things Jesus said would not be a great moral teacher. He would either be a lunatic – on a level with the man who says he is a poached egg – or else He would be the Devil of Hell. You must make your choice. Either this man was, and is, the Son of God: or else a madman or something worse.[149]

Lewis expressed things rather trenchantly, but is there really any satisfactory middle ground? That is the question every person needs to grapple with.[150]

One answer to Lewis's argument which has been proffered from time to time is that the historical Jesus did *not* claim to be divine.[151] But this contention seems weak, on several counts.[152] First and foremost, the Gospels record Jesus as having made such a claim several times, perhaps most directly when He was questioned by a doubting St Philip at the Last Supper: 'Anyone who has seen me has seen the Father' (John 14:9). St John's Gospel records a number of other like statements by Jesus (cf. John 5:16–30; 10:30; 12:49–50; 16:28). It is noteworthy, also, that on at least two of these occasions the Jewish people to whom Jesus spoke clearly understood Him to be claiming that He was divine; and they reacted with fierce hostility:

> 'We are not stoning you for any of these [i.e. the miracles],' replied the Jews, 'but for blasphemy, *because you, a mere man, claim to be God.*'
>
> (John 10:33, my emphasis. See also John 5:18)

It is then objected that most of Jesus's claims to divinity are recorded in John's Gospel, which (as I noted earlier) has traditionally been regarded as the least reliable of the four as an historical record. But what, then, of the claims recorded in the Synoptic Gospels? Two passages in Mark, the earliest Gospel, stand out for me. First, there is the one in which Jesus asks the Disciples, 'Who do people say I am?' Various answers are proffered, but in the end Jesus does not contradict Peter's exclamation – 'You are the Christ!' [i.e. the Jewish Messiah foreshadowed by the Old Testament prophets]. He then swears the Disciples to secrecy (Mark 8:27–30). Later, at his trial, Jesus is asked directly by the chief priest whether he is 'the Christ'. Jesus replies: 'I am' (Mark 14:61-2), or, as it appears in Matthew's and Luke's Gospels respectively, 'Yes, it is as you say'/ 'You are right in saying I am'. It has been convincingly argued that the more guarded phrases used by the authors of Matthew and Luke must be closer to Jesus's exact words.[153] Just a little later that same morning, even Mark's Gospel has Jesus responding in this rather cryptic way ('Yes, it is as you say') when asked by Pontius Pilate 'Are you the King of the Jews?' (See Mark 15:2; cf. Matthew 27:11; Luke 23:3) The slight ambiguity of all these passages lends them authenticity, because a Christ concocted by early Christian apologists would surely have spoken unequivocally.

The Synoptic Gospels contain other important evidence concerning Jesus's 'incarnational' identity.[154] Both Matthew and Luke attest that He was born of a virgin and the Holy Spirit. Jesus often addresses God as 'Father' and speaks of himself as having been 'sent' by God. There are a few passages in which Jesus refers to himself as 'the Son' or 'the Son of God', and many passages in which he calls himself 'the Son of Man'. Although there is debate as to the precise meaning of each of these titles[155], taken collectively they create a most powerful impression. The title 'the Son of Man' seems to have been favoured by Jesus because it was *not* associated with the long-popular idea of a Jewish political-military conqueror, and because it 'was sufficiently ambiguous to allow him to invest it with his own distinctive understanding of his mission'.[156] The term is used in the Old Testament Book of Ezekiel as a symbol of the idea that, through and by the will of God the Father, 'man feels within himself the birth of a new life of the spirit'.[157]

Also relevant are the claims that Jesus made about his capacities and authority.[158] The most inexplicable claim, if Jesus was not divine, may be that which He made to scoffers before curing a paralytic: 'So that you may know the Son of Man has authority on earth to forgive sins…' (Matthew 9:6; see also Mark 2:5–12). This 'throwaway line' amounted to an explicit claim that Jesus could forgive sins committed, not against him, but against other people. Why would a sane man say a thing like that? The same question arises as regards other statements attributed to Jesus in the Synoptics (see, for example, Matthew 10:40; Matthew 11:27; Luke 10:16).

There is another argument sometimes raised against Jesus's claims to divinity: the Gospels themselves contradict them, because Jesus's words and actions are often those of a man aware of, or constrained by, the limitations imposed by Nature. This raises the mysterious issue of Jesus's own self-consciousness. Could Jesus have been God without, in some sense, fully knowing it? Marcus Braybrooke is one who suggests such middle ground: 'I have come to think that Jesus was indeed aware of a unique vocation, even if he did not think of himself as the unique Son of God'[159].

There is a typically captivating discussion of this question by C.S. Lewis, in *Miracles*.[160] But the most helpful treatment I have read appears in G. Campbell Morgan's disarmingly eloquent book, *The Teachings of Christ*. His textual analysis of the Gospels persuades me of the strange truth of the conventional Christian position, which is that Jesus must have somehow been both God and a man simultaneously. Jesus said things 'which reveal the consciousness of a Being both superior to His own age, and subsisting in all ages; and therefore, ageless, timeless, age-abiding, eternal'. But Jesus said other things that reveal a consciousness of the limitations of time and space, and personal knowledge of poverty, loneliness, sorrow, and weakness – 'all of the things of one age, its limitations and its human experiences'[161].

This controversy can never be settled definitively. There is no authenticated document on which Jesus wrote: 'I am God', or anything else. We must contend, in the words of Joachim Kahl, with 'the fundamental historical fact that Jesus himself did not leave behind any written records'[162].

This stark fact raises a broader issue. Does the total absence of documents in Jesus's own hand clinch the argument, made by Kahl and many others, that the historical Jesus is unknowable? Does it tend to support the more radical theory that he did not exist at all?[163]

I draw a different conclusion. The fact that Jesus did *not* write down his teachings or an explanation of His true nature seems to me another essential concomitant of the Christian faith, like the time in history when Jesus lived. Had such a documentary record been left, it must be doubtful that the Gospels would ever have been written, and the letters of St Paul and others would have been considerably different from what they were.

Try to imagine the following possible scenarios.[164] Jesus might have written his treatise *before* the Crucifixion. He could have concluded it by recording the date and predicting His own Resurrection, and then left the document with (say) Peter for safe-keeping. Alternatively, He might have written his treatise *after* the Crucifixion, including details of events that had happened since that date, and handed over the document to the Disciples during one of His appearances to them. In either scenario, each of which seems strange indeed, the authenticity of the document itself would have been the key evidence for or against Christianity – the circumstances in which the document was written and delivered, and its persuasiveness as a treatise. Jesus's life and his inspirational effect on others interpreted through the efforts of the Apostles would not have been determinative. Faith would not have had so vital a part to play in the development of Christianity, from the first century until today. So I am left with the conviction that Jesus was right not to have left documents behind Him; their absence is, in a curious way, further evidence of His divinity.

Another aspect of Jesus's conduct is even more important to my belief: His holiness and righteousness as a man. We all know how hard it is to live even one day, one hour, without sinning. Many people today object to the word 'sin', but they ought not to. When used in the New Testament, it is most often a translation from the Greek *hamartia*, meaning 'failure' or 'the missing of a mark'. Jesus used the word to connote any moral or ethical imperfection.[165] In saying that it is hard to live without sinning, what I mean is this: each of us is aware, to a greater or lesser extent, if one is being honest, that there is an ideal of human behaviour that we consistently and repeatedly do not meet.

Yet the Jesus described in the Gospels *did* meet that standard. According to the people who knew Him best, He consistently demonstrated 'the highest pattern of virtue'[166] and a 'contagious holiness'[167]. Very few people today attack Christianity on the grounds that Jesus's conduct was evil or ill-motivated, or even flawed. To the contrary, even some of history's most urbane sceptics – Rousseau, J.S. Mill, Goethe, H.G. Wells, Ralph Waldo Emerson – acknowledged Jesus's sinless perfection. So does the Qur'an (*Mary*, verse 19; *Al-Imran*, verse 45).[168] A rare exception was Bertrand Russell, who, while granting Jesus 'a very high degree of moral goodness', purported to detect various 'defects' in Him too, one or two of them 'very serious'. Jesus lacked 'a proper degree of kindliness' because He believed in Hell[169], and He was not 'supremely wise' because He predicted – wrongly – that the Second Coming would occur during His hearers' lifetimes[170].

Russell was grasping at straws. His arguments were weak on both counts. The first was merely tautologous, because it assumed, as a matter of course, that Hell does not exist (or, if it does exist, that it is a Hell of an unreasonably monstrous kind – an assumption I will challenge in Chapter 10). Russell's second argument was based on a dubious reading of Scripture: although some of Jesus's followers may have thought that His return to Earth was imminent, and interpreted a few of His statements that way, it is quite unsound to conclude that Jesus Himself believed this. Most indications are to the contrary.[171]

For myself, I can discern no genuine defects in Jesus's character. His conduct, *as a man*, was exemplary, even in the face of temptation of every kind (cf. Hebrews 4:15). It may be conceded that the aim of the Gospel authors was to glorify Him, but I cannot agree with critics such as Joachim Kahl that they 'were most anxious to avoid reporting anything that might do him harm'[172]. The inference is that somehow there were disreputable incidents to report. I do not get any such sense from the Gospels, which are in fact rather candid when it comes to Jesus's moods. The truth is that Jesus not infrequently got angry with people, and rebuked them. He had a temper (see, e.g., Mark 1:41; Matthew 15:21–8); He was not, as Bertrand Russell complained He ought to have been, 'bland and urbane towards the people who would not listen to him'[173]; in that sense he was not merely a 'nice guy'. But His anger, like that of a fiercely devoted parent towards a recalcitrant child, was a manifestation of deep love – He *worried and cared*, and tried occasionally to shock people into obedience. If a child is about to walk over a cliff, blandness and urbanity are not virtues.

Similarly, there is an impressive candour in the Gospel accounts of Jesus's behaviour in the Garden of Gethsemane. He is described as having been agitated, uncertain and afraid – details which seem unlikely to have been invented by authors seeking to proclaim a New Messiah. But, equally, they are details which, properly understood, tell in Jesus's favour. Because Jesus was fully a man as well as divine, He knew that He would experience dreadful suffering – but went through with it anyway.

Jesus was fair, incorruptible and courageous. He never caused harm to anyone other than the hurt pride caused when one is told a home truth. He lived cleanly and simply; He was quite immune to flattery. He was also, as William Blake recognised, superbly energetic and creative. Above all, He was serenely sure of Himself, but at the same time humble. He is the best exemplar by far of Shakespeare's peerless advice (through Polonius to Laertes) as to how a man should conduct himself: 'This above all: to thine own self be true.' And it is worth remembering Polonius's reason for laying down this injunction: the man who is true to himself 'canst not then be false to any man'. Jesus, as I read the Gospels, was honest with everybody, sometimes brutally so.

Jesus's reported perfection as a human being seems to me an extraordinary fact – perhaps a *greater* miracle than the turning of water into wine or the healing of a leper. The way Jesus lived His life may be the best evidence of His divinity. In the words of G. Campbell Morgan, Jesus's revelation as God 'is not to be found finally in what He said, but in what He was, and in what He did'[174]. John Spong is at his most eloquent in describing the nature of Jesus's perfection – 'so whole, so open, so free, so at one with himself'[175] – but he persists steadfastly in the notion that Jesus was no more than a 'fully human [being]'. I just cannot accept that interpretation, because it flies in the face of the harsh reality of human nature. Nor can I accept that the evangelists somehow imagined such a character: 'Only a Christ could have conceived a Christ'[176].

On this issue – Jesus's conduct as a man – I have also been influenced by the writings of a Scottish theologian, Donald Baillee. Baillee sought to explain the significance of Jesus's life (and death) in terms of the concept of grace. Some of my beliefs on this key Christian concept are dealt with in Chapter 7. There my emphasis is upon grace as a force controlled by God operating for the overall benefit of Man – including the manifestation of grace in the lives of individual men and women.

Another (closely related) aspect of the concept of grace is, in Baillee's words, 'the conviction which a Christian man possesses that every good thing in him, every good thing he does, is somehow not wrought by himself but by God'. Baillee called this phenomenon 'the paradox of grace'. He averred:

> [T]his paradox … points the way more clearly and makes a better approach than any-
> thing else in our experience to the mystery of the Incarnation itself; and this paradox
> in its fragmentary form in our own Christian lives is a reflection of that perfect union
> of God and man in the Incarnation on which our whole Christian life depends, *and*
> *may therefore be our best clue to our understanding of it.*[177]

I have emphasised the concluding words in this passage because they go to the heart of the issue at hand. What evidence is there that Jesus was divine? Is there something to go on which any person can relate to – male or female, adult or child, whatever their station in life? My understanding of Baillee's essential point is this. When you feel yourself doing good, and at the same time are genuinely (not falsely) humble about the fact, you are in a state of grace, and close to God. *Jesus lived his whole life that way.* Try to imagine living your own life that way – all of the time. No mere man or woman can do so, nor any boy or girl: it is impossible. Yet Jesus managed it. How? Like Baillee, I am convinced that it was possible only because Jesus was divine. In the words of St Paul, 'God was reconciling the world to himself in Christ' (2 Corinthians 5:19).

In other words, Jesus of Nazareth could not have lived the life that he did unless he was God.

Many people still insist that there must be some middle ground: that Jesus lived a magnificent life, but was not God. Speaking for myself, the more I have read about Jesus, and the more I have thought about Him, the harder it is to imagine any coherent middle ground, let alone believe in it. If Jesus was not divine, as (probably) he claimed to be, then who was he? How did he live as he did? Why did so many of the common people of first-century Judea follow him so avidly? Why did his life and his teachings so profoundly disturb the powers that be? What motivated the Apostles and the authors of the Gospels? Any 'practical' answers to these questions seem hopelessly impracticable. One is left (remembering Brian Davies' words regarding the absolute rejection of the miraculous) with more problems than one set out to solve.

I concede that I am approaching the issue from the point of view of one who already had come independently to a belief in God. If you believe in God, a God with a special interest in Man, then it is completely logical also to believe that God would wish to communicate with Man, in a such way that maximised each person's chances of making a free (but not coerced or inevitable) decision to find God. For the reasons I have outlined, that is my own conception of Jesus: God's clearest sign yet – through the example of the perfect man – that He (God) exists. The matter seems exquisitely right, and there is no need to make it difficult.

If you do not independently believe in God – if the reasons that I and countless others have proffered remain unconvincing – then Jesus of Nazareth becomes a 'problem' who must be explained away, somehow, in ordinary human terms. At first blush this may not seem much of a challenge. But it is still a challenge that should be honestly taken up. Most people do not appear to try; they just assume that there must be an explanation, but regard the task of finding it as one for others to attempt. As far as I can discover, no one has done so in any intellectually satisfying fashion, in the same way that few people have proposed any alternative explanation for the ordered complexity of the physical Universe, or for the existence of love.

Jesus's own suggestion

It may be that almost everything written in this chapter is beside the point. According to John's Gospel, Jesus proposed a simple test for assessing His divinity. It is a test that anyone can begin to take, anywhere and at any time:

> If anyone chooses to do God's will, he will find out whether my teaching comes from God or whether I speak on my own.
>
> (John 7:17)

In other words, try to do what Jesus taught, and then decide. The secret of developing belief in His divine authority is, initially, obedience to His advice and imitation of His example. I venture to agree with G. Campbell Morgan that '[n]o man ever tried and tested Christ's teaching in that way, and decided that it was untrue'[178].

CHAPTER 6

THE RESURRECTION

They were startled and frightened, thinking they saw a ghost. He said to them, 'Why are you troubled, and why do doubts rise in your minds? Look at my hands and my feet. It is I myself! Touch me and see; a ghost does not have flesh and bones, as you see I have.'

Luke 24:37–39

The first fact in the history of Christendom is a number of people who say they have seen the Resurrection. If they had died without making anyone else believe this 'gospel' no gospels would ever have been written. It is very important to be clear about what these people meant.

C.S. Lewis, *Miracles*

This is, perhaps, the most important issue of all. The Christian religion was founded on the belief that the man Jesus of Nazareth was crucified, died and was buried, but three days later was alive again – 'resurrected'. More specifically, Christians claim that Jesus escaped from the sealed and guarded tomb in which His dead body had been interred. Subsequently, over a period of several weeks, He appeared *in bodily form* to hundreds of people, including the Disciples and Mary Magdalene. These people touched Him and spoke with Him and ate with Him.

This claim is utterly central to Christianity, to the idea that Jesus was not merely a mortal man, but also was God – and hence that everything He did and said must be understood in that context.

St Paul did not mince words on this subject. He bluntly conceded to sceptics of his day that if the Apostles' claims about the Resurrection were untrue, then the Christian religion was worthless and their conduct amounted to blasphemy:

[I]f Christ has not been raised, our preaching is *useless* and so is your faith. More than that, we are then found to be false witnesses about God, for we have testified about God that he raised Christ from the dead.

(1 Corinthians 15:14-5. My emphasis.)

St Paul concluded that Christians 'were to be pitied more than all men' (1 Corinthians 15:19) if they had placed their faith in a mortal man whose teachings applied only to this earthly life.

It may be objected that St Paul overstated the matter: quite a large number of people today who practise the Christian religion profess that they do not believe in the Resurrection as an actual historical event. Such people argue that we are not supposed to take the Resurrection story literally; that the Resurrection is a sort of grand metaphor for the change ('new life') that comes upon any person who truly tries to live by the teachings of Jesus. Sceptics and opponents of Christianity are usually not so charitable, but they arrive at the same conclusion. They assert with varying degrees of sanctimony, sarcasm and bile that the Resurrection cannot be understood literally. Some reject the event entirely. The Resurrection has been variously described as 'the central myth of the New Testament'[1] and as 'the defining heresy of traditional Protestant and Catholic Christianity'[2]. Christopher Hitchens has averred that 'we have a right, if not an obligation, to respect ourselves enough to disbelieve the whole thing'[3].

As I have made clear, I am certainly not one who considers that every word of the Bible should be read literally or that every passage should be accorded equal importance. There is good sense in many of the arguments advanced by John Spong and other 'liberal' Christians: in some respects the Bible does need to be 'rescued from fundamentalism'. When reading any given passage, you must consider the context in which it was written and ask yourself what the author of the passage must have been intending to convey.

When it comes to the Resurrection, however, it seems to me quite clear that St Paul in his letters – and the authors of the Gospels and Acts – intended what they wrote to be taken literally. They were recording their version of a real event; at the least, they all sincerely believed that the Resurrection actually happened. Even Joachim Kahl acknowledged this: 'The resurrection is regarded *everywhere* in the New Testament as a historical fact to which eyewitnesses bear authentic testimony'[4]. But Kahl rejected the accuracy of that testimony, as do many others like him today.

It is convenient, at this point, to describe the Resurrection claim in a little more detail. The 'tomb' was in the nature of a small cavern, hewn horizontally out of a rockface, on the outskirts of Jerusalem.[5] Jesus's body was placed inside it late on the afternoon of His death (a Friday), and the entrance was closed up with a very large stone (the *Golel*). At least three strong men were required to manoeuvre it into position.[6] A length of cord or thread was then strung across the entrance, and sealed at both ends[7], a security measure akin to the winding of plastic tape around a modern-day crime scene. The Jewish authorities had made arrangements with Pontius Pilate for a posse of soldiers (probably four Roman centurions) to keep guard there.[8] Saturday, a holy day for the Jews, passed uneventfully. At dawn on Sunday, a small group of women came to visit the tomb. They found it unguarded. The stone was some distance away from the tomb's entrance, and the seal was broken. The body of Jesus was missing.

There are many other salient facts, and a host of arguments and counter-arguments. I will come to these shortly. But most of the things I have stated in the preceding paragraph are relatively uncontroversial. On the other hand, the alleged resurrection appearances of Jesus are hotly disputed – and have been for two millennia. According to the New Testament, several appearances took place on that first Sunday. There were, ultimately, some fifteen of them[9], involving, in total, more than 500 men and women. Let it be said again: these people insisted that they saw, heard and/or touched the man Jesus of Nazareth.

If the Resurrection did actually happen, then clearly enough it was a miracle. The question, then, is whether that miracle did actually occur.

St Paul's seminal account of the event in his first letter to the Corinthians made a deep impression upon me when I first heard it read and explained during a sermon. It is to be borne in mind that this letter is one of the very earliest documents in the New Testament, written around AD 50 to 55 (about twenty to twenty-five years after the Crucifixion). The salient passage was based upon a creed first passed on to Paul around AD 35 (only five years after the Crucifixion and three years after Paul's own conversion). The words still resonate with me each time I consider them:

> Now, brothers, I want to *remind* you of the gospel I preached to you, which you received and on which you have taken your stand. By this gospel you are saved, if you hold firmly to the word I preached to you. Otherwise, you have believed in vain.
>
> For what I received I passed on to you as of first importance: that Christ died for our sins according to the Scriptures, that he was buried, that he was raised on the third day according to the Scriptures, and that he appeared to Peter, and then to the Twelve. After that, he appeared to more than five hundred of the brothers at the same time, *most of whom are still living*, though some have fallen asleep. Then he appeared to James, then to all the apostles, and last of all he appeared to me also …
>
> (1 Corinthians 15:1–8. My emphasis)

The extraordinary force of this famous passage is derived, for me, from its matter-of-fact tone. Evidently St Paul was reiterating to the Corinthians certain basic things that he and others had already told them many times. He was telling them *again* in summary form the essence of the Resurrection story, and incidentally reminding them that of the approximately 500 people who, in a group, saw Jesus after He rose from the dead, most were still alive to verify the matter if need be. It was as if Paul was saying: 'You don't need to take my word for it, or even that of the other Apostles; ask any of the 500 who are still alive.' The whole passage strikes me forcibly as a plainly truthful contemporary account of an extraordinary event. (See also 1 Thessalonians 4:14, Galatians 1:1.)

St Paul's own encounter with the risen Christ occurred a few years after the Crucifixion, and seems to have been an event of a somewhat different nature to that attested to by the other Apostles. It happened, as everyone knows, on the road to Damascus. According to the account in Acts 9:3–19, Paul was blinded temporarily by a powerful light. He fell to the ground, and then heard Jesus speak to him. The men travelling with Paul 'heard the sound but did not see anyone', and, after their stricken leader got up from the ground, they led him into Damascus. For three days Paul remained blind and could not eat or drink. Then his sight was restored to him by a Christian named Ananais, and Paul soon regained his strength. (Compare Acts 22:3:16, 26:12–18.)

It is a weird tale, but can there be any serious doubt that some such event occurred? After his strange experience, Paul renounced everything he had ever stood for. Until then he had been a doctrinaire Pharisee, steeped in Jewish tradition, and by his own admission a ruthless foe of the Apostles (Galatians 1:13). He had been chosen by the chief priests to lead the Great Persecution, and had supervised the stoning of Stephen, one of the leaders of the Hellenist wing of the early church. The reason Paul was travelling to Damascus was to seek out Christians in the synagogues there and bring them back to Jerusalem as prisoners (Acts 9:1–2).

Is there any reason to disbelieve the account in Acts of St Paul's conversion? That he was converted is incontestable.[10] Could St Luke, the author of Acts, have invented the story from scratch, a generation after the incident was said to have occurred? It seems highly unlikely. Could the story have been invented earlier by Paul himself, some time after his conversion? That too seems unlikely. Paul's own account of the aftermath of his experience strikes me, 2,000 years later, as singularly blunt, and anything but self-serving:

> [W]hen God … was pleased to reveal his Son in me … I did not consult any man,
> nor did I go up to Jerusalem to see those who were apostles before I was, but I went
> immediately into Arabia and later returned to Damascus. Then after three years, I went
> up to Jerusalem to get acquainted with Peter and stayed with him fifteen days. I saw
> none of the other apostles – only James, the Lord's brother. I assure you before God
> that what I am writing to you is no lie.
>
> (Galatians 1:16–20. See also 1 Corinthians 9:1)

In other words, Paul first went away for a while to reflect in peace upon a life-shattering event. It is now known that he made some early converts while in 'Arabia' (the Nabataean kingdom southeast of Judea), but that in the process he fell out with the local ruler, Aretus IV. He escaped, and came back to Damascus. After a lengthy stay in that city to contemplate his position and to plan his future, Paul decided to risk returning to the 'centre' of events, Jerusalem. He must have known that he would be *persona non grata* with the Jewish establishment and that, at least initially, he would also be distrusted by the followers of Jesus. However, he wanted to meet and talk with the men most likely to be 'in the know'. With the help of a prominent Jewish Christian named Barnabas, Paul gained access to Peter, the leader of the Apostles, and James, Jesus's brother. He stayed with Peter for a fortnight, but received death threats. Eventually it was decided that

Paul should return to his place of birth, Tarsus, in southern Asia Minor. He was to base himself there for eleven years. During that period, in AD 41 or 42, Barnabas sought Paul's help in establishing a Christian community in Antioch. That project took a year, and must have stimulated Paul's zeal for evangelism. Shortly afterwards he embarked upon his life's mission – 'That I might preach the Good News to the Gentiles'. He made three long and successful missionary tours into Asia Minor and Europe, before being executed in Rome in or about AD 63 on the order of Emperor Nero.[11]

The various attempts which have been made to undermine St Paul's credibility, by atheists and others, appear to me hopelessly lame. They amount to a mean-spirited denigration of the man. Michel Onfray alleges that Paul was a 'masochist' and a 'weakling', a hysterical sexual deviant, 'driven by a host of psychological problems'[12]. Others charge that the conduct Paul described in Galatians was stupid and irrational: he ought to have consulted the Apostles much sooner, and much more fully. Perhaps, but does not the fact that Paul behaved rather scattily in the period immediately following his conversion demonstrate the powerful and disconcerting character of the experience he had been through? In any case, the criticisms made of Paul's personality and conduct – fair or unfair – do not ultimately go to the question of *why* he behaved as he did. Why did he come to believe in Jesus as the Son of God? Why did he seek out the leaders of the Apostles, and work courageously for their cause? Whatever else he was, Paul was a man of high intellect. In my judgment, he 'came over at last because he was convinced not only that the disciples were honest, but that they were right'.[13]

Of course, St Paul's life and testimony is only one piece of the jigsaw. A huge amount of historical scholarship has been devoted to the events surrounding the Resurrection, and its aftermath. No one can read more than a small portion of the relevant literature. The best and most comprehensive scholarly treatment of the subject is N.T. Wright's magisterial twenty-first century work, *The Resurrection of the Son of God*[14]. However, Wright's masterpiece is caviar to the general, and it is probably not the best place for the curious lay reader to begin.

My own education about the Resurrection began with two short and accessible books. One of them, *The Case for Christ*[15], by American journalist Lee Strobel, is a good contemporary guide to the key issues. The other, Frank Morison's 1930 classic, *Who Moved the Stone?*[16] is a must-read. 'Frank Morison' was the pseudonym of Albert Henry Ross (1881–1950), an English lawyer. Ross was a sceptic. He set out to write a book *dis*proving the Resurrection. Instead, the more he looked at the evidence, the more he became convinced that the events described in the Gospels could not have been made up. His book is like a densely plotted detective story. The first time I read it, the details did not fully sink in; but on a second reading some years later, after I had become convinced for other reasons of the reality of the Resurrection, the book was revelatory. Especially persuasive is the analysis of the specific charges laid against Jesus by the Jewish authorities, and the conduct of the trials before the Great Sanhedrin and Pontius Pilate.

These and other works[17] have impressed upon me the importance of conceptualising the life and death of Jesus, the Resurrection, and the work of the Apostles as real historical events, rather than as mythical stories. The point – a simple but surprisingly subtle one – was brought home to me when I visited the Vatican in May 2004. Amidst all of the gilt and the splendour, the object that interested me the most was a plain plaque listing the names of the Popes, from St Peter onwards. I can remember thinking along these lines: 'Of course … St Peter was a real person, just like John Paul II. And that person – St Peter – was Christ's chosen apostle. That is how all of this started… St Peter probably spoke to his successor and that Pope with his successor, and so on.' Thus did the list of names seem to me to represent a simple but tangible link with Jesus Himself. (I have since learned that the notion of 'apostolic succession' was instituted some centuries after Peter[18], but that does not invalidate my original experience.)

The apologetic historical literature reminds us – like that plaque at the Vatican – that the story of Christianity is not some quaint fictional invention, albeit realised on a grand scale. And yet that is how I, for one, used to think of it. It seems probable that many people think that way, at least unconsciously. Such a trap is easy to fall into. If you do not believe, or do not want to believe, the more amazing claims of Christianity – such as the miracles or the Resurrection – then it is easy to forget that much of the *rest* of the story remains relatively uncontroversial historical fact.

On any view, a great many of the events recorded in the New Testament actually happened. The Apostles' work in establishing the Christian Church, the spread of the Gospel message throughout the Roman Empire, the persecution of the early Christians – these are facts of human history, just like Alexander's conquests, or Julius Caesar's, or Napoleon's*, facts that few people would think of challenging or could credibly challenge. Jesus's association with the man known as John the Baptist is similarly close to a bedrock historical fact.[19] So too, according to modern scholarly consensus, are a number of the seminal events of the Passion narrative: Jesus's creation of a disturbance at the Temple in Jerusalem during Passover week in AD 30, the Last Supper, Jesus's betrayal by one of the Disciples, His arrest in the garden by the Temple guard, the trial before Pontius Pilate, and the desertion of the Disciples.[20] The Crucifixion is in the same category. Frank Morison called it 'one of the certainties of history'[21]. Even so vehement a critic of Christianity as Joachim Kahl accepted that the Crucifixion was 'a probable historical fact', and referred his readers to another source for a comprehensive outline of the evidence.[22]

The very fact that Jesus was executed is, of itself, crucially important, as Morison in particular appreciated.[23] The Jewish authorities would not have wanted Jesus dead – and the Romans would not have carried out the execution – unless He had said and done things which alienated, even frightened, some powerful people. What were those things? As Craig L. Blomberg has written: 'Above all, one question must be answerable: why was Jesus executed?'[24] I will come to that issue presently. For present purposes, my point is that real historical events need sober historical explanations.

---

* In 1819, the Anglican Archbishop of Durham, Richard Whately, published a book entitled *Historic Doubts Relative to Napoleon Bonaparte*. It was, and remains, a clever piece of satire. Whately's point was that almost any fact of history could be 'disproved' by the application of fanatical scepticism – including the career of Napoleon. I am indebted to Timothy McGrew for drawing Whately's book to my attention.

Likewise, most of the denominations of the Christian Church that exist today were not founded upon arbitrary flights of fancy, made up by charlatans on a whim. Each major denomination is the product of important historical events and sober, reasoned choices. You may not care for some of the different 'takes' upon Jesus and His teachings that, down the centuries, different societies and cultures have adopted. But that is a far cry from assuming (as, it seems, do many atheists and disinterested sceptics) that such differences were plucked out of the air.

Some events in the history of Christianity were unquestionably real. *Was the Resurrection one of them?* That is the key issue. After years of anxious thought, I have come to believe that the Resurrection did actually happen. It may be that the body of the risen Jesus, as seen and touched by the eyewitnesses, was not strictly a *human* body any longer but some kind of 'spiritual' or 'numinous' body which gave every appearance of being a human body (see Paul's discussion of the 'how' of resurrection in 1 Corinthians 15:35–58).[25] But these people were not hallucinating. The event, I believe, happened as reported. My reasons are a mixture of the deductive, the intuitive and the personal.

The Resurrection makes sense

First, to put the matter broadly, the Resurrection now makes sense to me as an intellectual proposition. John Spong and others like him may choose to dismiss it as 'theological gobbledygook'[26], but more and more it just seems 'right'.

My main contention in the previous chapter was that God evidently decided to send into the world a 'perfect man', in order that every person might have a fair opportunity to come to understand – by the concrete example of what that man did and said during his life – that God really does exist, and that God hopes for a certain kind of behaviour from each of us. In sending Jesus to Earth, God in effect conceded that it was too much to expect Man fully to comprehend His nature by the sort of reasoning that I have attempted in Part One of this book. So-called 'general revelation' ('God's constant disclosing of Himself to every one of us … through Nature, providence and the workings of our own mind and conscience'[27]) can only go so far. God decided that it was also necessary that He appear in written form (through Scripture) and in human form (through Jesus) – so-called 'special revelation'. However, even the example of Jesus's life was not enough. To be as fair as possible to the human race, God decided that the circumstances of Jesus's death had to be even more extraordinary.

First, in the manner of his death, Jesus (the man) had to suffer excruciating mental and physical pain. He was betrayed by one of his closest colleagues, abandoned by several others, and then convicted on trumped-up charges by corrupt officials pandering to a cowardly mob. Then He was tortured. The Romans devised crucifixion as a method of slow and agonising public execution, to seek to deter rebellion. It was the ancient world's 'ultimate penalty'[28] and 'involved a whole galaxy of horrors'[29]. Extend your arms horizontally while holding in each hand an object of any significant weight. I cannot do it for more than fifteen or twenty seconds before my muscles screech. Sometimes I try to imagine how it must have felt for Jesus, hanging for many hours on the Cross in such a pose, but with the weight of His body supported by nails in the hands and feet rather than by his own legs. He had first received a vicious flogging, and lugged the heavy horizontal section of the Cross to Calvary Hill. There He was stripped naked before being nailed to the Cross. He was taunted as he suffered. Death, in the end, came by gradual asphyxiation or, possibly[30], a rupture of the heart.

Perhaps worst of all, suggests Timothy Keller, Jesus seems in his final agonies to have imagined that He had been forsaken by God – *His* beloved Father.[31] Jesus believed – like a man betrayed by his wife or his best friend (compare Chapter 3) – that He had been cut off from the love which had always sustained Him.

What were God's reasons for the horrific circumstances of Jesus's death? Why could Jesus not have died 'normally'? These questions trouble many people, especially non-Western religious people, some of whom perceive the crucifix 'as a violently obscene icon'.[32] At a practical level, it might be said in response that, when Jesus's mutilated body was taken down from the Cross, it needed to be demonstrably clear that He was really (physically) dead.[33] But I suggest there were other, much deeper reasons. God regarded Jesus's agonies as necessary and appropriate, in order to demonstrate to Man, in as vivid a way as possible, two crucial things. First, the full measure of God's love for us, and, second, His empathy for the pain and suffering which is a fundamental feature of the human condition. It has been suggested that, '[t]heologically speaking, the world is overshadowed by the scandal that it might never have happened'.[34] True enough, but surely the greater scandal was, and is, that the world did happen – and that (as Simone Weil argued) the inevitable result was suffering. That suffering serves many essential purposes, as I will argue in Chapter 7, but it is dreadful nonetheless, and all of it stems from God's 'one primal offense', the act of Creation. In short, God knows that He is 'the ultimately responsible party'.[35]

The Crucifixion brought Jesus's experience of suffering *as a man* to a level comparable with the most hideous suffering endured by any ordinary person on Earth. It was God's way of 'coming with us'[36], of 'giving us an opportunity to make Divine contact in a way not otherwise possible'[37]. Further, the vile conduct of the Roman and Jewish authorities compared at least in kind with the vileness of Man's collective sins – past and future – the atonement for which was a key purpose of Jesus's death and resurrection.[38] In short, as St Paul put it, 'God presented [Jesus] as a sacrifice of atonement … to demonstrate his justice' (Romans 3:25; see also Hebrews 9:26-8; 1 Peter 3:18). Importantly, Jesus had the (supernatural) power to save Himself, but He deliberately refrained from doing so – a kind of miracle in itself. (These notions were, in my view, at the centre of Mel Gibson's graphic film *The Passion of the Christ*.)

So, that aspect of the Resurrection story seems to me 'right'. But the second key aspect of the story makes even clearer sense to me – and was, perhaps, yet more important to God. Man had to be shown that death was not final. Why? Because death is the ultimate mystery, the undiscovered country from whose bourn no traveller returns. It is and always has been the common denominator for everyone on Earth, regardless of their personal circumstances. From Charlemagne in his pomp to the most penurious beggar, everyone must die. This, the most brutal fact of all, was peerlessly dramatised by Shakespeare – in the gravedigger scene in *Hamlet*. God's conception was to show

Man that it is possible to 'conquer death'. It was and remains the most striking way to demonstrate the reality of His power to *everyone*, because it was and is a universal example that everyone can understand.

These two key features of the Resurrection – atonement for Man's wrongs and triumph over death itself – distil, for me, the meaning of the Cross. The first focuses attention on the sacrificial element of the Crucifixion. For those wanting to understand this concept fully, I recommend reading and re-reading the parable of the unmerciful servant (Matthew 18:21–35). Jesus told the Disciples the story of a servant who begged his master to forego a debt, the payment of which would have ruined the servant and his family. The master relented, in effect granting the servant a fresh chance in life. But not long afterwards the servant ruthlessly enforced a much smaller debt owed *to him* by a fellow servant; the unfortunate man was jailed because he could not pay. Hearing of this, the master was furious and reinstated in full the larger debt he had earlier forgiven. The unmerciful servant was jailed and tortured.

G. Campbell Morgan regarded this parable as 'one of the most singularly fine illustrations of what the Cross is'. He explained:

> When a man forgives debt what does he do? He bears the loss resulting from another's wrongdoing. It is his personal loss, and he suffers it, in order to forgive. If God so forgives, by suffering loss on our behalf, He does it in order that we also may forgive, by suffering loss; and if we will not so forgive, then He will re-arrest us, *and claim the utmost penalty.*[39]

The words I have emphasised are a chilling warning. In Chapter 10, I will come to a fuller discussion of the way that God may judge individual souls, and my conception of Hell as 'the utmost penalty' for those judged adversely. For the moment, let us rather focus upon the other, joyful element of the meaning of the Cross: Jesus's defeat of death.

Again, I will quote some words of G. Campbell Morgan, because they have been influential for me. Dr Morgan explained why, conceptually, the Resurrection was so critical. Without it, he pointed out, 'the Cross would be a forlorn hope, the heroism of an utmost despair, the splendid dream of a misguided enthusiast, and nothing more'. But, he continued:

> [W]hen, according to [Jesus's] own constantly repeated affirmation that He would rise again, I see Him rise again; then I discover that in the mystery of the Cross He was not only the Sin-bearer; in the activities of that dark hour, He was the Sin-destroyer; in some infinite transaction beyond human power of thought, He destroyed the works of the devil...[40]

By 'the works of the devil', Dr Morgan meant sin, i.e. all human imperfection, individual and collective, including bodily death itself. Jesus's task was to 'grapple with [sin], master it, negative it; and, emerging from the struggle victorious, *communicate life*, in the power of which other souls shall be able to enter into the same struggle, and with like result'[410]. (My emphasis).

That, then, is my basic understanding of the Resurrection's meaning. It was the communication by God to Man – the fantastic demonstration by God to Man – that life on Earth is not futile. God exists, and God loves us. 'He is [our] champion, not [our] punisher'[42]. The closest thing we have to 'proof' is Jesus: the example of His life, the circumstances of His death, and – the clincher – the miracle of His Resurrection, which serves to make sense in retrospect of everything that He said and did.

When and if you come to believe that the Resurrection makes sense conceptually, you may also come to look less sceptically at the other evidence for it. You will be looking for *corroborative* evidence, rather than cast-iron proof of an otherwise inexplicable event. As C.S. Lewis wrote of the Incarnation in general:

> Whether the thing really happened is a historical question. But when you turn to history, you will not demand for it that kind and degree of evidence which you would rightly demand for something intrinsically improbable; only that kind and degree which you demand for something which, if accepted, illuminates and orders all other phenomena.[43]

Unbelievers may object that this is special pleading. So let us turn to the other evidence. It is persuasive but, necessarily, not definitive. If Christ had appeared in bodily form to *everybody*, both people at the time in Judea and since, there would be no such thing as faith – a point already laboured. St Luke may well have been alive to it (see Acts 10:41).

The eyewitnesses

I have argued that Man had to be shown by God that death is not final. But, strictly, only certain men and women were shown this directly: there were a relatively tiny number of original eyewitnesses to the risen Christ. Apart from the 520 or so people mentioned by St Paul in his first letter to the Corinthians, everyone else has had to take the Resurrection story on trust, as hearsay evidence, and to make of it what they can.

Why should we believe that the people who first reported the story may be relied upon? Is it not more likely that the whole thing was a mistake, or a myth, or wish-fulfilment, or a hoax? For some years, as I inched my way toward Christian belief in other less important respects, these doubts about the Resurrection often returned to me. Ultimately, though, I have come to the firm conclusion that none of these alternative explanations hold up – and not merely because the Resurrection makes sense intellectually. There are other, more prosaic considerations.

I will mention only in passing, and then put to one side, a number of fascinating lines of claim and counter-claim. There are contentions that Jesus survived the Crucifixion (merely having lost consciousness when His body was taken down) and later made a natural physical recovery. There are contentions that, even if Jesus did die on the Cross, the supposed disappearance of His body from the tomb can be otherwise explained – the body was never placed in a tomb, by Joseph of Arimathea or anyone else, but was buried in a common grave and later forgotten, or dug up and eaten by wild dogs; the tomb was not guarded by Roman centurions or Jews from the Temple, and was not otherwise secure, so the body could have been stolen from it; the guards fell asleep or were bribed to say that they had (cf. Matthew 28:11-15); the women and/or the Disciples came to the wrong tomb. A related argument is that the various accounts in the Gospels of the discovery of the empty tomb, and Jesus's later appearances, are so contradictory in certain details – and, in the case of Mark's Gospel, so remarkably *lacking* in detail – as to cast doubt on the whole story.[44]

Many of these issues are – factually and historically – rather complicated. But the various Christian explanations of them that I have read and absorbed appear generally convincing.[45] Three points of detail seem especially significant.

First, there is no record anywhere in the literature of a denial by the Jewish or Roman authorities that the tomb was empty. The fact was notorious. Various attempts were made to explain it away, but the one absolutely certain thing is that Jesus's dead body was never produced. If the powers that be had been able to produce the body they would surely have done so, because Christianity would have been stopped stone dead; and it would have been a simple and straightforward thing to do if the body had still been there, because the tomb was close by and its location well known.[46] Frank Morison's theory was that the authorities *knew* that the body was gone: the guards who had been stationed there on Saturday night must have experienced something weird, rolled back the large stone that sealed the tomb, and found the body missing. They reported back to their superiors and/or raised a general commotion in the streets of Jerusalem.[47]

There is a second and related detail of significance. The Gospels record that the tomb was visited at dawn on Easter Sunday by a small party of women – Mary Magdalene and one or two others – who had gone there to anoint Jesus's body. They discovered the tomb open and the body missing. They were terribly frightened*, and fled to report their find to the Disciples. Yet the role of the women is nowhere mentioned in any of the Epistles or in Acts. It appears that the first generation of Christians did not bother to cite the women's testimony, even during their first speeches in Jerusalem seven weeks after the Crucifixion. Why?

The Disciples may well have been loath to admit that any of their party had secretly visited the tomb, especially as they had been accused of stealing the body. But the best answer is that the women's evidence was unnecessary: within days it was common knowledge in Jerusalem that the tomb was empty.[48] No one needed persuasion of *that* fact. The real bombshell was the claim by the Apostles that they had seen the

---

* According to Morison, the women's terror could best be explained by the surprising presence in the empty tomb, *when they first arrived*, of a young man dressed in a white robe (see Mark 16:5–7). This young man must have decided to visit the tomb when he heard the guards' news that the body was missing. Morison suggested that he was the same unidentified young man present in the Garden of Gethsemane on the preceding Thursday night, when Jesus was arrested. On that occasion the young man 'was wearing nothing but a 'linen garment' (Mark 14:51–2).

risen Jesus. It was only when the Gospels came to be written a generation later that the full story was recorded for posterity, including the women's early-morning visit to the tomb.

These aspects of the story ring true and in any case seem most unlikely have been invented, given the lowly status of women in first-century Palestine. In Jewish legal proceedings of the time, a woman's evidence carried little or no weight. One is driven to conclude that this was simply the way it really happened.[49]

A third point of detail, exquisitely telling, is to be found near the end of John's Gospel – the account of John and Peter's visit to the tomb.[50] It is necessary to understand that, before being interred, Jesus's corpse was wrapped in strips of linen. The strips were impregnated with a copious mixture of myrrh and aloes; myrrh was used to ensure that the strips adhered closely to the body and would be difficult to remove. 'This was in accordance with Jewish burial customs' (John 19:39–40).

Crucially, on Easter Sunday, the body was gone but the strips of linen were still there. *And they were lying intact.* Moreover – the cherry on the cake – the cloth which had been wrapped around Jesus's head was '*folded* up by itself, separate from the linen' (John 20:6–7). There was, it seems, a gap between the linen and the headcloth, in the very place where the bare neck of Jesus had previously been resting.[51]

As soon as he took in this scene, John 'believed'. He must have reasoned instantly that the body had not been removed by human hands. In those circumstances, the whole mummy would have been missing, and the tomb in a state of disorder and disarray. Would thieves have risked capture by lingering at the scene? Would they – *could* they – have unwound all of the heavy linen strips, extracted the corpse, and then carefully rewound the linen strips to restore them to their original state? Would they have unwound and neatly refolded the head-cloth? Even if thieves had stolen the body alone, the linen strips and the headcloth must surely have have been left strewn about.

Read this passage in John and dwell upon it. It is 'powerfully understated'.[52] If these details were concocted for effect, then the author was a genius and a fiend. It reads to me like John's candid recollection, related as an old man, of the staggering moment when he first believed. The impression he got was that the body of Jesus 'had simply withdrawn itself'[53]. Everything else in the tomb was undisturbed.

Three vital matters

These are all important pieces of the puzzle. However, there are three more basal considerations that override the others. They have the virtue of simplicity.

The conduct of the Apostles

On any view of the relevant events, *something changed the Disciples*. Something caused them – with the essential aid of St Paul and St James – to create the Christian Church. This was an extraordinary achievement given their small numbers, their modest station in life, the hostile opposition of the all-powerful Roman Empire and the Jewish authorities, and their own patchy track record of devotion to the cause prior to Jesus's death. The last point seems to me highly significant, if not as often stressed. During Jesus's life, the Disciples had revealed themselves a somewhat unimpressive and unreliable group: Judas a traitor, the rest variously mistrustful, flighty or slow on the uptake. Within hours of Jesus's arrest even Peter three times denied any connection with his admired friend and leader, because he feared for his own safety – an episode, incidentally, which was most unlikely to have been invented by the early Christians. Like several others reported in the Gospels and Acts, it told badly against one of their leaders.

After the Crucifixion, the Disciples dispersed. Yet within weeks these same hitherto rather ordinary men emerged from hiding, gave up their occupations, and spent the rest of their lives proclaiming what was, on the face of it, an outlandish story. Relatives of Jesus were likewise transformed. James, one of Jesus's brothers, became a leader of the early Church. Yet James and other members of the family had evidently been highly sceptical of Jesus during His lifetime, at one stage declaring that He was 'out of his mind' (Mark 3:2; see also John 7:5). Jesus lamented that he was a prophet without honour 'among his relatives and in his own house' (Mark 6:4).[54]

It was this motley bunch that established one of the world's greatest religions – in my opinion, *the* greatest. No motive of personal gain can begin to explain their conduct. They had no prospect of achieving political or military power. All of them took on a life of strenuous labour and personal danger, travelling the Mediterranean diaspora and beyond. They frequently went hungry, or were persecuted, or beaten; and ultimately most of them were executed for their beliefs. To give the flavour: James was stoned to death, Paul was beheaded, and Peter (at least according to folklore) was crucified upside-down *at his own request*. Some of their lesser-known colleagues met even more grisly ends. Infamously, the Roman Emperor Nero arranged public spectacles at which Christians were torched alive, torn apart by wild beasts, or thrown (wrapped in animal skins) to packs of dogs.[55]

What motivated the Apostles? Frank Morison called this 'the historic crux of the problem'[56].

One possible answer – or part of the answer – is that they were reassured and emboldened by the happening of other miracles. The Apostles began their mission seven weeks after the Crucifixion, in Jerusalem, on the occasion of the Feast of Weeks. The urban metropolis of Jerusalem had not been a fertile recruiting ground for Jesus; his popularity, such as it was, was highest in the rural areas to the north, in Galilee. But the Feast of Weeks was a special occasion of remembrance, and the Apostles evidently sensed an opportunity. Jews from many nations had come to Jerusalem to celebrate the anniversary of the passing down of Moses' Law on Mount Sinai. According to Acts these visitors spoke many foreign languages, and to general astonishment the Apostles were able to preach to them *in those languages* (Acts 2:1–13). This experience must have had a profound effect on the Apostles themselves.

The account of the Apostles 'speaking in tongues' is frequently scoffed at by sceptics. But there is irrefutable evidence that speaking in tongues is a real-life phenomenon today in Pentecostal churches[57], just as it was in St Paul's day (see 1 Corinthians 14:1–40). As far as the events described in Acts 2 are concerned, to me they make more and more sense. Something must explain how the Apostles 'got their start' and how they overcame the practical problem of communicating their message to foreigners. The Apostles may not all have been the simple yokels of lore – in first-century Palestine, fishermen were fairly affluent merchants. It is likely that at least some of the Apostles were fairly well educated, and able to converse in Greek as well as Aramaic.[58] But that would not begin to explain the events described in Acts 2, and it does not seem a fully adequate explanation for the rapid spread of the Gospel.

Personally, I am inclined to agree with this reconstruction of what happened:

> The story does not appear to mean that the speakers of different languages were assembled and spoken to in separate groups, each in his own language, which *considering the habits of crowds seems highly unlikely. Silently the thoughts were received by the multitudes by super-sensory means; and when appearing in their own consciousness naturally did so in their own languages.[59]

So understood, St Luke's version of the relevant events in Acts 2 is logically satisfying, and yet seems too bizarre to have been invented. Later in Acts, there are reports of further miracles having been performed by the Apostles, under power granted them through the Holy Spirit. St Peter and St John cured a crippled beggar (Acts 3:1–10), and there were many other 'miraculous signs and wonders among the people' (Acts 5:12–16).

These events, too, help to explain the Apostles' zeal – they must have been astounded by their own feats. They knew, not only that Jesus had been resurrected, but that they themselves were now imbued with supernatural gifts. They could heal the sick and – perhaps even more miraculously – explain the Gospel with hitherto unglimpsed eloquence, fearlessness and insight.[60] This was exactly what Jesus had promised them at the Last Supper (see John 14:26).

But I suspect that some readers will not regard the evidence for these claims as sufficiently persuasive, and will object that invoking further miracles to establish the reality of the great miracle, the Resurrection, is not playing fair.

What, then, to return to my essential point, *originally* changed the Disciples, and members of Jesus's family? What was their primary motivation? Even John Spong has acknowledged that these questions demand an answer:

> Obviously something happened after the death of Jesus that had startling and enormous power … [I]t created a new holy day, the first day of the week, and in turn a new liturgical act, the breaking of bread, turning both into a weekly celebration of the presence of the living Lord in their midst. Easter was of such power that Jewish disciples taught from the time of their cradle that God alone was holy, that God alone was to be venerated, prayed to, and worshiped *now could no longer conceive of God without Jesus of Nazareth.*[61] (My emphasis)

There are those who contend that the 'something' which happened after the death of Jesus cannot have been his physical resurrection. Such things, in their worldview, simply do not happen – and therefore cannot have happened even in the case of Jesus. Bishop Spong's suggestion is that the Disciples had a 'life-changing inner experience'[62] as a result of reflecting upon Jesus's example and teachings for some six to twelve months after the Crucifixion[63]. According to Spong, they agonised about their betrayal of Jesus and eventually came to the realisation that his had been a life 'fully human', worthy of being equated with a theistic God.

Such 'realistic' suggestions just do not convince me. For the reasons I discussed in Chapter 5, it is necessary to keep an open mind about miracles. The question is: What explanation best fits the facts? Is it possible that *everything* written about the Resurrection in the Gospels, the Epistles, and Acts was intended to be understood figuratively?[64] I suppose it is barely possible, and I do not profess to be a biblical scholar. On the face of it, however, the proposal is self-contradictory. It requires you to accept that the testimony of the church fathers should be revered as to matters of *theology*, but discarded as to matters of *fact*.[65] In any event, it seems to me highly unlikely that any group of men and women – from any epoch – would subject themselves to the things the Apostles did merely as a result of having developed a collective guilty conscience about a fine man. If you read the relevant passages in the New Testament in their straightforward sense, there is a more plausible explanation, namely the one that the Apostles gave themselves.

In the words of Frank Morison:

> We cannot insist upon the strict reign of causality in the physical world, and deny it in the psychological. The phenomenon which here confronts us is one of the biggest dislodgements of events in the world's history, and it can only really be accounted for by an initial impact of colossal range and power.[66]

It is to be remembered that the very definition of an Apostle – the qualification for membership – was to have been an eyewitness (cf. Acts 1:22, 2:32; 1 Corinthians 1:9). The Apostles were emissaries or ambassadors[67], and the Resurrection was their key talking point, over and above anything else that Jesus said or did during His life. Furthermore, despite sceptics' arguments to the contrary, 'the Jews had no pre-existing expectation about a 'risen messiah' which might have inspired [such] claims'[68]. The reverse is true. In the words of C.S. Lewis, the Resurrection was an 'absolute novelty'[69]. And, significantly, the risen Jesus described by all eyewitnesses was neither a scarred and haggard cripple (as must have been the case if a mere man had somehow survived crucifixion by the Romans) nor a disembodied ghost. He was tangible, healthy and composed.

I conclude, then, that the Apostles should be taken at their word. They sincerely believed that they had seen, spoken with and even touched the risen Christ. They also sincerely believed that the purpose of Jesus's death and resurrection was to atone for Man's sins. That is the best explanation for their change of heart and for their subsequent conduct. It also explains why, virtually from the first, the Cross became the dominant symbol of their mission, and Communion their most distinctive ritual.[70] There is, however, a possible objection, apparently strong, even to these arguments. It leads me to the second of my three considerations.

Even if the Apostles were sincere, does that prove the truth of what they preached?

In my opinion, the Apostles' brave and tireless conduct proves beyond reasonable doubt that they believed the Resurrection really happened. The vast majority of professional New Testament historians concur in that view.[71] However, at least one sceptical objection remains open: the Apostles' conduct proves only the fact of their sincerity. It does not prove that what they believed was, in fact, true. After all, followers of other religions and creeds – Muslims are the obvious contemporary example – also have been willing to struggle and die for their beliefs. Presumably, they too were and are sincere, but that does not mean that all their beliefs are true either. Why should the Apostles' sincere belief in the Resurrection be regarded any differently?

There is a crucial difference between the Apostles' state of mind and that of even the most fanatical believer in Islam. The difference has been explained this way by the American philosopher and theologian, J.P. Moreland:

> Muslims might be willing to die for their belief that Allah revealed himself to Muhammad, but this revelation was not done in any publicly observable way. So they could be wrong about it. They may sincerely think it's true, but they can't know for a fact, because they didn't witness it themselves.[72]

It may here be interpolated – the same of course applies to almost all believers in the Resurrection of Jesus. You may sincerely believe in the reality of the Resurrection, but you cannot know it for a fact, because you were not there, at the empty tomb or on the occasion of any of His later appearances. But Moreland defines the key distinction in relation to the Apostles (the emphasis is mine):

> People will die for their religious beliefs if they sincerely believe they're true but people won't die for their religious beliefs *if they know their beliefs are false.*
>
> While most people can only have *faith* that their beliefs are true, the disciples were in a position to *know* without a doubt whether or not Jesus had risen from the dead. They claimed that they saw him, talked with him, and ate with him. If they weren't absolutely certain, they wouldn't have allowed themselves to be tortured to death for proclaiming that the Resurrection had happened.[73]

In short, people will not die for a lie. In this connection, it is important to note that none of the early Christians ever confessed to knowing involvement in a conspiracy. Some cracked under torture, denied Christ and worshipped Caesar, but there is no suggestion of admitted fraud anywhere in the historical record.[74]

Mass hallucination has been proposed occasionally, but the idea is ridiculous.[75] So too is any suggestion that the Apostles were labouring under some kind of innocent mistake. In the sardonic words of the great American jurist Simon Greenleaf: 'If it were morally possible for them to have been deceived in this matter, every human motive operated to lead them to discover and avow their error'.[76]

St Paul wrote contemporaneously to the Corinthians on this theme. He seemed to perceive that many people would doubt his motives; that his own words and conduct would not be taken at face value. In the course of urging people to listen to him and the other Apostles rather than those who preached a more 'conventional' message about Jesus, he wrote passionately about his own unique credentials. He reminded people that he had endured prison, floggings, beatings, a stoning, shipwrecks, banditry, sleeplessness, hunger, thirst, cold, exhaustion and near-constant anxiety. The point of doing so was not to boast, but to try to convince people he was sincere: 'I repeat: Let no-one take me for a fool … If I must boast, I will boast of the things that show my weakness. The God and Father of the Lord Jesus … *knows that I am not lying*' (2 Corinthians 11:16–31 My emphasis).

Could St Paul have been lying when he wrote those words? I do not believe so. He had laboured and suffered a great deal, and was attempting to explain why. When he was accused of being 'out of [his] mind' by the Roman governor Festus, for claiming that Jesus 'rose from the dead', he stood his ground gamely. The other Apostles were in a similar situation, and no doubt they responded to any questioning of their motives or their sanity with the same earnest indignation. They were all begging to be taken seriously.

But there is a third consideration, perhaps the most compelling of all.

The Apostles succeeded

The Apostles' message did not fall on deaf ears. They did not die as heroic but failed martyrs; they succeeded, overcoming all the barriers that stood in their way. Starting in Jerusalem, they managed to convert a substantial number of contemporary Jews to the new Christian faith. How was that possible?

Judaism was, and still is, an enormously durable religion. Since the Exodus from Egypt around 1300 BC, the Jewish people had suffered terrible persecution from the Babylonians, the Assyrians, the Persians, the Greeks and the Romans. The nadir was the sacking of Jerusalem by the Babylonians in 587 BC, when their sacred Temple was destroyed. Yet Judaism survived. At the time of Jesus's birth it had just survived the reign of Herod (37 BC to 4 BC), an amoral tyrant installed as king of Judea by the occupying Roman powers. Herod had presided over a period of considerable economic affluence, but he left behind him a corrupt Church hierarchy, largely controlled by the aristocratic and ultra-wealthy Sadducees. Up until the sacking of Jerusalem in AD 70, the Sadducees successfully collaborated with the Romans to maintain their own economic power and political influence. The effect of these developments was to energise the 'threatened remnant' of *genuine* religious Judaism – the highly-observant Pharisees, and the radical Zealots. During the later half of the first century these groups were 'fighting a spiritual battle against … paganism'.[77]

Placed in this context, the achievement of the Apostles seems all the more remarkable. They were up against highly motivated opposition, secular and religious. As far as practising Jews were concerned, the Apostles had to persuade them not only about the reality of the Resurrection as a physical event; they also had to persuade them that certain key aspects of orthodox Judaism were superfluous or wrong – that animal sacrifice was unnecessary, that ritual (rather than sincere) adherence to Moses' laws was inadequate, that Sunday rather than Saturday was the Sabbath, that Jesus was divine but that his purpose in coming to Earth was not as a political conqueror on behalf of the Jews. Most radically of all, they had to persuade devout Jews that Jesus should be worshipped 'in ways historically reserved for the Creator himself'[78].

These were all challenges to long-held and fundamental customs and beliefs – to a way of life – with which most practising Jews were content. The Apostles were not trying to galvanise an already disaffected populace, like the leaders of the Reformation. They did not offer any material inducements – quite the opposite. Nor were they spreading their creed by the use of force, like the founders of Islam (and, it must be conceded, many post-Constantine Christian rulers[79]). The Apostles relied on words alone, not coercion. The safer and apparently saner option would have been to ignore them.

Despite the monumental nature of the task they faced, the Apostles still won over many converts among the Jews, beginning in Jerusalem within seven weeks of the Crucifixion. The converts themselves, like the Apostles, faced the prospect of persecution from the Romans as well as ostracism or worse from their fellow Jews. Yet the faith spread steadily. None of this can credibly be squared with normal human behaviour, unless the message that was preached was extraordinary and compelling. More than that, I believe it was essential that at least a modest number of Jews, other than the Apostles themselves, had also to have seen the risen Jesus – including people previously unimpressed by, or opposed to, His teachings. Those people (the 500 or so mentioned by St Paul) were thus able to persuade at least their own close relatives and friends, who in turn must have spoken to others – and so on.

It is also to be emphasised that these eyewitnesses, like the Apostles, *realised the significance of what they had seen*. Another telling point for me is that Jesus appeared after the Crucifixion in and around the geographical areas where people had heard him preach and/or had been aware of his public execution. A number of common people in that vicinity had already been beneficiaries of the miracles, or had witnessed them. In short, a legend was not invented out of nothing. In the words of Ken Handley, a former judge of the New South Wales Court of Appeal and a thoughtful Christian author, the Resurrection story 'was not something that emerged at a time and place remote from the scene of the events'[80].

The success of Christianity in its early decades is proof of its truth – in particular, the truth of the Resurrection, which was the Apostles' main talking point. If the Apostles had been phonies, or deluded crazies, it is hard to imagine how they would have got anywhere. Yet it is estimated that by AD 100, when the last of the original church fathers died, there were some 50,000 Christians across the Roman Empire – Jews and

Gentiles among them.[81] Today, the number of Christians stands in the billions, and it is no exaggeration to say that 'measured by His effect on history, Jesus is the most influential life ever lived on this planet'[82].

In retrospect, one appreciates the wisdom and the prescience of the advice given by Gamaliel, a much-respected Pharisee, to the Sanhedrin. He persuaded the full assembly of the elders of Israel not to execute the Apostles, by reminding them of the failure of two previous uprisings once its leader had died:

> Men of Israel, consider carefully what you intend to do with these men. Some time ago Theudas appeared, claiming to be somebody, and about four hundred men rallied to him. He was killed, all his followers dispersed, and it all came to nothing. After him, Judas the Galilean appeared in the days of the Census and led a band of people in revolt. He too was killed and all his followers were scattered …

Having laid out these recent histories (or precedents, as I like as a lawyer to think of them), Gamaliel continued as regards the Apostles:

> Therefore in the present case I advise you: Leave these men alone! Let them go! *For if their purpose is of human origin, it will fail.* But if it is from God, you will not be able to stop these men; you will only find yourselves fighting against God.
>
> (Acts 5:35–39. My emphasis)

After Gamiliel's plea, the Apostles' lives were spared. (Their punishment on this occasion was 'merely' a severe flogging, and yet they rejoiced in it, because they believed themselves to have been counted worthy of suffering disgrace for Christ.) They continued their mission, and they did not fail. Ultimately, nothing could stop them. If Gamaliel's reasoning and precedents were sound, then this tends to suggest that their purpose was not of human origin. Their message was 'from God'.

A personal religious experience

At this stage, I will record an entirely personal experience. Make of it what you will. I have said earlier in this book that my own faith has developed fitfully – almost imperceptibly – over a period of some years. In that sense, I did not enjoy a sudden conversion, like that described by St Paul and countless others. However, I do recall one special moment, quite unexpected, when I suddenly became overwhelmed by the feeling that Jesus's love was – there and then – coursing through me, and healing me. (This was also the moment that led me to appreciate the unique and special place of music in God's Creation, an issue I have already discussed.)

It was on Good Friday 2003. In the morning I went to church alone, dispirited and troubled. The previous few days at work had been especially stressful and trying. The problems seemed intractable. There were other black thoughts, personal and emotional, flickering around in my head. Without realising it at the time, I was chronically exhausted, and probably already sinking into a state of clinical depression, though the condition was not to be diagnosed until the following year. I did not especially want to be in church. The congregation was small, and most of the people (though familiar friends) were much older than me. The early phases of the service did not stir me – and I recall thinking, guiltily, that this was supposed to be one of the most important days of the Christian year. Then, the Minister asked us to stand for a hymn – a hymn not then familiar to me, though I may have sung it once or twice before. The organ music began, and we started to sing:

We sing the praise of Him who died,
of Him who died upon the cross;
the sinner's hope let men deride:
for this we count the world but loss.

Inscribed upon the cross we see
in shining letters: 'God is Love'
He bears our sins upon the tree
He brings us mercy from above.

The cross – it takes our guilt away,
It holds the fainting spirit up;
it cheers with hope the gloomy day
and sweetens every bitter cup.

It makes the coward spirit brave
and nerves the feeble arm for fight;
it takes the terror from the grave
and gilds the bed of death with light.

The balm of life, the cure of woe,
the measure and the pledge of love;
the sinner's refuge here below,
the angel's theme in heaven above.[83]

The words that I have italicised in the third stanza indicate the point at which I began to cry. I had rarely cried since childhood; and I have not cried since. These were tears not of grief or sorrow or sentimentality, or even of happiness, but somehow of exquisite relief. My throat ached and tears streamed down my face. It might be said that this was simply my body's (or my psyche's) way of responding to beautiful music (William Gardner's 'Sacred Melody') or of releasing stress. Perhaps these were factors, but such prosaic explanations do not satisfactorily explain the intensity of the experience. Nor do they explain the timing of it, or the spiritual aspect of it. The tears were accompanied by a sudden sense of revelation. It was a revelation that I now understood more fully the significance of Jesus Christ's life and death and the meaning of the Resurrection: not just as the best and most accessible demonstration of the power of God – another reason, intellectually, to accept His existence – but as a *living force* capable in the here and now of providing consolation. For the first time in my life, I *felt* truly 'in Christ'. I knew exactly what Jesus meant when He gently urged, 'Come unto Me, all ye that labour and are heavy laden, and I will give you rest' (Matthew 11:28–9; KJV). At that moment, the Cross became a symbol with genuine meaning.

My experience was not, of course, in any sense unique. Throughout history, millions of people of all faiths have reported similar experiences, including many that were much more bizarre – and much more consequential – than mine.[84] Why is it that so many people relate such experiences, if not because they really happened – and really mean something? St Paul's conversion on the road to Damascus changed the world. So did Muhammad's revelation at Mount Hira.[85] As Herbert Butterfield pointed out:

> The phenomenon of religious experience is a thing which appears with indubitable power in history; and the question is: do the people who claim to possess this experience interpret it properly when they describe it as spiritual, or are they to be regarded as being under some illusion concerning their character?[86]

As we saw in Chapter 4, there are atheists like Richard Dawkins who insist that these experiences *are* illusions, like all things supposedly supernatural. Personally I am unconvinced by their theories, which seem to me to overemphasise the role of the material in life and to underplay if not deny entirely the role of the spiritual. I do not think it is safe to dismiss this realm of human experience so superciliously; rather, like Butterfield, 'I cannot tell what limits to set to the vision which is open to the spiritual mind in a state of exaltation'[87]. Moreover, I am inclined to believe that the sheer number of such experiences must count for something. Collectively they may properly be regarded as another pointer to the existence of God.

My own experience would seem to point in a more specific direction, to the reality of the Resurrection. Cynics may scoff, but that is how I feel. And I am not alone, even among those from what may loosely be termed the Christian Left. Commenting on 'the liberal/evangelical debate about the resurrection', in which liberals often question whether it is in order for them to believe in the Resurrection metaphorically, the American preacher/activist Jim Wallis has observed:

> [T]hat debate is often a mostly intellectual one, with heady arguments flying back and forth, and usually ends up quite unresolved. Their [i.e. the liberals'] sincere question prompted a different response in me. I simply asked a question back: 'In the heat of South Africa's oppression and the heart of apartheid's despair, do you think that a merely metaphorical resurrection would have been enough for Archbishop Desmond Tutu? It wouldn't have been for me.' Mere intellectual debates aren't enough when it comes to faith. It is what we face in our real lives and in the real world that has the most capacity to deepen our faith.[88]

Wallis nominates Desmond Tutu as an example of a courageous, non-violent Christian who believed in the Resurrection as a supernatural event. So he was, but there have been a great many others throughout history. What of Vibia Perpetua of Carthage, and her slave-girl Felicity, who, in AD 203, were arrested, incarcerated, and sent to ghastly deaths in the arena? Both of them were young mothers who had recently given birth. Perpetua's contemporaneous diary (a *real* historical document, let it be noted) reveals a patently sane woman of astonishing strength, humility and faith. All of the Christian martyrs, and there were thousands, proclaimed the crucified, risen Jesus as both their example and the source of their bravery.[89]

A mere metaphorical explanation of the Resurrection was surely not enough for the Christian martyrs, and it is not enough for me. I believe that the Apostles were affected by a real-life experience, as I was on Good Friday 2003.

The Resurrection: further conclusions

My conclusion that the Resurrection did in fact take place has led me, inexorably, to other conclusions.

The first is this. Although personally I believe in the Resurrection as a real historical event that took place in space and time, it is not, and never will be, susceptible to definitive proof. Moreover, God is content for things to be that way. Only the people privileged to have been eyewitnesses to those astounding events experienced the Resurrection as a matter of knowledge. The rest of humanity must take it on (reasoned) faith. We rely on the circumstantial evidence that I have attempted to summarise as, in the words of Paul Althaus, 'historical "signs" behind which lies the mystery of the resurrection'[90].

There is a second conclusion to which I have come. If you accept that the story of the Resurrection – the central plank of Christian theology – is true or even possibly true, then all other aspects of the Christian religion must deserve the most careful and sombre appraisal. Everything reportedly said and done by Jesus must be considered with an open mind. The reality of the miracles, if previously unbelievable in isolation, needs to be reassessed. Personally, I have become more open to believing in the Virgin Birth, and other miraculous aspects of the Nativity story, as well as the Transfiguration and the Ascension. There are sound theological reasons for accepting these events as literally true[91], and, in the case of the Ascension, a practical reason as well: how else to account for the disappearance of the risen Jesus's physical body?[92] (Puzzles remain, of course. The reason I am still undecided about the Virgin Birth is that there are references elsewhere in the Gospels to Jesus's family having doubted Him during His lifetime, behaviour which is very hard to reconcile with Mary and Joseph's certain knowledge of His true nature.[93])

The prophecies of the Old Testament must be scrutinised again. I would not go as far as saying that 'the chief proof of the divine origin of Christianity [lies] in its fulfilment of the prophetic Scriptures'[94]. However, this unfashionable issue needs to be considered carefully. Jesus seems to have understood that He was 'fulfilling' all Scripture (Matthew 5:17; Luke 24:27). The arch-agnostic Bertrand Russell nominated fulfilled prophecy – of a highly specific kind – as the kind of evidence which could convince him of God's existence.[95] Evidently none of the Biblical prophecies fitted Russell's criteria, but for many people they are persuasive. In my view this attitude is not unreasonable, especially if Old Testament prophecies are correctly to be regarded not 'as mere predictions but as anticipations'[96]. The position is deeply intriguing. For if you accept that the Resurrection occurred, it is hard to escape the further conclusion that the prophets correctly foretold (centuries in advance) at least the basic facets of that seminal event. Old Testament passages such as Chapter 53 of Isaiah, and the Twenty-second Psalm, assume a heightened significance. There are over 300 references in the Old Testament to the future coming of Christ, some striking in their similarity to the events described in the New Testament.[97]

The Old Testament prophecies could not themselves have been invented after Jesus's death: they had been 'in print' for centuries before then, a fact confirmed in 1947 by the discovery of the Dead Sea Scrolls near the ruins of the desert city of Qumran. Among some 800 separate documents written between 200 BC and AD 50 was a copy of the Book of Isaiah pre-dating Christ by some 150 years![98] This find was enormously important. Before 1947, the oldest complete copy of Isaiah was the so-called Masoretic Text of AD 916. Incredibly, despite being over a thousand years older, the words appearing on the Isaiah scroll are virtually identical to those in the Masoretic Text – including the prophecies about the Resurrection in Chapter 53.[99]

Retrospective concoction of the Old Testament prophecies can therefore be ruled out. However, another possibility remains intriguingly open. Unlike some Christians[100], I am not offended by this idea. Jesus Himself may have consciously done certain things which were prophesised in the Hebrew Scriptures, in order to strengthen the case for His own divinity. His entry into Jerusalem during Passover week AD 30 while riding on a donkey, an event recorded in all four Gospels, would appear to have been in this category. It reflected a famous prophecy of Zechariah.[101]

There is another, more sordid, possibility which must be considered. Could the story of Jesus have been wholly or mainly invented by the authors of the New Testament, in order that the Old Testament prophecies should be 'fulfilled'? This is another common argument, but it appears to me to be full of holes. It may be conceded that the New Testament authors assumed detailed knowledge of the ancient Jewish scriptures on the part of their readers, and that they sought to link their new teaching 'demonstrably with God's earlier work in the world'.[102] Some of the incidental details in the Gospels may thus have been added by their authors to heighten the connection between the prophecies and the events that had happened. It is also conceivable that the Gospel authors wished to shift responsibility for Jesus's death from the Romans to the Jews, to appease the Roman occupiers.[103] But is it conceivable that *all* or even *most* of the essential facts about Jesus's life and death were concocted, in order to play some kind of elaborate theological confidence trick? If so, Christianity is the product of the strangest and most successful conspiracy in human history, a conspiracy originally hatched by people lacking any of the usual motives (greed, fear, lust for power) and employing none of the usual methods (secrecy, bribery, violence).

There are two other flaws in this argument. First, at least some of the key events recorded in the New Testament which closely mirror Old Testament prophecies – such as Jesus's entry into Jerusalem on a donkey – are accepted by most scholars as being near to historical certainties. Simply, they happened. Second, and even more fundamentally, it is an undoubted fact that first-century Jewish authors really *did*, from time to time, 'invent unhistorical narratives inspired by Old Testament texts'[104]. But when this was done, the unhistorical narratives were tailored exactly to passages from Hebrew Scripture. The authors of the Gospels almost always did the reverse. It is the *Old Testament* references which were frequently reworded or reapplied.

As Craig L. Blomberg observes, this 'make[s] it much more likely that the Gospel writers were trying to show how the Old Testament fitted the events of Jesus' life and not the other way around'.[105] To a degree, this may 'devalue' some of the Old Testament prophecies *as prophecies* (i.e. their accuracy and specificity when compared to the events which happened). But it substantially strengthens the conclusion that the first-century events against which they were being 'compared' must really have happened – including the Resurrection. Just by undertaking the exercise of seeking parallels for them in the Old Testament prophecies, the Gospel authors *indirectly* attested to those events having happened. Otherwise, why would they have bothered? An analogy may help. If a town is flattened by a once-in-a-century tornado, the local meteorologist will very likely go back and scrutinise his weather forecasts of the preceding days. Did he 'get it right'? If, a week earlier, he had forecast 'strong winds' for the day in question, it would be debateable whether that constituted a proper 'prediction'. But no one would question the occurrence of the tornado.

The 'conspiracy' hypothesis is so unlikely that it can be eliminated. So we are left with the evidence of the Old Testament, and there emerges further corroboration of the Gospels – 'we have the word of the prophets made more certain' (2 Peter 1:19).

And the Old Testament prophecies do not stand alone. Also deserving of the most serious study are the predictions recorded in the Gospels as having been made by Jesus Himself – of His betrayal by Judas, of the future work of the Apostles, and (centrally) of His death and resurrection. St Matthew's Gospel says this:

> From that time on [i.e. after Peter's confession of faith] Jesus began to explain to his disciples that he must go to Jerusalem and suffer many things at the hands of the elders, chief priests and teachers of the law, and that he must be killed and on the third day be raised to life.
>
> (Matthew 16:21. See also Matthew 26:60–63; Mark 8:31–32; Mark 10:32–34; Mark 14:57–59; Luke 9:22–27; Luke 18:31–34; John 12:31–33.)

The traditional Christian claim is that these prophecies constitute further proof of Jesus's divinity, and of the reality of the Resurrection.[106] Witnesses heard Jesus describe, in advance, what was going to happen to Him – not only His death, but the events leading up to it, including His trial. Moreover, and this is vital, Jesus used language that was understandable only *after the event*; at the time, '[t]he disciples did not understand any of this. Its meaning was hidden from them, and they did not know what he was talking about' (Luke 19:34).

Sceptics argue that Jesus's prophecies must have been invented after His death by the early Christians and/or the authors of the Gospels. There is an intricate analysis of these and associated issues in Frank Morison's *Who Moved the Stone?* One of Morison's most thought-provoking arguments concerns Jesus's famous prophecy that He would be raised to life 'on the third day'. The Gospels record that the charge initially brought against Jesus at the preliminary trial before the chief priests was of a rather bizarre nature. He was alleged to have declared publicly an intention to 'destroy the temple' and to 'rebuild it within three days', or words to that effect (Mark 14:58, Matthew 26:61; see also John 2:19–21, Acts 6:13–4). The Jews understood this as a threat somehow to tear down and then reconstruct the sacred Temple building in Jerusalem – which would have been a heinous act. However, this charge failed before the chief priests because the two witnesses could not agree on precisely what Jesus said.

Now, Morison's key point was this. If the charge had been wholly invented as part of a plot, the witnesses would have got their stories straight; the fact that the charge was made by people *hostile* to Jesus, and that all three Gospel accounts include the singular expression 'in three days', is inverse proof that the witnesses based their testimony on words that Jesus had actually said. 'It would have been a strange coincidence indeed if the one sentence chosen by the enemies of Christ upon which to base the most deadly charge … found no counterpart or parallel whatever in all the varied teaching of the two preceding years'.[107] It seems certain, then, that Jesus said *something* along the general lines alleged. But what message was He trying to convey?

The Jews' assumption that His words amounted to a threat directed at the Temple building was understandable enough, because there is plenty of evidence that Jesus disapproved strongly of the commercial activities carried on there. His highly provocative action of overturning the moneychangers' tables during Passover week AD 30 is regarded by most contemporary scholars as 'the immediate cause of his demise'[108]. It is also possible that Jesus was alluding, prophet-like, to the Romans' destruction of the Temple building some forty years later in AD 70.[109] But neither of these interpretations is wholly satisfying. Morison's view, with which I agree, is that the author of John's Gospel 'got it right'. Only after Jesus's death did it become apparent that, by those strange words, Jesus had been referring to His own body (John 2:18–22).

There is a saying that the thirteenth stroke of a clock must cast doubt upon the whole device, and everything that has come before. The Resurrection is – in reverse – like the thirteenth stroke of a clock. If it really happened, then everything else in the Bible deserves to be considered in a different light: not automatically accepted as literally true, but treated with open-minded seriousness.

This seems to have been the way that the Resurrection affected the Apostles. They worked backwards from the primary fact they knew to be true (that they had seen Jesus alive after he had been crucified) and reinterpreted everything else in their experience accordingly. In that respect, I agree with the Protestant theologian Martin Kahler that the Gospels may be regarded as 'stories of the Passion with a detailed introduction'[110].

In my own case, belief in the reality of the Resurrection came after, rather than before, belief in God. I came initially to an emergent belief in God as the Creator of the physical Universe. It may be, however, that there are other people who will find it easier first to believe in the Resurrection – or at least to accept that, on the historical evidence, it constitutes an extremely curious mystery. Anyone of that mind should set their thinking beyond the Resurrection alone and also toward some of the other issues discussed in this book. You may find that, having cleared one hurdle, it is easier to attempt to clear others.

Here is one example of what I mean. Jesus taught that God directs all natural processes – He '[feeds] the birds of the air' and He 'clothes the grass of the field' (Matthew 6:26, 30). If you now believe, or suspect, that Jesus really was raised from the dead – that Jesus was God – why not go back to Chapter 1 and reconsider the arguments about Creation? For if Jesus's word now seems to you more trustworthy, you may find it easier to accept that the author of the book of Genesis was not 'childishly describing the waving of a magician's wand'. Rather, he was introducing us to 'the deepest mystery of religious principles'[111]. In effect, Jesus told us that God directed the formation of the stars and the process of Darwinian evolution, and that He is still doing so today.

PART THREE

ANSWERS TO SOME COMMON OBJECTIONS

CHAPTER 7

SUFFERING

My God, my God, why have you forsaken me?

Matthew 27:46

Sweet are the uses of adversity.

William Shakespeare, *As You Like It*

The prevalence of suffering in the world – especially suffering by the innocent – may be the most understandable reason to deny the existence of a loving God. Any God, so the argument goes, must be malevolent, or at best indifferent; thus it is preferable to believe that there is no God at all.

Many sincere people think this way. Even so, after careful thought, I am convinced they are mistaken. The existence of suffering can be reconciled with the existence of a loving God. More than that, suffering is an integral aspect of God's Creation.

At the outset of this discussion on suffering, it is only fair to make a blunt acknowledgment. In my own life, I have not experienced suffering of anything like the intensity that other people over the ages have endured, and that many still endure today. As an Australian born in 1963, to devoted parents blessed with affluence, I have enjoyed a most fortunate life. War, famine, disease, bereavement, homelessness: these and other horrors have thus far not touched me closely, or at all. It may therefore be objected that I have no real authority to speak on this issue.

Yet I am not deterred from embarking upon it, and for a number of reasons.

First, the existence of suffering is just too big an issue for anyone to ignore. The American science writer and thinker, John Horgan, has gone as far as to say that 'there is only one theological question that really matters: If there is a God, why has he created a world with so much suffering?'[1] This is not the only important question, but it is certainly one that any believer or inquisitive non-believer must confront – whatever his or her own personal circumstances. Indeed, it behoves the more fortunate to consider the issue the more carefully. As Jesus warned, 'From everyone who has been given much, much will be demanded; and from one who has been entrusted with much, much more will be asked' (Luke 12:48).

Second, I believe that I am 'qualified' to talk about suffering. Although I have lived a most fortunate life, I have still experienced suffering. No doubt it has not been as severe as that endured by many other people, but it has been suffering nonetheless – the same in kind, if not the same in degree or duration. The period of most intense suffering has, indeed, coincided with my emergent belief in Christianity, and with the writing of this book.

Third, and most importantly, I have reached the conclusion that, far from casting doubt on the existence of God or the doctrines of Christianity, the phenomena of suffering – and its by-product, grace – are among the strongest pointers to the truth. Suffering is not something that a Christian need shy away from or merely explain away. It should be a central plank in your argument.

Atheism arising from repugnance at suffering in the world is understandable, but illogical. C.S. Lewis explained why by tying the issue back to conscience. Anyone who feels about suffering a sense of outrage, or something akin to it, is really saying that much in the world offends his or her notion of justice. But to believe in justice necessarily involves acceptance of an ideal of right and wrong – an absolute standard against which events and human conduct are to be judged. The existence of that standard is of itself suggestive of the existence of God as the setter and enforcer of that standard, and as the Creator of each of our consciences.[2] The current Archbishop of Canterbury, Dr Rowan Williams, has made the same point. In his words, if you are an unbeliever who regularly challenges suffering and injustice, 'you have more faith than you think you have … [b]ecause actually you want to believe in a just world, and that is the first movement of faith, the belief that what we do on this earth is not insignificant.'[3]

To put the matter more bluntly still: In an atheist's world, why does evil matter? Why does the fate of human beings matter any more than the dinosaurs' 'pointless bellowing rivalr[ies] across primeval swamps'?[4] The atheist's indignant complaints about evil are hollow. Indeed, the existence and incidence of evil is 'at least as big a problem for nonbelief in God as for belief'[5]. James Franklin, Associate Professor of Mathematics and Statistics at the University of New South Wales, and an incisive writer on theology, has explained why:

> Ordinarily one thinks that the suffering of a human is a tragedy but the explosion of a dead galaxy is just a firework. Materialism, though, denies the distinction between the two, since it takes humans to be the same kind of things as galaxies, namely, moderately complicated heaps of matter. If the fate of a galaxy cannot give rise to a problem of evil, because its fate cannot in any absolute sense matter, then neither can the fate of a brain. In posing the problem of evil, a materialist who does not really believe in positive worth is cynically trading on our sense of the importance of those who suffer, *knowing he will undermine it later.*[6] (My emphasis)

If there is meaning to life, it must be derived from something more than matter. Eventually the Earth itself 'will be no more than a whiff of smoke drifting in desolate skies'. It follows that people 'who rest their ultimate beliefs in [human] progress are climbing a ladder which may be as vertical as they claim it to be, but which in reality is resting on nothing at all'[7]. Such people may not realise it, but logically their arguments lead to the conclusion that suffering is meaningless.

These arguments are, I now think, compelling. But I did not arrive at my own views about suffering as a result of theological or other academic reading. Of all the subjects canvassed in this book, suffering is the one that lends itself the least to theoretical analysis. Speaking for myself, it was necessary to experience sustained *personal* suffering – and then to reflect upon that experience – before biblical and other teachings on the subject made much of an impact. This, I have since learned, is a very 'Jewish' idea: 'the Hebrew way of understanding suggests that we really don't know the truth until it has affected our lives in some way'[8]. The Old Testament books of Job and Ecclesiastes now seem to me hauntingly perceptive; but that realisation was many years in coming.

Anyone who has lived a relatively happy, carefree life may find it difficult to empathise with some of the forthcoming discussion. And because this chapter is predominantly personal and emotional, rather than intellectual, it may seem to the reader somewhat more 'homespun' than most of the others. I am afraid that is unavoidable. I am honestly trying to explain the reasons for my own hope.

That said, I will attempt to make an argument 'for' suffering – and God – that is based on reason. My central thesis is that, in a number of ways, suffering is a fundamental and unavoidable feature of Man's Universe. Suffering is not – as the Gnostics believed – a colossal mistake flowing from the original divine 'error' of Creation.[9] It is a key part of God's deep-laid scheme.

Suffering begets wisdom

I will begin by relating a favourite historical anecdote.[10]

On 4 April 1968, Robert F. Kennedy was campaigning for the Democratic Party's nomination for President of the United States. Kennedy was in Indianapolis when he learned that, a few hours earlier, Martin Luther King had been murdered. It was evening, and Kennedy was scheduled to give a campaign speech a little later that night in a black ghetto. In 1968, civil rights, along with Vietnam, were among the most highly emotive issues. It was the year of George Wallace, the populist Governor of Alabama, who ran in the Democratic primaries (and, later in the year, as a third-party candidate for President) on an unashamedly racist platform. Richard Nixon was elected President in November that year, and early in his first term he began to employ his own less blatant rhetoric – a cunning appeal to the 'Silent Majority'. This was the phrase that marked the birth of modern 'dog-whistle' politics.

Kennedy was advised by Indianapolis police not to appear at the rally; riots were feared. But Kennedy insisted on going there, and without a police escort. He discarded his prepared speech, and spoke off the cuff. Many in the crowd of some 2,000 people, gathered in the open air, had not yet heard the news of King's death. Kennedy told them the awful news at the beginning of his speech. There were cries of anguish, but there was no riot.

Kennedy spoke, in his distinctive Yankee voice, both masculine and empathetic. The sound recording of the speech, which I have listened to many times, is much more evocative than words on a page. But the words themselves are great. Here is a selected portion of them:

Martin Luther King dedicated his life to love and to justice for his fellow human beings, and he died because of that effort.

In this difficult day, in this difficult time for the United States, it is perhaps well to ask what kind of a nation we are and what direction we want to move in. For those of you who are black – considering the evidence there evidently is that there were white people that were responsible – you can be filled with bitterness, with hatred, and a desire for revenge. We can move in that direction as a country, with great polarisation – black people among black, white people among white, filled with hatred toward one another.

Or we can make an effort, as Martin Luther King did, to understand and to comprehend, and to replace that violence, that stain of bloodshed that has spread across our land, with an effort to understand with compassion and love.

For those of you who are black and are tempted to be filled with hatred and distrust at the injustice of such an act, against all white people, I can only say that I feel in my own heart the same kind of feeling. I had a member of my own family killed, but he was killed by a white man. But we have to make an effort in the United States, we have to make an effort to understand, to go beyond these rather difficult times.

My favourite poet was Aeschylus. He wrote: 'In our sleep, pain which cannot forget falls drop by drop upon the heart until, in our own despair, against our will, comes wisdom through the awful grace of God.'

A little later, Kennedy concluded with these words:

Let us dedicate ourselves to what the Greeks wrote so many years ago: To tame the savageness of man and to make gentle the life of this world. Let us dedicate ourselves to that, and say a prayer for our country and for our people.

Kennedy's fundamental point was the same one made by Aeschylus, writing in the fifth century before Christ. It is only through suffering that Man *learns*. There are many, many dangers in the world, and suffering is the mechanism through which each of us is gradually taught how to recognise and cope with those dangers. The human body's capacity to perceive pain is essential to survival – because pain alerts us to internal and external physical dangers, such as disease or infection, fire or violent force. The rare medical condition of congenital insensivity to pain and anhydrosis (CIPA) is almost always fatal by the age of twenty-five. People with CIPA often injure themselves because they do not know they are hurt until too late. In the same way, our experiences of emotional and spiritual pain alert us to the vissisitudes of real life, and are essential to the process of maturity. A 'spoilt' child is one who has not been allowed to experience a sufficient amount of suffering, and to learn from it.

In short, suffering begets wisdom.

This point is made again and again in the Bible. Luke's and Matthew's Gospels record that Jesus Himself, as a young man, underwent rigorous 'testing' in preparation for His mission – the metaphorical forty-day trial in the desert.[11] 'He learned obedience from what he suffered' (Hebrews 5:8). The Apostles, also, regarded their many ordeals as beneficial. St Paul, in his letter to the Romans, was quite direct: 'We also rejoice in our sufferings, because we know that suffering produces perseverance; perseverance, character; and character, hope' (Romans 5:3; see also Hebrews 12:1–14; James 1:2–4). Many of the books of the Old Testament are inspired by the same theme. The greatest of them, perhaps, is Job, though many people find it unrelentingly grim. My own preference is for Ecclesiastes: 'Sorrow is better than laughter, because a sad face is good for the heart' (7:3), is the advice of the Teacher. The genius of this doleful but magnificent work lies in the author's recognition that suffering is as integral a part of the world as happiness. It is a mistake, if a natural mistake, to regard suffering as abnormal. Some suffering may be so intense when first experienced as to appear pointless; but in fact it has an effect, 'against our will'. We are 'refined … [and] tested in the furnace of affliction' (Isaiah 48:10).

And thus we learn. Perhaps we learn that we must strive to do better; perhaps we learn to value more highly the blessings that we already enjoy. Whatever we learn, we are thereby better able to pass on that learning to others. So is Man improved, collectively and (in most cases) individually.

Franz Schubert, the great nineteenth-century Austrian composer, seems to have understood this truth. His beautiful song cycle *Die Winterreise* (The Winter Journey) is a musical evocation of melancholy and depression springing from rejected love. Yet listening to these songs is uplifting, even pleasurable, in the way of all good tearjerkers. Why? And how? One critic, Lawrence Kramer, has suggested that Schubert's immortal achievement may have been to 'dramatize … the bottomless resistance of a human psyche that, though it sees no limit to its suffering, refuses to collapse into immobility'[12]. Even in the face of such suffering – indeed, because of it – the psyche 'keeps on wandering and, more, keeps on finding creative ways to reflect upon its own condition, *to turn its suffering into knowledge*'[13].

Think of the turning points in your own life, the scathing experiences that brought you to maturity. In retrospect, do they not seem to have done you at least some good?

On the night of the assassination of President John F. Kennedy, his brother Robert was overheard sobbing in a darkened room. He was asking, 'Why God? Why, God, why? … What possible reason could there be in this?'[14] I believe that, in time, RFK came to receive an answer. The assassination was *the* critical event in his development as a man. On the night of Martin Luther King's murder five years later, Kennedy was uniquely well placed to empathise with King's followers because he could truly speak from personal experience. More generally, Kennedy was a far more compassionate person in the last few years of his life, which was also cut short (only two months later in 1968) by assassination. His untimely death was tragic, but not futile. In the long run it proved to be a force for good, because, like Martin Luther King, RFK left behind his wisdom, his ideals and his followers. There can be little doubt that the still-potent legend of the Kennedys – the muscular liberal creed it represents – derives much of its power from the suffering and grief associated with the Kennedy name.

All of these themes were superbly elucidated by Herbert Butterfield. 'One of the clearest and most concrete facts of history,' he wrote, 'is the fact that men may not only redeem catastrophe, but turn it into a grand creative moment'[15]. Sometimes it is the victims of suffering who do so: Butterfield cited as examples the aftermaths of the Great Fire of London and the Reformation. Neither the huge loss of life and property caused by the fire, nor the brutal wars spawned by the split in the medieval Church between Catholics and Protestants, can have been regarded other than with horror by those who suffered through them at the time. But the consequence of each was that survivors were confronted by a new situation; and eventually, they learned to make a virtue of necessity. London was rebuilt to a much superior plan, and the doctrine of religious toleration was born.[16] Similar examples could be multiplied many times. The Black Plague of 1347–50 wiped out one-third of Europe's population, but it also severly undermined feudalism and led directly to the Renaissance. Australia was settled by the British as a dumping ground for convicts; by the mid-twentieth century it had become a great democratic country.

Sometimes it is the *perpetrators* of suffering who – after a process of self-reflection – make good out of evil. Germany and Japan seemed to learn practical and moral lessons from their defeat in the Second World War, and quickly became two of the most prosperous and civilised countries in the world. Ultimately, it was not for the victorious Allies to judge them in their shame and regret – the truths that each learned needed to be 'adopted and taken to heart by the nation concerned, as a matter between itself and God'[17].

The greatest tragedy of 9/11 was not the loss of innocent human life, dreadful though that was, but the fact that the leadership of the United States did not appear to learn from it. The unpalatable Christian lesson from 9/11 which stood clearly to be drawn by superpower America was that 'such a nation only suffers, in reality, for its part in man's original sin'[18]. In the modern jargon, it was 'blowback'. The weeks and months following 9/11 were a rare opportunity for America to demonstrate it had learned that lesson and to 'redeem catastrophe' by reaching out to its friends and foes in the world. Instead, its leaders indulged in self-deception and self-aggrandisement, and alienated almost everybody by repaying evil with evil. In the astoundingly prescient words of Rienhold Niebuhr, ruminating in 1952 upon the dangers which might be posed in the future by American exceptionalism: '[A]n hysterical statesman [will] suggest that we must increase our power and use it in order to gain the ideal ends, of which providence has made us the trustees'. And: '[T]he strength of a giant nation [will be] directed by eyes too blind to see all the hazards of struggle; and the blindness [will be] induced not by some accident of Nature or history but by hatred and vainglory'.[19]

Suffering draws us to God

As well as forcing us to learn, suffering also forces Man to think about God. In saying this I rely primarily on my own experience, but it seems to be a near universal phenomenon. Man's extremity is God's opportunity.

At times of the greatest distress, most people's instinct is to turn to God. Throughout my life, on the occasions when I felt most intensely afraid for my health or safety, or that of a relative or friend, my first thought was to pray. Tellingly, this happened *even when I was not a believer.* Prayer is the natural response of most people in extremis – those on death row, those on an apparently doomed aeroplane, those diagnosed with terminal illness. It is also the natural response of people who fear for the health or safety of someone they love. These examples are rather extreme but they serve to make the point: 'When I am afraid, I will trust in [God]' (Psalm 56:3). Many former atheists have acknowledged this ubiquitous phenomenon.[20]

Suffering is one of the few things in the world capable of discouraging the most deadly of sins: pride. In *Paradise Lost*, Satan's manically destructive conduct is driven by a sense of 'injur'd merit'. C.S. Lewis described pride as 'the great sin' and as 'the complete anti-God state of mind'[21]. He considered – and, more and more, I agree – that pride is the root cause of all sin. This is because pride is essentially competitive in nature. The proud person, to a greater or lesser extent (for the fault lies in each of us), is concerned most of all to outdo other people. Buddhists call it 'craving'. In those circumstances the 'golden rule' of proper conduct goes out the window, because the well-being of other people becomes secondary to the proud person's need to feel superior. This is one of the key themes of the book of Job: pride can beget an enormous amount of suffering for others.

But as the author of Job understood, this is also where a strange paradox of the world is discernible. Pride, the sin that God most abhors, the sin that is most inimical to love, causes suffering; and frequently it can backfire upon the proud themselves. But at times of greatest suffering, of most intense desperation, even the most proud among us tend to be driven instinctively – and sometimes against our conscious will – away from ourselves and back towards God. Two of the most venerated of the psalms recognise and celebrate this truth. Psalm 46 pronounces that 'God is our refuge and strength, an ever-present help in trouble'. Psalm 121 begins even more stirringly: 'I lift up my eyes to the hills – where does my help come from? My help comes from the Lord'. Who has not, at least a few times in their life, when things looked especially bleak, appealed to God for strength or for aid?

D.A. Carson, addressing himself to complacent Christians, has articulated the point bluntly:

> If Christians who shelter beneath such self-assurance do not learn better ways by
> listening to the Scriptures, God may address them in the terrible language of tragedy.
> We serve a God who delights to disclose himself to the contrite, to the lowly of heart,
> to the meek. When God finds us so puffed up that we do not feel our need for him,

it is an act of kindness on his part to take us down a peg or two; it would be an act of judgment to leave us in our vaulting self-esteem.[22]

The idea that God *actively* causes really dire tragedies for this sort of reason is rather grotesque, though it may be so as regards 'lower-level' misfortune or misadventure. In the case of cataclysmic events such as wars, I prefer to think that God may sometimes 'withhold His protection and let events take their course … [so that] the penalty comes from His formidable non-intervention'[23]. God does so, I believe, because in the long run it is the wise thing to do. '[S]ometimes … it is only by a cataclysm that man can make his escape from the net which he has taken so much trouble to weave around himself'[24].

Robert Winston has made the same point even more sweepingly. The overall message of the Old Testament, he argues, boils down to this: '[T]he ruination of their homeland and the repeated exiles they experience eventually results in the Israelites arriving at a fresh understanding of God … Their tortuous journey has taught them the truth of monotheism.'[25] Winston is Jewish, and many Christians today would dispute the idea that the religious education of the ancient Hebrews is, or ever was, the overriding preoccupation of the Old Testament. But the basic insight is correct. Prolonged or intense suffering often does beget humility and reflection, and a yearning for transcendence.

Now, this phenomenon is important in more ways than one. Not only does it help to 'justify' suffering; in my view it goes to the ultimate issue, the question whether God does or does not exist. I would pose this question: If God does not exist, then why and how – *even in our most unguarded state* – are we drawn towards Him? It is hard to think of any good reason. Modern research shows that some fatalities resulting from 'crisis situations' are avoidable, if the person involved focuses his or her mind on the immediate practicalities of minimising risk.[26] If God is a chimera, then praying to Him in crisis situations will not merely be unavailing; it is a waste of precious time and positively dangerous. Why would evolution select for such a trait? I am bound to conclude that the fact we ask God for help in hard times is further evidence that He is there.

It is critical to note *why* we are drawn toward God in hard times. The answer lies in another line from Psalm 121: 'My help comes from the Lord, the Maker of heaven and earth'. The same answer is to be found in Ecclesiastes: 'When times are good, be happy; but when times are bad, consider: God has made the one as well as the other.' (7:14). The greatest of the Old Testament prophets put it this way:

I form the light and create darkness,
   I bring prosperity *and create disaster*;
I, the Lord, do all these things.

(Isaiah 45:7. My emphasis)

The assumption implicit in any appeal to God for help is that God is *capable* of giving help. The reason we assume that God is capable of giving help – of solving any problem – is a belief that He controls everything, including all events on Earth and our individual fates in any afterlife. (Presumably, some people on a doomed aeroplane pray that the crash will be averted; others assume the crash is inevitable, and pray for forgiveness of their and their loved ones' souls; still others must do both.) But why do we believe that God controls everything? Underlying that belief must be a further belief – that God *made* everything. Thus, the desperate person's unguarded cry for help is really an unstated acknowledgment that God is his or her Creator.

So understood, the arguments for Design in relation to the physical and moral Universe may assume, for some, added significance. So too the arguments for the existence of the afterlife (see Chapter 10). If you are persuaded or half-persuaded by any of those arguments, the next time you ask God for help you may do so with greater confidence that the plea will be heard – and even answered, whether in this life or the next.

Two other issues concerning suffering

At this point, the sceptic might concede that suffering may sometimes cause people – even nations – to learn, or to contemplate God. But he would then pose a series of questions. Why would a loving God construct things in such a tortuous way? Why must pain be inflicted on anyone, or on anything? Why must there be evil in the world? Does the end (wisdom or faith) justify the means? To use an almost hackneyed, but entirely valid, example: What about the starving child in Africa who has never done anyone any harm? What about the Holocaust?

Many theologians and philosophers have devoted their careers to these extremely deep questions. For the layman searching for a good place to start, I would break my own rule and suggest going straight to the Bible – Chapters 38–42 of the book of Job. The author of Job tackled this vexing subject not by providing explicit answers, but by asking further questions. He assumed the existence of an all-powerful Designing God, and (in a variant on the clay pot metaphor) scorned Man's qualifications to doubt God's methods. God's famous monologue challenges Man's ignorance:

> Who is this that darkens my counsel with words without knowledge? Brace yourself like a man; I will question you, and you shall answer me. Where were you when I laid the earth's foundation? Tell me, if you understand… Have you ever given orders to the morning, or shown the dawn its place…? Have the gates of death been shown to you? … Can you bring forth the constellations in their seasons…? Do you send the lightning bolts on their way…? Who endowed the heart with wisdom or gave understanding to the mind?
>
> (Job 38:2–4, 12, 32, 35–36).

In other words, Man is in no position to talk back to God, about suffering or anything else. To do so is akin to a toddler who has learnt how to count to ten challenging Einstein on the laws of physics.

But many sceptics and unbelievers may not be moved by this answer. For a long time, it did not satisfy me; and, as I have said, my eventual acceptance of the place of suffering in the world was not due to the study of theology. In this chapter, my primary purpose is to explain my own personal feelings and deductions about the matter. I have cited the example of Robert Kennedy's speech in Indianapolis because it moves me so much, and taught me a lot.

In reaching my own position on the phenomenon of suffering, I found it important to return to basics. There seemed to me to be two essential questions, which I tried to work through.

First, would it have been possible to construct a world in which there was no suffering at all; or, at least, a world in which suffering was 'limited' so as to spare the innocent? Second, if the answer to the first question is 'no' – if God had no alternative but to create a world in which suffering exists – what happens to the innocent (or relatively innocent) victims?

A world without suffering?

What could have been the alternative to a world in which suffering and evil exist? It is crucial to come to grips with this issue. Much modern-day hostility toward religion seems to be grounded on a pivotal assumption, that any God who chooses to permit suffering is not worthy of worship, and should be repudiated. But implicit in that assumption is a further assumption – that God, if He exists, would have had viable alternatives to choose from.

It is conceivable that God could have created Man to live in a kind of blissful ignorance; as automata who would go safely and uneventfully through the motions of daily life, perhaps experiencing some basic physical pleasures, but having no real *choice* as to their conduct. Of course, the world is not like that. Man has free will, and free will – the capacity to choose – necessarily carries with it the potential for the choice of evil rather than good. That potential for choice in each of us is fundamental to what it is to be human.

C.S. Lewis went so far as to say that a world without suffering would be insufferable. His point was that there must be some inequality in the world – of virtue, wealth, health, happiness, intellect and so on – in order for Man as a whole, and people as individuals, to 'be'. The salient passage (from Lewis's book *Miracles*) is as follows:

> This selective or undemocratic quality in Nature, at least in so far as it affects human life, is neither good nor evil. According as spirit [i.e. each person's will] exploits or fails to exploit this Natural situation, it gives rise to one or the other [i.e. good or evil]. It permits, on the one hand, ruthless competition, arrogance and envy; it permits on the other modesty and (one of our greatest pleasures) admiration. A world in which I was *really* (and not merely by a useful legal fiction) 'as good as everyone else', in which I never looked up to anyone wiser or cleverer or braver or more learned than I, would be insufferable.[27]

In short, without free will, life would not be life.

Paul Johnson has helped me to understand this truth even more clearly. In *The Quest for God* he grapples with the old question whether God intended from the first to create a world with suffering in it, or whether the existence of suffering only came about as a result of 'the Fall' in the (metaphorical) Garden of Eden – i.e. as a result of the conscious rebellion of Man. Johnson convinces me that suffering must always have been part of God's plan:

> [God] knew his creatures would sin and thus invoke misery on themselves – but…he wished to create a moral drama … The sinless, deathless Adam and Eve in their semi-celestial garden are of little moral interest or significance … On the other hand, an imperfect, frail-willed man, a flawed creature, born in sin, living in suffering, exposed to all the evils and temptations of a rugged, dangerous world, who nonetheless, with the help of God's grace and mercy, and by virtue of the supreme sacrifice of his only son, manages to struggle successfully against his sinful nature and contrives in the end – just – to make himself worthy of joining God in Paradise: that is indeed a tale worth telling.[28]

Other Christian writers have echoed Johnson's idea that human life makes sense only if understood as a kind of 'moral drama'. J.I. Packer has described life on Earth as like 'an ante-chamber, dressing room and moral gymnasium'[29]. Herbert Butterfield thought it an inescapable conclusion that '[t]he world is not merely to be enjoyed but is an *arena* for moral striving'[30].

These metaphors (drama, tale, arena) carry with them notions of conflict and pain – and of a meaningful *outcome*. It follows, Johnson argues, that death is 'an indispensable element … a crucial function of the mechanism of salvation and redemption'. Accordingly, 'the fact of death is not an accident, a modification of God's original plan, but absolutely central to his concept of creation'[31]. Soren Kierkegaard held a similar view of death – the positive (i.e. life) is meaningful and comprehensible only because we are aware of the existence of the negative (death).

Likewise, it seems to me, suffering in general is neither an accident nor a modification of God's original plan. A third writer, D.A. Carson, clinched this issue in my mind. Carson has addressed the thorny question of why, if God is merciful and just, He does not answer all the prayers of good people in distress. Why does God allow such people to suffer, even when they have actively sought His help? Carson's answer is this:

> Suppose, for argument's sake, that every time we asked God for something and ended our prayers with some appropriate formula, such as 'in Jesus's name', we immediately received what we asked for. How would we view prayer? How would we view God? Wouldn't prayer become a bit of clever magic? Wouldn't God himself become nothing more than an extraordinarily powerful genie? … [God] may give us what we ask for; he may make us wait; he may decline. He may give us the goal of what we ask for, but by quite another means …[32]

So far so good. Free will must carry with it the capacity for Man to choose evil over good, and hence to inflict suffering on others. There must, then, be *some* suffering; death must come in the end; and God is wise not to accede to every prayer He hears. But these conclusions are not the end of the matter. There are still more troubling issues. Why, in so many cases, must suffering be so horrible? How can anyone begin to rationalise the Holocaust, the kinds of atrocities described by concentration camp survivors like Eli Wiesel: men and women thrown alive into furnaces, babies pitchforked in front of their parents, children gassed and hanged?

And why – added to the suffering caused by Man's choices – must there also be suffering caused by Nature? What is the explanation for God permitting a tsunami in an already poverty-stricken country? The existence of the poverty may be explainable by God's desire to see Man choose (through love of neighbour) to seek to alleviate it, but why the need for both poverty and a tsunami? Or, to employ another frequently used example: Why is it necessary for, say, a three-year-old-child to die a painful death from cancer, or starvation? For that matter, why is it necessary for any three-year-olds to die at all?

Here one is apparently in more difficult territory. I agree with Sam Harris that it is insufficient for Christians to fall back on God's 'inscrutability', or simplistically to attribute such dreadful events to divine wrath, as some do.[33] Nor am I satisfied with Hegel's view that, in retrospect, everything which has happened – good and bad – must now be considered to have been 'necessary'. These issues deserve treatment that is both responsive and intellectually coherent.

At the risk of sounding vain, I have come to believe that there is a fairly simple answer to the problem of suffering. Despite what atheists say, it is not necessary as regards this issue to 'indulge in every kind of metaphysical contortion'[34]. It is more productive to go back to the essential question: What could be the *alternative* to the precarious world in which we find ourselves? Let us confront the issue head on by taking the example of innocent children who die young.

Imagine a world in which, say, no one could die before the age of twelve; a world in which a supposedly more loving God 'spared the innocent', at least for this fixed time. Would that be a better world? No. The possibility that such a world could work satisfactorily really does not hold up for a moment. Children of a certain age would be known to be indestructible, and with what results? Parents would not care for them so painstakingly, nor love them with such protective tenderness; all kinds of monstrous evils (short of death) would be all the more likely to be visited upon them, by their parents and by others. And what would happen on the day when the child turned twelve, and was all of a sudden subject to the same risk of death as everyone else? How would the child cope with that situation? How would anyone go about the attempt to *prepare* the child for that situation?

There are no good answers to those questions. And that may well give us a clue to reconciling the existence of a loving God with other hideous – and seemingly capricious – events. Most Australians are familiar with the story of Sydney girl Sophie Delezio. As a toddler she was terribly injured when a car crashed into her day care Centre. She lost both feet, an ear, several fingers; and was permanently disfigured by burns. Then, a few years later, after a long and painful process of recuperation, she was struck by a car while on a pedestrian crossing, and suffered yet more physical trauma – broken ribs, a bruised lung, serious head injuries. Why would a loving God allow that?

Some might respond that Sophie did, at least, survive both incidents, and that she has set an example of courage for us all. They are valid observations, but the theological justification for her (and her parents') ordeal is, I suggest, more straightforward than that.

There is an obvious question: Why should someone like Sophie have suffered so terribly not once, but *twice*? My answer is: such awful possibilities must remain open, for the same reason that no one can ever be immune from death. Try to picture a world constructed by God in a way that ensured that, if someone had already suffered once from a terrible injury (or disease or deprivation or bereavement), he or she would be immune to any further misfortune (or misfortune of a like kind). It just would not work. We would return to a world of unimaginable exploitation of people known to be 'indestructible', at least in certain circumstances.

Put aside the Sophie Delezio example and consider the problem another way – from the perspective not of sparing 'innocent' children from suffering, but of minimising the amount of suffering inflicted *by* children. If any child up to the age of twelve (or eight, or five) knew that he or she was indestructible, what evils would that child inflict upon others? The implications of such a state of affairs become even more horrible to contemplate if adults up to a certain age were likewise immune.

The more I think about it, the clearer it seems: from the instant each of us is born, our mortality has to be uncertain. There are, in Umberto Eco's elegant phrasing, 'advantages of death' and 'disadvantages of immortality'.[35] It must be so in order to avoid much greater collective evil, and much greater individual and collective suffering. Unless we go back to the sterile theoretical world of automata, our lives must always be threatened, at least as a theoretical possibility. Each of us must live knowing, usually in the back of our minds, that we are vulnerable to many dangers: as Seneca observed, death opens to a thousand doors. Each of us must also live knowing that death will certainly come one day (cf. 1 Samuel 20:3). Most of us are spared knowledge of the how and the when of death – but not of the 'that'. We are never completely safe, even in our sleep; we are never utterly doomed, even in the direst extremity.

What all this means is that the consequences at any given moment of Nature inflicting harm upon Man by its outworkings, or of Man choosing evil over good, can be limited only by the fixed laws of the physical Universe. Those laws determine, for example, that there will from time to time be undersea earthquakes. Undersea earthquakes are crucial for sustaining all life on Earth, but occasionally they will cause tsunamis that wreak awful human suffering.

Many unbelievers assert that a loving God should and would 'step in' from time to time to prevent such things happening. If there must be undersea earthquakes, God should ensure there are no tsunamis. If it must rain, there should be no floods. If human beings must die, because our bodies must deteriorate, then the process should always be painless. This kind of argument is superficially attractive, given God's omnipotence, but it is also badly flawed. As the American writer John Blanchard has pointed out, God's frequent interference with the harmful outworkings of Nature would create many more problems than it would solve:

> Do we really want God to prevent things happening (or cause other things to happen) by manipulating the laws of physics in such a way that we would never know from one moment to another which were working which had been suspended? If God tweaked the laws of nature billions of times a day merely to ensure everybody's safety, comfort or success, science would be impossible and … [we] should be reduced to such a state of physical, social and psychological instability that life would fall apart, paradoxically bringing even more suffering in its train.[36]

The same objection applies to evil wrought by Man in the exercise of free will. An atheist would argue that if a burglar fires a gun at a panicky child, a loving God would stop the bullet from being ejected from the gun, as the laws of physics otherwise require. Or God would change the burglar's decision to fire the gun. Either way, suffering would be averted. Because suffering is often *not* averted in such situations, the atheist then reasons, God cannot exist. At least, any God who would permit such suffering does not merit the description 'loving'.

But as Blanchard explains, things are not so simple:

> [At] what level should God intervene? We might say that he should not have allowed the worst offenders – the Hitlers, Pol Pots and Mao Tse-tungs of this world – to do what they did. But what about the next level – say, thugs, sadists, rapists, child abusers and drug pushers – should God step in and stop them? If he did, another 'layer' of offenders would become the worst – say, drunk drivers, shoplifters, burglars and the like. If we argued like this we would soon get to the point at which we would be demanding that God should intervene to prevent *all* evil. Would you settle for that, even if it meant having your own thoughts, words and actions controlled by a cosmic puppet-master, robbing you of all freedom and responsibility?[37]

So, Nature and free will must be left to do their worst. Yet experience tells us that, astoundingly, such a system 'works'. Yes, there is undoubtedly a great deal of awful human suffering in the world, but there is also an enormous amount of joy, and beauty, and love, and all of the other wonderful things that make human life meaningful. It appears that precariousness (the ever-present possibility of suffering or evil) is the basis of order.

Suffering, then, is not merely necessary – it is desirable. Our freedom depends upon its ever-present potentiality and its limited actuality: it is proof not of God's non-existence, but of His wisdom. In the words of John Polkinghorne, God 'is a lawgiver, but he is not a tyrant'.[38] Those conclusions do, however, give rise to another crucial question.

What happens to the victims of suffering, especially those who die young and 'innocent'?

This question leads inevitably to another: Is there life after death? That subject is addressed fully in Chapter 10. For present purposes, I confine myself to stating my belief that there is an afterlife. On that premise, it follows that the long-term fate of individual victims of suffering hinges on the notion of divine justice. As to that, I have come to believe in two things.

First, that ultimately God will judge everyone fairly. I share the conviction of Jonah that God is gracious and merciful, slow to anger, and of great kindness (Jonah 4:2). Above all, I believe that God is just in all His ways (Psalm 145:17). It seems to me to follow that if a person has suffered greatly on Earth through little or no 'fault' of their own, then God will be fully aware of all the circumstances, and take them into account. Likewise, a person who has lived a fortunate life on Earth will be judged the more strictly.

I believe, moreover, that there are very few truly 'innocent' people on Earth: with the exception of very young children, each of us, to a greater or lesser extent, does not even approach the ideal. As St Paul wrote, 'There is no difference, for all have sinned and fall short of the glory of God' (Romans 3:23). For this reason, I am attracted to the Catholic doctrine of purgatory (as the intermediate punishment for those sinners ultimately bound for Heaven, on a scale commensurate with their sins on Earth). The notion strikes me as essentially right – and, if true, immensely comforting.

My second belief about divine justice is that our notion of what is just – or 'fair' – is likely to be rather different from God's. Even Christians have a tendency to judge everything that happens by the material standards of life on Earth. Atheists like Sam Harris implicitly assume that death, or at least 'early' death, is the ultimate misfortune; for Harris, the tragedy of natural catastrophes such as the 2004 Boxing Day tsunami is that 'human beings suffer the most harrowing abridgements of their happiness for no good reason at all'.[39] That statement assumes, among other things, that when you die you will never again experience happiness, because death is the end of consciousness. The statement also assumes that when you die there is no further suffering either; it follows that the tragedy of dying young consists of the 'lost years'. But if there is an afterlife, quite different conclusions follow. The Christian position is that life on Earth, 'however good and desirable in itself, is not the final purpose for which man is created'[40].

Similar considerations apply as regards suffering caused by human evil. The average right-thinking person feels sympathy for the person who is wronged and enmity toward the wrongdoer. But that sympathy may – in a subtle but profoundly important way – be misplaced. Who is really the more blessed or the more to be pitied – the murderer or his victim? The murderer is likely to spend the rest of his life on Earth in torment of one kind or another, suffering punishment meted out by Man and/or agonies of conscience. And if there is an afterlife, the murderer also faces judgment by God. The victim, on the other hand, may be positively fortunate. He or she may have been delivered from all kinds of troubles that would have come on Earth – not least the desire to exact violent revenge upon his or tormentors – and may experience Heaven earlier than expected.

This thought suddenly occurred to me a few years ago as I watched Alan Parker's moving film about racism in the American South, *Mississippi Burning* (1988). There is a blood-curdling sequence in which a kindly Negro man, trying to protect his family at night from a raid by the local Klan, is overpowered and strung up on a noose. His young son has to hide and watch as his father's body twitches in its death throes. On the face of it, the murdered Negro man deserves all of our pity, and the murderers none. But the opposite may be closer to the truth, if one believes in divine justice – that each of us after we die (if not also before) will eventually receive our due. Anyone watching that scene would know in their heart that, if there were a God, then the Negro man would be treated mercifully and that his murderers were, at the least, in grave danger of losing their immortal souls.

This is a stark example. Most situations in real life are not nearly so clear-cut. Human behaviour is rarely entirely good or entirely bad. There are always shades of guilt in any situation. Even a murderer may be able to point to factors that explain, if not excuse, his or her conduct. If a sane civilian shoots another dead in cold blood, he is guilty in law. That much is straightforward. But the chain of causation may be long, and the scales of moral justice finely balanced. The shooter may have acted on a spur-of-the-moment impulse that was the culmination of many years of accumulated cruelty towards him by the apparently 'innocent' victim. In short, worldly appearances may be deceiving.

The world would be a far more frightening place if each of us could rely only upon the justice meted out by Man. As everyone knows, man-made justice is usually imperfect, and often grossly so. Sometimes it appears non-existent. There are 'righteous men who get what the wicked deserve, and wicked men who get what the righteous deserve' (Ecclesiastes 8:14). Think of Jesus, who died on the Cross, and Stalin, who died in his bed. The Teacher pronounced this state of affairs 'meaningless', and so it would be if the earthly world were all that there is. However, if you believe in God, a God who knows the whole truth of every situation, it is possible to see things in a different perspective, and to derive comfort thereby. As Warwick Fairfax contended, there is a sense in which 'ill-treatment by others ... can be borne with greater fortitude *if undeserved*'.[41]

This was another of Jesus's main themes in the Beatitudes. The poor in spirit, those who mourn, the meek, the persecuted – none of them need despair of relying upon human justice alone. A contemporary Croatian theologian, Miroslav Volf, has developed this idea. Volf argues that sincere belief in divine justice should be, and often is, a deterrent to aggressive violence – and especially to *retaliatory* violence by victims of suffering who are enraged and/or bereaved.[42] A man who does not believe in God may be more inclined to take justice into his own hands. The ghost of Hamlet's father quelled his son's rage towards the feckless Gertrude by exhorting Hamlet to 'leave her to heaven'.[43]

Of course, God desires that we should try – without using violence – to correct worldly injustice ourselves. He deplores injustice wrought by any conscious decision of

Man. Those things cannot be stressed enough. But there is a 'backstop' for those who suffer: God Himself. God may choose to repay the proud and wicked with suffering on Earth (cf. Isaiah 10). Further or alternatively, He may choose to reward the humble and good with happiness on Earth. (In this connection, it is a mistake to suppose that the 'rewards' which Jesus promised in the Beatitudes are necessarily for the afterlife *only*. Those who suffer on Earth may enjoy spiritual succour in the here and now.[44]) But, in any event, God will impose justice in the next world. One of the few fairly certain opinions which I hold about the nature of Heaven is that 'all suffering will be vindicated', an idea propagated amongst the early Christians by Irenaeus, the late second-century bishop of Lyons, in his highly influential five-volume treatise *Against Heresies*.[45]

Another way of looking at suffering

So far I have defended the existence of suffering on pragmatic grounds. God 'got it right' because, without suffering, Man would develop neither wisdom nor faith; and, more broadly, there is no workable alternative to a world with suffering in it. Moreover, God protects the victims of suffering in the afterlife.

But I now believe that there is another reason for the existence of suffering, which is still more fundamental: suffering was and is an inevitable feature of the Universe, given the nature of the God who created it.

The twentieth-century French philosopher and Christian mystic, Simone Weil, also struggled with the problem of suffering. The answer she eventually proposed is compelling. For her, the key lay in fully conceptualising the nature of God. God – as I have already sought to describe Him – is the explanation for everything. He is all-knowing and all-powerful. He is perfect. It follows, argued Weil, that such a God, if He is to create anything, can only create something *inferior* to Himself. Suffering and evil (imperfection) are therefore an inevitable consequence of Creation.

The basal question, then, is why God would decide to create a Universe in which there must be suffering and evil, as opposed to creating nothing at all. This was Weil's answer:

> On God's part creation is not an act of self-expansion but of restraint and renunciation. God and all his creatures are less than God alone. God accepted this diminution. He emptied a part of his being from himself. He had already emptied himself in this act of his divinity; that is why Saint John says that the Lamb had been slain from the beginning of the world. God permitted the existence of things distinct from himself and worth infinitely less than himself. But through this creative act he denied himself, as Christ has told us to deny ourselves. God denied himself for our sakes in order to give us the possibility of denying ourselves for him. This response, this echo, which it is in our power to refuse, is the only possible justification for the folly of love of the creative act.[46]

The implications of this passage are profound. The explanation for the 'problem' of suffering is not that God chose to do things that way from a range of possible alternatives that did not involve the existence of suffering; rather, having decided to create *something*, and more particularly to create matter[47], it was inevitable that the thing created would be less than perfect (i.e. that suffering would exist). As Warwick Fairfax put it: 'To create something and to give it nothing to do, no difficulties to triumph over, no chance of creating evil or fallibility would seem to be meaningless.'[48]

Moreover, understood in that way, the act of Creation was an act of forbearing love, because it would have been easier for God, in the exercise of His power, to do nothing. Like a parent who – *out of love* – steps back and permits a child to make mistakes so that the child may learn for itself, God steps back and, by His absence from the world, permits us to learn how to live and how to find Him. However, also like a loving parent, God does not leave Man completely to his own devices. God remains ever-present, but in the background, protecting most of us individually and all of us collectively from much greater suffering than does, in fact, occur.

That brings me to the subject of grace.

Grace

For a long time I did not fully comprehend this key Christian concept. Broadly, it is the idea that *everything*, each moment of our existence, should be regarded as a gift from God. No state of affairs should be taken for granted or regarded as a product solely of your own efforts – especially not faith itself. God's most generous act of grace – by far – was to become a man, Jesus of Nazareth, and to suffer and die on the Cross as atonement for Man's otherwise irredeemable sins, individual and collective. (See John 3:16, the most famous verse in the Bible.) This notion is basic to Christianity[49], and especially to the streams of Protestant theology that began in the sixteenth century with John Calvin and Martin Luther.

That is the most important aspect of grace, using the word in a strictly Christian sense, and that is why I have devoted Part Two of this book completely to Jesus. However, there are other aspects of grace which are worth considering. For some readers, especially agnostics or atheists, these may be easier to understand and relate to.

Grace manifests itself in the world in many ways. It is a multifaceted thing that bobs up everywhere. And, for reasons I will try to explain, grace is another sharp pointer towards the existence of God. The very existence of the phenomenon of grace – as Man experiences it – should be another string in the bow of any Christian evangelist. Speaking for myself, it was grasping the concept of grace that helped to clinch my belief in Christianity.

I will start with those aspects of grace which are the best known and the least controversial.

Grace in Man: thankfulness and humility

Thankfulness is a key aspect of grace, and it was laboured repeatedly by St Paul. D.A. Carson has suggested that it is worth reading all of the varied expressions of thanksgiving in St Paul's prayers. One lesson they teach us is that thankfulness is a manifestation of grace in Man. Another lesson is that thankfulness in Man is most likely to be sincere if it truly springs from recognition of *God's* grace, rather than convention, flattery or other baser human motives.

When we are expressing thanks or praise openly to others (rather than in silent prayer to God) it can be especially constructive to acknowledge the role of God's grace. Citing a verse from St Paul's prayer for the Thessalonians (3:9), Carson has explained why this is so. In thanking the Thessalonians, 'Paul … simultaneously drew attention to [their] spiritual growth, thereby encouraging them, and insisted that God [was] the one to be thanked for it, thereby humbling them'. While the Thessalonians would be bound to have taken heart from the great Apostle's pleasure at their progress, 'there [was] simply no way that these believers [could] thoughtfully listen to what Paul [said] and then smugly pat themselves on the back: God and God alone [was] to be praised for the signs of grace in their lives'.[50]

In case this explanation seems somewhat overblown, I will try to make the point another way by describing a feeling I have had. Many other people must also have experienced it. On fairly rare occasions, people have told me that they had been or would be praying for me, either to thank God for something I had done or to ask God to help me during a difficult period. Each time, I was extraordinarily moved to hear such a thing said; and I had that feeling just as strongly on the occasions *before* I believed in God as on the occasions after.

Thankfulness for our obvious blessings, then, is an integral aspect of grace, and I have always been at least dimly aware of that fact. But what I ought to have realised sooner is that grace is an even more sweeping and precious thing. To appreciate it fully or, better still, to be able to put it into practice, can be an enormous comfort. Learning about grace helped me to understand some things I could never previously understand, such as why the survivors of a flood or a bushfire, all their worldly possessions destroyed, or the parents of a severely handicapped child, could actually *thank* God for their good fortune.

After Sophie Delezio was injured a second time, her father said:

A lot of people think we might be the most unlucky family in the world … but I like to think the other way. We're probably the luckiest parents alive today with having Sophie survive a second accident.[51]

That is grace.

Another well-known aspect of grace – closely linked to thankfulness – is humility. If pride is the worst of human sins, and one of the greatest evils, then pride's antithesis, humility, must be one of the greatest virtues. This is made explicit in many passages of the Bible (cf. Proverbs 22:4; Isaiah 66:2; James 4:6).

But humility, paradoxically, is often wrought by suffering – including suffering brought about by Man's evil. This now seems to me another crucial truth. The parable of the prodigal son (Luke 15:11–32) has thus become, for me, one of the most important in the Gospels. The prodigal son, after experiencing suffering, demonstrates grace by returning, humbled, to his father; the father demonstrates grace by welcoming him back despite all of the suffering that his son has caused him; the 'good' son is graceless because he cannot see that the worthy (and generally happy) life he has led should in itself be reward enough for him – he resents his father's joy because he is not, for once, the object of it, and so commits the sin of pride.

The grace of God: Providence

Thus far I have focused on the manifestations of grace in Man. The other side of the same coin is the grace of God or, to give the concept its old-fashioned label, Providence.

One of the most profound and comprehensive attempts to explain Providence was undertaken by the great German theologian Karl Rahner; but no one should start with him. Rahner's body of work is dense and challenging. For the uninitiated, there are a number of more readily accessible discussions of the subject.[52] Years before I had heard of Rahner, I chanced across one of the clearest elucidations of the concept of grace, in an unlikely place. A close friend recommended *The Road Less Travelled*, a well-known 'self-help' book written in the 1970s by M. Scott Peck. As a self-help book understood in the secular sense it is justly admired, but for my own part the highlight of the book is the eloquent discussion of the Christian concept of grace. (Peck used the term grace rather than Providence, and I will do so too in the discussion that follows.)

Peck defined grace as 'the powerful force originating outside human consciousness that nurtures human life and the spiritual growth of human beings.'[53] Grace, Peck argued, is the force that accounts for a range of commonplace but fundamental events (and non-events) in each of our lives. It accounts for the fact that so many of us, even those living in difficult circumstances, do not fall victim at an early age to disease, mental illness, accident or any of the myriad other dangers that potentially confront us. It accounts for the fact that such events do not occur nearly as often as seemingly they might.

Peck drew particular attention to the fact that we have all experienced 'near misses'. In thinking back on my own life, I can recall many occasions when, for no apparent reason, and certainly without any conscious action of mine, my life was 'spared' by the intervention of a force that I now believe to have been divine grace.

For example, have you ever momentarily slept at the wheel of a car, but awoken just in time to avoid a collision? Have you ever been in a car crash that left the car badly damaged, but you and your passengers unhurt? Have you ever been struck by the realisation that you just walked across a road without looking at the traffic? Has a car ever swerved or braked sharply to avoid hitting you?

Such sensations are, of course, nothing out of the ordinary. Many people would be able to recount similar experiences in their own lives. One thinks not merely of cars and roads, but of close shaves of many other kinds, especially those involving children – falls, drownings, collisions, poisonings, scaldings, electrocutions, swallowings of foreign objects: all the thousand natural shocks that flesh is heir to. These sorts of near misses occur routinely. Very rarely does the worst actually happen.

And that is exactly the point. The force of grace seems to be all-pervasive, operating as it does to protect the majority of the human race from misadventure. Moreover, the fact that all of us experience the near misses – personally, and vicariously through loved ones, especially children – reminds us from time to time of the preciousness of life. The fifteenth-century Jewish ethicist Orchoth Zaddikkim identified this phenomenon:

> Be grateful for, not blind to the many, many sufferings which thou art spared; thou art no better than those who have been searched out and wracked by them.[54]
>
> (See also Luke 13:4–5)

Grace manifests itself not only in the countless sufferings from which we are spared, but also in many of the sufferings which we must endure. Illness, even serious illness, can be a blessing. For some time I have suffered quite severely from anxiety and depression. In many respects, the experience has been, and still remains, distinctly unpleasant. It certainly slowed down the writing of this book. In the worst periods (before and after diagnosis) I sank into a bleak despair. Occasionally, I would feel a pent-up fury welling inside, but more often there was merely a dull ache. At other times, which were all too frequent, a dismal feeling of anxiety consumed me. Any amount of stress became hard to bear, and I would do strange things to avoid the risk of it becoming unmanageable. I experienced insomnia and near-constant fatigue. I have had to take anti-depressant drugs, which have helped to relieve some of the worst symptoms but produced debilitating side effects and, later, ghastly withdrawal symptoms.

Taken on the whole, however, I am thankful for having become ill. It has brought me closer to many of the people I love. It has shown me just how deeply unhappy I was and has forced me to train my mind to better ways of thinking. It has caused me to face up to my character flaws and to reconsider my priorities. It has made me realise the essential importance in life of courage.

(There is a revelatory song about depression, called 'The Valley'. It was written by a remarkable Canadian woman named Jane Siberry. The song was popularised by k.d. lang, who included it in her 2004 album, *Hymns of the 49th Parallel*. The lyrics reveal, on Siberry's part, both empathy for the sufferer's experience and a realisation of the essential role of love and grace in lifting him out of it. She invokes some of the most beautiful and best-known Biblical metaphors of all, from the Twenty-third Psalm. The sufferer of depression 'live[s] in the valley', 'walk[s] through the shadows' and feels 'deserted by the staccato of the staff'. But it is possible, through the consoling power of supportive love, for the sufferer to come into the light. The song ends on a hopeful note: 'The shepherd upright, and flowing/You see …')

Before being diagnosed with depression, I knew next to nothing about the condition. In retrospect, I expect I would now be ashamed of whatever views I might previously have expressed about the subject, had it ever arisen. Certainly, I now understand (as I did not on an earlier reading) the wisdom in M. Scott Peck's views about the link between mental illness, suffering and grace:

> We live our lives in a real world. To live them well it is necessary that we come to understand the reality of the world as best we can. But such understanding does not

come easily. Many aspects of the reality of the world and of our relationship to the world are painful to us. We can understand them *only through effort and suffering*. All of us, to a greater or lesser extent, attempt to avoid this effort and suffering. We ignore certain painful aspects of reality by thrusting certain unpleasant facts out of our awareness. In other words, we attempt to defend our consciousness, our awareness, against reality. We do this by a variety of means which psychiatrists call defence mechanisms. All of us employ such defences, thereby limiting our awareness. If in our laziness and fear of suffering we massively defend our awareness, then it will come to pass that our understanding of the world will bear little or no relation to reality. Because our actions are based on our understanding, our behaviour will then become unrealistic. When this occurs to a sufficient degree our fellow citizens will recognise that we are 'out of touch with reality', and will deem us mentally ill even though we ourselves are most likely convinced of our sanity.[55]

(I interpolate here that this was exactly my own experience. Before suffering the panic attack at work that left me unable to function and precipitated the diagnosis of my depression, I had no inkling that I was mentally ill; I had long been aware of unhappiness and acute anxiety but these feelings were 'normal' for me, a part of daily life. Even *after* suffering the panic attack, it came as a surprise to hear the senior partner of my law firm talking about me in terms of being sick and needing medical help.)

Peck went on:

But long before matters have proceeded to this extreme, and we have been served notice of our illness by our fellow citizens, we are served notice by our unconscious of our increasing maladjustment. Such notice is served by our unconscious through a variety of means: bad dreams, anxiety attacks, depressions and other symptoms. Although our conscious mind has denied reality, our unconscious, which is omniscient, knows the true score and attempts to help us by stimulating, through symptom formation, our conscious mind to the awareness that something is wrong. In other words, *the painful and unwanted symptoms of mental illness are manifestations of grace.*[56] (My emphasis)

This is a remarkably acute description of the onset of mental illness. It exemplifies an extraordinary thing about the world, the first of the two things that demonstrate to me the reality of God's grace. The world is full of suffering – it must be, if Nature is to 'work' and the gift of free will is to have meaning – but even much of that suffering of itself begets something good. Often that thing is wisdom or faith. But there is a broader sense in which suffering operates as a 'positive'. Despite and indeed *because of* suffering, Man – taken on the whole – relishes life: much more so than would be possible if there were no such thing as suffering, because without suffering we could not appreciate all that is worthwhile and precious. Crucially, the suffering that there is does not completely engulf, nor render nugatory, the good that it produces. C.S. Lewis called this the principle of Vicariousness.[57]

This principle underlies the parable of the lost sheep (Luke 15:1–10). The shepherd's anguish is only temporary, and it is not pointless. He feels the joy of *relief* in finding the lost sheep, which he had feared might be gone forever. As a result, he values it – and his other ninety-nine sheep – all the more. It is true that if he had failed to find the lost sheep, some good might still have resulted. He would probably have been more careful in future. But in the events that occur in this parable the shepherd learns that same lesson, *and* experiences the joy of relief, *and* reclaims the object of his search.

This is a metaphor, not only for the nature of God's love, but for how most human beings live their lives. We make mistakes, incur setbacks, suffer illness, and experience accidents and near misses. But most of us – at least for a reasonable time – survive and learn, and experience our share of happiness. Somehow, despite all of the things that do go wrong, and the many more things that we fear *might* go wrong, meaningful life continues.

It might be objected that this proposition applies only to life in the West – that most of the billions of people in the Third World must be desperately unhappy, and cannot be regarded as recipients of God's grace. I do not accept this contention. The opposite may be closer to the truth. Worldwide surveys of public opinion consistently show that (above a level of bare subsistence) people's happiness does not increase commensurate with material wealth. In fact, happiness tends to *decrease* at the higher end of the scale.[58] There is plenty of anecdotal evidence to back this up. One only has to observe the faces of the people in Sydney's Central Business District on a weekday morning – the grim suits and the harried shopkeepers – to know that it is so. I would imagine it is the same in London or New York. But most people in the world do not live this way, despite the insidious effects of globalism and free-market economics. A close friend who had just returned from a trip to India once told me how she was struck by the evident contentment of the people she saw in the rural areas and market towns, cheerfully going about their simple lives.

According to almost every statistical measure, most Australians today are healthier and wealthier – by far – than ever before. But many of those statistics are misleading; indeed, they are as much a measure of our *problems* as our blessings. This phenomenon of 'affluenza', a term coined by the Australian commentator Clive Hamilton[59], is another manifestation of the biblical teaching that the accumulation of riches on Earth is no guarantee of happiness, let alone any reliable sign of virtue. For what good is it for a man to gain the whole world, yet forfeit his soul (cf. Mark 8:36)?

I am convinced that, on the whole, and in the absence of extraordinary circumstances such as war or famine, people in Third World countries are as happy as people in the West. Indeed many must tend to resent well-meaning attempts to impose Western standards and culture upon them. That, of course, is not to say that efforts to relieve dire poverty and to preach Christianity are not worthwhile and right. But, through the ages, people have adapted to the conditions in which they found themselves. Meaningful life has persisted, even in conditions that today's Western sophisticate would regard as almost sub-human.

One of the hardest things for people in the Western world today to understand, it seems to me, is that 'real life' did not begin sometime in the nineteenth or the twentieth century, or even during the Renaissance. The ancient Middle Eastern people who wrote the Bible were *human beings* like us, struggling to come to grips with the universal challenges of life. Man's use of technology has become much more advanced since then, and so to a lesser degree have the laws and assumptions underpinning the organisation of mass society. The total sum of human knowledge has hugely expanded. But I venture to say that the things that really make people tick as individuals – family, friends, a worthwhile vocation in the home or out – have not changed for many, many centuries.[60] That is why the Bible and other ancient texts are still capable of speaking to us so powerfully. Pick up and read the Old Testament book of Proverbs. There are few pieces of advice in it that do not hold true in 2008.

For thousands of years the formative experiences and lessons of life have remained, at core, the same. Like Herbert Butterfield, 'I [do not] know of any mundane fullness of life which we could pretend to possess and which was not open to people in the age of Isaiah or Plato, Dante or Shakespeare.'[61] Accordingly, it makes sense to regard the phenomenon of grace as we now experience it not as a recent by-product of 'advanced civilisation', but as a fundamental feature of the human condition.

Grace thus points to God.

Other manifestations of grace

In *The Road Less Travelled*, M. Scott Peck linked the concept of grace to two other phenomena: the process of Darwinian evolution, and suffering. His observations about each are well worth contemplating.

As to evolution, a subject I sought to tackle in Chapter 1, Peck observed that the process appears to run counter to one of the most basic laws of science, the Second Law of Thermodynamics. That law holds in substance that the natural 'flow' of energy in any closed system in the Universe is from a state of organisation to a state of disorganisation (known as 'entropy'). In short, like a cottage garden, most things if left alone will run down over time; it takes another source of energy to organise and prevent dissipation. Yet the process of evolution, at least as it is understood according to conventional Darwinian theory, seems to defy this law. It flows against the force of entropy. Life on earth has progressed from microbe to man, through higher and higher states of complexity. In Peck's words, 'the process of evolution is a miracle, because in so far as it is a process of increasing organisation and differentiation, it runs counter to natural law. In the ordinary course of things, we who read and write this book should not exist'.[62]

A number of eminent scientists have also made observations along these lines, including Hermann von Helmhotz (one of the founders of the science of thermodynamics), Sir Arthur Eddington (who was a devout Quaker) and Edwin Schrödinger. A twentieth-century French philosopher and cleric, Teilhard de Chardin, who trained as a geologist and paleontologist, wrote a notable book devoted to this theme. Entitled *The Phenomenon of Man*, and published posthumously in 1955, it is an extended argument for the existence of an all-pervading teleological force (ultimately, God) which counteracts the force of entropy.

These arguments are far from being mainstream. Many other eminent scientists – in including men and woman of strong faith – have disputed that there is any conflict between evolution and the Second Law.[63] Further or alternatively, they have sought to explain its more puzzling aspects in terms of the phenomenon of 'emergent complexity', whereby Nature somehow seems to produce increasingly complex phenomena which are not reducible to the sum of their constituent parts.[64]

My own untutored view is that the whole issue is, from a scientific perspective, a deep mystery. But that very mysteriousness is suggestive. Before Darwin's discoveries, most people regarded complex life as a miracle, requiring a supernatural explanation (God). Now, even after Darwin, complex life *still* appears to be a miracle – but for different reasons. Why? Because (assuming Darwin's theory to be essentially correct) there is now the question how evolution can be squared with the Second Law and – one of my main points in Chapter 1 – the even deeper question how the finely tuned process of evolution itself came into being.

The very fact that life *appears* to be a miracle – and has always appeared to be a miracle – is indicative of Design. It is as though Man is supposed to speculate about the matter, to wonder at the origins and the preciousness of life. One is driven to believe, not only in evolution, but in so-called 'involution' – the idea that 'what has been produced by the universe must somehow have previously been in it'[65]. This looks like God's grace in action again.

M. Scott Peck's views about grace and evolution got me thinking. Later in his book, Peck went on to discuss grace in a quite different context: the functioning of evil in the world:

[E]vil backfires in the big picture of human evolution. For every soul that it destroys – and there are many – it is instrumental in the salvation of others. Unwittingly, evil serves as a beacon to warn others away from its shoals. Because most of us have been graced by an almost instinctive sense of horror at the outrageousness of evil, when we recognise its presence, our own personalities are honed by the awareness of its existence. Our consciousness of it is a signal to purify ourselves.[66]

This, too, struck me on first reading as a well-drawn observation. It also is not original (cf. Proverbs 11), but it helped at the time to hone my thinking. The notion that a certain amount of evil and suffering often prevents even *greater* evil and suffering is a key fact about the world. It is another facet of grace, and it is discernible both at the level of individual lives and in the broad sweep of human history.

At the personal level, this idea received memorable treatment in one of the best mainstream English-language films of the last generation, *American Beauty* (1999). The pivotal scene occurs near the end. The central character, Lester Burnham (Kevin Spacey), a dejected and embittered middle-American Everyman, finds himself in a position to fulfil the sexual fantasy that has sustained his broken life for months. A beautiful blonde teenage girl (one of his daughter's friends) lies underneath him, urging him on. But Lester senses, finally, the evil that would be wrought by his living out his dream. He hesitates. He realises in an instant, though this is not made explicit in the film, that the evils that have been previously inflicted *upon him* – by a frigid, manipulative wife; by the soulless, material culture that produced those flaws in a once lovely woman – would only be further perpetuated by his taking advantage of the girl. He now really understands why evil must not be repaid with evil. He realises, also, that to do so in this case would mean the death of his own already deeply sick soul.

A little later, Lester sits in his kitchen thinking, wistful and serene. Then he is murdered – by a repressed gay neighbour, who is himself a victim of evil. But Lester dies in a state of grace. Like the criminal on the Cross next to Jesus on Calvary, his last act has redeemed him. The viewer of the film is asked to assume that the suffering inflicted upon and by Lester has not been degrading and futile, but ennobling and significant. Carolyn, his wife – who is *not* an unmitigated monster, but also a victim – is briefly seen sobbing in guilt and despair. She had contemplated killing Lester herself, and had bought a gun to do it with. Now she, too, assumes a state of grace, a reconciliation with herself made possible, we realise, only through Lester's death. The beautiful teenage girl has her life ahead of her. Lester's life has been lost, but his soul has been saved; Carolyn and girl have been given another chance. A certain amount of evil has prevented much greater evil.

These patterns are discernible not only at the level of individual lives, but in the history of nations and empires. I have already discussed the idea that whole races of people, entire nations, have from time to time in history learned from their suffering, and set about actively atoning for their collective mistakes. But there is a sense in which the force of grace (or Providence) operates even more profoundly. As Herbert Butterfield explained, 'there is a kind of progress which comes from no merit of ours and implies no necessary improvement in our essential personalities'[67]. It is the progress that simply *happens* as the natural and logical result of changed circumstances or the effluxion of time. Butterfield used the examples of the fall of the Roman Empire and the Norman Conquest of England. Both events were, at the time, catastrophic for countless individual men and women and for many organised societies. But in the long run each event was the catalyst for 'a new world order' which, in retrospect, few would wish away.[68]

Nuclear weapons

That brings me to one final consideration in this sequence of argument concerning grace, a consideration that any sceptic of God ought carefully to ponder. There is one potential event – nuclear holocaust – that would *not* lead to a 'new world order'. If it ever happened, human life would almost certainly be rendered meaningless, if not extinct. For over sixty years Mankind has possessed the means to destroy itself. While this circumstance is extremely recent in the scheme of human history, I cannot help but think it has great theological significance. The fact that Mankind has not yet destroyed itself is positively extraordinary. Indeed, our survival since 1945 suggests to me more strongly than anything else the reality of God's grace.

One of the most frightening books ever written is Jonathan Schell's masterpiece

The Fate of the Earth, first published in 1982 and updated in 2000.[69] Schell described in exhaustive but compelling detail the consequences that would follow – for Mankind, and the Earth itself – in the event of nuclear war. The picture that he painted is utterly dire: under at least some scenarios, the destruction *forever* of most, if not all, life on Earth. The United States would be reduced, in Schell's imperishable phrase, to 'a Republic of insects and grass'. In *The Road* (2006), a magisterial novel by Cormac McCarthy, the author's vision of a post-Apocalypse America is only slightly less desolate. A few people survive, scavenging a ghastly existence in the dead, grey remains of civilisation.

A number of other books and films dealing with this subject have likewise made a searing impression upon me. Especially resonant were certain scenes in Nicholas Meyer's 1983 film *The Day After*, which depicts events from the perspective of ordinary citizens and low-level military personnel in Missouri and Kansas. There is a chilling moment when one of the central characters, a young farmer's wife, feels a violent rumble when sitting at her dressing table. She rushes to the window, and sees that missiles have just been launched from a nearby American base. The expression on her face tells us that she knows, then and there, that it is the end of everything.

Other works of art have imagined the way in which a nuclear exchange might be brought about. In *Fail-Safe*, a novel written in 1964 by Eugene Burdick and Harvey Wheeler, and subsequently filmed, a malfunction in a small but vital piece of machinery – a transistor – results in six American bombers being sent on an unstoppable course to Russian cities. The *Terminator* films proceed on the assumption that computers have reached such a level of sophistication as to usurp the control of Man. The same notion is at the heart of Kubrick's masterpiece about human and artificial intelligence, *2001: A Space Odyssey* (1968). Kubrick's film explicitly about the nuclear issue, the black comedy *Dr. Strangelove* (1962), focuses upon the potential fallibility of human decision-makers in times of crisis.

Of course, no work of art can adequately convey the scale of such a calamity. But for me these works resonated, and still do. The subject has always held a grim fascination. I can remember, as a young man, during the era of Ronald Reagan, being genuinely fearful that a nuclear war might begin at any time. Once, I awoke during the night to an ear-splitting roar, and for a moment believed that the awful moment might have come. It was only a summer thunderstorm.

My fears were not unfounded. We now know that, during the first term of Reagan's presidency, on the night of 8–9 November 1983, the Soviet Union came extremely close to launching its arsenal. Members of its high command mistakenly believed that a NATO training exercise ('Able Archer 83') was the prelude to a real attack by the US.[70] This was before Mikhael Gorbachev and *perestroika*, and enmity between the superpowers ran deep. In the early 1980s there had been a huge military build-up on both sides; in March 1983, Reagan famously denounced the Soviets as 'the focus of evil in the modern world'. As tensions were raised, public fears grew, in both eastern and western Europe as well as North America. The anti-nuclear movement – with strong backing from Pope John Paul II – gained strength throughout the West. On 5 May 1983, the US House of Representatives passed a 'nuclear freeze' resolution.

To his great credit, and whether for electoral or other reasons, President Reagan responded. During 1984 he toned down his rhetoric substantially, and, while still championing the so-called 'Star Wars' programme, stressed its *defensive* purpose. At the outset of his second term, in January 1985, Reagan committed himself to the goal of large-scale arms reduction, including the 'elimination' of nuclear weapons. When Gorbachev came to power later in 1985, Reagan worked with him to end the Cold War. Often, along the way, he overruled hawkish advisers in the White House and the Pentagon.[71]

In retrospect, the early 1980s were truly frightening. But it is generally acknowledged that the Earth came closest to nuclear war during the so-called Cuban missile crisis, in October 1962. This is not a matter of speculation or opinion: there are hundreds of pages of verbatim transcripts of the conversations that took place in the White House between President Kennedy and his military and civilian advisers.[72] To read these transcripts is to realise just how forbiddingly real the possibility of imminent catastrophe was. It seems clear that, at various points in the drama, if Kennedy had followed the advice urged upon him by members of the Joint Chiefs of Staff and/or his Cabinet, nuclear war must almost inevitably have been the result. Like several of Reagan's conciliatory moves towards Gorbachev after 1985, most of Kennedy's key decisions on Cuba were opposed by the majority of his own advisers. To nominate three: the decision to establish a naval blockade of Cuba rather than invade; the decision *not* to invade despite the shooting down of an American reconnaissance jet; and the decision to offer an exchange of American missiles in Turkey for the Soviet missiles in Cuba. On each occasion, Kennedy stood down the hawks. Their instinct was almost always for more aggression, for more brinkmanship. They frequently displayed a frightening faith in violence and technology, when those very things were the root cause of the predicament.

The Soviet leader, Khrushchev, also emerges from the historical record with considerable credit. The exchanges between Khrushchev and his own advisers were not recorded verbatim, as were the White House deliberations. But enough is now known of the Soviets' side of the matter to conclude that Khrushchev, like Kennedy, rejected much of the advice he was getting. In the end, it was Khrushchev who made the crucial decision to back down. Of course, he caused the crisis in the first place by ordering the secret construction of the missiles in Cuba; but that fact can only have made his ultimate decision the more difficult, because his pride was on the line. Khrushchev's great achievement was that he swallowed his and his nation's pride. In later defending the Soviet retreat, Khrushchev hit the nail on the head: 'They talk about who won and who lost. Human reason won. Mankind won.'[73]

What, it may be asked, does all this have to do with grace, and the existence or otherwise of God? There are three considerations of importance.

First, it is significant that Man, alone of all creatures, has been able to harness the awesome power of the nuclear forces of Nature. This demonstrates definitively the fact of Man's dominion over the Earth. There is also a mystical symmetry about the fact of Man's achievement. The Universe began at the moment of the Big Bang with the creation of the four fundamental forces of Nature. Billions of years later, it is Man who has learnt enough about the Universe to understand those forces, and to seek to utilise them for his own ends, both good and evil. Does that not tell us that there is something quite special about Man?

Second, one must try to discern how and why Mankind survived the Cuban crisis in October 1962. My belief is that a calamity must have been much more likely but for two key historical events, both of which were still fresh in Kennedy's mind: the botched invasion of Cuba in April 1961 at the Bay of Pigs; and the bombings of Hiroshima and Nagasaki in August 1945.

The Bay of Pigs fiasco taught the then-inexperienced President to be wary of cocky assurances by his military and intelligence advisers. All had predicted an easy victory by the CIA-backed Cuban rebels, and the swift ousting of Fidel Castro by sympathetic locals. The operation was badly planned and ended in a rout. Kennedy had the good sense not to allow events to escalate by sending in American forces, as the top brass had urged him to do, and he took the blame politically. But the event scarred him.

The bombings of Hiroshima and Nagasaki were, I suspect, even more pivotal to Kennedy's decision-making process during the missile crisis. Some have argued (with considerable force) that President Truman's decision to authorise those bombings was morally wrong. In 1946 the US Federal Council of Churches issued a statement (drafted by Rienhold Niebuhr) in which America was judged to have 'sinned grievously against the laws of God and against the peoples of Japan'[74]. The official justification for the bombings at the time, and frequently since, was that such a grisly demonstration was required in order to force the Japanese to surrender, thereby saving the lives of many American soldiers and many more Japanese soldiers and civilians; and it is true that, after Nagasaki, the Pacific War was brought swiftly to an end. But could not the same point have been made by a detonation over an uninhabited area of Japan? Or a military rather than a civilian target? At the least, why was more than one bomb required?

These questions could be debated *ad infinitum*. But they are incidental to my present point, which is that the longer-term safety of Mankind seems to have been secured – albeit precariously – only because Truman had wreaked such appalling suffering on those two occasions. Man thus came to understand the reality of nuclear weapons not merely in theory, but by reference to a concrete, tragic example. Suffering begat wisdom.

The Cuban crisis was over forty-five years ago. The world's arsenals are now much more powerful than they were in 1962. How is it that Man has not, by now, been obliterated by nuclear holocaust? This to me is the third and most important consideration as regards nuclear weapons, for on the face of it Man's survival is highly improbable.

Experience tells us that if something can go wrong then, eventually, it will. Granted, things do not go wrong all of the time, or even most of the time, and the consequences of things going wrong are not usually especially bad. But all of us – individually and collectively – are fallible. There are no exceptions to this truism, even for people utterly pre-eminent in their own field: Caesar trusted his senators; Einstein wasted the last forty years of his life on a 'theory of everything' that went nowhere; Bradman made seven Test ducks.

Collectively, too, people can and do make the gravest mistakes: the inhabitants of

Easter Island harvested it and themselves to death; the German people – 43.9 per cent of them at the federal election of 1933 – *elected* the Nazis. No technology is foolproof, even (perhaps especially) the most elaborate or heralded or expensive technology: the *Titanic* sank on its first voyage, without enough lifeboats; the wonder drug Thalidomide maimed a generation; the *Challenger* and *Columbia* space shuttles disintegrated in mid-air, killing all on board.

Similar examples, from the trivial to the momentous, could be multiplied indefinitely.[75] Yet against all of the odds, Mankind has been spared from nuclear catastrophe. In Khrushchev's phrase, Mankind continues to 'win'. This is positively extraordinary. Indeed, I believe it is nothing less than a miracle. Consider the technical and operational complexity of the weapons systems described by Jonathan Schell and others; the often bellicose, craven or unstable leadership of the countries possessing that weaponry – not least Khrushchev himself in October 1962; the high potential for deliberate acts of evil, for human error, for technological failure of some kind or another – all of these things lead me to believe that a holocaust must already have occurred but for some greater force preventing it.

What force? In Andrei Tartovsky's masterful film *The Sacrifice* (1986), perhaps the most profound artistic treatment of this mesmerising subject, a small group of people is gathered at a house in the Swedish countryside. News comes through on a crackling television set that a nuclear war is unfolding in Europe. The people at the house variously react with disbelief, anger, resignation, terror, despair. The main character, an elderly man, promises God that if only He will undo what has happened, he (the man) will give up everything he holds dear. After a strange series of events normality is restored, though the man now appears to be insane and is carted away to a mental asylum. This bare outline does no justice to the surreal beauty of the film, which may be interpreted in many possible ways: the man dreamt it all; the news of the holocaust was real, after which the man went mad and was hallucinating; it was all real, including the divine intervention.

It is debatable whether Tartovsky intended the events depicted in the film to be understood in any one way. But contemplation of his film has confirmed my own belief. It is this: since the invention of nuclear weapons, the survival of the human race has been due, not to good luck or good management, but to God's grace. As Scripture says, 'Because of the Lord's great love we are not consumed' (Lamentations 3:22).

Conclusion: the vital link between suffering and grace

Suffering is an essential concomitant of two kinds of grace, and thereby points to the existence of God.

First, suffering gives rise to grace on the part of Man. This was Christ's insight in the parable of the prodigal son, and the theme of *American Beauty*. Suffering promotes wisdom and humility, and true thankfulness for the things that make life worthwhile. It challenges each of us to show forgiveness for the measure of suffering that is inflicted on us by others. It enables us appreciate the meaning of Christ's suffering. And, especially when it is most extreme, suffering draws us closer to God.

In short, suffering forces us to look beyond ourselves. As ever, Shakespeare[76] got it right:

> Thou seeest we are not all alone unhappy:
>> This wide and universal theatre
> Presents more woeful pageants than the scene
>> Wherein we play in.

Suffering also reveals the grace of God. The suffering that there is demonstrates what can happen, but usually does *not* happen, at least on the scale that we fear. Taken on the whole, there is just enough suffering to make life meaningful, but not so much that life itself loses meaning.

The great German philosopher, Gottfried Leibniz, reached broadly similar conclusions. Leibniz's theory was that we live in the 'Best of All Possible Worlds'. He did not mean that the world is perfect – far from it – but that God did not create a *better* world because there isn't one. As Franklin has explained it:

> [C]ontrary to appearances … if one part of the world were improved, the ramifica-
> tions would result in it being worse elsewhere, and worse overall. It is a 'bump in the
> carpet' theory: push evil down here, and it pops up over there.[77]

If you think hard enough about this state of affairs, it should not turn you away from God but give rise to a heightened appreciation of the genius of His Creation.

CHAPTER 8

CHRISTIANITY AND POLITICS

Whoever wants to become great among you must be your servant, and whoever wants to be first must be your slave.

Matthew 20:26–27

The Christian ideal has not been tried and found wanting. It has been found difficult; and left untried.

G.K. Chesterton

For many people in the West of left-wing ideological persuasion, there is an obstacle to Christian faith even more formidable than the existence of suffering. That is the association in their minds between Christianity and right-wing politics. The former leader of the Australian Labor Party (ALP), Mark Latham, is representative of this mindset: 'Organised religion: just another form of conservative command and control in our society'[1]. A lot of people who are close to me also think in this way; and I once did myself.

The more you learn about Christianity, however, the more evident it becomes that the Latham view is shallow and simplistic. It is not entirely wrong: there is no doubt that some denominations of the Christian church, especially in the United States, have aligned themselves with right-wing political parties. In addition, many aspects of Christian theology are aptly described as conservative. But in saying that, I do not use the word 'conservative' as a synonym for right-wing ideology in general, as I suspect Latham did. Rather, Christianity is conservative in this commendable sense: it teaches that we should place a high value on certain long-established moral and ethical precepts, and be wary of any form of change that threatens the primacy of those precepts.

In other respects, Christianity is anything but conservative. At a personal level, it challenges people to change the way they live their lives, to make what Kierkegaard called an act of 'infinite resignation'. Sometimes the change that results from following Christianity is radical, as it was for the Disciples called at the Lake of Gennesaret. Jesus was blunt about the disruption that such change may cause (see Luke 14:26; Matthew 10:34), though He was most certainly *not* saying, as is too often claimed, that His followers should hate their own families.[2]

At a political level, too, Christianity is (or should be) a dynamic force. It should not be equated with timid preservation of the status quo, nor with what 'works' in some pragmatic sense, but with what is proper and just. In my judgment, Christianity is more 'left-wing' than 'right-wing' in emphasis; but ultimately it is a set of beliefs that, as a whole, defies such labelling.

After a lifetime of immersion in politics, and a decade of learning about Christianity, I have reached six broad conclusions. The following explanations of them may assist other people to overcome any prejudice against Christianity that is based on political ideology. My purpose is not to espouse a party-political message. I want to encourage people on both the Left and the Right to think again about some of their political views in the light of Christian principles, and to think again about Christianity in the light of their political principles.

Christianity reflects some seminal 'left-wing' values

The Jesus of the Gospels was an agitator, a pacifist and a champion of the lowly. He was quite disinterested in the accumulation of wealth. He espoused principles that are in many ways unrecognisable in the views of some modern-day adherents of Christianity.

So-called religious 'conservatives' in the United States, and increasingly in Australia, are regularly to be heard invoking Jesus's name. Yet it is hard to escape the conclusion that, if Jesus were alive today, some of those same people would label Him a dangerous radical, an appeaser and a 'bleeding heart'. It is fair to ask, if only rhetorically: '[H]ow did the message of Jesus ever become aligned with big business, military spending, gun ownership, tax cuts and disdain for the environment?'[3] The situation is sad and perplexing. It is as if some Christians just have not read the Gospels.

Jesus regarded *agape* – the practice of charity toward one's fellow man – as fundamental to right behaviour. He emphasised time and again that each of us would be judged by how we have treated the weakest people in society. According to Matthew's Gospel, this was the very last thought that Jesus left with the Disciples. In the account of the Final Judgment, Jesus explicitly equated helping the needy with having helped *Him*:

> '...For I was hungry and you gave me something to eat, I was thirsty and you gave me something to drink, I was a stranger and you invited me in, I needed clothes and you clothed me, I was sick and you looked after me, I was in prison and you came to visit me.' Then the righteous will answer him, 'Lord, when did we see you hungry and feed

you, or thirsty and give you something to drink? When did we see you a stranger and invite you in, or needing clothes and clothe you? When did we see you sick or in prison and go to visit you?' The King will reply, 'I tell you the truth, whatever you did for one of the least of these brothers of mine, you did for me.'

(Matthew 25:35–40)

This was not an isolated thought but a central theme of Jesus's teaching, also reflected in the parables of the rich fool (Luke 12:13–21) and of the rich man and Lazarus (Luke 16:19–31).

The same idea is consistently reiterated in the rest of the New Testament. St Paul declared bluntly that 'nobody should seek his own good, but the good of others' (1 Corinthians 10:24), and St Peter expressed similar sentiments. But the theme receives its most powerful treatment in the letter of James. As I have earlier noted, St James was Jesus's brother. He was a formidable leader of the early Church in Jerusalem (assuming full authority there after Peter's departure from the city in AD 43–44) and his epistle is probably the oldest of all the New Testament writings. It is thus strong evidence of the priorities of the Church's founders.

What were those priorities? James stressed the importance of good works as well as faith. He defined 'pure and faultless' religion as taking care of orphans and widows in their suffering; its antithesis, he said, was to allow yourself to be corrupted by the world (James 1:27, 2:14–26). James directed a tirade against rich people who hoarded their wealth, exploited their workers, 'fattened [them]selves' by over-eating, and/or wallowed in 'luxury and self-indulgence' (5:1–6).

This social justice tradition in Christianity did not begin with Jesus. It can be traced to some of the greatest of the Old Testament prophets, who saw their role as challenging the rich and powerful, exposing their cruelty and excesses, and encouraging a simple piety.[4] Micah asked rhetorically: 'What does the Lord require of you but to do justice, and to love kindness and to walk humbly with your God?' (Micah 5:2–3). Amos denounced those who 'sell the needy for a pair of sandals [and] trample on the heads of the poor as upon the dust of the ground' (Amos 2:6–7). And Solomon stated things more bluntly still: 'He who gives to the poor will lack nothing, but he who closes his eyes to them receives many curses.' (Proverbs 28:27)

These are not the sentiments exhibited in recent decades by welfare-slashers and bean-counters, obsessive tax-cutters and ruthless profiteers.

Throughout recorded history, socio-political change that advantages the poor over the wealthy has never been easy to accomplish. Those in positions of power and influence tend to oppose it, and their views disproportionately sway the opinions of others, so there is rarely a peaceful consensus in favour of reforming the status quo. Partly for that reason, in the words of Martin Luther King, '[a]lmost always the creative dedicated minority has made the world better'[5].

Sometimes, these dedicated minorities have been inspired by people of faith – such as King himself. Catholic social justice teaching has long emphasised the right of all people to petition government for the redress of grievances.[6] But, more often, pious religious people have retreated from the sullied milieu of secular politics. Jesus, however, rejected any suggestion that man should 'live by bread alone' – i.e. entirely spiritually.[7] As we shall see, He also lambasted religious officials who closed their eyes to the plight of the needy *in this earthly life*. It is therefore regrettable in the extreme that, over the centuries, some religious leaders and institutions have actively opposed socio-political change aimed at helping the poor and oppressed.

The situation today is, in some ways, as bad as ever. Throughout the West, for at least the last thirty years, right-wing political parties espousing neo-liberal, market-driven economic policies have been supported disproportionately by Christian voters. Frequently, Christian people of this kind are exemplary in their own personal lives; they exhibit kindness and generosity to family and friends. But there it seems to end.

The fault does not lie with Christian theology, but with fallible human beings. Most of us have not truly taken to heart Jesus's admonition to the Pharisees: it is just not enough to be kind to your family and friends (cf. Luke 14:12–14). To do so is to lack the imagination to place yourself (or your family or friends) in the same situation as others less fortunate than you. To do so is also, unconsciously or not, to regard your own good fortune (and that of your family and friends) as no more than a just reward for effort, as though luck and circumstance never play a role in human affairs. It is to forget that your own material blessings – even if they truly are, in some sense, a reward for effort – usually are made possible only because of the gifts of nationality, or intelligence, or personality, or talent, or stamina, or physical beauty, all of which are themselves bestowed by God.

The matter is stated plainly in the Old Testament:

> You may say to yourself, 'My power and the strength of my hands have produced this wealth for me.' But remember the Lord your God, for it is he who gives you the ability to produce wealth.
>
> (Deuteronomy 8:17–18)

Too many right-wing Christians seem oblivious, even hostile, to this teaching. They forget that it was Friedrich Nietzsche, the arch-atheist of the late nineteenth century, who lambasted Christianity as a 'cult of resentment'. Nietzsche sneered at Christianity's heavy emphasis on charity, 'its active pity for all the failures and all the weak'.[8] Yet, today, such an attitude seems to inform the political views of a significant number of people on the Religious Right, and their faulty example accounts in no small part for the secular Left's hostility to Christianity. But that is not a good reason to reject Christianity holus bolus, especially as the Gospels provide strong support for many of the principles that the Left holds dear.

The great Australian Labor prime minister from 1945–49, Ben Chifley, cast his and his party's aspirations explicitly in terms of social justice:

We have a great objective – the light on the hill – which we aim to reach by working for the betterment of mankind not only here but anywhere we may give a helping hand.[9]

Chifley's famous image of 'the light on the hill' was, of course, taken from Scripture.[*] It appears in the Sermon on the Mount (Matthew 5:14).

Those of the Left who scorn Christianity should go back to the Gospels, and the example of Jesus. They might also usefully read any of a number of books that explore political issues from a 'liberal' Christian perspective. Among the best from the United States are *The Politics of Jesus* (1972) by John Howard Yoder[10], a seminal work, and, more recently, two books by the well-known preacher/activist Jim Wallis (*God's Politics* (2005) and *The Great Awakening: Seven Ways to Change the World* (2008)). Wallis is also the editor-in-chief of *Sojourners*, which has been an indispensible monthly journal of the Christian Left since the 1970s.

My own purpose in this section is to briefly examine four of the most vexed and important political issues. My contention – broadly speaking – is that on these four issues the 'left-wing' position is considerably closer to Christian teaching than the 'right-wing' position.

War and peace

In *God's Politics*, Jim Wallis points out that there are only two legitimate Christian traditions regarding war: pacifism and the just-war doctrine[11]. As I get older, I lean more and more towards the Quakers' stance of strict pacifism and non-violence, but it is not necessary to be a pacifist to believe that war is the ultimate evil. Once the dogs of war are unleashed, the vilest of human sins are inevitable – usually on a worse scale than any sins of the enemy that precipitated war in the first place. Almost every political and military leader pays lip service to this sentiment, but few really live by it.

The Christian position on war comes down to a question of emphasis. No reasonable person can deny that there are great dangers in the world and that every government has a duty to protect its citizens (cf. 1 Timothy 2:2). But the question is how to provide the most effective protection, consistently with Christian ethics. Should governments concentrate their efforts on preparing to fight wars, or on tackling the problems that cause them? Is it wise to promote fear in the hearts and minds of the enemy, in the hope of deterring them from aggression? Is it right to promote fear and hatred of the enemy among one's own people, if necessary by dishonest propaganda, in order to galvanise them to fight? Or is it better to encourage, if not love and understanding, then at least hard-headed compromise, between peoples with grievances against each other?

The Christian position is clear. The emphasis must not be upon fear and intimida-

---

[*] Chifley is not the only leader to have invoked this biblical metaphor. So too did John Winthrop, the Puritan governor of the Massachusetts Bay Colony, in a sermon to his fellow pilgrims shortly before they sailed from England to the New World in 1630. Winthrop envisaged that the society they were to create would be 'as a Citty upon a Hill, [with] the eies of all people … upon us.'

tion but upon love, understanding and compromise: the non-violent resolution of conflict. God's way, His ultimate vision, is evoked in these words of the Old Testament prophet Micah:

> He will judge between many peoples and will settle disputes for strong nations far and wide. They will beat their swords into ploughshares and their spears into pruning hooks. Nation will not take up sword against nation, nor will they train for war any more. Every man will sit under his own vine and under his own fig-tree, and no-one will make them afraid any more.
>
> (Micah 4:3–4; see also Isaiah 2:4)

At the heart of this teaching is the basal truth that wars are very rarely 'clear straight conflicts of right against wrong'[12]. Political and military leaders almost always depict wars that way, but usually their root causes are murky and mixed. As Herbert Butterfield observed, 'Though one side may have more justice than another in the particular occasion of a conflict, there is a sense in which war as such is a judgment on all of us'[13]. Most wars are the result of a failure of imagination on both sides, an inability or unwillingness to find a better way than rape, pillage and bloodshed.

The New Testament is also clear on this issue. The universal symbol of peace is derived from the Gospels – at Jesus's baptism, 'the Spirit of God descended like a dove' (Matthew 3:16). Jesus was sometimes known as the Prince of Peace, and His teachings about loving one's enemies are paramount. These teachings apply not merely in our personal lives but also at the level of governments and nations.

One reason for treating enemies with decency and respect – for eschewing retaliatory violence – is that it may shame and embarrass them. St Paul likened it to 'heaping burning coals on their heads' (see Romans 12:14–21). In the twentieth century, Rienhold Niebuhr contended that it 'rob[s] the opponent of the moral conceit by which he identifies his interests with the peace and order of society'[14]. Occasionally, this strategy may kindle remorse in the enemy and bring about a change in their conduct. If that sounds utopian, consider a more nakedly pragmatic argument: it is not merely wrong but *impossible* to 'rid the world of evil' (in George W. Bush's phrase) by the use of force. Violence begets more violence, and hate more hate. Moreover, history shows that violence and hate will only be exacerbated if a war is depicted as a 'battle for righteousness', because to do so inflames passions on both sides and makes compromise more difficult. If any war truly *must* be fought, it is better that each participant honestly acknowledges its own pragmatic motives and those of both its allies and its enemies.[15]

In the Sermon on the Mount, Jesus said: 'Blessed are the peacemakers, for they will be called Sons of God' (Matthew 5:9). On any fair interpretation, that pronouncement requires every country, every leader, every soldier and every citizen to strive to avoid war if there is any tolerable alternative. We should, in consequence, be extremely wary of questioning the 'strength' or the 'realism' of leaders who in good faith seek alternatives to war, even if those alternatives are themselves far from satisfactory. Usually such leaders are the strongest and most realistic. They do not have short memories, and they measure 'honour' in a different way. As Milton wrote, 'Peace hath her victories/No less renowned than war'[16]. In the same vein, Benjamin Franklin remarked, 'There never was a good war, or a bad peace.'[17]

The reality of war – for soldiers and civilians directly affected – is almost inconceivably appalling. One of the greatest achievements of the cinema has been to represent that reality, in all its squalid horror, to people who have never experienced war for themselves. Still, even the most graphic and moving films – Peter Weir's *Gallipoli* (1981), Oliver Stone's *Born On the Fourth of July* (1989), Terence Malick's *The Thin Red Line* (1998), to name three that especially shocked me – can convey (I would guess) only a faint sense of the barbarity of the experience.

Wars are fought by *individual* human beings, who love and are loved. Christian teaching about love generally – and not merely the need to love one's enemies – is pertinent to a consideration of war. There is a tendency to depersonalise the consequences of war (before or after the event) by thinking of it as something, albeit horrible, that happens only to strangers. The antidote to such thinking must be to put yourself in the place of the soldier, the stretcher-bearer, the terrified civilian. Jesus's teachings require any political leader to try to imagine – *before* committing to war – that it will be his son's guts spilling to the ground in front of his eyes after the shrapnel has flown, his daughter's skin melting off her face after the bomb explodes, his wife's grief on hearing the news of a husband's or a child's death or mutilation.

Robert Walpole, the first British Prime Minister, may have been thinking in this way in 1774, when he defended to Queen Caroline his decision not to send English troops to intervene in a now long-forgotten Polish war: 'Madam, there are fifty thousand men slain this year in Europe, and not one Englishman.'[18]

There is one other reason why militarism and war are an affront to Christianity as much as 'left-wing' values. The proliferation of armies and arsenals, and the reliance upon actual or implicit threats to deploy them, amounts to a form of idolatry. Rather than placing trust in God, Man relies anxiously upon military might. But as I have argued as regards nuclear weapons, there is ultimately no safety in military might. 'No king is saved by the size of his army,' says the Thirty-third Psalm.

Piling up arms, and curtailing human rights and freedoms in the name of 'security', is counterproductive and wrong. Herbert Butterfield thought that Man's gravest collective sin in the first half of the twentieth century was 'distrust of Providence'. He feared that 'by an excessive desire to control the destiny of mankind we may create disaster and only enlarge the area of the original disorder'[19]. The second half of the twentieth century would only have confirmed Butterfield in this view. Vietnam and Iraq were prime examples of 'enlarging the area of the original disorder'. The Cold War ended peacefully, but by arming itself to the teeth the human race has vastly increased its own vulnerability, to the extent that our existence now depends, more than ever, on God's grace. If you do not believe in God, then you must hope for the indefinite continuation of what has been, so far, over sixty years of inexplicable good luck.

The precarious state of the world today had its origins in the First World War. It weakened Britain and France irrevocably, left Germany embittered, and led directly to the Second World War. The unprecedented slaughter was brought about in large part by the incompetence of military and political leaders before, during and immediately after the event. That collective failure undermined all forms of authority, including that of the churches. The War thus accelerated the decline of organised religion in the West, a process that had already begun well before 1914. Indeed, as Paul Johnson has eloquently argued, the War itself can be attributed to that decline, and more specifically to another form of idolatry:

> The detonator of the modern tragedy of humankind was the First World War ... Its destructive impact on established and improving notions of human behaviour and international morality was immeasurable and we are still suffering from its consequences. This war was not merely without reason, it was plainly avoidable. What caused it? I suggest it was, above all, the worship of money and still more power which already, by 1914, was becoming for many people a substitute for the worship of God.[20]

Johnson's observation as to 'the worship of money' leads to the second of my four issues.

The distribution of wealth

In *God's Politics*, Jim Wallis points out that there are several thousand verses in the Bible dealing with poverty, injustice and God's injunctions about them. It is the second-most prominent subject in the Old Testament (behind idolatry) and a central concern of the Gospels.[21] (It was also a central concern of Muhammad, who, like Jesus, enjoyed his greatest initial success among slaves, women and the underprivileged – those who were not sharing in seventh-century Mecca's burgeoning commercial prosperity.[22])

I have already set out some of the key passages from the Bible which stress the importance of charity toward the afflicted. Another key Christian teaching centres upon the dangers *for the rich* of accumulating inordinate wealth. Schopenhauer compared wealth with sea water: 'The more we drink, the thirstier we become'[23]. Perhaps the best known biblical passage on this theme is this one:

> For we brought nothing into the world, and can take nothing out of it. But if we have food and clothing, we will be content with that. People who want to get rich fall into temptation and a trap and into many foolish and harmful desires that plunge men into ruin and destruction. For the love of money is a root of all kinds of evil.
>
> (1 Timothy 6:7–10)

For the privileged, it is salutary also to recall Jesus's prophecy that, at the Final Judgment, 'many who are first will be last, and many who are last will be first' (Matthew 19:30).

Despite these and other similar biblical warnings (see, for example, Luke 12:33–34), there remain, in the West today, significant numbers of apparently sincere Christians who vehemently oppose the central tenets of the Left's economic agenda. Many more

Christians remain, if not actively hostile, then at least stubbornly indifferent to these causes.

That situation may finally be starting to change[24], but, if so, it is not before time. From the late 1970s onwards, blocks of Christian voters regularly helped right-wing candidates to win high political office – and stay there. US Presidents Ronald Reagan, George H. W. Bush and George W. Bush all relied on this electoral 'base', and so, to a lesser extent, have right-wing politicians in other countries. But the end-result has not been the furtherance of Christian values in any meaningful sense. The changes effected by or from the Right over the last generation have been almost solely economic.

Throughout the West, a certain orthodoxy – a 'responsible' way of doing things – gradually became entrenched. It has been dubbed 'neo-liberalism' or (the term I prefer) 'supercapitalism'.[25] Its articles of faith are – or were – wholesale deregulation of markets, both within and across national borders; much-reduced personal and corporate tax rates; and the maintenance of constant 'economic growth'. By various statistical measures, these policies 'succeeded' – and for a remarkably long time. There was a sustained rise in almost everybody's material living standards. Now, in early 2009, the Global Financial Crisis is upon us, and at the time of writing it is hard to say how it will play out. But, that consideration aside, there was always a darker side to the story.

I am not an economist. Accordingly, it would be silly to attempt any technical discussion of the relative merits of economic rationalism* on the one hand and Keynesianism** on the other, as regards the *creation* of wealth. In any event, the Bible does not teach that wealth in itself is an evil. More relevant for present purposes are the moral arguments advanced by people (including Christians) who routinely oppose efforts to bring about the more equal *distribution* of wealth. I speak here of the whole gamut of measures calculated to improve the material welfare of the less prosperous men, women *and children* on Earth, in areas such as progressive taxation, minimum wages, workplace conditions, housing, healthcare, access to education, foreign aid, and so on.

Broadly speaking, those who oppose systematic State-sponsored charity (*agape* in political-economic terms) advance two arguments. Neither stands up well to Christian analysis.

The first argument is that any such measures amount to an infringement upon personal freedom; or, as it is sometimes put, a 'disincentive' to individual effort and hard work. This sort of assertion has never seemed to me at all convincing. If life as a commercial lawyer taught me anything, it is that there will never be any shortage in the

---

* The term 'economic rationalism' means different things to different people, but I use it in the sense defined by Professor John Quiggin in 1997: 'The view that commercial activity ... represents a sphere of activity in which moral considerations, beyond the rule of business probity dictated by enlightened self-interest, have no role to play [or have as limited a role to play as is politically possible].' The qualifying words in square brackets are mine. See at http://en.wikipedia.org/wiki/Economic rationalism.

** I use the term 'Keynesianism' to describe the economic doctrine pioneered in the 1930s by John Maynard Keynes. It 'promotes a mixed economy, where both the state and the private sector play an important role. Instead of the economic process being based on continuous improvement in potential output... [Keynesianism] assert[s] the importance of aggregate demand for goods as the driving factor of the economy especially in periods of downturn.' See at http://en.wikipedia.org/wiki/Keynesianism.

world of people with ambition and a desire for self-advancement – and that is a necessary thing. But in my observation such people are almost always driven by something quite innate. God has blessed them with resourcefulness, reasonable luck and (sometimes) talent. They work hard for a mixture of motives – enjoyment, desire for wealth or status, a sense of duty – and nothing would be likely to deter them. Self-interest is the rule, self-sacrifice the exception.

It may seem a harsh thing to say, but I believe that in opposing measures by the State to help people who are not as prosperous as they are, the true motivation of many successful people is an inverted sense of grievance. It is an idea that, having struggled themselves to succeed, they 'deserve' reward from the State more than those who (as they see it) have not done the requisite hard work. Such an attitude does not conform with the Christian concept of grace. It directly flouts Moses' teaching in Deuteronomy as well as Jesus's startling advice to the rich young man (Matthew 19:16–22) and the thrust of the parable of the workers in the vineyard (Matthew 20:1–16).

The second argument advanced by those seeking to justify large disparities of wealth admits of the existence of the 'deserving poor'. But the argument then proceeds on the basis that the amelioration of their condition is best achieved by harder individual effort, or private charity, rather than through the State. The Brazilian archbishop, Dom Helder Camara, famously lamented this attitude: 'If I give food to the poor, they call me a saint. If I ask why the poor have no food, they call me a communist.'[26]

Right-wing Christians frequently argue that the State's role is to encourage the strong to help the weak, and that this is best achieved by better 'incentivising' the strong. The wealthier the rich get, the more will 'trickle down' to everyone else; and in any case the poor must learn to help themselves. Apart from being extremely convenient, this sort of argument always strikes me as dissembling, as passing the buck. Some people can help themselves only up to a certain point. And private charities – admirable as they mostly are – have never been anywhere near capable of meeting all of the genuine material needs of the citizenry. The dreadful deprivation wrought by the Industrial Revolution, or the Great Depression, would not have been satisfactorily alleviated by private charity: *agape* on a much more systematic scale was required. The calamity of the Irish potato famine (1845–9) showed what can happen when Western governments decline to act on these sorts of grounds. Indeed, it is not necessary to go so far back in history. You need only look at the United States today with its obscene extremes of rich and poor, so sadly highlighted by the devastation of New Orleans in 2005 by Hurricane Katrina.

Where material wealth is concerned, the dictates of Christian love boil down to a question of priorities. Toward what kinds of goals should the efforts and talents of believers – and secular idealists – primarily be directed? To making life yet more comfortable and prosperous for those who already enjoy a fair measure of comfort and prosperity? Or to ameliorating suffering and injustice?

It may be conceded that the two goals are not always mutually exclusive and that a certain degree of inequality is inevitable – indeed, desirable – in any free society. It is also true that some people exploit charity, whether it is privately given or sponsored by the State. But the central issue is clear. In the service of what cause should political efforts be exerted: at reducing material inequality between human beings, or increasing it? At more charity, or less?

It is not really an answer for the wealthy to say that the poor 'have enough to get by' or 'are better off than they were'. Of course, depending on circumstances, some governments and countries will have less capacity to correct inequality than others. But the test is one of generosity of spirit. As St Paul said of giving in general: 'If the willingness is there, the gift is acceptable according to what one has, not according to what one does not have' (2 Corinthians 8:12).

The sad fact is that, when one examines the record of right-wing political forces down the ages, the 'willingness' has not often been there. The Right has tended to defend or even exacerbate existing inequality and to favour less charity rather than more.

Human rights

One can discern similar themes in the history of human rights: due process; the abolition of slavery; the extension of the franchise to the middle and working classes, and then to women; protection of racial, ethnic and religious minorities; respect for the physically handicapped and mentally ill; humane treatment of immigrants, refugees, felons and prisoners of war. All of these causes and others like them were opposed, at least initially, and often violently, by the powers that be. To a considerable extent, the modern equivalents of these causes are still opposed by some on the Right, in Australia and elsewhere; and some of the hard-won advances that were achieved in the past are undermined or resented.

The Bible teaches not only that the poor and afflicted should be helped materially and treated with kindness. It teaches also that God is vitally *and equally* interested in every individual person, be he or she rich, poor, or anything in between. This was one of the key insights developed by the authors of the Old Testament. In exile, the scattered and embattled Jewish people began to perceive that God might be primarily concerned not with nations or communities but with people *as people*[27]; that righteousness in God's eyes might ultimately depend not upon membership of a 'successful' group but upon personal thoughts and personal conduct.

This idea – that God 'sees each individual as a creature of eternal moment' – was entrenched in Christianity by the New Testament authors. It is a fact of history that the early Christians preached the radically egalitarian, other-regarding 'love-ethic' taught by Jesus. They placed a high value upon the quality of mercy, which in the first century was a notion 'striking and subversive'[28]. So was Jesus's frequent practice of dining with people from the lower orders of society[29].

St Paul understood his own mission as preaching the Gospel not merely to his own 'elect' race, the Jews, but to all other peoples. He regarded Christ as having 'made the two one and [as having] destroyed the barrier, the dividing wall of hostility' (Ephesians 2:14). Jesus, he believed, had come to earth to unite Mankind:

He came and preached peace to you who were far away and peace to those who were near. For through Him we both have access to the Father by one Spirit. Consequently, you are no longer foreigners and aliens, but fellow-citizens with God's people and members of God's household…

In his letter to the Galatians (3:28), Paul was even more explicit: 'There is neither Jew nor Greek, slave nor free, male nor female, for you are all one in Jesus Christ.' (See also Romans 1:16; 2:11; 10:12–3.) The earliest Christian communities were unique in human history for the way in which strikingly diverse groups of people were suddenly thrown together – and managed to get along. Today, Christianity is practised extensively in almost all nations on Earth, across a wide range of cultures and political systems; all other religions remain, to a greater or lesser extent, localised in their places of origin.[30] Indeed, since the Second World War, Christianity has proved much easier to 'export' than liberal democracy. But in countries where *both* Christianity and liberal democracy have become entrenched, human rights have tended to flourish.

Of course, the Bible has been used perversely and unscrupulously down the ages to *justify* racism, slavery, sexism and other such vices. St Paul, for instance, like most of the other biblical authors, assumed the existence of institutionalised human inequality – it was a fact of his times. But Paul was certainly no racist. And, as Timothy Keller has observed, the indentured servitude of the Roman Empire was, in practice, a good deal more humane than the brutal 'chattel' slavery of the New World. Paul could live with the former, as his letter to Philemon shows, but he unequivocally condemned the latter: 1 Timothy 1:9–11.[31] Even so, it must be allowed that some of Paul's opinions, especially as regards women, seem repugnant today. Does anyone now seriously contend that a woman should never speak at any church meeting? (see 1 Corinthians 14:33–5).

But this is where it becomes important to discern the overall spirit of Christ's message, to educate yourself about the early Church, and to listen to your conscience. Jesus spoke decisively against tribalism, racism and religious bigotry. He also mixed freely with women – from all walks of life – and was prepared to teach them as well as men. A group of especially loyal women accompanied Jesus during His travels – they may even have 'bankrolled' His mission[32] – and Mary Magdalene was the first person to see Jesus alive after His crucifixion. St Peter travelled everywhere with his wife, as did a number of the other Apostles. St Philip had four daughters, three of whom were extremely prominent in the young church in Asia Minor, which was dominated by women. Paul's letters name several women who were, evidently, key players in early church communities.[33] Among them was Phoebe of Cenchrea, a deaconess, who was said by Paul to have 'been a great help to many people, including me' (Romans 16:2). It is possible that one of the two people referred to by Paul in Romans 16:7 – *as a fellow apostle* – was a woman. Some translations use the feminine name 'Junia', others the masculine name, 'Junias'.[34]

Especially noteworthy is the fact that many of the most famous Christian martyrs were women. The early Christian communities saved, and raised to adulthood, many baby girls who had been abandoned at or shortly after birth by citizens of the

Roman Empire. (The authorities in Rome rewarded couples who had sons, and, in any event, female infants were valued much less than males in many cultures of the day.) As a result, there were substantially more women than men in first- and second-century Christian churches, and many of these women were quite remarkably brave and virtuous.[35]

All this may partly explain why, by the second century, Mother Mary had become an increasingly revered figure in Christian theology. It also helps to account for an important historical fact, which feminists today would do well to remember, viz. that the early Christians pioneered fundamental changes in the nature of marriage. For the first time, a man and his wife were to be considered equals, even if their individual roles were not identical. Husbands as well as wives were required to be loving, devoted, and sexually faithful. All this was most unusual by the misogynistic standards of the times.[36]

All in all, the early Christians extended far more respect and practical compassion to women and girls – as well as to slaves, the sick, the poor, and people of marginalised races – than any society in the ancient classical world.[37] And as regards the development and recognition of the right of free assembly, the Church, for obvious pragmatic reasons, has had an especially important role.[38]

It is true that, since the third century AD, the Church has had a chequered record as regards human rights, an issue to which I will come in more detail in Chapter 9. But it is also true that, down the centuries, and on the whole, the Church has been the 'one major institution defending the objectivity of rights all along'. The theological basis for that stance is and always has been, at core, 'the irreducible worth of persons – the irreducible equal worth of persons – and what follows from that'[39]. Human rights must ultimately be derived from the Moral Law, a concept I sought to explain in Chapter 2. In short, human rights come from God. They cannot come from Nature, which, at the biological level, operates on the amoral utilitarian principle that only the fittest survive. Nor are individual human rights the creation of, or effectively guaranteed by, legislative or other human majorities. Majorities can, and often do, behave immorally and capriciously when it suits.[40] I will come shortly to an infamous Australian example.

The exemplar of modern day human rights was, and is, Jesus Christ. I defy anyone to read the New Testament and honestly come away with the notion that, if Jesus had been alive on Earth during the relevant periods in history – say, the 1970s in South Africa, the 1850s in America, the 1900s in Britain – He would have condoned Apartheid, or the institution of black slavery, or the disenfranchisement of women. In each case I have no doubt that He would have been on the side of equality and human dignity. In the words of Martin Luther King, Jesus would not have 'slept through a revolution'[41]. He would have led the revolution, just as Dietrich Bonhoeffer, the great German theologian and pastor, led the internal resistance against the foul Nazi State.

Those of right-wing political persuasion in respect of these kinds of issues often bridle at the suggestion that their contemporary positions may be in any way comparable to reactionary, cowardly and now-discredited positions of the past. But it is often sobering to remember the past, including the not very distant past. As recently as the mid-1980s, Western appeasers of Apartheid were vociferous in their support of Springbok Rugby tours and the like. They condoned the imprisonment of Nelson Mandela as befitting of a dangerous terrorist. How do such arguments look today?

To take a more contemporary example, from my home country Australia: would Jesus have turned back the *Tampa*?* Or would He have shown mercy for people in distress? Would Jesus not, at least, have taken them in to His country, listened to each one of their stories, and then decided upon the fair thing to do? Or would He have done as the Australian Government did[42], with the support of most of the populace: rejected

---

* For people of other nationalities who are unacquainted with the story, the *Tampa* was a 44,000-tonne Norwegian cargo ship which, in August/September 2001, became the subject of a momentous episode in Australian domestic and international politics. On 26 August 2001, the *Tampa* was on a voyage through the Far East to China and Japan, carrying a crew of twenty-seven. The Norwegian captain of the vessel, a 61-year-old veteran seaman named Arne Rinnan, responded to a mayday call from Australian authorities about a stricken vessel in the vicinity. The *Tampa* diverted course and rescued 438 people from a 20-metre Indonesian fishing boat, the *Palapa*, which was drifting in the Indian Ocean about eighty-five nautical miles from Christmas Island. Christmas Island is an Australian territory some 1,500 kilometres north-west of the nearest Australian mainland, and over 2,500 kilometres from the nearest Australian city, Perth. The 438 people rescued from the Palapa included twenty-six women (two pregnant) and forty-six children. All but a few were asylum-seekers, mostly Afghanis fleeing from the brutal regime of the Taliban. When rescued by the *Tampa*, the asylum-seekers had already been at sea for three days and were in various states of mental and physical distress. Conditions on board the *Tampa* were cramped and unhygienic, and provisions were insufficient. Captain Rinnan soon feared for the health and safety of those on his ship. In accordance with standard maritime practice, he sought urgent permission to enter Australian waters and to come ashore at Christmas Island, the nearest land. Indonesia was about 400 kilometres and a further six hours away, and, in any event, the people on board wished to have their claims for asylum assessed in Australia. The Australian Government bluntly refused. It asserted with indecent relish that it had a duty to 'protect Australia's borders' from 'illegals'. It ordered SAS troops to board the *Tampa*, detain the ship, and pressure Captain Rinnan to leave Australian waters – a stance that was questionable under international law, but instantly popular with a large majority of Australians. Electorally, the arrival of the *Tampa* proved a godsend for the Government. It faced an election later in the year, and for some months had been trailing the Opposition in public opinion polls. Now its stocks soared. When Rinnan, backed by his Norwegian employers, refused to accede to the Government's directives, a diplomatic stand-off ensued between Australia, Norway and the United Nations. Legal proceedings were commenced in the Federal Court of Australia on behalf of the asylum-seekers by a Victorian civil liberties group and a concerned lawyer. All the while, conditions worsened appreciably on the vessel. Many people fell ill, but the Government remained desperate to prevent the *Tampa* – and any and all other vessels carrying asylum-seekers – from landing in Australia. Hastily, it negotiated the so-called 'Pacific Solution'. This entailed the transfer of the asylum-seekers to an Australian naval vessel, the HMAS *Manoora*, and their transportation to destinations many thousands of kilometres away. 150 would go to New Zealand, whose government had offered them protection. The rest would be transported to Nauru, a tiny island-nation in the Pacific, where their claims for asylum would eventually be processed by the United Nations. The transfer of the asylum-seekers to the *Manoora* took place on 3 September 2001, and the ship set course for Nauru. On 11 September 2001, a Federal Court judge (North J) held that the asylum-seekers had been unlawfully detained on the *Tampa*, and were entitled to enter Australia. The Government appealed that decision to the Full Bench. The appeal was argued on 13 September 2001, less than forty-eight hours after the 9/11 terrorist attacks in the United States. The Government's counsel referred the court to 9/11, and categorised both the perpetrators of those evil attacks and the asylum-seekers on the *Tampa* as, in law, 'friendly aliens'. He asked the appellate judges to envisage a situation in which a vessel arrived in Australia with terrorists and weapons aboard, and then submitted that the Australian Government had prerogative power to 'stop' such people. On 17 September, a 2:1 majority of the Full Bench overturned North J's decision. On 19 September, the *Manoora* docked in Nauru. Almost all of the people from the *Tampa* who were put off in Nauru eventually had their claims for asylum upheld. Also upheld were most of the claims made by people who arrived subsequently, on other vessels, and who were also transported to Nauru as part of the 'Pacific Solution'.

their cries for help, vilified all of them collectively, and sent them far away, by force, to countries much less prosperous than His own?

The Christian answers to these questions are straightforward.[43] It has been rightly said that Christianity's 'supreme challenge', at least as regards inter-human relationships, 'is to see God's image in one who is not in our image'[44]. The ancient Hebrews were themselves refugees and outcasts; not surprisingly, the Old Testament takes their side. The prophet Jeremiah taught that those in political power should 'do no wrong or violence to the alien' (Jeremiah 22:3; see also Leviticus 19:34).

This injunction – that desperate outsiders should be welcomed and assisted – is reiterated forcefully in the New Testament. Joseph and the heavily pregnant Mary, strangers in Bethlehem, needed somewhere safe to take shelter. The parable of the Good Samaritan (Luke 10:25–37) might have been written for the *Tampa* episode, and its message is as clear now as it was in 2001. The Norwegian captain who rescued the asylum seekers at sea behaved like the Good Samaritan, who attended to the beaten man and brought him to an inn on his own donkey. The vast majority of Australians, led astray by their Government, behaved like the priest and the Levite, who had earlier passed by the beaten man on the other side of the road. Indeed, Australia's conduct was crueler still: it was as if the innkeeper to whom the Good Samaritan delivered the beaten man had called in security guards to remove 'the evil wretch' from his premises.

Most politicians went missing during the *Tampa* affair. By and large, the Australian churches did not, and their forthright conduct at that time ought not to be forgotten by the Left.

The environment

Man has dominion over the Earth. The fact of that dominion has given rise, in the last fifty years, to two grave threats. The first is that posed by nuclear weapons, a subject I have dealt with. The other threat is that posed by global warming; and it is in the context of this momentous issue that I will briefly discuss Christian teaching on environmental matters.

The scientific evidence for global warming – the recent sharp increase in the average temperature of the Earth's atmosphere – now seems to be overwhelming. Also strong is the evidence of the root cause of this phenomenon: greenhouse gas emissions, mainly carbon dioxide, produced by industrialised and developing nations. The solution, however unpalatable, is obvious: reducing the level of those emissions substantially, and as soon as possible, by whatever means necessary. That, at least, is – and has been for a long time – the 'left-wing' position.

There is still room for debate as to the best methods of achieving that goal. And there is still uncertainty as to how much time Man has to act before truly catastrophic and irreversible consequences will manifest themselves. The consensus seems to be somewhere between five and thirty years. But the potential perils are well known. At risk is the exquisitely delicate balance of the world's ecosystem. In 2005, in his groundbreaking book *The Weather Makers*, Tim Flannery made this prediction: 'In the years to come this issue will dwarf all others combined. It will become the *only* issue.'[45]

The stakes, then, say most experts, could not be higher: the future habitability of the planet. Yet for many years there were those in positions of political and commercial power (most conspicuously in the United States, but, also, in other nations across the West) who denied the problem or obstructed well-meaning efforts to take it seriously. Almost all of them were from the Right. Even now, many downplay the evidence, pick on trivial side issues, rant against 'doomsayers', and complain about the 'impracticality' of changing our energy consumption habits. They get support from prominent and intelligent journalists, themselves from the Right, who seem to be playing a strange game of inverse political correctness. All of these people call themselves 'conservatives', yet they are prepared to play dice with the Earth itself.

Of course, scientists have been wrong before – one thinks of Thomas Malthus's excessively dire predictions in 1798 about European population growth – and we all hope that on global warming they have erred on the side of pessimism. But do the 'pragmatists' ever pause to think what may happen if *they*, not the scientists, are wrong? Even worse, do some of them obstruct the search for truth and for tough solutions knowing that the scientists are probably right? Or even partly right? (Malthus, by the way, was far from wholly wrong. By drawing attention to the very real threat of over-population he sparked intellectual debate on several key fronts, including economic growth, evolutionary theory, and birth control.[46])

What, as regards climate change, and care for the environment generally, are the dictates of the Christian faith? In general, I believe that they require Man to honour and preserve God's Creation – not least the human species itself. 'The Earth is *the Lord's*, and the fullness thereof', says the Twenty-fourth Psalm. Man has a duty of stewardship. It is a duty that arises from the fact that God, not Man, created the Earth – 'He set the Earth on its foundations' (Psalm 104:5).

Not only did God create the Earth; He regards that which He created as 'very good' (Genesis 1:31). 'It was made in joy and therefore is good in and of itself.'[47] Accordingly, out of love and respect for God, Man ought to strive to preserve His Creation for as long as possible. In the beautiful words of the psalmist:

> May the glory of the Lord endure for ever;
>   may the Lord rejoice in his works.
>
> (Psalm 104:31)

All over the world there are increasing numbers of 'Christian environmentalists' who take these teachings seriously.[48] Many people of other religions share the same beliefs: that the Earth, in all its vast array, is a precious thing, and that it is not Man's to destroy. To do so is to breach the Seventh Commandment, thou shalt not steal, in the most heinous possible way. In *Paradise Lost*, one of Satan's most despicable crimes is the desecration of no less than three 'landscapes': Heaven, Hell and the Garden of Eden. One modern-day Milton scholar, Charlotte Clutterbuck, has drawn attention to the great poet's uncannily 'green' sensibilities. A lot of the imagery in *Paradise Lost* is apt to describe the modern-day activities of many property developers, mining magnates, and industrial polluters.[49]

It may be objected that if God is all-powerful, He would not permit Man to destroy the Earth; that God's love for Man will ensure that He continues to extend His grace towards us. Indeed, for the reasons discussed in Chapter 7, there are powerful reasons to conclude that God has done so already as regards nuclear weapons. But it would be immensely unwise and immoral for human beings to abdicate responsibility for our own safety. God's grace ought not to be taken for granted: we must do our best to deserve it.

Some 'left-wing' values cannot be reconciled with Christianity

On four seminal issues, then – war and peace, the distribution of wealth, human rights, the environment – it is my contention that Christian teaching supports a 'left-wing' perspective. But at this stage, for a left-wing sympathiser like me, the position becomes much more complicated. Important as the 'Big Four' issues are, they are not the only issues that matter. And on many of those other issues, most particularly 'moral' or 'social' issues, Christian teaching supports a (for want of a better generalisation) conservative perspective.

In one sense, this should not be surprising. Religion and politics are different discourses. What sort of a religion would Christianity be if it were accessible only to people on the Left of politics, or only to people on the Right? St Paul wrote that he (i.e. St Paul) became 'all things to all men so that by all possible means I might save some' (1 Corinthians 9:22). Without compromising the Gospel, he tried to appeal to all manner of people with (presumably) a wide range of temperaments and preoccupations.

Christianity has pushed me further to the left on some issues, especially war and peace, but on many so-called 'social' issues it has had the opposite effect. The principal determinant is *agape*. It now seems to me that (speaking generally) the cause of love of neighbour is better served by protecting the weak or the innocent, or by promoting the 'public good', than by encouraging or facilitating the indulgence of the selfish individual. Moreover, to do so is ultimately better *for the individual*. Of course, in real life situations, such judgments are not necessarily clear-cut – as Frank Brennan has put it, often 'the moral calculus is complex'[50]. In general, however, difficult judgments should err on the side of self-control.

More often than not, in the West today, people seem to err on the side of self-gratification. To list a hotchpotch of concrete examples, major and minor, I am now far from convinced that widespread societal acceptance of speedily obtainable 'no-fault' divorce, or pornography, or 'recreational' drugs, or habit-forming gambling, or casual sex, or cloning, or de facto relationships, or the depiction of explicit sex and violence on television and the Internet, or profane language, or discourtesy, or euthanasia, or abortion, have been good things for the Western world. Even the contraceptive pill has been, at best, a mixed blessing. To a greater or lesser extent, all these things have contributed to the entrenchment of a culture of licentiousness and materialism, to the weakening of the institution of family (especially the extended family), and/or the debasement of public and private manners. The deleterious effects of these trends have been most acute among the least wealthy members of society, and especially their children, though far from confined to them.

That last paragraph is a mouthful. It covers a lot of ground. But there is a common thread. It was identified by no less a left-wing icon than Martin Luther King, whose views on 'the Big Four' issues are revered today by 'progressives' but whose views on most other issues tend to be forgotten:

> [W]e have adopted in the modern world a sort of relativistic ethic ... Most people can't stand up for their convictions, because the majority of people might not be doing it. See, everybody's not doing it, so it must be wrong. And since everybody is doing it, it must be right. So [it's] a sort of numerical interpretation of what's right.[51]

Dr King was complaining about 'the permissive society'.

Now, it is true that many people who vote for left-wing political parties live morally upright private lives; and many people who vote for right-wing political parties live morally lax private lives. And everyone is a sinner. But it is also fair to say that *on the whole* – and except as regards insistence upon the virtue of truthfulness, in both private and public life – right-wing parties and voters tend to place more emphasis on issues of personal morality. In my opinion this is a perfectly legitimate attitude, especially when it comes to choosing between political candidates: a politician's character is vitally important, especially in this age of near-untrammeled executive power. I agree with Jim Wallis that 'a firewall between the personal and public dimensions of our lives is a secular fiction'[52].

The response of the cultural Left is often to deride these concerns, especially those relating to sex. Some of the most vocal modern-day atheists seem quite preoccupied with sexual libertarianism. Michel Onfray asserts that Christians have always had a 'loathing of women and the flesh', directly traceable to the story of Adam and Eve and to St Paul's '[inability] to lead a sex life worthy of the name'![53] Onfray appears to yearn for a world free of sexual taboos. Likewise, Christopher Hitchens argues that one of the four 'irreducible objections' to religious faith is that 'it is both the result and the cause of dangerous sexual repression'[54]. Both Hitchens and Onfray regard with disdain the Churches' support for the ideals of abstinence outside of marriage and monogamy and child-rearing within it.

The vast majority of Christians do not 'hate sex', let alone hate women. These generalised claims are absurd. Rather – for reasons I advanced in Chapter 3 – Christian theology tries to strike a sensible balance between individual sexual fulfilment, non-sexual forms of love, and the civilised functioning of society. It is not a question of naivety, or repression for its own sake. Nor is it part of a misogynist plot to oppress women. Quite the opposite: a society with no sexual rules would harm women – and children – much more than men. Put to one side the endemic problems of unwanted pregnancies and falling birth-rates. In the West today there are literally millions of unhappy thirty- and forty-something women who want to get married, or to re-marry, but who cannot find a man who will 'commit'. The main reason is that men no longer need to marry women in order to enjoy regular loving sex and the comforts of domesticity.[55] (Another reason is that some modern women, once they *are* married, come to treat their husbands' sexual needs with indifference, if not disdain.[56] Young single men are scared of falling into the same trap, and many married men in this predicament either have illicit affairs or leave the marriage – usually with lamentable consequences for all concerned, including the women with whom they become sexually involved.)

These are highly important societal issues, and the Right is quite correct to be concerned about them. The Left is wrong to trivialise their concerns as inevitably motivated by cruel and pointless prudery. Even the *Christian* Left is prone to this mistake. For instance, Kevin Rudd, the Labor prime minister of Australia since November 2007 and a committed Anglican, has written that he 'see[s] very little evidence that this preoccupation with sexual morality is consistent with the spirit and content of the Gospels'[57].

In one sense, Rudd is correct. Sins against chastity (to use the old-fashioned term) are not the focus of the Gospels. Such sins spring not from pride or malice, but from weakness: the inability to resist the alluring pull of lust or *eros*, as is required by the hierarchy of love. As C.S. Lewis, a conservative in most things, rightly observed:

> [T]he centre of Christian morality is not here … The sins of the flesh are bad, but they are the least bad of all sins. All the worst pleasures are purely spiritual: the pleasure of putting other people in the wrong, of bossing and patronising and spoiling sport, and back-biting; the pleasures of power, of hatred.[58]

Nevertheless, arguments to the effect that the Gospels are not much concerned with issues of 'private' morality are less than satisfying, for at least four reasons.

First, as to sexual morality, the authors of the Gospels (and the rest of the Bible) did, unequivocally, stress its importance (see, for example, Matthew 5:27–32,19:9–12; Mark 7:21; 1 Corinthians 5:9–11; Romans 13:9; 1 Peter 4:3–4; Acts 15:20; some 'liberated' young women might also take heed of Proverbs 11:22).[59] It is a fact of history that the early Christians were widely admired for their self-discipline and self-control, which contrasted starkly with the lewd excesses of the Romans and of other pagan societies. Evidently the Apostles regarded sexual ethics as important, and I have tried to explain why. Second, to return to the present, the concerns of the Religious Right are far from confined to issues of sexuality; its principal concerns are the not unrelated 'sanctity of life' issues: euthanasia, abortion, cloning and so on. Third, on any view, these are weighty concerns, arguably of at least equal importance to 'material' issues such as poverty. And fourth, the Left's record on sanctity of life issues is just as selective as the Right's.

Kevin Rudd, for example, has contended that Christian theology supports the proposition that 'capital punishment is unacceptable in all circumstances and in all jurisdictions'[60]. I am inclined to agree. Rudd has also ably enunciated the link between poverty – which *kills* people – and respect for life. But to date he has been much more equivocal – indeed, largely silent – about the other, less fashionable 'sanctity of life' issues, those which are anathema to many left-wing voters. Most other political leaders on the Left are similarly reticent, however able and decent they may be, and however spotless their own private lives. In part, this reticence is due to the fact that these issues are less readily amenable to legislative solutions; the relationship between jurisprudence and morality is 'difficult ground'[61]. But there is a large degree of electoral calculation involved in the Left's approach to these issues. (The Right's too.) This is not entirely illegitimate, but it is less than edifying.

When people judge political parties on particular issues ('health', say, or 'family values') they mostly do so *not* by reference to considered analysis of policy platforms and electoral promises, or even the parties' records. Rather, they assess *sincerity*. In the Australian vernacular, they ask themselves (consciously or unconsciously) which party is 'fair dinkum' about a certain cause. Do many Americans join the Republican Party nowadays because they are passionate about the environment, or the fairer redistribution of wealth? Do many join the Democratic Party because they are worried about the tragically high rates of abortion, divorce, drug use, violent crime? The same questions could be asked in respect of the equivalent parties of right and left in Europe, Britain, Canada and elsewhere.

Voters cannot be blamed for sniffing out where their elected representatives' real passions lie. The Left needs to face the sad fact that, in the words of Jim Wallis, it has a 'cultural disconnect with too many [people], including many people of faith'[62]. The Democratic Party in the United States, like the ALP in Australia, alienates many voters 'who would naturally vote for them except for the cultural and moral divide they feel with [left-wing] language and policies'[63].

Recent developments in American and Australian national politics have not fundamentally altered this fact. Given the historically high disapproval ratings of former President George W. Bush among American voters, and the dire economic circumstances pertaining in the US, the relative *narrowness* of Barack Obama's victory at the polls in November 2008 says a great deal. The Republican ticket's respectable showing in the two-party vote (53.5 to 46.5 per cent) cannot be explained adequately by John McCain's candidacy. McCain was and is a decent man. But a Democratic candidate in McCain's position, running against a Republican opponent possessing all of Obama's myriad advantages, must have been annihilated in a 40:60 landslide – or worse. My theory from afar is that McCain, and many Republicans in Congress, were spared humiliation because Christian voters, especially in the South, remain wedded to the 'conservative' cause. But that should not, and need not, be so. It must be doubtful whether any significant number of Christians who voted Republican in 2008 did so to endorse the Iraq war, or to deny climate change, or to usher in yet another round of tax cuts for the richest 1 per cent of citizens. The reasons were *cultural*. Bizarre as it may sound, I am convinced that an Obama/Mike Huckabee ticket – perhaps even an Obama/Sarah Palin ticket – could have gone close to carrying all 50 states for the Democrats, provided it could have been 'sold' with the requisite skill. More importantly, such a ticket would have been broadly representative of the will of the people.

Neither the 'left-wing' issues nor the 'right-wing' issues are clear-cut

The discerning reader will already have noted that, so far in this chapter, my arguments have been rather one-sided. It is time squarely to acknowledge that, consistently with Christian teaching, there are legitimate 'right-wing' qualifications to the left-wing issues, and legitimate 'left-wing' qualifications to the right-wing issues. These reveal the intellectual and moral depth of Christian theology.

The 'Big Four' left-wing issues

On war and peace, there is a respectable Christian case against pacifism and non-violence.

For a start, as John Howard Yoder has argued, there is a valid distinction to be drawn between war – even just war – and 'a limited and focused use of force, administered within the rule of law'[64]. Thus, a persuasive moral case can be made for strong-armed police action, or even military-style intervention, in order to curtail genocide or ethnic cleansing – and to capture and punish the perpetrators. In such circumstances, targeted violence is morally defensible if, and because, it is motivated by a demonstrated and urgent need to save innocent human lives. Full-scale war, on the other hand, inevitably snuffs it out ('collateral damage').

What, then, of war proper? The doctrine of 'just war' sanctions the use of military force in extreme circumstances. The four criteria are: that there is a just cause; that war is initiated by a legitimate authority; that there is 'right intention' on the part of those involved; and that any force used is proportional. Cruelty must also be eliminated to the extent possible.[65] The Iraq War failed on most if not all counts; it is at least arguable that the Second World War met most of them.

Charles de Gaulle put the case for just war as follows:

> War stirs in men's hearts the mud of their worst instincts. It puts a premium on violence, nourishes hatred, and gives free reign to cupidity. It crushes the weak, exalts the unworthy, bolsters tyranny… [but] had not innumerable soldiers shed their blood there would have been no Hellenism, no Roman civilisation, no Christianity, no Rights of Man. … War is the worst of plagues but has made the world as we know it.[66]

It is hard to disagree with the general sentiment, if not all the specifics. Some fine Christian thinkers have argued against blanket pacifism, including Reinhold Niebuhr during the 1930s. Yet there are great difficulties with the just war doctrine, because it is so open to manipulation by the bloodthirsty and unscrupulous and leads so frequently to the consequences that both de Gaulle and Niebuhr deplored. As Warwick Fairfax observed, in *every* war there are cries on all sides that '[i]f we do not do this, that or the other … civilization, democracy, freedom or something else will never survive'. I agree with Fairfax that, for Jesus, 'the collapse of one particular civilization would be quite a secondary consideration alongside greater moral issues'[67].

Nevertheless, it must be acknowledged that the just war doctrine, in its purest form, springs from a basal Christian truth: that the death of the human body is not the supreme calamity. As G. Campbell Morgan explained, 'Christ treats it as an incident merely, something about which a man need not be careful under certain circumstances'[68]. For Jesus taught, 'Do not be afraid of those who kill the body but cannot kill the soul. Rather, be afraid of the One who can destroy both soul and body in hell' (Matthew 10:28).

On the second of my 'Big Four' issues, wealth, there are also important Christian teachings that must temper an extreme left-wing position. First and foremost, 'the practice of all ages has consecrated the principle of private ownership, as being pre-eminently in conformity with human nature'.[69] So much is clearly implied in the Seventh Commandment ('thou shalt not steal'). Accordingly, property is not theft, and rich people can go to Heaven. It is not wealth *per se* that God abhors, but the love of wealth – the horrible, warping things that it can do to people (Ecclesiastes 5:10–17; 1 Timothy 6:10). Sometimes, perhaps most of the time, people pursue wealth not for the good things they can do with it, but as an end in itself. Wealth becomes the measure of success and virtue or, worse, an instrument of evil. In those circumstances material progress becomes no more than, in Thoreau's words, 'improved means to an unimproved end'[70].

But properly used, wealth can be a means to great good. St Clement of Alexandria, a wise and moderate man, stressed this theme in the second century. He was right to do so. Jesus taught in the parable of the talents that God expects us to use our abilities, our opportunities *and our money* to best advantage (Matthew 25:14). God dislikes idleness and waste (Proverbs 19:15; Matthew 20:6) and He does not object to a measure of 'rational self-interest'[71]. The so-called 'Christian work ethic' which emerged from the Reformation reflects the key Protestant idea that God may be worshipped through ordinary daily life, so that work becomes a form of spiritual activity. If in the course of doing worthwhile work a person earns money and spends it wisely (or, better still, charitably), then God is pleased. According to Robert Winston:

In its dislike of luxury and opulence, and its insistence on simple, hard-working piety, Protestantism encouraged capitalists to acquire more and more profit, but also to reinvest it in their businesses rather than squandering it on showy displays of wealth and status. Protestantism did not fuel capitalism, or vice versa, but there was a perfect fit between the two ideas, and both benefited from it.[72]

Money – wealth – is necessary for human civilisation. Science, architecture, philosophy, hospitality, the arts: none can flourish if most members of society are concerned with bare subsistence. Not only that, a reasonable degree of material comfort is necessary for individual peace of mind, and is something to be thankful for: 'When God gives any man wealth and possessions, and enables him to enjoy them, to accept his lot and be happy in his work – this is a gift of God' (Ecclesiastes 5:19; see also Matthew 6:19–34). In short, wealth can be a means to do great good; it is greed, leading to all manner of other sins, which is bad. The distinction is a fine but utterly critical one.

On the third of the 'Big Four' issues, human rights, there are also qualifying Christian principles to consider. Put to one side the Bible's alleged 'support' for slavery and the subjugation of women. Also put to one side the very real contemporary phenomenon of political correctness, and the Left's tendency to elevate what are, at best, desirable outcomes (say, free tertiary education) to the status of genuinely inalienable *rights*, such as freedom of worship.[73]

The overriding biblical principle of relevance here is that – in practice – individual rights must frequently yield to the rights of others. It is has been aptly said that 'rights without responsibilities are pure abstractions'[74]. This was a persistent theme of the successful 'Third Way' politicians of the 1990s, such as Bill Clinton and Tony Blair. It has, too, been one of my main themes in this book: the hierarchy of love often requires people to forsake their own freedom or enjoyment (i.e. to deny themselves) for the good of others, people both known and unknown to them. That is what morality is. Many on the Left tend to treat human rights in isolation, as a set of absolutes, rather than as an integrated whole; the corresponding duties which attach to all rights are downplayed or ignored. (Those who are passionate about certain right-wing causes also fall into this trap sometimes, as in the United States in relation to the constitutional right to bear arms.) But no man is an island; as Donne went on to say, 'Every man is a piece of the continent, a part of the main'[75].

On the environment, too, the last of my 'Big Four' issues, the Christian position is not as doctrinaire as that held many people in the conservation movement. Certainly, Man has a duty of stewardship. But that does not mean that Man should not make substantial use of the Earth for his own good purposes. God commands that Man 'fill the earth and subdue it' (Genesis 1:28). God made the Earth in such a way that there is food to eat, liquid to drink, wood to craft, minerals to mine – and so on. Further, Man has a unique cognitive capacity to utilise these resources.

The Christian case against radical left-wing environmentalism has been eloquently made by Paul Johnson. I am far from agreeing with everything Johnson has written on the subject, but his main point is right: love of Nature can sometimes become worship of Nature. Johnson points out that many of the earliest voices raised against rampantly destructive industrial capitalism – people like William Blake, Edmund Burke, Samuel Coleridge, John Henry Newman – were those of the conservative and religious establishment. They and the environmentalists of their day 'always brought God into the argument'.

> [T]hey never fell into the trap of pantheism or paganism, or invested inanimate nature itself with rights which properly belong to God alone. Nor did they ignore the rights of man, as tenant-in-chief and, under God's law, ruler of creation in this world.[76]

The right-wing social issues

It is not only the 'Big Four' left-wing issues that have a Christian flipside. So too do many of the seminal right-wing social causes. The Religious Right's position on these issues is generally closer to Christian teaching, which is, in a nutshell, that '[s]ocial life should, if properly ordered, conduce to virtue, at least to the extent that conspicuous inducements to vice are prudently limited and even, in appropriate circumstances, legally suppressed'[77]. That is the general principle, but there are valid and important left-wing (or libertarian) qualifications, which stem in part from the undoubted fact that it is harder to legislate for social and moral ends than for economic or political ends. For the sake of demonstration I will look briefly at two representative issues.

The first is 'family values' – a catch-all term for the Religious Right's conviction that children should be conceived and raised by a man and a woman who are, and remain, married to each other. Another related conviction is that, at least while any children are young, their mother should be at home looking after them. My own view is that these are ideals to be encouraged as much as possible. In the words of Mary Eberstadt:

> [T]hough it is politically charged to say so … a generation of social science has established that children do best when they grow up with married, biological parents in the home and that children who do not enjoy that advantage are at higher risk of a large number of problems.[78]

Not only do young children do best when the mother is in the home; recent research suggests that religious faith may do better too. According to a British academic, Professor Callum Brown, the entry of women into the paid workforce in Britain in the 1960s coincided with a further sharp decline in religious observance. Fewer women any longer considered it part of their role to promote piety in the family.[79]

For all these reasons, it might be expected that most people on the Right – and especially the religious Right – would support all 'family friendly' measures. It is not so. In many respects the Right's positions are hopelessly inconsistent and hypocritical.

First and foremost, the pervasive effects of neo-liberal economic policies are quite antithetical to traditional family life and legitimate family aspirations. Longer and more unpredictable working hours for both parents; less secure employment; spiralling housing prices in the cities; an increasingly unequal education system, especially at the secondary and tertiary levels – these are a few of its manifestations in modern Australia. The Prime Minister, Kevin Rudd, has written persuasively on this theme, as have other senior members of the new Labor Government, and there is a lot of empirical research supporting their arguments.[80]

Another effect of neo-liberal economic policies, less often commented upon, is the declining rate of marriage in the West among the working and lower-middle classes. This phenomenon first manifested itself in the 1970s, when the broad-based prosperity that followed the Second World War began to be replaced by much greater disparities of wealth and income. The effects of these disparities on marriage have been exacerbated by another closely related trend: well-educated young men, with high or potentially high earning power, more and more often marry well-educated young women possessing similarly high earning power. Dual-income couples become richer still; and, statistically, there is much less chance than there used to be for less prosperous women, even those who are very beautiful, to 'marry up'. Marriage is thus becoming a luxury for the well-off. According to one American expert, 'We seem to be reverting to a much older pattern, when elites marry and a great many others live together and have kids'.[81]

Yet another unwelcome by-product of plutocracy is sensationalism, vulgarity and obscenity in the media, including the sexualisation of children. These techniques make big money – they are the product, largely, of corporate greed. As Thomas Frank has written:

> [I]t is business that speaks to us over the TV set, always in the throbbing tones of cultural insurgency, forever shocking the squares, humiliating the pious, queering tradition, and crushing patriarchy. It is because of the market that our TV is such a sharp-tongued insulter of 'family values' and such a zealous promoter of every species of social deviance.[82]

Especially in the United States, the Religious Right seems most unwilling to criticise big business or its hard-line political supporters, even if the effects of unrestrained capitalism are often contrary to their own much-touted 'family values'. But while the Religious Right is soft on the excesses of big business, it can be as hard as nails when it comes to relatively powerless individuals, whose lifestyles do not tightly conform to those values. Gays and single mothers are often singled out for harsh treatment, even those of them who try their best to live worthy, family-based lives. I believe that the traditional nuclear family is the best way to raise children, and that for those people to whom that option is available it is to be encouraged strongly. But for some people the best option is just not available, often through no fault of their own.

Homosexuality is still a vexed issue in the Christian church. Considering the heavy emphasis placed upon it by many right-wing Christians, there are surprisingly few mentions of it in the Bible. There are, it is true, certain passages in the Old Testament in which the practice of homosexual intercourse is denounced as such (e.g. Leviticus 18:22 and 20:13). St Paul also condemned it (Romans 1:26–7). However, after careful thought I have come to agree with John Spong that these passages must be seen as reflecting the *human* superstitions of a different era, when it was not known that homosexuality is genetically influenced.[83] The Bible, it has frequently been noted, 'does not necessarily approve of all it records'[84], and this may well be one of those instances.

St Paul's views on the subject were undoubtedly shaped by his strict Judaic upbringing. The Holiness Code of the Book of Leviticus contained a clear injunction against homosexuality. But, as Garry Wills has pointed out, that Code included many other injunctions which are now universally regarded as defunct. For instance, there were prohibitions upon such high crimes as: contact with a menstruating woman, the eating of shellfish, the possession of slaves not purchased from a neighbouring nation, the trimming of one's hair around the temples, and the planting of two kinds of crops in the same field.[85] Christians who condemn homosexuality *per se* usually skip over Leviticus, and base their argument on certain passages in Genesis. Specifically, they point out that God expects the human race to 'be fruitful and multiply' (Genesis 1:28 (KJV)); and that man and wife are to be considered 'one flesh' (Genesis 2:24).

But must these verses necessarily be read as a blanket ban on gay sex? On any non-reproductive sex? I think such arguments are a big stretch.[86] These and related passages seem rather to be about the husband/wife relationship and the desirability of wives having babies. True, there is an underlying assumption that most sexual relationships will be between a man and a woman. But Genesis 1, read as a whole, is a metaphorical celebration of *all* the wonders of God's Creation.

Importantly, Jesus is not recorded as having had anything to say on the subject. Perhaps that was because, being God, He knew that for most people homosexuality is much more than a preference or a whim. Rather, Jesus directed His teachings about sexual conduct to everyone, making no distinctions. Some people argue that it may be 'taken as read' that Jesus abhorred homosexuality; it 'went without saying'. This seems an extremely weak argument to me: the phenomenon was well known (as St Paul's letters show) and Jesus was not slow to weigh in on most other moral issues – at least, those which He regarded as important. According to the Gospels, He also said nothing about circumcision, which was a 'hot button' issue of the day. Evidently, as regards circumcision, the Gospel authors did not feel free 'to put words in Jesus's mouth that he didn't utter'[87]; it seems reasonable to conclude that Jesus did not say anything about homosexuality either. At the least, His priorities were most certainly elsewhere.

Knowing what we know today about the nature of homosexuality, and bearing in mind Jesus's support generally for the 'unclean', the excluded and the oppressed, I believe that He would now be sympathetic to the cause of gay and lesbian rights, including – possibly – their right to marry.[88] At a minimum, He would support civil unions: a public institution by which the State formally recognises the rights *and responsibilities* of committed homosexual couples.

There is a respectable argument (no more) that the word 'marriage' has acquired over the centuries a certain fixed meaning, exclusively heterosexual, and that another word needs to be found to describe any gay and lesbian equivalent. But that is semantics. To my mind, the key point is that the expression of homosexual love should not be confined to the ephemeral realms of lust or *eros*. Rather, homosexual love should be elevated to the civilising influence of *philia*. What is more consistent with 'family values'?

Jesus, of course, would expect homosexual people to adhere to the dictates of filial love between spouses, including the promise of monogamy. He would deplore salaciousness and promiscuity in homosexual people, in or out of marriage, just as He deplores it among heterosexuals. I am not sure what view He would take as regards gay and lesbian couples adopting babies, let alone their utilising surrogacy arrangements or artificial insemination – personally, I think those issues are much more complicated, and not only as regards homosexuals. But Jesus would not condemn gay and lesbian people *per se*.

On 'sanctity of life' issues – abortion, euthanasia, cloning – there is a lot to be said for the Religious Right's catchcry that if you are in doubt, 'choose life' (cf. Deuteronomy 30:20). But there are also important Christian qualifications to any hard-line position. As far as abortion is concerned, there is the vexed theological question whether a foetus is, from the moment of conception, or at some later stage during pregnancy, equivalent to a fully-fledged human life. The Christian churches themselves have held a wide variety of positions on that question over the last 2,000 years, no doubt because the Bible is far from explicit.* However, it is not necessary to equate a foetus with a fully fledged human life in order to conclude that, generally speaking, abortion is something to be strongly discouraged. It is enough that, on any view, a foetus is at least a *potential*

---

* There is a dearth of clear scriptural guidance on abortion. The Sixth Commandment ('Thou shalt not kill' (Exodus 5:17)) is, I think, relevant; but it cannot fairly be regarded as decisive because it assumes the killing of a human being, and begs the question whether and, if so, when a foetus is a human being. Judaism contains no blanket prohibition against abortion, on the basis that the foetus does not become a fully fledged human being unless and until it breathes. One of the biblical passages said to support this view is Genesis 2:7, which states that God made man 'from the dust of the ground and breathed into his nostrils the breath of life, and the man became a living being'. The New Testament contains nothing directly on point. Neither Jesus nor St Paul are recorded as having had anything to say on the subject, and throughout human history both religious and secular views have differed markedly. Some of the early founders of Christianity spoke strongly against abortion, and in 1869 the Vatican adopted what remains its firm position (that human life begins at conception). On the other hand, the ancient Greeks and Romans practised abortion freely, and for many centuries before 1869 the Catholic Church was relatively liberal in its attitudes. As strict a theologian as St Thomas Aquinas considered that the foetus became a human being only after forty days in a male and ninety days in a female. Many Protestant denominations adopted a similar compromise position until the mid-nineteenth century, and some still do. A half-way approach was taken in the English common law. Abortion performed before 'quickening' (the first discernible movement of the foetus in the womb, usually occurring at between sixteen to eighteen weeks) was not an offence; and abortion performed after quickening was not murder, but a lesser offence. It was not until the nineteenth century that the British Parliament made abortion illegal in most circumstances; at around the same time, the British colonies and most American states did likewise. That development, it should be emphasised, was brought about *not* primarily as a result of changed religious thinking but as a response to falling birth rates and hazardous medical procedures at that time. This hard-line legal position prevailed in the United States until the seminal decision of the Supreme Court in *Roe v Wade* 410 U.S. 113 (1973). (I have drawn some of my information about the history of abortion from the majority judgments in that case.) The Court decided that a woman's right to privacy, guaranteed by the Fourteenth Amendment to the US Constitution, accorded her a 'qualified right' to terminate her pregnancy. The right was held to be unqualifiable by the State for the stage until the end of the first trimester and qualifiable by the State only in the interests of the mother's health for the stage subsequent to the end of the first trimester. The Court held that the State may regulate or proscribe abortion for the stage subsequent to 'viability' (the time, at about the twenty-fourth week, when the foetus is capable of existing outside of the mother's womb). Even during that period, however, the Court held, abortion may be permissible if it is necessary for the preservation of the life or health of the mother. Subsequent decisions have not substantially changed the law in the United States. In Australia, the legal position across the states and territories is not dissimilar: see Natasha Cica, 'Abortion Law in Australia' (Australian Parliamentary Library Research Paper 1, 1998–99). Meanwhile, debate continues on the issue that many people regard as pivotal, morally if not legally: defining the moment at which the foetus is rightly to be regarded as a fully fledged human being. There is an interesting analysis of that issue by Carl Sagan in his book *Billions and Billions: Thoughts on Life and Death at the Brink of the Millennium*, Headline (1997), chapter 15, and esp. pp.179–80. Sagan approached the issue of abortion by reference to the uniquely human characteristics of Man. He rejected the idea that a foetus's 'humanity' should be assessed against purely physiological criteria such as facial appearance, the ability to move or to respond to stimuli, or viability outside of the womb. They are all arbitrary, and the last (viability) is determined by the technology of the day. He preferred a test tied to the essence of what it is to be human: the ability to think things through or, in short, cognition – a phenomenon I discussed in Chapter 2. According to Sagan, 'Thought is our blessing and our curse, and it makes us who we are'. It is not an easy matter to assess when the foetus is capable of thought. Conservatively, however, it is believed from the results of neurological examination that brain waves with regular patterns typical of adult human brains begin to be discernible around the thirtieth week of pregnancy. In short, by about the end of the second trimester or early in the third, a foetus can think. That, according to Sagan's thesis, is the moment at which it can fairly be said that a foetus really is a fully fledged human being, with legal rights of its own independent of the mother's. It would follow that so-called 'partial birth' and other late-term abortions are not only morally wrong but should be prohibited by law.

human life and (as pre-natal photographs show) a beautiful thing in itself. For present purposes, my main point is a different one. I support the traditional Christian view that abortion, euthanasia, cloning – and all other practices that tend to devalue human life, including capital punishment and war – are essentially wrong. Whether and in what circumstances they ought to be prohibited by domestic or international law is another thing. But, at least, the emphasis of churches, governments and individuals should be upon preventing or minimising their occurrence. That seems a sound general rule. But the general rule still needs to be applied to individual circumstances in the real world. Those who believe in these causes, however passionately, must strive to temper their behaviour with mercy and love.

Too often, public spokespeople for these causes, and people peripherally affected by them in real-life situations, display neither mercy nor love. Their approach is simply to vilify any person who, usually for understandable reasons, has taken the easier way out of a terrible dilemma, or who supports the legal right of others to do so if they choose. Consider the pregnant teenager (abortion), the sympathetic doctor (abortion and euthanasia), the parents of a homicide or rape victim (capital punishment), the spouse of someone in terminal pain (euthanasia and cloning), the political leader who decides to wage war because he honestly and reasonably believes his country to be in peril. Very rarely, if ever, are such people fairly described as 'murderers' or as 'condoning murder'. Very rarely is it fair to ostracise them. That sort of conduct does no one any good.

Take abortion, for example. I am inclined to agree with Christopher Hitchens that 'the whole case for extending protection to the unborn, and to expressing a bias in favour of life, has been wrecked by those who use unborn children … as mere manipulable objects of their doctrine'[89]. Let me invoke an analogy, admittedly imperfect but one which I have found helpful.

When a kidnapper is holding a child as a hostage, the first priority of the police is *to save the child*, not to punish the kidnapper or to threaten or vilify him. The police will usually try to reassure and reason with the kidnapper, even to praise him, because they know that the child's immediate fate lies in the kidnapper's hands. In that situation, honey tends to work better than vinegar. Similarly, in the case of an unwanted pregnancy, it seems to me that from the standpoint of everyone other than the pregnant woman, the dictates of Christian love point primarily in the direction of showing compassion and concern for the welfare of the woman. That is certainly not to say that women with unwanted pregnancies should usually (or ever) be encouraged to have an abortion, any more than it means that all such woman should be forced (on pain of prosecution and conviction) to carry a foetus to term.[90] It means that, if the pregnant woman comes asking for help or advice, you should treat her as a vulnerable person faced with an especially difficult moral choice. You should be kind and not judgmental, and to the extent possible offer practical help. You should extol the joys and consolations of parenthood, and promise to provide whatever help you can in raising the child, should the mother choose to go to term. If more people behaved that way, there would be many fewer abortions.

Some critics in Australia have accused me of 'soft pedalling' on this issue. But I am sincerely convinced that the blunt instrument of the criminal law is not the solution to the tragedy of abortion. Criminalising abortion *per se* might deter a few women and some doctors, at least if the laws were enforced, but it would also make many more pregnant women (especially those of low socio-economic status) even less likely to seek responsible advice and guidance. Many more would resort, as in the past, to dangerous forms of self-help. If the State has a useful role to play in the area of public policy, I believe it lies in much greater support for, and encouragement of, the institution of adoption.

In short, in my opinion, abortion should be 'permitted but disdained'[91]. On this and other like issues the Right is essentially correct in religious and moral terms, but has generally failed to realise its aims. More often than not, its efforts have been counterproductive. It would do well to humanise its approach both in public and in private by reference to Christ's teachings.

Some issues defy a 'left-wing' or a 'right-wing' interpretation

So far I have discussed political issues that, while nuanced, admit of a left-wing or right-wing emphasis. But there are certain political issues that, regarded from a Christian perspective, just cannot be so categorised. They are evenly balanced and defy any attempt at generalisation. I will briefly discuss two such issues that are close to my own heart.

Crime and punishment

This is a quintessential 'halfway' issue. As a lawyer, I have great admiration for the Anglo-American system of laws. The institution of trial by jury and the civil law principles of common law and equity are among the greatest achievements of the human mind. And legislation enacted by a democratically elected Parliament should always be accorded deference, whatever your opinion of the government of the day.

In addition, for the reasons discussed in Chapter 2, I also now believe in a universal higher law, a set of standards of moral conduct that most people know, at core, to be right (honesty, non-violence, etc.). In the Judeo-Christian West, most of our criminal and civil laws reflect that set of standards. One seventeenth-century English judge, Lord Chief Justice Sir Matthew Hale, went as far as to say that 'Christianity is parcel of the laws of England'[92], a proposition repeated many times by English and American jurists until the early twentieth century. That proposition is not accepted today, at least as a formal statement of the common law, and it may readily be conceded that Western legal systems – to a greater or lesser extent from jurisdiction to jurisdiction – owe more to ancient Roman and Germanic sources than to Mosaic (i.e. Old Testament) tradition.[93] Nevertheless, I take as my starting point the proposition that *all* systems of law – nomocratic or theocratic – are ultimately grounded upon universal precepts of proper conduct.[94]

Where, generally, should a Christian stand with regard to issues of crime and punishment? On the one hand, the Bible stresses again and again the fallibility of every human being. Accordingly, we should be very slow to judge the conduct of others adversely; if we do, we should expect the same standards to be applied ruthlessly to ourselves, and the results are unlikely to be welcome (see Luke 6:37). In short, the quality of mercy should be very highly valued.

Another recurrent theme, especially in the Gospels, is that while everyone is morally flawed, no-one is entirely beyond redemption. God alone is the proper judge of each of our consciences. These considerations, and especially the last, seem to me decisive with regard to the issue of capital punishment: its brutal finality usurps the place of God, even if some grossly evil individuals 'deserve', by any reasonable standards, to die. But the issues then get much harder.

Two other fundamental themes of the Bible are that we are all commanded to show love to one another, and that the failure to so – by preferring one's own selfish wishes to those of others – is sin in God's eyes. Perhaps the most conspicuous message of the Old Testament is that 'human sin [is] a serious affair'[95].

Each polity's system of criminal and civil laws formalises this value system – the demarcation of right and wrong. On this point, I find myself in rare agreement with arch-atheist Michel Onfray – 'the very foundations of judicial logic proceed from chapter 3 of Genesis'. The reason is this:

> The premise that human beings have free will is the key to the cause-and-effect relationship between crime and punishment. For eating the forbidden fruit [and] disobedience … flow from an act of will, and therefore from an act that can be reproved and punished. Adam and Eve could have refrained from sinning, for they had been created free, but they chose vice over virtue.[96]

Onfray correctly identifies the theological precepts inherent in the judicial method, while strongly disapproving of them. I subscribe to them wholeheartedly as, I believe, would most people, if they applied their minds to the issue. To put things bluntly: 'If we cannot help being what we are then no one can blame us.'[97]

It follows that however imperfect any particular legal system may be, any crime or breach of civil law is an inherently serious matter. Human nature being as it is, Man's methods of detecting and punishing sinful conduct must be effective, and must be seen to be effective, or notions of right and wrong may soon become blurred or forgotten. That means that crime or civil wrongdoing of any sort cannot simply be 'tolerated' by the State. Although victims of civil wrongs should be encouraged to settle their disputes 'out of court' (see Matthew 5:25), the State must deal soberly and deferentially with any suit that reaches a court of law. So too any criminal prosecution. The relevant conduct must be investigated and adjudicated upon in as scrupulously fair a way as possible, and (if guilt or liability is ascertained) punished or redressed in some way.

The English statesman George Halifax remarked in 1685: 'Men are not hanged for stealing horses, but that horses may not be stolen'.[98] No one would support capital punishment for horse-theft nowadays, but Halifax's main point is still sound. As a matter of principle, all crime should be detected and confronted; the alternative is lawlessness. As Warwick Fairfax correctly understood, 'This is not morality, it is jurisprudence; the law in the interests of society has no choice but to prescribe that certain actions in certain circumstances are legal or illegal.'[99]. In short, the State must be a 'terror' to criminal conduct (see Romans 13:1–5).

Deciding the nature and extent of the punishment in a given case is usually the hardest question. In respect of criminal matters, public opinion (at least in Western countries) tends overwhelmingly to favour harsher punishments than the courts routinely impose. This is partly due to the inability or unwillingness of most people to try to put themselves in the position of the individual perpetrator, to imagine that 'there but for the grace of God go I' (or goes my child, or someone I know). Most crimes are not committed out of pure irrational evil, in the manner of Iago, but for some banal combination of motives: laziness, cynicism, anger, greed, or even misplaced altruism.

Like Dostoyevsky, who explored the theme in his great novel *Crime and Punishment*, I am convinced that the capacity for really serious crime lies somewhere quite near the surface in each of us. Whether, when and in what way this capacity is ever realised, however, depends upon upbringing and fortune. Herbert Butterfield once observed astutely that in the modern world, Christian and secular thinkers alike 'in practice ascribe rather too little than too much to conditioning circumstances'[100]. Butterfield was, I think, quite right in believing that '[the] same human nature which in happy conditions is frail … [is] in other conditions capable of becoming hideous'[101]. Yet most people cannot or will not make this judgment against themselves. They can easily picture themselves as the victim of crime, but rarely as the perpetrator and almost never as a perpetrator who would be undeserving of leniency.

The desire that most people have for harsher criminal punishments – on others – does not usually spring from an inability to love. Nor much of the time are such people principally motivated by an ugly desire for vengeance. I suspect that far more often they are motivated by fear – for themselves or, sometimes even more acutely, for those they love. Their attitude demonstrates that almost all of us give much less priority to love of neighbour (*agape*) than we do to *eros* or to *philia*. In the words of John MacMurray, an influential Scottish theologian of the mid-twentieth century: 'Hatred is love frustrated by fear'[102].

Thus, the average person fears that it may be his or her spouse or child or lover or friend who could fall victim to crime. They reason to themselves (motivated by love) that everything should be done to prevent or, at least, to reduce the risk of such an awful event occurring. They place faith in deterrence or the brute fact of incarceration, and it follows from either thought process that criminals should spend as long as possible away from the community. Moreover, it is often said, convicted criminals should not expect to receive any amenity or kindness in the process.

Where would Jesus stand today on these issues? I will hazard a guess: somewhere in between the standard right-wing and left-wing positions.

For a start, Jesus would reject vengeance as a proper basis for any kind of punishment. He would also be doubtful about the value of 'deterrence', in the limited sense of trying to scare other potential criminals (i.e. as individuals) into 'good' behaviour.

He would, however, accept the broader notion that the community must not tolerate or condone wrongdoing, and thus that punishment for wrongdoing must be meted out.

In meting out punishment, Jesus would not always be lenient or always be harsh: some of His verdicts would be likely to elicit surprise in both respects. He would, I believe, place much more emphasis upon the perpetrator's motives than most human judges do; in any event, He would regard it as obvious that the punishment should be commensurate with the crime, and that every individual's case should be considered on its own facts. Further, He would regard just punishment as something fundamentally of benefit to the wrongdoer; indeed, He would believe that the truly repentant wrongdoer should in a real sense welcome punishment (even harsh punishment) as an opportunity to show that repentance.

Jesus would also have accepted that there is – legitimately – such a thing as the protection of the community. There are a small number of individuals who simply pose too great a risk to others to be released into society, at the least until many years have passed and, perhaps, not ever. But Jesus would insist that even those people should be treated with a measure of kindness and dignity.

As regards the vast majority of criminals, whose crimes are serious but not heinous, Jesus would be wise enough to recognise the practical reality that such people cannot be kept incarcerated forever. Sooner or later these people must go back into the community, and it is overwhelmingly in the community's interests (as much as theirs) that, when this happens, they are not more alienated from the world than they were before.

Jesus would recognise that the best, the *only* way to try to bring about the rehabilitation of criminals is to extend *agape* towards them – by keeping them safe, caring for their physical and mental health, and affording them reasonable opportunity to nurture (by access to books, television, music, sport, further education and so on) their useful skills and interests. Jesus would also permit them regular contact with family and friends (cf. Hebrews 13:3), and would insist that their spiritual needs be kindled and nurtured by exposure to religious teaching.

Censorship

This issue, for Christians, may be the most problematic of all.

On the one hand, history shows that the repression of free speech – especially religious speech – leads to all kinds of terrible evils. Christianity itself was threatened at the outset by attempts on the part of the Roman and Jewish authorities to suppress the Apostles' message. For nearly 2,000 years, Christians in their millions have suffered dreadfully in resisting such attempts; and so down the ages have people of most other religions, in the face of similar oppression. The principle is the same in respect of secular as well as religious speech. 'Wherever books will be burned,' cautioned Heinrich Heine, 'men also, in the end, are burned'.[103]

There is a strong case to be made that, as far as adults are concerned, permitting access to and discussion of any kind of matter – however contemptible, crazy or worthless it may appear – is the least of the possible evils. The reason is that no human being or organised group of human beings can be trusted as the absolute arbiter of what is or is not 'fit' matter for any other adult human being. There must clearly be exceptions to this principle in respect of children, to minimise atrocities such as child pornography and, more generally, to avoid exposing unformed and immature minds to certain material. The latter aim does, it is true, pose difficult practical problems arising from children's ability to access newspapers, magazines, television and the Internet; but with responsible parenting and modern technology these problems ought not to be insuperable.

In short, putting to one side the special position of children, Censorship *by law* should be minimised as much as possible. Apart from anything else, banning films or books rarely works in the long term. The Church itself learnt that lesson the hard way as regards Tyndale's and Coverdale's English translations of the Bible.

All that said, as a Christian, I fervently believe that in the Western world today much of the information and other material to which adults expose themselves is vulgar, degrading and obscene. The churches have an entirely valid role to play in warning people of the profound dangers of such material. People should be shamed, if necessary, into rethinking their attitude to much of they read, watch and listen to. Violence, pornography, profanity, blasphemy, consumerism – much of our daily diet of information is gratuitous and perverted. Those of the educated cultural Left should more often be prepared to admit this – to themselves if not publicly. In this sphere, conscience has a key role to play. Conscience, indeed, may well in the long run be the best if not the only effective weapon against these evils.

But, again, it is necessary to caution yourself and others against superficial judgments. Some (not all) of the publicly distributed matter that is today routinely derided by the religious Right as 'immoral' is actually among the most moral. As one twentieth-century Christian writer, Harry Blamires, once insisted, 'the moral quality of a piece of literature is the extent to which it *recommends* moral as opposed to immoral behaviour'[104]. I have emphasised the word 'recommends' to highlight the fact that Blamires (who was a very conservative man) did not use the word 'depicts'. Thus, for example, on television or in the cinema, works that explicitly depict casual sex or drug-taking or gambling or violence can be – though fairly rarely – the most effective in exploring or denouncing the evils involved. Conversely, works that appear on the surface to be fairly harmless escapism can, sometimes, provide subtle but insidious reinforcement of societal trends that any Christian should deplore.

Films such as Ang Lee's *The Ice Storm* (1997) or Clint Eastwood's *Mystic River* (2003), while graphic and confronting, are most certainly not immoral. In fact, they are infinitely more morally serious – and less morally harmful – than many Hollywood 'action' films or soft-porn melodramas, or for that matter many advertisements for shoddy or frivolous products. What matters is the message, not the mere images on the screen divorced from the message. The Bible, after all, depicts human nature with 'merciless realism'[105]; it contains explicit accounts of every kind of immorality, cruelty and brutality. It is not possible to face up honestly to the myriad challenges of Christian ethics without permitting the fullest and frankest discussion of the real world, good and bad.

The amazing balance between conservatism and reform: further evidence of Design?

It has taken me many years to grapple my way towards this amalgam of views. What I have tried to do is assess how Christian teaching should shape both individual behaviour and public policy. In the course of doing so I have become increasingly conscious of a sense of isolation. In current-day Australia, and the West in general, what I now believe is more or the less the exact opposite of majority opinion – or, at least, majority opinion among the powers that be. When Nathanael West wrote *Miss Lonelyhearts* in 1933, to highlight Christianity's problematic place in the modern world, he could not have envisaged where things stand today.

For want of a better generalisation, the trend of 'elite' modern opinion over the last thirty years has been increasingly to the Right in respect of economic issues and increasingly to the Left in respect of social issues (at least until the onset of the Global Financial Crisis in 2008). The common thread is worship of individualism – an insistence upon 'the supremacy of the individual over all personal, communal and civic attachments'.[106] I used to stand on the Left in respect of most social issues, and for a long time I found it hard to give up my reflexively held opinions. I was happy to have some of my existing political views supported by Christian teaching but rather uncomfortable to have others undermined.

My discomfort was largely a product of societal conditioning. Michel Onfray is correct when he observes in *The Atheist Manifesto* that Christian teachings are often at odds with a libertarian view of the world. People like Onfray complain that – because of what they see as the still-insidious influence of religion – the free-market, socially permissive West is not yet *sufficiently* respectful of individual autonomy: '[W]e…denounce the individual, deny him rights, and heap him with duties by the shovelful. We celebrate collectivity over the singular, [and] plead for transcendence'[107].

As I have tried to demonstrate, Christians generally believe in a greater not reduced emphasis on duty, transcendence and practical love of neighbour. Even so, the starting point is individual salvation. A person who is free of inner burdens is more likely to sustain the passion and integrity needed in long-term work for the 'common good'.[108] People who pursue worthy causes for reasons of personal pride, political ideology or worldly self-interest are prone to cynicism, burnout and corruption. They are also more likely to become blinkered and hidebound – a charge frequently levelled against Christians, but only occasionally with justification.

It is a mistake to regard Christian theology in black-and-white terms. As regards most issues, there are nuances. The more I ponder Christian teaching, the more I find myself gleaning fresh and surprising political insights.

Take the distribution of wealth. I have come to believe that many people on both the Right and the Left of politics are prone to misunderstand the attitude to wealth of a good proportion of voters on the other side. Many partisans are stuck in a sort of Marxist belief that, if everyone behaved rationally, the wealthy would always vote for more economic liberty and the poor always for more economic equality. Of course, the electorate does not behave that way. It is still the rough general rule, at least in Australia, that people vote according to the twitch of their 'hip pocket nerve'. But there are countless individual exceptions to that rule – and always have been. Earl Mountbatten of Burma, Queen Elizabeth II's late cousin, once quipped that while he voted Labour, his butler was a staunch Tory.

This phenomenon peeves many on both sides of politics. On the Right, there are those who snarl at 'chardonnay socialists' – comparatively wealthy people who vote against their own financial interests. For those right-wing voters who are motivated primarily by a desire to make money, and to protect it once they have it, the notion that anyone *with* money would wish to give it away – of their own accord! – is extremely hard to fathom. They are peeved, even affronted, when affluent people like them advocate higher and more progressive taxation, or increased government regulation, or higher public spending for broad-based social purposes.

Some on the Left are guilty of a similar vice. They regard less prosperous people who do *not* vote on the basis of economic issues as silly, duped or perverse. In Britain such people were known as 'working class Tories'. For a long time, however, this phenomenon has been most prevalent in the United States. Many of the poorest citizens, in many of the poorest states, overwhelmingly vote Republican, or fail to vote at all – often ensuring neo-liberal economic policies that are quite contrary to their own material interests. In his captivating 2004 book *What's the Matter With Kansas?* Thomas Frank tried to explain the causes of this 'derangement'. The book is variously sad, informative and hilarious; but it is also deeply, deeply patronising. The underlying assumption is that the voters are fools – or, worse, plain evil. They 'waste' their votes on religious, social and cultural issues.

Now, I yield to no one in disgust for the twentieth-first century version of the Republican Party, but my guess is that most of the Americans who vote for it on non-economic issues do not deserve to be demonised. By and large they are Christian people who do not especially care about money. They try to live by Jesus's injunction to consider the lilies of the field (Matthew 25:34). It must be remembered that, notwithstanding Jesus's fiercely egalitarian sympathies, He 'avoided all direct political action'[109]. Nor was He a social reformer. The purpose of His life was not 'satisfying earthly needs, making heavenly aspirations unnecessary, occluding broader horizons'[110]. Quite the opposite. Jesus's primary concern was, and is, individual salvation. That is the focus of most evangelical voters in their own personal and family lives, and, as a consequence, their political focus (such as it is) tends not be on matters economic. Their focus is on other issues, and on those issues the Republican Party at least speaks to them.[111] It is true, as Frank and others have ably demonstrated, that the Republicans' record of finite achievement on those issues is patchy at best; but at least they *say* the right things. The Democratic Party has not done so in a Presidential election (at least not with any conviction) since Jimmy Carter ran and won in 1976. Carter was the last Democrat to carry the South, and he did so because he won sufficient votes from the white Christian poor, in rural areas as well as the cities.

But Carter was a pragmatist. It is more than 100 years since the Democratic Party chose a presidential candidate who stood strongly and unashamedly to the Left on peace and social justice issues *and* strongly and unashamedly to the Right on Christian moral issues: William Jennings Bryan, an inspirational preacher from Nebraska. Bryan lost three times, though only narrowly on the first occasion he ran, in 1896. (In that year the Electoral College map was almost the exact reverse of what it was just over 100 years later, in 2004, when George W. Bush narrowly beat John Kerry. In 1896, the Democrat (Bryan) carried the poor, mainly rural states in the South, the prairies and across the Rocky Mountains, as Bush did; the Republican (William McKinley) carried the wealthier, more cosmopolitan states in the North East and along the Pacific coast, as Kerry did. The Mid-West was split, as in 2004.)

Today, it is inconceivable that a candidate like William Jennings Bryan would be selected by either of the two major parties to run for presidential or other high office. The same applies in all other Western democracies. Throughout the twentieth century, very few electorally successful politicians couched their message explicitly in Christian terms. A rare and honourable exception was Abraham Kuyper, the Prime Minister of the Netherlands from 1901–05. Kuyper was a Dutch Reformed Church minister who founded a new political movement, the Anti-Revolutionary Party. Kuyper based his message on a Calvinist view of Scripture; he advocated a quite radical role for the State in bringing about economic justice and maintaining a fair and just system of laws, but he held deeply conservative views as regards the family, the church and society.[112] But Kuyper was a very rare bird, and his term in office was short.

What does this tell us? That Christian values *as a whole political package* do not sell well in elections. More than that: most people find the whole package uncomfortable, even embarrassing, as I did when I first became serious about Christianity. I was, therefore, fascinated and encouraged when I came across the following passage in C.S. Lewis's *Mere Christianity*, because it recognised and tried to make sense of this phenomenon. Reading this passage for the first time was a 'Eureka!' moment in my journey to Christian belief. Lewis wrote:

[T]he New Testament, without going into details, gives us a pretty clear hint of what a fully Christian society would be like. Perhaps it gives us more than we can take. It tells us that there are to be no passengers or parasites … Every one is to work with his own hands, and what is more, every one's work is to produce something good: there will be no manufacture of silly luxuries and then of sillier advertisements to persuade us to buy them. And there is to be no 'swank' or 'side', no putting on airs … If there were such a society in existence and you or I visited it, I think we should come away with a curious impression. We should feel that its economic life was very socialistic and, in that sense, 'advanced', but that its family life and its code of manners were rather old-fashioned – even perhaps ceremonious and aristocratic. Each of us would like some bits of it, but I am afraid very few of us would like the whole thing. *That is just what one would expect if Christianity is the total plan for the human machine.* We have all departed from that total plan in different ways …[113] (My emphasis)

Lewis's point now seems to me a profound one. The fact that most people find it hard to accept all the teachings of Christianity – the whole thing – indicates its universal rightness. It is a set of beliefs capable of appealing to most people in some particulars but to very few people in all particulars. Accordingly, 'like [all] the greatest teachings of the past, [Christianity] cannot be used as a basis for a political party.'[114]

This looks to me like another sign of God's designing hand. Furthermore, it may be the best answer to the not-unjustified complaint of atheists that '[p]eople have been cherry-picking the Bible for millennia to justify their every impulse, moral and other-wise'[115]. Strictly, Christian teaching requires that 'the Word of God and His plan of salvation trump all political and social values'[116]. Nevertheless, I believe that, because God understands the vagaries of human nature, He tolerates *sincere* cherry-picking. God does so because it enables most people to relate to, and expound, at least *some* of His tenets.

I believe, too, that down the ages, in fits and starts, Man as a whole has inched somewhat closer to the Christian ideal, at least in certain respects. Back in 1891, in the encyclical *Rerum Novarum*, Pope Leo XIII urged that modern societies should eschew the extremes of both state socialism and unchecked *laissez faire* capitalism. Just over one hundred years later, I agree with James Franklin's assessment that 'the 'regulated capitalism' or 'market socialism' of the present day is much closer to Leo XIII's plan than to the socialist or capitalist rivals of his time'.[117] That seems to me a remarkable thing, because most of the economic and socio-political change which has taken place in the West since 1891 was implemented not by the churches, but by secular political movements. Progress has come through the collective pull of conscience, expressed at the ballot box and in the actions of law-makers.

Democratic politics provides other indications of Design, of Fred Hoyle's 'deep-laid scheme'. Consider, for instance, the amazing *closeness* of almost all fairly conducted elections. Why is it that the voters split so near to 50/50 between Right and Left, thus ensuring the survival of the two-party system which is the key to political stability? It looks contrived, and yet no individual can know in advance any vote but his own. (There are psephological explanations, but these explain the how and the immediate why – not the ultimate why.)

A related phenomenon is the regularity with which parties of the Right and Left go in and out of power. This ensures that, in most Western countries, both parties remain viable, motivated and effective in opposition, a prerequisite to functional democracy. The stability of the system seems (like the forces of Nature or the process of evolution) to hang by a thread – the small percentage margin by which almost all elections are decided. Just enough people change their minds at each election, but (and this too is crucial) it is never the same group of people from one election to the next. All these factors contribute to the efficacy and perceived legitimacy of the electoral process. And surprisingly often, with the benefit of hindsight, it is possible to say with some meas-ure of objectivity that the people 'got it right'. (A former Australian Prime Minister, R.J.L. (Bob) Hawke, has made this observation as regards national elections here since Federation in 1901, and I agree with him. Although I would not personally have voted with the winning party or parties on each occasion, I think it is fair to say that, in the sweep of history, the Australian people collectively made a legitimate and understandable choice almost every time. The one glaring exception, in my view, was the racially charged election of 2001.)

And consider another phenomenon. History shows that, not infrequently, and whether for good or ill, important left-wing change is effected by governments of the Right, and important right-wing change by governments of the Left. In nineteenth-century Britain, it was the Tories who ultimately abolished slavery and extended the franchise to the middle and working classes. Bismarck did the same in Germany. In twentieth-century America, it was Richard Nixon who first went to China. It was Ronald Reagan who responded to Mikhail Gorbachev's proposals for nuclear disarmament, culminating in the seminal INF (intermediate-range nuclear missiles) Treaty of 1987 that did much to precipitate the end of the Cold War.[118] Likewise, it was Bill Clinton who balanced America's massive budget and (because he did much to improve the economic position of low-income women) presided over a large fall in America's abortion rate[119].

True, such change is often the culmination of many years of pressure from the other side of politics. But when change is effected by the party which might notionally be expected to oppose it, the measures are given crucial legitimacy. Change may be less likely to endure if it is imposed by one side or the other of politics for the benefit of its own supporters.

And that leads to my final point in this sequence. It is a point that ties in with the arguments developed in Chapter 2 concerning conscience and the universal standard of right conduct. I think that the vast majority of voters, both right-wing and left-wing inclined, sincerely believe that they vote the morally 'correct' way. In other words, they vote in good conscience. Although partisans on both sides of politics tend to behave as though they hold a monopoly on virtue, the truth is that demonstrably 'good' people vote in huge numbers for both sides, and in roughly similar proportions. How is that possible if, as I believe, Christian theology clearly dictates certain approaches or emphasises as regards particular issues?

It is not enough to argue that one side or the other is honestly mistaken, or even that each side is honestly mistaken as regards certain issues. That is part of the answer, but it does not fully account for the *clear conscience* of kind-hearted people who vote for plutocratic economic policies or of highly ethical people who vote for permissive social policies. Those people, by and large, believe sincerely that they are supporting the *right* causes, and not merely turning a blind eye to the 'rough edges' of their favoured party for reasons of self-interest.

The answer, I submit, is that everyone understands deep down the primacy of certain bedrock virtues: love, joy, peace, patience, kindness, goodness, faithfulness, humility and self-control, to repeat St Paul's list in Galatians 5:22. Democratic politics is never truly a contest between 'good and evil', but between two sets of people – good and bad and everything in between – who hold different opinions as to how best to go about realising these virtues in socio-political terms. They may be awfully mistaken, but most economic rationalists truly believe that their policies are not just more efficient, but *more compassionate*. Likewise, libertarians truly believe that it is not just kinder but *more responsible* to maximise people's freedom to have sex, to take drugs, to gamble money, to abort babies and to assist the terminally ill to die quickly. And both camps' arguments, although in my view misguided, are not completely untenable.

This phenomenon seems to me a remarkable thing. If it were otherwise, democratic politics would quickly descend into ugly and unmanageable chaos.[120] Instead, we live in a world where there is room for rational argument about means, in the context of near universally accepted ends.

Some things are more important than politics

My argument so far in this chapter is that Christianity has a critical role to play in politics – on the Left no less than the Right – but that its tenets do not neatly conform to any party-political philosophy. In addition, certain features of democratic politics provide yet more evidence of a wise Designer. Our system of government may properly be regarded as a gift from God, as another manifestation of divine grace. Like all forms of government down the ages, however imperfect they may now appear to us, democracy 'produces a world in which men can live and gradually improve their external conditions, in spite of sin – in other words it does the best that human beings have left possible for it at any [given] time [in history]'[121].

Ultimately, though, there is a sense in which Christianity – all religions – must stand separate from politics and government. I do not speak here of the conventional notion of the separation of church and state – though that notion is critical. It is largely forgotten today that the 'separation' was initiated, in the eleventh century, by none other than Pope Gregory VII. He saw it as a way of preserving the independence of the Roman Catholic Church from 'emperors and empires'[122]. The arrangement worked, until the Enlightenment, in the Church's favour. However, the conduct of the ecclesiastical authorities was all too often appalling while ever they and their leaders remained closely aligned with the established political order, whether monarchy, aristocracy or democracy.[123]

That problem, however, is not so nearly so acute today, at least in the West; and my present point is a somewhat different one. If and when the churches become partisan cheerleaders for any political party or nation, they lose the very quality that should inform their role in public affairs: fearlessness. Worse, if individual Christians try to manipulate Christ's teachings for political ends, by saying things in the name of God that they do not truly believe, then they commit a grave sin. You must go where your Christian conscience leads you, rather than pick and choose the teachings that may please or advantage you in a given situation. Ultimately, your duties to God trump any and all duties to the State, which are insignificant by comparison. This, as I read the passage in context, was Jesus's main point in advising the Pharisees and the Herodians to pay their taxes to Caesar (Mark 12:13–17).

Politics is important, but it is not all-important. It is easy for politicians and the political class to talk of the 'general good', while forgetting the vital place in life of individual kindnesses. William Blake contended that the 'general good' is too often the plea of the scoundrel, the hypocrite or the flatterer: 'He who would do good to another,' Blake thought, 'must do it in minute particulars'[124]. As a general rule, that is probably right. Some prosperous people who vote for left-wing political parties seem to regard the mere casting of their vote as the be-all and end-all of charitable duty. I now tend to think that a vote for the Left is the very least you should do. Far more important is the charity which you, yourself, extend to others. Politicians can effect great change, and sometimes it truly is for the general good. But just as often they merely muddle through, or make things worse.

Politicians are, in the end, fallible men and woman. As the psalmist urged, 'Put not your trust in princes' (Psalm 146:3; KJV). The prophet Jeremiah went further, declaring that 'cursed is the man who trusts in man' (Jeremiah 17:5). The advice is sound, if understood as a warning against investing any human leader or institution with unfettered power. That is not so much a theological truth as an anthropological and historical one.[125] More broadly, however, I think that these and other Old Testament passages are also a warning against elevating Man to the status of a god. The horrors of Soviet and Chinese Communism – the purges, the gulags, the systematic suppression of human rights – showed what happens when politics is deified, and the State attempts, formally or informally, to prohibit religion. Communism began, ostensibly, as an effort to implement a practical vision of neighbourly love. Its dreadful failure was due to an obsession with Man's material needs at the expense of his emotional and spiritual needs.

Yet, in the Soviet Union, the Communist system eventually collapsed because it could not provide adequately even for the people's *material* needs. This strikes me as a spectacular inverse proof of one of Jesus's most famous teachings. In the Sermon on the Mount, He urged that we should not worry about material things. He did not mean that such things are unimportant, but that to treat them as paramount is counterproductive:

> For the pagans run after all these things, and your Heavenly Father knows that you
> need them. But seek first his kingdom and his righteousness, and all these things will
> be given to you *as well.*
>
> (Matthew 6:32–33. My emphasis)

At the level of personal relationships, too, some things are much more important than politics. One of them is love. Many people have at least a few dear relatives or close friends with whom they do not agree on political matters. Such relationships can prosper even between people who are completely immersed in political issues and engaged in political conflict. Churchill paid generous tribute to David Lloyd George in the House of Commons after the death of his long-standing rival in March 1945 ('the greatest Welshman … since the age of the Tudors'). An even more touching example, from the contemporary United States, is the marriage of James Carville and Mary Matalin. Carville was and is a fiercely combative Democratic Party activist (he was Bill Clinton's campaign director) and Matalin was and is a fiercely combative Republican

Party activist (she worked closely with both of the Bush Administrations). Yet they love each other.

The secret of these kinds of relationships, I imagine, is not preparedness to compromise on strongly held political convictions. It is, rather, the capacity to open one's heart to the best human qualities in the other person and to search for common ground outside of politics. Sometimes it may be very hard to find common ground, but it can usually be done. As Richard Nixon once wrote, of a meeting he had with Todor Zhikov, the former Communist dictator of Bulgaria:

> [We] had very little in common politically. But there was one thing on which we completely agreed … [H]e asked me how many grandchildren I had. When I told him three, he said, 'You are a very rich man. Having grandchildren is the greatest wealth a man can have.'[126]

If Nixon and Zhikov could find common ground, the same should be possible for people in the West today from the Left and the Right of politics. Rather than routinely demonising each other, they might try to see the other's point of view. This attitude comes naturally to the vast majority of citizens, for whom politics is not a major interest, let alone a vocation.

Conclusion

I am convinced that God does not judge us by our politics as such. He judges us by our faithfulness to Him and to His commandments. Some of those commandments are 'left-wing' in emphasis – a significant majority of them, I think. But other commandments are decidedly 'right-wing' in emphasis, and there are some that defy any political categorisation. All of them have at least a few left-wing or right-wing twists.

We can come to appreciate the things that are most important to God by trying to follow Jesus's peerless example and by trying to understand why God sent Jesus to Earth. Politics should not be the lodestar. As D.A. Carson has written:

> If God had perceived that our greatest need was political stability, he would have sent us a politician … But he perceived that our greatest need involved our sin, our alienation from him, our profound rebellion, our death; and he sent us a Saviour.[127]

CHAPTER 9

OTHER RELIGIONS

Jesus Christ of Nazareth … is 'the stone you builders rejected, which has become the capstone'. Salvation is found in no-one else, for there is no other name under heaven given to men by which we must be saved.

Acts 4:10–12

Religion? Yes; but which of all her sects?

Lord Byron, *Don Juan*

Many sincere people say that they cannot believe in any one religion – be it Christianity or any other – because not all religious beliefs can be correct. They point to the contradictions between the many faiths, and question how any one group can credibly claim to hold a monopoly upon spiritual and metaphysical truth. Some people regard such absolutism as the height of arrogance. Others think it absurd: 'One religion is as true as another,' quipped Robert Burton in his seventeenth-century classic, *The Anatomy of Melancholy*.[1]

Another common claim is that a disproportionate amount of evil has been wrought throughout history by proponents of some of the major faiths – in particular, Christianity – in their attempts to convert people. There is no denying that many wars of conquest and other forms of violence and coercion have been perpetrated in the cause of religion.

These are serious issues. For a long time I struggled to come grips with them, and there are probably no definitive answers capable of satisfying those who find them intractable. Nevertheless, in this chapter, I will attempt to explain my thinking about them. I have come to the view that most of these objections are either misconceived or exaggerated. To the extent that they have some validity, none shakes me in my main reasons for belief.

The first point that requires making is this. Atheism – not religiosity of some sort – is the loneliest spiritual position that any person can hold. Christians and Muslims and Hindus have much more in common with each other than they do with atheists. An atheist is required to believe that *everybody* else is fundamentally wrong; that all of the world's religions are based upon a false premise. Throughout human history, atheists have been in a small minority, and they still are. As one American writer has pointed out:

> Angels, demons, spirits, wizards, gods and witches have peppered folk religions since mankind first started telling stories … According to anthropologists, religions that share certain supernatural features – belief in a noncorporeal God or gods, belief in the afterlife, belief in the ability of prayer or ritual to change the course of human events – are found in virtually every culture on earth.[2]

From this incontrovertible fact, atheists do not conclude that, perhaps, there may be something in religion after all. Rather, they deride *all* faiths by lumping them together in the one basket. The posthumous 'founder' of modern atheism, the French priest Jean Maslier (1664–1729), sub-titled his book 'Clear and Evident Demonstrations of the Vanity of All the Religions of the World'.[3] Many others have since followed suit. Their reasoning is that all religious beliefs cannot be true, and some have been proved definitely false; therefore religion *per se* is utter nonsense. But that conclusion is a non sequitur. It is a bit like saying that all current scientific theories are worthless because many scientists got things wrong in the past and some still get things wrong today.

A Christian does not need to believe – and I certainly do not believe – that all other religions are entirely wrong. I look at the matter the other way around: the fact that there are and always have been many shades of religious belief is reassuring. It strengthens my conviction that *all religions are at least partly right*. They are all partly right to the extent that they posit a reality outside of Man and the material Universe. It is true that there are substantial differences between the various religions as regards the nature of that reality and what it requires of Man. However, these differences are less fundamental than the atheistic alternative. The biggest gap lies between those who claim that Man and the material Universe is all that there is and those who believe that there is – or must be – something more.

I will try to explain the matter another way. It helps me to imagine 'the Truth' – in theological terms – as lying on a scale of 0 to 100. Zero represents atheism and 100 represents everything that there is to know about the other reality that lies outside of Man and the physical Universe. It must be very doubtful whether, in this life, Man's knowledge is capable of approaching anything near 100. We see, as St Paul thought, through a glass darkly; or, as Plato believed, mere shadows on a cave wall.

Nevertheless, through the discipline of practising one or more of the world's religions, each of us can and must aspire to attain the greatest degree of enlightenment that is possible. But which religion? Is one as good as another? An American theologian, John D. Caputo, has suggested that 'there is not a reason on earth (or in heaven) why many different religious narratives cannot all be true'[4]. I cannot accept that all of them can be *completely* true; there is no doubt in my mind that some religions have much more to offer than others. Some might score only 20 or 30 on the scale of Truth, others considerably higher. But no religion is entirely without value, even those developed long ago in 'cultures untouched by civilized rationalism'[5], and I believe that God takes into account the local circumstances in which particular religions are (or were) practised.

A short overview of other religions

It is legitimate to seek to categorise the world's major religions.[6] At least, I have found it useful to do so in order to clarify my own thinking. While I do not pretend to detailed knowledge of any faith but Christianity, acquiring an understanding of the place of Christianity in the scheme of the other major faiths has helped me to overcome lingering doubts about the apparent 'problems' posed by the existence of those other faiths.

First, there are the creeds that contain much valuable worldly wisdom but that, at core, really amount to secular philosophy. They do not posit theism, but they do recognise the crucial importance to meaningful and civilised human life of adherence to a universal standard of morality – in particular, respect for key human relationships, such as father/son and husband/wife. Confucianism is perhaps the best and most important example. It extols the twin virtues of *jen* (altruistic concern for others, i.e. neighbourly love) and *li* (a formal, ritualistic notion of proper conduct).[7] Taoism – at least in its original form – is another example of such a creed.

Second, there are the religions 'of the way'. These involve adherence to an integrated and unified set of beliefs about proper conduct and ultimate wisdom – or true enlightenment. Buddhism – with its Four Noble Truths and Eight-fold Path – is the prime example. In its emphasis upon right *thought* as well as right behaviour, and strict pacifism, Buddhism echoes much of Christ's most radical teaching. But, like Confucianism, Buddhism is not a theistic doctrine.

Third, there are those religions that conceive of the world (or the Universe) as the venue for a sort of ongoing war between the forces of good and the forces of evil. They are all forms of what is sometimes generically called dualism. The most important religion of this kind in human history was Manichaeism, although it is now virtually extinct. Zoroastrianism, which is still quite extensively practised today, is a variant form of dualism – though it combines elements of monotheism as well.[8] The term 'dualism' can also applied more generally, to any religion or philosophy which conceives of the world as something more than matter. On this worldview – which has been aptly described as 'the default human conviction'[9] – our personal thoughts and values, and the Moral Law, have some sort of independent existence separate from the stuff of our brains. Interestingly, C.S. Lewis regarded dualism as the most coherent alternative to Christianity.

Fourth, there are the polytheistic religions. Throughout history, these have been perhaps the most common. One thinks of the famous gods of the ancient Egyptians,

Greeks and Romans, and the many faiths of 'primitive' indigenous civilisations such as the Native Americans or the Australian Aboriginals. Sometimes these took the form of worship of natural phenomena *as gods* – such as the Sun in the case of the Egyptians, or plants and animals in the case of the Aborigines. Anthropologists have established, however, that most tribal peoples do not worship objects as such: their idols represent spiritual or ethical principles.[10]

The major polytheistic religions in the world today are Shinto (the indigenous religion of Japan) and, of course, Hinduism. Hinduism is the main religion of India, the basis of the caste system. It postulates many divinities, of which the highest are *Brahma* (the creator of the Universe), *Vishnu* (its preserver) and *Shiva* (its destroyer). The wife of *Shiva*, a sort of dualistic goddess, is also highly sacred to many believers. Hindus also worship certain animals as gods.

I have used the terms 'divinities' and 'gods' but, strictly, Hindus do not believe in the supernatural. Rather, they posit 'a spiritual reality within the empirical [world]'[11]. The central tenets of Hinduism are summarised in the Bhagavad-Gita, a profoundly beautiful ancient Sanskrit text written sometime between the fifth and second centuries BC. Gandhi wrote a magnificent commentary on the Gita, in the teachings of which he found 'a solace ... that I miss even in the Sermon on the Mount'[12].

Although it is impossible for me to do justice to them, two key Hindu beliefs are worth noting. The first is the concept of *karma*, pursuant to which everything done by a person during his or her life, good and bad, determines the fate of the soul in the next life. The other is reincarnation, the belief that the soul never dies but is reborn continuously into the body of a new person or animal, unless and until the soul enters a perfect (eternal) state, called *moksha*. The three possible ways to *moksha* are conduct (*karma*), wisdom (*jnana*) or devotion (*bhakti*).[13]

At this point, it is worth taking stock. Many of the religions I have mentioned so far – especially the ancient forms of polytheism – now seem to be regarded in the West (among both Christians and secular humanists) as quaint absurdities. Such an attitude is, I think, profoundly mistaken. For a start, it is wrong to regard the history of religion as 'a slow progression from ignorance to wisdom'[14]. Man has not been 'getting better' at religion over time; and God was vitally interested in the activities of even primitive Man. True, the appearance of Jesus was relatively recent, and an event of unique theological importance. But the Incarnation did not render all religious thought before Jesus, and all non-Christian thought since, entirely otiose. I believe that Warwick Fairfax came closer to the truth, when he described the history of religion as being 'a series of flashes of light, often [though not always] becoming increasingly dim'.[15] Plato (428–348 BC) articulated concepts essentially common to both pre-Christian Eastern mysticism and post-Reformation Christianity.

Fairfax also contended that many of the great religions of the past almost certainly 'contain[ed] far more than we realize, because the innermost secrets of the fully initiated are seldom or never committed to writing even where writing existed'[16]. It is a simple point, easily forgotten. Even so, based on what is written down, it is possible to say that most, if not all, of the belief systems which I have mentioned so far exhibit certain underlying similarities. The most striking in the case of nearly all of them is a set of moral rules that do not fundamentally differ from the rules that underpin Western morality today. It is a fallacy, as C.S. Lewis stressed, that the *ideals* of basic human morality – as distinct from customs and social practices, and actual human conduct – have changed through history or across cultures. What is amazing is their essential uniformity.[17]

Four other features are common to most of these religions. First, an explanation for the creation of the world and/or for the state of the world that is somehow greater than the world itself. Second, a belief that something in Man survives bodily death, whether that happens by way of a form of reincarnation (Buddhism, Hinduism), or by some other less precisely specified means (Confucianism, Shinto, Taoism). Third, belief in the happening of certain miracles – events unexplainable by natural causes.

The polytheistic faiths share a fourth similarity. They posit a collection of gods that to a greater or lesser extent determine the course of natural and human events and/or supervise human behaviour.

When other religions are stripped to these kinds of essentials, it seems evident that they cannot and should not be regarded as providing some kind of wholesale disproof of Christianity, or of religion in general. On the contrary, the accumulated theological wisdom of Man reveals a consistent preoccupation with certain basic concerns – creation, the soul[18], 'right' conduct, the existence of evil. There are also revealed, in many instances, similar answers to these concerns, in particular as regards the rules of 'right' conduct. It has been credibly suggested that '[w]hat all religions are looking for is inner peace that translates into living peaceably with other people'.[19] As for reports of miracles from many different religions, I cannot agree with David Hume's view that such reports are necessarily contradictory, and of themselves somehow disprove *every* religion (including Christianity). My own view is that the consistency of such reports through human history is suggestive that miracles do – rarely – occur.[20] Has the Catholic Church *always* been wrong when, as a precondition to conferring sainthoods, it has accepted reports of miracles? I doubt it. And I agree with Richard Swinburne that 'evidence for a miracle 'wrought in one religion' is only evidence against the occurrence of a miracle 'wrought in another religion' if the two miracles, if they occurred, would be evidence for propositions of the two religious systems incompatible with each other'[21]. I do not understand that the miracles reported in the New Testament can be so categorised.

My point at this stage is that Christianity is not so very different from some of the other, non-monotheistic faiths as many people seem to assume. Indeed, modern research shows that 'there is a limited storehouse of supernatural ideas from which humans construct their religious belief' – 'people do not just believe anything'[22]. As I have said, there is a much bigger difference between Christianity and atheism. I believe that any moderately intelligent, open-minded and religiously uninstructed person, living anywhere on Earth, could by some process of thought not dissimilar to that set out in Part One of this book, arrive at roughly the same conclusions as I have. Which organised religion, if any, such a person then practised would to a large extent depend upon circumstances, and God's will.

This is not to say that one religion is as good as another. There are some important differences between the faiths. According to Robert Winston, views about theism down the ages have differed most crucially on one key question: is God transcendent (outside the Universe), immanent (present within the Universe) or both?[23] Most religions proffer a hybrid solution of some sort, but these solutions all differ from each other in some aspects. Two other issues on which religions differ are the how and the why of worship. It has been a characteristic of many of the polytheistic belief systems throughout history that the relevant gods must be *appeased*. Such appeasement could take the form of offerings, sacrifices, or 'good' human conduct (good in the sense that the conduct is motivated by desire for reward from the gods rather than goodness for its own sake wrought by belief in God). That concept is quite alien to Christianity, as I understand the New Testament. Further, and in any event, the polytheistic religions have logical problems: the multiplication of deities 'implies a conflict of legislation in the natural world' and leads to 'a spawning of unnecessary complexity'.[24]

That brings me to the fifth and final category, which is comprised of the three great monotheistic religions of the world: Judaism, Christianity and Islam. They developed, of course, in that order. All share the commonalties already identified in respect of most other faiths: a supernatural explanation for Creation, a firm moral code of proper human conduct, reports of miracles, and a belief that something in Man survives bodily death.

Even more fundamentally, however, these three religions all postulate the existence of one personal Creator-God: an all-powerful, all-knowing and righteous supernatural being who is vitally interested in the soul of every single person. This God – Yahweh, the God of Abraham – neither needs nor wants to be appeased by Man. He created Man in His own image, in the sense of possession of an immortal soul, and possession of the capacity to give and receive love. This God also granted Man the precious but dangerous gift of free will, and a conscience to go with it. For the reasons set out in Part One, I believe in a God who was and is capable of doing these things. A monotheistic loving God is, in my view, the best and most coherent conception of such a deity. In holding this opinion I am happy to find myself in a substantial majority of the world's several billion religious people. There is comfort to be derived from sheer weight of numbers.

Judaism, Christianity and Islam have several other points of 'unexpected agreement'.[25] It is a tenet of all three that God inspired Moses, the Old Testament prophets, and the psalms of David. Even an ardent atheist like Michel Onfray can recognise – albeit archly – that these faiths are 'variations on one and the same theme' and display 'shared fundamentals'.*[26]

---

* The five 'shared fundamentals' identified by Onfray are: 'First, a sequence of waves of hatred set in violent motion throughout history by men claiming to be repositories and interpreters of God's word – the priestly castes. Second, hatred of intelligence, which monotheists reject in favour of submission and obedience; hatred of life coupled with a passionate and unshakable obsession with death; hatred of the here and now, consistently undervalued in favour of a beyond, the only possible reservoir of sense, truth, certainty and bliss; hatred of the corruptible body, disparaged in every aspect, while the soul – eternal, immortal, divine – is invested with all the higher qualities and all the virtues; and, finally, hatred of women, condemnation of liberated sexuality and sex for pleasure.'

Ultimately, the commonalties between Judaism, Christianity and Islam can be traced back to a common source, the ancient Hebrews. Their Exodus from Egypt in or about 1300 BC was, perhaps, *the* seminal event for Mankind. As Herbert Butterfield once observed, it is remarkable that the ancient Hebrews should be remembered at all, let alone that 'so small a nation should have come to occupy so great a place in the history of the world'[27]. Yet these things are so.

The principal reason that the ancient Hebrews are remembered is that their finest minds discovered a new way of conceiving God – the monotheistic conception. Strictly speaking, the world's first monotheistic religion was Zoroastrianism (it having been founded in Persia in the eighteenth to fifteenth centuries BC), but the Hebrews broke new ground. They developed a tradition of scrutinising and examining God, of reflecting closely on His nature, and of debating vigorously amongst themselves. At the same time they saw a new way of understanding history, according to which 'the might and grandeur of the human drama' took precedence over mere triumphalism and the recording of events for posterity. The concept of justice became central. Calamity, they thought, was properly to be attributed to lack of righteousness, and success to the favour of God.[28] These were epoch-making theological insights.

The distinguishing factors in favour of Christianity

The three monotheistic religions share one other remarkable central feature, not already mentioned: 'The man Jesus of Nazareth is associated in a vital way with all three'[29]. He is mentioned extensively in post-Crucifixion rabbinic literature, and also in the Qur'an.[30] This of itself is significant because it underscores the reality of the historical Jesus. But it also provides the best clue to answering the obvious question: Why believe in Christianity as opposed to Judaism or Islam? Choosing, as it were, between these three religions necessarily involves deciding which of the three most cogently explains what Jesus said and did, and his ultimate significance.

Historical factors

Christianity is differentiated from all other faiths by the fact that it is pre-eminently an *historical* religion. It is historical 'in a particularly technical sense that the term possesses – it presents us with religious doctrines which are at the same time historical events or historical interpretations'[31]. Events such as the Crucifixion and the Resurrection 'are considered to have a spiritual content and to represent the divine breaking in upon history'[32]. As Craig L. Blomberg has written, 'no religion stands or falls with a claim about the resurrection of its founder in the way that Christianity does'[33]. Only two other major world religions are based on a personality rather than mere philosophical propositions: Buddhism and Islam. But both Buddha and Muhammad died unremarkable and *final* deaths.[34] Their bodies – like those of Abraham, Zoroaster and Confucius – stayed buried in the earth. '[Only] Jesus's tomb is empty'[35].

How does this help the waverer today? In this crucial way: up to a point, the unique claims of Christianity can be tested using historical methodology. We are not confined to 'a religion of nebulous love and mere sentimental good fellowship ... of disembodied truths and abstract nouns'[36]. Christianity is a religion allegedly based upon real people, real places, real events. Using reason and commonsense, we can assess the probabilities.

In Part Two, I surveyed some of the evidence about the historical Jesus and the work of the Apostles, a 'narrative that knits itself into the story of the Roman Empire'[37]. I did my best to elucidate the case for the Christian account of Jesus. In my view, the evidence suggests that Jesus was not a gifted charlatan, an imposter, as people of Jewish faith must maintain. Nor can I accept that he was merely a human prophet like Moses or Muhammad, as Muslims believe. (So, incidentally, did Manichaeans.) Muhammad's own personal understanding of orthodox Christian theology has been shown to have been limited, and in some respects flawed.[38] It seems to me that the most credible explanation of Jesus's life and death is the Christian explanation – that Jesus was sent by God and was God.

There is another historical consideration that inclines me toward Christianity – the way in which the early Church was established. It was achieved peaceably, and often in the face of violent retaliation. This is the factor that most clearly sets apart the early history of Christianity from that of Islam. It is worth examining this issue at a little length, not only for what it says about Christianity but also for what it can teach us about the origins and true nature of Islam. Both religions come out well, though the story of Christianity is, I believe, the more extraordinary.

Islam began its life in seventh-century Arabia not so much as a new religious movement than as a socio-economic and spiritual protest, 'a reaction against urban living'[39]. Muhammad ibn Abdullah, its founder, was a prosperous merchant from Mecca. He was a devout man who worshipped the pantheon of Arab gods, of which Al-Lah was the highest. Many Arabs already believed that Al-Lah was the same God as the one worshipped in neighbouring lands by Jews and Christians, but their faith was waning. The various Arab tribes fought murderously with one another. The Quraysh tribe of Mecca, of which Muhammad was a distinguished member, had become wealthy through trade with surrounding nations, and many had fallen into the perennial trap: indifference to God, and selfish preoccupation with material possessions and high living. Mecca had become a discontented society of haves and have-nots, and this deeply troubled Muhammad.[40]

It was in this context, in AD 610, that Muhammad experienced his first great revelation at Mount Hira. He was convinced that the One God had been revealed to him, and that he had received a direction to restore all of the Arab people to a more traditional way of life, one consistent with God's intentions for Mankind – 'to share wealth and create a society where the weak and vulnerable were treated with respect'[41]. Personally, I have little doubt that Muhammad's experience was real. Over the next twenty-one years he was inspired to write the Qur'an. Within only a few years he had converted to his cause some of Mecca's most underprivileged inhabitants, including slaves and women, as well as a modest number from the aristocracy and loyal members of his own family. But soon Muhammad and these early followers faced strong opposition in Mecca from the powers that be, and their position in that city eventually became untenable. In AD 620 Muhammad met with a delegation of Arab tribal chiefs from Yathrib, a struggling agricultural settlement 250 miles north. It was agreed that Muhammad would move his followers there and join with the other tribes in establishing a peaceful community (*ummah*) organised on principles of social justice. In AD 622, the new community was founded. It was called al-Medinah (Medina), *the* City.[42]

With this background in mind, it is instructive to look at the next phase of the development of the Islamic religion. The comparison with Christianity is revealing. Remember that in its first 300 hundred years Christianity was spread by its adherents without the use of violence, though violence was used extensively *against* them. The nature and extent of that violence varied considerably from time to time, but, during the reigns of the worst of the Roman emperors, it was bestial. Major persecutions of Christians took place under Nero (a monster), Domitian, Trajan, Septimius Severus (another monster), Maximinus, Decius (the worst and most effective persecutor of all), Valerian, Diocletion, and Galerius. In all, between AD 30 and 311, up to 100,000 Christians are estimated to have been murdered for their faith; Christians murdered no one.

A little more Christian history is in order.[43] Galerius died in AD 311, having issued an Edict of Toleration on his deathbed. But he left behind an unstable political situation, and, at this point in history, the future of both the Roman Empire and Christianity lay in the balance. The chief rivals for the leadership of the western Empire were Flavius Constantinus (later 'Constantine') and Augustus Maxentius. The following year, on 28 October AD 312, their armies met in battle just outside Rome, near Milvean Bridge. Though rarely mentioned in the West today, this was one of the most fateful battles in human history. For reasons which remain disputed, Constantine's army fought under the banner of the Cross – and it prevailed. Constantine himself, until then a pagan, became the world's leading patron of Christianity. How sincere his personal conversion really was – whether it happened just before or just after his victory, on his deathbed, or at all – is still debated. But, in any event, Constantine proceeded to make amends to the Christian church. By the Edict of Milan in AD 313, he and his then-ally in the eastern part of the Empire, Licinius Augustus, returned confiscated land and property and finally outlawed violent persecution. Almost immediately, wealthy people began to join Christian churches in much greater numbers than ever before. This was critical a turning point, and, in AD 317, there came another. Constantine sent forces to Carthage to intervene in a bitter dispute within the local church. Thus, *for the first time*, 'Christians used the [military] power of the state'.[44] It had taken almost 300 years.

The early history of Islam was very different. The rapid spread of that faith after AD 622 was achieved in significant part by military methods, on the part of those doing the converting as well as those who resisted them.[45] It would be inaccurate to say that Islam was founded exclusively or even mainly by force, and quite wrong to label Islam as a 'warlike' creed, then or now. (I put to one side modern-day Islamic extremism, which most mainstream Muslims seem to regard as a perversion, and which is better understood as a consequence of post-colonial political failure in the Middle East. Islam, like all non-Christian faiths, must not be assessed 'by reference to features which their own best teachers see as abuses'.[46]) As we have seen, in the first dozen or so years after his revelation in AD 610, Muhammad employed exclusively non-violent methods. He was a peace-loving man who yearned to see an end to inter-tribal warfare among the Arab peoples. But from about AD 623–632, his *ummah* faced fierce opposition from various quarters – the Quraysh tribe back in Mecca, Arab pagans in Medina, and three hostile Jewish tribes in Medina (the Qaynuqah, Nadir and Qurayzah). Much of the ensuing violence was not initiated by Muhammad, but it is an historical fact that that the *ummah* had to 'fight its way to peace'[47]. There was a great deal of bloodshed, as well as skilful diplomacy. By the time of his death in AD 632 Muhammad had defeated all comers and united most of the tribes of Arabia. This was as much a political as a religious achievement. Muhammad's primary motive was not evangelical, even among his fellow Arabs – he permitted some of the Bedouin tribes to join the *ummah* for pragmatic economic reasons. Inevitably, however, the faith took hold.[48]

After Muhammad's death, the spread of Islam into non-Muslim territories was rapid. Iraq, Syria, Egypt, Palestine, North Africa – all were conquered within twenty years by Muslim armies, with substantial loss of life. Within one hundred years the Islamic empire extended from the Pyrenees to the Himalayas. Karen Armstrong has contended that these wars were not primarily motivated by religion; they were undertaken, at least in the earlier phases, to keep the Islamic confederacy together as a political entity and to supply its material needs. Some of the conquered peoples actually welcomed the end of Persian or Byzantian rule, and most of them were not forcibly converted to Islam. It was Muslim policy to permit their subjects to continue to practise their own faiths; indeed, until the eighth century, even non-violent attempts at conversion were not encouraged.[49]

So much may be conceded. It may also be conceded that many of the basic tenets of Islam were then, and are still today, worthy and inspiring. As Robert Winston has observed, Muhammad's core message of simple piety, austerity and social justice was not unlike that of Jesus.[50] Those teachings deserved to be accepted. Nonetheless, it is impossible to discount the 'fear factor', which operated in favour of the spread of Islam in its first hundred years. Many conquered peoples must have found it convenient to adopt the new faith, and rebellion within the *ummah* itself was ruthlessly suppressed. There was also violent in-fighting at the top: two of Muhammad's earliest successors as caliph, Uthman ibn Affan and Ali ibn Abi Talib, were assassinated by fellow Muslims.[51]

Compare the early history of Christianity. As we have seen, the fear factor operated from the first *against* its establishment. To a greater or lesser extent that situation lasted until AD 312, when Constantine was converted – or, at any rate, was brought 'onside'. A little over a decade later, by AD 324, Constantine had become the undisputed ruler of the whole Roman Empire, and the full-scale Christianisation of Europe, northern Africa and central Asia had begun.[52] Thereafter, the massive resources of the state, and the tide of public opinion, worked inexorably in the Church's favour. And – inevitably – conflict, corruption and sheer institutional incompetence soon set in.

But – and to my mind this point cannot be emphasised enough – the era *before*

Constantine was quite remarkably different. The myriad challenges which Christians faced and overcame in that 300-year period were very much greater than those faced by either post-Constantine Christians or by the founders of Islam in the years after AD 623. Prosaic explanations for their success will not suffice. For almost three centuries, the best thing that the Apostles and their successors had going for them was their message – and the central focus of their message was the Resurrection. Jesus's appeal during His lifetime – like Muhammad's – might be attributable in no small part to His concern for the poor, the sick and the oppressed. Not so the original Apostles. True, they and their early followers shared those general sentiments, and the first Christian communities were run along the lines of 'primitive communism'[53]. (See Acts 4:32–7: 'No-one claimed that any of his possessions was his own, but they shared everything they had … There were no needy persons among them.') Later, in the second and third centuries, Christians became renowned across the Roman Empire not only for caring devotedly for each other, but also for extending generous charity to widows, the sick, and other despised minorities. Rich Christians (there were not many) opened up their homes to poorer members of their congregations.

But these factors were incidental and consequential. They do not account, adequately or at all, for the Church's beginnings. Even Jesus Himself made only a small number of true converts during His lifetime on Earth.[54] Yet in the first twenty or thirty years after Jesus's death, the Apostles attracted many thousands.

The Apostles' base motives were neither political nor philanthropic. Their preoccupation was with a specific supernatural claim, a claim regarded with hostility by the powers that be (see, e.g., Acts 4:1–4, 5:25–33). Their success in the teeth of the odds – without resort to violence – suggests to me that the evidence they presented for that claim must have been compelling. And they must have come across to others as utterly sincere. That could not have been so unless they wholeheartedly believed in their own message and, as I argued in Chapter 6, the Apostles were in a unique position to know whether what they preached about the Resurrection was true or false. Later, during the second and third centuries, prominent Christians continued to emulate the Apostles' example. Some of them – Quadrates, Aristides, Justin Martyr, Tatian of Assyria, Tertullian of Carthage and Melito of Sardis, to mention a few – wrote elaborate apologetics defending the faith.[55] Many others died as martyrs. Until the seminal battle at Milvean Bridge in AD 312, almost no one calling himself or herself a Christian resorted to aggressive violence.

In short, unlike at least some other major religions – and many disreputable cults – Christianity did not have 'corrupt beginnings'. The motives of its founders were pure. While atheists are entitled to point out that 'people are always free to make up a religion that suits or gratifies or flatters them'[56], that charge cannot fairly be leveled at the early Christians. It makes their achievement all the more remarkable.

Theological considerations

In addition to these historical factors, there are two issues of theology that, to my mind, favourably distinguish Christianity from Islam and Judaism, and all other religions.

The first is the doctrine of the Trinity. Richard Dawkins ridicules it in *The God Delusion* as obscurantist nonsense; he quotes Thomas Jefferson's mischievous assertion that 'no man ever had a distinct idea of the trinity'[57]. The concept of the three-personed God is subtle and difficult, to be sure – differences concerning it were a major cause of the schism in the eleventh century between the Roman and Eastern Orthodox churches[58] – but that is hardly a good reason for dismissing the doctrine out of hand. Darwinists squabble among themselves on issues big and small; does that discredit the entire theory? It is childish to denounce something that you self-evidently do not understand and have not tried to understand. Speaking for myself, the Trinity helps to make sense of many things.

It is necessary to place the doctrine of the Trinity in its context, like all other events in the history of Christianity. The bishops who met at Nicea in AD 325 did not pluck the idea out of the ether. For almost three centuries, people had been trying to come to grips with Jesus; how his life and death fitted in to the scheme of monotheistic theology. St Paul, in the 50s AD, had conceived of Jesus as being divine in nature and yet distinct from both God and the Holy Spirit (cf. 2 Corinthians 13:14). So too the author of Matthew's Gospel (Matthew 28:19). But this was not the only possible way of looking at things. Since the Crucifixion, different Christian sects (among them the Gnostics and the Marcionites) had, understandably, interpreted Jesus's nature and significance in different ways. Some thought that Jesus was God; others were not sure; still others denied his divinity, while granting him exalted status. It was Tertullian of Carthage, a brilliant but eccentric Christian scholar of the early third century, who first used the Latin term *trinitas*.[59]

Debates about theological and other issues continued into the fourth century, though by that time 'belief in the divinity of Jesus was as mainstream as it got in the Christian community'.[60] By AD 325 Constantine was the sole ruler of the Roman Empire, and he had been a convert to the faith for over a decade. Roman persecution of Christians had ceased (though it continued elsewhere, notably in Persia) and the Church was growing apace. But another fierce theological schism had developed within the church hierarchy, this time over an issue concerning Jesus's exact nature as the Word of God. There was a real risk of a serious split. Constantine was anxious to unify the Church and solidify his authority. He convened a council of some 250 to 300 bishops to thrash out the matter, rather like a prime minister today would appoint a Royal Commission to tackle a big issue such as climate change. The best minds went to work, and came up with a serious answer. The dispute was resolved, and, in the process, the doctrine of the Trinity was written down in the form of the so-called Nicene Creed.[61]

The following is a useful, if simplified, outline of the three-fold conception of God:

Man knows the Father when he knows God as infinitely distant, he knows the Son when he knows God as absolutely close, and he knows the Holy Spirit when he knows God as penetrating existence and history.[62]

C.S. Lewis regarded what he termed 'the dance or drama' between the three aspects of the Trinity as 'perhaps the most important difference between Christian and all other religions', because it meant that God always remained a vibrant and not static entity in his mind.[63] In my view this observation applies with the greatest force to Christ. Jesus enables us to know God personally; He is 'the Way' to God.[64] Anyone in any circumstances at any time (at least, anyone who has been taught the rudiments about Jesus) can conceive of the question: What would Jesus do? That is possible only because God came to the world as a man. Christ continues by His example and living presence to mediate through us, via the Spirit, especially if we encourage Him to do so by prayer (See 1 John 5:1–12).

Paradoxically, perhaps, the doctrine of the Trinity can also serve as a bridge to many of the other great religions. It is a way for Christians to try to understand them better; and it may also be a way for sceptics of all religions – many of whom dimly perceive only a mass of contradictory mumbo jumbo – to understand the essential commonalities of religious experience.

This idea has been eloquently articulated by the Indian-Spanish theologian, Raimundo Panikkar. Having at various stages of my life been in both camps – cynical agnostic and confused Christian – I have found Panikkar's ideas most illuminating. They have been summarised as follows:

> [Panikkar] has developed the doctrine of the Trinity as a framework for Christians to relate to other religions. He describes three aspects of the divinity and three corresponding forms of spirituality. The first is the silent apophatic dimension, which transcends any human concepts, which he relates to the Father who expresses himself only through the Son. The second is the personalistic dimension, which Panikkar relates to the Son, who is the personal mediator between God and man. The third is the immanent dimension, which relates to the Spirit. Panikkar suggests that the apophatic spirituality of the Father is similar to the Buddhist experience of Nirvana, whilst the personalistic approach relates to the Jewish and Muslim stress on the Word of God. The immanent spirituality of the Spirit resonates with the Hindu sense of the non-duality of the self and the Absolute.[65]

In addition to the doctrine of the Trinity, there is a second theological feature of Christianity that, for me, distinguishes it favourably from all other religions. Christianity identifies correctly the essentially flawed character of human nature. At various points in this book I have touched upon the idea that pride – or self-righteousness – is the most deadly of human sins. Pride is destructive at both the individual and collective levels because it prevents people from engaging in honest self-analysis. Pride thus perpetuates wrongdoing by people who are too convinced of their own rectitude and too set in their own ways. It also perpetuates, among people who imagine themselves to be 'idealists', a naïve sort of wishful thinking that can be just as harmful in the long run as outright wrongdoing. At the extreme end of the scale, the combinative effect of these kinds of pride produces monsters like Hitler and Stalin, prime examples of those upon whom 'judgment in history falls heaviest'. Such are the men 'who come to think themselves gods, who fly in the face of Providence and history, who put their trust in man-made systems and worship the work of their own hands'[66].

Christianity addresses these awful truths directly, in the doctrine of original sin. It is not necessary to accept every aspect of that doctrine (let alone to believe literally in the story of Adam's temptation by Eve) in order to recognise that Christianity of all religions *takes the world seriously*. It teaches us always to be on our guard against the evil that lurks in every human, group and national soul – without exception. This was a consistent theme in Reinhold Niebuhr's writings. Christianity requires each of us humbly to admit that we are flawed, and that to have a chance of redemption we need to look to a higher power than ourselves. This message was uniquely communicated to Man in the person, the teachings, and the death and Resurrection of Jesus. As Herbert Butterfield wrote:

> In one fundamental sense … Christianity alone attacks the seat of evil in the kind of world we have been considering, and has a solvent for the intellectual predicaments which arise in such a world. It addresses itself precisely to that crust of self-righteousness which, by the nature of its teaching, it has to dissolve before it can do anything else with a man.[67]

There is a third aspect of Christianity which distinguishes it from all other faiths. Some people regard it as *the* distinguishing feature, 'the fundamental difference between the gospel and religion'.[68] It is the notion that individual salvation comes solely through God's grace, rather than moral effort by human beings. I confess that I continue to struggle with all the ramifications of this radical idea, and will discuss it more fully in Chapter 10 in the context of Heaven and Hell.

To summarise, then, my argument so far in this chapter. I believe that each of the world's major religions, and probably also a number of the minor ones, contain a portion of the whole truth. There are many points of similarity between religions, including reports of miracles, and that fact strengthens my conviction that God exists. Atheism is the really radical creed.

Of the main religions, I believe that Christianity is the closest to the whole truth, to the extent that the truth is accessible to Man in this life. A monotheistic conception of God seems to me to be the one most consistent with the views to which I have come about the nature of the physical Universe and Man's place in it. Of the three great monotheistic faiths, Christianity stands out for me, because it best explains the life and death of Jesus of Nazareth, and because the conduct of its founders in the first 300 years was uniquely and amazingly admirable. It is also the most realistic of the faiths in the way it recognises both the good and the bad in human nature.

The ways to God

The question may then be posed: Is it necessary to believe that Christianity is the *only* way to reconciliation with God? Further, even within Christianity itself, are there 'right' ways and 'wrong' ways to worship? Few subjects give rise to greater rancour than these ones, so it is as well that I state my position candidly at the outset: I am what is called an inclusivist.

Choices between belief systems

There are some kinds of Christians who insist that their way is the only way. Such people argue with stubborn certainty that even if some other faiths may teach a few things of value, ultimately there is only one worthwhile religious position.[69] On this reasoning, you might just as well be an implacable atheist and a mass murderer as (say) a devout Buddhist who spends her life caring for the sick. You might just as well score 0 per cent in the religious examination of life as (say) 65 per cent. The end result is the same: complete failure, and damnation of the soul – 'a poignant kind of tragedy'[70].

In *Letter to a Christian Nation*, atheist Sam Harris endorses this dichotomy:

> The Bible is either the Word of God, or it isn't. Either Jesus offers humanity the one, true path to salvation (John 14:6) or he does not. We agree that to be a true Christian is to believe that all other faiths are mistaken, and profoundly so.[71]

But Harris sets up a false choice. Without even beginning to come to grips with the substantive arguments, he mocks the idea that 'there is ... a vast and beautiful terrain between atheism and religious fundamentalism that generations of thoughtful Christians have explored'[72]. The bottom line for Harris is that *all* religions are 'absurd' and that *all* religious people are 'fooling themselves'[73]. Christopher Hitchens has advanced similar arguments, with his usual rhetorical flair.[74]

There is, however, some rational middle ground. Christian theologians have been grappling with this issue for centuries, notably at the Council of Trent from 1545 to 1563. The idea that salvation may be available to non-Christians is not new. I am broadly attracted to the Judaic approach to this issue, which is that 'the righteous of all nations shall inherit the world to come'[75]. In my judgment, for the reasons which follow, that approach is not inconsistent with Christian teaching.

The Christian conception of God is the one I believe in, but to assume that anyone of a (formally) different belief is necessarily doomed – and for eternity, at that – seems to me quite unnecessarily presumptuous. Salvation is a gift of God; who God decides to save, and precisely why and when, is up to Him. Some Christians may like to believe that they, and they alone, are the 'chosen ones'. But such a state of affairs just does not square with my notion of a loving and just God. Rather, I agree wholeheartedly with Warwick Fairfax:

> The claim of any race, people or religious body to be the sole repository of Divine Truth is contrary to all metaphysical principles, to the greatest religious traditions, and to the teaching of the New Testament.[76]

The New Testament contains a number of reminders that the Christian Bible is not the only way that God communicates with Man. In his letter to the Romans, St Paul wrote:

> For since the creation of the world God's invisible qualities – his eternal power and
> divine nature – have been clearly seen, being understood from what has been made.
>
> (Romans 1:20)

Paul was speaking here, as I read him, of the organised complexity of the physical Universe: the sorts of considerations canvassed in Chapter 1. As I noted there, the wonders of the physical world have moved Man to religious belief since the beginning of recorded history, long before Moses and the Law and long before Christ.[77] Those wonders – enlarged rather than diminished by modern scientific knowledge – remain a key pointer to God. They are accessible in some form or another to everyone, from the most primitive tribesman to the most learned Western sophisticate.

Later in Romans (at 2:13–15), Paul alluded to another way by which God communicates with all people: through their conscience. I have already quoted this passage in Chapter 2. It seems to me a vitally important passage in many ways. Not only is my own conscience evidence of the existence of a personal God; the fact that other people also possess a conscience helps me to reconcile my belief in the truth of the Christian religion with the idea that all other people – whatever their circumstances – have had or do have a 'fair chance' of finding God, *perhaps whether they are aware of the fact or not.*

In this regard, I share Warwick Fairfax's view that it is possible to be 'unconsciously religious'[78]. As Fairfax pointed out, 'highly intelligent people can deny strenuously with their reason a faith which the whole course of their nature shows that they are really following'[79]. The great Karl Rahner used the term 'anonymous Christians' to describe such people, or, at least, those of them who are conscientious adherents of non-Christian faiths. Many of my closest relatives and friends do not practise the Christian religion in any formal sense. But I love and admire them because of the ethical way in which they live their lives. I comfort myself with believing (on the basis of passages such as Romans 2:13–15) that God may already have touched their souls; in any event, God misses nothing and will judge them accordingly.

Paul Johnson has written eloquently on this theme.[80] He directs attention to the opening words of St Peter's great speech in Caesarea:

> I now realise how true it is that God does not show favouritism but accepts men from
> every nation who fear him and do what is right.
>
> (Acts 10:34–5)

In other words: everybody has a conscience. To fear God is to act according to its dictates. As Johnson says, 'That conscience is the instrument of absolute morality, of Natural Law, and if we follow it, we cannot go wrong'[81]. It does not much matter where you live, or who you are, or even what you do provided it is done for the right reasons. What matters is faithfulness to the Spirit (cf. 2 Corinthians 3:6). So I believe that it may be possible for a person who does not practise any religion, or even to have heard of the Christian Church, to achieve a state of grace that is acceptable to God. God does not judge on the basis of outward appearances; He is, to use the words of the King James Version, 'no respecter of persons'. What he respects is sincere effort to comply with universal moral principles, bearing in mind the difficulties that each particular individual has had to confront and the opportunities (or lack of them) that the individual has enjoyed. He judges each of us by, in Martin Luther King's immortal words, the content of our character. Or, to bring the solution to this 'problem' back to Scripture: a person is put right with God if and when – and because – he or she is 'in Christ' (see 1 Thessalonians 4:13–18).

It will be objected: But what about John 14:6, and Acts 4:12? These famous verses are routinely relied upon by Christians holding exclusivist beliefs. There are a few others as well, but those two are the ones most frequently invoked. John 14:6 appears in the fourth evangelist's lengthy account of the Last Supper ('I am the way and the truth and the life. No-one comes to the Father, except through me.') Acts 4:12 is a line from St Peter's speech to the Sanhedrin, following his and John's arrest by the Temple guard, as recorded by St Luke. ('Salvation is found in no one else, for there is no other name under heaven given to men by which we must be saved.')

Does either verse compel the conclusion that knowledge of Jesus of Nazareth or of Christian doctrine *per se* – i.e. knowledge acquired in this earthly life – is a precondition to salvation? The issue is couched fairly in the following passage:

> There are two ways of understanding this. The God we see in Jesus is the true God, and we may recognise God on that basis in many places, even in other cultures and religions; or: God is only to be seen and known in Jesus and nowhere else; there is no other way.[82]

In my view the first of the two positions must be the correct one. Jesus is the best starting point for thinking about God, and He is *the* end point of religious experience for all of us. It is Jesus who will judge our souls in the afterlife (see John 5:22), and in that sense He is the indispensible 'instrument' of salvation. However, to attain salvation, it is not strictly necessary for someone to have 'named His name' during their earthly life.[83] The God which Christians see in Jesus is the true God, but we may recognise God *on that basis* in many places – the beauty of Nature, the pull of conscience, and (pre-eminently) the experience of love. We may also, like Raimundo Panikkar, recognise Jesus in other cultures and religions. Non-Christians may not be aware that they have recognised 'Jesus' in these other things, but many believe that they have recognised God. As I conceive things, they have therefore recognised Jesus. At all events, in good conscience, I am quite unable to believe anything else.

True, there are passages in St Paul's letters which admit of the exclusivist position (see, e.g. Romans 10:1–21). But, likewise, there are plausible textual arguments for a 'liberal' approach. One of them is that the 'I' in John 14:6 is a reference to the Word – or Christ the *Logos* – rather than Jesus the man or even Jesus the Son of God. The

Word was a concept known to Neo-Platonist Greek philosophy, and a central aim of John's Gospel was to effect a theological reconciliation between thinkers from that tradition and adherents of post-Resurrection Judaism. St Augustine was schooled in both, and he was not an exclusivist.[84]

There is a risk, in this controversy, of becoming mired in abstruse theology. Some common sense also needs to be utilised. God knows full well that vast numbers of people throughout human history who have already lived and died were ignorant of the Bible and (in the centuries before Christ) ignorant of the Law of Moses. God knows that, even today, in spite of the missionary efforts of the Church, there are many millions of people on Earth who have had little or no exposure to Christian teaching. He knows that people of all faiths hold their views sincerely and that many of them live generally upright lives, often in conditions of material deprivation. For all the reasons discussed, it seems to me a monstrous jump of logic to assert that God would be so unjust as to condemn or forsake such people on the basis that they were not or are not practising Christians.

Dogma, ceremony and ritual

Let us turn from one touchy subject to another. How important to God are the formalities of religious observance – whatever the religion in question? In my opinion: not very important at all.

In a Christian context, that places me, I suppose, in the Protestant rather than the Catholic tradition. Even so, I do not believe that God favours the members of any particular denomination of the Christian Church over the members of any other denomination. I do not believe that God takes much notice of the seemingly endless 'doctrinal' arguments that appear to preoccupy certain kinds of religious officeholders and public spokespeople. This is not to underestimate the importance of at least some of the key doctrinal issues[85], such as free will versus predestination. Nor would I wish to belittle the achievements of some of the theological giants of history, men like Martin Luther, John Calvin, John Wesley and George Fox. Or, for the matter of that, those of men such as Joseph Smith Jr and Brigham Young. All these people created their own versions of the Christian religion and brought millions along with them, including many new converts who were dissatisfied with elements of the (man-made) status quo. It is a tremendous thing that there are now thousands of Christian denominations world-wide. There is strength in diversity.

All that said, the differences between the denominations should properly be regarded as matters of emphasis and/or of adaptation to local circumstances. Christians are entitled to differ about many things; in part, those differences reflect the ubiquitous uncertainty to which the human mind is wont. As I have argued, God permits and even encourages uncertainty. But ultimately, what are most important are the points on which all Christians can agree. In 2009, I expect that God considers that far too much time is taken up by all denominations of the Church in arguing amongst themselves, and that far too much time is taken up by most congregations in discussing administrative trivia. The division and discord to which such activities often give rise is profoundly unattractive and distracts attention from the main game. At an individual level, people should concentrate on the plank in their own eye (cf. Matthew 7:3); at a collective level, churches should concentrate on tending to their own flocks, fighting for social justice, and spreading the core Gospel message to the populace (cf. Amos 5:21–4). There are huge numbers of people who are clueless; they have not yet asked themselves the most basic spiritual questions. The churches will not reach them by bickering about fine details.

Many people in the West who profess not to believe in God, or who cannot bring themselves to take the Christian Church seriously, seem to equate religious faith with dogma, ceremony and ritual. In fact, they are – or should be – quite peripheral to it. Jesus hammered this theme (cf. Mark 2:23–4 and 3:1–6), and so did St Paul, a man who before his conversion had been immersed in such matters. In his letter to the Romans, St Paul counselled vigorously against judging fellow-Christians on the basis of fourth-level issues such as dietary rules: 'Do not destroy the work of God for the sake of food' (Romans 14:20), he pleaded. Likewise, in his letter to the Colossians, St Paul emphasised the dangers for any believer of not seeing the wood for the trees, and of being overborne by bullies in authority:

> Therefore do not let anyone judge you by what you eat or drink, or with regard to a
> religious festival, a New Moon celebration or a Sabbath day. These are a shadow of the
> things that were to come; the reality, however, is found in Christ … Since you died with
> Christ to the basic principles of this world, why, as though you still belonged to it, do you
> submit to its rules: 'Do not handle! Do not taste! Do not touch!'? These are all destined
> to perish with use, because they are based on human commands and teachings. Such
> regulations indeed have an appearance of wisdom, with their self-imposed worship,
> their false humility and their harsh treatment of the body, but they lack any value…
>
> (Colossians 2:16–23)

The same point was made nearly 2,000 years later by D.A. Carson: '[G]enuine godliness is so easily aped, its place usurped by its barren cousin, formal religion.'[86]

These and other similar passages resonate strongly with me. It is dispiriting so often to confront Christians who seem far more interested in form or style than in what St Paul called the 'basic principles' – and who try to foist their petty foibles on to others. One of the reasons for the Apostles' early success in recruiting converts was their complete disinterest in the trappings of formal religion. Their bold message resonated strongly among Greek-speaking people, many of whom were inclined to believe in the monotheistic God of the Jews but were turned off by rituals such as compulsory circumcision and bewildering dietary laws. Similarly, in Samaria (the region between Galilee in the north and Judea in the south), the local people were particularly receptive to the Apostles' message. St Philip, one of the leaders of the Hellenist wing of the early church, enjoyed considerable success among them. The Samaritans had long been reviled by the hidebound Jewish authorities in Jerusalem. Although they followed

Mosaic law faithfully, the Samaritans used a slightly different version of the Hebrew Scriptures and, until 129 BC, had worshipped at their own Temple.[87]

I do not contend that form and style are entirely unimportant. Ritual is a prominent feature of all religions.[88] Individual worshippers can draw great comfort from rituals with which they are familiar, especially if they grew up with them. And rituals serve the purpose of fostering community spirit. There is nothing wrong with that, and it is positively cruel to deny people the pleasure that these practices afford, provided that adherence to them does not become an end in itself, the main point of the whole exercise.

Ultimately, I do not believe that God is much interested in the particular choices that people make in these matters. He does not care whether you prefer the King James Version of the Bible or the Good News Version. He does not care whether you like to sing Wesleyan hymns or to rock along with the Planetshakers. He does not care whether you adopt the Catholic or the Protestant rites of Communion. He cares about the quality and the sincerity of your love for Him and your love for other people. He cares whether you really strive to be like Christ. The author of St John's first letter put it this way: 'He who has the Son has life; he who does not have the Son of God does not have life' (1 John 5:12).

William Temple, the great twentieth-century English theologian and Archbishop of Canterbury, summed things up this way: 'It is a mistake to suppose that God is only, or even chiefly, concerned with religion.'[89] They are supremely wise words.

Temple was not using the term 'religion' in a wholly pejorative sense, but his observation highlights the fact that 'religion' is a loose term. Psychologists recognise at least two kinds of religion, 'extrinsic' and 'intrinsic'. These terms were coined in the 1950s by the American researcher Thomas Bouchard. Extrinsic religion was the label he gave to 'religious self-centeredness' – religion practised insincerely for reasons of social convention or personal advancement (often by people with a propensity for prejudice). On the other hand, 'intrinsic' religion is practised sincerely as an end in itself; it becomes the central organising principle of a believer's life. According to Bouchard's research, extrinsic religion tends to be the product of a person's environment (direct parental influence, schooling, etc.) whereas intrinsic religion is something innate.[90] Bouchard's theories as to the causes of these twin phenomena were and are highly controversial, but there can be little doubt that each form of religion exists. There can also be little doubt that extrinsic religion flourishes within established churches.

And yet, organised religion is essential. According to the New Testament, Jesus Himself directed the establishment of the Christian Church (Matthew 16:18; 18:17). The authenticity and meaning of these passages are hotly disputed[91], but no one can doubt that group solidarity was critical to the Church's growth – its very survival – in the first and second centuries. Operating at its best, the Church – or any congregation – is an emblem of everything that Jesus stood for. I have suggested that human friendship may be the purest form of filial love. In the same way, fellowship within a congregation is, or ought to be, one of the purest forms of worship. D.A. Carson has explained why:

It is made up of people who are as varied as can be: rich and poor, learned and unlearned, practical and impractical, sophisticated and unsophisticated, aristocratic and plebian, disciplined and flighty, intense and carefree, extrovert and introvert – and everything in between. The *only* thing that holds such people together is their shared allegiance to Jesus Christ …[92]

So I have now reached this position. Christianity is the creed that most comprehensively satisfies my own religious sensibilities. But many other religions contain at least a portion of the truth, and even people who do not practise any religion may be able to put themselves right with God by perceiving His presence in Creation, by listening to their conscience, and by loving well. In sending Jesus to Earth, God tried to make it easier for Man to know and understand Him, but in so doing I doubt very much that God intended to cut off all other possible ways of reaching that state of mind. God prefers us to worship in an organised way, but ultimately the form of worship is secondary.

I certainly cannot believe that God judges people primarily or at all by reference to man-made criteria (of the Christian or any other religion) with which many people in human history were and are ignorant. The Bible makes clear distinction between wilful sin and sin committed unintentionally or through ignorance (e.g. Ezekiel 45:20). St Paul taught that God may be prepared to overlook honest ignorance, though turning a blind eye to the evidence is something quite different (Acts 17:30).

These tentative conclusions are, I realise, quite at odds with the views of some conservative Christians. They would accuse me of 'Renaisance theology'[93]. One, J.I. Packer, has mocked the idea that Christianity is merely 'the Rolls-Royce among religions, the best of its kind, but [that] the same basic sense of oneness with God underlies them all'.[94] Nevertheless, that is essentially my belief. As I have said, I would label my own position as inclusivist (though with a few extra twists). I think it is consistent with a broader idea already touched upon in various parts of this book. The existence of some element of doubt or uncertainty – as a precondition to order – seems to be a recurring theme in the Universe. Matter obeys certain fixed laws, but some kinds of events and phenomena cannot be predicted. Human beings are subject to universal rules of right conduct, but these may at any time be flouted through the exercise of free will. Faith itself is possible only because of the *im*possibility of knowing God fully or proving His existence in any definitive way. Similarly, the fact that we cannot be *sure* of knowing of all the ways to God is a necessary and desirable feature of the human spiritual condition. It helps to promote tolerance and humility.

Unfortunately, however, religious belief does not always manifest itself in benign ways. That brings me to another important issue, the last to be addressed in this chapter.

Absolutism and evil perpetrated in the name of religion

It is undeniable that many people throughout human history have asserted claims to knowledge of absolute religious truth. There is no question that much evil has been wrought as a result. I use the word 'evil' quite deliberately, in the sense of conduct that is odds with the universal standard of proper conduct and, accordingly, wrong in God's eyes. It is hard to disagree with John Spong's assessment:

> [W]henever a group of religious folk begin to believe that they possess God's truth, almost inevitably they become those who in the name of their version of that truth persecute, excommunicate, purge, burn at the stake, or justify cruel religious wars against any who will not salute their tradition or acknowledge their rightness in things religious.[95]

In his book *The Misery of Christianity*, Joachim Kahl expanded on this theme. In clinical and sometimes grisly detail, he tracked through the sorry history of wars and persecutions fought in its name – the Crusades, the Thirty Years War, the Inquisition, and many other comparable atrocities. Christopher Hitchens adopts a similar approach in *God Is Not Great*, focusing not merely on Christianity but religion in general. Some of his more original examples from the modern era – Imperial Japan, Sri Lanka, Rwanda – are especially shocking.

Almost as bad as religiously motivated violence is secular violence sanctioned or encouraged by the churches. As Jim Wallis has written: 'The Pentagon cannot be expected to be faithful to the teachings of Jesus, but the church should be.'[96] Martin Luther King took up this subject in one of his most famous sermons:

> In the terrible midnight of war men have knocked on the door of the church to ask for the bread of peace, but the church has often disappointed them … During the last two world wars, national churches even functioned as the ready lackeys of the state, sprinkling holy water upon the battleships and joining the mighty armies in singing 'Praise the Lord and pass the ammunition'.[97]

Dr King also pointed to the failures of the churches on other issues, such as economic justice: the Greek Orthodox Church in Czarist Russia was so closely aligned with the despotic status quo that the Bolsheviks tried to eliminate it.[98] Joachim Kahl likewise lamented the Church's long history of support for the institution of slavery, its anti-Semitism, and its oppression of women. He referred with evident agreement to the assessment of another scholar, William E.H. Lecky, that 'the Christian Church has caused a greater measure of undeserved human suffering than any other religion'[99].

These considerations must give pause to anyone who seeks to defend Christianity, or any religion. But having considered them, they do not shake my own faith. One reason is that there is another – noble – side to the historical and human story: inspirational people down the centuries who did not resort to violence or other evils but, rather, devoted their lives to peaceful evangelism or other good works. The Apostles, St Clement of Alexandria, St Francis of Assisi, William Jennings Bryan, Martin Luther King, Australia's own John Flynn – these are my own Christian heroes. And for 2,000 years there have been countless millions of Christians of more modest accomplishment, people who spent their lives extolling the faith and extending practical love to others. Their conduct and the *motivation* for their conduct should not lightly be forgotten. The atheist's common retort – that such people are 'a compliment to humanism, not to religion'[100] – seems to me patronising in the extreme. Christopher Hitchens takes the argument to absurd lengths, claiming that Martin Luther King was '[i]n no real as opposed to nominal sense ... a Christian'[101]. That would have been news to Dr King.

I do not think that people like Hitchens have really tried to imagine what the world would be like today if not for the influence of Christianity (and religion in general) on the inner lives of ordinary human beings. Even Bertrand Russell conceded that '[a] man's anti-social wishes may be restrained by a wish to please God'[102]. Herbert Butterfield suggested that doubters and cynics of his time should try to imagine (say) the year 1800, and 'the thousands and thousands of priests and ministers [who] were preaching the Gospel week in and week out, constantly reminding the farmer and the shopkeeper of charity and humility, persuading them to think for a moment about the great issues of life, and inducing them to confess their sins'.[103] Butterfield's point was that this sort of unnoticed Christian work never stopped, even during the reigns of the worst of the popes; he contended that in the total scheme of history such work had had a much greater cumulative impact on the quality and texture of human life than the wars and other atrocities waged by the institutional churches.[104] In short, taken on the whole, 'the spread of piety *does* mean a growth in charity'[105]. The proposition is impossible to prove in any definitive way, but I am convinced it is correct.

But leave aside the beneficial aspects of religion in practice. There are better reasons for concluding that evil wrought in the name of Christianity (or excused by the Church) does not invalidate the faith itself, let alone somehow disprove the existence of God. For one thing, it is overly simplistic to ascribe certain tumultuous world events solely or even mainly to 'religion'. 9/11, for instance, had many causes. So too did the Crusades, fought sporadically from the eleventh to the thirteenth centuries, and frequently held up as the archetypal example of religiously-motivated conflict. In fact, according to one expert, '[t]here are serious difficulties in categorising the crusades as wars of religion'.[106] They were fought for myriad reasons – ethnic, dynastic, economic, political, historical and military. 'On neither side was there interest in, or even awareness of, religious specifics'.[107] Of course, there was an underlying 'religious' subtext: between the seventh and eleventh centuries, the Ottoman Empire, which was predominantly Muslim, had expanded into most of the Middle East and significant parts of Europe – areas which, previously, had been predominantly Christian. If the Crusades had not been fought, Islam may well have spread further, at least in the short term. Even so, it is important to distinguish causes from effects.

Ever since the Treaty of Westphalia in 1648, which entrenched the system of sovereign nation states, most wars have not been waged even notionally for purposes 'religious'. National leaders have had no difficulty in finding other reasons to fight – especially in more recent times. As the English agnostic John Humphrys has justly written, 'the bloodiest century in the history of mankind [the twentieth century AD] can be blamed on many things but religion comes some way down the list'[108].

It must nevertheless be granted that, sometimes, religion has been, and still is, an important factor in starting wars, and in other dreadful events in human history. But what does that really teach us?

I return to some of my earlier themes. If there is a God who created Man, then there is nothing to be gained by wishing away His existence because you disapprove strongly of some of Man's conduct on Earth. You must try to understand the place of evil. To my mind, evil committed by people who call themselves Christians (or Muslims or Hindus) is just more evidence of the inherent fallibility of human nature, which is the inevitable by-product of God's gift of free will. That gift extends to conduct motivated by religious belief. Inevitably, many people who are so motivated will exploit the gift, some in a well-meaning way, others maliciously. To classify their conduct as wrong is of itself to acknowledge the existence of an absolute morality – which prohibits aggressive violence and (most of all) pride. I have already discussed pride. It is the worst of sins, and religious intolerance is, regrettably, one of its most poisonous manifestations. But to abhor religious pride is a poor reason for ignoring religion.

Nor should people of faith be deterred from enthusiastic evangelism. It is true that, in the secular West today, one's efforts will often be greeted with puzzlement, embarrassment or distaste – sometimes naked aggression. Michel Onfray's atheism 'leaps to life when private belief becomes a public matter, when in the name of a personal mental pathology we organize the world for others'[109]. There is nothing new about this phenomenon. In similar vein, Lord Melbourne once complained: 'Things have come to a pretty pass when religion is allowed to invade the sphere of private life.'[110]

Christians should also not be deterred from evangelism among peoples of other faiths. On that score, I part company with the Judaic tradition and with liberal Christians such as John Spong. There is no escaping the duty laid down in the Gospels to 'make disciples of all nations' (Matthew 28:19), and this command need not be understood in the discredited sense of forcibly converting the heathen. What needs to be encouraged is open and vigorous debate between proponents of different religions, with all parties putting aside irrelevant prejudices based on gender, nationality, race, sexuality or class. Any such process – *if conducted with humility* – may well lead all concerned to a deeper appreciation of the transcendent wonders of God, and greater respect for each other. I feel quite certain that God means it to be this way. God wants the debate about Him to continue. He has left room for uncertainty. He has not closed off the debate – as, surely, He could have done.

God has, though, provided Christians with the best single argument: the example of Jesus. And as C.S. Lewis observed, if you continue to harbour doubts as to whether people other than Christians are capable of being put right with God, there is only one right course of conduct. It is not to throw up your hands at the apparent injustice of the situation, and to do nothing to help the 'people outside'. Rather, you must intensify your own efforts to know Christ:

> [If] you are worried about the people outside, the most unreasonable thing you can do is to remain outside yourself. Christians are Christ's body, the organism through which He works. Every addition to that body enables Him to do more. If you want to help

those outside you must add your own little cell to the Body of Christ who alone can help them. Cutting off a man's fingers would be an odd way of getting him to do more work.[111]

This book is my attempt to do Christ's work. I hope in this chapter not to have offended people of other faiths, or of no faith. My purpose has been to explain why the existence of other faiths is not a sound argument against the truth of Christianity.

CHAPTER 10

HEAVEN AND HELL

What must I do to inherit eternal life?

Mark 10:17

Parting is all we know of heaven,
And all we need of hell.

Emily Dickinson

Is there life after death? There is no escaping this question in any hard-headed discussion of Christian belief. I have already touched upon the matter in places, but will now tackle it in detail. It is a subject of high importance and an appropriate subject with which to conclude this book.

The afterlife has become a distinctly unfashionable subject, even in some religious circles. A number of the more liberal Protestant denominations of the Church – whose views I share on a good many issues – seem especially reticent when it comes to grappling with it, particularly the notion of Hell. In some ways this is understandable. The sane mind seems to recoil instinctively from conscious thoughts of eternity – not because the idea is absurd, but because it is unsettling.

Atheists are generally not shy about addressing this critical issue. They will assert plainly that the concept of an afterlife is an infantile invention of Man, 'a cognitive illusion'[1]. Michel Onfray devotes a great deal of attention to this issue in *The Atheist Manifesto*. He pities the 'naïve and foolish believer' who has swallowed the idea that Man can 'ward off death by abolishing it'[2]. In Onfray's view, which was also that of Bertrand Russell[3], the 'religious impulse' ultimately stems from fear of death, from an 'inability to look death in the face … and distress at the realisation that human life is finite'[4]. Concepts of heaven and hell are imagined, Onfray argues, as a source of comfort.

It has been suggested that the rage exhibited by radical atheists like Onfray may itself be a product of the fear of death – of a truly uncanny fear that death *is* the end, and that there is no 'big vague thing … going to happen'. The rage of such a person 'is so huge and so personally felt that he craves the vindication of repudiating the God in whom he does not believe'[5].

This suggestion is interesting, because it recognises an undeniable fact. Most of us do, indeed, fear death. Consequently, for many people, dwelling on the afterlife is much less often a source of comfort than it is a source of *dis*comfort. And it is not 'silly', as Cicero tried fruitlessly to argue, that this should be so.[6] There are good and rational reasons to fear death. For some people (the poet Philip Larkin was one) the prospect most to be dreaded is eternal oblivion. But for others – a majority of the human race, I dare say – it is the alternative prospect, that of 'living on' after death, which is the *more* frightening. That is why I am unconvinced by arguments such as Onfray's. Contemplating the possibility of Hell – as many believers do – seems a strange sort of wish-fulfilment.

The whole subject of the afterlife is not one calculated to brighten dinner table conversation, in part because it is so mysterious and – let it be said – frightening. I can remember as a child of ten or eleven, during the phase when I attended a Bible study group, being terrified by the idea of Hell. From memory we had been subjected to the 'fire and brimstone' version. It horrified me to think that my mother and father, who were not practising Christians, might be separated from me one day and pitched into such a dreadful place. I soon stopped going to the Bible study group, and these feelings passed.

My childhood experience reflected a common human attitude. Most people prefer to dwell on the more congenial and accessible aspects of religion, or to put the whole subject of what happens after death out of their minds entirely. Belief in an afterlife is, though, a common feature of many faiths. It is integral to Christianity, which shares with Islam and Zoroastrianism a conception of both Heaven and Hell. Now that I am no longer a child, there is no option but to face up to the issue. It is not a question of seeking comfort, but of asking the hard questions. It can plausibly be argued that *atheists* are the ones really trying to comfort themselves, by pretending to be certain that death is mere nothingness and should therefore hold no fears.

I believe that there *is* life after death, and will attempt to explain why. I also believe in both Heaven and Hell, though my conception of each is decidedly hazy, and quite possibly in conflict with more orthodox Christian teaching. I will try to describe what I imagine both places to be like, and how God will decide who goes where. My aim is to demonstrate that there is much comfort to be derived from belief in an afterlife, as well as much to be feared.

Why I believe in the afterlife

It is necessary to emphasise one point at the outset. Whatever claims may sometimes be made to the contrary, neither the existence nor the non-existence of the afterlife can be proved to a level of scientific certainty. But I agree with Bertrand Russell that '[t]he question whether people survive death is one as to which evidence is possible'[7].

The closest thing we have to 'evidence' (in a secular sense) is the phenomenon of near-death experiences – the visions described by people who have been resuscitated after cardiac arrest, i.e. who 'survived' clinical death. Most of these people are regarded by researchers as honest and reliable witnesses; not a few were atheists before their experience. The classic NDE is this:

> As well as ... bright light and [an] out-of-body experience...people, while clinically dead, see a tunnel, deceased relatives and divine figures. They may be guided by one of these spirits through a life review in which, some report, they feel again every emotion the past events aroused. Though they believe themselves to be dead, this cascade of feelings typically occurs against a prevailing sense of euphoria. At some point, they're told it's not their time and they return to the confinement of their body.[8]

As well as 'positive' NDEs such as these, an increasing number of 'negative' NDEs are now being reported. Numerous people revived after clinical death have relayed horrifying stories of torture, panic, shrieking and despair. It has been suggested that this kind of NDE is under-reported, because the people who have them are usually reluctant to relive their experience. According to one expert, all these stories 'have one thing in common: they leave the revived patient frantic for a second chance at redemption'.[9] A NDE of this sort was recorded by the 'venerable' eighth-century scholar St Bede, in his magisterial work *Ecclesiastical History of the English Nation*. A Northumbrian landowner named Drithelm claimed, after coming out of a coma, to have visited both Hell and Purgatory. After this scarifying experience Drithelm gave away his fortune and thereafter lived a life of piety and good works.[10] Similar experiences are attributed to St Christina Mirabilis, a twelfth-century Belgian nun.

These stories are intriguing. Modern research into NDEs will, and should, continue, like research about evolutionary processes and quantum physics. However, I very much doubt that any definitive metaphysical 'answers' will emerge. For the Christian apologist, most accounts of NDEs might properly be regarded as broadly consistent with church teachings about the immortality of the soul – or, at least, as not inconsistent with those teachings. But accounts of NDEs are also not inconsistent with atheism: my brother, a model of open-mindedness on most things, concluded after researching the matter thoroughly that 'on balance, it's almost certain that NDEs happen in the theatre of one's mind, and that in the absence of resuscitation, it's the brain's final sound and light show, followed by oblivion'[11].

Needless to say, I disagree with my brother on this one. And I believe that the mystery of the afterlife is best approached not through empirical science but philosophy. The starting point for me is belief in justice.

I have argued that God, in granting human beings the gift of free will, must have appreciated that a great deal of suffering would be caused as a result. Suffering is the inevitable consequence of each and every person having the freedom to choose wrong over right, to disregard (whether deliberately or negligently) the universal standard of right conduct which is a basic feature of the Universe. As I have tried to demonstrate, it is that kind of suffering, together with the suffering caused by the outworkings of the physical laws of Nature, that makes human life meaningful.

Conceivably, the collective richness of Man's life on Earth could provide sufficient justification for God's creation of a world containing so much suffering. Some religious people believe that. Atheists *must* believe that what happens during our lives on Earth is the be all and the end all: that you simply draw a straw in the lottery of life. Be that straw long, short or somewhere in between, the rest is silence. But my conception of God as loving and just does not permit me to believe any such thing. Moreover, the evidence is against it.

Man does not live only or even mainly in a collective way; we are each of us individuals, with a conscience. It is that faculty that enables each of us to extend love to other people and (if we so choose) to enjoy 'fellowship' with God during the time of our bodily life on Earth. God loves each of us individually, and scrutinises each of us individually. I do not believe that God would create a Universe in which there was no mechanism for the rectification of suffering on Earth and no mechanism for individual assessment of each one of us against His universal standard of right conduct. There is and always has been too much horrible suffering and evil in the world that goes uncompensated and unpunished by Man.

In short, I believe in divine judgment. And in order to believe in divine judgment, it follows that you must believe in an afterlife. It also follows, though even many Christians express unease as to the concept, that God is a 'record-keeping deity'[12]. I do not know whether the description in the Bible of 'the book of life' reflects a literal truth – probably not – but it seems right that each of us will be judged according to what we have done (Revelation 20:12–13). God 'will bring every deed into judgment, including every hidden thing, whether it is good or evil' (Ecclesiastes 12:14). This theme of divine judgment was stressed many times by Jesus Himself. Jesus also taught that God is concerned not primarily with a person's outward deeds but with his or her state of mind – those who do evil *knowing* it to be wrong will be judged more harshly than those whose evil conduct is born of ignorance. (see Luke 12:47–48). Conversely, those who do apparently good deeds for reasons of pride or self-aggrandisement will not win favour from God. Such deeds may bring the doer condemnation (see Matthew 6:1–4).

Thus, the existence of suffering and evil in the world is my first reason for belief in an afterlife. I touched upon this subject in Chapter 7. To put the matter plainly, it is God's way of rewarding those people who – for the right motives – have done a disproportionate amount of good during their earthly lives. There is honest horse-sense in these words of D.A. Carson:

> Christians are not masochists: they do not want to suffer out of some forlorn but stupid belief that suffering is intrinsically good. They are prepared to suffer and to endure because they keep their eye on the goal.[13]

The flipside, of course, is that God will punish those who have wrought a disproportionate amount of evil. It is also His way of squaring the ledger, as it were, between those who have enjoyed a disproportionate amount of His grace and those who have been less fortunate. That is my own instinctive view, and it is a view which has been shared by the majority of human beings throughout history.[14] It is also an inescapable theme in the New Testament (see, for instance, 2 Thessalonians 1:6–10). I will come presently, and in some detail, to my conception of the 'how' of these notions.

My second reason for believing in the afterlife – and it is related to the first – is the existence of love. Love in all its manifestations is a magnificent and complicated thing. It may be the most wondrous of God's creations. I have tried to explain how love operates as an integrated force on Earth and why, in my opinion, the experience of human love can help us to understand the nature of God's love for Man, and God's expectations concerning our love for Him.

One feature of love that I have not so far commented upon is its relationship with time. This theme has been taken up by countless poets, novelists and other artists. Love between human beings exists in time but, like suffering, it also exists in memory. Anyone who has experienced the death of a loved one will understand what this means: the person who has died does not simply cease to exist but 'lives on' in the hearts and minds of those who remember and mourn. Hamlet, for instance, was never really separated from his father: the ghostly visitations on the battlements and in Gertrude's bedchamber are best understood as a product of Hamlet's loving, idealised memory. Likewise, Hamlet's grief and anger at Ophelia's funeral is motivated by a still-extant love for her.

When I was growing up and my grandmother was alive she often talked about her husband, even though he had died many years before. 'Nev', as she always called him (not 'your grandfather' or some such) remained for her an actuality, a person who continued to influence her own conduct in many aspects of life. When, in turn, my grandmother died, she lived on (and still does) in my heart and mind – and in those of others. There are still occasions when I can still see her and hear her, and imagine what she would have done in my place.

My conception of the afterlife is not confined to the notion that people who die remain a part of the lives of those who loved them. Far from it. But this phenomenon bears out the comment of the English priest Marcus Braybrooke that human love has 'an inherently deathless quality'[15]. As Dylan Thomas put it: 'Though lovers be lost love shall not'[16]. Philip Larkin enunciated the point more plainly still: 'What will survive of us is love.'[17]

The contemporary American writer Mary Eberstadt, whose thoughtful views about love and family I referred to in Chapters 3 and 8, has gone a step further. She suggests that love within families is '*literally* death-defying' because it 'bind[s] those alive to relatives both past and yet to come'. This feature of family life, she argues, 'might make it easier for those living in families to make related transcendental leaps of the religious variety'[18].

St Paul also wrote on this theme:

> Love never fails. But where there are prophecies, they will cease; where there are tongues, they will be stilled; where there is knowledge it will pass away. For we know in part and we prophesy in part, but when perfection comes, the imperfect disappears.
>
> (1 Corinthians 13:8–10)

Love never fails – or, as the idea is expressed in other translations of this passage, *love is eternal*. There are various aspects to this notion. One is that human love – the love that we give and receive during our earthly lives – survives our bodily death in some extraordinary way. This can only be possible if divine love is also eternal.

In Chapter 3, I developed the idea that love must have been God's motive for the creative act. In the words of Julian of Norwich, the fourteenth-century English anchoress, 'Before God made us, God loved us ... Our beginning was when we were made, but the love in which He made us never had a beginning'[19]. In short, divine love existed *before* Creation. The corollary of this idea is that divine love will continue to exist *after* the physical products of God's Creation, including Man, have ceased to be. God's love for Man will persist. Julian of Norwich was alive to this idea as well. She believed that God's love had 'never faltered, nor ever will'. Thus, God's love is the source of our immortality: 'He has done everything for our benefit; *in this love* our life is everlasting'[20].

What do these ideas suggest as regards God's love for individual human beings? To my mind, they suggest that divine love does not cease when your body dies; its influence will continue to be felt, indeed it will be felt the more strongly when you confront God face to face. As St Paul wrote in a different letter:

> For I am convinced that neither death nor life, nor angels nor demons, neither the present nor the future, nor any powers, neither height nor depth, nor anything else in all creation, will be able to separate us from the love of God that is in Christ Jesus our Lord.
>
> (Romans 8:38–39)

That puts the matter plainly enough. If death will not separate any of us from God's love, it follows that something (the soul) must live on after death – for even God's love must have an object.

There is a third reason why I believe in the afterlife. It has to do with an argument advanced at various points in this book: that not only Christianity, but secular life itself, depends upon there operating in the Universe some element of uncertainty or unpredictability. If bodily death were truly the end for each individual person – *and everyone knew it for certain* – then the world would be a much more terrifying place. I am convinced that a lot of potential evil in the world is prevented only because, somewhere in the recesses if not at the forefront of our minds, we harbour at least the suspicion that one day we will be called to account. Uncertainty about the afterlife also forces people to battle on in life when things go badly wrong, rather than taking the extreme but logical route of suicide. Thus, as Hamlet lamented, conscience makes cowards of us all.

It is true that some people profess to be convinced there is no afterlife, and that many of them are reasonably law-abiding citizens. But I suspect that such people are, in fact, rather rare. Most people, I would guess, take a version of Pascal's wager; they are at least uncertain whether there is an afterlife, and that uncertainty affects their conduct – for the better. In the words of Czeslaw Milosc, an eminent Polish poet, the greatest danger lies in 'a belief in nothingness after death – the huge solace of thinking that our betrayals, greed, cowardice, murders are *not* going to be judged'.[21]

Atheists may complain that a system of morality based on fear of an authority figure is vulnerable to '[d]eceit and self-deception'[22], and is far from foolproof. But *all* effective systems of law – including nonocratic systems – involve investing power in a person or institution. That person or institution must be able to decide between right and wrong, to administer punishment to the guilty, and/or to award compensation to the wronged. The strength of any such system depends in large part on the awe in which it is held – or, if you like, the extent to which the wrongdoer *fears* justice and (just as important) the person wronged *expects* justice. There is nothing corrupt about such a system, and a system of divine justice is simply the ultimate manifestation of those principles.

It may be objected that the existence of the theoretical possibility of an afterlife does not amount to proof, or even good evidence, than an afterlife in fact exists. As a matter of strict logic, that is probably right. But in this regard I hark back to my argument in Chapter 2 about cognition. Why does Man possess the capacity to speculate about the possibility of God if, in fact, God does not exist? There seems to me no credible reason in purely materialistic terms; it would be a distraction from the main game of Darwinian survival.

Similarly, if there is no afterlife, I do not understand why Man has the capacity to imagine it. If God does not exist, then our ability to speculate about both Him *and* the afterlife seems – at least at the level of individual survival – doubly superfluous. Assuming that God does exist, one must ask why God would permit Man to speculate about the afterlife if, in fact, the afterlife does *not* exist. One answer might be this: it keeps the human race collectively 'in check', but ultimately it is just a trick. On balance – and bearing in mind the other three reasons why I believe in the afterlife – I cannot agree with that contention. I do not believe that God would conduct Himself in that way.

That brings me to the fourth and final reason why I believe that there is an afterlife. Jesus of Nazareth said so. Generally, in this book, I have tried to avoid arguing my thesis on the basis *solely* of appeals to biblical authority. Where I have quoted from the Gospels or the epistles, it has usually been because the author was able to express a concept or an argument more eloquently than I could myself. But in this instance, I think it is legitimate to rely upon the words of Christ (i.e. of God) Himself. True, Jesus's exact words on the matter have probably been lost in the mists of time. But for the reasons earlier discussed, the Gospels are sufficiently reliable as an historical record of Jesus's words and deeds to permit one to conclude that He did, in fact, address the question directly. One or two of the relevant passages in the Gospels have that strange quality of verisimilitude about which A.N. Wilson has commented. And the gist of what Jesus said is fairly clear.

Most of Jesus's allusions to the afterlife are found in St Matthew's Gospel, the first of them in the Sermon on the Mount. Heaven is referred to twice in the Lord's Prayer, though it is not described (Matthew 6:9–10). Elsewhere, however, Jesus does paint a picture of Hell, and a dreadful picture it is: a place of fire and pain and despair. I cannot bring myself to take all of these descriptive phrases literally. It has been suggested that the Qur'an depicts Heaven and Hell in more obviously symbolic terms than does the Christian Bible.[23] I must confess that I empathise with that approach. Perhaps it is wishful thinking, but the notion of Hell as a place of eternal physical suffering is just not credible to me. It is at odds with my belief in a just and loving God.

Reading the relevant New Testament passages between the lines, I suspect that Jesus tried to make His point with a degree of metaphorical flamboyance – as he was wont to do. The image of Hell as a fiery, putrid chasm was one familiar to most people in Jesus's day. It was derived by the Old Testament prophets from a real-life place, Gehenna, a canyon just south of Jerusalem which was once used by pagans for human sacrifice. The Hebrews converted it into a place for burning all kinds of stinking rubbish.[24] I expect that Jesus made use of this well-known image in order to relate to His contemporary audiences.[25] Jesus abhorred evil-doing, and wanted everyone to understand that, in the afterlife, there *is* a Final Judgment. He also wanted everyone to understand that there is an experience called Heaven and an experience called Hell.

In short, Jesus spoke with a sense of urgency. He wished to emphasise that the stakes are high. So too did the authors of the Gospels and the Epistles in which these images are occasionally invoked.

In any event, for present purposes, the key point is that Jesus taught that there is life after death; that the afterlife is eternal; and that each of us will be judged according to what we have done on Earth. If you believe that Jesus was God – or that 'God was in Christ' – then what Jesus is recorded as having said on the matter is of the highest importance. From a personal point of view, I must also take notice of the fact that what Jesus said is broadly consistent with my own reasoning about the existence and nature of an afterlife. Lastly, and to my mind conclusively, what Jesus said about the afterlife is supported by what He did – rise from the dead.

On what basis will God judge us?

This is a difficult question, one with which I had trouble for a long time. Divine judgment is widely regarded today as 'one of Christianity's most offensive doctrines'[26]. Many people deride it, and/or say that they disbelieve it, often in insistent terms. However, I suspect (like Timothy Keller) that this attitude often stems 'more [from] a feeling of revulsion than a doubt'[27]. I feel queasy about the doctrine myself. Nonetheless, because I now believe it to be essentially true, it becomes necessary to grapple with the 'nuts and bolts'. How will God judge us? How is a Christian expected to know what is required of him or her in order that he or she may go to Heaven and not to Hell?

Many unbelievers in the West today hold a generalised notion that God – if He exists – must simply cast an overall judgment upon the worthiness of each of our lives. Zoroastrians believe that there is literally a 'weighing' of the soul (the *urvan*) upon death: God takes every word, thought and action carefully into account.[28] Superficially that sounds a fair thing, but it is not what orthodox Christianity teaches. God does take cognisance of all our behaviour, but divine judgment is not ultimately a matter of the grading and tabulation of all the 'good' and 'bad' episodes in a person's life. If it were, many people might reach a point later in life when it would become too late to save (or to lose) their soul. They would pass a point of no return.

Most Christians believe something different. It sounds unfair, but in fact it is not. As St Paul famously insisted, 'It is by *grace* you have been saved, through faith – and this not from yourselves, it is the gift of God – not by works, so that no-one can boast' (Ephesians 2:8–9; see also Titus 3:4–6; Romans 10:10–13). In other words, you will go to Heaven not because you have 'morally outperform[ed] others'[29], still less because, having been an objectively 'good' person, you deserve to. You will go to Heaven if, when and because you have admitted that you *deserve* nothing; that you cannot save yourself by your own efforts; and that you need God. Your soul must be in a right relationship with God. In some sense you must believe in Him, and He in you.

Some atheists (Richard Dawkins among them) argue that mere belief or unbelief in anything is a ridiculously unjust basis on which to judge someone. Bertrand Russell, an agnostic, once wrote that 'if there [is] a God, I think it very unlikely that He would be offended by those who doubt His existence'[30]. But this is to misunderstand the subtle concepts at play here. I do not want to get bogged down in the old argument about faith and works. Reconciling all of the relevant passages in the New Testament on that subject is a task beyond my knowledge and expertise. But the issue is too important to be ignored, and I will state what I believe.

God is vitally interested in *both* the sincerity of our relationship with Him (faith) and in the practical way in which we demonstrate that faith on Earth (works). 'Faith without deeds is dead' (James 2:26). In St Paul's expression, faith is 'a calling'. Any good works that result from positive belief in God are evidence of a resolve 'to live a life worthy of the calling you have received' (Ephesians 4:1). In the end, Paul thought, 'the only thing that counts is faith expressing itself through love' (Galatians 5:6). Faith without deeds too often morphs into 'Christian narcissism' or 'Christian triumphalism'[31].

I noted in Chapter 9 that, according to John's Gospel, it is *Jesus* who will judge us, not God the Father (John 5:22). Personally I take great comfort from that fact, because the Gospels provide us with many examples of Jesus in judgment mode. We should know what to expect! Plainly enough, the sin which Jesus detested most of all was self-righteousness. He rarely quizzed people about theology; he demanded the so-called 'twin loves', of both God *and* neighbour. As John Dickson has astutely observed, Jesus 'left no room for the neighbourly agnostic *or* for the spiritually minded hypocrite'[32]

G. Campbell Morgan understood these ideas as follows:

Not only is it true that men are not saved by holding a theory; it is equally true that He [i.e. Christ] never on any single occasion made it necessary that a man should hold any theory concerning Him; but that men should believe in Him… [P]erhaps we should be nearer the word of Christ if we read, That you should believe *into* Him Whom He hath sent. That lifts belief far higher than the intellectual realm, making it a volitional act by which a man abandons himself to the truth of which he is convinced. There are men who question as to whether it is possible to choose their beliefs. There are senses in which it is not. No man can choose a conviction. Conviction is necessary to faith; but faith is more than conviction; it is conviction followed.[33]

Dr Morgan went on:

The unbelief that robs a man of peace and power, and prevents him from coming into living association with Christ is not intellectual doubt or intellectual difficulty. The unbelief that shuts a man away from Christ is that man's *refusal to act upon the conviction that has gripped his soul.* And consequently the belief that saves is an action of the will.[34] (My emphasis)

The point so far is that what saves one's soul is not mere belief, nor mere acts, but acting upon belief. But, Dawkins and others would object, what if you have not got to the stage of belief in the first place? What are you expected to do then?

It has been suggested that the early Christians would have scoffed at this sort of plea. D.A. Carson has written:

We are inclined to buy into the modern view that 'belief' is simply a matter of opinion. Whether or not you are a believer is a private matter. It has to do with your disposition and conditioning; no matters of ultimate truth are at stake. The New Testament writers, however, including Paul, never see things that way. They hold that God has objectively revealed himself – not only in the distant past, but now decisively in his Son, Jesus Christ, whom he raised from the dead. Not to trust him totally is not merely a matter of religious preference, not a matter of 'unbelief' in the modern sense, but willful disobedience, moral rebellion.[35]

These are tough words, and although I agree with them in part I do not share Carson's underlying assumption that anything less than 'total' belief during this earthly life amounts to damning rebellion. There is no doubt that much alleged 'unbelief' in the West today is really no more than laziness, a myopic and convenient refusal to take the biggest issues seriously, rather than a properly considered position. Belief requires hard work: in extolling the 'Kingdom of God', Jesus and the Gospel authors often placed emphasis not only on 'God's initiative in bringing the kingdom, but on the 'effort' needed on the part of the individual seeking the kingdom'.[36]

There is, however, a crucial difference between never engaging in the quest for God and struggling in that quest. It is perfectly understandable that many, perhaps most, believers struggle with their faith. My own view is that faith is *not* the equivalent of intellectual acceptance or positive (let alone 'total') belief, though some people of faith do enjoy those states of mind. I think that faith, as God understands it, must be a somewhat broader concept. To regard faith as mere belief that God exists may be the most common mistake that modern-day people make as regards religion. It is a natural mistake, but a grave one, because to adopt this mindset is simultaneously to set the bar too low and too high. Too low because some of the most evil people in history probably believed in God as a logical proposition (cf. James 2:19). Too high because it excludes people who are conscientiously *seeking* God but who still harbour doubts and uncertainties. It is now known, from her private diaries, that Mother Teresa was one such person. Is it likely she would be in Hell?

In my opinion, faith is better understood, at least in its initial stages, as a 'venture' or a 'choice of direction'. It is 'a certain way of setting our personalities and confronting the universe'[37]. At the behavioural level, we must listen to our conscience and do good works, because 'there is a moral basis to the knowledge of God'[38]. At the intellectual level we must eschew arrogance, keep our minds open at all times, and search constantly for signs of the ineffable. As St Paul said in his speech to the councillors of the Areopagus in Athens, God made us so that we 'would seek him and perhaps reach out for him and find him' (Acts 17:27). In short, we must at the least be sincerely *trying* to reach God. That was the view held by St Anselm[39] (and, more or less, by the author(s) of the Upanishad, one of most sacred of Hindu texts (see Chand. III, 14, 1).[40] It is evidently the view of the current Archbishop of Canterbury, Dr Rowan Williams, who has likened faith to being in a close personal relationship such as marriage. The essential thing is to commit to the relationship and to grow in it. Likewise, when and if you commit to seeking God, deeper and deeper knowledge of God will follow – not knowledge in the sense of 'acquaintance with a particular fact or state of affairs' but 'knowledge that comes from relation and takes time'[41].

That leaves one further question. What will be the fate of apparently conscientious people who are convinced, having thought about the issues, that God does not exist? I do not refer here to people who are unsure, but who still truly want to find God. (They should be fine.) Nor do I refer to people who have given up seeking God or (worse) who now actively seek reasons only to *dis*believe. (They are in danger.) I am talking about people who retain an open mind and who still want to find God but who, as things stand, believe positively that God does *not* exist. My suspicion is that such people are very rare, but the issue is still a most important one. What can you do if you are such a person?

One option is to suspend your disbelief as best you can and ask God in prayer to grant you belief. You should also ask others, those who *do* believe in God, to pray for you. St Paul frequently prayed that God might strengthen his own faith, and the faith of others. In his letter to the Philippians he told them that he prayed 'that your love may abound more and more in knowledge and depth of insight, so that you may be able to discern what is best' (Philippians 1:9–10).

Another option for unbelievers is to do what Jesus recommended. He urged anyone in intellectual difficulty about His true nature – anyone unable to make up their mind – to 'put what He said to the test of doing it'[42]. If you obey God's will, Jesus promised, you 'will find out whether my teaching comes from God or whether I speak on my own' (John 7:17). In other words, give Christ the benefit of any doubt and behave accordingly. *Then* decide. This may be the best, the only answer to the faith/works conundrum. It has the virtues of fairness and of glorious uncertainty. Anyone can try to obey Christ's teaching, but no one can be sure if they have done so to God's satisfaction.

This leads to another issue concerning Heaven and Hell. I believe, with Paul Johnson[43], that it is an essential feature of God's grand plan that no one can be certain how they – or anyone else – will be judged by God at any given time. We all sin, and none of us knows when our day and hour will come (cf. Matthew 24:36, 42).

We can be sure that we will be judged fairly, but we cannot be sure of the outcome. There are no precise criteria, no set of boxes to be ticked. We cannot be absolutely positive that even the likes of Stalin and Hitler are in Hell, though the overwhelming probability must be that they are. There is, however, always time and opportunity for sincere repentance. As St Paul wrote, 'God has mercy on whom he wants to have mercy' (Romans 9:18). When Christ was dying on the Cross, He asked His Father to forgive the executioners, for they knew not what they did (Luke 23:34). Who can know whether or not that prayer was answered?

This, again, is an example of the uncertainty principle. Everyone on Earth, whatever their station in life, must be left in some doubt about God's intentions. This is just as important for 'good' people as it is for the obviously vile. If we truly take to heart the Christian message that everyone is flawed, and that everyone is at risk of going to Hell, our pride is less likely to lead us astray, and we are less likely to judge others. As far as the obviously evil are concerned, the position is not hopeless. They too are given every chance to reform their ways, for the benefit not merely of themselves but of everyone else.

One of the most persuasive descriptions that I know of God's likely approach to the judging of our souls is to be found in a sermon of Martin Luther King. I find these words immensely comforting. Dr King preached:

> In the final analysis, God does not judge us by the separate incidents or the separate mistakes that we make, but by the total bent of our lives. In the final analysis, God knows that his children are weak and they are frail. In the final analysis, what God requires is that your heart is right. Salvation isn't reaching the destination of absolute morality, but it's being in the process and on the right road.[44]

Herbert Butterfield had a similar conception of the criteria for salvation. All in all, it is the most satisfactory one that I know. Butterfield was convinced that the mere *doing* of apparently 'good' or 'bad' acts cannot be the test, because the morality of any given example of human behaviour depends so heavily on circumstances and motive. It is easy for the rich to appear virtuous, for the flatterer to appear kind, for the intelligent and well-educated to appear wise, and so on. Yet Butterfield accepted the Christian idea that 'in the course of ages there must be a division between the sheep and the goats amongst the race of men'. The only test which seemed to him 'to be fair all round' was one centred upon a person's 'capacity to attain a certain childlike quality'[45]. In sum, what God is looking for is a tendency to *humility* in thought, word and deed, as regards both God and your fellow human beings. That is what it is to be 'in Christ', a notion I discussed in Chapter 9. I am strengthened in these conclusions by a little-known historical fact, rightly emphasised by John Dickson: it was the authors of the New Testament who elevated humility to the status of a great human virtue.[46] The early Christians drew this lesson from the example of Jesus.

What will Heaven and Hell be like?

It seems incumbent upon me to explain in more detail my conception of what Heaven and Hell may be like, and the sorts of people who may well be bound for each.

Before doing so, I need briefly to mention a theological issue of some controversy: whether after death only our souls survive, or whether our bodies will also undergo some kind of resurrection. Over the centuries there have been theologians in both camps.[47] St Paul famously wrote that 'flesh and blood cannot inherit the kingdom of God' (1 Corinthians 15:50). Nevertheless, the more orthodox Christian conception of the afterlife is as of a 'restoration' of the material world to its state of intended perfection.[48] I am inclined to agree that the orthodox position is right, for the reason given by St Thomas Aquinas, namely that 'the natural condition of the human soul is to be united with the body ... Hence the will cannot be perfectly at rest until the soul is again joined to the body ... Therefore man's final happiness requires the soul to be again joined with the body'[49]. In other words, in order to make sense of Heaven, it is necessary to believe in bodily as well as spiritual rebirth of some sort. Precisely how it works – for example, what age one's body will assume in Heaven (or in Hell) – I simply do not know. In Hell, it may be that the soul is not rejoined with the body, and one thing that makes the place so wretched is that the disembodied soul is aware of the fact. Again, I do not know, but it seems a possibility.

Hell

There are, indeed, almost endless possibilities when it comes to imagining Hell. The lurid descriptions in St John's Revelation bear an eerie similarity to some contemporary depictions of nuclear holocaust. But, if anything, the images of fire and darkness and torment that are invoked in the Revelation and elsewhere in the New Testament seem rather to trivialise the concept of Hell. Many theologians, writers and painters down the ages have also imagined Hell in this way, but I am bound to say that their work leaves me largely unmoved. St Augustine (*City of God*), Dante (*Divine Comedy: The Inferno*), Hieronymus Bosch, Rubens (*The Fall of the Damned*), John Bunyan (*The Pilgrim's Progress*) and Michelangelo (*Last Judgment*) – none of their portraits of Hell satisfies or even much interests me.

Considerably more fascinating, I think, are the real-life 'visions' of Hell recounted throughout history by many ordinary, and apparently credible, men and women. Among the most famous is that of St Teresa of Avila, a sixteenth-century Spanish nun. According to one contemporary expert, 'Church scholars have speculated that

[St Teresa's account of Hell] is perhaps the most accurate description of the inferno known to humanity'[50]. It is worth reading in full.[*]

I do not doubt that people such as St Teresa really believed they had had these experiences, but I cannot accept that the 'fire and brimstone' images which they recounted reflect a literal truth. The scholarly consensus is that '[a]ll descriptions of heaven and hell in the Bible are symbolic and metaphorical'[51]. On the other hand, 'the Bible clearly proposes that heaven and hell are actual realities'[52]. My personal belief is that Hell is a real – supernatural – place, and not merely (as some theologians suggest) a label for the miseries that people bring upon themselves on Earth by their wrongdoing.[53] There are too many people on Earth who seem not to suffer much at all while visiting pain upon others.

D.A. Carson has this conception of Hell:

> The final picture is not a pretty one. Some people think of hell as a place where sinners will be crying out for another chance, begging for the opportunity to repent, with God somehow taking on a 'tough guy' stance and declaring, 'Sorry. You had your chance. Too late.' But the reality is infinitely more sobering. There is no evidence that there is any repentance in hell. The biblical pictures suggest that evil and self-centeredness persist and persist – and so does the judgment.[54]

For reasons to which I will come shortly, I do not share Carson's vision of lost souls left *indefinitely* to stew in their own juices, but I agree that the final picture (whatever it is) will not be pretty. Hell has frightening possibilities. Those that strike me as being plausible are as follows.

First, I imagine the gut-wrenching shock that must come to those who learn that they are bound for Hell. There is a vivid passage from a sermon of John Henry Newman, quoted in Paul Johnson's book *The Quest for God*, in which this moment is described. One may choose to ignore the nineteenth-century flourishes about demons and hellfire, but the gravamen of the passage is chilling.

> Oh, what a moment for the poor soul, when it comes to itself, and finds itself suddenly before the judgment seat of Christ! Oh what a moment, when breathless with the journey and dizzy with the brightness, and overwhelmed with the strangeness of what

---

[*] 'The entrance resembled a very long narrow passage, like a furnace, very low, dark and closely confined; the ground seemed to be full of water which looked like filthy, evil-smelling mud, and in it were many wicked-looking reptiles. At the end there was a hollow place scooped out of a wall, and it was here that I found myself in this close confinement ... I felt a fire within my soul the nature of which I am utterly unable to describe. My bodily sufferings were so intolerable that, though in my life I have endured the severest sufferings of this kind – the worst that it is possible to endure, the doctors say, such as the shrinking of the nerves during my paralysis – ... the knowledge that they would be endless and unremitting. And even these are nothing by comparison with the agony of my soul ... To say that it is as if the soul were continually being torn from the body is very little ... in this case, the soul itself is tearing itself to pieces ... I felt, I think, as if I were being both burned and dismembered; and I repeat that the interior fire and despair are the worst things of all ... There was no light and everything was in the blackest darkness ... and my burning on earth is a small matter compared with that fire.' Quoted in Van Scott, *Encyclopedia of Hell*, op. cit., p. 274.

is happening to him, and unable to realise where he is, the sinner hears the voice of the accusing spirit, bringing up all the sins of his past life, which he has forgotten or which he has explained away, which he would not allow to be sins, though he suspected that they were … And, oh! still more terrible, still more distressing, when the judge speaks and consigns it to the jailors, till it shall pay the endless debt which lies against it! And the poor soul struggles and wrestles in the grasp of the mighty demon which has hold of it, and whose every touch is torment. 'Oh, atrocious!' it shrieks in agony, and in anger too, as if the very keenness of its affliction were proof of its injustice. 'A second! and a third! I can bear it no more! Stop, horrible fiend, give over; I am a man and not such as thou, I have not on me the smell of fire, nor the taint of the charnel house … I know what human feelings are; I have taught religion; I have a conscience; I have a cultivated mind; I am well versed in science and art…[55]

As Paul Johnson has remarked, this passage draws its disturbing power from Newman's evocation of a 'soul's realisation that it is not dreaming, that its life on earth has gone, irrevocably, and that it is now on its own, without friends, relations, possessions or claims to importance of any kind'[56]. Among other things, the passage also brings home a point that I suspect escapes most unbelievers and even many believers: at least as a *possibility*, Hell exists for the many, and not merely for the exclusive few. As a child I can remember thinking that, surely, only murderers, rapists, robbers and their ilk were really 'sinners'; most people just occasionally do bad things, so why would they go to Hell? This now strikes me as a fundamental misconception.

D.A. Carson's description of Hell is surely accurate in one key respect. Whatever the experience may entail, it will be the culmination of an individual's behaviour on Earth. At death, your soul will be in the state in which you have left it, through the exercise of free will during your life on Earth. If Hell is your fate, then you will have brought it upon yourself, by ignoring God and pursuing your own selfish ends. In the trenchant words of Warwick Fairfax, 'If anyone with even the slightest degree of insight into the teachings of Jesus and the meaning of God will look at himself he will see that this hell is of his own making.'[57]

All people are sinners, and it is only pride that leads us to assume that our own sins are trivial compared to those of most others. That is one reason why, in the New Testament, we are repeatedly told not to judge other people but to worry about our own transgressions. God wants us to understand, I think, that we cannot blithely assume that Hell is exclusively for the Charles Mansons and Myra Hindleys of the world. In St Matthew's Gospel, the people who suffer in Hell are generally those who enjoyed good fortune on Earth, but who mistreated, exploited or neglected the poor and the weak. But the author of Matthew almost certainly did not intend to suggest any exclusive criteria. Rather, as Johnson puts it, Hell may also be for the 'mixed-up person, ill-informed, inattentive, weak, silly, vain … and shallow', the person who is 'not a monster… [and] who, given the choice, would [not] choose evil in preference for good'. Such people – and we all know them – would enter Hell only because of what they would regard as 'a colossal misunderstanding'[58].

My own belief about the likely fate of 'ordinary' sinners is this. They will not be thrown into everlasting fire and torment, in any literal sense. I hold on to one of my firmest beliefs, which is that God is wise and just. Accordingly, not only will everyone be fairly *judged*; once judgment is passed, everyone will also be fairly *dealt with*. There will be no cruel or unusual punishment; indeed, I have come to believe that the notion of retributive punishment scarcely enters the equation. This does not mean, however, that the sinner's experience in the afterlife will be easy or congenial.

Nobody can expect to enter Heaven unless and until he is worthy – or not unworthy – of dwelling in God's presence. How likely is it that anyone will be in such a state at the moment of death? As Warwick Fairfax observed, there is great difficulty involved in 'expecting any soul to prepare itself for Heaven *in one lifetime*'[59]. Fairfax posed this rhetorical question: 'Are the imperfectly prepared souls even of the best of us immediately ready for the full awareness of the perfect God?'[60] Personally, I doubt it very much.

What follows from this? Not, surely, that only a handful of saints will be spared from eternal Hell. God is much more merciful than that. But nor will huge numbers of deeply flawed individuals breeze straight into Heaven, merely because they 'believed' in God and/or in Christ. I do not think that Jesus's sacrifice of atonement can be regarded as a 'free pass' of that sort. Rather, at death, each one of us will be forced to examine – rigorously and unflinchingly – the state of our soul (our Self). The time for self-delusion will be over. It will then be obligatory to attempt a total reconciliation with God.[61]

How will that reconciliation be effected? The Hindu answer – indeed, the answer of many Eastern faiths – is reincarnation of some kind. The soul will, as it were, be given the chance to purify itself, back on Earth, over as many lifetimes as it takes to be rendered 'fit' for eternity. But that notion is very hard to reconcile with the New Testament. My own view is that there will be no 'returning' to the earthly realm. Instead, God – or, rather Jesus Christ – will in some manner 'supervise' this process of reconciliation. Remember: Jesus is the ultimate judge of our souls. He, and only He, can decide when a person is 'in Christ'. It is possible that those who judged other people harshly on Earth will be judged the more harshly by Jesus (cf. Matthew 7:2).

This process of reconciliation must, I imagine, vary substantially from person to person, both in character and duration – possibly even in outcome. I share Fairfax's conception (borrowed, of course, from Catholic theology) that '[t]o the extent that [the sinner] can effect a reconciliation, it will be purgatory; to the extent that he cannot it will be hell'[62]. If Martin Luther King was right, and God's interest is in the essence of a person, then Jesus will concentrate upon each sinner's worst flaws – the vicious moles of Nature in them. His ultimate aim will be to rehabilitate, if and to the extent this is possible, but as part of that process each sinner will be 'repaid in kind'. The bullies of the world will endure some time being bullied themselves, but then they will spend a great deal more time learning how to be kind. The deceitful will be made to feel what it is like to be conned and lied to, and then will be taught the value of honesty. The rude will be treated contemptuously for a good while, but then will be taught some manners.

The greedy will spend some time in hunger and want. The lazy will be put to useful work. And so on. Some sinners, perhaps most, will be 'treated' for more than one vice. Throughout this process, each sinner will be burdened by the knowledge that the process which he or she is enduring need not have been necessary at all, or at least not as agonising. Each sinner – by now fully aware of God's righteousness – will feel dreadful shame in the realisation that his or her soul, in its original state, was not fit for Heaven. And, worst of all, every sinner will feel intense shame for his or her lack of faith while alive on Earth, and will feel intense deprivation for being 'shut out from the presence of the Lord and from the majesty of his power' (2 Thessalonians 1:9).

I imagine, too, like Newman, that the experience of Hell will be made worse by the fact that each sinner will be alone. Friends, family and other familiar faces will be absent, at least for a time. The sinner will be thrown onto his or her own resources, without the comfort that comes from human solidarity. Moreover – and this feature of Hell is clearly suggested by the parable of the rich man and Lazarus (Luke 16:19–37) – I imagine that the sinner will also feel a sense of helpless despair in being unable to warn loved ones back on Earth that the same fate awaits them unless they turn from their sins.

My conception of Hell is terrible enough, but of course it is not the traditional conception. On this issue, I believe that a minority branch of the Church may be closest to the truth – the Unitarians. Like them, I simply cannot believe in a God who would consign any sinner to Hell *for eternity*. Hell itself, like Heaven, may well be eternal. (This would be consistent with Plato's view that ultimate reality is timeless.) But I do not believe that any individual sinner, however black the state of his or her soul at the moment of death, will be required to stay in Hell forever – at least, not a Hell in which the sinner is aware of, and resigned to, its eternal nature. If that were so, suffering in Hell would be pointless and sadistic rather than – as it is on Earth – redemptive and instructive.[63] In short, Hell is purgatorial – a tenet, incidentally, of both Islam and Zoroastrianism.

For similar reasons, I cannot believe in the somewhat more palatable concept of 'annihilation'. This idea – that all souls sent to Hell will be dispatched into oblivion – was advanced by Origen, the second-century Christian philosopher.[64] Arguably, there is support for this theory in the Bible (see Ezekiel 18:4 and Matthew 10:28), but, again, it does not seem consistent with God's methods and purposes, as I conceive them. That said, there may possibly be cases where a person's soul is in so dreadful a condition when it enters the afterlife that reconciliation with God, of the kind I have described, proves impossible. In such cases, if there are any, 'Hell is the entanglement of of the soul in fallacious or evil earthly ends from which it cannot disassociate itself and which are *completely irreconcilable* with the spiritual realms in which it finds itself, and even more so with God'.[65] In those (rare) circumstances, the individual in question might properly be regarded as having killed his own soul, and to have 'descended … to the level of a souless animal'[66]. This would be a kind of annihilation.

Conservative Christians will object – many in Australia already have! – that to deny eternal Hell is to fall into the trap of moral relativism. It is, they claim, another manifestation of the underlying ethos of Western modernity, whereby Man is obsessed with 'seeking power and control rather than wisdom and glad enjoyment of the "givenness" of God's creation'.[67] We must, they say, 'learn to live in conformity with this unyielding reality'[68] – which includes *eternal* Hell. But does it? How can anyone be so sure? And how can some people defend the idea of eternal Hell with such unseemly relish?

I accept that to deny divine judgment entirely would be to deny 'unyielding reality'. But why is some middle ground so unthinkable? Timothy Keller is one writer I generally admire who staunchly defends the notion of eternal Hell. Yet Keller has also recognised the unique graciousness displayed by Jesus toward *all* the people who wronged Him, even His executioners – 'Father, forgive them; for they know not what they do' (Luke 23:34 (KJV)). '[Jesus's] resistence to their evil-doing,' notes Keller, 'was measured and courageous, not venomous and cruel'.[69]

As a lawyer, I hold firm to the fundamental notions of fair compensation and proportionate punishment. These principles are basic to any just system of laws, and it is inconceivable to me that God would not abide by them. On the one hand, God's 'judgments are true and just' (Revelation 19:2). On the other hand, the exacting of excessive compensation or the imposition of disproportionate punishment is unfair and unjust. Even the notoriously stern God of the Old Testament demanded but 'an eye for an eye', and Jesus Himself explicitly invoked the principle of proportionate punishment ('With what measure ye mete, it shall be measured to ye.' (Mark 4:24). Consigning any conscious soul to eternal Hell would be unfair and unjust ('venomous and cruel'), so I cannot believe that God would ever do it. In holding that view, I sincerely believe that I am not shying away from a difficult truth. I am trying to conceive what the truth is, measuring the possibilities against the knowledge that there is to be had of God's nature, especially as shown in the human person of Jesus. Jesus was a tough but forgiving man.

In the end, I find myself in partial agreement with Marcus Braybrooke. He does not believe in Hell. He does believe that, because God wills *all* people to be saved (cf. 1 Timothy 2:4), there must be a process by which 'all souls come to a true knowledge of themselves and are opened to divine love'. Braybrooke hopes that 'in the end all souls will recognise and accept the gracious love of God'[70]. This idea, sometimes called Universalism, is neither new nor especially radical. My belief is that the afterlife must provide a mechanism – fearful but fair – through which that process will take place. The Mormons hold a not dissimilar belief.[71]

Heaven

The New Testament leaves the precise nature of Hell uncertain, but it is almost silent in relation to Heaven. The word itself is used often, but there is little elaboration. That may be further proof of the wisdom of the men who wrote the Christian Bible. Most of them did not attempt to describe the indescribable. St Paul confined himself to this:

> [N]o eye has seen, no ear has heard, no mind has conceived, what God has prepared for those who love Him.
>
> (1 Corinthians 2:9; cf. Isaiah 64:4)

This suggests that even our most hopeful imaginings are likely to be wide of the mark. Perhaps the only certainty about Heaven is that you will experience the 'Beatific Vision' – seeing God face to face. And Christ will somehow be there. Otherwise, if you try to conjure up a mental picture of Heaven utilising worldly objects and constructs, the result will probably seem lame, even silly. I confess to drawing little of much help from the description of the New Jerusalem in Chapter 21 of St John's Revelation, other than the general averment that 'there will be no more death or mourning or crying or pain, for the old order of things has passed away' (Revelation 21:4). It has been suggested that Jesus clearly intended the Last Supper to be 'the principal image of the afterlife', and that He confirmed this after the Resurrection by appearing to the wayfarers at Emmaus while they were breaking bread (Luke 24:30).[72] That seems to me to be drawing a long bow.

Likewise, and as in the case of Hell, I have rarely derived personal inspiration about Heaven from theologians, writers or painters. Many have tried to imagine it, including several men and women of genius: St Thomas Aquinas (in *Summa Theologica*), Albrecht Durer (*The Adoration of the Trinity*), St Francis of Sales, John Milton (*Paradise Lost*). A number of the most beloved Church figures down the centuries – St Monica, St Bridget of Sweden, St Catherine of Siena, St Hildegard of Bingen – claimed to have experienced real-life visions of Heaven. All of these accounts are worth reading, and not a few are very beautiful. But none of them is, for me, really satisfying.

For what they may be worth, I proffer some personal thoughts as to what Heaven may be like. Most of my ideas concern the *feelings* that being in Heaven may generate. First, I imagine experiencing a massive sense of relief, at the moment of realisation that one is – how extraordinary! – actually in Heaven. For most people this moment will occur only after the scathing experience of Hell. The contrast between the two feelings will be, I venture to guess, sublime.

Shortly thereafter, other emotions will take hold. There will be gratitude that God has extended His mercy. There will be an overwhelming sense of humility. There will also be a surge of curiosity, an intense desire to learn all that there is to know about Heaven, accompanied by happy expectation that one's curiosity will, in good time, be satisfied.

What will happen then? One can only speculate, but it is fun to try. One thing I believe firmly is that Heaven will be a place of ecstatic reunion with loved ones. Many people seem impassionedly to think so, and to derive much solace thereby. It is common to hear the bereaved being reassured that they will one day be with the deceased again, in the next life. St Chad, a seventh-century Northumbrian monk, told shortly before his death of being comforted by a vision of his beloved brother, Cedd, safely and happily in Heaven. At the time of Chad's vision the brothers had not seen each other for two years, as Cedd was serving as Bishop of Mercia, but Chad died reassured he would meet his brother again.[73]

In writing of death, the Chilean novelist, Isabel Allende, has emphasised the notion of reunion:

What will it be like to die? What is on the other side? Only night and silence? It occurs to me that to die is to fly like an arrow through dark reaches toward the firmament toward infinite space, where I must look for my loved ones, one by one.[74]

So might Ruth have spoken about Naomi.

I believe that even now there are people in Heaven whom I will see again in the next life: my grandparents, several friends, perhaps even my favourite childhood cat. Ultimately – if God's grace shines upon me – I would hope to be reunited again with *all* of the people dearest to me. Indeed, my list of names would be quite a long one. Perhaps it is simply a failure of my imagination, but I cannot but think that their presence with me in Heaven would be essential for my happiness. Why do I believe that reunion with all of them is possible, even likely? Because the greatest of all God's creations is love, and love is eternal. Heaven makes no sense to me without the love of all these people, and the love that I am able to give to them. For even one of them to be absent would be unendurable. If I am fortunate enough one day to reach Heaven, I cannot imagine God inflicting that sort of suffering upon me.

How otherwise will the whole set-up work? Will those in Heaven have any conception of time? Or space? If there is bodily as well as spiritual resurrection, what age will we all be? Will there be food to eat and tasks to perform? Will there be sex? As to sex, St Paul thought not (cf. Galatians 3:28; 2 Corinthians 5:1ff), but if there is bodily resurrection it is hard to see why that joy would be denied to us.

Heaven must also, I would like to think, be a place of *intellectual* pleasures. Giles of Rome, a thirteenth-century theologian, envisioned a realm free of language barriers where people could converse freely and graciously about all subjects, including the deepest mysteries of the Universe. If that is right, Heaven is a place where people 'delight in knowledge for its own sake'[75]. I love that idea.

These are all personal ruminations. No doubt other people have their own, quite different conceptions of Heaven. It is best that way. God evidently decided that the details of Heaven ought not to be spelt out clearly, or at all. Perhaps God reasoned that to do so would inevitably trivialise – even debase – the concept, or (as C.S. Lewis thought) distract us from our more immediate and important Christian responsibilities. Perhaps Heaven is indescribable in human language.

At all events, Heaven is thus left to the imagination of each individual believer. In that respect, the principle dwelt upon several times in this book – that some things in the Universe work best when and because there is an element of uncertainty attaching to them – seems to be at play again.

As a believer, it is enough to feel sure that anyone who reaches Heaven will, as King David imagined, 'dwell in the house of the Lord for ever' (Psalm 23:6).

WHAT IS YOUR VERDICT?

I press on towards the goal to win the prize for which God has called me heavenwards in Christ Jesus. All of us who are mature should take such a view of things. And if on some point you think differently, that too God will make clear to you.

Philippians 3:14–15

Hope is definitely not the same thing as optimism. It is not the conviction that something will turn out well, but the certainty that something makes sense, regardless of how it turns out.

Vaclav Havel, *Disturbing the Peace*

My hope in Christianity is of the sort articulated by Vaclav Havel: to me, Christianity makes sense. It 'leads us to expect the things we observe'[1]. Some readers may well remain unconvinced, and that is their right. But this book will have fulfilled its purpose if you are now persuaded that there is at least a tenable case for Christianity, and that the motives of Christian evangelists are in the main honourable. For, in the words of D.A. Carson, 'Christianity is not interested in tempting you to believe contradictory nonsense. It invokes mystery now and then; it does not invoke nonsense.'[2]

I hope also to have demonstrated that there are very real problems with the case *against* Christianity, and religion in general. Anyone who wishes to postulate atheism as a serious alternative explanation for the how and the why of Man's existence faces a formidable challenge. It is just not sufficient for the atheist to declare that 'we have only the scantiest reasons for thinking that there are [supernatural objects] – and powerful reasons for thinking that there are not'[3]. The opposite may be closer to the truth. The evidence for the existence of something supernatural, i.e. God, is not scant but considerable — I would say imposing. True it is that the evidence is capable of being interpreted in different ways; the atheistic hypothesis is open. But all of the following questions, and others, need credible answers:

- Why is there something rather than nothing?
- How did that something come into being?
- Why are the fundamental physical laws that govern the Universe just right for life?
- How and why did life on Earth begin?
- Does Darwinian evolutionary theory fully explain the organised complexity of life on Earth?
- Why is the incidence of genetic mutation just right to enable the process of Darwinian evolution to work?
- Why are human beings able to decode Nature?
- Why do human beings have a conscience?
- Why are there basic moral laws which all human beings recognise?
- Is free will an illusion? Can any of us ever do anything other than what we end up doing?
- Why can human beings make and respond to music?
- Is faith a mere incidental by-product of Nature?
- Is love a mere incidental by-product of Nature?
- Will science ever be able explain everything?
- Was Jesus of Nazareth merely an invention of human minds?
- If Jesus lived, then who or what was he, if he was not divine?
- How otherwise do you explain the reports of Jesus's perfect, sinless life?
- How otherwise do you explain the reports of Jesus's miracles?
- How otherwise do you explain the reports of Jesus's significant following among the common people, and the conversion even of some Jews and Romans in positions of authority?
- How otherwise do you explain the reports of Jesus's arrest, trial and crucifixion?
- How otherwise do you explain the reports of the Resurrection?
- If the Resurrection did not happen, how do you explain the Apostles' conduct, St Paul's conversion, and the establishment of the Christian Church in the face of overwhelming odds?
- How do you explain the corrolations, which are sometimes striking, between many of the prophecies of the Old Testament and certain key events described in the New Testament?
- How do you explain the corrolations between many of Jesus's prophecies, as recorded in the Gospels, and certain key events described in the New Testament?
- How do you explain the reports of personal religious experiences by many millions of people down the ages?
- How do you account for the nature and incidence of suffering, and its many beneficial by-products?
- If there is no God, why do people pray when their lives are in imminent danger, including many unbelievers?

- How do you account for the phenomenon of grace?
- Why has Man not yet been destroyed by nuclear holocaust?
- Is there really a fundamental dichotomy between Christianity and left-wing politics, or does Christianity reflect some seminal left-wing principles?
- Why is it that Christianity as a whole does not conform to either left-wing or right-wing ideology?
- Is there further evidence of Design in the operation of the democratic system of government?
- How do you account for the fact that atheism is, and always has been, an unpopular minority creed?
- How do you account for the many commonalities between different religions, and in particular the commonalities between Judaism, Islam and Christianity? Is it more likely that all people of faith are completely wrong, or that they are all (to varying degrees) partly right?
- If you now better understand the Christian doctrine of the Trinity, would you at least agree that it represents a comprehensive attempt to explain God, and many earthly phenomena besides?
- Is there an afterlife, or is the rough 'justice' meted out by Nature and by Man all that we can ever hope for?
- Is there an afterlife, or does love die with our bodies? Will we never be reunited with our loved ones once we or they die?
- If there is no afterlife, why is Man capable of imagining it?
- If there is no afterlife, why did Jesus say that there was?
- How do you explain the consistency of the visions of the afterlife reported by people down the ages, including people revived after clinical death?

In this book I have suggested answers to all these questions. You may have been impressed by some of my answers, but less so by others. Please do not cling to the points on which I have failed to persuade you, and use those as an excuse for putting Christianity out of your mind. When you find yourself stuck on a difficult point, try to adopt St Paul's advice to the Philippians and trust that God will eventually resolve the difficulty for you. But bear in mind that it is not necessary to solve every problem. Accept that there must – necessarily – be some uncertainty in this world. As John Blanchard has written, 'It is less important to know all the answers than to know and trust the one who does.'[4]

Take strength from your clearest insights. Ponder them even more carefully, and then re-examine some of the harder issues in a new light. There is a useful parallel with the way in which juries are instructed to carry out their task. The High Court of Australia has endorsed this approach:

> At the end of the trial the jury must consider all the evidence, and in doing so they may find that one piece of evidence resolves their doubts as to another.[5]

I suggest that you pause, reread that last sentence, and ponder its implications for Christianity. The High Court then continued:

> For example, the jury, considering the evidence of one witness by itself, may doubt whether it is truthful, but other evidence may provide corroboration, and when the jury considers the evidence as a whole they may decide that the witness should be believed. Again, the quality of evidence of identification may be poor, but other evidence may support its correctness; in such a case the jury should not be told to look at the evidence of each witness 'separately in, so to speak, a hermetically sealed compartment'; they should consider the *accumulation of the evidence*.[6]

Thus, you may not be persuaded of the truth of Christianity by, say, the evidence of the Resurrection alone. But that evidence when assessed *in combination* with the other main 'pointers' to God – the ordered complexity of the Universe, cognition, conscience, love, the Incarnation, grace – may then seem to you much more persuasive and, perhaps, decisive. In the same way, a passage in the Bible may seem quaint or obscure when read for the first time, especially if it is considered in isolation. But repeated study of the whole text will – I promise you – yield understanding in the end: 'The point of each part only becomes fully clear when seen in relation to all the rest'[7]. That said, many Biblical passages can easily – and profitably – be read in isolation, and by people of all ages, intellect and temperament. In the words of Warwick Fairfax: 'The miracle of the Bible is that it gives at the same time milk for the innocent child and wine too strong for the hardiest hero'[8].

It may take a long time before your state of mind rises to the level of certainty. While ever you remain in doubt, bear in mind that the world seems to function because, in most if not all things, there subsists an element of *un*certainty. It is useful to bear in the mind J.I. Packer's insight that 'all the writers of both [the Old and the New] Testaments are constantly telling us more than they themselves ever knew'.[9] St Paul himself conceded that 'great ... is the mystery of our religion' (1 Timothy 3:16; KJV).

But this above all: retain an open mind, and never stop seeking. The early twenty-first century is, it seems to me, an especially apt time in history for anyone to be seeking the truth about Christianity. Civilisation stands at the crossroads; in some ways we are in a comparable position to the people who lived in the first few centuries after Christ. The opportunity exists to contemplate old doctrines with a fresh and informed eye, and to shape the future accordingly. This is already happening in North America, in the growing movement known as the 'Great Emergence'.

In 1949, Herbert Butterfield thought that Man had reached the point where, for the first time in 1,500 years, 'we can just about begin to say that no man is now a Christian because of government compulsion, or because it is the way to procure favour in court, or because it is necessary in order to qualify for public office, or because public opinion demands conformity, or because he would lose customers if he did not go to church, or even because habit and intellectual indolence keep the mind in the appointed groove'[10]. In retrospect Butterfield may have been premature in that assessment (especially as regards qualification for high public office in the United States), but his words apply with singular aptness to contemporary Australia. The absence here of what Butterfield called the 'many kinds of inducement and compulsion'[11] makes the search for Christian (or any) faith a more meaningful and exciting exercise. No one is forcing you to do it.

Of course, this circumstance also poses a challenge for twenty-first century Christians, especially those with an evangelistic streak. How can the Gospel message be taught effectively or extensively in the West, when so many people are under no compulsion to listen? And when so many people have ceased to read words on a printed page? In my view, the Internet will have a major role to play. Like the Church itself, the Internet is a fantastically powerful 'self-organizing system of relations … between inumerable member parts'. Also like the Church, 'no one of the member parts or connecting networks has the whole or entire "truth" of anything'.[12] The American writer Phyllis Tickle, who has written a book on this subject, contends that the Internet is a system employing 'total egalitarianism'. In her view, it manifests respect for the ordinary citizen 'that even pure democracy never had, and a complete indifference to capitalism as a virtue or to individualism as a godly circumstance'.[13]

They are strong words. Nevertheless, there can be little doubt that the Internet is a tool superbly suited for the spreading of the Gospel – indeed, almost any religious message – to a world of over six billion people. As a self-organising, evolving form of communication, it is certainly superior to radio and television. Is its emergence at this moment in history another example of Providence in action?

The Internet will help, but in the end it is up to individual human beings to make the effort to learn. I believe that if you search long enough and sincerely enough, then you *will* find God (cf. Jeremiah 29:13). But making the effort is critical. If you do not seek, you almost certainly will not find. For the first thirty years of my life, I was not seeking. When I did begin to seek, thoroughly and sincerely, I found God. But therein lies, not only a spur to action, but another lesson – perhaps a warning. As Warwick Fairfax noted, 'it is no use asking for wisdom unless [you] are ready to follow the truth when you find it, and that is precisely why [many people in] the modern world [do] not find it.'[14]

The prize of faith is precious. It is difficult to attain and – Fairfax's point – sometimes even more difficult to maintain. God has no choice but to hide Himself, not so completely that to find and stay faithful to Him is impossible, but sufficiently well that doing so is not automatic. Solomon was right:

It is the glory of God to conceal a matter;
To search out a matter is the glory of kings.

(Proverbs 25:2)

ENDNOTES

Preface
1. Bertrand Russell, 'Why I am not a Christian' (1927), reproduced in Robert E. Egner and Lester E. Denonn (ed.), *The Basic Writings of Bertrand Russell 1903-1959*, George Allen & Unwin Ltd (1961), p. 596. 'Why I am not a Christian' was first delivered by Russell as a public lecture, on 6 March 1927. In that same year it was published as a monograph by C.A. Watts & Co., and was subsequently reprinted in *Why I am not a Christian*, ed. by Paul Edwards, Allen & Unwin (1957).
2. Evelyn Waugh, *Brideshead Revisited*, first published by Chapman & Hall (1945), Penguin Books (1981), p. 331.
3. Quoted at www.keepmedia.com/pubs/RoughGuides Music/2001/11/01/284598.
4. Quoted in Peter Watson, *A Terrible Beauty: The People and Ideas that Shaped the Modern Mind*, Phoenix Press (2000), p. 703.
5. Two highly valuable Christian apologetics written by lesser-known lawyers are Edmund Bennett's *The Four Gospels from a Lawyer's Standpoint* (1893) and John Warwick Montgomery's *The Law Above the Law* (1975). See generally Timothy McGrew's collected materials at www. lydiamcgrew.com/Historicalapologeticsreading and an article by Ross Clifford, 'Justification of the Legal Apologetic of John Warwick Montgomery: An Apologetic for all Seasons', at www.trinitysem.edu/journal/cliffordpap.html. Clifford has been the Principal of Morling Theological College in Sydney since 1997. Like me, he was formerly a solicitor of the Supreme Court of New South Wales.
6. Richard Dawkins, *The God Delusion*, Bantam Press (2006), p. 50.
7. Among the recent spate of books scorning religion are Dawkins, *The God Delusion*, ibid.; Sam Harris, *Letter to a Christian Nation*, Bantam Press (2006); Christopher Hitchens, *God is Not Great: How Religion Poisons Everything*, Allen & Unwin (2007); Michel Onfray, *The Atheist Manifesto: The Case Against Christianity, Judaism and Islam*, Melbourne University Press (2007); Tamas Pataki, *Against Religion*, Scribe (2007); Phillip Adams, *Adams Vs God: The Rematch*, Melbourne University Press (2007). There is a considerably more balanced discussion of most of the 'anti-religion' arguments in John Humphrys, *In God We Doubt: Confessions of a Failed Atheist*, Hodder & Stoughton (2007); the author describes himself as a 'devout sceptic' and defends reasoned agnosticism.

Introduction – A DEDUCTIVE APPROACH TO CHRISTIANITY
1. Onfray, *The Atheist Manifesto*, op. cit., p. 1.
2. Pataki, *Against Religion*, op. cit., p. 8.
3. Paul Collins, 'Believe it or not', *The Australian Review of Books*, May 1998, volume 3, issue 4, p. 19.
4. Hitchens, *God is Not Great*, op. cit., p. 10. Original emphasis.
5. H. Griffith-Thomas, quoted in Alister McGrath, *Dawkins' God*, Blackwell Publishing (2005), p. 86.
6. Onfray, *The Atheist Manifesto*, op. cit., p. 68.
7. Dawkins, *The God Delusion*, op. cit., pp. 49-50. See also Bertrand Russell, 'What Is an Agnostic?' (1953), reproduced in Egner and Denonn (eds.), *The Basic Writings of Bertrand Russell*, op. cit., pp. 577-84 esp at p. 583; Josh McDowell, *Evidence for Christianity*, Thomas Nelson (2006), pp. 4-5, 15-16.
8. Steven Weinberg, 'Without God', *New York Review of Books*, Volume 55, Number 14, September 25, 2008.

9. Compare Warwick Fairfax, *The Triple Abyss: Towards a Modern Synthesis*, Geoffrey Bles Ltd (1965), p. 239.

10. Robert Winston, *The Story of God*, Bantam Books (2005), p. 262.

11. Albert Schweitzer, *Out of My Life and Thought*, Mentor (1953), p. 182.

12. Hitchens, *God is Not Great*, op. cit., p. 63.

13. Frank Morison, *Who Moved the Stone?* first published by Faber and Faber Ltd (1930), Authentic Media (2006), p. 125.

14. Fairfax, *The Triple Abyss*, op. cit., pp. 82-3.

15. Joachim Kahl, *The Misery of Christianity, or a Plea for a Humanity Without God*, translated by N.D. Smith, Pelican Books (1971), p. 143. Compare J.I. Packer, *God has Spoken*, Hodder & Stoughton (1979), p. 25 ('We know in our bones that we were made for certainty, and we cannot be happy without it.').

16. Timothy Keller, *The Reason for God: Belief in an Age of Scepticism*, Dutton (2008), p. xvii.

17. Ibid., p. xviii.

18. Dawkins, *The God Delusion*, op. cit., p. 65.

19. See Pataki, *Against Religion*, op. cit., p. 89; Hitchens, *God is Not Great*, op. cit., pp. 232-4.

20. Robert M. Sapolsky in John Brockman (ed.) *What We Believe But Cannot Prove: Today's Leading Thinkers on Science in the Age of Certainty*, Pocket Books (2006), p. 31. Sapolsky is an atheist, but he neatly distils an argument often employed by believers. Compare Fairfax, *The Triple Abyss*, op. cit., p. 446 ('Our knowledge of Divine aims in spheres above earthly life *must*, despite religious revelation, be very limited.').

21. Fairfax, *The Triple Abyss*, ibid., p. 384.

22. Jim Wallis, *Seven Ways to Change the World: Reviving Faith and Politics*, Lion Books (2008), p. 5.

23. Harry Blamires, *The Christian Mind*, first published by SPCK (1963), fifth edition (1974), pp. 122-3. See also Packer, *God has Spoken*, op. cit., p. 123: '[T]he assumption that one cannot study the Bible effectively without a mass of technical theological equipment is false.'

24. Fairfax, *The Triple Abyss*, op. cit., p. 214.

25. Ibid., p. 240.

26. Pataki, *Against Religion*, op. cit., p. 9.

27. Humphrys, *In God We Doubt*, op. cit., pp. 66-7.

28. Alister McGrath, *In the Beginning: The Story of the King James Bible and How it Changed a Nation, a Language and a Culture*, Hodder & Stoughton (2001), p. 3.

29. Herbert Butterfield, *Christianity and History*, first published by G. Bell & Sons Ltd (1949), third Fontana Books impression (1964), p. 151.

30. Jack Miles, *Christ: A Crisis in the Life of God*, Arrow Books (2001), p. 44.

31. See Robert Adler, 'Committee Speak', *London Review of Books*, 19 July 2007, pp. 16-7. The piece is a review of Karel van der Toorn's *Scribal Culture and the Making of the Hebrew Bible*, Harvard (2007).

32. Jack Miles, *God: A Biography*, Arrow Books (1996); Jack Miles, *Christ*, op. cit. (note 30). See generally as regards the 'literary' approach to Biblical criticism, Craig L. Blomberg, *The Historical Reliability of the Gospels* (Intervarsity Press), 2007, pp. 87-96

33. Miles, *Christ*, ibid., p. 292.

34. Ibid., p. 309. See also Blomberg, *The Historical Reliability of the Gospels*, op. cit., pp. 89, 98.

35. See McDowell, *Evidence for Christianity*, op. cit., pp. 493ff. A starting date of around 1300 BC is consistent with the traditional view that the Pentateuch was written by Moses, substantially if not in whole. The alternative view is that these texts were not written until the ninth to eighth centuries BC, well after the Exodus of the Jews from Egypt.

36. Winston, *The Story of God*, op. cit., p. 157. See also McDowell, *Evidence for Christianity*, ibid., pp. 480-4.
37. Miles, *Christ*, op. cit., p. 275.
38. McDowell, *Evidence for Christianity*, op. cit., p. 22.
39. Ibid., p. 26.
40. Ibid., pp. 60-75 (as to the New Testament), pp. 103-13 (as to the Old Testament).
41. See, for example, as regards the King James Version, McGrath, *In the Beginning*, op. cit., passim.
42. Packer, *God Has Spoken*, op. cit., p. 85; see also at pp. 94-5, 97-102. See also Keller, *The Reason for God*, op. cit., p. 93; Blomberg, *The Historical Reliability of the Gospels*, op. cit., p. 51.
43. Packer, *God has Spoken*, op. cit., pp. 76-7. My emphasis.
44. Ibid., p. 103.
45. See Blomberg, *The Historical Reliability of the Gospels*, op. cit., p. 60.
46. See, for a discussion of the various objections which can be raised to the terms 'infallible' and 'inerrant', Packer, *God has Spoken*, op. cit., pp. 105-6.
47. Ibid., p. 34.
48. Quoted in Francis Collins, *The Language of God*, Free Press (2007), p. 157.
49. J. Michael Matkin, *The Complete Idiot's Guide to Early Christianity*, Alpha Books (2008), pp. 206-9. (Yes, I used this source! I found it most valuable.) Compare Fairfax, *The Triple Abyss*, op. cit., p. 239.
50. Keller, *The Reason for God*, op. cit., pp. 92-3.
51. McGrath, *In the Beginning*, op. cit., p. 161.
52. Packer, *God has Spoken*, op. cit., p. 44.
53. Mary Eberstadt, 'How the West Really Lost God', *Policy Review*, No. 143, June and July 2007, p. 1. Available online at www.hoover.org/publications. See also McDowell, *Evidence for Christianity*, op. cit., pp. 29-30.
54. See generally McGrath, *In the Beginning*, op. cit, passim. One gentleman of my acquaintance has gone as far as insisting that other translations of the Bible, in particular the New Revised Standard Version, are so inferior to the King James Version as to be blasphemous. He has written a scholarly paper on the issue: Graham Harman, 'The Gordon Uniting Church Pew Bible (NRSV): Is it an anti-Christian document?', unpublished, copy supplied to the author.
55. 'Leaves of Grass' (1855).
56. Dawkins, *The God Delusion*, op. cit., p. 13. Compare John Shelby Spong, *Jesus for the Non-Religious: Recovering the Divine at the Heart of the Human*, HarperCollins (2007), p. 214. Bishop Spong wants to re-define Christianity into a non-theistic religion, but that is not my purpose.
57. Hitchens, *God is Not Great*, op. cit., p. 4.
58. See generally Victor J. Stenger, *God: The Failed Hypothesis: How Science Shows That God Does Not Exist*, Prometheus Books (2008); compare John Lennox, *God's Undertaker: Has Science Buried God?* Lion Publishing (2007).
59. Weinberg, 'Without God', op. cit., (note 8 above).

Part One: Reasons to Believe in God

Chapter 1 – THE PHYSICAL UNIVERSE

1. Harris, Letter to a *Christian Nation*, op. cit., p. xiv.
2. See Jonathan Barnes, 'What, even bedbugs?' *London Review of Books*, 5 June 2008, p. 30. This piece was a review of a book by David Smedley entitled *Creationism and its Critics in Antiquity*, California (2008).
3. Antony Flew, 'The Atheist Delusion of Richard Dawkins', *Quadrant*, October 2008, No. 450 (Volume LII, Number 10), p. 48.
4. Compare Fairfax, *The Triple Abyss*, op. cit., p. 289.
5. Dawkins, *The God Delusion*, op. cit., p. 347.

6.   See Isaac Asimov, *The Secret of the Universe*, Oxford University Press (1992), pp. 117-135.

7.   John D. Barrow, *New Theories of Everything*, Oxford University Press (2007), pp. 5-6. See also Collins, *The Language of God*, op. cit., pp. 176-7. But compare Roger Carswell, *Why believe?* OM Publishing (1990), 1999 reprint, p. 28.

8.   Paul Davies, *The Fifth Miracle*, Penguin Books (1999), pp. 45-52; Bill Bryson, *A Short History of Nearly Everything*, illustrated edition, Doubleday (2005), pp. 367-77, 403-17. See generally Collins, *The Language of God*, ibid., pp. 88-96.

9.   Winston, *The Story of God*, op. cit., pp. 70-6.

10.   For a concise and well-structured exposition of the 'young Earth' case, see Todd S. Beall, 'Christians in the Public Square: How Far Should Evangelicals Go in the Creation/ Evolution Debate?' Address to the 58th Annual Meeting of the Evangelical Theological Society, Washington DC, November 15, 2006. Available online at www.wordmp3.com/ groupitem.aspx?pg=145.

11.   Winston, *The Story of God*, op. cit., pp. 335-6.

12.   Beall, 'Christians in the Public Square', op. cit., passim.

13.   Fairfax, *The Triple Abyss*, op. cit., p. 272.

14.   Paul Collins, 'Believe it or not', op. cit., p.19. Compare Fairfax, *The Triple Abyss*, ibid., pp. 250, 271-3, 439. See generally Ronald F. Youngblood (ed.), *The Genesis Debate: Persistent Questions About Creation and the Flood*, Baker (1990).

15.   Quoted in John Horgan, *The End of Science*, Little, Brown and Company (1997), p. 266.

16.   See, e.g., Hitchens, *God is Not Great*, op. cit., p. 65.

17.   Barrow, *New Theories of Everything*, op. cit., p. 194. See generally Simon Singh, *The Big Bang*, Fourth Estate (2005).

18.   Paul Davies, *Are We Alone?* Penguin Books (1995), p.69.

19.   Bryson, *A Short History of Nearly Everything*, op. cit., p. 21.

20.   Paul Davies, *The Goldilocks Enigma: Why is the Universe Just Right for Life?* Allen Lane (2006), pp. 69-70.

21.   Bryson, *A Short History of Nearly Everything*, op. cit., p. 16.

22.   Russell, 'Why I am not a Christian', op. cit., p. 587. Compare Fairfax, *The Triple Abyss*, op. cit., p. 244. Writing in 1965, Fairfax – who was a deeply religious man – favoured the Steady State theory over the Big Bang theory! He was wrong, but he followed the technical evidence as he saw it. Crucially, he demonstrated sincere faith; he had the imagination to realise that, whichever scientific account of the formation of the Universe being might turn out to be correct, God must lie behind things somehow.

23.   Bryson, *A Short History of Nearly Everything*, op. cit., p. 16.

24.   John D. Barrow, *The Book of Nothing*, Vintage (2001), p. 226. See also Barrow, *New Theories of Everything*, op. cit., pp. 106-7.

25.   Barrow, *New Theories of Everything*, ibid., p. 226.

26.   John D. Barrow, *The Constants of Nature*, Vintage (2003), p. 3.

27.   Ibid., p. 165. See also Barrow, *New Theories of Everything*, op. cit., p. 117.

28.   Barrow, *The Constants of Nature*, op.cit., p. 46. See also Barrow, *New Theories of Everything*, ibid., pp. 117-9, 134.

29.   Barrow, *The Constants of Nature*, ibid., p. 259ff. See further Barrow, *New Theories of Everything*, ibid., pp. 124-8.

30.   Barrow, *New Theories of Everything*, ibid., p.92.

31.   Davies, *The Mind of God*, Simon & Schuster (1992), pp. 61-72. See also Barrow, *New Theories of Everything*, ibid., pp.23, 36-9, 69, 85ff.

32.   Alan Lightman, quoted in Bryson, *A Short History of Nearly Everything*, op. cit., p. 180.

33.   Davies, *The Mind of God*, op. cit., p. 62.

34.   Michael J. Behe, *The Edge of Evolution: The Search for the Limits of Darwinism*, Free Press (2007), pp. 234-5.

35.   Barrow, *New Theories of Everything*, op. cit., p. 70.

36.   Ibid., p. 75. See also Keller, *The Reason for God*, op. cit., pp. 128-9; Collins, *The Language of God*, op. cit., p. 67: 'The Big Bang cries out for a divine explanation.'

37.   Barrow, *New Theories of Everything*, ibid., p. 12. See also at p. 147: 'it [is] a mystery that there are such a reasonable number of *linear and simple* phenomena in Nature.'

38. Barrow, *The Constants of Nature*, op. cit., p. 222. See further Barrow, pp. 33, 226.
39. Davies, *The Fifth Miracle*, op. cit., p. 113.
40. See Barrow, *The Constants of Nature*, op. cit., pp. 152-5; see also Davies, *Are We Alone?* op. cit., pp. 76-7.
41. Barrow, *The Constants of Nature*, op. cit., p. 154.
42. Quoted in Barrow, ibid., p. 157.
43. See, e.g., Hitchens, *God Is Not Great*, op. cit., p. 65.
44. Barrow, *The Constants of Nature*, op. cit., pp. 154-5.
45. Ibid, p. 183; Barrow, *New Theories of Everything*, op. cit., p. 70.
46. Ibid, p. 186.
47. Ibid, pp. 183-4.
48. Ibid, p. 187. See further Barrow, *New Theories of Everything*, op. cit., pp. 143-5, 189 ('our Universe appears to be far more orderly than we have any right to expect'), 225.
49. Richard Dawkins, *Climbing Mount Improbable*, first published by Viking (1996), Penguin Books (2006), p. 69. My emphasis.
50. Asimov, *The Secret of the Universe*, op. cit., p. 95.
51. Davies, *Are We Alone?* op. cit., pp. 78-9.
52. Tim Flannery, *The Weather Makers: The History and Future Impact of Climate Change*, Text Publishing (2005), pp. 5, 21-2.
53. Anthony Flew with Roy Abraham Varghese, *There is a God: How the World's Most Notorious Atheist Changed His Mind*, HarperCollins (2007). See also Mark Oppenheimer, 'The Turning of an Atheist', *The New York Times*, November 4, 2007.
54. Oppenheimer, ibid., p. 1.
55. Davies, *The Goldilocks Enigma*, op. cit., p. 167. For another useful collection of examples, see Lee Strobel, *The Case for a Creator*, Zondervan (2004).
56. Davies, *The Goldilocks Enigma*, ibid., pp. 166-70.
57. Quoted in Winston, *The Story of God*, op. cit., p. 369.
58. Dinesh D'Souza, interview with Dr. Paul Kengor for FrontPageMagazine.com, October 31, 2007. Available at www.frontpagemagazine.com/Articles/Read.aspx?GUID=2F74C381-8239-4FA2-B775-1FDAB1E...
59. Davies, *Are We Alone?* op. cit., p. 80.
60. Davies, *The Mind of God*, op. cit., p. 220. As regards Occam's razor, see also Collins, *The Language of God*, op. cit., p. 76.
61. See generally, Davies, *The Goldilocks Enigma*, op. cit., pp. 172-216; Behe, *The Edge of Evolution*, op. cit., pp. 220-7.
62. Hitchens, *God is Not Great*, op. cit., pp. 68-71. See also Dawkins, *The God Delusion*, op. cit., p. 147. Incidentally, William of Ockham (or Occam, as the place name is sometimes spelt), was not an atheist. He was a Christian theologian who lived from c.1285-1347. His famous 'razor' is also known as 'the principle of parsimony'. Ockham's basic insight was that, in framing any explanation (theological or scientific), all hypotheses and assumptions which are not strictly necessary should be eliminated. In short, keep it simple, stupid.
63. Davies, *The Goldilocks Enigma*, op. cit., p. 292.
64. Ibid., p. 226.
65. Horgan, *The End of Science*, op. cit., p. 138.
66. Davies, *The Fifth Miracle*, op. cit., p. 53. See generally on the demise of the theory of spontaneous generation, M.J. Whitten, 'The Conceptual Basis for Genetic Control' in *Comprehensive Insect Physiology Biochemistry and Pharmacology*, Pergamon Press (1982), chapter 14, p. 480. Mr Whitten kindly supplied a copy to the author.
67. Quoted in Davies, *The Fifth Miracle*, ibid., p.53.
68. Stephen Jay Gould, *Life's Grandeur: The Spread of Excellence from Plato to Darwin*, Vintage (1997), p.169.
69. Ibid., p.155.
70. Collins, *The Language of God*, op. cit., p. 90. See also Roger Forster and Paul Marston, Christianity, Evidence and Truth, Monarch Publications (1995), p. 36ff; Michael Behe, *Darwin's Black Box: The Biochemical Challenge to Evolution*, first published by The Free Press

(1996), First Free Press paperback edition (2003), p.166ff; Fairfax, *The Triple Abyss*, op. cit., pp. 182, 252-3.

71. Dawkins, *The God Delusion*, op. cit., pp. 135, 140. See also Dawkins, *Climbing Mount Improbable*, op. cit., pp. 259-63.
72. Bryson, *A Short History of Nearly Everything*, op. cit., p. 367.
73. See Collins, *The Language of God*, op. cit., p. 68.
74. Ibid., p.102.
75. Carl Sagan, *Cosmos*, Futura Publications (1983), p. 52.
76. Ibid., p. 50. See also Collins, *The Language of God*, op. cit., pp. 1-2, 102-4.
77. Collins, *The Language of God*, ibid., p. 102.
78. Ibid., pp. 90-1.
79. Ibid., p. 109.
80. Davies, *Are We Alone?* op. cit., p. 19.
81. Sagan, *Cosmos*, op. cit., p. 45.
82. Forster and Marston, *Christianity, Evidence and Truth*, op. cit., p. 38; Davies, *The Fifth Miracle*, op. cit., p. 92ff. See further Collins, *The Language of God*, op. cit., pp. 90-1.
83. McDowell, *Evidence for Christianity*, op. cit., p. 468.
84. Davies, *Are We Alone?* op. cit., pp. 52-3, 55. See also Behe, *The Edge of Evolution*, op. cit., p. 159, repudiating this idea.
85. Fairfax, *The Triple Abyss*, op. cit., p. 182; see also at pp. 252-3.
86. See generally, Daniel M. Harrell, *Nature's Witness: How Evolution Can Inspire Faith*, Abingdon Press (2008).
87. Flew, 'The Atheist Delusion of Richard Dawkins', op. cit., p. 48.
88. See James McLaurin and Kim Sterelny, *What Is Biodiversity?* University of Chicago Press (2008), pp. 84-105, esp at p.104
89. Phillip E. Johnson, *Darwin on Trial*, revised edition, InterVarsity Press (1993).
90. Michael Denton, *Evolution: A Theory in Crisis*, Adler & Adler (1996).
91. Behe, *Darwin's Black Box*, op. cit. (note 55).
92. Jonathan Sarfati, 'Misotheist's misology: Dawkins attacks Behe but digs himself into logical potholes' at www.creationontheweb.com/content/view/5213, p.7.
93. Behe, *The Edge of Evolution*, op. cit. (note 34). For a recent discussion of ID, see also William A. Demski and Jonathon Wells, *The Design of Life: Discovering Signs of Intelligent Design in Biological Systems*, Foundation for Thought and Ethics (2007).
94. Dawkins, *The God Delusion*, op. cit., pp. 129-32. See also Richard Dawkins, 'Inferior Design', *The New York Times*, July 1, 2007. Compare Collins, *The Language of God*, op. cit., pp. 182-95.
95. See Fairfax, *The Triple Abyss*, op. cit., pp. 186-7, for a more than usually persuasive version of this argument.
96. Behe, *The Edge of Evolution*, op. cit., p. 72. See also pp. 69-72, 95, 165. Evidently, Behe's views on this issue changed somwhat after 1996, when he published *Darwin's Black Box*. See also Collins, *The Language of God* , op. cit., p. 134
97. Davies, *The Goldilocks Enigma*, op. cit., p. 218.
98. Behe, *Darwin's Black Box*, op. cit., p.193.
99. Behe, *The Edge of Evolution*, op. cit., p. 95.
100. Maclaurin and Sterelny, *What is Biodiversity?* op. cit., p. 102.
101. See Dawkins, *The Blind Watchmaker*, op. cit., pp. 123-6.
102. Maclaurin and Sterelny, *What is Biodiversity?* op. cit., p. 88.
103. Behe, *The Edge of Evolution*, op. cit., pp. 11, 110.
104. Maclaurin and Sterelny, *What is Biodiversity?* op. cit., p.90.
105. Behe, *The Edge of Evolution*, op. cit., p. 111.
106. See generally on mutation rates, Dawkins, *The Blind Watchmaker*, op. cit., pp. 73, 123ff, 306ff; Davies, *The Fifth Miracle*, op. cit., pp. 16, 31, 89; Bryson, *A Short History of Nearly Everything*, op. cit., p. 511.
107. Behe, *The Edge of Evolution*, op. cit., p. 162.
108. Ibid., pp. 17-43.
109. Ibid., pp. 34, 52.
110. Ibid., p. 59.

111. Ibid., pp. 60-1.
112. Ibid., p. 139.
113. Ibid., p. 165.
114. Ibid., p. 220.
115. Quoted in Deborah Smith, 'Intelligent design not science: experts', *The Sydney Morning Herald*, 21 October 2005. See at www.smh.com.au/news/national/intelligent-design-not-science-experts/2005/10/20/1129775902661.html.
116. See, for a useful summary of the main counter-arguments to ID, Jerry Coyne, 'The Faith That Dare Not Speak Its Name: The case against intelligent design', *The New Republic*, August 22 and 29, 2005. I am indebted to the author of this piece.
117. See generally Donald R. Prothero, *Evolution: What the Fossils Say and Why It Matters*, Columbia University Press (2007). See also Richard Dawkins, *Climbing Mount Improbable*, op. cit., pp. 81-2, 95; Collins, *The Language of God*, op. cit., pp. 94-5.
118. Ernst Mayr, '80 years of watching the evolutionary scenery', *Journal of Genetics*, Vol. 84, No. 1, April 2005, 91, at p. 93. See also Maclaurin and Sterelny, *What Is Biodiversity?* op. cit., pp. 35-6.
119. Dawkins, *Climbing Mount Improbable*, op. cit., passim; Collins, *The Language of God*, op. cit., pp. 188-95.
120. See Sarfati, 'Misotheist's misology', op. cit., p. 4.
121. See Watson, *A Terrible Beauty*, op. cit., pp. 207-8.
122. Behe, *The Edge of Evolution*, op. cit., p. 228.
123. Ibid., p. 229.
124. See Barrow, *New Theories of Everything*, op. cit., pp. 140-3; Collins, *The Language of God*, op. cit., pp. 199-210; Keller, *The Reason for God*, op. cit., p.87.
125. Maclaurin and Sterelny, *What Is Biodiversity?* op. cit., p. 64.
126. Dawkins, *Climbing Mount Improbable*, op. cit., pp. 70-4.
127. Davies, *The Fifth Miracle*, op. cit., p. 30. Compare Collins, *The Language of God*, op. cit., p. 95.
128. Dawkins, *Climbing Mount Improbable*, op. cit., p. 181.
129. Davies, *The Fifth Miracle*, op. cit., p. 30; Dawkins, *Climbing Mount Improbable*, ibid., pp. 76, 181.
130. Sagan, *Cosmos*, op. cit., p. 51. My emphasis.
131. Carl Zimmer, 'In Games, an Insight Into the Rules of Evolution', *The New York Times*, July 31, 2007. Available at www.nytimes.com/2007/07/31/science/31prof.html?ei=5070&en=4031aeea8c683b.
132. See, e.g., Dawkins, *Climbing Mount Improbable*, op. cit., pp. 66, 70. Daniel Dennett has argued that the 'extraordinary richness' and 'open-endedness' of the natural world (as distinct from the comparative 'simplicity' of the virtual world of computers) accounts for the extraordinary fact that there are 'an appropriate number of mutations'. See Dennett, *Freedom Evolves*, op. cit., p. 50. This explanation seems to me to beg further questions.
133. Dawkins, *The Blind Watchmaker*, op. cit., p. 306; Dawkins, *Climbing Mount Improbable*, ibid., pp. 71-3.
134. Dawkins, *Climbing Mount Improbable*, ibid., p. 71.
135. Ibid., p. 70. Original emphasis.
136. Ibid., pp. 72-4.
137. Barrow, *New Theories of Everything*, op. cit., p. 144.
138. Maclaurin and Sterelny, *What Is Biodiversity?* op. cit., p. 96.
139. Ibid., p. 91.
140. Ibid., p. 92. My emphasis.
141. Dawkins, *Climbing Mount Improbable*, op. cit., p. 204ff.
142. Maclaurin and Sterelny, *What Is Biodiversity?* op. cit., p. 102.
143. McGrath, *Dawkins' God*, op. cit., p. 72.

144. Extracts from Charles Darwin's *Autobiography* (1876), quoted in Gertrude Himmelfarb, 'Monkeys and Morals', *The New Republic*, December 12, 2005. See also Collins, *The Language of God*, op. cit., p. 99.

145. See at http://en.wikipedia.org/wiki/James_Jeans.

146. Ibid.

147. Umberto Eco, *Turning Back the Clock*, translated from the Italian by Alastair McEwen, Harvill Secker (2007), p. 282. See also Fairfax, *The Triple Abyss*, op. cit., pp. 274-5.

148. Harris, *Letter to a Christian Nation*, op. cit., p. 63.

Chapter 2 – THE HUMAN MIND: COGNITION AND CONSCIENCE

1. Dawkins, *The God Delusion*, op. cit., p. 61.

2. Hitchens, *God is Not Great*, op. cit., p .4.

3. Pataki, *Against Religion*, op. cit., p. 63.

4. Collins, *The Language of God*, op. cit., p. 136; Robyn Williams, *Unintelligent Design: Why God isn't as smart as she thinks she is*, Allen & Unwin (2006), p.49.

5. Williams, *Unintelligent Design*, ibid., p. 49.

6. Butterfield, *Christianity and History*, op. cit., p. 149.

7. Ibid., p. 150. See also Fairfax, *The Triple Abyss*, op. cit., pp. 183-4.

8. Fairfax, *The Triple Abyss*, ibid., p. 183.

9. Butterfield, *Christianity and History*, op. cit., p. 150.

10. Maclaurin and Sterelny, *What is Biodiversity?* op. cit., p. 144.

11. Ibid., p.63.

12. Barrow, *New Theories of Everything*, op. cit., p. 161. See also Fairfax, *The Triple Abyss*, op. cit., pp. 60-1, 331 ('Animals accept themselves as they are, and we do not.'; '[An animal] lives in the present, neither brooding about the past nor worrying for the future … it lacks capacity to observe its own consciousness, to alter what is at the focus of consciousness.')

13. Fairfax, *The Triple Abyss*, ibid., p. 190, citing Robert Broom, *The Coming of Man – Was it Accident or Design?* Witherby (1933).

14. *Hamlet*, II, ii, 309-13

15. *Hamlet*, IV, iv, 33-9.

16. On the issue of climate change, an excellent starting point is Tim Flannery's much-discussed book, *The Weather Makers*, op. cit. (note 52 to Chapter 1).

17. Paul C.W. Davies, in Brockman (ed.), *What We Believe But Cannot Prove*, op. cit., p. 18.

18. See Behe, *The Edge of Evolution*, op. cit., pp. 210-1. See also Fairfax, *The Triple Abyss*, op. cit., p. 195.

19. Barrow, *New Theories of Everything*, op. cit., p. 28 ('the finiteness of the speed of light insulates us from contact'). See also Collins, *The Language of God*, op. cit., pp. 69-71. See generally Jean Heidmann, *Extraterrestrial Intelligence*, translated by Storm Dunlop, Cambridge University Press, second edition (1997); Ben Bova and Byron Priess (eds), *Are We Alone in the Cosmos? The Search for Alien Contact in the New Millennium*, ibooks (1999); Paul Davies, *Are We Alone?* op. cit. (note 18 to Chapter 1).

20. Cf. Barrow, *The Constants of Nature*, op. cit., p. 145. See further Barrow, *New Theories of Everything*, op. cit., p. 166. Complex life, suggests Barrow, is 'a rather parochial affair'.

21. Fairfax, *The Triple Abyss*, op. cit., p. 4.

22. Ibid., pp. 16-17, 22, 26.

23. Sir Francis Crick, quoted in Horgan, *The End of Science*, op. cit., p. 164. See also Onfray, *The Atheist Manifesto*, op. cit., p. 84.

24. Michael Shermer, in Brockman, *What We Believe But Cannot Prove*, op. cit., pp. 38-9.

25. Horgan, *The End of Science*, op. cit., p. 173.

26. Fairfax, *The Triple Abyss*, op. cit., p. 22.

27. See Stefan Anitei, 'Why is Memory so Mysterious?' at http://news.softpedia.com/news/Why-Memory-is-so-Mysterious-59904.shtml.

28. Steve Grand, quoted in Dawkins, *The God Delusion*, op. cit., p. 371. Original emphasis.
29. See Fairfax, *The Triple Abyss*, op. cit., p. 297.
30. Lewis, *Miracles*, op. cit., p. 204. Original emphasis. See also Fairfax, *The Triple Abyss*, ibid., pp. 394-5, 408-9.
31. Fairfax, *The Triple Abyss*, ibid., p. 70. See further the discussions at pp. 17-19, 64-76.
32. See Watson, *A Terrible Beauty*, op. cit., p. 673. See also Amanda Lohrey, 'Letter to a Young Friend on God and the Question of a Good Lunch', *The Monthly*, June 2007, p. 62; see also Keller, *The Reason for God*, op. cit., pp. 91-2.
33. Fairfax, *The Triple Abyss*, ibid., p. 318.
34. Davies, *Are We Alone?* op. cit., p. 82. See also pp. 57-8; Barrow, *New Theories of Everything*, op. cit., pp. 202-3.
35. Quoted in Watson, *A Terrible Beauty*, op. cit., pp. 673-4.
36. Davies, *Are We Alone?* op. cit., p. 84. See also Davies, *The Mind of God*, op. cit., pp. 149, 151-6.
37. Albert Einstein, 'Physics and Reality', *Franklin Institute Journal*, March 1936.
38. John Polkinghorne, 'God's Action in the World', 1990 J.K. Russell Fellowship Lecture, pp. 3-4. Reproduced at www.starcourse.org/jcp/action.html. See also Barrow, *New Theories of Everything*, op. cit., pp. 12, 203, 213.
39. Robert Winston, *The Human Mind: and how to make the most of it*, Bantam Books (2004), p. 413.
40. Agatha Christie, *An Autobiography*, Collins/Fontana (1977), p. 518.
41. Packer, *God has Spoken*, op. cit., p. 72. See also Fairfax, *The Triple Abyss*, op. cit., pp. 349, 351-2.
42. Davies, *The Mind of God*, op. cit., pp. 107-8.
43. Barrow, *New Theories of Everything*, op. cit., pp. 12-3.
44. Ibid., pp. 149-50.
45. Stephen Jay Gould, *Dinosaur in a Haystack*, Penguin Books (1997), p.4.
46. See Behe, *The Edge of Evolution*, op. cit., p. 213.
47. Singh, *The Big Bang*, op. cit., pp. 131-2. My emphasis, except on 'appears'.
48. Don DeYoung and John Whitcomb, *Our Created Moon: Earth's Fascinating Neighbour*, Master Books (2003), pp. 71-84. The authors are of the 'young Earth' school, but many of their observations are fascinating nonetheless.
49. See, e.g., Behe, *The Edge of Evolution*, op. cit., pp. 212-3.
50. De Young and Whitcomb, *Our Created Moon*, op. cit., pp. 83-4.
51. Davies, *Are We Alone?* op. cit., pp. 84-5.
52. Polkinghorne, 'God's Action in the World', op. cit., p. 4.
53. Keller, *The Reason for God*, op. cit., p. 135.
54. Humphrys, *In God We Doubt*, op. cit., pp. 242, 243. See also p. 261: '[conscience's] existence is proof of something transcendent, beyond the material'. See also Fairfax, pp.101-2, 397-8.
55. Bertrand Russell, 'Why I am not a Christian', op. cit., p. 595.
56. Ibid.
57. D.A. Carson, *A Call to Spiritual Reformation: Priorities from Paul and His Prayers*, first published Baker Books (1992), seventh printing (2000), p. 135. My emphasis. See also Keller, *The Reason for God*, op. cit., p. 54.
58. Elizabeth Spelke, in Brockman (ed.), *What We Believe But Cannot Prove*, op. cit., p. 74. See also Dawkins, *The God Delusion*, op. cit., pp. 222-6; Humphrys, *In God We Doubt*, pp. 245-6, 277-9.
59. Martin Luther King, 'Rediscovering Lost Values' (1954), reproduced in Clayborne Carson and Peter Holloran (eds.), *A Knock at Midnight: Inspiration from the Great Sermons of Martin Luther King, Jr.*, Abacus (2000), p. 12.
60. Carson, *A Call to Spiritual Reformation*, op. cit., p. 128. Compare Fairfax, *The Triple Abyss*, op. cit., pp. 176, 425-6.
61. See Fairfax, *The Triple Abyss*, op. cit., p. 177.
62. Winston, *The Story of God*, op. cit., p. 409.
63. See Packer, *God has Spoken*, op. cit., p. 67; Keller, *The Reason for God*, op. cit., p. 112.
64. See John Dickson, *Jesus: A Short Life*, Lion Hudson (2008), pp. 55-8.
65. Fairfax, *The Triple Abyss*, op. cit., p. 426.

66. Martin Luther King, 'Unfulfilled Dreams' (1968), reproduced in Carson and Holloran (eds.), *A Knock at Midnight*, op. cit., p. 192.

67. Quoted in Frank Brennan, *Acting on Conscience: How can we responsibly mix law, religion and politics?* University of Queensland Press (2007), p. 33.

68. Barrow, *New Theories of Everything*, op. cit., p. 209. Barrow was describing mathematical laws.

69. Fairfax, *The Triple Abyss*, op. cit., pp. 104-5.

70. Ibid., p. 157.

71. Ibid., p. 173.

72. Keller, *The Reason for God*, op. cit., p. 147.

73. Compare Fairfax, *The Triple Abyss*, op. cit., p. 107.

74. Bertrand Russell, 'The Essence of Religion' (1912), reproduced in Egner and Denonn (eds), *The Basic Writings of Bertrand Russell*, op. cit., p. 565; see also Fairfax, *The Triple Abyss*, ibid., p. 335.

75. Margaret Symons, *Faith, Money and Power: What the Religious Revival Means for Politics*, Pluto Press Australia (2007), p. 1.

76. *Macbeth*, III, ii, 6-9.

77. See Fairfax, *The Triple Abyss*, op. cit., pp. 88-92, 191-2.

78. *Othello*, I, iii, 320-1. See also Russell, 'The Essence of Religion', op. cit., p. 575: 'The essence of religion … lies in subordination of the finite part of our life to the infinite part'. Russell, however, denied that the 'infinite part' of Man's soul either is, or eminates from, a Deity.

79. C.S. Lewis, *Mere Christianity*, first published William Collins (1952), thirty-seventh impression, Fount Paperbacks (1983), p. 32.

80. Paul Johnson, *The Quest for God: A Personal Pilgrimage*, Phoenix (1997), pp. 2-3. My emphasis.

81. See generally Winston, *The Human Mind*, op. cit., pp. 409-13.

82. Dawkins, *Climbing Mount Improbable*, op. cit., pp. 80-1.

83. Collins, *The Language of God*, op. cit., p. 28. But see also Dawkins, *Climbing Mount Improbable*, ibid., p.77.

84. Dawkins, *Climbing Mount Improbable*, ibid., p. 279.

85. For example, Dr. Francis S. Collins, quoted in Zimmer, 'In Games, an Insight Into the Rules of Evolution', op. cit., p. 4. See further Collins, *The Language of God*, op. cit., pp. 24-8; Keller, *The Reason for God* , op. cit., pp. 147-8; Fairfax, *The Triple Abyss*, op. cit., pp. 80-1.

86. Dawkins, *The God Delusion*, op. cit., pp. 214-20.

87. See also Winston, *The Human Mind*, op. cit., pp. 408-9. According to Winston, 'at one base level, morality is likely to be a hangover from our evolutionary past … [but] human morality goes way beyond the simple survival needs of the group.'

88. Dawkins, *The God Delusion*, op. cit., p. 221.

89. Fairfax, *The Triple Abyss*, op. cit., p. 84.

90. Ibid., p. 98.

91. Quoted in Forster and Marston, *Christianity, Evidence and Truth*, op. cit., pp. 26-7.

92. Fairfax, *The Triple Abyss*, op. cit., p. 84.

93. C.S. Lewis, *Miracles: A Preliminary Study*, first published by Geoffrey Bles. (1947), C.S. Lewis Signature Classics Edition, HarperCollins (2002), p. 205.

94. Fairfax, *The Triple Abyss*, op. cit., p. 40. My emphasis. See also pp. 61-2.

95. Ibid., p. 128.

96. Ibid., p.62.

97. Simon Nowell-Smith, quoted in Fairfax, *The Triple Abyss*, op. cit., p. 162.

98. Winston, *The Story of God*, op. cit., p. 111.

99. Ibid., p. 157.

100. Hitchens, *God is Not Great*, op. cit., p. 257.

101. Quoted in Brian Davies, *An Introduction to the Philosophy of Religion*, Oxford University Press (1982), p. 93. See also Fairfax, *The Triple Abyss*, op. cit., p. 279.

102. Donald D. Palmer, *Kierkegaard for Beginners*, Writers and Readers Publishing Inc. (1996), p. 61. Original emphasis.

103. Terry Eagleton, 'Does a donkey have to bray?' *London Review of Books*, 25 September 2008, p. 7. Eagleton's piece was a review of a book by Ross Hamilton, *Accident: A Philosophical and Literary History*, Chicago (2008).

104. See further Fairfax, *The Triple Abyss*, op. cit., pp. 79-88.

105. Ibid., p.280ff.

106. See generally Frank Brennan, *Acting on Conscience*, op. cit. (note 67), esp. at pp. 28-49.

107. Quoted in Brennan, *Acting on Conscience*, ibid., pp. 30-1.

108. Ibid, p. 31.

109. G. Campbell Morgan, *The Teaching of Christ*, Pickering & Inglis Ltd. (1946), p. 28.

110. Collins, *The Language of God*, op. cit., p. 205. See also Fairfax, *The Triple Abyss*, op. cit., p. 275.

111. Martin Luther King, 'The American Dream' (1965), reproduced in Carson and Holloran (eds.), *A Knock at Midnight*, op. cit., p. 88.

112. Lawrence Kramer, *Why Classical Music Still Matters*, University of California Press (2007), p. 33.

113. Paul Johnson, 'The profound mysteries of why we enjoy music', *The Spectator*, 30 September 2006, p. 31.

114. Daniel J. Levitin, *This Is Your Brain On Music: The Science of a Musical Obsession*, Penguin (2007).

115. Johnson, 'The profound mysteries of why we enjoy music', op. cit., p. 31.

116. Kramer, *Why Classical Music Still Matters*, op. cit., p. 211.

117. John Polkinghorne, quoted in Collins, *The Language of God*, op. cit., p. 228.

118. Kramer, *Why Classical Music Still Matters*, op. cit., p. 33.

119. Quoted in Watson, *A Terrible Beauty*, op. cit., p. 56.

120. Kramer, *Why Classical Music Still Matters*, op. cit., p. 211.

121. Ibid, p. 210.

122. Matkin, *Early Christianity*, op. cit. (note 49 to Introduction), pp. 212-3.

123. Packer, *God has Spoken*, op. cit., p. 7.

124. Lecture given at the New York City YMCA in 1970. Collected in *The Oxford Dictionary of Phrase, Saying and Quotation*, edited by Susan Ratcliffe, Third Edition (2006), p. 418.

Chapter 3 – LOVE

1. Fairfax, *The Triple Abyss*, op. cit., p.221.

2. My knowledge of Spinoza has been acquired from secondary sources, principally Antonio Damasio, *Looking for Spinoza: Joy, Sorrow and the Human Brain*, Vintage (2003) and Andre Comte-Sponville, *A Short Treatise on the Great Virtues: The Uses of Philosophy in Everyday Life*, translated from the French by Catherine Temorson, Vintage (2003). Comte-Sponville draws frequently from Spinoza. The quoted definition of love appears on page 11 of Damasio's book.

3. Comte-Sponville, *A Short Treatise on the Great Virtues*, ibid., p. 226ff.

4. See Fairfax, *The Triple Abyss*, op. cit., p. 95.

5. Quoted in Plato, *Republic*. For the full quotation see *The Oxford Dictionary of Phrase, Saying and Quotation*, op. cit., p. 410. See generally, for a lucid conservative analysis of the sexual instinct, Roger Scruton, *An Intelligent Person's Guide to Philosophy*, Duckworth (1996), pp. 127-40.

6. Garry Wills, *What Jesus Meant*, Viking (2006), p. 36.

7. *Romeo and Juliet*, II, ii, 132-5.

8. Ibid., II, ii, 143-8.

9. Fairfax, *The Triple Abyss*, op. cit., p. 221.

10. *As You Like It*, I, ii, 247.

11. Fairfax, *The Triple Abyss*, op. cit., p. 220.

12. Martin Boyd, *Lucinda Brayford*, first published 1946, Landsdowne Press (1980 reprint), p. 118.

13. Recalled on his death. See www.bartleby.com/63/86/3986. And see generally Gregory Hart, *Unrequited Love: On Stalking and Being Stalked, a story of obsessive passion*, Short Books (2003).

14. Fairfax, *The Triple Abyss*, op. cit., p. 221.

15. From Ian Hamilton (ed.), *Robert Frost: Selected Poems*, Penguin Books (1984), p. 213.

16. William Bayer, *The Great Movies*, Grosset & Dunlap, Inc. (1973), p. 40.

17. Fairfax, *The Triple Abyss*, op. cit., p. 227.

18. Comte-Sponville, *A Short Treatise on the Great Virtues*, op. cit., p. 254.

19. See, e.g., Caitlin Flanagan, 'The Wifely Duty', *Atlantic Monthly*, January/February 2003.

20. Symons, *Faith, Money and Power*, op. cit., p.94.

21. Eberstadt, 'How the West Really Lost God', op. cit., p. 6.

22. Matkin, *Early Christianity*, op. cit., p. 162.

23. Iris Murdoch, 'The Sublime and the Good', *Chicago Review* 13 (1959).

24. See generally on Bryan: Michael Kazin, *A Godly Hero: The Life of William Jennings Bryan*, Alfred A. Knopf (2006). See also the brilliant review of Kazin's book by Jackson Lears, 'When Jesus Was a Democrat', *The New Republic*, 10 April 2006. Available online at www.powells.com/review/2006_04_13html.

25. See generally on McGovern: Theodore H. White, *The Making of the President 1972*, Jonathan Cape (1974); Hunter S. Thompson, *Fear and Loathing on the Campaign Trail '72*, first published 1973, Warner Books Edition (1983); Richard Michael Marano, *Vote Your Conscience: The Last Campaign of George McGovern*, Praeger (2003).

26. See generally J.L. Jowell and J.P.W.B. McAuslan (eds), *Lord Denning: The Judge and the Law*, Sweet & Maxwell (1984); Lord Denning, *The Due Process of Law*, Butterworths (1980).

27. Wallis, *Seven Ways to Change the World*, op. cit. (note 2 to Introduction), p. 212. See also Wills, *What Jesus Meant*, op. cit., pp. 52-4.

28. Martin Luther King, 'Loving Your Enemies' (1957), reproduced in Carson and Holloran, *A Knock at Midnight*, op. cit., pp. 41-60, especially at pp. 49-50.

29. Ibid., pp. 51-5. Compare Fairfax, *The Triple Abyss*, op.cit., pp. 391-2.

30. Quoted in Johnson, *The Quest for God*, op. cit., p. 93.

31. Reinhold Niebuhr, *Moral Man and Immoral Society* (1932), quoted in David Bromwich, 'Self-Deceptions of Empire', *London Review of Books*, 23 October 2008, p. 11.

32. Roger Scruton, *England: An Elegy*, Pimlico (2001).

33. Fairfax, *The Triple Abyss*, op. cit., p. 168.

34. See Don Watson, *Death Sentence: The Decay of Public Language*, Knopf (2003). Two other perceptive (and funny) books, on related themes – the decline of public and private manners, and the ever-increasing thoughtlessness that pervades all spheres of life – are Lynne Truss, *Talk to the Hand: The Utter Bloody Rudeness of Everyday Life (or six good reasons to stay home and bolt the door)*, Profile Books (2005); and Shelley Gare, *The Triumph of the Airheads and the Retreat from Commonsense*, Park Street Press (2006).

35. Reproduced in Geoffrey Summerfield (ed.), *Voices: The third book*, Penguin Books (1972), p. 57.

36. Collected in *The Oxford Dictionary of Phrase, Saying and Quotation*, op. cit., p. 263. Solzhenitsyn's views about the Soviet Union were not dissimilar to the views held by many people about the Bush administration in the United States. The misdeeds of Team Bush can hardly be compared with those of Stalin/Brezhnev et al., but a common thread was disdain for truth: see, for example, Frank Rich, *The Greatest Story Ever Sold: The Decline and Fall of Truth – The Real History of the Bush Administration*, Viking (2006); Al Franken, *Lies and the Lying Liars Who Tell Them: A Fair and Balanced Look at the Right*, Allen Lane (2003).

37. Brian Coman, 'The right to personal ownership, use and disposal of property subject to the right of others', in James Franklin (ed.), *Life to the Full: Rights and Social Justice in Australia*, Connor Court Publishing (2007), p. 95. Compare Fairfax, *The Triple Abyss*, op. cit., p. 417: 'Perception of truth is in itself an awareness of God'.

38. See generally Kevin Donnelly, *Dumbing Down: Outcomes-Based and Politically Correct: The Impact of the Culture Wars on Our Schools*, Hardie Grant (2006). See also Gare, *The Triumph of the Airheads and the Retreat from Commonsense*, op. cit., pp. 125-52; Eco, *Turning Back the Clock*, op. cit., pp. 97-102; Anthony Cleary, 'The right to education', in Franklin (ed.), *Life to the Full*, op. cit., pp. 57-62.

39. *Sermons* 358, 1.

40. Pataki, *Against Religion*, op. cit., p.107.

41. Fairfax, *The Triple Abyss*, op. cit., p. 229. See also at pp. 97-8, 204, 228-9.

42. Eberstadt, 'How the West Really Lost God', op. cit., note 13.

43. Graham N. Stanton, *The Gospels and Jesus*, Oxford University Press (1999), pp. 244-6.

44. Ibid., p. 246. And see 1 Corinthians 7:10-15.

45. Comte-Sponville, *A Short Treatise on the Great Virtues*, op. cit., p. 226.

46. Fairfax, *The Triple Abyss*, op. cit., pp. 99, 162.

47. M. Scott Peck, *The Road Less Travelled*, first published in 1978, Arrow Books edition (1990), p. 298.

48. Reproduced in A.R. Chisholm (ed.), *Shaw Nielsen: Selected Poems*, first published by Angus & Robertson Publishers (1965), First A & R Modern Poets edition, reprinted (1980), p. 179.

49. Terry Eagleton, 'Does a donkey have to bray?' *London Review of Books*, 25 September 2008, p.7.

50. Fairfax, *The Triple Abyss*, op. cit., p. 279.

51. *Revelations of Divine Love* (the long text), Chapter 86, Revelation 16. Penguin Classics edition (1966).

52. Quoted in Humphrys, *In God We Doubt*, op. cit., pp. 82-3. See also Keller, *The Reason for God*, op. cit., p. 214.

53. Keller, *The Reason for God*, ibid., pp. 218-9.

54. Ibid., p. 216.

55. See Pataki, *Against Religion*, op. cit., pp. 49-53. See also Winston, *The Human Mind*, op. cit., pp. 369-97.

56. *Measure for Measure*, I, ii, 7-11.

57. Cf. Butterfield, *Christianity and History*, op. cit., p. 47.

58. See Stanton, *The Gospels and Jesus*, op. cit., p. 191. See also Dickson, *Jesus: A Short Life*, op. cit., pp. 59-60, 133; Wills, *What Jesus Meant*, pp. 84-91.

59. Damosio, *Looking for Spinoza*, op. cit., p. 274.

60. See Bertrand Russell, 'The Essence of Religion', op. cit., passim.

61. Spong, *Jesus for the Non-Religious*, op. cit., p. 246.

62. Eberstadt, 'How the West Really Lost God', op. cit., p. 4.

63. Ibid., p. 6.

64. Ibid.

65. Ibid., pp. 9-10.

66. King, 'The American Dream', op. cit., p. 98. Compare Keller, *The Reason for God*, op. cit., pp. 216-7: 'Ultimate reality is a community of persons who know and love one another. That is what the universe, God, history and life is all about.'

67. Keller, *The Reason for God*, ibid., p.162.

68. There is a lovely short poem on this theme by a twentieth-century New Zealander, Basil Downing, entitled 'As Others See Us'. It is reproduced in Summerfield (ed.), *Voices: The third book*, op. cit., pp. 22-4.

69. Eberstadt, 'How the West Really Lost God', op. cit., p. 7.

70. Onfray, *The Atheist Manifesto*, op. cit., p. 66.

71. Packer, *God has Spoken*, op. cit., p.79.

72. Barbara Brown Taylor, quoted in Keller, *The Reason for God*, ibid., p. 160.

Chapter 4 – TACKLING ARGUMENTS AGAINST A DESIGNING GOD

1. Butterfield, *Christianity and History*, op. cit., p. 162.

2. Ibid.

3. Ibid., p. 20.

4. See Collins, *The Language of God*, op. cit., pp. 83 (note 13), 156-7.

5. C.J.S. Purdy, *How Fischer Won: World Chess Championship – 1972*, E.J. Dwyer (1972), p. 34.

6. Johnson, *The Quest for God*, op. cit., pp. 77-8.

7. Fairfax, *The Triple Abyss*, op. cit., p. 218.

8. Barrow, *New Theories of Everything*, op. cit., p. 18. See also Keller, *The Reason for God*, op. cit., p. 132.

9. Martin Rees, *Our Cosmic Habitat*, Phoenix (2003), p. 164.

10. Ibid. See also Barrow, *New Theories of Everything*, ibid., p. 141.

11. Polkinghorne, 'God's Action in the World', op. cit., p. 3.

12. Dawkins, *The Blind Watchmaker*, op. cit., p. 5.

13. Ibid., p. 15.

14. Quoted in Horgan, *The End of Science*, op. cit., p. 19.

15. Ibid., pp. 30-1.

16. Ibid., p. 31.

17. See Barrow, *New Theories of Everything*, op. cit., p .67.

18. Bryson, *A Short History of Nearly Everything*, op. cit., pp. 178-9. See also Polkinghorne, 'God's Action in the World', op. cit., p. 7.

19. See Barrow, *New Theories of Everything*, op. cit., pp. 60-1, 137-9.

20. Polkinghorne, 'God's Action in the World', ibid., pp. 7-8.

21. Russell, 'Why I am not a Christian', op. cit., p. 589.

22. Robyn Williams, *Unintelligent Design: Why God isn't as smart as she thinks she is*, Allen & Unwin (2006), p. 59. See also Hitchens, *God is Not Great*, op. cit., p. 82.

23. C.S. Lewis, *The Problem of Pain*, first published by Geoffrey Bles. (1940), C.S. Lewis Signature Classics Edition, HarperCollins (2002).

24. Williams, *Unintelligent Design*, op. cit., p. 57ff. See also Harris, *Letter to a Christian Nation*, op. cit., pp. 75-9.

25. See, for example, as to the eye, Sarfati, 'Misotheist's misology', op. cit., p. 2.

26. Behe, *The Edge of Evolution*, op. cit., pp. 237-9.

27. See generally Maclaurin and Sterelny, *What Is Biodiversity?* op. cit., esp. at p. 174.

28. *Novum Organum* (1620), translated by James Spedding.

29. Fairfax, *The Triple Abyss*, op. cit., pp. 48-9, 352.

30. Quoted in Davies, *The Goldilocks Enigma*, op. cit., p. 251. For a typical and very recent example of the argument that Man has no special role in the Universe, see also Weinberg, 'Without God', op. cit. (note 8 to the Introduction).

31. For a representative example of this sort of 'common sense' objection to God's methods, see Humphrys, *In God We Doubt*, op. cit., p. 40ff.

32. Barrow, *The Constants of Nature*, op. cit., pp. 109-10.

33. Ibid., p. 113.

34. Ibid., pp. 145-6.

35. See Russell, 'Why I am not a Christian', op. cit., p. 588.

36. Compare Fairfax, *The Triple Abyss*, op. cit., p. 251: 'And if God is infinite it must be theologically impossible for an event to be no longer a part of God's cosmic manifestation because it is past nor to be not a part of it because it has not yet happened.'

37. Polkinghorne, 'God's Action in the World', op. cit., p. 5. See also Winston, *The Story of God*, op. cit., p. 335.

38. C.S. Lewis, *Miracles*, op. cit., p. 195.

39. Hitchens, *God is Not Great*, op. cit., p. 85.

40. See Behe, *The Edge of Evolution*, op. cit., pp. 224-30.

41. Fairfax, *The Triple Abyss*, op. cit., p. 195.

42. Dawkins, *The God Delusion*, op. cit., p. 166.

43. Collins, *The Language of God*, op. cit., p. 38. See also Fairfax, *The Triple Abyss*, op. cit., p. 4: '[O]ur belief in religion, even if a delusion, is so close to being universal, that it should be accounted for.'

44. For an overview of the competing theories, see also Winston, *The Story of God*, op. cit., pp. 90-127; Robin Marantz Henig, 'Darwin's God', *The New York Times*, March 4, 2007, available at www.nytimes.com/2007/03/04/magazine/04evolution.t.html?ei=5070&en=622a31be.

45. Randolph M. Nesse, quoted in Brockman (ed.), *What We Believe But Cannot Prove*, op. cit., p. 43.

46. Cf. Winston, *The Story of God*, op. cit., pp. 176-7.

47. Dawkins, *The God Delusion*, op. cit., pp. 166-9. See also Winston, *The Story of God*, op. cit., pp. 108-12.

48. Winston, *The Story of God*, op. cit., p. 112.

49. Dawkins, *The God Delusion*, op. cit., pp. 169-72; see also Henig, 'Darwin's God', op. cit., p. 11.

50. Dawkins, *The God Delusion*, ibid, p. 173.

51. Ibid, pp. 172-9. See also Henig, 'Darwin's God', op. cit., p. 5.

52. Henig, 'Darwin's God', op. cit., pp. 4-5.

53. Behe, *The Edge of Evolution*, op. cit., pp. 202-3.

54. E.O. Wilson, quoted in Collins, *The Language of God*, op. cit., p. 163.

55. Dawkins, *The God Delusion*, op. cit., pp. 179-90. See also Winston, *The Story of God*, op. cit., p. 91ff.

56. Richard Dawkins, *The Devil's Chaplain*, Wiedenfeld & Nicholson (2003), p. 135.

57. Dawkins, *The God Delusion*, op. cit., p. 201.

58. McGrath, *Dawkins' God*, op. cit., chapter 4 passim.

59. See Pataki, *Against Religion*, op. cit., pp. 49-53.

60. Keller, *The Reason for God*, op. cit., p.138.

61. McGrath, *Dawkins' God*, op. cit., p. 137.

62. Spong, *Jesus for the Non-Religious*, op. cit., p. 220ff.

63. Pataki, *Against Religion*, op. cit., p. 16.

64. Collins, *The Language of God*, op. cit., p.37.

65. Fairfax, *The Triple Abyss*, op. cit., p. 4.

66. Pataki, *Against Religion*, op. cit., pp. 8-9.

67. McGrath, *Dawkins' God*, op. cit., p. 123.

68. Quoted in Henig, 'Darwin's God', op. cit., p. 13. See also Collins, *The Language of God*, op. cit., p.38.

69. See, e.g., Humphrys, *In God We Doubt*, op. cit., p. 77ff.

70. See Russell, 'Why I am not a Christian', op. cit., p. 587.

71. Dawkins, *The God Delusion*, op. cit., p. 149.

72. Ibid., p. 147.

73. Behe, *The Edge of Evolution*, op. cit., pp. 224-7.

74. Ibid., p. 226.

75. Dawkins, *The God Delusion*, op. cit., p. 150.

76. See generally, on the nature of God, Fairfax, *The Triple Abyss*, op. cit., pp. 289-306.

77. Ibid., p. 251; see also p. 298.

78. Ibid., p. 293

79. See generally McGrath, *Dawkins' God*, op. cit., p. 94.

80. Quoted at www.christianitytoday.com/ch/2002/003/9.28.html.

81. Martin Luther King, 'The Three Dimensions of a Complete Life' (1967), reproduced in Carson and Holloran (eds), *A Knock at Midnight*, op. cit., p. 135.

Part Two: Reasons to Believe in Christianity

Chapter 5 – JESUS

1. See Fairfax, *The Triple Abyss*, op. cit., p. 152. Although he strongly disagreed with much of what they said, Fairfax thought that Marx and Sartre 'ha[d] made suggestions that [were] coherent and constructive'. I would say the same as regards some of Richard Dawkins' ideas.

2. Winston, *The Story of God*, op. cit., pp. 183-4.

3. Fairfax, *The Triple Abyss*, op. cit., p. 295.

4. See Miles, *Christ*, op. cit., pp. 284-5. Timothy Grew, an American academic, has compiled an excellent list of historical Christian apologetics published in the period 1697-1893. McGrew modestly calls his list 'An Introductory Bibliography', but it is imposing enough. See at www.lydiamcgrew.com/Historicalapologeticsreading.

5. See Marcus Braybrooke, *The Explorer's Guide to Christianity*, Hodder & Stoughton (1998), pp. 13-4. See also Roger Carswell, *Why Believe?* first published 1990, OM Publishing (1999), pp. 123-5; Packer, *God has Spoken*, op. cit., p. 53: 'No one knows God apart from revelation.'

6. Butterfield, *Christianity and History*, op. cit., p. 156.

7. Quoted in Amanda Lohrey, *Voting for Jesus*, Black Inc. (2006).

8. Lewis, *Miracles*, op. cit., p. 229.

9. Braybrooke, *The Explorer's Guide to Christianity*, op. cit., pp. 13, 75. My emphasis.

10. Butterfield, *Christianity and History*, op. cit., pp. 155-6.

11. Onfray, *The Atheist Manifesto*, op. cit., pp. 60-1, 117-21. Onfray refers approvingly to the work of two 'ultra-rationalists', Prosper Alfaric and Raoul Vaneigem. See also Earl Doherty, 'The Jesus Puzzle: Was There No Historical Jesus?' reproduced at http://jesuspuzzle.humanists.net/partone.htm.

12. Kahl, *The Misery of Christianity*, op. cit., p. 102. See also A.N. Wilson, *Jesus*, Pimlico (2003), p. 57; Spong, *Jesus for the Non-Religious*, op. cit., pp. 207-11; Miles, *Christ*, op. cit., p. 307.

13. See generally Dickson, *Jesus: A Short Life*, op. cit., pp. 7-14.

14. Ibid., pp. 46-7.

15. Ibid., p. 17.

16. Ibid., p. 23.

17. See Stanton, *The Gospels and Jesus*, op. cit., pp. 141-3; Forster and Marston, *Christianity, Evidence and Truth*, op. cit., pp. 64-5; McDowell, *Evidence for Christianity*, op. cit., pp. 82-4, 88, 171-9; Dickson, *Jesus: A Short Life*, op. cit., pp. 18-22. Dickson identifies eleven Greco-Roman texts of the first and second centuries in which Jesus is mentioned.

18. Quoted in Stanton, *The Gospels and Jesus*, op. cit., p. 143. See further as to this famous passage, Blomberg, *The Historical Reliability of the Gospels*, op. cit., pp. 254-6; McDowell, *Evidence for Christianity*, op. cit., pp. 85-6.

19. Stanton, *The Gospels and Jesus*, op. cit., pp. 144-5; Forster and Marston, *Christianity, Evidence and Truth*, op. cit., pp. 65-7; Winston, *The Story of God*, op. cit., pp. 163-4, 250.

20. Dickson, *Jesus: A Short Life*, op. cit., p. 83. See also Blomberg, *The Historical Reliability of the Gospels*, op. cit., p. 112; McDowell, *Evidence for Christianity*, op. cit., p. 419.

21. Stanton, *The Gospels and Jesus*, op. cit., p. 141. See also Blomberg, *The Historical Reliability of the Gospels*, ibid., pp. 252-4; McDowell, *Evidence for Christianity*, ibid., pp. 87-8.

22. Dickson, *Jesus: A Short Life*, op. cit., pp. 40-2.

23. Stanton, *The Gospels and Jesus*, op. cit., pp. 145-8. See also Forster and Marston, *Christianity, Evidence and Truth*, op cit., pp. 61-2; Ken Handley, 'A lawyer looks at the resurrection', *Kategoria*, 15 (1999) 11-21, note 16; Butterfield, *Christianity and History*, op. cit., p. 29. For an example of archeological evidence of an Old Testament story, see Winston, *The Story of God*, op. cit., pp. 171-3.

24. Blomberg, *The Historical Reliability of the Gospels*, op. cit., p. 20.

25. McDowell, *Evidence for Christianity*, op. cit., p. 60.

26. Matkin, *Early Christianity*, op. cit., p. 129.

27. McDowell, *Evidence for Christianity*, op. cit., p. 66; Matkin, *Early Christianity*, ibid., p. 73.

28. McDowell, *Evidence for Christianity*, ibid., p. 62.

29. Blomberg, *The Historical Reliability of the Gospels*, op. cit., p. 20. My emphasis. See also McDowell, *Evidence for Christianity*, ibid., p. 28.
30. McDowell, *Evidence for Christianity*, ibid., pp. 93-7.
31. Stanton, *The Gospels and Jesus*, op. cit., pp. 147-8; Blomberg, *The Historical Reliability of the Gospels*, op. cit., p. 329; McDowell, *Evidence for Christianity*, ibid., p. 99.
32. Blomberg, *The Historical Reliability of the Gospels*, ibid., pp. 206, 326-31; McDowell, *Evidence for Christianity*, ibid., pp. 98-100.
33. McDowell, *Evidence for Christianity*, ibid., pp. 131-64.
34. See generally Blomberg, *The Historical Reliability of the Gospels*, op. cit., pp. 256-80; McDowell, *Evidence for Christianity*, ibid., pp. 42-9.
35. See Dickson, *Jesus: A Short Life*, op. cit., pp. 25-6, Blomberg, *The Historical Reliability of the Gospels*, ibid., pp. 264-80, esp. at p. 279.
36. See generally Blomberg, *The Historical Reliability of the Gospels*, ibid., pp. 258-63; McDowell, *Evidence for Christianity*, op. cit., pp. 185-92.
37. McDowell, *Evidence for Christianity*, ibid., pp. 81, 256.
38. See Blomberg, *The Historical Reliability of the Gospels*, op. cit., pp. 292-3.
39. Chase, *The Bible and the Common Reader*, op. cit., p. 240; Blomberg, *The Historical Reliability of the Gospels*, ibid., p. 289.
40. McDowell, *Evidence for Christianity*, op. cit., p. 258.
41. See Blomberg, *The Historical Reliability of the Gospels*, op. cit., pp. 283-94.
42. Dickson, *Jesus: A Short Life*, op. cit., p. 31; Blomberg, *The Historical Reliability of the Gospels*, ibid., p. 25.
43. See Blomberg, *The Historical Reliability of the Gospels*, ibid., pp. 40-3, 45, 281; McDowell, *Evidence for Christianity*, op. cit., p. 81.
44. Blomberg, *The Historical Reliability of the Gospels*, ibid., p. 205; but compare McDowell, *Evidence for Christianity*, ibid., pp. 80-1; Fairfax, *The Triple Abyss*, op. cit., pp. 350-1.
45. See generally McDowell, *Evidence for Christianity*, ibid., p. 79.
46. Forster and Marston, *Christianity, Evidence and Truth*, op. cit., p. 63.
47. See generally Blomberg, *The Historical Reliability of the Gospels*, op. cit., pp. 37-47.
48. McDowell, *Evidence for Christianity*, op. cit., p. 180.
49. Keller, *The Reason for God*, op. cit., p. 101.
50. See Blomberg, *The Historical Reliability of the Gospels*, op. cit., p. 53; McDowell, *Evidence for Christianity*, op. cit., pp. 77-9.
51. Dawkins, *The God Delusion*, op. cit., pp. 96-7.
52. Wills, *What Jesus Meant*, op. cit., p. xxx.
53. C.S. Lewis, quoted in Keller, *The Reason for God*, op. cit., p. 106.
54. Keller, *The Reason for God*, ibid., pp. 101-4; Blomberg, *The Historical Reliability of the Gospels*, op. cit., p. 53.
55. Blomberg, *The Historical Reliability of the Gospels*, ibid., p. 54.
56. See Dickson, *Jesus: A Short Life*, op. cit., pp. 31-5.
57. A.E. Harvey, 'What He Said', *Times Literary Supplement*, 4 April 2007, p. 4. The piece is a review of Richard Bauckham's book, *Jesus and the Eyewitnesses: The Gospels as eyewitness testimony*, Eerdmans (2007). See also Keller, *The Reason for God*, op. cit., p.101.
58. Dickson, *Jesus: A Short Life*, op. cit., p. 33; though compare Blomberg, *The Historical Reliability of the Gospels*, op. cit., p.54.
59. Stanton, *The Gospels and Jesus*, op. cit., pp. 158-9. See also Blomberg, *The Historical Reliability of the Gospels*, ibid., pp. 55-6.
60. Blomberg, *The Historical Reliability of the Gospels*, ibid., pp. 58-62.
61. Ibid., p. 56.
62. Harvey, 'What He Said', op. cit., p. 2.
63. Blomberg, *The Historical Reliability of the Gospels*, op. cit., p. 75.
64. Ibid., p. 69.
65. Ibid., p. 162.
66. Dickson, *Jesus: A Short Life*, op. cit., p. 24.
67. See Fairfax, *The Triple Abyss*, op. cit., p. 381.

68. John Shelby Spong, *Rescuing the Bible from Fundamentalism: A Bishop Rethinks the Meaning of Scripture*, HarperSanFrancisco (1992), p. 16.
69. Onfray, *The Atheist Manifesto*, op. cit., p. 125.
70. Chase, *The Bible and the Common Reader*, op. cit., p. 241. But compare Miles, *Christ*, op. cit., passim. Miles argues that all four of the authors of the Gospels were literary geniuses.
71. Chase, *The Bible and the Common Reader*, op. cit., p. 242; cf. Miles, *Christ*, op. cit., p. 288. See also Blomberg, *The Historical Reliability of the Gospels*, op. cit., p. 303. Blomberg advocates 'the presumption of an intention on the part of the Gospel writers to record historically accurate information'.
72. Butterfield, *Christianity and History*, op. cit., p. 163.
73. Spong, *Jesus for the Non-Religious*, op. cit., p. 104.
74. Spong, *Rescuing the Bible from Fundamentalism*, op. cit., p. 144.
75. See generally Miles, *Christ*, op. cit., passim. Miles concludes that not everything in the New Testament was intended to be understood figuratively, but that much of it was: '[T]he New Testament does sometimes report historical events, but we can open ourselves to its power in a new way if we can respond to the fantastical and the fictive within it as equal in importance to the historical' (p. 307).
76. Stanton, *The Gospels and Jesus*, op. cit., pp. 102-24, especially at p. 108.
77. Wilson, *Jesus*, op. cit., p. 67.
78. Ibid. See also at p. 153.
79. Ibid., pp. 67-8.
80. Ibid., p. 68.
81. Ibid.
82. Ibid., pp. 68-9. See also Keller, *The Reason for God*, op. cit., pp. 106-7.
83. Hitchens, *God is Not Great*, op. cit., p. 118.
84. Blomberg, *The Historical Reliability of the Gospels*, op. cit., pp. 242-9.
85. Ibid., p. 233.
86. Ibid., pp. 25-37.
87. Braybrooke, *An Explorer's Guide to Christianity*, op. cit., pp. 60-1. See also Spong, *Jesus for the Non-Religious*, op. cit., pp. 15-24; Miles, *Christ*, op. cit., pp. 267-8; Wills, *What Jesus Meant*, op. cit., p. xxx. But compare McDowell, *Evidence for Christianity*, op. cit., pp. 390-410.
88. Dickson, *Jesus: A Short Life*, op. cit., pp. 12, 37-9. See generally Raymond E. Brown, *The Birth of the Messiah*, Cassell & Collier Macmillan (1977).
89. See Wills, *What Jesus Meant*, op. cit., pp. 11-12.
90. Stanton, *The Gospels and Jesus*, op. cit., pp. 160-3. See also Blomberg, *The Historical Reliability of the Gospels*, op. cit., pp. 310-12.
91. Butterfield, *Christianity and History*, op. cit., p. 163; Stanton, *The Gospels and Jesus*, ibid., p. 163. See generally Blomberg, *The Historical Reliability of the Gospels*, ibid., especially at p. 103; McDowell, *Evidence for Christianity*, op. cit., pp. 594-607
92. Butterfield, ibid., p.164.
93. Onfray, *The Atheist Manifesto*, op. cit., pp. 55-7.
94. Blomberg, *The Historical Reliability of the Gospels*, op. cit., p. 16; Spong, *Jesus for the Non-Religious*, op. cit., p. 191; McDowell, *Evidence for Christianity*, op. cit., p. 622.
95. Blomberg, *The Historical Reliability of the Gospels*, ibid., p. 239. See generally McDowell, *Evidence for Christianity*, ibid., pp. 620-8.
96. Wills, *What Jesus Meant*, op. cit., p.xxvi.
97. Ibid., p.xxv.
98. Lewis, *Miracles*, op. cit., p. 174.
99. Quoted in Davies, *An Introduction to the Philosophy of Religion*, op. cit., p. 106.
100. Ibid., p. 107.
101. Hitchens, *God is Not Great*, op. cit., p. 47.
102. See Stanton, *The Gospels and Jesus*, op. cit., p. 214. Stanton himself rejects this idea.
103. Blomberg, *The Historical Reliability of the Gospels*, op. cit., p. 105.
104. Stanton, *The Gospels and Jesus*, op. cit., p. 214.
105. Ibid., p. 218.

106. Quoted in Davies, *An Introduction to the Philosophy of Religion*, op. cit., p. 108. Compare Spong, *Jesus for the Non-Religious*, op. cit., p. 54.

107. Quoted in Davies, *An Introduction to the Philosophy of Religion*, ibid., p. 113.

108. See, e.g. William Adams, *An Essay on Mr. Hume's Essay on Miracles* (1752); George Campbell, *A Dissertation on Miracles* (1762). There are links to online copies of these and other works on miracles at www.lydiamcgrew.com/Historicalapologeticsreading. And see generally on Hume, McDowell, *Evidence for Christianity*, op. cit., pp. 463-7.

109. See generally Blomberg, *The Historical Reliability of the Gospels*, op. cit., pp. 105-8.

110. McDowell, *Evidence for Christianity*, op. cit., p. 447. See generally pp. 447-73.

111. Ibid., pp. 623-4.

112. Davies, *An Introduction to the Philosophy of Religion*, op. cit., pp. 109-10. See also McDowell, *Evidence for Christianity*, op. cit., pp. 9-12.

113. See, e.g., Keller, *The Reason for God*, op. cit., p. 86.

114. Spong, *Jesus for the Non-Religious*, op. cit., p. 69.

115. Ibid., p. 81.

116. Dickson, *Jesus: A Short Life*, op. cit., p. 9.

117. Spong, *Jesus for the Non-Religious*, op. cit., p. 87. But see also Blomberg, *The Historical Reliability of the Gospels*, op. cit., p. 173. Blomberg argues that such omissions 'should occasion no surprise'.

118. Blomberg, *The Historical Reliability of the Gospels*, ibid., p. 111.

119. Ibid., p. 113.

120. Quoted in Blomberg, *The Historical Reliability of the Gospels*, op. cit., p. 126.

121. Hitchens, *God is Not Great*, op. cit., p. 140. Compare Humphrys, *In God We Doubt*, op. cit., p. 159.

122. Stanton, *The Gospels and Jesus*, op. cit., p. 216. See also Wills, *What Jesus Meant*, op. cit., p. 28; Blomberg, *The Historical Reliability of the Gospels*, op. cit., p.127; Fairfax, *The Triple Abyss*, op. cit., pp. 385-6.

123. Dickson, *Jesus: A Short Life*, op. cit., p. 87. Original emphasis. See also Keller, *The Reason for God*, op. cit., pp. 95-6; McDowell, *Evidence for Christianity*, op. cit., pp. 418-19.

124. Fairfax, *The Triple Abyss*, op. cit., pp. 374-5.

125. Lewis, *Miracles*, op. cit., p. 218. See also Packer, *God has Spoken*, op. cit., p. 94, as regards 'the lyrical drama of Job'; and the sources quoted in McDowell, pp. 522-3, 609-15 (though McDowell himself does not subscribe to a legendary view of the patriarchal narratives). Compare Spong, *Jesus for the Non-Religious*, op. cit., pp. 55-62.

126. See Dickson, *Jesus: A Short Life*, op. cit., p. 65; though compare McDowell, *Evidence for Christianity*, op. cit., pp. 425-7.

127. Collins, *The Language of God*, op. cit., p. 53; see also Wills, *What Jesus Meant*, op. cit., p. 29.

128. See Fairfax, *The Triple Abyss*, op. cit., p. 420; cf. Spong, *Jesus for the Non-Religious*, op. cit., p. 60.

129. Fairfax, *The Triple Abyss*, op. cit., p. 374-375

130. Compare Spong, *Jesus for the Non-Religious*, op. cit., p. 87.

131. Tom Frame, 'The Future of Easter in a Secular Society', *Quadrant*, March 2008, Volume LII, Number 3. See also Fairfax, *The Triple Abyss*, op. cit., p. 381: '[I]n the nature of things there can never be proof that will satisfy the sceptic since he must cease being a sceptic before he can find it.'

132. See McDowell, *Evidence for Christianity*, op. cit., pp. 247-52.

133. See, e.g., Blomberg, *The Historical Reliability of the Gospels*, op. cit., pp. 134-5, in connection with the account in Luke 7:11-17 of the raising of the son of Nain's widow.

134. Ibid., p. 152ff.

135. See Packer, *God has Spoken*, op. cit., pp. 77-8.

136. Fairfax, *The Triple Abyss*, op. cit., p. 360.

137. Matkin, *Early Christianity*, op. cit., p. 10.

138. See also Fairfax, *The Triple Abyss*, op. cit., p. 360.

139. Weinberg, 'Without God', op. cit. (note 8 to Introduction), p. 3.

140. Morison, *Who Moved the Stone?* op. cit., pp. 29-30. See also Fairfax, *The Triple Abyss*, op. cit., p. 364ff.

141. Wills, *What Jesus Meant*, op. cit., pp. 67, 92-6; cf. Fairfax, *The Triple Abyss*, ibid., pp. 432-3.
142. See Blomberg, *The Historical Reliability of the Gospels*, op. cit., p. 229.
143. Ibid., p. 226 ('the arresting party thought it was confronting a dangerous person').
144. See generally on this issue, McDowell, *Evidence for Christianity*, op. cit., pp. 410-16.
145. Morgan, *The Teaching of Christ*, op. cit., p. 9.
146. Fairfax, *The Triple Abyss*, op. cit., p. 363.
147. Ibid., p. 363.
148. See Blomberg, *The Historical Reliability of the Gospels*, op. cit., p. 22.
149. Lewis, *Mere Christianity*, op. cit., p. 52. Compare Wills, *What Jesus Meant*, op. cit., p.xxi: 'If [Jesus] was not God, he was a standing blasphemy against God'; Fairfax, *The Triple Abyss*, op. cit., p. 349: '[W]ho else has claimed to be God Himself? If not true this would imply a mind so completely unhinged that we could take little account of his teaching.'
150. See generally McDowell, *Evidence for Christianity*, op. cit., pp. 375-83.
151. See Stanton, *The Gospels and Jesus*, op. cit., pp. 220-34.
152. See generally McDowell, *Evidence for Christianity*, op. cit., pp. 353-60.
153. Blomberg, *The Historical Reliability of the Gospels*, op. cit., pp. 166-7.
154. Ibid., p. 209.
155. See e.g. Stanton, *The Gospels and Jesus*, op. cit., p. 220ff; Wilson, *Jesus*, op. cit., passim. See also Blomberg, *The Historical Reliability of the Gospels*, op. cit., pp. 314-16; McDowell, *Evidence for Christianity*, op. cit., pp. 367-9; Fairfax, *The Triple Abyss*, op. cit., pp. 370-1.
156. Blomberg, *The Historical Reliability of the Gospels*, ibid., p. 315.
157. Fairfax, *The Triple Abyss*, op. cit., pp. 370-1.
158. See generally McDowell, *Evidence for Christianity*, op. cit., pp. 362-4.
159. Braybrooke, *An Explorer's Guide to Christianity*, op. cit., p. 61.
160. Lewis, *Miracles*, op. cit., pp. 173-213. See also Stanton, *The Gospels and Jesus*, op. cit., pp. 177-8.
161. Morgan, *The Teaching of Christ*, op. cit., p. 36. See also Wills, *What Jesus Meant*, op. cit., p. xxiii; Blomberg, *The Historical Reliability of the Gospels*, op. cit., pp. 208-12; Fairfax, *The Triple Abyss*, op. cit., pp. 376-7
162. Kahl, *The Misery of Christianity*, op. cit., p. 103.
163. Onfray, *The Atheist Manifesto*, op. cit., p. 123.
164. See also Butterfield, *Christianity and History*, op. cit., p. 164.
165. Morgan, *The Teaching of Christ*, op. cit., p. 106.
166. Williams H. Lecky, quoted in McDowell, *Evidence for Christianity*, op. cit., p. 416.
167. Craig L. Blomberg, quoted in Dickson, *Jesus: A Short Life*, op. cit., p. 80, note 24.
168. See McDowell, *Evidence for Christianity*, op. cit., pp. 415-16, 423-4.
169. Russell, 'Why I am not a Christian', op. cit., pp. 586, 593-4.
170. Ibid., pp. 592-3.
171. See Blomberg, *The Historical Reliability of the Gospels*, op. cit., pp. 64-6.
172. Kahl, *The Misery of Christianity*, op. cit., p. 118.
173. Russell, 'Why I am not a Christian', op. cit., p. 593.
174. Morgan, *The Teaching of Christ*, op. cit., p. 22.
175. Spong, *Jesus for the Non-Religious*, op. cit., p. 178.
176. Joseph Parker, quoted in McDowell, *Evidence for Christianity*, op. cit., p. 422.
177. Quoted in Braybrooke, *An Explorer's Guide to Christianity*, op. cit., p. 78. My emphasis.
178. Morgan, *The Teaching of Christ*, op. cit., p. 16.

Chapter 6 – THE RESURRECTION
1. Kahl, *The Misery of Christianity*, op. cit., p. 164.
2. Spong, *Jesus for the Non-Religious*, op. cit., p. 127.
3. Hitchens, *God is Not Great*, op. cit., p. 143.
4. Kahl, *The Misery of Christianity*, op. cit., p. 164.
5. McDowell, *Evidence for Christianity*, op. cit., pp. 275-7.
6. Ibid., pp. 283-5.
7. Ibid., pp.285-6.
8. Ibid., pp. 286-93.

9.   Ibid., p. 305.
10. Spong, *Jesus for the Non-Religious*, op. cit., p. 210.
11. Matkin, *Early Christianity*, op. cit., pp. 54-61.
12. Onfray, *The Atheist Manifesto*, op. cit., pp. 60, 134-5, 136.
13. Morison, *Who Moved the Stone?* op. cit., p. 173.
14. N.T. Wright, *The Resurrection of the Son of God*, SPCK (2003).
15. Lee Strobel, *The Case for Christ: A Journalist's Personal Investigation of the Evidence for Jesus*, Zondervan Publishing House (1998).
16. See note 11 to the Introduction.
17. I derived considerable help from Ken Handley's article, 'A lawyer looks at the resurrection', op. cit. (see note 23 to Chapter 5). For a comprehensive historiographical treatment of the faith, see Paul Johnson, *A History of Christianity*, Touchstone Simon & Schuster (1976). Johnson divides the history of Christianity into eight parts.
18. Wills, *What Jesus Meant*, op. cit., p. 81.
19. Spong, *Jesus for the Non-Religious*, op. cit., pp. 107, 208-9. See also Dickson, *Jesus: A Short Life*, op. cit., pp. 49-55; Wills, *What Jesus Meant*, op. cit., pp. 9-11. As regards John the Baptist, see also Stanton, *The Gospels and Jesus*, op. cit., pp. 165-76.
20. See Dickson, *Jesus: A Short Life*, ibid., p. 110; Spong, *Jesus for the Non-Religious*, ibid., pp. 30, 107 (desertion of the Disciples).
21. Morison, *Who Moved the Stone?* op. cit., p. 66.
22. Kahl, *The Misery of Christianity*, op. cit., p. 119; Spong, *Jesus for the Non-Religious*, op. cit., pp. 98, 115 ('[The Crucifixion] is surely one of the most certain historical memories.'). But compare Onfray, *The Atheist Manifesto*, op. cit., p. 128 ('Another improbability: the Crucifixion').
23. Morison, *Who Moved the Stone?* op. cit., pp. 6-7.
24. Blomberg, *The Historical Reliability of the Gospels*, op. cit., p. 312.
25. See also Wills, *What Jesus Meant*, op. cit., pp. 124-8.
26. Spong, *Jesus for the Non-Religious*, op. cit., p. 8.
27. Packer, *Jesus has Spoken*, op. cit., p. 54.
28. Dickson, *Jesus: A Short Life*, op. cit., p. 112, note 10; see also Carswell, *Why believe?* op. cit., pp. 136-7.
29. Wills, *What Jesus Meant*, op. cit., p. 111.
30. McDowell, *Evidence for Christianity*, op. cit., pp. 272-3.
31. Keller, *The Reason for God*, op. cit., pp. 29-30.
32. Miles, *Christ*, op. cit., p. 3. See further Wills, *What Jesus Meant*, op. cit., pp. 108-23.
33. See McDowell, *Evidence for Christianity*, op. cit., pp. 268-74; Fairfax, *The Triple Abyss*, op. cit., p. 444.
34. Eagleton, 'Does a donkey have to bray?' op. cit. (note 103 to Chapter 2), p. 7.
35. Miles, *Christ*, op. cit., pp. 9-10.
36. Wills, *What Jesus Meant*, op. cit., p.118. Compare Keller, *The Reason for God*, op. cit., p. 195.
37. Fairfax, *The Triple Abyss*, op. cit., p. 441.
38. See generally Martin Hengel, *The Atonement: The Origins of the Doctrine in the New Testament*, Wipf & Stock (1985), a book described by John Dickson as '[t]he unsurpassed historical study of this theme'.
39. Morgan, *The Teaching of Christ*, op. cit., p. 200. My emphasis. See also Dickson, *Jesus: A Short Life*, op. cit., pp. 105-7; Keller, *The Reason for God*, op. cit., pp. 187-8.
40. Morgan, *The Teaching of Christ*, op. cit., p. 197.
41. Ibid., pp. 197-8.
42. Wills, *What Jesus Meant*, op. cit., p. 119.
43. Lewis, *Miracles*, op. cit., pp. 212-3.
44. See Morison, *Who Moved the Stone?* op. cit., pp. 95-113; Strobel, *The Case for Christ*, op. cit., pp. 255-302. Cf. Onfray, *The Atheist Manifesto*, op. cit., pp. 125-9.
45. See generally McDowell, *Evidence for Christianity*, op. cit., pp. 315-48. On the alleged 'contradictions' between the various Gospel accounts of the Resurrection, and the lack of detail about the Resurrection in Mark's Gospel, see also Blomberg, *The Historical Reliability of the Gospels*, op. cit., pp. 140-1. See also Peter Kreeft and Fr. Ronald Tacelli, SJ, *Handbook of*

Christian Apologetics, Intervarsity Press (1994), chapter 8. Reproduced at http://hometown. aol.com/philvaz/articles/num9.htm.

46. Morison, *Who Moved the Stone?* op. cit., pp. 123, 129, 199-202. See also Wills, *What Jesus Meant*, op. cit., p. 124; McDowell, *Evidence for Christianity*, ibid., p. 279 (the tomb was 'in a garden nigh to the place where He was crucified, outside [Jerusalem's] city walls').
47. Morison, *Who Moved the Stone?* ibid., pp. 180-90.
48. See McDowell, *Evidence for Christianity*, op. cit., pp. 297-301.
49. Ibid., pp. 135-40. See also Wilson, *Jesus*, op. cit., p. 241; Dickson, *Jesus: A Short Life*, op. cit., pp. 124-6.
50. See generally McDowell, *Evidence for Christianity*, op. cit., pp. 301-3, 329-31; see also Handley, 'A Lawyer Looks at the Resurrection', op. cit. (note 23 to Chapter 5). Handley's article first brought this point to my attention.
51. See McDowell, *Evidence for Christianity*, ibid., pp. 302, 321.
52. Handley, 'A lawyer looks at the resurrection', op. cit.
53. J.N.D. Anderson, quoted in McDowell, *Evidence for Christianity*, ibid., p. 302.
54. See also Strobel, *The Case for Christ*, op. cit., pp. 116, 202, 323-4, 325, 344, 355; Wills, *What Jesus Meant*, op. cit., pp. 5-8; McDowell, *Evidence for Christianity*, op. cit., p. 310.
55. Matkin, *Early Christianity*, op. cit., pp. 65-7.
56. Morison, *Who Moved the Stone?* op. cit., p. 114.
57. See, e.g., Symons, *Faith, Money and Power*, op. cit., pp. 5, 8-9, 32-3; Tanya Levin, *People in Glass Houses: An Insider's Story of a Life In & Out of Hillsong*, Black Inc (2007), pp. 21, 31, 57-8, 68.
58. Stanton, *The Gospels and Jesus*, op. cit., p. 186.
59. Fairfax, *The Triple Abyss*, op. cit., p. 448.
60. Ibid., pp. 450-1.
61. Spong, *Rescuing the Bible from Fundamentalism*, op. cit., pp. 222-3.
62. Spong, *Jesus for the Non-Religious*, op. cit., p. 123.
63. Ibid., p. 283.
64. Ibid., pp. 107-16.
65. See McDowell, *Evidence for Christianity*, op. cit., p. 268. This point was first made by Bernard Ramm.
66. Morison, *Who Moved the Stone?* op. cit., p. 115.
67. Wills, *What Jesus Meant*, op. cit., pp. 78-9.
68. Dickson, *Jesus: A Short Life*, op. cit., p. 121.
69. Lewis, *Miracles*, op. cit., p. 238. See generally Keller, *The Reason for God*, op. cit., pp. 206-8; Blomberg, *The Historical Reliability of the Gospels*, op. cit., pp. 138-9.
70. Dickson, *Jesus: A Short Life*, op. cit., pp. 115-8, 123.
71. Ibid., p. 120. See also McDowell, *Evidence for Christianity*, op. cit., pp. 332-3.
72. Quoted in Strobel, *The Case for Christ*, op. cit., p. 333.
73. Ibid., p. 334. My emphasis. See also McDowell, *Evidence for Christianity*, op. cit., pp. 333-4.
74. Doherty, 'The Jesus Puzzle', op. cit. (note 11 to Chapter 5), p. 3.
75. See generally McDowell, *Evidence for Christianity*, op. cit., pp. 335-43.
76. Quoted in McDowell, *Evidence for Christianity*, ibid., p. 264.
77. Winston, *The Story of God*, op. cit., pp. 203-7. See also Stanton, *The Gospels and Jesus*, op. cit., pp. 235-41.
78. Dickson, *Jesus: A Short Life*, op. cit., p. 134; see also Keller, *The Reason for God*, op. cit., pp. 208-10.
79. See Onfray, *The Atheist Manifesto*, op. cit., pp. 149-52.
80. Handley, 'A lawyer looks at the resurrection', op. cit.; see also Kreeft and Tacelli, *Handbook of Christian Apologetics*, op. cit., quoting from William Lane Craig's book *Knowing the Truth About the Resurrection*.
81. Matkin, *Early Christianity*, op. cit., p. 86.
82. Kenneth Scott Lautorette, quoted in McDowell, *Evidence for Christianity*, op. cit., p. 428.
83. Reproduced in *Rejoice!* Presbyterian Church of Australia (1987), Hymn no. 213.
84. See Winston, *The Story of God*, op. cit., pp. 246, 317-8.
85. Ibid., pp. 244-6.

86. Butterfield, *Christianity and History*, op. cit., pp. 151-2. See also Collins, *The Language of God*, op. cit., pp. 35-6.
87. Butterfield, *Christianity and History*, op. cit., p. 154. See also Fairfax, *The Triple Abyss*, op. cit., pp. 329, 333.
88. Jim Wallis, *God's Politics: Why the American Right Gets It Wrong and the Left Doesn't Get It*, Lion Books (2005), p. 349.
89. Matkin, *Early Christianity*, op. cit., pp. 98, 100-1, 187-8.
90. Quoted in Kahl, *The Misery of Christianity*, op. cit., p. 140.
91. See McDowell, *Evidence for Christianity*, op. cit., pp. 390-400; Fairfax, *The Triple Abyss*, op. cit., pp. 371-4, 430-1.
92. Fairfax, *The Triple Abyss*, ibid., p. 453.
93. See Spong, *Jesus for the Non-Religious*, op. cit., p.29.
94. Packer, *God has Spoken*, op. cit., p. 65. See also at pp. 68-9, 75.
95. Russell, 'What Is an Agnostic?' op. cit. (note 7 to Introduction), p. 584.
96. Colin Brown, quoted in Blomberg, *The Historical Reliability of the Gospels*, op. cit., p. 86.
97. See Roger Carswell, *Why Believe?* op. cit., pp. 21-4. See also Packer, *God has Spoken*, op. cit., p. 65-6; McDowell, *Evidence for Christianity*, op. cit., pp. 32, 193-243, especially the summary at pp. 241-3.
98. Forster and Marston, *Christianity, Evidence and Truth*, op. cit., pp. 55-6. See also Blomberg, *The Historical Reliability of the Gospels*, op. cit., p. 83; McDowell, *Evidence for Christianity*, ibid., pp. 104, 107, 113-19.
99. McDowell, *Evidence for Christianity*, ibid., p. 115.
100. See, e.g., McDowell, *Evidence for Christianity*, ibid., p. 230.
101. Dickson, *Jesus: A Short Life*, op. cit., pp. 93-5.
102. See Miles, *Christ*, op. cit., especially at pp. 281-2. See also Blomberg, *The Historical Reliability of the Gospels*, op. cit., pp. 75-87
103. Braybrooke, *An Explorer's Guide to Christianity*, op. cit., pp. 52-4.
104. Blomberg, *The Historical Reliability of the Gospels*, op. cit., p. 78.
105. Ibid., p. 79.
106. See McDowell, *Evidence for Christianity*, op. cit., pp. 253-5.
107. Morison, *Who Moved the Stone?* op. cit., pp. 19-20. See also Stanton, *The Gospels and Jesus*, op. cit., pp. 182, 263-7.
108. Dickson, *Jesus: A Short Life*, op. cit., p. 110.
109. Ibid., pp. 99-100.
110. Quoted in Kahl, *The Misery of Christianity*, op. cit., p. 111.
111. Fairfax, *The Triple Abyss*, op. cit., p. 274.

Part Three: Answers to Some Common Objections

Chapter 7 – SUFFERING

1. Horgan, *The End of Science*, op. cit., p. 281.
2. Lewis, *Mere Christianity*, op. cit., pp. 41-2. See also John Blanchard, *Where Was God on September 11?* Evangelical Press (2002), pp. 10-13; Keller, *The Reason for God*, op. cit., pp. 25-6.
3. Quoted in Humphrys, *In God We Doubt*, op. cit., p. 166.
4. Hitchens, *God is Not Great*, op. cit., p. 80.
5. Keller, *The Reason for God*, op. cit., p. 27.
6. James Franklin, 'Leibniz's solution to the problem of evil', *Think* (Autumn 2003), 97-101 at p. 100.
7. Butterfield, *Christianity and History*, op. cit., p. 90.
8. Wallis, *Seven Ways to Change the World*, op. cit., p. 226.
9. Winston, *The Story of God*, op. cit., p. 299.
10. The following account is distilled from C. David Heymann, *RFK: A Candid Biography of Robert F. Kennedy*, Arrow (1999), pp. 460-2. My favourite books on Bobby Kennedy are

Theodore H. White, *The Making of the President 1960*, Jonathan Cape (1962); Robert F. Kennedy, *To Seek a Newer World*, Bantam Books (1968); Lewis Chester, Godfrey Hodgson and Bruce Page, *An American Melodrama: The Presidential Campaign of 1968*, Penguin Books (1970); David Talbot, *Brothers: The Hidden Story of the Kennedy Years*, Free Press (2007).

11. See generally Wills, *What Jesus Meant*, op. cit., pp. 11-18.
12. Kramer, *Why Classical Music Still Matters*, op. cit., p. 123.
13. Ibid., pp. 123-4. My emphasis.
14. Talbot, *Brothers*, op. cit., p. 17.
15. Butterfield, *Christianity and History*, op. cit., p. 101.
16. See further on the Reformation, Winston, *The Story of God*, op. cit., pp. 307-15.
17. Butterfield, *Christianity and History*, op. cit., p. 86.
18. Ibid.
19. Quoted in Bromwich, 'Self-Deceptions of Empire', op. cit. (note 31 to Chapter 3), pp. 12, 14.
20. See, e.g., Symons, *Faith, Money and Power*, op. cit., p. 1.
21. C.S. Lewis, *Mere Christianity*, op. cit., p. 107.
22. Carson, *A Call for Spiritual Reformation*, op. cit., p. 117. Cf. generally Butterfield, *Christianity and History*, op. cit., pp. 67-91.
23. Butterfield, ibid., p. 80.
24. Ibid., p. 83.
25. Winston, *The Story of God*, op. cit., p. 160.
26. Amanda Ripley, *The Unthinkable: who survives when disaster strikes – and why*, Arrow (2008). See also Rosemary A. Thompson, *Crisis Intervention and Crisis Management*, Routledge (2004).
27. Lewis, *Miracles*, op. cit., p. 189. See also Fairfax, *The Triple Abyss*, op. cit., p. 100.
28. Johnson, *The Quest for God*, op. cit., p. 132. Compare Fairfax, *The Triple Abyss*, ibid., p. 326: 'To create something and to give it nothing to do, no difficulties to triumph over, no chance of creating evil or fallibility would seem to be meaningless.' See further the discussion later in Chapter 7 about Simone Weil's explanation for the existence of suffering.
29. Packer, *God has Spoken*, op. cit., p. 16.
30. Butterfield, *Christianity and History*, op. cit., p. 102. My emphasis. Compare Fairfax, *The Triple Abyss*, op. cit., p. 418.
31. Johnson, *The Quest for God*, op. cit., p. 132.
32. Carson, *A Call for Spiritual Reformation*, op. cit., pp. 222-3.
33. Harris, *Letter to a Christian Nation*, op. cit., pp. 47-8.
34. Onfray, *The Atheist Manifesto*, op. cit., p. 43.
35. Eco, *Turning Back the Clock*, op. cit., pp. 360-2. See also Barrow, *New Theories of Everything*, op. cit., p. 29: 'In the long run, living forever might not prove as attractive as it seems at first.'
36. Blanchard, *Where was God on September 11?* op. cit., pp. 18-9.
37. Ibid., p. 19. The Archbishop of Canterbury, Dr Rowan Williams, has made the same point: 'I can't quite see how a universe could be constructed in which some people's free will was, if you like, guaranteed to be aborted at certain points so that it wouldn't damage others.' Quoted in Humphrys, *In God We Doubt*, op. cit., p. 157.
38. Polkinghorne, 'God's Action in the World', op. cit., p. 5.
39. Harris, *Letter to a Christian Nation*, op. cit., p. 54.
40. Pope Leo XIII, *Rerum Novarum*, paragraphs 40-1. Quoted in John Sharpe, 'The right to worship God in public and private', in Franklin (ed.), *Life to the Full*, op. cit., p. 19.
41. Fairfax, *The Triple Abyss*, op. cit., p. 425. My emphasis.
42. See Keller, *The Reason for God*, op. cit., pp. 74-5.
43. *Hamlet*, I, v, 86.
44. See Fairfax, *The Triple Abyss*, op. cit., p. 417.
45. See Miriam Van Scott, *Encyclopedia of Heaven*, Thomas Dunne Books (1998), p. 9.
46. Quoted in Comte-Sponville, *A Short Treatise on the Great Virtues*, op. cit., pp. 272-4. See also Fairfax, *The Triple Abyss*, op. cit., p. 338 ('The first impression is that God has sullied Himself in activities which we cannot help regarding as unGod-like') and p. 435 ('In one sense the entire creation is a sacrifice – the descent of the Infinite into the limited.')

47. Fairfax, *The Triple Abyss*, ibid., pp. 319-21, 325-7.

48. Ibid., p. 326. See also p. 327 ('Matter is the abrasive without which our soul cannot be the jewel which was intended.') and p. 328 ('Matter is God's challenge to Himself. He calls us in to overcome it, not as pawns or satellites but as partners of equal right.')

49. See, e.g., Keller, *The Reason for God*, op. cit., p. 57 ('The essence of Christianity is salvation by grace'). One of the classic explanations of this concept was given by C.H. Spurgeon in his sermon 'All of Grace' (7 October 1915). It is widely available today in book form.

50. Carson, *A Call to Spiritual Reformation*, op. cit., p. 87.

51. Quoted in 'Brave Sophie Leaves Hospital', *The Age*, 8 June 2006 (AAP).

52. See generally, McGrath, Christian Theology, op. cit., chapters 13 and 14. See also Philip Yancey, *What's So Amazing About Grace?* Zondervan Publishing House (1997).

53. M. Scott Peck, *The Road Less Travelled: A New Psychology of Love, Traditional Values and Spiritual Growth*, first published by Hutchinson & Co (1983), Arrow edition (1990), p. 279. Compare Fairfax, pp. 253-4. Fairfax used the term 'the Law of Cosmic Force' to describe the same idea.

54. From *The Ways of the Righteous*. Collected in *The Oxford Dictionary of Phrase, Saying and Quotation*, op. cit., p. 438.

55. Peck, *The Road Less Travelled*, op. cit., pp. 310-1.

56. Ibid, p. 311. My emphasis. Compare Fairfax, *The Triple Abyss*, op. cit., p. 344 ('There would be nothing surprising in the soul … leading the subject into severe trials, into illnesses, … in order to serve its own spiritual purpose. Five other books about mental illness have helped me to understand and come to terms with my condition and to begin to recover from it: Susan Tanner and Jillian Ball, *Beating the Blues: A Self-Help Approach to Overcoming Depression*, first published by the authors in Australia and New Zealand in 1989, fifteenth reprint, Southwood Press; Tracy Thompson, *The Beast: A Journey Through Depression*, Plume (1996); William Styron, *Darkness Visible: A Memoir of Madness*, Vintage Books (1992); Dr Gina Glouberman, *The Joy of Burnout: How the End of the World Can Be a New Beginning*, first published by Hodder and Stoughton (2000), Inner Ocean Publishing (2003); and (best of all) Dr Lisa Lampe, *Take Control of Your Worry: Managing Generalised Anxiety Disorder*, Simon & Schuster (2004).

57. Lewis, *Miracles*, op. cit., p. 191.

58. See, for example, research by the London School of Economics, reported at www.inspirationalstories.com/3/302/ht.

59. Clive Hamilton and Richard Dennis, *Affluenza: When Too Much is Never Enough*, Allen & Unwin (2006).

60. Compare Fairfax, *The Triple Abyss*, op. cit., pp. 357-8, for a somewhat different view.

61. Butterfield, *Christianity and History*, op. cit., p. 89. See also pp. 88, 96, 118, 127.

62. Peck, *The Road Less Travelled*, op. cit., p. 283. Compare Fairfax, *The Triple Abyss*, op. cit., pp. 252-6, 270-1.

63. Davies, *The Fifth Miracle*, op. cit., p. 25. See also, Stephen Jay Gould, *Life's Grandeur: The Spread of Excellence from Plato to Darwin*, Vintage (1997), pp. 23-7; Collins, *The Language of God*, op. cit., p. 173.

64. See Barrow, *New Theories of Everything*, op. cit., pp. 183-5.

65. Fairfax, *The Triple Abyss*, op. cit., p. 270.

66. Peck, *The Road Less Travelled*, op. cit., p. 299.

67. Butterfield, *Christianity and History*, op. cit., p. 128.

68. Ibid., p. 95.

69. Jonathon Schell, *The Fate of the Earth*, first published by Knopf (1982), 2nd edition, Stanford University Press (2000).

70. See Nathan Bennett Jones, 'Operation RYAN, Able Archer 83, and Miscalculation: The War Scare of 1983', paper delivered at the International Graduate Conference on the Cold War, University of California, Santa Barbara, April 2008, available online at www.wilsoncenter.org/index.cfm?topic_id=1409&fuseaction=topics.item&news_id=400459.

71. James Carroll, *House of War: The Pentagon and the Rise of American Power*, Scribe (2006), pp. 381-418.

72. See Ernest R. May and Philip Zelikow (eds), *The Kennedy Tapes: Inside the White House During the Cuban Missile Crisis*, The Belknap Press (1997); see also Robert Kennedy, *Thirteen Days: A Memoir of the Cuban Missile Crisis*, W.W. Norton and Company (1999); and Robert S. McNamara's recollections in the documentary film *The Fog of War* (2003). Another source worth going to – it influenced me, and is entertaining as well – is Roger Donaldson's film, *Thirteen Days* (2000). Considerable dramatic license is taken with the role of the Kevin Costner character (JFK's childhood buddy and White House appointments secretary, Kenny O'Donnell), who narrates the film, but otherwise the film holds up well, I think, as dramatised history.

73. Quoted in *The Observer*, 11 November 1962. See also at http://education.yahoo.com/reference/quotations/author/Khrushchev,%20Nikita.

74. Quoted in Bromwich, 'Self-Deceptions of Empire', op. cit., p.11.

75. See, for a sobering list of examples, Stephen Weir, *History's Worst Decisions and the People Who Made Them*, Pier 9 (2006); Jared Diamond, *Collapse: How Societies Choose to Fail or Survive*, Penguin Books (2005).

76. *As You Like It*, II, vii, 135-8. Consider also Edgar's observation: '[T]he worst is not, / So long as we can say "This is the worst"…' (*King Lear*, IV, i, 27-8).

77. Franklin, 'Leibniz's solution to the problem of evil', op. cit., p. 97.

Chapter 8 – CHRISTIANITY AND POLITICS

1. Quoted in Brennan, *Acting on Conscience*, op. cit., p. 218.
2. See Blomberg, *The Historical Reliability of the Gospels*, op. cit., p. 161.
3. Rev. Tim Costello, Foreword to Wallis, *God's Politics*, op. cit., p. xv. Costello was formerly a Baptist minister and is currently the Director of World Vision Australia. He is a prominent religious spokesman in Australia and the brother of Peter Costello, who was Federal Treasurer in the Howard Government from 1996-2007.
4. See Winston, *The Story of God*, op. cit., pp. 186-96. See also Keller, *The Reason for God*, op. cit., pp. 58-61.
5. Martin Luther King, 'A Knock at Midnight' (1963), reproduced in Carson and Holloran (eds), *A Knock at Midnight*, op. cit., p. 69.
6. Paul Russell, 'The right to petition government for the redress of grievances', in Franklin (ed.), *Life to the Full*, op. cit., pp. 63-8.
7. See Fairfax, *The Triple Abyss*, op. cit., p. 434.
8. Quoted in Miles, *Christ*, op. cit., p. 6.
9. Quoted in Sally *Monthly* Warhaft (ed.), *Well May We Say…The Speeches That Made Australia*, Black Inc. (2004), p. 169.
10. John Howard Yoder, *The Politics of Jesus*, first published 1972, Wm. B. Eerdmans (1994).
11. Wallis, *God's Politics*, op. cit., p. 109.
12. Butterfield, *Christianity and History*, op. cit., p. 120.
13. Ibid.
14. Quoted in Bromwich, 'Self-Deceptions of Empire', op. cit., p. 11.
15. Butterfield, *Christianity and History*, op. cit., pp. 179-80. See also Bromwich, 'Self-Deceptions of Empire', ibid., pp. 12-13.
16. 'To the Lord General Cromwell' (1652).
17. Letter to Josiah Quincy, 11 September 1783. Compare the Qur'an 8:16-17.
18. Quoted in John Hervey, *Memoirs* (1848).
19. Butterfield, *Christianity and History*, op. cit., p. 140.
20. Johnson, *The Quest for God*, op. cit., p. 23. Compare Fairfax, *The Triple Abyss*, op. cit., p. 7.
21. Wallis, *God's Politics*, op. cit., p. 212.
22. Winston, *The Story of God*, op. cit., p. 252. See also Wallis, *Seven Ways to Change the World*, op. cit., p. 74.
23. Quoted at http://thinkexist.com/quotation/wealth.
24. As to the situation in the US, see Wallis, *Seven Ways to Change the World*, op. cit., passim.
25. See generally Robert Reich, *Supercapitalism: the transformation of business, democracy, and everyday life*, Scribe (2008). For a prescient discussion, written in 1992, of where trends were then heading, see John Ralston Saul, *Voltaire's Bastards*, Penguin Books (1993).

26. Attributed. Collected in *The Oxford Dictionary of Quotations*, Fifth Edition, edited by Elizabeth Knowles, Oxford University Press (1999), p. 182.

27. Butterfield, *Christianity and History*, op. cit., p. 103.

28. Dickson, *Jesus: A Short Life*, op. cit., pp. 68-9. See also Keller, *The Reason for God*, op. cit., pp. 60-1.

29. Dickson, *Jesus: A Short Life*, op. cit., pp. 76-80.

30. Keller, *The Reason for God*, op. cit., pp. 41-5.

31. Ibid., pp. 110-1; Matkin, *Early Christianity*, op. cit., pp. 194-5.

32. Dickson, *Jesus: A Short Life*, op. cit., p.75, citing Luke 8:3.

33. Wills, *What Jesus Meant*, op. cit., p. 50.

34. Matkin, *Early Christianity*, op. cit., p.184.

35. Ibid., pp. 166-7.

36. Stanton, *The Gospels and Jesus*, op. cit., p. 202. See also Dickson, *Jesus: A Short Life*, op. cit., pp. 73-6; Wills, *What Jesus Meant*, op. cit., pp. 48-51; Matkin, *Early Christianity*, op. cit., pp. 170-1.

37. Keller, *The Reason for God*, op. cit., p. 20; Matkin, *Early Christianity*, ibid., pp. 166-7, 198.

38. Michael Hogan, 'The right of association and peaceful assembly', in Franklin (ed.), ibid., p. 84.

39. James Franklin, introduction to Franklin (ed.), *Life to the Full*, op. cit., p. 2.

40. See generally Keller, *The Reason for God*, op. cit., pp. 150-6.

41. Martin Luther King, 'Remaining Awake Through a Great Revolution' (1968), reproduced in Carson and Holloran (eds), *A Knock at Midnight*, op. cit., p. 206.

42. There is a comprehensive and utterly damning account of the *Tampa* episode and related events (including the tragic sinking of the vessel known as SIEV X with the loss of 353 lives) in David Marr & Marion Wilkinson, *Dark Victory*, Allen & Unwin (2003).

43. See Wallis, *Seven Ways to Change the World*, op. cit., pp. 138-41. See generally, on Christianity and immigration, M. Daniel Carroll R., *Christians at the Border: Immigration, the Church and the Bible*, Baker (2008).

44. Jonathon Sacks, *The Dignity of Difference: How to Avoid the Clash of Civilizations*, Continuum (2002), p. 60.

45. Flannery, *The Weather Makers*, op. cit., p. 8.

46. See Michael Hart, *The 100: A Ranking of the Most Influential Persons in History*, Simon & Schuster (1993), pp. 395-8.

47. Keller, *The Reason for God*, op. cit., p. 219.

48. See generally Wallis, *Seven Ways to Change the World*, op. cit., pp. 111-28.

49. Charlotte Clutterbuck, 'Satan, the first polluter', *The Sydney Morning Herald*, Weekend Edition, December 19-21, p. 26.

50. Brennan, *Acting on Conscience*, op. cit., p. 78.

51. Martin Luther King, 'Rediscovering Lost Values' (1954), reproduced in Carson and Holloran, *A Knock at Midnight*, op. cit., p. 11.

52. Wallis, *Seven Ways to Change the World*, op. cit., p. 228.

53. Onfray, *The Atheist Manifesto*, op. cit., pp. 71, 134.

54. Ibid., p. 4.

55. See generally, Angela Shanahan, 'The sexual revolution robbed us of our fertility', *The Weekend Australian*, September 15-16 2007, p. 27. See also Kay S. Hymowitz, 'Love in the Time of Darwinism: A report from the chaotic postfeminist dating scene, where only the strong survive', *City Journal*, Autumn 2008, available online at www.city-journal.org/printable.php?id=3093.

56. See, e.g., Caitlin Flanagan, 'The Wifely Duty', op. cit., passim (note 19 to chapter 3).

57. Kevin Rudd, 'Faith in Politics', October 2006, p. 26.

58. Lewis, *Mere Christianity*, op. cit., p. 92. See also Fairfax, *The Triple Abyss*, op. cit., p. 403; Wills, *What Jesus Meant*, op. cit., pp. 35-9. Wills questions the view that Jesus would have regarded all non-procreative sex, even that within marriage, as sin.

59. See Andrew Cameron, 'Do we have a sex problem?' (13/10/08) at www.sydneyanglicans.net/indepth/articles/do_we_have_a_sex_problem.

60. Rudd, 'Faith in Politics', op. cit., p. 26.

61. Fairfax, *The Triple Abyss*, op. cit., pp. 203-4
62. Wallis, *God's Politics*, op. cit., p. 9.
63. Ibid, p. 11.
64. Quoted in Wallis, *Seven Ways to Change the World*, op. cit., p. 212.
65. Braybrooke, *An Explorer's Guide to Christianity*, op. cit., pp. 220-1.
66. Quoted in Richard Nixon, *In the Arena*, Pocket Books (1990), p. 405.
67. Fairfax, *The Triple Abyss*, op. cit., p. 420.
68. Morgan, *The Teaching of Christ*, op. cit., p. 96.
69. Pope Leo XIII, *Rerum Novarum*, quoted in Coman, 'The right to personal ownership, use and disposal of property subject to the right of others', op. cit., pp. 94-5.
70. Quoted by Martin Luther King in 'Paul's Letter to American Christians' (1956), reproduced in Carson and Holloran (eds), *A Knock at Midnight*, op. cit., p. 27.
71. Martin Luther King, 'The Three Dimensions of a Complete Life' (1967), reproduced in Carson and Holloran (eds.), *A Knock at Midnight*, ibid., p. 139.
72. Winston, *The Story of God*, op. cit., p. 313. See also pp. 364, 404. For a Catholic take on the same issue, see Franklin (ed.), *Life to the Full*, op. cit., pp. 10, 87-91. There is another, more specifically theological explanation for the 'fit' between capitalism and Protestantism – or, at least, its Calvinist strains. Famously, Calvin taught that believers are justified by faith alone – the doing of good works, while admirable, is not necessary for salvation. Many of Calvin's followers were thereby 'enabled to engage in worldly activity without serious anxiety regarding their salvation as a consequence': McGrath, Christian Theology, op. cit., p. 386. In short, the importance of charity was de-emphasised. This development troubled other Christian thinkers of the time, and for good reason, but there can be little doubt that Calvin's influence fuelled economic growth in Reformation Europe and beyond. And that of itself was no bad thing.
73. See Eco, *Turning Back the Clock*, op. cit., pp. 80-96; and see generally Franklin (ed.), *Life to the Full*, ibid., passim. A few of the 'rights' identified in Franklin's book seem to me to lie close to the borderline.
74. Professor Geoff Gallop, 'Rights and responsibilities: towards a genuinely Australian understanding', 2006 Sambell Oration, delivered on 30 August 2006 at the Social Rights and Responsibilities Conference of the Brotherhood of St Laurence. Copy supplied to the author.
75. Meditation XVII, *Devotions Upon Emergent Occasions* (1624).
76. Johnson, *The Quest for God*, op. cit., p. 87.
77. Sharpe, 'The right to serve and worship God in public and private', in Franklin (ed.), Life to the Full, op. cit., p. 23.
78. Eberstadt, 'How the West Really Lost God', op. cit., p. 8.
79. See Humphrys, *In God We Doubt*, op. cit., pp. 124-6.
80. See Kevin Rudd, 'The Global Financial Crisis', *The Monthly*, February 2009, p. 20. See also Rudd, 'Faith in Politics', op. cit., p. 28; Mark Latham, *The Latham Diaries*, Allen & Unwin (2005); Lindsay Tanner, *Crowded Lives*, Pluto Press (2003). Tanner's is not an explicitly Christian analysis. Latham would appear to be an atheist. See also the Report of the Australian Human Rights and Equal Opportunities Commission, *It's About Time: Women, men work and family* (2007), at http://hreoc.gov.au/sex_discrimination/its_about_time/index.html.
81. Blaine Harden, 'Poor shun the luxury of marriage', *The Sydney Morning Herald*, 8 March 2007.
82. Thomas Frank, *What's the Matter With Kansas? How Conservatives Won the Heart of America*, Owl Books (2005), p. 133.
83. John Spong, *Living In Sin? A Bishop Rethinks Human Sexuality*, HarperSanFrancisco (1990), p. 135ff. See also Collins, *The Language of God*, op. cit., p. 260.
84. McDowell, *Evidence for Christianity*, op. cit., p. 77.
85. Wills, *What Jesus Meant*, op. cit., pp. 33-5.
86. For a forthright discussion of these issues, read the 2006 Pride Sermon, delivered by Rev. Geoffrey Vine on 3 September 2006 in Glenaven, New Zealand. Available at http://homepages.ihug.co.nz/~Serlewis/mtke/gaypride06.html.

87. Keller, *The Reason for God*, op. cit., p. 104.

88. For a well-argued contrary view, from a Catholic social justice perspective, see Marita Waters, 'The right to choose and maintain a state of life, married or single, lay or religious', in Franklin (ed.), *Life to the Full*, op. cit., pp. 51-6.

89. Hitchens, *God is Not Great*, op. cit., p. 223.

90. See generally Michael Casey, 'The right to personal liberty under just law', in Franklin (ed.), *Life to the Full*, op. cit., p. 35. See also Gideon Haigh, 'Justice Menhennit & Australia's Roe v Wade', *The Monthly*, November 2007, pp. 28-38.

91. Chris Gacek, quoted in Wallis, *Seven Ways to Change the World*, op. cit., p. 161.

92. *Rex v. Taylor* (1676) 1 Vent 293.

93. Pataki, *Against Religion*, op. cit., p. 90.

94. See also Onfray, *The Atheist Manifesto*, op. cit., pp. 49-51 where the author makes essentially same point; see also Franklin, introduction to *Life to the Full*, op. cit., pp. 7-9.

95. Forster and Marston, *Christianity, Evidence and Truth*, op. cit., p. 51.

96. Onfray, *The Atheist Manifesto*, op. cit., pp. 49-50.

97. Fairfax, *The Triple Abyss*, op. cit., p. 233.

98. 'Of Punishment', *Political, Moral and Miscellaneous Thoughts and Reflections* (1750).

99. Fairfax, *The Triple Abyss*, op. cit., p. 100.

100. Butterfield, *Christianity and History*, op. cit., p. 62.

101. Ibid, p. 63.

102. See Frank G. Kirkpatrick, *John Macmurray: Community Beyond Political Philosophy*, Rowman & Littlefield (2005), p. 107ff.

103. 'Almansor' (1823). Compare Acts 19:19, which is occasionally cited by atheists as some kind of Christian endorsement of enforced book-burning. In fact, it is a description of a *voluntary* act of redemption by people who had been converted to Christianity by peaceful methods and who had come themselves to see the evils of 'sorcery'.

104. Blamires, *The Christian Mind*, op. cit., p. 98. My emphasis.

105. Fairfax, *The Triple Abyss*, op. cit., p. 181.

106. Casey, 'The right to personal liberty under just law', op. cit., p. 36. See also Wallis, *Seven Ways to Change the World*, op. cit., p. 76. Wallis decries 'market individualism' from the Right and 'lifestyle individualism' from the Left. Compare Fairfax, *The Triple Abyss*, ibid., pp. 357-9. Fairfax argued that a critical difference between ancient and modern civilisations was that the former were based upon the 'group ego' while the latter give precedence to the 'personal' or 'individual' ego.

107. Onfray, *The Atheist Manifesto*, op. cit., p. 36.

108. Wallis, *Seven Ways to Change the World*, op. cit., p. 11.

109. Wills, *What Jesus Meant*, op. cit., p. 43.

110. Ibid., p. 14.

111. See Brad Carson, 'Vote Righteously', *The New Republic*, November 22, 2004, p. 34. Carson was the unsuccessful Democratic senatorial candidate in 2004 in the US state of Oklahoma. A fortnight after his defeat at the polls, which many on the Left regarded as inexplicable, Carson graciously and perceptively defended the people of his native state against charges of stupidity and bigotry.

112. For a good summary of Kuyper's views and achievements, see Irving Hexman, 'Christian Politics according to Abraham Kuyper', *CRUX*, Vol. XIX, No. 1, March 1983:2-7; available online at www.ucalcary.ca/~nurelweb/papers/irving/kuyperp.html.

113. Lewis, *Mere Christianity*, op. cit., pp. 76-7. My emphasis.

114. Fairfax, *The Triple Abyss*, op. cit., p. 152.

115. Harris, *Letter to a Christian Nation*, op. cit., p. 18. See also Onfray, *The Atheist Manifesto*, op. cit., p. 161.

116. Damian Grace, 'The right to freedom of expression', in Franklin (ed.), *Life to the Full*, op. cit., p. 47.

117. Franklin, introduction to *Life to the Full*, ibid., p. 3.

118. James Carroll, *House of War: The Pentagon and the Rise of American Power*, Scribe (2006), pp. 411-4. Carroll's book contains a superb analysis of the nuclear arms build-up since 1945, written from an informed liberal Christian perspective.

119. Brennan, *Acting on Conscience*, op. cit., p. 76.
120. Butterfield, *Christianity and History*, op. cit., pp. 50-2.
121. Ibid, p. 51. See also p. 75.
122. Tom Holland, 'Secularism: the unlikely but valuable legacy of Christianity', *The Australian Financial Review*, 12 December 2008, p. 5 (Review section).
123. Ibid, pp. 176-7.
124. 'Jerusalem' (1815).
125. Butterfield, *Christianity and History*, op. cit., p. 64. See also Fairfax, *The Triple Abyss*, op. cit., pp. 418-19.
126. Nixon, *In the Arena*, op. cit., p. 430.
127. Carson, *A Call to Spiritual Reformation*, op. cit., p. 109. Compare Wills, *What Jesus Meant*, op. cit., p. 13: 'Jesus [did] not come to bring mankind a higher politics'.

Chapter 9 – OTHER RELIGIONS

1. *The Anatomy of Melancholy* (1621), Part III, Section 4, Member 1, Subsection 1. Michel Onfray echoes the same theme: 'None of them is truer than another'. See Onfray, *The Atheist Manifesto*, op. cit., p. 17.
2. Henig, 'Darwin's God', op. cit., p. 3. See also Fairfax, *The Triple Abyss*, op. cit., pp. 4, 257-70.
3. See Onfray, *The Atheist Manifesto*, op. cit., p. 29.
4. Quoted in Pataki, *Against Religion*, op. cit., p. 120. See also Keller, *The Reason for God*, op. cit., pp. 11-13. This school of thought is sometimes called 'parallelism', and it has a certain superficial attraction. But it also ignores, if not denies, the possibility of ultimate religious Truth. See generally, McGrath, Christian Theology, op. cit., pp. 462-3.
5. Fairfax, *The Triple Abyss*, op. cit., p. 262. And see generally at pp. 356-7.
6. The sources I have used for own quite rudimentary survey include Karen Armstrong, *Islam: A Short History*, Phoenix Press (2001); Winston, *The Story of God*, op. cit.; Michael Hart, *The 100: A Ranking of the Most Influential Persons in History*, op. cit., especially chapters 1, 3, 4, 5, 6, 83, 93 and 100; and *The World Book Encyclopedia*, Field Enterprises Educational Corporation (1975), entry on 'Religion'. See also, for an Australian take, John Dickson, *A spectator's guide to world religions – an introduction to the big five*, Blue Bottle Press (2004). As for the differences between the many Christian denominations, I confess to having obtained considerable help from Jeffrey B. Webb, *The Complete Idiot's Guide to Christianity*, Alpha Books (2004).
7. Hart, *The 100*, op. cit., p. 28.
8. See generally on Zoroastrianism, Winston, *The Story of God*, op. cit., pp. 129-38; Hart, *The 100*, op. cit., pp. 464-7.
9. Bryan Appleyard, 'Life After Life', *The Weekend Australian Magazine*, January 17-18 2009, p. 19.
10. See Fairfax, *The Triple Abyss*, op. cit., p. 261.
11. Keller, *The Reason for God*, op. cit., p. 15. On Hinduism, see generally Fairfax, *The Triple Abyss*, ibid., passim.
12. Quoted in S. Rhadhakrishnan, 'Introductory Essay', *The Baghvad Gita*, Harper Collins (2002), pp. 14-15.
13. *The World Book Encyclopedia*, entry on 'Religion'; Winston, *The Story of God*, op. cit., p. 151.
14. Fairfax, *The Triple Abyss*, op. cit., p. 262.
15. Ibid.
16. Ibid., p. 356.
17. Lewis, *Mere Christianity*, op. cit., pp. 17-8. See further my discussion in Chapter 2.
18. See Fairfax, *The Triple Abyss*, op. cit., pp. 313-4: 'The individual soul is much the same in the Christian and Moslem religions and in Platonic, Neo-Platonist and Hindu teaching, as something apart from the body, from the mind with its cognitive and emotional aspects, and from all other aspects of the human organism.'
19. Kathleen Norris, quoted in Julie Polter, 'Why Bother?' *Sojourners*, September-October 2008, p. 48.
20. Winston, *The Story of God*, op. cit., pp. 82-90; Fairfax, *The Triple Abyss*, op. cit., pp. 263-9.
21. Quoted in Davies, *An Introduction to the Philosophy of Religion*, op. cit., p. 117.

22. Winston, *The Story of God*, op. cit., p. 119. Winston's observation is yet another reminder that there are many similarities between the world's religions. But what conclusions can validly be drawn from this fact? It is an old question. Two philosophers of the Enlightenment, Englishmen John Toland and Matthew Tindal, propounded the idea that all religions are just 'a rational reaffirmation of moral truths already available to enlightened reason'. (McGrath, Christian Theology, op. cit., p.67, my emphasis.) Man, they claimed, is capable of discovering 'ultimate reality' acting entirely on his own; and all religious traditions lead to the same thing, whether that thing is called 'God' or something else. In the twentieth century this philosophy came to be known as 'pluralism'. It has been subjected to some trenchant criticism in recent decades, primarily on the grounds that it trivialises the real differences between religions and that it devalues, or denies, the importance of divine revelation – above all, the coming of Jesus Christ. See McGrath, Christian Theology, op. cit., pp. 143, 448, 455-7, 460-2.

23. Ibid., p. 184.

24. Barrow, *New Theories of Everything*, op. cit., pp. 6-7. See also Fairfax, *The Triple Abyss*, op. cit., pp. 265-6.

25. Forster and Marston, *Christianity, Evidence and Truth*, op. cit., pp. 50-1.

26. Onfray, *The Atheist Manifesto*, op. cit., p. 59.

27. Butterfield, *Christianity and History*, op. cit., p. 99.

28. Ibid., pp. 97-100. See also Winston, *The Story of God*, op. cit., pp. 163-4, 174-5.

29. Forster and Marston, *Christianity, Evidence and Truth*, op. cit., p. 45.

30. See Blomberg, *The Historical Reliability of the Gospels*, op. cit., pp. 278-85.

31. Butterfield, *Christianity and History*, op. cit., p. 12.

32. Ibid., p. 156.

33. Blomberg, *The Historical Reliability of the Gospels*, op. cit., p. 109.

34. McDowell, *Evidence for Christianity*, op. cit., p. 247.

35. Ibid., p. 252.

36. Butterfield, *Christianity and History*, op. cit., p. 157. See also Blomberg, *The Historical Reliability of the Gospels*, op. cit., pp. 17-19.

37. Butterfield, *Christianity and History*, op. cit., p. 12.

38. See Blomberg, *The Historical Reliability of the Gospels*, op. cit., pp. 273-4, and the source cited at note 91.

39. Winston, *The Story of God*, op. cit., p. 244.

40. Armstrong, *Islam*, op. cit., pp. 3-4.

41. Ibid., p. 4.

42. Ibid., pp. 4-14.

43. My source for what follows is Matkin, *Early Christianity*, op. cit., pp. 228-36.

44. Ibid., p. 234.

45. Hart, *The 100*, op. cit., p. 4. Compare Winston, *The Story of God*, op. cit., pp. 253-5, 269-79.

46. Packer, *God has Spoken*, op. cit., p. 59. As to modern Islamic extremism, see Winston, *The Story of God*, op. cit., pp. 262-7; Humphrys, *In God We Doubt*, op. cit., p. 290.

47. Armstrong, *Islam*, op. cit., p. 19.

48. Ibid., pp. 19-22.

49. Ibid., pp. 22-7.

50. Winston, *The Story of God*, op. cit., p. 252.

51. Armstrong, *Islam*, op. cit., pp. 25-31.

52. Braybrooke, *An Explorer's Guide to Christianity*, op. cit., pp. 120-3. See also Onfray, *The Atheist Manifesto*, op. cit., pp. 141-50; Matkin, *Early Christianity*, op. cit., p. 235.

53. Wills, *What Jesus Meant*, op. cit., p. 52.

54. Fairfax, *The Triple Abyss*, op. cit., p. 449.

55. Matkin, *Early Christianity*, op. cit., pp. 104-9.

56. Hitchens, *God is Not Great*, op. cit., p. 156. See also p. 192.

57. Quoted in Dawkins, *The God Delusion*, op. cit., p. 34.

58. See Winston, *The Story of God*, op. cit., p. 295; Fairfax, *The Triple Abyss*, op. cit., p. 446.

59. Matkin, *Early Christianity*, op. cit., pp. 130-1.

60. Ibid., p. 242.

61. Ibid., pp. 239-44.

62. Thomas Sheehan, 'The Dream of Karl Rahner', *The New York Review of Books*, Volume 29 Number 1, 4 January 1982. J.I. Packer has proposed this summary of the Trinity: 'God the Father is the giver of Holy Scripture; God the Son is the theme of Holy Scripture; and God the Spirit, as the Father's appointed agent in witnessing to the Son, is the author, authenticator, and interpreter, of Holy Scripture.' *God has Spoken*, op. cit., p. 91. And see generally on the Trinity, Fairfax, *The Triple Abyss*, op. cit., pp. 299-301, 353-5.

63. Lewis, *Mere Christianity*, op. cit., pp. 148-9.

64. See Keller, *The Reason for God*, op. cit., p. 82.

65. Braybrooke, *An Explorer's Guide to Christianity*, op. cit., pp. 71-2.

66. Butterfield, *Christianity and History*, op. cit., p. 82.

67. Ibid., p. 58.

68. Keller, *The Reason for God*, op. cit., p. 185. See also at pp. 174-5.

69. See, for example, Packer, *God has Spoken*, op. cit., pp. 56-9.

70. Ibid., p. 59.

71. Harris, *Letter to a Christian Nation*, op. cit., p. 3.

72. Ibid, p. 4. Compare Humphrys, *In God We Doubt*, op. cit., p. 171.

73. Ibid, pp. 6, 7.

74. Hitchens, *God is Not Great*, op. cit., pp. 167-8.

75. Winston, *The Story of God*, op. cit., p. 179.

76. Fairfax, *The Triple Abyss*, op. cit., p. 356. See also at p. 239 ('My view is Christian, but it does not support the exclusivist pretensions of any religion or religious sect.')

77. Ibid., p. 356.

78. Ibid., p. 410.

79. Ibid.

80. Johnson, *The Quest for God*, op. cit., p. 110.

81. Ibid.

82. Revd. Professor William R.G. Loader, 'First Thoughts on Year C Gospel Passages from the Lectionary: Pentecost', at www.staff.murdoch.edu.au/~loader/LkPent.htm.

83. See the discussions of John 14:6, Acts 4:12 and other relevant Biblical verses at www. biblegateway.com.

84. Fairfax, *The Triple Abyss*, op. cit., pp. 365-8; Wills, *What Jesus Meant*, op. cit., pp. 89-91. See generally John Hick and Paul Knitter (eds), *The Myth of Christian Uniqueness: Towards a Pluralistic Theology of Religion*, Orbis (1987). A non-exclusivist construction of John 14:6 seems to me highly plausible for other reasons. It is consistent with certain passages in the New Testament in which Jesus is referred to as a sort of 'mediator' between God and Man (cf. 1 Timothy 2:5; 2 Peter 1:4). More importantly, it takes account of the historical context in which John's Gospel was written, and the literary approach adopted by the author. In the opening chapter, which sets the scene for everything which follows, heavy emphasis is laid upon the Word. Jesus is 'the Word made flesh' (John 1:14). See generally McGrath, Christian Theology, op. cit., p. 296. See also Hall, "Interreligious Perspectives on Incarnation", op. cit., pp. 431-2.

85. See Keller, *The Reason for God*, op. cit., pp. 7-8, 116-7.

86. Carson, *A Call to Spiritual Transformation*, op. cit., p. 20. See also Wills, *What Jesus Meant*, op. cit., pp. 59-77. Compare Onfray, *The Atheist Manifesto*, op. cit., pp. 71, 74.

87. Matkin, *Early Christianity*, op. cit., pp. 42-3.

88. See Winston, *The Story of God*, op. cit., p.105ff.

89. William Temple, *In Search of Serenity*, R.V.C. Bodley (1955), chapter 12.

90. Winston, *The Story of God*, op. cit., pp. 93-4.

91. See Blomberg, *The Historical Reliability of the Gospels*, op. cit., p. 318.

92. Carson, *A Call to Spiritual Transformation*, op. cit., p. 42.

93. Packer, *God has Spoken*, op. cit., p. 88.

94. Ibid., p. 57. See also Keller, *The Reason for God*, op. cit., pp. 8-9.

95. Spong, *Rescuing the Bible from Fundamentalism*, op. cit., p. 170. See also Keller, *The Reason for God*, op. cit., p. 4. Compare Russell, 'Why I am not a Christian', op. cit., pp. 595-6.

96. Wallis, *Seven Ways to Change the World*, op. cit., p. 59.

97. King, 'A Knock at Midnight', op. cit., p. 72.
98. Ibid.
99. Quoted in Kahl, *The Misery of Christianity*, op. cit., p. 94.
100. Hitchens, *God is Not Great*, op. cit., p. 27.
101. Ibid., p. 176.
102. Russell, 'What Is an Agnostic?' op. cit., p. 578
103. Butterfield, *Christianity and History*, op. cit., p. 170.
104. Ibid., pp. 170-1.
105. Ibid., p. 177.
106. J.L. Nelson, 'Eastern Promises', *London Review of Books*, volume 29, number 23, 29 November 2007, p. 31. Nelson's piece was a review of Christopher Tyerman's book *God's War: A New History of the Crusades*, Penguin (2007).
107. Ibid.
108. Humphrys, *In God We Doubt*, op. cit., p. 288. See also Keller, *The Reason for God*, op. cit., p. 56.
109. Onfray, *The Atheist Manifesto*, op. cit., p. 3.
110. Collected in *The Oxford Dictionary of Quotations*, op. cit., p. 504.
111. Lewis, *Mere Christianity*, op. cit., p. 62.

Chapter 10 – HEAVEN AND HELL
1. Jesse Bering, in Brockman (ed.), *What We Believe But Cannot Prove*, op. cit., p. 35.
2. Onfray, *The Atheist Manifesto*, op. cit., p. 2.
3. Russell, 'Why I am not a Christian', op. cit., p. 596.
4. Onfray, *The Atheist Manifesto*, op. cit., p. 39. See also p. 65ff.
5. Miles, *Christ*, op. cit., p. 11.
6. See Steven Weinberg, 'Without God', op. cit. (note 8 to Introduction).
7. Russell, 'What Is an Agnostic', op. cit., p. 580.
8. Daniel Williams, 'At the Hour of Our Death', *Time*, 10 September 2007, p. 36.
9. Miriam Van Scott, *Encyclopedia of Hell*, St. Martin's Press (1998), pp. 214-5.
10. Ibid., p. 38.
11. Williams, 'At the Hour of Our Death', op. cit., p. 36.
12. John Spong, *Why Christianity Must Change or Die: A Bishop Speaks to Believers in Exile*, HarperSanFrancisco (1999), p. 210. See also Braybrooke, *An Explorer's Guide to Christianity*, op. cit., p. 111. Both Spong and Braybrooke reject the notion of a record-keeping deity.
13. Carson, *A Call to Spiritual Transformation*, op. cit., p. 45. See also Packer, *God has Spoken*, op. cit., p. 17.
14. See Keller, *The Reason for God*, op. cit., p. 72.
15. Braybrooke, *An Explorer's Guide to Christianity*, op. cit., p. 113.
16. 'And death shall have no dominion' (1936).
17. 'An Arundel Tomb' (1964).
18. Eberstadt, 'How the West Really Lost God', op. cit., p. 6.
19. *Revelations of Divine Love*, chapter 86, revelation 16. Penguin Classics edition (1966)
20. Ibid.
21. Quoted in Keller, *The Reason for God*, op. cit., p. 75. My emphasis.
22. Pataki, *Against Religion*, op. cit., p. 77.
23. Winston, *The Story of God*, op. cit., p. 256.
24. Van Scott, *Encyclopedia of Hell*, op. cit., pp. 123, 132-3.
25. See Blomberg, *The Historical Reliability of the Gospels*, op. cit., pp. 51-2.
26. Keller, *The Reason for God*, op. cit., p. 69.
27. Ibid.
28. Winston, *The Story of God*, op. cit., p. 133.
29. Keller, *The Reason for God*, op. cit., p. 18.
30. Russell, 'What Is an Agnostic?' op. cit., p. 581. See generally Keller, *The Reason for God*, ibid., p.70ff.
31. Wallis, *Seven Ways to Change the World*, op. cit., pp. 27, 150.

32. Dickson, *Jesus: A Short Life*, op. cit., p. 64. My emphasis. See also, on the faith/works question, Packer, *God has Spoken*, op. cit., p. 113.
33. Morgan, *The Teaching of Christ*, op. cit., p. 143.
34. Ibid., pp. 143-4. My emphasis. See also Dickson, *Jesus: A Short Life*, op. cit., p. 64: 'The curious upshot of Jesus' emphasis on the twin loves is that the 'religious' and the 'moral' can prove themselves sinners just as easily as the irreligious and the immoral.'
35. Carson, *A Call to Spiritual Transformation*, op. cit., p. 215.
36. Stanton, *The Gospels and Jesus*, op. cit., p. 193.
37. Butterfield, *Christianity and History*, op. cit., pp. 148-9.
38. Carson, *A Call to Spiritual Transformation*, op. cit., p. 108.
39. See Wills, *What Jesus Meant*, op. cit., p. xxx.
40. The relevant passage is quoted in Fairfax, *The Triple Abyss*, op. cit., p. 167: 'Now verily a person consists of purpose. According to the purpose which a person has in this world, *so does he become on departing hence.*' My emphasis. Fairfax's own view was similar: 'The individual … can choose to … open himself to God's purpose or shut it out.' (p. 311)
41. Quoted in Humphrys, *In God We Doubt*, op. cit., p. 69. See also at p. 182.
42. See further Morgan, *The Teaching of Christ*, op. cit., pp. 144-5.
43. Johnson, *The Quest for God*, op. cit., p. 171. See also Keller, *The Reason for God*, op. cit., p. 80: 'No one can … be sure of who is ultimately going to arrive in heaven or hell'.
44. King, 'Unfulfilled Dreams', op. cit., p. 196. See also Fairfax, *The Triple Abyss*, op. cit., pp. 422, 431 ('we must learn to understand and watch the spiritual pattern which our lives are creating').
45. Butterfield, *Christianity and History*, op. cit., p. 152.
46. Dickson, *Jesus: A Short Life*, op. cit., p. 117.
47. For an interesting version of the argument that the afterlife is spiritual only, see Fairfax, *The Triple Abyss*, op. cit., pp. 284, 443.
48. Keller, *The Reason for God*, op. cit., pp. 31-4.
49. Quoted in Davies, *An Introduction to the Philosophy of Religion*, op. cit., p. 121. See also Keller, *The Reason for God*, ibid., p. 223.
50. Van Scott, *Encyclopedia of Hell*, op. cit., p. 273.
51. Keller, *The Reason for God*, op. cit., p. 260, note 10.
52. Ibid.
53. See, for example, Braybrooke, *An Explorer's Guide to Christianity*, op. cit., p. 111.
54. Carson, *A Call for Spiritual Transformation*, op. cit., p. 49. Compare Packer, *God has Spoken*, op. cit., p. 16; Keller, *The Reason for God*, op. cit., pp. 76-9.
55. Quoted in Johnson, *The Quest for God*, op. cit., pp. 165-6.
56. Ibid., p. 166.
57. Fairfax, *The Triple Abyss*, op. cit., p. 443. See also at p. 311.
58. Johnson, *The Quest for God*, op. cit., p. 168.
59. Fairfax, *The Triple Abyss*, op. cit., p. 446. My emphasis.
60. Ibid., p. 284.
61. Compare Fairfax, *The Triple Abyss*, ibid., p. 443.
62. Ibid.
63. Compare Fairfax, *The Triple Abyss*, ibid., p. 443: 'I do not believe that the grace of God would ever permit a soul … to kill itself beyond hope of redemption'.
64. Van Scott, *Encyclopedia of Hell*, op. cit., p. 20.
65. Fairfax, *The Triple Abyss*, op. cit., p. 443. My emphasis.
66. Ibid., p. 311.
67. Keller, *The Reason for God*, op. cit., p. 71.
68. Ibid.
69. Ibid., p. 191.
70. Braybrooke, *An Explorer's Guide to Christianity*, op. cit., p. 111. The idea that all souls will eventually be saved is sometimes called Universalism. Despite its immense unpopularity in certain Protestant circles in Sydney, it is an idea which is neither 'modern' nor especially radical. Theologians as diverse as Origen, Huldrych Zwingli, Karl Barth and John A.T. Robinson composed variations on the same theme. Universalism strikes me as

quintessentially 'right', but, that said, I am highly conscious that I may be wrong. Within the upper echelons of most Christian denominations, Universalism is frowned upon. It is sensible to acknowledge that some of the giants of Christian theology – including St Augustine, Aquinas, Calvin, Jonathon Edwards and C.S. Lewis – believed in eternal Hell. On this issue, the prudent course for any believer (or waverer) must be to assume that physical death is the cut-off point at which divine judgment is handed down – for eternity. Although that idea appalls me, and I doubt very much that it is true, it is the basis upon which I now approach life.

71.   See Webb, Christianity, op. cit., pp. 217-8.
72.   Wills, *What Jesus Meant*, op. cit., p. 131.
73.   Van Scott, *Encyclopedia of Heaven*, op. cit., pp. 59-60.
74.   Quoted in Antonella Gambotto-Burke, 'Ines of my soul', *The Weekend Australian*, 23 December 2006, p.10r.
75.   Van Scott, *Encyclopedia of Heaven*, op. cit., p. 121.

Epilogue – WHAT IS YOUR VERDICT?

1.   Richard Swinburne, quoted in Keller, *The Reason for God*, op.cit. p. 121. See also Keller's own discussion at pp. 140-1.
2.   Carson, *A Call to Spiritual Reformation*, op. cit., p. 157.
3.   Pataki, *Against Religion*, op. cit., p. 56. Compare Keller, *The Reason for God*, op. cit., pp. 117-21.
4.   Blanchard, *Where Was God on September 11?* op. cit., p. 23.
5.   *Chamberlain v. The Queen (No. 2)* (1984) 153 CLR 521 at [14], citing *Reg. v. Beble* [1979] Qd. R. 278 at 289.
6.   Ibid.
7.   Packer, *God has Spoken*, op. cit., p. 99.
8.   Fairfax, *The Triple Abyss*, op. cit., p. 385.
9.   Packer, *God has Spoken*, op. cit., p. 99.
10.   Butterfield, *Christianity and History*, op. cit., p. 175.
11.   Ibid., p. 176. See also Humphrys, *In God We Doubt*, op. cit., pp. 59-60; Humphrys makes the same point as regards contemporary Britain.
12.   Phyllis Tickle, 'The Great Emergence', *Sojourners*, August 2008, p. 28, at p. 33.
13.   Ibid., p. 35.
14.   Fairfax, *The Triple Abyss*, op. cit., p. 346.

ACKNOWLEDGMENTS

Writing a book is in large part a solitary exercise, but it cannot be done without help and encouragement from others. Many people contributed to *God, Actually*, some more than they might have realised, and perhaps a few without realising it at all.

On the winding road to publication in Australasia, which finally took place in June 2008, I received a great deal of moral support, practical assistance, sage advice and/or friendly cajolement. I cannot name everyone, but prominent among those who helped me in these ways were: Daniel Williams, my most excellent brother (whom I still hope to convince one day), Alec Leopold, Lynne Harman, James Franklin, Rev. Niall Reid, Jessica Maish, Janet Hutchinson, Adrian Chek, Debra Bowers, Antonella Gambotto-Burke, Peter Kirkwood, Duncan Graham, Kim Beazley (my mate from Milperra, not the former federal Opposition Leader), Georgina Garrett, the late Rev. Lewis Robins, Max Whitten, Graem Sims, Sandra Lee, Jim Thynne, Michael Rose, Liisa Hiltunen, Alex Finley, Greg Burton, Rev. Graham Spence, Rebecca Kaiser, Peter Luck, Shirley Trembath, Gideon Haigh, Graham Harman, Meredith Curnow, Tony Stephens, Murray Waldren, Mandy Mitchell, Virginia Taylor, Kenneth Davidson, Lesley Vick, Guy Foster, Martin Drevikovsky, Carolyn Williams, Warwick Bowd, Nicola Shew, Dr Peter Ross, Kylie Virtue, Cath Keenan, Ros Rossettin, Philip Long, Vivienne Skinner, Rae Williams, Kylie Giblett, Sally Jeffrey, Liza Yates, the late Ian Yates, and my wonderful and extraordinary parents, Evan and Janet Williams.

Likewise, over the last year, through the process of promoting *God, Actually* in Australia, I have been greatly assisted by other people. In addition to many of those already listed above, who have continued to bless my life, I am very grateful to Scott Whitmont, Peter Kaldor, Michael Quinlan, Polly Seidler, Miriam Cosic, Mark Wormell, Andrew Wiseman, Talitha Fishburn, Ken Harman, Anne Day, Frank Sheehan, Scott McKinley, and Arina Usikov.

In conclusion, I wish to make five other very special mentions.

Margaret Kennedy, my wise and tenacious agent, without whom the book would almost certainly have disappeared without trace in a mountain of slush piles.

Shelley Gare, a kindred spirit, who convinced me when my stocks were low that it was worth pressing on, and selflessly gave of her vast knowledge and expertise.

The fantastic team at ABC Books in Sydney, but especially Jacqueline Kent, Jane

Finemore, Anastasia Konstantinos and Susan Morris-Yates. Susan understood what I was trying to do and gave me my chance.

Tony Collins, Simon Cox and the rest of their sterling team at Lion Hudson in Oxford, England. Tony's offer to publish *God, Actually* in Britain and North America came like manna from heaven.

Most of all, my dear, dear wife, Suzanne, and our two beautiful daughters, Hope and Violet. The three of them coped daily with my many failings, frailties and foibles. Their love, devotion and challenging wit was, and is, a constant source of inspiration.

Thank you, everybody. I will always be extremely grateful.

Roy Williams
Sydney, April 2009

INDEX